Peter Harry Brown is a journalist and the author of the bestselling book *Marilyn: The Last Take*. He lives in Cardiff-by-the-Sea, California.

Pat H. Broeske is a veteran entertainment reporter who writes for *Entertainment Weekly*, the *Washington Post* and the *New York Times*. She lives in Santa Ana, California.

HOWARD HUGHES

THE UNTOLD STORY

PETER HARRY BROWN

—— AND ——

PAT H. BROESKE

WARNER BOOKS

A *Warner* Book

First published in Great Britain in 1996
by Little, Brown and Company
This edition published in 1997 by Warner Books
Reprinted 1998, 1999, 2001 (twice)

Copyright © 1996 by Peter Harry Brown and Pat H. Broeske

The moral right of the authors has been asserted.

A CIP catalogue record for this book
is available from the British Library.

ISBN: 0 7515 1597 3

Typeset in Bembo by M Rules
Printed and bound in Great Britain by
Clays Ltd, St Ives plc

Warner Books
A Division of
Little, Brown and Company (UK)
Brettenham House
Lancaster Place
London WC2E 7EN

For my mother, Frances Saunders Brown,
And my mother-in-law, Helen Holgate Twedell
—Peter Harry Brown

For my parents, Claude and Hazel Hague
—Pat H. Broeske

CONTENTS

Prologue: Storming the Fortress   1

1. Crown Prince   6
2. Shadow of Death   21
3. The Bartered Bride   32
4. Going Hollywood   47
5. An Affair to Remember   56
6. Applause   66
7. Adrift   78
8. Coming of Age   88
9. Cary and Kate   98
10. Katharine the Great   111
11. Highway in the Sky   119
12. He's in the Money   126
13. The Parade's Gone By   132
14. Way Out West   143
15. The Blue Prince   149
16. Brainstorms   165

17. The Great Escape   180
18. The Lone Wolf   193
19. Fall from Grace   204
20. Hide-and-Seek   225
21. Hollywood Confidential   236
22. September Song   246
23. Secret Police   256
24. Girls, Girls, Girls   264
25. Tycoon   275
26. Wedding Bell Blues   285
27. Shotgun Wedding   300
28. Refuge   315
29. The Mask of Sanity   321
30. Orphan of the Storm   330
31. The Captive   344
32. Howardgate   361
33. Evil Under the Sun   368
     Epilogue: Legacy   376

     Howard Hughes: Aviation Highlights   384
     Filmography   388
     The Women in Hughes's Life   394
     Source Notes   400
     Bibliography   430
     Acknowledgments   457
     Index   463

HOWARD HUGHES

PROLOGUE

STORMING THE FORTRESS

HOLLYWOOD, CALIFORNIA, JUNE 5, 1974

A COASTAL MIST SHROUDED THE HULKING ART DECO BUILDING AT 7000 Romaine Street, making the corporate fortress appear even more sinister than it was. Security guard Mike Davis shivered in his aviator jacket as he systematically checked each outside door and window, though all of them had been sealed shut four decades earlier. As he reached the front entrance, he glanced at his watch. It was about 12:45 A.M.—right on schedule.

Just as Davis opened a side door he felt "something hard" jammed into his back. He didn't put up a fight. "I just assumed they were armed. I knew I wasn't," he later recounted.

"We're going in," said a voice behind Davis. Then the burglars—at least two, perhaps as many as four—entered a structure previously thought to be impregnable. A Davis co-worker had dubbed it "the Bastille."

"Be quiet and don't look around," Davis was told. At their orders he lowered himself to the floor on his belly. While one man bound his hands, another tied a loose blindfold over his eyes. A thick rectangle of duct tape was placed over his mouth.

Part one of this beautifully planned heist had proceeded without a glitch.

Without triggering an alarm, without encountering a single video monitor, without attracting a single glance from anyone wandering the streets of late-night Hollywood, a group of men had effortlessly invaded the legendary castle keep of the phantom billionaire, Howard Robard Hughes. Once considered the most impenetrable commercial building in Los Angeles, once guarded by an army of secret police, it proved as simple to breach as a skid-row pawnshop.

Davis listened as the men wheeled in a handcart carrying a pair of acetylene torches. Peering down through a gap in the blindfold, he glimpsed the words UNITED STATES NAVY on the side of one of them.

The burglars appeared to know where they were going as they made their way through the building that so few had ever been permitted to enter. They stormed through the offices, breaking into hundreds of file cabinets and torching their way into walk-in vaults, many of which hadn't been opened in decades. The Los Angeles Police would later reveal that several offices were opened with keys. They spent four hours rifling through the dark hiding places that had protected Howard Hughes's deepest secrets for forty-five years.

After burning their way into the most personal of Howard's safes—dating back to the era of silent films and silver-screen vamps—the men pillaged the faded mementos of dozens of fabulous love affairs, touching keepsakes of Hollywood's most prolific Don Juan.

Passionate love letters from Katharine Hepburn were carelessly tossed onto the floor along with fiery telegrams from Ava Gardner, postcards from Yvonne De Carlo, and notes from Lana Turner.

A sweet, annotated children's book from Terry Moore tumbled to the floor among hundreds of close-up photos of Jane Russell's cleavage and a scented envelope of dried violets, a wistful gift from heiress Gloria Vanderbilt. They tossed a bundle of faded receipts into a corner, reminders of romantic escapades with Ginger Rogers, Ava Gardner, Susan Hayward, Vanderbilt, and Howard's most elusive lover, dark, sultry actress Faith Domergue.

In one crumbling dossier, the burglars flipped through picturesque hotel bills from the fabled Mexican resort Agua Caliente, where Hughes had wooed and bedded Jean Harlow, the hot blonde he had made into a superstar in his epic *Hell's Angels.*

Unnoticed was a velvet casket of engagement rings—accepted and then rejected by silent queen Billie Dove, Ginger, Ava, Kate, Lana, Faith, Kathryn Grayson, and the most famous debutante ever, Brenda Frazier.

The marauders uncovered the bulging contents of a polished mahogany cabinet jammed into the back of the vault. Thousands of folders spilled out—surveillance reports on hundreds of unknown but startlingly beautiful starlets who had been part of a secret harem of lovers collected by Howard during the fifties. Also listed and catalogued were apartments, mansions, beach hideaways, and hotels where the errant billionaire had housed this stable of paramours.

Scrapbooks—more than four hundred of them—bulged with yellowed clippings. Aviation trophies and keys to cities across the country, souvenirs of a hero's welcome decades past, lined the shelves.

The burglars, though, abandoned Hughes's private inner sanctum and burned their way into a more modern and efficient vault two doors down. As the smoke cleared, the men stirred with excitement. Here was their quarry. Within this vault the invaders spied a matching pair of blue leather file boxes, one of which bore the words FEDERAL BUREAU OF INVESTIGATION, DUPLICATED FILES.

"Here it is," Davis heard one of the men bellow. "This has to be it."

Breaking the thick wax seal on the dossiers, the men dumped the papers onto the carpet and began examining the reports under the dim light of a Tiffany lamp, a relic from *Hell's Angels*. But this was not what they were after.

The hoard, passed to Hughes by J. Edgar Hoover "because of my high regard for you," were the actual transcripts of one of the most audacious bugging operations in the history of domestic espionage: the 1943–46 bugging of Hughes's love nests and Manhattan hotel suites. This record detailed the billionaire's nights of passion with Lana Turner, Ava Gardner, and Yvonne De Carlo, a potent anthology of "the lone wolf" in action.

"Worthless," one burglar muttered.

Finally, in a tiny safe, they found what they had come for—an insignificant-looking pile of yellow legal pads, CIA contracts, and a fistful of quickly scrawled personal notes, all of them condensations of telephone conversations between Hughes's Las Vegas headquarters and select members of President Richard M. Nixon's "palace guard."

The men grabbed the CIA documents first, stuffing them hurriedly into the duffel bag. In their haste they failed to notice some of the key papers, including an actual contract between Howard Hughes and the CIA to plant an enormous spy station at the bottom of the ocean. That memorandum, in which Hughes agreed to be the front man for the most expensive CIA gambit in history, slid under the edge of a desk, where it remained hidden for days.

They pocketed the Nixon documents almost as an afterthought, failing to realize that these private white papers proved that Howard's tangled financial relationship with the president had actually resulted in the Watergate break-in and the tragedy that followed. Nor could they know that one note from Robert Bennett, a Hughes operative in Washington, proved conclusively that the eighteen-minute erasure of the Oval Office tapes included an explosive exchange between Nixon and his hard-nosed aide H. R. Haldeman over Howard's curious financial deals with Nixon—words that might have single-handedly destroyed the president. Yet another five-line message even suggested that Bennett was the infamous Deep Throat who had spilled his guts on Watergate to Bob Woodward and Carl Bernstein, the *Washington Post* reporters who authored the landmark exposé *All the President's Men*.

Whether they were interested in Watergate or the CIA connection may never be known. But the thieves were satisfied. They stuffed the contents of the safe, plus one hundred yellow legal tablets bearing Hughes's own handwriting, into their bag and unobtrusively slipped from the building and into history. The raid on Romaine remains an unsolved burglary.

When Hughes was informed that his sanctum had been invaded, he wasn't particularly interested that the burglars had pocketed more than $100,000 in cash or carted off a rare South American butterfly collection, or that his ties to Nixon and the CIA were in unsafe hands. Instead, he flew into a rage about the fate of his love letters, his surveillance logs, and the cache of telegrams that had flown back and forth between himself and his two wives, Houston socialite Ella Rice and actress Jean Peters. Informed that the personal mementos were intact, he had them carted off to a bank vault, where they rested safely for six years.

Through a grueling course of research lasting three years, we followed a trail of intimate passion. We obtained facsimiles of the CIA and Watergate documents, which gave us the framework for an exhaustive study of one man's far-reaching empire and his power. We delved through hundreds of thousands of documents, an avalanche assembled during the exhaustive battle over the Hughes estate. We spoke with more than six hundred people in fifteen states, Mexico, Canada, and Europe, in order to penetrate the heart and soul of the most secretive, reclusive man of the twentieth century.

This is an inside look at one man's rise to the heights of fame and his eventual fall from grace. It is a saga of Hollywood, from the gin-mill speakeasies of the Roaring Twenties through the chic and stylish forties, when Hughes was considered to be one of the sexiest and most irresistible men in Hollywood.

This story involves unbelievable wealth: millions of dollars worth of jewels, thrown at the feet of Ava Gardner, Elizabeth Taylor, and Ginger Rogers; the world's most luxurious yacht; and seduction in the skies.

And it's the story of a modern-day harem—exotic beauties, many of them just teenagers, who found themselves trapped in lavish prisons, waiting, often in vain, for the coveted summons from the distant and legendary billionaire.

It is the story of a man so powerful that Richard M. Nixon lost his presidency because he feared Hughes so irrationally, of an aeronautical swashbuckler who changed the face of aviation, and of a man in the public eye who was so consumed with shyness and fear that each step out of the house was an act of courage.

It is the story of a privileged and handsome heir who died like a derelict, of two ideal marriages shattered by infidelity, of teenage Lolitas and one man's relentless search for the ideal lover—a lover who could equal the beauty and sensuality of his own mother.

It is a story that has never been told.

CHAPTER 1

CROWN PRINCE

IT WAS THE MOST DIFFICULT BIRTH DR. OSCAR L. NORSWORTHY HAD EVER witnessed.

On Christmas Eve 1905, while most Houston families were making last-minute holiday preparations, Allene Gano Hughes was in labor for nine excruciating hours in the city's Baptist Hospital. Attended by an increasingly alarmed nurse, Allene lost consciousness several times and, just before dawn, began hemorrhaging. This prompted Norsworthy to notify two specialists that they might be needed at any minute.

During the ordeal, Howard Robard Hughes paced up and down a stark corridor. He was a lean, intense young man, impeccably dressed in a Brooks Brothers hand-tailored suit and rimless spectacles. Dr. Norsworthy slipped away several times and offered comforting words. But Hughes sensed the gravity of the situation. His wife of eighteen months lay dying while delivering his child—a child he had been desperate to have.

The surgeons saved her life by stemming the blood at the last minute. Finally her boy was born, but only after inflicting such damage on his mother's body that she would not give birth again. Howard Robard Hughes, Jr., would be an only child.

Howard Sr. was allowed a few minutes with his wife as she lay in the recovery room, her deep brown hair tumbling around her pale face. The sight of his ravaged wife and a fleeting glimpse of his robust son would prove to be the defining moment of his life, giving him the impetus "to finally make something of himself," as his novelist-screenwriter brother, Rupert Hughes, later wrote. "For he had absolutely no prospects then to speak of."

At the age of thirty-six, Hughes, who had been born into a family of overachievers, did not have a steady job. In the ten years since he had bolted from a lackluster legal practice, he had jumped from job to job: telegraph operator in Iowa, newspaper reporter in Colorado, zinc miner in Oklahoma and Missouri. Like a latter-day Mississippi riverboat gambler, he had survived on his gregarious charm and good looks. But several thousand grimy days and whiskey-soaked nights in a dreary string of boomtowns had netted Hughes nothing more than fool's gold, a polished flair with saloon girls, and a practiced way with a deck of cards.

It was four years earlier, in 1901, when he was working as a Missouri ore crusher, that a band of Texans sunk a drill into the black shale at Spindletop, Texas, and tapped into an underground sea of petroleum—which, in turn, reinvented the Lone Star State. That strike would also change the course of Hughes's life.

"I heard the roar in Joplin," wrote Hughes, who flung down his pickax and headed for south Texas. As he later chronicled, "I turned greaser and sank into the thick of it. Roughneck, well owner, disowner [sic], promoter, capitalist, and mark; with each I claim kin for I have stood in the steps of each." Skilled as a drill master, he had an uncanny ability to pinpoint the "soft spot," the hole leading to vast petroleum pools, but his paychecks were erratic. "One month he had fifty thousand in the bank; the next he owed the bank fifty thousand," wrote his brother Rupert.

Fortunately, he was flush the night he walked into a Dallas ballroom and caught sight of Allene Gano, one of the most sought-after debutantes in the state. Her flowing dark hair, grace, and flair for fashion brought a steady parade of swains to her door. The daughter of a social register Dallas judge and granddaughter of a legendary Confederate general, Allene had a pedigree that spanned the annals of American history. The first Ganos had been French Huguenots who settled in New York in the seventeenth century. Like the other young ladies in the Dallas Blue Book, she was bred to grace the arm of a rich and powerful husband. "Instead, she married a man with no discernible future," recalled her younger sister, Annette. "But my sister was stubborn—she married for love in an era when few married for that reason."

Howard Sr. not only swept her off her feet but to the European continent—Britain, France, and Italy on $2,000 a day. The 1904 honeymoon cost $49,100, stripping Hughes of his wildcatter wealth. He came home with a steamer trunk full of Savile Row suits, a set of diamond studs, and a platinum pocket watch—but nearly flat broke.

The first Hughes residence was a prefabricated, four-room structure at the end of a dirt lane, deep within Houston's unfashionable east side. It was to this house—a reminder of his failure—at 1404 Crawford Street, that Hughes returned, following the Christmas Eve birth of his son in 1905. Around him was a boomtown that was growing so rapidly that many of the streets and boulevards hadn't even been named. Banks and hotels lined the streets, as did mansions for the nouveau riche oil barons who had been living in tents six months earlier. Over the Houston Ship Channel was a glowing mist, the aerial outflow from fleets of oil tankers. Sixty thousand barrels a minute were being poured into the bowels of these enormous ships twenty-four hours a day, even on Christmas Eve.

Everyone Hughes knew was getting rich. Men who'd wielded a shovel alongside him just months earlier were wearing cashmere coats and fine wool suits. His erstwhile poker partners were now dressing their wives in Parisian gowns and ostrich plume hats. With the birth of his son, Hughes realized that he had been little more than a camp follower, contenting himself with the fancy women and gambling parlors of the derrick camps that clustered about the drilling towers like Lilliputian villages.

All that would change, he told himself as he grabbed a handful of Havana cigars and a bottle of brandy, which he had tucked away for this occasion. Then he dashed next door to one of his hangouts: the poker table at Houston's Fire Station No. 8. The fire captain eyed the cigars, smiled at Hughes, and turned to his crew, yelling, "Ring the bells, boys." The station's shrill brass chimes began to peal, echoing up and down the lower-middle-class neighborhood, bringing residents out into the damp, chilly night.

As the firemen gathered around for cigars and brandy, Hughes hoisted his glass and offered the toast, "To my son." Then he took a horse cab to the Western Union office in downtown Houston and dispatched dozens of telegrams to his family in Keokuk, Iowa, and to Allene's in Dallas. The congratulations sped back, accompanied by floral tributes, silver mugs, and trappings for the nursery.

In the hours following the birth of his son, Hughes told his fellow wildcatter Walter Sharp that his profligate days were at an end. He could no longer sweat his leisurely way along oil country, hoping the next hole he dug would finally make his fortune. Now he had to find a sure thing.

Three years would pass, however, before his lucky break: the invention of a newfangled tool that changed the nature of oil drilling.

Until this innovation, when oilmen attempted to reach the truly vast reservoirs of black gold, they were stymied by the unyielding granite shelf that lay underneath two thousand square miles of Louisiana and Texas. Their two-pronged drills were usually ground into nubbins as soon as they chewed into the bedrock. Yet just beneath lay an underground sea of petroleum that would pave the way for the era of the automobile, the age of the jet plane, and eventually, the exploration of space.

By 1908 more than a dozen inventors were racing to build a bedrock-piercing drill when Howard Hughes Sr. struck gold.

While some of the highest-paid engineers in America were searching for the perfect drill bit, Hughes realized that a series of bits, working off a single shaft, was the answer. He purchased a rudimentary prototype that had failed in field tests from an inventor named Granville A. Humason. But Hughes felt it could be perfected.

Hughes went home to his father's farm house in Keokuk, Iowa. On November 20, 1908, he sat at his childhood breakfast table with ten blocks of soft pine and a carving knife. The result was a drill prototype with a series of cone-shaped bits with 166 cutting edges—with the cones all rotating and scooping separately.

After patenting the drill bit, Hughes and his new partner Sharp, who had invested $1,500 and his own exhaustive expertise into the project, fashioned a metal version that they tested in a deserted Houston warehouse in mid-1909. As the rotating teeth tore through a ten-inch slab of granite, the two men whooped with glee. Their delight turned to astonishment when the bit pierced through the table it was sitting on and then ate through the concrete floor of the warehouse.

Shortly before dawn on a summer morning in 1909, Hughes and his crew loaded a locked wooden box onto a horse-drawn coach and disguised it under layers of burlap. They took it to a field at Goose Creek, not far from Houston. They removed the odd-looking metal device, attached it to a drill stem, and let it rip. For eleven hours it bore through fourteen feet of solid rock, cutting a thousand-foot well at a location given up as hopeless by all the major oil companies.

Their discovery would change the nature of oil exploration the world over.

Within ten years, the Hughes rock bit—also known as the Hughes rollerbit—would be used in 75 per cent of the world's oil wells. The drill bit would be the foundation of the Hughes family fortune, for a time the richest in Texas history. To broaden the base of his wealth even further, Hughes refused to sell the drill bits. Oil explorers large and small had to lease them at $30,000 per well. (Standard Oil would use fifteen thousand of the drills in its first decade.) Once a well was gushing, the bits were returned to the Sharp-Hughes Tool Company, where they were cleaned, sharpened, and leased again to other corporations. "Sheer genius," proclaimed William Stamps Farish, president of Standard Oil. "It was highway robbery, of course, but genius all the same."

Howard Sr. couldn't have known that his infant son would one day rule a billion-dollar empire. But he was all too aware of the power of money to corrupt. Even before the tool company's first major factory was built in 1909, Howard Sr. spent weeks drafting a clever will. It left his wife fully in charge—with mandated guidance from Howard Sr.'s brothers. The share for his only son, Howard Jr., was a fourth, to be held in trust until he turned twenty-one. As Hughes Sr. confessed to his sister-in-law, Annette, he feared his son would become a petroleum playboy—of the sort Houston was then fashioning by the hundreds.

He certainly wasn't shaping his son by hands-on parenting. During those first years of Howard Jr.'s life he had continued wandering from strike to strike. Despite his vow the night of his son's birth to give up carousing, Howard Sr. had returned to womanizing, and this would continue during the years he traveled to sell his drill bit. He was gone so often that by the time he decided to become a husband and father he found he was an intruder in a self-contained family of two.

"Allene and her son shared a bond so strong and so intimate that I never saw anything to equal it—before or since," recalled Dudley Sharp, Howard Jr.'s boyhood friend and the son of Walter Sharp. After grimy years in tent cities and a lonely existence in the Crawford Street house, Allene's son was the only secure touchstone of her life. While her husband gambled through the nights and raced from coast to coast hawking the drill bit, Allene pampered Howard Jr. as if he were a prize colt. The closeness was physical as well. From infancy, Howard often slept in his mother's room on a small trundle bed. At the least hint of a fever or the slightest sign of a rash, physicians were rushed to the house, no matter what hour.

Most mothers had abandoned Victorian health rituals in the nineteenth century. Not so Allene. "Stand still, Howard," she ordered each morning and evening. Surveying her naked son, she exhaustively checked his teeth, ears, genitals, elbows, and kneecaps. Then she checked the contents of his toilet. "Now you can flush," she would tell him. She saw to it that he had cod liver oil and Russian mineral oil in the morning and used Epsom salts in the evening. And each day she bathed him, from his toes to his ears, using strong lye soap.

It was a dark, troubling relationship that a psychologist would later describe as "emotionally incestuous."

In 1910, when profits from the tool company reached $500,000 a year, Hughes moved his family to a brick home on Yoakum Boulevard on the fashionable south side—an area of colonnaded mansions and rolling hills of lush green lawns. They joined the elite congregation of Christ Church Cathedral and became stalwarts of the Houston Country Club. They hosted elaborate formal dinners and summer garden parties. When Howard was old enough for school, he was sent to Houston's Prosso Academy, the school of the wealthy.

Howard Sr.'s spectacular rise as one of Texas's great tycoons made him a key player in the expanding universe of the oil and gas industry, especially when he became the sole owner of the tool company in 1915, after the death of Walter Sharp. From then on it was the Hughes Tool Company.

Chartered railroad cars carried Howard Sr. from boomtown to boomtown on marketing excursions that featured French champagne and gorgeously costumed party girls. He was soon lured into the rich old boys' network that was helping to make Houston an industrial center. Always the dandy, Howard Sr.'s wardrobe soon filled an entire room, replete with pinstriped business suits and linen and cavalry twill outfits for the summer.

For Allene, the trappings of wealth and entrée into all the correct clubs meant little. She was, after all, a daughter of one of the first families of Texas. But riches provided her with the means to mold her son into a Little Lord Fauntleroy, a misfit among the brash, hell-raising sons of most oil barons. Neighbors remembered him riding his first bicycle around and around his circular driveway, glancing enviously as boys sped past toward summer adventures on the bayou.

Allene knew she couldn't keep her husband by the hearth, but young Howard had no choice. He was soon enmeshed in a web of formality spun by his lonely mother. "Howard didn't treat his mother the way all of us treated our mothers," said a Dallas cousin, Martha Potts, who recalled a trip Allene organized for Howard and his cousins—a jaunt to the seaside in nearby Galveston. "When we returned and all started to scatter to our rooms, Howard came up to his mother and said, 'Thank you, Mother, for so much fun today.' It made the rest of us feel like country bumpkins."

Allene's possessiveness kept Howard alienated from many of his class-mates. According to Prosso director James R. Richardson, Howard was taunted by the other boys, who called him "sissy." Maintaining that Howard had been "brought up to feel his superiority," Richardson urged Howard Sr. to extract his son from his mother's side. "He needs to feel he is a part of the world, instead of the larger or better parts."

When Howard was ten, Allene used her social clout to have him crowned King of the May at Christ Church Cathedral's annual spring car-nival. Average upper-class boys scorned that sissified honor. Howard endured it. A surviving photo of the event captures his disdain as he glares from beneath his paper-crown—awkward in a dandified toga.

Only a few children broke through the wall of loneliness Allene had built around her "only chick." Those who did saw early flashes of both genius and deep emotional turmoil. "You can always notice differences in children, and Howard was different," surmised Elva Kalb Dumas, who used to look on as her younger brother played with six-year-old Howard. "Howard was a strange boy. Very shy and very lonely," echoed Dudley Sharp.

What he lacked on the playground, though, he made up for by being highly inventive. Taking note of her son's mechanical prowess, Allene once said proudly, "He thought a puppy dog was a machine of some sort." During his years at the Prosso elementary school, Howard turned ordinary childhood games into experiments.

"One afternoon we were using a great, high swing in Dudley Sharp's backyard," recalled Mary Cullinan Cravens. "Dudley and I were trying to see who could go the highest without jumping out." Looking down from her dizzy perch in the air, Mary Cullinan saw that Howard was making calculations after every jump. "The rest of us were doing it for fun," Mrs. Cravens recalled. "But Howard was trying to work out the curve of where you would land. He wanted to know the mechanics of everything, even at that early age."

At the age of eleven, Howard Hughes built the first wireless broadcasting set in Houston so that he could communicate with ships in the Gulf of Mexico. As Dudley Sharp discovered, Howard tracked and recorded sounds from these ships, found out that these bleeps and dashes were part of the Morse code, and then taught himself the code overnight. "He was talking to ships' officers the very next day," Sharp recalled.

According to Sharp, Hughes's interests often became all-consuming. "One day we both decided to buy saxophones and started taking lessons. At first all Howard could do was make weird noises, but he practiced night and day and became proficient in a number of weeks."

It was during his saxophone epoch that Howard took a pair of the instruments to a camp for boys on the Brazos River. The saxes were well disguised in his gear, and no one noticed him sneak them into his tent. Then at three o'clock on the first night out, camp director Robert Bryson heard a loud, insistent wailing that sounded like the cries of some odd animal. On investigating, he found Howard sitting erect in his small tent, practicing chords on his sax.

Bryson gave Hughes four demerits and ordered him to stand guard alone the next night. "This time play your sax very quietly," Bryson warned Howard.

Hughes Sr. built his son a workshop behind the big house—a dim, oily haven with both woodworking and electronic equipment. There was but one standing rule: Howard had to leave the shop spotless after every time he used it. Even one thing out of order and he was locked out for a week. Violations occurred only twice.

But this shop, while allowing Howard to sharpen his precocious engineering skills, also isolated him further from his contemporaries. "He spent weeks amusing himself with these little inventions. That meant he was in a world by himself even when his parents were still living, even when he was a young boy," Sharp remembered.

Hughes's adolescent creations included a motorized bicycle (a twelve-year-old Howard posed solemnly by his invention for a photographer from the *Houston Post*), an intercom system for the Yoakum Boulevard mansion, and a telegraph connection between his home and Dudley's four blocks away. "My son is going to be a genius," Allene would gloat. "Little Howard is going to be outstanding in some field."

As the Hughes family fortunes rose, Howard's mechanical passions escalated. One day when he was fourteen he showed up at the Stutz agency in downtown Houston to see the latest Bearcat. In 1919, it was one of the country's most glamorous cars. He paced around the gleaming motorcar, deep in thought. Finally, he turned to salesman Jack Horner and said, "I want this. Will you please send it out to my house today?"

The startled salesman nodded and disappeared into a back room where he telephoned Howard Sr. and asked for approval. Told the price, a then hefty $7,000, and the speed potential, a very racy ninety miles an hour, Howard Sr. merely asked, "Did my son say what he wanted to do with it?"

"Yes, sir," said Horner. "He said he wanted to tear it down and put it back together again."

"Very well," said Big Howard, as he had come to be known. "Send it out."

Howard took apart the roadster and reassembled it in less than a month.

Another hallmark of Howard's childhood, one that would cast long shadows into the future, was his repeated bouts of ill health. He became a uniquely talented hypochondriac.

Soon, Allene was regularly spiriting her son away from Houston's vile heat and humidity. Of course, these emotionally charged journeys to faraway resorts further isolated Howard from companions of his own age.

His versatile repertoire of ailments, including chills and strange episodes of malaise, stumped even the best physicians. They also allowed him to cling to the sheets in his corner room. By the age of ten, Howard had become what modern psychoanalysts call "an avoider," a person who uses psychosomatic illnesses to escape from life.

Hughes's hypochondria served Allene's purposes as well. When Howard Sr.'s womanizing escalated, she used her son's health as a bargaining tool to bring the philanderer to her side. If Howard Jr. contracted a cold or broke out in hives, Senior came running home from Manhattan or from the oil fields of Louisiana or from Los Angeles, where the tool company had recently opened a new branch.

Howard Jr. learned early that the way to get what he wanted was to feign illness. Both parents rushed to his side at the mere suggestion of it.

But Allene was more than a protective mother: she was a phobic, hysterical overseer. "Her reactions weren't normal," said Dr. Raymond Fowler, who worked for three years to provide a psychological profile of Howard Hughes for his estate after his death. Explained Fowler, "A normal mother would take her son's temperature or check his symptoms and then decide whether or not to send him to school. But she kept him home at the slightest complaint."

Fowler, who reconstructed Hughes's life from hundreds of documents and interviews, noted, "He was not a robust child, didn't gain weight like other children. So that frightened her. Because she couldn't have another child, her worry was even more intense."

Allene used her son's "delicate constitution" to bind him, keeping him by her side at all times. Most nights Howard slept in his mother's room, whereas his father bunked in an upstairs study. On their frequent trips to the East Coast, Howard Jr. also shared a room with Allene. Howard's father often took another suite—sometimes down the hall.

Allene's sister Annette noted, "Sonny [young Howard's nickname] did not spend a single night away from his mother until he was ten years old. Even on trips to relatives, he slept in whatever room she occupied." If anyone spoke out about this tendency to overprotect, Allene launched into a diatribe about little Howard's susceptibility to germs.

This unhealthy bond was broken for the first time in 1916, when Howard Jr., then eleven, surprisingly asked permission to attend a boys' camp in the Pocono Mountains of Pennsylvania. It was founded by former U.S. Army Rough Rider Daniel Carter Beard (who also helped to found the Boy Scouts). Beard transformed it into a survival school of sorts for eastern preppies who had been pampered from birth.

These scions of some of America's top families were thrown together in a six-week course designed to turn them into Buckskin Men. "We took these silver-spooners and roughed them up," Beard later wrote. "They had to get along or they wouldn't make it through the course."

Allene and Howard Sr. reluctantly entrusted their son to Beard and his camp—just barely. With little reason, both hovered nearby in the East: Senior making work for himself in Manhattan and Allene stopping at a series of resorts close to the Poconos. Both corresponded daily with Beard.

Ten days after the camp opened, Howard Sr. sent Beard a clipping about a polio epidemic in New York state. "These clippings show you how easily these violent germs are carried even by a well person," Howard Sr. wrote.

Even before Beard could answer, Howard Sr. had heard rumors that a boy in camp had contracted a "flulike virus." Both parents were ready to yank Howard out when Beard assured them by wire: "You can be satisfied that the boy has been adequately quarantined. Don't worry about little Howard."

Three days later, Allene wrote: "I know my dear boy must be lonely for me, and I would appreciate it if you can help him over his homesickness and his super sensitiveness."

Beard's matter-of-fact reply must have been unwelcome. "He is an interesting little chap . . . he has shown no signs of homesickness at all and seems very happy."

Allene was outraged. She refused to believe that her "one little chick" could survive without her. On August 9 she wrote, asking to break the camp's rules and see Howard for a "few precious hours." Explained Allene: "His letters are so short and unsatisfactory that I feel I must see him. Otherwise I cannot let him remain any longer in your camp." She gave no credence to a previous report from the camp doctor, who declared Howard in tip-top shape.

After nearly six weeks away from home, Howard had become sun-bronzed and sturdy. With the rest of the camp's first-timers—the "tenderfoots"—he had boated on Lake Teedyuskung and camped out overnight. He had learned to make fires without matches and, no small feat for a boy of privilege, to fry up a breakfast of bacon and flapjacks over an open fire. In "scoutcraft," he excelled in bird studies.

Nevertheless, his mother ignored Dan Beard's protests and pulled him from the camp, fleeing to the Cleveland estate of her brother-in-law, Felix Hughes. She explained to a crestfallen Howard that she had barely rescued him from the ravages of a polio epidemic "raging across the country." She sobbed, "It could kill you. You don't understand the danger you were in at that camp."

What Howard did understand was the humiliation of being pulled from an overnight trek and of hearing the snickering of the other boys as he packed up his clothes, his mineral oil, his fussy and elaborate wardrobe, and his unnecessary satchel of patent medicines.

Soon even Cleveland and Uncle Felix's immaculate house were deemed potential health hazards. So mother and son continued their flight from noxious clouds of imaginary germs sweeping across America. One evening Allene sat Howard down and graphically described the physical horrors he would endure if the polio virus were to catch up with him. With his photographic memory, Howard absorbed every detail and retained them until the end of his life.

But he still begged to return to Beard's camp the following summer. "This year I'll get my woodcrafter's badge," he told Dudley Sharp. "And I could even become a junior counselor." Sharp had never heard such independence and joy from his friend.

Allene reluctantly sent him back to camp. She had no plausible excuse not to; the outbreak of infantile paralysis had abated. But she immediately posted another pitiful letter to Beard. "Have the doctor keep an eye on little Howard. And particularly watch his teeth and his feet." She also forbade the camp to let Howard eat any flapjacks.

She was not unaware that her suffocating love was making her son the constant target of derision. The day Howard arrived at the mountain camp she wrote, "Please help Howard take all the teasing which he gets from the other boys. It must be terrible for him."

By the time Howard entered South End Junior High in the fall of 1919, he had grown tall, filled out, and was developing broad shoulders. He also had the beginnings of dark, brooding good looks. Still regarded as a loner and a mechanical wizard by his classmates, he nonetheless made efforts to branch out. He joined the YMCA basketball team and practiced swimming and diving.

But he could not shake his mother's firmly instilled phobias. His neurotic dependence on infirmity turned deadly serious on the morning of April 10, 1920, when he was fourteen.

When he failed to appear for breakfast, Allene called for him. Sonny didn't answer—a breach of Hughes family etiquette. Rushing upstairs, she found Howard moaning and delirious. Allene began a probing inspection of her son's body, starting with his eyes and teeth, working downward. When she came to his legs, she noticed that the left dangled as if lifeless and that the other was entangled in the sheets. "Son, can you stand up?" Allene asked.

"My legs won't move," Howard answered.

In many ways, Allene's relationship with both Howard Sr. and her son had been careening toward this tragic moment for more than a decade. Her prophecy of doom had been fulfilled. She rushed into action.

The payoff for Howard was immediate. His father hastily returned from a gambling palace on the Mississippi; Allene cleared her substantial social calendar; concerned relatives converged on the Yoakum Boulevard mansion. Houston's Dr. Frederick Lummis, who was then courting Annette, was summoned to Howard's bedside but was bewildered by a singular absence of any real symptoms. The boy had no fever, no swelling, no abnormalities in his blood work. Yet he couldn't walk. A steady parade of eminent Texas medics, with Allene hovering over their shoulders, were equally puzzled.

Both Allene and Howard Sr. believed that the polio virus they had been trying to outrun since 1912 had caught up with them at last. Howard Sr. wired the eminent Rockefeller Institute for Medical Research and offered its director, Dr. Simon Flexner, "any amount of money to cure our dear boy." Flexner dispatched his right-hand man, Dr. H. T. Chickering, a pioneer in polio research, to Houston. He moved into the bedroom next to Howard's and subjected the stricken young man to a regimen of drugs and physical therapy.

For eight harrowing weeks, the Hugheses, the Ganos, and the Lummises lived in a state of suspended animation as Chickering coaxed Howard out of his stupor. It took three weeks to lure him into a wheelchair for trips up and down Yoakum Boulevard. When Houston's crushing summer heat and humidity descended, Allene and Chickering escaped with their patient to Mackinac Island in Michigan for a month of even more intense therapy.

According to Howard's Dallas cousin Mrs. John Wharton, it was this mystery illness that brought about the deafness that would plague Howard his entire life—in effect, cutting him off socially from those around him, leading many to wrongly think of him as cool and aloof. (The adult Hughes confided to his lovers, including Katharine Hepburn and Faith Domergue, that a diving accident during his teenage years triggered the deafness. But the trait may have been inherited; other members of his family, including Rupert Hughes, were hard of hearing.)

Some Hughes relatives later believed he had been stricken with diphtheria, scarlet fever, or possibly meningitis. But Dr. Chickering suspected Howard was feigning illness and that there was no physiological cause for "this hysterical paralysis."

When Howard Sr. saw the diagnosis, it jolted him into action. Perhaps too late, he decided to weaken the dangerous bond between Allene and their son. Thinking his son would do better away from home, Howard Sr.

packed him off to the Fessenden Academy, a prestigious prep school outside of Boston. While Allene remained in Houston, Howard Sr. personally escorted his son to the school.

Not surprisingly, Howard's greatest obstacle was his shyness. For the first few months he retreated whenever he was approached by other boys who populated the elite academy. Classmates later depicted him as awkward, shy, and lonely at Fessenden. When called upon to recite poetry in class—a Fessenden essential—he stuttered and mumbled with hands trembling at his sides. On one occasion he chose Oliver Wendell Holmes's "Old Ironsides," the shortest poem he could find. He started out whispering, and when the teacher said, "Speak up, I can't hear you," Howard started shouting.

Perhaps from this shyness, his affinity for late-night hours began at Fessenden, where he would sneak out of the dorm at one or two in the morning and climb through a basement window in the gymnasium. Once inside, he paced back and forth, sometimes working out his homework on a small pocket notebook. Sometimes he repeated over and over again: "You can do it, Howard. You can do it." An instructor once found him in the center of the basketball court with his fists clenched at his sides screaming out his French homework and listening as it echoed off the walls.

In the beginning he also continued to ask for the sort of preferential treatment he was accustomed to. First, he demanded unlimited funds. A compliant Howard Sr. sent a letter of credit: "Please allow Howard to purchase anything he desires . . . charge my account liberally for such." The headmaster would later convince Senior to limit his son's spending to the level of his fellow students.

Accustomed to indulgent tutors, Howard also complained about "the crushing loads of homework" required at the academy. Allene pleaded with the headmaster to ease up. Frederick James Fessenden replied: "It's important for Howard to do what's required of him. It isn't easy for a boy who has never attended boarding school and who has been so indulged at home."

Though he would spend only a year at Fessenden, it was there that Howard was introduced to what would become an all-consuming passion. During a weekend visit he talked his father into taking him to a New England river where a seaplane bobbed. Reluctantly, Howard Sr. let his son take a brief flight—at a cost of $5. A defining moment, it changed Howard's life—and, in years to come, the very course of aviation.

When Howard graduated from the equivalent of Fessenden's eighth grade with "distinction," Howard Sr. felt his experiment had succeeded. The process of weaning his son from Allene's domination had taken its first strides forward.

To finish the job, Howard Sr. enrolled his son in the Thacher School, near Santa Barbara, California. Before the school year was out, though, the mother-son bond would be irretrievably broken—by tragedy.

CHAPTER 2

SHADOW OF DEATH

ON AN AUGUST DAY IN 1921, HOWARD JUMPED ABOARD THE SANTA FE Zephyr and settled into a private compartment. He wore khaki pants, a sports shirt, and cowboy boots. In his monogrammed suitcases were Levi's, sweatshirts, a baseball mitt, and cleated track shoes. Finally, at age sixteen, he was outfitted like any other Texas boy. These were only outer trappings, but they signified steps toward real emancipation from his mother's smothering love and control.

During the summer, despite Allene's disapproval, a brigade of tutors had coached him in baseball and basketball to prepare him for his new school, force-feeding him skills that most boys learn at the corner sandlot.

As his train chugged away from the swelter of Houston, Howard smiled. Ahead lay Southern California—that exotic playground of Spanish tiled villas, pounding azure waves, and movie stars.

Located in Ojai Valley, just inland from the coast, the Thacher School had once been a ranch of orange and avocado trees. But Sherman Day Thacher, a rugged footballer from Yale, couldn't eke a living from the 168 acres of sagebrush. So he founded a prep school instead. This spartan ranch was a fitting site for an academy that was geared to disciplining rich boys. This was one reason Howard Sr. chose it.

Getting his son accepted, though, hadn't been easy. When Howard Sr.

first approached Thacher about his son, the school was full, with a substantial waiting list. "I can't accept that," Howard Sr. told Thacher. "My own life has been a constant uphill fight. I'm determined to see Howard into Thacher." He offered to build a new dormitory or a gymnasium. Sherman Day Thacher declined, but money probably changed hands in some manner. In any case, Howard became the sixty-first Thacher preppie in an institution that guaranteed "no more than sixty students per quarter."

Senior also had an unwritten agreement with Thacher: Howard was to finally stand on his own two feet. There would be no more special treatment, no more health alerts, no more scholastic dispensations.

Thrown into a room with three others, Howard formed tentative friendships. He bought a horse, played a little polo, and performed in the first school play of the season. When evening came, he sometimes galloped off into the scrub oak-filled ravines.

When Thacher informed Howard Sr. that the prescription was working, the elder Hughes was delighted. In late fall, however, Allene broke her promise and began to interfere once again. She insisted on special medical checkups and lobbied constantly for her son to receive preferential treatment. "I think it is awfully hard for an only child to adjust himself in school and to make friends as he should," she wrote Thacher.

When Allene learned that her son had suffered an insignificant boil and a minor scratch on one of his rides, none other than the esteemed Dr. Chickering was rushed from the Rockefeller Institute to the campus in Ojai. "I found Howard quite well and happy," Dr. Chickering wrote. "He was not in the least ill."

Allene's renewed preoccupation with Howard's health came at a time when she herself was adrift, both physically and emotionally. She wandered the Yoakum Boulevard house all alone. Howard Sr.'s private railroad car continued to speed from Houston to Manhattan, from Chicago to Los Angeles on sales expeditions. With two dozen varieties of the rock bit in production and another dozen in development, he was in demand everywhere.

On the West Coast, his tool company soirees were aided by contacts provided by his brother Rupert. The physical opposite of the tall, lean, anxious-looking Howard Sr., Rupert was short and plump with cherubic features. A prolific writer for magazines and newspapers, Rupert had found success as a screenwriter in Hollywood. During his visits to Southern California, Hughes Sr. was a frequent guest at Rupert's *Arabian Nights*-style home on Los Feliz Boulevard. So were countless glamorous actresses of the day.

Rumors soon made their way back to Houston about Senior's dalliances with silent stars Mae Murray, "the girl with the bee-stung lips," and Eleanor Boardman, the former Kodak Girl on advertising posters. Hughes Sr. was even said to have carried on with bewitching screen temptress Alla Nazimova, the wild-eyed Russian émigrée whose sprawling Sunset Boulevard estate was known as a setting for her dalliances with other women. The tool company's parties at the Ambassador Hotel often lasted until dawn, fueled by Hughes's fabled pre-Prohibition wine cellar and a lifetime stock of prime 1915 bourbon whiskey.

Still, during the Christmas of 1921, the dutiful Allene presided over a warm family gathering at the Yoakum mansion, fully decorated for the first time since it was built. Though Allene and Howard Sr. had been growing apart, the holiday was an occasion for them to renew their ties. Their reunion brought an unexpected result: in February doctors informed Allene that she was pregnant.

Howard Sr. was initially elated. He had come to believe that his wife needed another child to compensate for Howard's absence. He also felt his son needed a sibling—that the burden of being a cosseted only child was stifling him.

But the pregnancy became a cause for alarm; the rigors of Howard's birth had ravaged Allene's system. Worse, it was discovered to be a tubular pregnancy. With the baby developing outside the uterus, there was danger of rupture and internal bleeding. Imminently life-threatening, the pregnancy had to be terminated.

Relatives, even Allene's sister, Annette, were informed only that Allene was entering the hospital for "minor" surgery. Howard Jr. wasn't informed at all. At 2:47 on the afternoon of March 29, 1922, after Dr. Gavin Hamilton administered a gas anesthetic to Howard's mother, her heart stopped. Allene was just thirty-nine years old.

Less than an hour after his wife died, Howard Sr. met with his sister-in-law and exacted a vow of silence from her. The real reason for Allene's emergency operation and the rushed nature of the proceedings were to remain a secret—particularly from his son.

A shaken and grieving Howard Sr. dispatched two telegrams, one to his brother Rupert, the other to Howard. He also telephoned Sherman Day Thacher, who personally took his cablegram to Howard's bunk room.

"Mother is ill," the cable read. "Rupert will bring you home to Houston. Love Howard R. Hughes."

Young Howard did his best to be strong, but he sensed tragedy. His face revealed his unspoken fears as he climbed into his uncle's Hollywood limousine. Shortly before they caught the train for Houston, Rupert put his hand on his nephew's shoulder. "I hate to be the one to tell you, but you have to know. Your mother is dead." Seeing the look of shock on his nephew's face, Rupert explained, "She didn't survive an operation."

Howard hunched down and looked at the floor. He fought back tears.

"My poor brother had suffered so much that telling Howard would be too much for him," Rupert said later. "So I did it as gently as possible."

Howard Sr. had chased furiously after wealth and position in order to give the genteel Allene all the trappings so prized in southern society. Now he sat in the sprawling Yoakum Boulevard mansion with its Georgian silver, Viennese crystal, and lush damask draperies. Traces of Allene's flowered perfumes hung in the air.

Her all-pervading presence was too much. Howard Sr. packed up his closetful of hand-tailored suits, his gleaming Oxford shoes, his scores of Egyptian-made cotton shirts, his platinum and gold watches, and his sterling silver brushes and combs. He had to leave Yoakum.

For the rest of his life, the imposing but impersonal Rice Hotel served as his official Houston address—on those occasions that he was in town. "Houston haunted him and so did the Yoakum Boulevard house," Annette recalled. "My sister's death left him with a collection of phobias he could not seem to overcome." Some felt Hughes Sr. was too heartbroken to return. Others thought he was too guilt-ridden.

Still, Hughes Sr. was a realist. He knew he would need help in raising Howard.

So he climbed the stairs at Yoakum to Annette Gano's suite of rooms. She had joined the Hughes household back in 1919. Eight years younger than Allene, she was a dauntless adventuress who had graduated from Wellesley College and followed the World War I troops to the western front, where she ran an early USO outpost and nurses' aid station. In Houston, she had become a tireless philanthropist. It must have been a humbling experience for Hughes Sr. to have to woo his sister-in-law to be a substitute mother for Howard. Annette had been a confidante to her older sister, witness to Allene's heartbreak during Howard's philandering.

Now he was asking her not just to give up her life in Houston but to leave the side of her fiancé, Dr. Lummis, and move with Howard to California. Howard Sr. begged Annette, who was thirty-one, to remain single, "and devote the rest of your life to raising Howard."

"He was frantic, emotional, and possessed," she recalled. "I told him I would give him one year. Then I would marry. I also told him it wasn't good to let this boy live with a little old lady, which I considered myself to be."

At the funeral, held in the muted splendor of Allene's house, father and son, in matching black suits, stood between Annette Gano and the flamboyant Rupert.

Howard returned to Thacher, but his father, once so strong and self-contained, collapsed under the weight of this separation. He telephoned Thacher several days later, requesting Howard's return. "I'm terribly lonely without him," he confessed. "I can't get a grip on myself."

Thacher was sympathetic but firm. "I feel it would be the very worst thing for this young man," he wrote Howard Sr. Privately, Thacher, who had been redeeming spoiled young men for two decades, believed that the academy was Howard's last chance to become a socially well-integrated young man.

Remarkably, in the months following Allene's death, Howard Jr. appeared to recover rapidly from his sorrow. His professors noted that his mother's death seemed to have freed him from a great emotional burden. One pointed out that even his intense shyness began to abate.

A powerful tug-of-war erupted as Thacher fought Hughes Sr. to keep Howard in school through the end of the school year. Thacher convened a meeting of the teachers closest to Howard, and after listening to their counsel, he wrote Howard Sr. that his son, "needs more than most boys the contact with other fellows such as he gets here." Added Thacher, "I think your desire and tendency to indulge him in every way would probably be very hard for him to resist."

Six Thacher professors signed a petition in an attempt to rescue Howard. It concluded: "This boy truly needs to remain in school."

Thacher's final letter stated, "Pulling Howard from school would be treating him in a special and peculiar manner, and he needs to be treated like any other boy."

Thacher was trying to throw this emotionally churning student a life raft, but Howard Sr. was either too selfish or too distraught to respond. He removed his son from Thacher anyway.

*   *   *

Father, son, and aunt began new lives in Southern California.

Howard Jr. and Annette settled into a Spanish colonial bungalow surrounded by orchids and bougainvillea, tucked into the lush gardens of Pasadena's Vista Del Arroyo, a hotel retreat for blue bloods and polo players. At night, waiters appeared, pushing carts piled with sumptuous dishes. In the morning, a full-time maid bustled about the rooms, changing sheets and bringing in fresh floral arrangements.

Senior summoned tailors and had his son outfitted in formal suits, tennis clothes, a golfing wardrobe, and dozens of pairs of shoes, all of them specifically made for Howard.

Howard Sr. also looked for a new school for his son. And once again he bought what others less wealthy and powerful couldn't. He offered rich donations to the prestigious California Institute of Technology on the condition that they accept Howard as an unaccredited student. Soon several of the nation's leading engineers and scientists were tutoring the rich kid from Texas. "Mr. Hughes bribed the school," Annette later admitted. "Howard took regular upper-division classes despite his lack of a high school diploma." She also commented dryly, "I don't know how much he learned there."

Howard was learning one lesson, though: money could buy almost anything. At a time when middle-class families lived on $5,000 a year, Howard received a check for that amount as his monthly allowance. His clothes, living expenses, food, and entertainment were paid for separately. In addition, a black Duesenberg limo and chauffeur were at his disposal.

Annette persuaded Howard's favorite Dallas cousin, Kitty Callaway, to leave Dallas and move into the Arroyo for a while, "so that poor Howard wouldn't be all alone." Howard and Kitty spent hours together going to silent-picture houses.

Howard soon adopted a leisurely routine: tinkering with Cal Tech scientists all morning, tennis at noon, golf in the early afternoon, and movies for the rest of the day—sometimes triple features. And three days a week, Howard—who still cherished the memory of the $5 plane trip he had taken while at Fessenden—went to flight school. "He exhausted the aviators with pressing questions about the theory and dynamics of flight," Annette remembered. "We only guessed at how serious this would become."

The teenager stuffed his pockets with small brown notebooks in which he recorded the gist of what he learned in the laboratory, in the silent-film theaters, and in the air. At age seventeen, the great themes of Howard Hughes's life were already forming: movies and aviation.

In the meantime, once he established the ersatz family unit, Howard Sr. took lavish connecting suites at the Ambassador Hotel. It was a wild, posh gathering place of Los Angeles's Roaring Twenties, where Hughes Sr. quickly became the merriest widower in a town loaded with merry widowers.

He spent so wildly that Hughes Tool Company executives nervously watched the corporation's cash reserves dip below $100,000. "He spent gigantic sums on flowers, jewels, and clothing, all of them on glamorous women," said Suzanne Finstad, a lawyer and author who worked on the estate battle following Howard Jr.'s death.

At one point, Howard Sr. chartered three railroad cars and transported a party of fourteen to the Kentucky Derby. He would spend weeks in New York, and sailed his yacht, a monster with six staterooms, in leisurely fashion around the Caribbean Sea and through the Panama Canal.

All the while, the son he had pulled from Thacher to help him overcome his pangs of loss remained marooned at the Vista Del Arroyo—fatherless and directionless.

By the end of 1923, Howard Sr. roused himself from the endless party of the 1920s long enough to realize that he was leading his eighteen-year-old son down the same path. Hollywood and its intoxicating pleasures were having an effect on movie-mad Howard Jr.

Rupert Hughes was now directing movies as well as writing them. Whenever possible, Howard Jr. wangled invitations to his sets, where he invariably met the leading ladies. Junior also silently stargazed at the Sunday luncheons held at Rupert's home.

Life in Houston did not compare. Still, Hughes Sr. gave up his huge suites in Hollywood and New York and returned to bring new life to the tool company and to coerce his son into pursuing serious studies at Houston's prestigious Rice University. It didn't matter that Howard Jr. didn't quite have the required scholastic background; Howard Sr. reached into his pockets and poured money into a university building fund.

But once back in Houston, Howard Jr. didn't concentrate on studying engineering. Instead, he was spotted on the golf course and burning up the road in his Duesenberg. He certainly had the money to indulge himself. Houston society was stunned when Hughes increased his son's allowance from $5,000 per month to $5,000 a week. And society was bemused when

Howard Sr.'s yacht sailed into moonlit Sylvan Beach, where the dance pavilion, complete with sixty-piece orchestra, was rented for Howard Jr. to impress some visiting debutantes.

However much money he spent on his son, though, he was still unwilling to live with him at Yoakum. Once again he talked his sister-in-law Annette into playing parent. By this time she had married Lummis, despite Howard Sr.'s objections. He even cruelly boycotted her wedding after promising to be the one to give her away. Now he wanted her once again to put her life on hold, and that of her husband, to care for Howard Jr.

"After all that time, he still couldn't return to his own house," Annette said in a 1977 deposition. Once again she moved to Yoakum, this time accompanied by her husband.

Senior's return to the tool company, Howard's curriculum at Rice, the instant family at Yoakum, the cars, the golfing weekends: they all turned out to be parts of an empty facade.

On January 14, 1924, Hughes Sr. attended a luncheon with half a dozen oil barons to discuss the expanding oil fields in Southern California, where the tool company, or Toolco as it was called, was opening a factory. Senior's right-hand man, R. C. Kuldell, a former army colonel, said later that his boss seemed particularly driven that winter and "was only beginning to deal with the taxing new demands for the drill bit in Europe and the Middle East."

After the business luncheon Hughes spent more than an hour with S. P. Brown, the Toolco sales manager, discussing ways to speed up manufacture of the drill bits (there were now more than 150 sizes and types). For most of the meeting Hughes paced back and forth, reading aloud from reams of sales data. Then he sank into his large leather chair, gasping for air.

Before Brown could rush to his side, Hughes rose to his feet, grabbed for the arm of his chair, then crumpled to the floor with the sales papers still in his hands.

"He died instantly," the *Houston Post* reported in a page-one story. At fifty-four, Hughes Sr. had suffered a fatal heart attack.

A who's who of petroleum executives converged on Houston for the funeral, but Howard Jr. withdrew from the pomp surrounding his father's death. He closeted himself in his corner room at Yoakum, surrounded by his youthful trappings—the ham radio set that had so impressed his father, parts from the Stutz Bearcat, and the family photos he had taken with his own box camera while still a toddler.

Howard was a pale presence at the funeral on January 16, his six-foot-three frame towering above the other mourners in the library of the family house. Massive floral arrangements, including one from the local police department, surrounded the gray casket. A church quartet sang, and according to the *Houston Press*, a mockingbird outside a window "sang a farewell melody." The Reverend Peter Gray Sears, the Christ Church director who had buried Howard's mother less than two years ago, performed similarly sad duties again.

Later that day, while Annette dealt with a steady stream of mourners, Howard retreated to his father's study. The night before, he had found two wills in his father's safe. The first, signed only weeks after his mother's death, gave him 75 per cent of the estate and a million-dollar package of stocks and bonds. Twenty-five per cent went to the other relatives.

The second, which Howard Sr. had hidden from his son, cut Howard's share to slightly less than 50 per cent. The remainder and controlling interest in the tool company empire were divided among Howard's relatives.

To Hughes's relief, his father had not signed the revised document. He slipped the new codicil into a pile of his own papers, where it was found three decades later.

Still, the young man felt betrayed by his father's last, unsigned will. He had long felt like a pawn of both parents and resented his father's last attempt to manipulate him. "My father never suggested that I do something; he just told me. He shoved things down my throat, and I had to like it," Howard once said.

On this afternoon, he unleashed years of pent-up frustration and anger. As mourners milled about the rooms of Yoakum, speaking in hushed voices, Howard slid behind his father's mahogany desk and yanked open drawer after drawer, rifling the contents and tossing reams of notes and mementos into a roaring fire nearby.

He was unprepared for the discovery he made in a small locked black box, hidden behind a bulging collection of files. In the bottom, underneath his parents' marriage license and a scattering of yellowed love letters, was a letter his mother had written to his father the night before her death.

In it Allene indicated that she had had a premonition of her own mortality. And in her elegant, slanting hand, Howard's mother expressed her continued and "eternal love" for Howard Sr. Writing that she knew about her husband's relationship with movie actress Eleanor Boardman, Allene sincerely added, "I understand and totally forgive you."

Howard tucked the letter away. He later admitted that he was haunted by his mother's stoic pain over his father's infidelity.

"He told Dudley Sharp and myself that he would never speak of this again, and I never heard him do so," said Noah Dietrich, the accountant who became Hughes's right-hand man shortly afterward. Dietrich would never forget the "intense sorrow" in Hughes's eyes when he had talked of the letter.

After a tour of Europe with Dudley Sharp, Howard returned to Houston for a showdown with his relatives, especially Uncle Rupert, who wanted to assume the role of guardian to the eighteen-year-old. Howard now saw his relatives as potential gold diggers. "I want them out of my life," he raged at his friend Sharp. "And I'm gonna find somebody to run that damn tool company as well." It was, after all, his father's—not his.

He hauled out the massive tool company ledgers and pored over the columns to determine how much ready cash was available. He had a bold plan, one that belied his years and experience. By mortgaging the Yoakum Boulevard mansion and borrowing on the tool company's considerable assets, Hughes could buy out his relatives, with their permission.

He headed for Hollywood, where he had a series of ugly arguments with his grandparents and Rupert. During one standoff Howard vehemently insisted to Rupert, "I will not return to school! And I will not accept a guardian. In fact, I'm prepared to buy you all out and to assume control of the tool company."

A long silence followed.

Rupert finally spoke: "You can't buy us out. You're still a minor."

"Not for long," Hughes responded. "I'll have myself declared an adult."

"He was obsessed with this," Annette recalled. "And he paid no attention to any of us."

Rupert and the other relatives indulged the young heir. Initially, there seemed to be little chance that he would be declared an adult at eighteen. But with the help of his father's attorney, Frank Andrews, Hughes had discovered a peculiar provision in the Texas civil code that allowed a minor (over eighteen) to be declared an adult if he could convince the court he could handle his own affairs.

Hughes unleashed a clever, persistent campaign by prevailing upon

Superior Court Judge Walter Montieth, a well-connected socialite who had known Howard as a child. Over leisurely games of golf at the Houston Country Club and lavish lunches at the city's Rice Hotel, Howard pleaded his case. Montieth questioned Hughes endlessly: about the oil industry, about future technology that might affect the drill bit, and about the hundreds of intricacies necessary to run an economic empire. "There wasn't a single question he couldn't answer," Montieth told Annette. "I was absolutely convinced." Montieth was also assured that the young heir would carry out his father's final wishes, detailed in his will, and continue with his schooling.

On December 24, 1924, his nineteenth birthday, Hughes stepped before Judge Montieth. He spoke briefly, "All I want is something I'm going to get anyway. I just want it three years earlier." Then he looked up at Judge Montieth and lied earnestly, "And I plan to return to Rice University to complete my education."

A series of family conferences followed. One by one, the other heirs accepted cash for their shares in the Hughes Tool Company. The total buy-out cost Hughes $325,000, all the cash reserves that the corporation possessed.

Only one hurdle remained: Hughes needed the blessing of his mother's two sisters, Janet Houstoun and the indomitable Annette. "I was dead set against it," Annette later recalled. Like Rupert, she challenged her nephew, at one point even declaring, "You will never amount to anything unless you get an education!"

Annette knew her nephew wasn't going to return to class or make his career at the tool company: "I knew his intention was to go to Hollywood." And so she agreed to give her blessing if he would agree to a compromise.

Explained Annette: "I could not send him with all that money to Hollywood alone. Not with all those vampire movie people."

Howard Hughes, Jr., was to be married.

CHAPTER 3

THE BARTERED BRIDE

EARLY ON THE STEAMY MORNING OF JUNE 2, 1925, A BRIGADE OF florists descended upon the Houston mansion of oil magnate William Stamps Farish on fashionable Remington Lane. They bustled in and out of the English garden, bearing great bunches of pink hydrangeas and tub after tub of blush-colored roses that were fashioned into a nuptial bower and woven into a celebratory arch. Other technicians strung dozens of smilax blossoms into feathery ropes and hung them on either side of a garden walkway.

Overseeing this rapidly assembled pomp and circumstance was a large, handsome woman named Libby Rice Farish, 39-year-old sister of the bride and a friend of Howard's Aunt Annette. As the matron of honor, she was already dressed in apple green chiffon and antique rose point lace— shades that precisely matched the hydrangeas. Thanks to the Rice family pedigree and the wealth of her husband, the chairman and founder of Standard Oil, Mrs. Farish summoned all the right people to this ceremony uniting her young sister to Howard Hughes, Jr.

By late afternoon, wedding presents were piling up in the foyer of the imposing home. Most were, however, mismatched pieces of china and silver. The haste of this wedding had not allowed the bride and groom to select patterns.

Guests arrived at six on the dot—the men in linen and cavalry twill, the women in chiffon and flowing silk. As Howard's best man, Dudley Sharp, recalled, "The weather was so stifling as the sun prepared to set that we thanked God for the lightness of our suits."

At a signal from Libby Farish, an orchestra launched into a medley of twenties love songs followed by snatches of Victorian wedding marches. The orchestral strains were punctuated by the thunder of a lightning storm out over the Texas plains.

The deacon of Christ Church, Reverend Peter Gray Sears, strode onto the terrace followed by Dudley Sharp and, finally, by Hughes in an ivory suit and dark tie. His hands were folded behind his back, and his dark hair fell over his eyes as he looked shyly out over the crowd. The guests were rapt with attention. Because he had attended schools in Massachusetts and California, Hughes was little known in his hometown. Now all eyes were on him.

"He was easily the best-looking man at the wedding, in the neighborhood, and in Houston—but was totally unaware of it," said Sharp.

The opening chords of *Lohengrin*'s Wedding March sounded.

First down the aisle were Mrs. Farish and Howard's stern-faced aunt Annette Lummis, the formidable architects of the marriage. They were followed by another of Ella's sisters, Laura Rice. And finally, by Howard's bride.

Ella Rice, dubbed by the press "the most sought-after debutante in Houston," had made her debut during the season of 1921–22, but her world was more closely allied with that of Scarlett O'Hara and the genteel reminders of the Old South than with the anything-goes Jazz Age of Zelda and F. Scott Fitzgerald.

With her dark, fine-edged features, she looked remarkably like Hughes's mother, Allene.

With her old family name, she moved gracefully through the diverse elements of south Texas society: the old mainstays and the brash new oil bunch. Ella was a grandniece of William Marsh Rice, one of Houston's founding fathers and the namesake of Houston's Rice University. Clearly, her branch of the family possessed a proud heritage. But according to her friend Laura Kirkland Bruce, it was also "a branch with hardly any money at all." This singular lack of affluence put Ella Rice in harm's way when her older sister Libby and Annette began negotiations for her marriage to Howard.

Howard was five and Ella was seven when they were classmates in kindergarten. They remained passing acquaintances. By the time others were plotting her future, Ella had been in love for several years with a dashing young financier, James Overton Winston. He was a comer but, like Ella, was from a family without substantial money. They had met on a blind date three years earlier and by 1925 considered themselves unofficially engaged.

Explaining why he stepped aside so that his sweetheart could marry another man, James Overton Winston said realistically, "In those days a man was expected to provide well for his wife, and I couldn't—not then."

But Ella didn't immediately agree to the arranged marriage. According to accounts by Howard's cousin Kitty Callaway and Noah Dietrich, Howard at last succeeded in winning her over by resorting to a familiar ploy: he got sick.

He claimed to have been stricken with an unnamed illness during an early 1925 trip to California. "The doctor called Ella, told her that Howard was extremely ill and that he kept calling out for her in his semiconscious state," Dietrich once wrote. "That proved irresistible to Ella." By the time Howard had returned to Houston, a devoted Ella was waiting.

Hughes betrayed his disdain for the union when he closeted himself with the divorce specialists at Houston's crack law firm Bryan, Dyess and Colgin just five days before the wedding. He charged them with researching the community property laws of both Texas and California so that he could protect his inheritance. The firm's fifty-page report coached Hughes on how to safeguard his rapidly expanding empire. It cautioned him against making substantial purchases. "Merchandise and real estate," the report said, "even if bought with separate funds, and with sale at a profit is legally community property." The report also warned: "The same is true for the profits of speculation in stocks and bonds." For the duration of his marriage, Hughes would make no major purchases.

Two nights before the wedding, when most young blades would have been reveling in bachelor parties, Hughes signed a new will instead. It made sure that the burgeoning Hughes Tool Company would not fall into the hands of his relatives or his new wife. His bequests included $75,000 to his aunt Janet Houstoun and $1,000 and the family home on Yoakum to Annette.

The bulk of the estate was to be held in trust for the establishment of "Howard R. Hughes Medical Research Laboratories," to be created "as soon after my death as practicable." He charged the foundation with "scientific research for discovery and development of antitoxins and specific remedies for the cure and prevention of dangerous diseases."

He also designated $500,000 "in first class, high grade securities to my wife, Ella Rice Hughes."

Arranged marriages were not uncommon in the South of the time. As Houston's historian Marguerite Johnston explained, "Houston is not typically Texan. It is part of the very deep South." So, Howard and Ella were united in a classic society wedding of the time, arranged out of concern for status and image, not affection—or sexual compatibility.

The *Houston Chronicle* gushed over Ella's appearance that day. The bride wore a gown of white chiffon with antique rose point lace. "Her tulle veil was held in place by a cap of rose point and seed pearls, adjusted with orange blossoms and gardenias. Her arms were filled with a bridal shower of lilies of the valley."

Howard Hughes was now bound to a patrician young woman who was virtually a stranger to him.

After honeymooning in Manhattan and the toniest beaches on Long Island, Mr. and Mrs. Howard Robard Hughes, Jr., arrived at Los Angeles's Union Station in late summer, when the air was heavy with the scent of gardenias, sweet olive, and night-blooming jasmine. Riding grandly in an open Phaeton, one of the great luxury cars of the day, they brought with them half a dozen trunks of clothes, a pair of town cars, and leather boxes from Cartier and Tiffany. Hughes had letters of credit from three banks, $50,000 in cash, and printed personal checks from two Houston banks. Ella, as carefully dictated by the marriage agreement, had her own accounts in both cities.

Two hotel limousines collected Howard and Ella, carrying them through the Art Deco downtown, past the Angel's Flight Trolley line and out sweeping Wilshire Boulevard to the rambling Ambassador Hotel, which was set in a park of rolling lawns and Tahitian hibiscus bushes. On the hotel's ground floor was the Cocoanut Grove, the jazzy nightclub home of silent-film society. Snappily dressed bellboys showed Howard and Ella to an expansive pair of suites that boasted brocade furniture, heavy starched draperies, and hothouse flowers that were brought in fresh each morning. Maids, valets, and masseuses bustled in and out at the touch of a button.

Howard and Ella were perfectly cast—he with his sharply cut linen suits, dark tousled hair, and deep brown eyes; she with her elegant beauty and flowing chiffon gowns. "Handsome enough to be film stars—the both," recalled journalist Adela Rogers St. Johns. But Howard and Ella were not fated to be co-stars in their dreamlike world.

Ella haunted her hotel suites or paid calls on society matrons far from Hollywood. Howard set about becoming a movie producer.

Within days of his arrival, all Hollywood society had heard of Hughes. "We heard he had just inherited millions, and that he was 'mysterious and wild,'" said Billie Dove, a leading movie queen of the silent era, whose confidantes included movie legends Mary Pickford and Gloria Swanson and actress Marion Davies, the mistress of publishing tycoon William Randolph Hearst.

Everywhere he went, from Hearst's magnificent castle, San Simeon, to gossip queen Louella Parsons's tea parties, Hughes earnestly stated that he planned to be Hollywood's next great film producer. Screenwriter Ben Hecht called him "the sucker with the money."

His first step in his new career was to shrug off the workaday cares of the oil industry—even though it was enriching him at the rate of $5,000 per day. Everyone had assumed, particularly his troublesome relatives, that he would occupy the throne left vacant by Howard Sr.'s death. When Dudley Sharp urged him to make it a lifetime career, Hughes snapped back, "It doesn't interest me." So determined was Hughes to create his own legacy that when asked what he wanted to do with his father's antique desk, he answered adamantly, "Sell it."

Hughes was cagey enough, though, to realize that he needed someone to harness this geyser of wealth generated by the Hughes Tool Company, someone not ashamed to dirty his hands on the Houston assembly line if necessary. Although itching to get into the motion picture business, Howard spent much of August 1925 receiving a steady stream of applicants. There were attorneys (he didn't trust them), slick young executives (he saw them as too glib and "too soft") and stockbrokers (too formal for the gritty world of petroleum).

Finally, a scrappy 36-year-old accountant and former prize fighter named Noah Dietrich appeared at the door of Howard's Ambassador suite and introduced himself to the fresh-faced Hughes with a firm handshake. Hughes laughed at the look of surprise on Dietrich's face, saying, "I'm the right guy—even if I am only nineteen."

Something in Dietrich's demeanor put Hughes at ease. He barely looked at the accountant's résumé before tossing it on the table. Instead he stared at Dietrich intently, as if he could read the man's soul. "His eyes showed a depth and a merriment I never saw before or since," Dietrich later recalled. "And he did have an uncanny talent at sizing up his friends and enemies, a skill that would make him a billionaire."

Hughes moved closer to Dietrich. "Could you tell me how a battleship finds its target?"

Noah didn't hesitate. "It is a matter of triangulation, Mr. Hughes."

Hughes moved even closer. "Could you explain for me the principles of the internal combustion engine?" Noah obliged confidently.

Then Hughes ordered drinks, and the two men talked away the afternoon, discussing motor cars, airplanes, and the pros and cons of investing in moving pictures.

Dietrich left the Ambassador wondering if he had impressed this "intriguing and brilliant young man." He was left in the dark until several weeks later, when Hughes's new Los Angeles attorney, Neil McCarthy, appeared at Noah's door to tell him that he was to join Hughes's team that very afternoon. Dietrich had no way of knowing that he would eventually become father, mother, psychoanalyst, and the closest of confidants to Hughes. Or that his tenure would last almost four decades.

Hughes installed Dietrich in yet another Ambassador suite—this one without a connecting door to the private rooms—and set about launching himself into Hollywood's pantheon of stars.

At first, Dietrich feared that he had placed his future in the giddy hands of a run-of-the-mill playboy, an aimless wastrel destined for bankruptcy before the end of the decade. It was a legitimate concern; many of America's greatest fortunes were squandered during the twenties.

During Noah's first twenty-four months as Howard's aide, the Hughes bank accounts hemorrhaged cash: $100,000 for a fleet of motor cars; $4 million in failed investments; $20,000 for clothes, furs and jewelry (with many of the baubles presented to a band of willing starlets); $20,000 for entertainment and hotel accommodations; $25,000 for a personal Wall Street ticker-tape machine; and $550,000 to build a steam-powered touring car.

Hughes also spent $80,000 to finance his first movie, a never released stinker called *Swell Hogan*. It was directed by an old Houston friend of Howard Sr.'s named Ralph Graves, who had been working in movies for almost a decade. All about a good-natured Bowery bum, played by Graves, it was originally supposed to cost $40,000. But when Hughes kept providing cash, Graves kept the cameras rolling. "Never again!" declared Hughes when he realized he had been taken. He was quick to flash his money in those early years. And to indulge himself.

Reminiscent of his father, Hughes never bought one pair of imported shoes when he could buy twenty, never purchased one car when he could have half a dozen. He bought up fancy watches by the tray and was fitted for twenty hand-cut Brooks Brothers suits in a single afternoon.

If Howard spent heedlessly, he was a true creature of the times.

It was a decade like no other before or since. Fraught with postwar cynicism and materialistic frenzy, the twenties gave birth to the Charleston, jazz babies who bobbed their hair and shortened their hemlines, and the rat-tat-tat-tat of mobsters' gunfire. Thanks to Sigmund Freud's newly discovered theories, sex was for the first time a topic of *public* discussion. Thanks to the Eighteenth Amendment banning alcohol, hooch was a must-have. But the thirst wasn't just for booze: the race was on for thrills. Making that pursuit all the easier was the suddenly accessible automobile. "Pay as you go," cooed the advertisements for the four-wheel dream machine.

Setting the trends were motion pictures. In a single year in the midtwenties, Hollywood put four hundred films on the country's nearly fifteen thousand theater screens. Garbo, Chaplin, Keaton, Fairbanks, Pickford—and countless others, many since forgotten—ruled over a powerful new kingdom. The mass hysteria triggered by Valentino's unexpected death in August 1926 was proof of the allure of America's new royalty.

They didn't reign over just the screen. They held court at the watering holes and swank eateries that were springing up on what had once been bean fields and pepper tree groves. At Hollywood's fashionable Montmartre the luncheon crowd that gathered in the 350-seat dining room was so starstudded that gawking tourists had to be cordoned off with a red velvet rope. At the Brown Derby, just opposite the Ambassador, anxious autograph seekers clustered at the doors.

It seemed that garish movie sets had spilled out beyond the sound stages. The Derby was hat-shaped, its waitresses garbed in billowy, hatshaped skirts. In downtown Los Angeles, The Paris Inn attempted to recreate the food, drink, and debauchery of the Left Bank. In Universal City, The Zulu Hut boasted an African village motif and waiters in black-face. The Hollywoodization of the landscape even spilled out over the Mexican border. Tijuana, just five hours away, lured the starry crowds with legal booze, a racetrack, and casinos. Then there was Agua Caliente with its spas, swimming pools, tennis courts—and a casino where players used only pieces of gold. The gin and glamour weren't confined to land: three miles offshore, in the waters between Santa Monica and Long Beach, bobbed gambling ships. Seafaring was never so sinful.

When Hughes entered this scene he was as good-looking as the matinee idols of the day. Yet he was still as demanding as a child.

At the Ambassador, his room service orders were often so precise that the hotel chefs could not meet his demands. Tomato slices had to be no thicker than a quarter of an inch; sandwiches had to be cut into precise triangles; lettuce had to be "shredded on the bias."

One morning waiters delivered four plates of scrambled eggs, all of which were rejected by Hughes. Noah Dietrich recalled that he and Ella watched in amusement as Hughes sent for the head chef and asked him to appear with a portable stove, eggs, milk, and a skillet. Throwing on an apron, Hughes poured milk into the already warm skillet, advised the chef to "never, never scald the milk" and then carefully scrambled the eggs. He would be equally demanding about the proper preparation of chocolate chip cookies, grilled cheese sandwiches, and green peas.

He was an expert at telling others what to do. Once stricken with a virulent form of flu, he summoned the hotel physician. When the doctor administered a hypodermic needle, Hughes said impatiently, 'You're just putting the needle in the wrong place. You have to get it right into the bloodstream.' Howard then plunged the needle deep into the fleshy part of his own arm. The next morning, he had a swelling the size of an egg. "I won't do that again," he told Noah Dietrich.

Dietrich remembered constantly being surprised by Hughes's impulses and obsessiveness. One morning Hughes burst into Dietrich's Ambassador Hotel office and said, "I want a stock ticker at my bedside. I'm about to make a killing on the market."

Dietrich protested, "But, Howard, there's a tape downstairs in the hotel arcade."

"Not good enough," said Hughes. "I want to sit up in bed at four in the morning, read the latest quotations from Wall Street, and start buying before everyone else does in this city."

"This will cost a lot of money," Noah replied.

"Damn the money," Hughes countered.

Dietrich finessed Western Union and charmed the Los Angeles Municipal Transit District to run a trunk line down the trolley poles and into his boss's bedroom. At 4 A.M. every day, Hughes bounded out of bed to read the tape as it spewed in wild swirls across the bed.

His compulsion to deal in the booming stock market of the mid-twenties would cost him plenty. In the years leading up to the Great Depression, Hughes squandered $8 million speculating on Wall Street.

He became equally obsessed with building a fleet of steam-powered automobiles. "Noah, I think we can develop a car that can travel from Los Angeles to San Francisco on a single tank of water."

Dietrich was skeptical: "How much will this car cost?"

Hughes doodled some quick algebraic equations on a scratch pad and said, "I think we could make them for somewhere between $25,000 and $30,000 apiece."

Dietrich laughed out loud. "Howard, who will be able to afford them?"

"Well, some of my sportsmen friends would want them. But if they don't, at least I'll have a dandy new car once every year."

A team of California Institute of Technology engineers produced a prototype with a price tag of $550,000. Their creation, a five-passenger open touring car, was sleek and efficient, capable of doing four hundred miles on a single tank of water.

But the body of the car was a tangled mass of radial tubing. When Howard studied the steam pipes running through the doors he warily asked an engineer, "What would happen if I got broadsided? I would get scalded, right?" The scientist nodded.

Hughes turned to Dietrich and said, "Noah, get some torches and cut this thing up." Then he added, "And, Noah, you see to it that it gets cut up in tiny, tiny pieces. Really small pieces."

At first, Dietrich stood back and allowed the headstrong young heir to spend at will. As long as Howard did not mortgage the tool company or dip into Howard Sr.'s carefully orchestrated portfolio of securities, the aide-de-camp remained bemused by the Texan's madcap schemes. But when he realized his prodigy was being seduced by the mere exhilaration of spending, Dietrich counseled Howard one morning that "all great men have goals which are clearly and sharply defined."

"So do I," Hughes said. "I intend to be the greatest golfer in the world, the finest film producer in Hollywood, the greatest pilot in the world, and the richest man in the world." With a grin he added, "But not in that order."

When he stormed the lush greens of Los Angeles's triumvirate of golf establishments, the Wilshire Country Club, the Los Angeles Country Club, and the Bel Air Country Club (despite exorbitant membership fees, he joined all three), his approach was equally scientific. He coaxed and coerced his way into the city's best foursomes, imported golf pros, and even had his practice sessions filmed—both at ground level and from above—in slow motion and pioneering Technicolor, using a blimp that circled overhead.

To strengthen his arms, a wrestling coach showed up before dawn each day to put him through a withering session on a rubber exercise mat. He was to lament, one afternoon, that he was too tired to make love.

But with his first film Hughes proved himself to be the rube with the cash. At the only screening of his bomb, *Swell Hogan*, the young heir's face reddened at the laughter from the audience.

After enduring the picture, his familial nemesis Rupert Hughes took him aside and said, "Give it up. You won't succeed, and you'll end up squandering your entire fortune."

A furious Howard instead launched his own movie company. The Caddo Company was a subsidiary of a Hughes Tool Company arm, the Caddo Rock Drill Bit Company of Louisiana. He also obtained better directors and haunted the sets of his next two films: *Everybody's Acting*, a comedy about five men and a baby, returned $160,000 on a $70,000 investment. *Two Arabian Knights*, about a pair of doughboys in an Arabian harem, cost $500,000 and earned nearly $800,000, plus an Academy Award for Lewis Milestone's direction of a comedy.

Hughes was so intent upon succeeding that he completely took apart one of his films and put it back together, re-editing it and slicing 10 per cent off every scene. Hughes also charmed his way onto every major film set in Hollywood, filling up another twenty of his notebooks on the ins and outs of big studio films.

Hughes was pursuing another goal as well: to romance and bed as many of the world's most beautiful women as possible, implemented as meticulously and fervently as he pursued his other professions.

He didn't arrive in Hollywood a seasoned Romeo. According to Dietrich, Howard was so awkward toward women in the beginning that Dietrich suspected he may not have consummated his marriage until after the honeymoon. Which means Howard may have been a virgin when he checked into the Ambassador Hotel—the virtual headquarters for Tinseltown's extramarital affairs. Gloria Swanson and swashbuckling silent star Rod La Rocque trysted there, as did Rudolph Valentino and Pola Negri. Charlie Chaplin maintained a love nest in a discreet corner of the hotel. So did Ramon Novarro, the first Ben-Hur (except Ramon's partners were pretty-boy extra players he brought home from MGM).

Hughes approached sex in the same scientific manner he would utilize to conquer the skies. He brought in a series of very high-class ladies of the evening who quickly showed him the ins and outs of liberated sexuality. He was particularly attracted to a voluptuous party girl who upped the sexual ante by arriving at the Ambassador wearing one of a series of her trademark fur coats—she had sable, ermine, or mink, depending upon the occasion.

An elevator flight down was the Cocoanut Grove, where he shyly looked on at the starlets under the papier-mâché palm trees—props left over from *The Sheik*. He would soon do more than look, courting former flapper Joan Crawford; Constance Bennett, who was looking to marry a millionaire; and Madge Bellamy, a fellow Texan whose most recent films were *The Reckless Sex* and *Havoc*.

"He was gorgeous," said Bellamy, who maintained one of the wittiest, wildest salons in Hollywood. She was perhaps the first, however, to discern the torment hidden by Hughes's open Texas charm. Whenever he came to visit Bellamy in her palazzo in the Hollywood foothills, she noticed that he walked slowly up the terrace looking over his shoulder as if "someone were following him—and he was just a kid."

By October 1925, Hughes wanted to hide his expenditures and escalating sexcapades from Ella. Her presence was uncomfortable at best and problematic at worst. He convinced her to return to Houston, insisting that the Yoakum Boulevard mansion needed to be opened and festooned for the upcoming holidays. He promised to join her there sometime before Thanksgiving.

Ella reluctantly returned home, taking with her a collection of seldom-worn couture gowns, an armload of rare furs, and a limitless line of credit. She had everything a young southern matron could desire, except a home of her own, a dashing husband on her arm, and companionship.

Hughes had spent $50,000 converting the Yoakum Boulevard mansion into a honeymoon home, and he staffed it with servants. But so strict were the southern codes of morality that Ella didn't dare stay there husbandless. Instead she moved into a spare wing of her sister Libby Farish's home in fashionable River Oaks. Oil town society buzzed with rumors that Hughes had sent his young wife away, but Ella brushed them off and glided through the holiday fetes with her socially prominent sister at her side.

As Christmas approached, however, Ella sent the first in a series of poignant telegrams begging her husband to join her. If only he would return to Houston, Ella felt, the marriage might work.

"I miss you horribly," she wired late on the afternoon of December 21, her second cable that day.

Ella was even more desperate by December 23: "Cannot understand why I have not heard from you. Am counting on you leaving Los Angeles tomorrow."

On Christmas Eve—Hughes's birthday—she cabled: "All my best wishes for a happy birthday but am thinking of you every minute."

Sometimes she showed her impatience. "Did you attend to my bank account? If not please do so as I want to give the servants their Christmas money . . . be sure and tell me you are leaving tomorrow." Signing off, she dropped her usual "love" and simply used "Ella."

Though Howard's telegrams were usually dictated by Noah with as much gallantry as possible, they were usually cold: "Still busy. No chance of leaving Los Angeles" was a typical reply.

Dietrich was ashamed to be a party to Howard's cruelty. Dietrich maintained that Howard never loved Ella but had only married her based on "a cold, calculated decision" to "get rid of his relatives." A psychologist who studied Howard's life said the early marriage also gave Hughes a psychological payoff. "He felt abandoned in the world, and he needed to have the security of marriage to help him cope with his loss," explained Dr. Raymond Fowler.

Among her friends back home in Houston, Ella never spoke unkindly of Howard. "But she didn't say what was in her innermost heart, either. She kept her feelings to herself," said Mary Cullinan Cravens. Ella felt so distant from Howard that she had to ask Dietrich if he could suggest a Christmas gift for Howard. Admitted Ella, "I've no idea."

While Ella was in Houston playing the role of a proper, albeit lonely wife, Dietrich anticipated scandal. "Howard is so swamped with girlfriends that anything could happen," he once told attorney Neil McCarthy.

Sure enough, in mid-December disaster struck—though with no

repercussions. Shortly before he was to take the train to Houston, Howard's favorite party girl, the redhead with those alluring fur coats, bade Hughes good night and slipped into her wrap and into the hands of Howard's chauffeur, a former police driver named Hal Connon.

Since Los Angeles was in the grip of a winter storm, Connon took the woman home in the sturdiest car in Hughes's fleet, an oversized Rolls-Royce. Ten minutes later, though, the car careened out of control on a rain-slick street and crashed into a power pole. The redhead, naked under her black mink, was killed instantly; Connon was knocked unconscious.

Connon refused to implicate his boss, allowing the traffic cops to believe the dead girl was his date. Even when police finally traced owner-ship of the Rolls to Hughes, the chauffeur pulled strings, and money from his pockets (provided by Dietrich), to see that his boss wasn't involved. Noah arranged for court costs, paid the fine, and saw to it that the driver received probation.

Hughes stayed in Los Angeles, and shortly before Christmas he had a high-flying affair with a blonde starlet at San Simeon. It was a double date: pal William Randolph Hearst, Jr., also brought a blonde. Howard spent Christmas Eve, his twentieth birthday, at a Los Angeles nightclub.

His aunt Annette Gano Lummis was not amused by his absence. On Christmas morning she ordered her nephew home to help Ella plan a gala New Year's celebration. Howard did as he was told. But he brought along a new bag of golf clubs and Noah Dietrich.

During the reunion with Ella and the rest of the family, Dietrich noted that his boss was "barely civil." He added, "He spent most of his time on the greens of the Houston Country Club or locked in his dad's old library talking on the phone to Hollywood."

By mid-January 1926, Hughes had returned to Los Angeles with Ella, but he felt the walls of the Ambassador Hotel closing in on him. Ella was always within earshot; her very presence reminded him that he was not the bachelor in paradise he wished to be. And Dietrich had taken over the neighboring suite as the West Coast base for Hughes Tool Company and Howard's other corporate operations. Noah constantly invaded his boss's privacy, bustling in and out with the latest figures. But the figures Hughes was interested in had nothing to do with the mechanics and hydraulics of drilling bits. So he banished both Dietrich and his wife: Dietrich to a new suite of offices in downtown Los Angeles; Ella to a sprawling, gloomy mansion in Hancock Park, a bastion of old Los Angeles society. Hughes had leased the mission-style estate at 211 Muirfield Drive, complete with furniture.

While his wife cultivated leaders of old and moneyed society, Hughes prowled the streets in a souped-up Rolls, flirting with all those wild young things who had flocked to Hollywood trying to break into the movies. Howard sauntered through the afternoon tea dances at the Cocoanut Grove. After midnight he prowled Fatty Arbuckle's Plantation Club. He was also far from unknown to the proprietress of Maude's House, a gilded den of prostitution that featured willing carbon copies of Joan Crawford, Norma Shearer, Gloria Swanson, and others. He even showed up at the opening of a transvestite revue just off West Hollywood's sizzling Sunset Strip.

In the meantime, Ella languished in her brocaded boudoir at Muirfield. On the rare occasions when Howard took her out into brassy Hollywood society, she appeared to be deferential, even frightened of her husband. Those who met her at actor Ben Lyon's beach house recalled her as perfectly typecast in her role as the shy, soft-speaking southern belle. Silent star Patsy Ruth Miller said she was "a sweet little wife who seemed thrilled when her husband pointed out film stars. I have been told that I could get conversation out of a sphinx, but even I had trouble getting more than a yes or a no out of Ella Hughes. And what she said . . . she only talked at all after looking up at her husband for permission."

James Overton Winston, Ella's eventual second husband, said her Hollywood life was that of "a bird in a gilded cage." Annette Lummis, one of those responsible for this marriage, later admitted, "It was a heck of a life for Ella . . . Howard would come home for an hour or so each day, wolf down a sandwich, and then leave." According to Annette, the marriage made Ella "terribly miserable." As for her nephew, Annette confessed, "I don't think Howard had any feelings for her."

Houstonian Elva Kalb Dumas, who knew Ella before and after her marriage, said, "Hughes sacrificed poor Ella." Added Dumas, "She was very fragile, not very assertive."

After less than a year of marriage, Hughes expressed his disdain by ordering Ella back to Houston in March 1926. They had spent only sixteen weeks together since Ella's fall banishment.

Three weeks later, Ella begged to come back to Los Angeles. On April 19, in the first of more than fifty telegrams, she wired: "Please try and phone me. I don't intend to stay here very long. Miss you terribly."

"Sorry you didn't have time to call me last night," she wrote on April 21. "Am sure you know why I didn't go to the Country Club dance."

Between April 19 and July 4, Ella begged twenty times to rejoin her husband in Los Angeles. "I shall stay here as long as you think best in spite of the fact it is against my judgment and my desire," she cabled in mid-May. As spring turned to summer, Ella became so desperate she sometimes sent as many as three wires a day.

Hughes's contempt for Ella's feelings and his deliberate, studied callousness are difficult to explain given his chivalrous treatment of the legions of Hollywood stars and starlets he would romance during the coming decades. Noah Dietrich, in his unpublished reminiscences, shrugged it off: "He was entirely incapable of living within a married state. Ella was a lovely, cultivated, affectionate woman, but she had been forced on Hughes. And he resented it."

In early July, a drift toward divorce was diverted by the combined efforts of Annette Lummis, her husband Dr. Frederick Lummis and Libby Farish, Ella's sister.

Howard finally granted her permission to return to the lonely existence as Mrs. Howard Hughes. "Will be happy to see you tomorrow," Ella had wired him on June 4—hours before she climbed onto Santa Fe's Zephyr and headed for Los Angeles.

Chastened by stern conversations with his aunt and by Noah's well-expressed disapproval, Hughes assumed the role of faithful husband for a brief period.

Ella had to have known about Howard's womanizing—it was the talk of Houston. Tool company executives, long disdainful of their "playboy boss," made certain that all the juiciest rumors emanating from the Los Angeles factory received full airing among the ruling classes of America's oil capital.

By the time Ella returned to Hancock Park, Hughes had rented another house five doors down. Nicknamed "Angelo," it was maintained as a lovers' hideaway and for entertaining the demi-monde of film society.

Ella would reinstall herself as mistress of Muirfield, but this would not bring an end to Hughes's womanizing or obsessive behavior. Indeed, in the coming years her primary rival would not be his other women but the grandest of dreams.

CHAPTER 4

GOING HOLLYWOOD

IN THE FALL OF 1927, HOWARD LOCKED ELLA AND HIS STAFF OUT OF THE downstairs suite of the Muirfield mansion, installing new double locks on the doors to the formal downstairs study and the magnificent Spanish colonial library beyond. Most afternoons Howard secreted himself in this locked wing as soon as he strolled off the green of the Wilshire Country Club. He muttered an occasional greeting to his wife and then vanished into the bizarre universe he was building in this somber formal parlor. Hughes, who was now avidly taking flying lessons, rapidly filled the rooms with towers of aviation books, faded Defense Department photos of war planes, and endless spools of newsreels depicting the great aerial battles of World War I.

After viewing the silent film masterpiece *Wings*, the World War I epic that won the first Academy Award for best picture, Hughes came to believe that he could do better. He would make the ultimate air epic. He also planned to make it using "at least $2 million of my own money" and without the power and protection of a major Hollywood studio.

Studio heads and columnists scoffed at the idea; not since the earliest days of the movie industry had one man challenged Hollywood's clubbish world of moguls. To quote Louella Parsons, the doyenne of movie columnists, "The brash young man, Mr. Howard Hughes, is going it alone. And he's calling his film *Hell's Angels*." But Hughes's film approach to World War I aviation would be unique. His film would chronicle the top guns of four nations: Great Britain, Germany, France, and America.

Noah Dietrich learned of the film and its scope when Hughes ordered him to transfer $700,000 into a special account to pay for used airplanes, set construction, and salaries for two dozen veteran fighter jocks and a hundred aircraft mechanics. Freeing this much cash forced Dietrich to seize all the reserves of the tool company. When a cadre of executives protested this second raid on the corporate treasury (the first had come when Howard had bought out his relatives), Hughes snapped at Dietrich, "It's my money. Just get it for me."

Howard soon spent half a million dollars to assemble a private air force of fighting planes, from all four countries. He wound up with more than forty warplanes—though breathless Hughes-orchestrated publicity accounts inflated the number to nearly one hundred. His team of scouts stormed through the mothballed fleets in Germany's Weimar Republic; in the dusty hangars outside of Paris; and the collections of America's daring barnstormers. They brought back nifty, snub-nosed Spodes; sinister SE-5s; sturdy Sopwith Camels; and World War I's top killer, the great Fokker airplanes. (Unable to locate a German Gotha, Hughes ordered a top-secret makeover of a hulking Sikorsky.) And he started the payroll clock ticking for the mechanics and the pilots, under the command of World War I aces Roscoe Turner and Paul Mantz, Hollywood's most daring and busiest fliers.

Hughes worked through the night, plotting the movie's aerial battles, including a spectacular special effects sequence, involving a raid on London, that utilized two sixty-foot models of zeppelins. Climaxing with an airship's fiery descent, the zeppelin episode alone cost $460,000—more than three times the budget of the average feature film. Meanwhile, director Marshall Neilan began filming the interior scenes, including a dazzling military ball requiring seventeen hundred lavishly costumed extras. Soon a sleep-starved Hughes began appearing at the set in a director's costume of cavalry britches, leather flight jacket, and boots with a mirror shine. When he overruled Neilan again and again, the veteran director stalked off the set. So Hughes imported Luther Reed, the former aviation editor of the *New York Herald Tribune* turned budding director. But Howard also interfered during Reed's direction.

Finally, Reed screamed, "If you know so much, why don't you direct this film yourself!"

Howard was silent for a few seconds. Finally he answered, "All right, I will."

For the next three years, this sweeping saga about the top guns of World War I became an obsession, shoving aside his private life, undermining his corporate image, and almost ruining his health.

When Dietrich tried to rein him in, Hughes warned, "I'll do whatever it takes to be the greatest movie producer in Hollywood history."

On January 10, 1928, Howard's air force taxied off the twin runways of Mines Field in Inglewood, California, to begin the aerial battles in the crystal clear skies over Santa Monica. It took two hours just for all the planes to take off.

Circling far above this diving, dueling army of fighter planes was Hughes, who directed the action using a sophisticated radio system that linked the pilots with their nominal commander.

But Hughes wasn't just content to play director. Like many fledgling fliers of the Roaring Twenties who had been too young to fly in the Great War, he ached to risk his life in combat stunts. Hughes grabbed his chance in early February.

While his pilots were performing some of the most dangerous aviation stunts ever filmed, Howard instructed Mantz in a scene that simulated a strafing raid. "And I want the pilot to dive toward the ground, but pull back up when he's just two hundred feet above the runway," said Hughes.

"That's a suicide mission," Mantz declared. "Dive lower than a thousand feet and the plane will crash."

Howard was stubborn. "That's ridiculous. Any good flier can do it."

"Yeah, well not one of my fliers," Mantz answered.

"Fine," Hughes said. "I'll do it myself."

Still in his modish movie director costume of wool breeches, argyle sweater, and socks to match, Howard leaped into the cockpit of a Thomas Morse Scout and soared into the sky. He lazily circled Inglewood several times, leaning out of the cockpit to study the seventy-eight-foot tower where he had installed a bank of cameras to record the stunt.

Then he signaled the cinematographer to start, and plunged toward the earth.

At fifteen hundred feet, the Scout's engine began to wail. Hughes pulled at the controls, frantic to slow the speed of the dive. At one thousand feet the plane plunged so fast that there was a roar as the wings cut through the coastal winds. From below, the ground crew watched anxiously. Wasn't it time for Hughes to pull upward? Hughes concentrated on guiding his camera into range instead of pulling up the Scout.

At 750 feet, he knew he was in trouble. Hughes grabbed the controls, trying to pull out of the dive. But the Scout continued its fall. The camera crew caught a last glimpse of their boss: Hughes had thrown off his leather helmet and was bracing himself with his feet against the dashboard. A crash was unavoidable.

The left wing folded first, like a Japanese fan. There was a scraping noise. Then the propellers screamed as they dug into the asphalt runway, kicking up grit and bits of glass.

As a cloud of dust blew up around the wreck, an ominous silence followed. Finally, Frank Clarke, one of the *Hell's Angels* squadron leaders, uttered, "Damn. We've just lost our meal ticket." Clarke, Mantz, and a pair of medics sprinted into the thick of the swirling dust. They found the ravaged cockpit and Hughes's leather jacket; they also found blood dripping down the side of the plane. But no Hughes.

A moan came from the direction of a newly constructed hangar. Through the murk they finally saw Howard grimacing and leaning against the wall. His clothes were tattered and bloody.

Hughes, in a state of shock, began babbling incoherently about his golf game. Then he collapsed, unconscious. An ambulance rushed him immediately to Inglewood Hospital, where an alarmed Noah Dietrich met his critically injured boss. Acting on prearranged instructions, he registered Hughes under an assumed name and swore the doctors and nurses to silence.

Howard had suffered a major concussion, a crack in his skull from the top of his head to just above his eyes, and unknown injuries at the top of his spinal cord. By the time he was shifted to the emergency room operating table he was in a coma. He would remain in that state for three days. "There may be brain damage. And he could lose the sight of his right eye," one doctor told Dietrich.

Inconceivably, the next morning Howard sat up in bed and claimed to be fully recovered.

"I want you to stay in this hospital room with the blinds closed," a doctor told him.

According to Dietrich, Howard actually replied, "Nonsense. What's my sight compared to my art?" The next day he was back on the set.

Only decades later did Howard understand that this crash probably had left behind lasting damage to his brain. Because of the time spent unconscious and because a shard of metal had lodged in his skull, he suffered scarring that went unnoticed until his death.

The *Hell's Angels* crash would be the first of many, all of them leading to a legacy of blinding migraines, strange memory lapses, irrational acts and, decades later, to an emotional illness which would erode his genius and his sanity. For now, the crash only resulted in a cosmetic change: Howard had to have minor facial surgery, which took away the cleft in his chin that the ladies had so favored.

As *Hell's Angels* pushed forward, the marriage that had been forced on Hughes continued to unravel.

By 1928 Hughes had banished his wife again. Against her will, Ella became a part of the Houston retinue of her wealthy older sister, Libby Farish, traveling with the Farishes from one social enclave to the next. She languished at polo tournaments, yachting parties and health spas, communicating with her husband through a sad litany of cablegrams brightened by the occasional phone call—always at Howard's convenience.

From Manhattan she once cabled, "Will see the international polo games. My sister has a box." Ella added wistfully, "Shall I hold a seat for you?" During a 1927 trip to Chicago for the headline-making Tunney–Dempsey fight, she asked hopefully, "Don't you think you could make it somehow?"

Citing business matters, Howard remained distant, in every sense. Ella grew angry and humiliated at her fate. In one wire she berated Hughes: "I cannot drift indefinitely, and from past experience I know how you postpone making any move. If this is going to be the case, please let me know, as I find all this so embarrassing." Hughes was unmoved.

In October 1928 Noah Dietrich was sent to escort Mrs. Hughes back to Houston where the Farishes' guest room waited. She collapsed there on October 5, a victim of exhaustion and stress.

Ella was checked into Houston's St. Joseph's Infirmary. The diagnosis: "ulcerated colitis," "nervous exhaustion," and "dehydration." Hughes, who had been hitting Hollywood night spots after spending the days shooting *Hell's Angels*, hadn't learned of her condition. While she was ill he sent one of his infrequent telegrams, casually informing her that he had a "new wrestling coach who is plenty tough." Added her errant husband: "I have to get up at 7:30 A.M. so I won't be making much whoopee."

But Hughes sent a second telegram that day, just four hours later, to

Ella's physician, Dr. Lummis. This time Hughes was contrite. "Please make a careful examination of Ella's health. Spare no expense. Terribly worried."

Ten days later, when Ella was back at the Farishes', Hughes sent an unusually genial wire: "Forgive me for being so non-communicative but am awfully busy with the picture. Am also stiff all over as the new wrestler is very rough on me—so much so that I could hardly play golf last Sunday."

On October 31, with Ella still wracked with cramps and now being fed intravenously, Hughes sent an angry telegram to Dr. Lummis, "Why isn't she improving? I think you'd better call in the specialists—damn the cost."

Howard also wired Ella at the Farish residence. "Still trying to shoot the big air scene from *Hell's Angels* with thirty-two airplanes in Oakland. Suffering under bad weather—hope you're feeling better."

Lummis had promising news on November 8. "Ella is cheerful again and now has very little pain . . . I'll keep on reporting to you." But on November 19, again on Thanksgiving, and on into December, Hughes was "too busy" to call his wife.

Hughes's Aunt Annette remembered Ella as "gray, sad, and wistful." This forced union had become a quiet tragedy. Despite these polite telegrams, elegant notes, and medical reports, no one voiced the obvious: Ella Rice had crumbled under the weight of her marital charade.

She and Hughes spent a second Christmas apart and, incredibly, Ella again appealed to Noah Dietrich with a telegram. "Have you heard Howard express a desire for anything he needs or would like that I can give him for Christmas? Maybe something for his office?"

Christmas 1928 was different for Ella. Houston boldly buzzed about the scandal involving the distant Mr. Hughes and the ever-present Ella Rice. For the first time marital infidelity was discussed. A name was even bandied about. "The first time I heard Billie Dove's name was when rumors cropped up that Ella's marriage was in trouble," said Laura Kirkland Bruce, one of Ella's closest friends.

The movie star's name, and others, also reached the ears of Ella's sister Libby and her husband, William Stamps Farish, chairman of the board of Standard Oil. Farish was the single largest customer of the Hughes Tool Company. Libby was determined that her younger sister not be upstaged by "an actress." In early 1929 she packed Ella's bags and put her on the train to Los Angeles for one last attempt to salvage the marriage.

Once back at Muirfield, Ella moved into one of the guest bedrooms, where she would sleep alone for the duration of her marriage.

In February 1929, a discouraged Hughes walked into Dietrich's office and sank into a chair. His face was a mask of exhaustion, his clothes rumpled from around-the-clock editing of *Hell's Angels.* The young would-be mogul had made a costly error in judgment. He hadn't taken sound seriously. Since starting as a novelty, as "pictures that talk," sound had virtually taken over the industry. Silent pictures were now playing to near empty houses. Already, the careers of Harold Lloyd, Buster Keaton, John Gilbert, and Clara Bow had turned to ashes, done in by their untrained voices. As Louella Parsons put it, talkies were "the eventual Waterloo" of actors. For directors, too.

Sitting facing Dietrich, Hughes cleared his throat, then admitted, "We have to convert *Hell's Angels* into a talkie." Dietrich's accountant mind reeled. His boss had already spent $2.2 million—an enormous budget at the time—on the epic. The movie was threatening to bring Hughes's financial empire to the threshold of ruin. Dietrich had already doused two revolts by Hughes Tool Company executives over their young boss's free-spending ways.

"How much is this going to cost?" groaned Dietrich. Howard had calculated to the last penny. The revamping would run to $1.7 million and include a new score, sound dubbing, and the restaging of some interiors. Fortunately, the lavish $100,000 ballroom sequence needed only new orchestration.

"He didn't ask me to find the money; he expected it to appear by magic," Dietrich later wrote.

Bringing sound to *Hell's Angels* meant bringing dialogue to its actors. That wasn't a problem for the two male leads. Ben Lyon and James Hall, playing brothers in the Royal Flying Corps, sounded stalwart. But statuesque Greta Nissen, playing the English hussy who comes between the brothers, had a thick Scandinavian accent. "We've got to get rid of her," Hughes insisted. Because of the cost of the sound conversion, Hughes couldn't afford a star name as a replacement. So he launched a search for someone new—and sexy.

The rush was on. Starlets and extras paraded past Hughes. He screened dozens of tests of up-and-comers, made by Metro-Goldwyn-Mayer, Paramount, and Warner Brothers. Nubile young actresses June Collyer, Thelma Todd, and Marian Marsh were considered, as was future star Carole Lombard, who was even announced for the role, then rejected several weeks later.

Actually, the part might have gone to Lombard if a pushy young agent named Arthur Landau hadn't stumbled onto the *Hell's Angels* set one Friday afternoon. On his arm was a brassy blonde wearing a cheap organdy dress and a splash of Jungle Gardenia toilet water. Thick mascara and Betty Boop lips completed the portrait of a girl who had looked just perfect in her last picture, opposite Laurel and Hardy. "My God, she's got a shape like a dust pan!" said Joseph Moncure March, the *Hell's Angels* dialogue writer.

Hughes wasn't impressed with the blonde who was brought to his office. In fact, he laughed the minute he caught sight of her. He remained disinterested after she did a screen test opposite star Ben Lyon. "In my opinion, she's nix," Hughes told her agent.

Landau pleaded with him: "She's a broad ready to put out for flyers. But she knows that after she's made them forget the war for a little while, they still have to take off and they might never come back. So her heart's breaking while she's screwing them."

Hughes, who had grown bored with the casting dilemma, countered, "But can she deliver this?"

"A cinch. She's just nervous now," Landau replied.

"One more thing," said Hughes. "How is she in the bomb department?" The slang expression referred to breasts. So far, he had only seen the girl modestly dressed.

"Big enough. Believe me!"

Hughes took a chance and cast Jean Harlow in her first major role.

"I suppose Howard Hughes was just so sick of looking at blondes, he was in a mood to give up," said a philosophic Harlow, who received the Guild minimum of $1,500 for six weeks' work and, it turned out, stardom.

Ella's future as Mrs. Hughes was not as promising. She joined the Los Angeles Junior League, plunged into charity work, and often drifted past her nocturnal husband as he was on his way out the door. According to Dietrich, the Muirfield house "echoed with silence." Very occasionally, Howard escorted Ella to the Brown Derby or to one of Louella Parsons's sedate dinner parties. "I don't even remember when Howard's lovely young wife stopped coming," Parsons admitted. "Certainly, Howard never mentioned her again."

Ella Rice Hughes decided to wage one final battle to save the marriage. If her patrician beauty failed to interest her husband, and if he still sought out starlets to sleep with, perhaps she could intrigue him with her considerable social skills.

In mid-March 1929, Ella prepared a series of dinners and receptions designed to unite Los Angeles society figures, her crowd, with Howard's, the ragtag film world. Ella planned a "white on white" sit-down dinner as the inaugural event. She consulted with Howard again and again to make sure he was free on the pertinent Saturday. Grumbling approval, he even genially supplied a guest list that included Louella Parsons, *Hell's Angels* star Ben Lyon and his actress wife Bebe Daniels, and the Dietrichs.

Suspicious of her husband's intentions, Ella reminded him as the date approached with a series of notes and telephone calls.

By Saturday at 7:00 P.M., the Muirfield house was a symphony of white. Wedgwood servers, thousands of gardenias, hundreds of pure white orchids, and Irish lace tablecloths graced the house. Uniformed valets parked the cars—the Pierce Arrows and the Rolls-Royces of the moneyed crowd and the garish Hollywood limos of Howard's guests.

"The two groups stood around almost silently, with nobody trying to bring them together," Dietrich later revealed. "And Howard was typically late, arriving at 9:30, when the guests were eating dessert—crepes suzette."

In rumpled corduroys and a soiled shirt, Hughes mumbled apologies and fell into his chair. With one leg over the arm, he wolfed down his food. Then, with a nod to Louella Parsons, he disappeared upstairs.

For Ella, the marriage was over the minute Howard turned his back on her guests. With tears in her eyes, she confessed her surrender to Dietrich. "You know, Mr. Dietrich, I tried. I really tried. But there's no point." The next day, she told Hughes she intended to file for divorce in Houston. Howard did not put up a fight.

Two days later, Ella's furious sister Libby Farish and Howard's troubled aunt Annette Lummis arrived at Muirfield to lend emotional support as Ella once again packed her belongings.

The official separation started the minute Ella stepped onto the Sunset Limited.

CHAPTER 5

AN AFFAIR TO REMEMBER

BY THE TIME ELLA RICE HUGHES CREPT OUT OF HOLLYWOOD TO BEGIN THE first stages of a divorce, a humiliation at the time, *Hell's Angels* was no longer her only rival. The gossip that was bandied about in Houston was true. Her husband was seeing the luminous Billie Dove, one of the great stars of the silent era.

When Hughes met Dove on the Starlight dance floor of the Biltmore Hotel, Hollywood gushed about "love at first sight." Louella Parsons, the town's first gossip columnist, described it as "divine fate." Actually, Hughes arranged it.

Using William Randolph Hearst's mistress, Marion Davies, as matchmaker, Hughes prowled through the Hollywood social calendar, searching for just the right moment. And timing was critical. They could approach the very married Dove only when she was out of earshot of her director husband, Irvin Willat, a man renowned for his jealousy and possessiveness. Hughes outfitted himself with new dinner clothes and tight ice cream suits, the beige-and-cream stud uniform of the Twenties, and lurked at the edges of the best soirees ready to pounce when Davies signaled that the time was right.

Hollywood high society (the Mary Pickford–Gloria Swanson crowd) must have scoffed at the very idea of a union between Hughes, still viewed as a Houston hayseed with a thick wad of dough, and Billie Dove, the ultimate Ziegfeld girl. While Hughes had been dodging bullies at the Fessenden School, Billie had been the centerpiece of the Ziegfeld Follies, dripping with beads and dancing to Irving Berlin's "A Pretty Girl Is Like a Melody." Her stage door Johnnies had included swains from the Vanderbilts and Rockefellers. When Hughes was struggling with his shyness at the Thacher School, Dove had already starred in thirty films and had been dubbed by critics "the most beautiful girl in the world."

Yet Marion Davies and Louella Parsons believed Howard and Billie were perfect for each other. "For one thing, he was as gorgeous as she. And they both shared a sad, inexplicable shyness," recalled columnist Dorothy Manners, Parsons's assistant in the twenties. "Their affair was unavoidable."

Their meeting took place at a white-tie ball at the Biltmore Hotel. All Hollywood was looking on. Billie Dove recalled it: "Suddenly everyone at the table was looking over my shoulders. I turned and saw Marion coming toward me with a tall, dark stranger on her arm. He was stone faced."

Davies tapped Dove's shoulder with a kid-gloved hand. "This is Howard Hughes, Billie. He's been asking to meet you." Billie flashed a radiant smile and tried to make conversation. "He just looked at me and looked at me, without saying a word," Dove remembered. Finally, after an uncomfortable silence, Hughes signaled Marion to escort him away.

Billie was amazed. "I thought, Surely, this can't be the young man they're raving about; the man with the millions. He was a zombie. I didn't like him at all."

Yet strangely, the brief, awkward meeting only increased Hughes's ardor.

Longtime agent Johnny Maschio, who was an assistant director for Cecil B. De Mille when he met Hughes in the late twenties, said, "He really thought Billie was going to be the great love of his life. And I think she was."

Hughes stumbled around "drunk with love," to quote Noah Dietrich. "Like an adolescent after his first kiss." And so, at twenty-three, Hughes began his very first real courtship, chasing his 24-year-old Ziegfeld girl through the glorious sunset of the silent era. He followed her from party to party, into and out of Hollywood's elegant speakeasies, and across the dance floors of the Cocoanut Grove and the Montmartre.

"Wherever I went, the door would open and in would come Howard to sit beside me, where he would remain for the rest of the evening. Our love developed slowly and quietly, the deepest love I would ever experience," remembered Dove.

Gardenias, yellow roses, and orchids by the hundreds rained down on Billie's home, followed by jewels and crystal decanters of perfume. Soon the courtship resembled a military campaign. Hughes even had detectives discreetly track the star's every movement and assemble a surveillance log, which he devoured every evening. When Billie filmed on location in central California, Hughes's plane often appeared and invariably dipped its wings in an aerial salute, which would soon become a trademark.

Howard confessed to Billie that his marriage was over. "He made it clear that the divorce was under way, and that no reconciliation was possible." Billie responded that her union with Willat existed "in name only," and promised to divorce the director, a difficult, angry man who vowed to fight her every step of the way.

Soon Willat put his own detectives on the case and ordered them to shadow Billie and Howard, no matter where they went. This caravan of sleuths, in their clunky roadsters, had Hollywood tittering, but Willat was building a strong case against the young lovers. At stake were Dove's burgeoning assets—for years she had been one of the highest-paid actresses of the silent screen. She had only recently signed a contract with Warner Brothers–First National that guaranteed her $100,000 per film.

The takeover by talkies only increased her price; Dove was one of the few leading actresses with a trained stage voice. Willat, on the other hand, was passé. The prolific director of silent films could not make the transition to talkies.

As Billie's marriage began to crumble, what was left of Hughes's marriage also gave way. It would end as it started: with a bout of illness. Just before dawn on June 1, 1929, Hughes stumbled home from the *Hell's Angels* edit bay and threw himself into bed without even taking off his leather flight jacket.

He thrashed around for hours, sweating through his clothes and skirting the edge of consciousness. The housekeeper found him in his bed at noon. His sweat had soaked through the bed linen. She alerted Dietrich. "I think he's dying," she said. "Hurry!"

Dietrich in turn alerted Dr. Verne Mason, the physician who had saved Hughes's life following the *Hell's Angels* plane crash. Both men rushed to the ornate master bedroom and kept a vigil there for forty-eight hours as Hughes suffered under the grip of spinal meningitis, a wasting disease that was frequently fatal in an era before the discovery of antibiotics.

Early on June 3, Mason pulled Dietrich into the hall. He informed him that his boss was only hours from death. "I think it's time to call Mrs. Hughes," Dr. Mason said.

Dietrich hesitated. Ella and Howard hadn't even spoken since March. He suspected that a divorce was imminent. He also believed that the union had become "loveless and strained: doomed to failure."

But with Mason predicting death, Dietrich wired Ella at the Ambassador Hotel in Manhattan. She was about to embark on a tour of Europe with the Farishes. "Howard dying," Dietrich cabled. "Dr. Mason advises return to Los Angeles."

Ella was skeptical. Thinking back to when Howard had feigned illness in the days when he was trying to convince her to marry him, she suspected this was a trick. But she was dutiful up to the end. She and her sister Libby pulled their trunks off the French liner *Normandie* and caught the train for Los Angeles. Ella wired, "Tell the doctor I am coming. Let him use his own judgment about telling Howard should Howard regain consciousness. Thanks for the message. Best wishes."

She noted in the telegram that she would change trains in Chicago. "Advise me there of Howard's condition."

Two hours later, Hughes startled Dietrich and Dr. Mason by coming to and groggily inquiring, "What's going on?"

Mason was dumbfounded. "You were so bad off that we called your wife. She's on her way here now."

Hughes groaned. "Why, why did you call her back?" Then he reached for the telephone.

Now that Billie Dove had moved to the center of his life, he was desperate to keep Ella from returning. Using the telephone with finesse, he fielded two teams to ambush Ella in Chicago and make sure that she returned to New York and from there sailed on to Europe. He enlisted the master of the Santa Fe Railroad Line's Dearborn Station and the chief of the Chicago Western Union office, Michael McCloud, and empowered them with duplicate copies of the personal telegram to Ella. The cablegram read: "Just heard you had left. Why didn't you let me know first? My temperature is down to one hundred today. I do not know why Dietrich wired you, but it is nothing serious. It is ridiculous for you to spend three days on the train so please go back to New York and call me from there.

By all means, don't come. Don't come until you talk with me on the phone."

The station master personally slid the cablegram under Ella's compartment door and a duplicate under Libby Farish's as well. He also stationed an orderly in the hall to see that the wires were retrieved from under the doors. They were. Hughes, however, was not convinced.

Paying double time and promising favors in return, he persuaded McCloud and agents Kebbele, Zimmerlee and a Miss Kumnick. It was Miss Kumnick who handed four duplicate telegrams to Mrs. Ella Rice Hughes personally at 7:45 A.M. as she returned from the dining car, but Ella did not get off the train. She continued west. The cables were the first communication she had received from Howard in months.

When she disembarked with her sister at the Pasadena train station, she was radiant with anticipation. Noah Dietrich, who met them there, realized she thought she was headed toward a reconciliation with her husband.

"I was so goddamn naive," Dietrich wrote. "When Ella's sister took me aside and asked if it was safe for Ella to return to Muirfield, I thought she meant was it contagious. So I said, sure, perfectly safe. Actually, Dove had darted out the back door with her clothes while I was collecting Ella and Mrs. Farish. In fact, that's how I found out that Howard was courting Billie and that it was serious."

When Ella arrived at Muirfield she discovered that Hughes was already converting a suite of rooms for someone else. She also discovered that Howard was the same as ever: callously indifferent. He was angry that she had read the possibility of a reconciliation into his telegrams. And he refused to be touched by the fact that his bartered bride had cared enough to come to his side.

As Ella sat in a guest bedroom weeping in the arms of her sister, Hughes made another phone call to Billie.

After a few days' recovery, he pulled himself from his bed, packed his yachting clothes, and sailed away to Santa Catalina Island with the other woman, Billie Dove. This brazenly public jaunt across the channel to Avalon Harbor, the azure blue haven for the idle rich, was a declaration of independence for the two lovers and a notice to Ella and to Dove's husband Irvin Willat that their marriages were over.

Gossip queen Louella Parsons tattled about the idyll to her national radio audience. She proclaimed Miss Dove to be "exhausted from the grueling demands of talking pictures." No need to worry about Billie's virtue on her trip with the elusive Mr. Hughes, Parsons assured her listeners. "Miss Dove's mother accompanied the couple."

But this romantic interlude almost ended in tragedy. During their return trip on Sunday afternoon a Pacific swell roared in, churning up twenty-foot waves and tossing the fifty-foot yacht up and down. Water poured into the ship's passageway and swirled around Billie's ankles. Panicked, she hoisted herself onto the deck. "I was desperately trying to return to my cabin," Dove recalled. "Suddenly a powerful wave hit me and knocked me down. I was in danger, about to be swept overboard." Hughes was inside, oblivious to the drama. Not so the ship's captain. "He grabbed me by the ankles and pulled me back on board," said Dove.

Hughes found Billie shivering on a couch. As the yacht fought its way back to Los Angeles Harbor, he embraced her tightly. "My God, I nearly lost you," Hughes said, shaking. He kissed her gently. "I don't know if I could go on without you."

A week after Santa Catalina Howard phoned Billie and told her to dress for an especially formal dinner, saying, "I've got a surprise for you."

His chauffeur drove them across Los Angeles, past hills dotted with trees and oil wells, to San Pedro. A gleaming white yacht awaited their arrival. In the formal dining room Howard presented her with a gold florist box. Inside was a spray of ten white orchids that were nestled atop fresh gardenias. Over a candlelit dinner in the yacht's formal dining room, Howard spread his arms to indicate the eighty-foot expanse of the floating palace. "It's ours," he said. "I bought it today."

They named it *Rodeo,* in honor of the character Dove was currently playing in the Jazz Age talkie *The Painted Angel.* Only hours earlier, Noah Dietrich had paid $350,000 cash for the cabin cruiser, plus a bonus that guaranteed Hughes's possession of the yacht that same evening.

Billie and Howard remained on the yacht till early in the morning, sitting on the deck, holding hands, and making love under the stars. "It was wildly romantic," Dove recalled. "The yacht became our love nest, a secret we shared with no one else."

This "sweet, secret romance," as columnist Dorothy Manners characterized it, now entered a dangerous phase, for the wounded Willat was bent on revenge against Hughes. If Willat couldn't have her, he would make Billie pay by making Hughes a co-respondent in a messy divorce. And

Hughes would pay through nasty publicity that could affect his delicate divorce agreement with Ella.

One afternoon as Hughes and Billie were driving down Hollywood Boulevard, he frowned. "I think someone's following us. Hang on tight." He sped around the corner to Las Palmas Avenue, a tiny street leading to a dead end in the backwash of Hollywood. The car behind them kept up the pace, finally trailing them to a dead-end alley. "Howard opened his door and so did the other man," Dove remembered.

Billie saw Howard sprinting down the alley a few paces behind his quarry, who soon disappeared. Howard returned to the car ten minutes later and banged his hand on the fender. "I lost him, but he was following us, dammit! He was absolutely following us!"

Billie frowned. "I suppose it's Irvin."

At eight o'clock the following morning Hughes summoned Noah Dietrich and his attorney Neil McCarthy to Muirfield. He commanded them to "find that son of a bitch Willat and ask him what he wants to divorce Billie and leave us alone."

Willat instantly dismissed the emissary. "Tell Howard to meet me face-to-face like a man," he said, "then I'll talk." Hughes appeared at Willat's bungalow the following afternoon.

The director told him that he had built Billie into a major star, that he had protected and nurtured her as both husband and manager. "I'm proposing a simple business arrangement," Willat said. "When you pay me $325,000, I'll agree to an uncontested divorce."

Billie was outraged. "I pleaded with Howard not to pay it," she said. "But he was determined to marry me as soon as possible. So he decided to go ahead." Noah delivered 325 thousand-dollar bills to Willat the next morning.

By this time Ella and Libby were in Houston, and Ella had filed for divorce—the first in the history of the esteemed Rice family. Ella and her attorneys, under the guidance of Ella's brother-in-law William Stamps Farish, negotiated a quiet, effective divorce that, nonetheless, favored Hughes. Ella accepted a $1.2 million settlement rather than the $10 million she could have expected by insisting on Texas law, which called for a fifty-fifty division of community property.

Ella's petition noted, "There is no community property and this settlement is in the form of a gift, not a claim against Hughes's community property." Ella even allowed Hughes to make payments: $250,000 per year until 1933.

In her divorce petition she called Hughes "irritable, cross, cruelly critical, and inconsiderate, rendering living together inappropriate."

She was a lady to the end.

Anxious to marry his Ziegfeld girl, Howard agreed to participate in a preposterous scheme to outwit the residency requirements of Nevada, where Billie's divorce could be carried out more quickly than in California.

"Operation Nevada" began Howard's fantastic flirtations with masquerades and false identities. In a scheme concocted by attorney Neil McCarthy, Hughes would become an average Joe. Not long after Hughes bought off Willat, he telephoned Billie early one morning. "Tell Mary [Billie's maid] to go out and buy you some countrified clothes. Farmer clothes. Things you wouldn't be caught in.

"I'll be there to pick you up at 8 A.M. Wear the clothes and remove all traces of makeup. Leave your hair just as it is when you wake up."

Shortly after, wearing her gingham dress, scuffed work shoes, and an atrocious bonnet, the most beautiful woman in Hollywood climbed into a limo with one of America's most dashing heirs, who greeted her in overalls, boots, and a sweat-lined hat that obscured his handsome features. The car delivered them to a side entrance at Los Angeles Union Station, where they bought economy seats to a small farming community in Nevada.

"We stopped at a very small station where a beat-up old car awaited," Dove said. "We went way way out into the desert, where we were deposited in front of a modest farmhouse surrounded by fields." Next to it was a small single-room structure—"a shed," according to Dove. It had corrugated metal walls, a window without a glass pane, and a dirt floor. Howard pointed to it. "Here is the residence I arranged for you. This will qualify you for a Nevada divorce." Both of them doubled over in laughter.

Hughes then told Billie the essentials of his plan. They were to pretend to be brother and sister and work for a farmer and his wife while the clock ticked away on Billie's residency requirement. That way they could be together without anyone in Hollywood, or Houston, knowing what they were doing. They didn't need any more scandal.

When they met the farmer they were to work for, Howard told Billie, "They think we're here to learn farming." Billie listened, astonished, as Hughes continued, "You'll work inside the farmhouse; I'll be out in the fields. But we've got to be careful—no slips."

"And boy did we work!" Dove recalled. 'We certainly didn't look like motion picture people, I call tell you. And I did my best. I started each day making 'my brother's' bed. When the farmer's wife was putting up vegetables for the winter, I would watch and then copy exactly what she was doing. Putting up the beets was the worst." When the farmer's wife washed dishes, it was Billie who dried them. "And my 'brother' was out slaving in the fields."

Every night just before sunset, Billie and Howard walked down a lane and beyond a gnarled windbreak of eucalyptus trees to hold hands, standing there in silence. "It was impossibly romantic," Dove recalled.

But Hughes's lawyers discovered the shed would not qualify as a legitimate residence for Billie Dove. The rural charade lasted less than two weeks. The "brother" and "sister" rode back to Los Angeles to engineer a California divorce—in full glare of the Hollywood press corps.

Years later, Dove recalled that Howard had seemed happier as a simple field hand than as the celebrated millionaire and film producer that he was.

The media circus over Dove's divorce began early on the morning of January 2, 1930, when Louella Parsons informed her readers that Billie Dove would appear in court that morning to divorce her husband of six years, Irvin Willat. Louella led off her column this way: "Instead of the dove of peace, the menace of a beating constantly hovered over the home of Billie Dove. Irvin Willat, in fact, walked right up to his wife at a party and knocked her down flat. I was there to see it."

There were other headlines that morning: BILLIE DOVE SAYS WILLAT SLUGGED HER screamed the *Hollywood Citizen-News,* and the *Examiner* trumpeted TERRIBLE CRUELTY ASSERTED BY INTERNATIONAL BEAUTY.

At 9:05 A.M. on the first work day of a new decade, Dove glided to the witness box in a black Chanel suit, a tight-fitting black straw toque, and matching black stockings. She quite naturally resembled a Ziegfeld girl in mourning.

She pled her case quietly, but the proceedings were recessed twice so that attorney Neil McCarthy could dash outside and telephone his boss, Howard Hughes, for instructions. Each time he returned, he whispered them to Billie.

At 10:10 A.M. the divorce was granted by Judge Henry R. Archbald, a golfing buddy of Howard's at the Los Angeles Country Club.

Billie was now free to become the second Mrs. Howard Hughes.

Outside in the hall, reporters cornered her. "Are you going to marry

Howard Hughes?" demanded one of them. Dove calmly adjusted her little hat and said, "Give me a cigarette please." The journalist persisted, "Are you *ever* going to marry Howard Hughes?"

"Give me a cigarette, someone," Billie said as she pressed through the crowd.

Then she turned and looked back over her shoulder. "I will say this: Howard is a brilliant air pilot and a first-class golfer."

With that Billie Dove tripped down the steps of Los Angeles Superior Court, into Howard Hughes's waiting limousine.

CHAPTER 6

APPLAUSE

BEATRICE DOWLER, RESIDENT HOUSEKEEPER AT THE MUIRFIELD MANSION, was awakened by a staccato burst of explosions. The wall next to her shook; the panes in the lead windows rattled. It sounded as if a fierce gun battle were underway in the wine cellar beneath her first-floor apartment. She reached for the phone and hesitated. There was a lengthy pause.

She heard the clattering of shell casings as they scattered across the terrazzo floor of the basement. It could only be Hughes. He was so paranoid about the cellar and its contents that he kept its only key.

When the explosions began again, Dowler grabbed the phone and alerted Noah Dietrich, just as she had been instructed to do whenever her employer changed from Jekyll to Hyde.

Noah drove across town from Westwood to sedate Hancock Park, where Hughes was easily the youngest homeowner. He was relieved to see that the lights of neighboring houses were still dark. He found his young boss careening about the fortresslike bunker, wielding a Thompson submachine gun, borrowed from the set of *Hell's Angels*, while surrounded by his father's rich collection of pre-Prohibition whiskey.

Hughes had shot craters into the ceiling and walls of the cellar, which had been specifically reinforced to protect Howard Sr.'s $50,000 cache of 1918 bourbon and Scotch. Howard appeared haggard, exhausted, and totally unaware of the commotion he had caused. Both men leaned against the walls of the cellar for a while. Dietrich waited to see if Howard would talk. He would not.

So Dietrich, like a caring father, got his employer into bed and then drove home, ending another crazy day in a jumble of crazy days and crazy nights that tumbled one over the other as spring turned to summer in 1930.

. Obsessed and bedeviled by the endless delays and mounting costs of *Hell's Angels,* and emotionally exhausted from his complicated campaign to marry Billie Dove, Hughes had suffered the first of many emotional collapses.

For the only time in his life, Howard drank heavily. After eighteen-hour days in the editing lab, he coaxed Dietrich to his wine cellar for company as he drank glass after glass of aged whiskey. Noah tried to keep his silence, but he gradually noticed that the alcohol, coupled with Hughes's troubled personality, was driving his boss toward near suicidal acts.

"What the hell are you trying to do?" he finally demanded.

Hughes regarded him with a smile. "I'm trying to become what every young man should become, a gentleman drinker."

"Bullshit," answered Dietrich. "You're just feeling sorry for yourself."

Hughes had gambled recklessly on the fate of *Hell's Angels*, draining millions from a fortune already ravaged by the Depression. The film had also taken a human toll. During filming, in separate incidents, three aviators had lost their lives.

With postproduction costs running at $25,000 per day, Hughes was under tremendous pressure. Hollywood columnists had made the film an industry joke. Even Louella Parsons, Howard's close friend, finally printed, "*Hells Angels* has become synonymous with delay and is the stock joke of Hollywood, one of those perennial things which flowers every few months."

Several weeks later, Parsons goaded her friend further: "In years to come, when we are talking to our grandchildren about Howard Hughes, some intrepid soul will finally release *Hell's Angels*." This attack in newsprint, the first Howard had ever experienced, made for tense times in the editing labs.

One night, screenwriter Joseph Moncure March, who was still writing new dialogue to be dubbed onto the soundtrack, noticed the door of the projection room being flung open as one of the *Hell's Angels* editors stumbled down the stairs. Hughes was just behind him, yelling and shaking his fist.

"Seeing his quarry elude him, Hughes picked up a heavy metal ashtray and hurled it at the retreating figure," March recalled. "It just missed the film editor's head by an inch and smashed one of the banisters." After which, Hughes stalked grimly back to his office, slamming the door behind him. "When Hughes's patience snapped, he could be formidable."

He spent hours walking after midnight on the velvet greens of the Wilshire Country Club. Other nights he carted out an enormous pile of golf balls and drove them out over the silent hills with a nine-iron.

Always infatuated with powerful machines, Hughes now became maniacal over speed, pushing his automobiles and planes to their limits. He wrecked his Duesenberg, repaired it, and then wrecked it again.

Because Billie was away, filming on Santa Catalina Island, he felt betrayed. Like a small child, he needed attention.

After endless hours at work on *Hell's Angels* he would jump into one of his cars and roar out Wilshire Boulevard and onto Pacific Coast Highway, past Malibu to the darkness of Point Dune. One night his powerful canvas-top Cord skidded on a hairpin turn and crashed into the side of a granite cliff. The impact pushed Howard's head into the windshield, knocking him out. When he came to in the emergency room of Santa Monica Hospital, he jumped up from his bed and ran to the door.

"Mr. Hughes, wait!" said a young physician. "You suffered a concussion."

"Nonsense," said Hughes, looking back over his shoulder. "If I had a concussion, I wouldn't be walking out this door."

During the final retakes for *Hell's Angels*, Hughes became intrigued with a specially souped-up World War I fighter. Since special training was needed to fly it, only veteran flier Paul Mantz had access to the plane. During a lull in filming, Hughes leaped in anyway and was taxiing down the runway when Mantz ran after him and jumped into the co-pilot's seat. "Howard, you can't fly this plane," he said.

"Paul, I already am," replied Hughes.

But landing the sophisticated aircraft wasn't so easy. After making three awkward passes at the field, once missing the camera tower by several feet, Hughes disgustedly surrendered the controls to Mantz. "I give up. You land the goddamned thing."

According to Dietrich, Hughes appeared to be saying, "Kill me, if you can!" The aide-de-camp felt that the only antidote for this emotional tur-moil would be the completion and release of *Hell's Angels*.

Easier said than done. By the time filming had wrapped, eight differ-ent flying locations had been used, including Oakland Airport, where pilots were holed up for weeks, waiting for cloud formations Hughes wanted as an aerial battle backdrop. As *Photoplay* noted, "If the clouds wouldn't come to Mr. Hughes, Mr. Hughes would go to the clouds."

Though he had proclaimed his love for Billie Dove, Hughes played the role of the director to the hilt—by having a brief fling with his leading lady, Jean Harlow. According to *Hell's Angels* star Ben Lyon, from the time Hughes met Harlow, "Sparks flew." Agent Johnny Maschio said the affair ensued despite the fact that Harlow "wasn't Howard's type—she was too hard-looking," and said Hughes took her to Agua Caliente. Journalist Adela Rogers St. Johns saw the two at William Randolph Hearst's San Simeon retreat. Actress Dorothy Lee remembered Hughes escorting Harlow at the Cocoanut Grove. Harlow would later claim that an irate Billie Dove put an end to the tryst.

Just nineteen, Harlow was at first uneasy in the role of the *Hell's Angels* temptress who is supposed to ooze wanton bliss. At one point she desper-ately turned to James Whale, who was directing her scenes, and asked, "Tell me exactly how you want me to do it."

Whale cruelly retorted, "I can tell you how to be an actress, but I can-not tell you how to be a woman."

But Hughes knew what he wanted her to do. In what would become a peculiar Hughes trademark, he got involved in the design of Harlow's costumes, including a gown so skintight that there were gasps when she sauntered on the set in it. Backless, it had a low-cut bodice held up by only the wispiest of rhinestone-studded straps.

Then there was the scene in which Harlow wore a gossamer, come-hither negligee. For Hughes, it wasn't come-hither enough. "Open it wider," he demanded. She obliged, by several inches. "Wider!" said Hughes. "Before they got through, the negligee was open practically to her navel, showing a generous view of her large breasts," wrote Joseph Moncure March.

Hughes would take further advantage of Harlow's breasts for the film's publicity stills. Publicist Wilson Heller took credit for putting Hughes in touch with a photographer whose work emphasized actresses' bustlines. He took a few shots of Harlow, with plunging and barely-there necklines, and "Howard was crazy about them." Added Heller,

"Those early tit pictures were delivered to papers across the whole country."

As the film's publicity rolled out, four editors toiled on an astounding twenty-five miles of film, 560 hours' worth.

Hughes finally booked the prestigious Grauman's Chinese Theater, the most expensive venue in America. Opening night was set for June 30, 1930.

At seven o'clock on that breezy evening, Hughes bounded through the front doors of the Muirfield house and lowered himself into the hired luxury of a traditional Hollywood limousine, with its silver vase of roses and crystal decanters of fine spirits. He pulled aside the tails of his hand-tailored dinner clothes and made last-minute adjustments to the white tie and starched shirt front. The dazzle of this formality contrasted with the look of earnest concern on his handsome face, making him appear far younger than his twenty-four years.

Clutched in one hand was a spray of pale violet orchids, chosen to match the powder blue gown of Billie Dove, who nestled beside him. With a nod from Hughes the limousine eased into place as part of a gleaming caravan of identical sedans, each equipped with a radiophone.

The car ahead carried an uncertain Jean Harlow, almost buried in the cascade of white orchids and gardenias Hughes had showered upon her.

As the parade turned onto fabled Vine Street and headed toward Hollywood Boulevard, a wall of searchlights came into view, three hundred columns of penetrating light, stretching from the foothills of Los Feliz to the forecourt of Grauman's with its famous footprints of Mary Pickford, Charlie Chaplin, and a pantheon of silent stars.

Because of the crush of the limousines and the pushing, surging crowd of fans, it took the Hughes contingent more than an hour to reach the boulevard. "There are at least forty-five thousand cars here, making the greatest traffic jam ever known in the west," declared one breathless newsreel announcer, who added, "Five hundred thousand people are prowling the streets to get a glimpse of the stars and celebrities." Three hundred and fifty Los Angeles policemen and one hundred United States Marines maintained tentative control.

When Hughes was a mile from Grauman's, he sent a message via radiophone, cueing an aerial pageant unequaled in Hollywood history. A squadron of vintage airplanes roared in from the San Fernando Valley, diving, zooming, and tumbling in mock warfare. Nine hundred gallons of liquid smoke left vivid ribbons of red, gray, and ocher in the foggy sky above the theater. The beams of the retreating sun glinted off the swirls so that, according to Jean Harlow, "they resembled streaks of oil paint."

Three of the planes painted a crimson arrow that ran the full length of Hollywood Boulevard, with the point hovering over the mock Chinese towers of the theater.

In the limousine, Howard was lost in his own thoughts. Bad reviews could literally ruin him. He had expressed deep fears the night before to Noah Dietrich. "If this doesn't work out and I go broke, I'm going to fly my plane as high as I can go and then dive into the ocean."

"It was tough," Dietrich later recalled. "He was out there alone with no studio behind him. They were counting on this 24-year-old kid to fail, hoping he would fail."

The jury that would decide his fate, the Hollywood press corps, was waiting in plush reserved seats inside the movie temple, buried in press releases and clutching limited edition leather-bound programs. Hughes had bravely confronted the issue of cost by releasing a breakdown of the $4.2 million budget, one of the biggest of the day, including the $40,000 spent on the premiere. Another press release, by Hughes's personal publicist, Lincoln Quarberg, coined the term "platinum blonde" to describe Harlow, a phrase that would help carry her to the first rank of film stars.

Outside Grauman's, a roar spread through the crowd as Howard's car moved into view of the searchlights. Marines, sprinting in formation in dress uniform, guided Hughes, Dove, and the incandescent Harlow, swathed in white fur, into the splendor of Grauman's, where a live hundred-piece orchestra was already playing rousing battle music from the film's soundtrack.

With the who's who of Hollywood finally seated, a glittery "prologue" show began. There were acrobats, intricate ballet numbers, a comedy troupe, and even an appearance by World War I ace Roscoe Turner, in full flier's uniform and accompanied by his trademark pet lion cub.

But what the assembled crowd really wanted was the long-awaited movie. At last, the chandeliers dimmed. And the title credits rolled. Three hours later, this jaded industry audience of two thousand stood and applauded. Hughes was awestruck. It appeared that he had created the one thing the studios had not achieved—the first potential blockbuster of the sound era.

"We all hoped this glamorous young man would lead the industry out of the slump brought on by the Depression and the universal popularity of radio," said columnist Adela Rogers St. Johns. "Hollywood would never see another night like this."

Seated in the last row, Howard and Billie slipped out of the theater while the crowd was still cheering and walked through the palm grove of the old Garden Court apartments to the Montmartre Cafe, where Dove was hosting a postpremiere party.

"He was never one to brag about his accomplishments," Dove recalled. "But he was immensely pleased." And with good reason. *Hell's Angels* had made him a major Hollywood player overnight.

He did not have to rewrite his reviews for *Hell's Angels*. "Beside this picture, *Wings* was but a feeble thing," wrote Harrison Carroll in the *Los Angeles Evening Herald*. The *Los Angeles Times*'s Edwin Schallert proclaimed, "Hughes's 'folly' is a magnificent picture." *Variety* declared, "As an air film, it's a pip." Even today *Hell's Angels* remains unsurpassed, with "the most spectacular flying scenes ever filmed," according to noted film historian Kevin Brownlow.

Critics and audiences were likewise taken with Jean Harlow. Never mind that *Hell's Angels* found her wildly miscast as a Britisher. Her revealing costumes and such lines as "Would you be terribly shocked if I slipped into something more comfortable?" made her the most sexquisite star of the day.

Hell's Angels made Hughes a celebrity producer. But it did not enhance his bank account. Noah Dietrich said the movie never did recoup its budget, ultimately leaving Howard $1.5 million in the red. But at the time it looked to be a moneymaker.

By that winter, Hughes had five motion pictures in various stages of development, making him the most important independent producer of the early talkies.

For Hughes, *Hell's Angels* was the cornerstone of what he envisioned would be a new film empire. During its filming, Hughes's production company, the Caddo Company, also made *The Racket*, a gritty underworld melodrama, and *The Mating Call*, about a marriage of convenience. Both were successful; *The Racket* was even named one of the year's top films by many of the country's critics.

Hughes continued to contract stars, though not always wisely. He signed Butterfly Wu, "the Mary Pickford of China," but never found another picture for his premier contract player, Harlow, whose contract he sold. He also became involved in a movie theater chain and an early color photography process. The color lab was located in an Art Deco building at 7000 Romaine Street in Hollywood. When the company folded, Hughes continued to use the unmarked, fortlike structure as his office. It came to be known as 7000 Romaine.

He scoured the theatrical and literary worlds and snared the rights to *The Front Page*, the zany Broadway hit written by Charles MacArthur and Ben Hecht. It was to be directed by Lewis Milestone, who won Academy Awards for directing Hughes's *Two Arabian Knights* and the great war drama *All Quiet on the Western Front*. Pat O'Brien and Adolph Menjou were cast in the tale of Chicago newspaper reporters, after Hughes voted thumbs-down to James Cagney (whom Hughes dubbed "a little runt") and Clark Gable (because "his ears are too big and his tits are too small").

Scarface was a fictionalized account of the rise and fall of notorious gangster Al "Scarface" Capone. Though Hughes was in the midst of a lawsuit with filmmaker Howard Hawks over his aviation picture, *The Dawn Patrol,* which Hughes claimed lifted scenes from *Hell's Angels,* he had the audacity to approach Hawks about directing the gangster opus.

"I was just teeing off at Lakeside Country Club, when the golf pro came up to me and said, 'Howard Hughes is on the phone,'" remembered Hawks. Hughes wondered if he could join Hawks for a game. "I said, 'Tell him I don't want to play golf with him.' "

After relaying that message to Hughes, the golf pro came back to report, "He says he'll call the suit off."

Hawks and Hughes played golf, and while on the green they agreed to team up for what would become a landmark film. Starring newcomer Paul Muni as the Chicago mobster, the movie ran into early problems with the era's moralistic censorship board known as the Hays Office. But just as Hughes went his own way with *Hell's Angels,* he stubbornly refused to bend to pressure.

"Screw the Hays Office," he told Hawks. "Start the picture and make it as realistic, as exciting, as grisly as possible."

Hughes had also purchased Billie's contract with Warner Brothers, and had her career to shoulder. *Sky Devils* was a comedy about fly boys that utilized leftover footage from *Hell's Angels* and starred a young Spencer Tracy. He sought to further enshrine Billie with starring roles in *The Age for Love* and *Cock of the Air.*

When he began to map the budgets of his films, Hughes was dumb-founded to learn that *Hell's Angels* had drained his production accounts dry. When he tried to dip into the reserves of the tool company, he discovered that the accounts had dwindled to less than $100,000. Yet he had an iron-clad deal for the five films with United Artists, which had already scheduled the movies for release.

As usual, he telephoned Noah in Houston and demanded a fresh infusion of cash.

"Howard, we've got to talk about this face-to-face."

Two days later Noah and Howard sat across from each other in the sunny breakfast room at Muirfield. A servant delivered an old-fashioned Texas breakfast of eggs, thick slices of toast, rib-eye steak, and scalding black coffee. They ate for a while in silence; Dietrich wasn't particularly anxious to deliver his news.

After some small talk about the success of new drill bits and the state of Howard's unlamented relatives, Dietrich finally gave it to him straight: "Essentially, Howard, you're broke. You haven't got a ready cent of cash to spare."

Dietrich spoke carefully. Howard Hughes was not accustomed to hearing the word no. Ever since being freed of his family ties, and his arranged marriage, Hughes had acted as if he owned the world. It was left to Dietrich to tell him that he didn't. In the next three months the full brunt of the Depression finally clobbered the Hughes Tool Company. It suffered losses for the first time since 1912.

Worse, the executives at the tool company were preparing to stage a mutiny to protest the "profligate ways" of the young heir. Adding to the embarrassment, Hughes was about to default on the next installment of Ella's divorce settlement. Her family, particularly William Stamps Farish, chairman of Standard Oil, and Hughes's Aunt Annette were outraged.

"You're only broke. You're not ruined. But you've got to stop spending," Noah warned.

Hughes spread out the accounting ledgers for the five films. He needed slightly more than $2 million. Noah realized he was treading on extremely sensitive ground: not only was Howard obsessed with his identity as a film producer, he was also planning to spend $550,000 on three films starring his paramour, Billie. In fact, he had already signed a distribution deal to deliver her first film, *The Age for Love*, within six months.

Dietrich was also aware, as were the social leaders of far-off Houston, that Hughes had spent $1.5 million on Dove, directly and indirectly. Though she herself had protested, Howard paid $500,000 for her contract from Warner Brothers; the $325,000 bribe to Irvin Willat to secure her divorce; $350,000, including remodeling, for the yacht *Rodeo*; $20,000 in fees to Neil McCarthy to process the divorce; $20,000 for a European tour they had taken that summer; and an unknown amount on jewels and gifts.

The money Howard spent on Billie was just a fraction of the $16 million the young heir tossed away between 1927 and 1930, $6 million of it on motion pictures and a crude experiment with a color film processing company. By 1930, Hughes was spending hundreds of thousands of dollars every month.

Dietrich's earlier warnings had been ignored. On the way back from Europe, when Hughes stopped briefly in New York, he cabled Noah that he planned to speculate on a series of stocks. "I've had an inside tip," he explained.

Realizing the market was still shaky, Dietrich begged leading broker Rudolph Cutton to speak with the heir. "Stay out of the market, kid," said Cutton. "This thing is far from stable."

Howard bought 70,000 shares of blue-chip stock anyway, including a massive package of Chrysler bonds.

Cutton woke Noah up the next morning. "What the hell has your boy done? The bottom has fallen out at Chrysler and three other firms." Noah blanched. Hughes had lost $4 million in less than an hour.

Dietrich called him off the greens of a Long Island golf club: "You've got to keep those seventy thousand shares and hope the market recovers; that could take years. *Why* did you ignore me?"

Hughes was embarrassed: "I got a tip from a guy on the golf course. It seemed like a sure thing."

During the time it took Howard and Billie to reach the West Coast, Dietrich devised a daring plan to finance the films and to prevent the sale of the Hughes Tool Company. "Our only choice is to mortgage the company," Dietrich explained. "We will turn over a large package of shares to the City Bank–Farmer's Trust Company, and they will advance us two-point-seven million dollars—enough for the films plus your own living expenses."

Hughes understood that it was a desperate gamble. Failure to repay the loan would cost him control of his father's legacy. He reluctantly agreed and also promised to reduce his living expenses to a "penurious"

$250,000 per year in 1931, a year in which the average family income in America was $4,000.

Dietrich also negotiated a humiliating accord with Ella Rice Hughes and her brother-in-law William Stamps Farish, who was pulling the strings. They allowed Hughes to default on his 1932 installment of $250,000 and to stagger the remaining $750,000 throughout the thirties, with the last payment coming in 1939. But Farish insisted on draconian conditions, stating flatly in letters that neither he nor the former Mrs. Hughes "trusted Hughes's financial responsibility." To satisfy these doubts, Farish forced Howard to sign over temporary title to seventeen hundred shares of the Hughes Tool Company, about 25 per cent of the corporation's stock, to Mrs. Hughes until she was paid in full. They also obtained a court order prohibiting Hughes from making any major expenditures of $100,000 or more "without written permission from Ella Rice Hughes." Other than the films already contracted for, Hughes could make no other films until 1939 nor could he invest heavily in the stock market.

As Noah succinctly put it: "Howard had enough money to be a playboy but not enough to be a film mogul or an entrepreneur."

Financially, the highest-flying heir of the Roaring Twenties was grounded.

However, the mutinous executives at the tool company had underestimated Howard. He ordered Noah to Houston to deal with "those overgrown functionaries." Added Hughes, "Remember, this is *my* company."

Meeting with every major officer in the drilling company, Dietrich discovered that they were disdainful of their young owner. Colonel R. C. Kuldell, the senior vice president, a key executive for ten years, who had been a close friend of Howard Sr., spoke for them all: "Howard has made absolutely no contribution to the company, yet we have given our life's blood. He's just a spendthrift kid who's draining all the money out of this company to spend it on wild living in Hollywood."

When Kuldell's remarks were repeated to Hughes, he erupted in fury. His first impulse was to fire them. "But they'll just go to your nearest competitor," Dietrich counseled. "It's better to placate them."

The executives offered a plan wherein they would take over control of the tool company, giving Hughes $500,000 a year for life. It was a proposal they had presented twice before but with lower payoff figures.

From Muirfield, Hughes expressed his amusement: "Hell, Noah, I plan on making a lot more off the tool company than five hundred thousand dollars a year. Instead, offer them stock options, to be instituted over a five-year period." As an additional peace offering, he paid the top five executives an additional $100,000 a year.

After the phone negotiations ended, Hughes icily told Dietrich that he never intended to lose control of the tool company. He had lied to his executives. There would be no stock options. "This is a cash cow," Dietrich later remembered Hughes telling him, "and it will eventually make me one of the richest men in the world."

To that end, he ordered Dietrich to Houston for half the year, establishing a two-man dictatorship of Hughes and Dietrich to build the Hughes Tool Company into the largest corporation of its type in the world, the cornerstone of a billion-dollar fortune. From that day forward, Howard no longer pushed aside the reports and figures and tallies from Houston; he studied them eagerly. During the next five years, as the Great Depression abated, the research staff at the tool company was doubled, the output quadrupled, the number of drills multiplied by ten, and the factory totally modernized.

In affairs of the heart, however, he was not going to do as well. His incessant skirt-chasing would cost him the love of his life, sending him into a tailspin in which he would desperately womanize his way from coast to coast, looking to recover what he had irretrievably lost.

CHAPTER 7

ADRIFT

BILLIE DOVE WOULD NEVER REVEAL WHY SHE LEFT HIM. CERTAINLY IN 1930 it seemed that their soaring romance would never end. In early July, Howard, Billie, and her maid-companion boarded the Santa Fe Chief for New York City, where *Hell's Angels* premiered in three movie theaters at once. The following day, they left on the *Europa*. Destination: Europe. Settled in matching suites, the most luxurious on the liner, they indulged in the romance of this unusual pre-honeymoon.

They strolled the deck late at night and normally had dinner in one of their suites, talking until dawn. "It was the most romantic time you can imagine," Dove recalled. One evening, as they were embracing passionately on the bank of the River Thames in London, a friendly bobby chided them. "He ended up taking us on a private tour of London, showing us things you usually cannot see," said Dove. On the last leg of the tour, they lingered in wintry Austria and finally went on to the Bruner Clinic in Prague.

It was Billie who insisted that they visit the world-famous Czechoslovakian clinic. "Howard was going deaf," explained Billie, "and it was getting worse every year. Consequently, he often had no idea what people were saying. I found that he could understand if I looked in his eyes and spoke very slowly. What he could not understand, he could deduce by reading my lips." Often, Dove would take his face in her hands, look directly into his eyes, and whisper to him very slowly. Sometimes she would indicate something across the room, and his eyes would follow hers. "We were deeply in love and on top of the world," recalled Dove. In a sad way they were also lost in their own world.

Though Hughes had at first tried to conceal it, his hearing problem had been evident by his early teenage years. Houston physicians, possessing only rudimentary knowledge of ear diseases, recommended hearing aids. He took that as an affront. "I will *never* wear a hearing aid," he told his Aunt Annette. He sent away for information on a lipreading course but never followed through. West Coast specialists were meanwhile mystified. By 1928, human voices had become garbled by static and an incessant whistling and buzzing. By 1930, Hughes suffered from constant ringing in both ears. This interrupted his sleep and had made it impossible for him to discern the editing cues as he dubbed *Hell's Angels*.

His only relief came when he was behind the wheel of his car or in the cockpit of an airplane. The regular drone of engines masked the ringing while encouraging his companions to raise their voices. He would embrace these enclosed places for the remainder of his life.

After ten days of testing, the Czech physicians informed Hughes that he had otosclerosis, a genetically transmitted disease of the bones inside the ear. They also told him the condition was largely incurable. "The bones will continue to grow," said one of the doctors, "slowly choking off the eardrum." Constant ringing was a torturous by-product of unnecessary bone and blood vessels throughout the ear. The doctors offered him a sophisticated series of hearing aids, which he refused.

"His damned vanity," Dietrich later said. "Pride prevented him from using the very thing which would have lessened his isolation from the rest of us."

The Czech doctors had one last bit of advice: "Learn to read lips."

In 1930, Los Angeles's cushy suburb Hancock Park was the preserve of the tastefully rich. It was singularly different in almost every way from Beverly Hills, the preserve of the flashy rich; from the Hollywood Hills, the preserve of the trashy rich; and from the hills of Bel Air, the preserve of the nouveau riche. Obscured behind the Art Deco commercial sprawl of Wilshire Boulevard, the neighborhood's tree-lined streets meandered up and down a series of knolls and centered on an upmarket shopping village where maids and butlers could procure fancy beef filets from Kansas City, raspberries out of season, and Scottish tea scones.

The raffish movieland press corps invaded Hancock Park only when specifically invited to the afternoon teas and extremely formal dinners that were the social mainstays of this insular community. Journalist Aggie Underwood wrote that "the dogs who bark in Hancock Park do so very quietly." And Katharine Hepburn was later to wonder why "the silence was so deafening."

It was to this oasis of respectability that Howard and Billie returned in the winter of 1930 to plan their wedding and a domesticated future.

The signs of Billie's influence pervaded the Muirfield mansion, from crystal bowls of roses in the entry way to the gleaming new piano in the parlor. Upstairs, carpenters, tile layers, and carvers were transforming a dingy series of rooms into an airy boudoir for Dove. Decorators had already descended upon Muirfield with swatches of carpeting, English wallpaper, and photos of furniture for her inspection.

She and Hughes shunned the industry's star-studded parties, avoided Hollywood's raucous night clubs, and almost always dined alone. "Ours had become a very deep, quiet love; the kind of love you only find once in a lifetime," Dove recalled with great emotion. "Many times I would play the piano and sing; sometimes Howard would play the saxophone. We didn't need all that glamorous stuff."

Dove was Howard's first soul mate, a lover who put his interests before hers. Her presence calmed him; she gave him a peace of mind he had never before known.

When his insomnia worsened, Billie sat by his side through the night, talking to him in her soothing voice. When he gave up on trying to sleep, she would accompany him to the Goldwyn Studios to screen the latest films. They often sat through more than one.

Yet when Hughes returned from the *Scarface* set late one afternoon in 1931, he discovered that Billie had left him. There had been no confrontation, no ugly scene, no hurtful words. She simply collected the few things she kept at Muirfield—perfume, sheet music, and her collection of notes from Howard. Then she returned to the house she had built for her parents around the corner.

They spoke on the telephone several times. Howard made promises. Dove remains too discreet to criticize Howard, even after six decades. But it seems certain that his philandering and his fits of jealousy doomed the relationship. Billie sensed what other women would come to realize about Hughes: he saw women as possessions. He had to have total control. They were under his command, like prisoners.

"He insisted upon knowing where she was every minute of the day," Dietrich recalled. "I don't think she knew it, but he had her followed, had the staff at Muirfield spying on her." In crowded night clubs, he sometimes even followed Billie to the door of the powder room, where he would wait to escort her back to the table.

Billie may also have discovered her fiancé's secret party house down the street. There, in a bordello-type atmosphere, he continued to occasionally sleep with the faceless, usually nameless (to history) starlets who drifted through his life like shadows. To meet his assignations, all Howard had to do was grab his golf clubs and disappear through the hedges toward the getaway house. Like Muirfield, it backed up against the golf course. "Not many people knew about it," said Johnny Maschio, who visited Howard at both houses.

"My reasons for breaking with him were intensely personal," Dove said. "It was what I would describe as a small thing. Some might call it insignificant." She added, "We both carried torches for a long, long time."

Howard was shaken: "Billie's left me," he told Noah. "I don't know what I'm going to do."

When Billie left, Hughes had been planning a dinner party to be held on the *Rodeo*. He went ahead and played host on his own. But he was distant with his guests. As the yacht cruised off Malibu, silent star Colleen Moore couldn't find Howard. So she went looking for him. He was at the very back of the ship, staring out at the moonlit Pacific. "It's a lovely night, isn't it," said Moore, offering up small talk. "Yes," said Hughes. "And I'm the unhappiest man in the whole world."

With Hughes producing Billie's films *Cock of the Air* and *The Age for Love*, he couldn't even run away from his memories of the leading lady. In the months following her departure, he would sometimes sit in his projection room, watching her image flicker across the screen. The first great love of his life was over.

For a few frantic years Howard dated girls by the score, as if sheer numbers could compensate for the intimacy he had lost when Billie deserted him. From 1931 through 1933, Hughes's name was linked to more than fifty actresses, debutantes, party girls, and chorines on both coasts.

In Hollywood, he was spotted in the company of actresses Dorothy Jordan (Ramon Novarro's frequent co-star, she went on to marry *King Kong* director Merian C. Cooper), Lillian Bond (who was often cast as a marriage-wrecker), and starlet June Lang (who went on to marry gangster Johnny Rosselli). He once sent MGM musical queen Jeanette MacDonald a note across a Hollywood dance floor. And he put the move on Joan Crawford, even though she was married, promising her "a *very* big present," if she would date him.

He squired up-and-coming teenage actress Ida Lupino, who stressed, six decades later, "my mum went along." For her sixteenth birthday, remembered Lupino, he wanted to give her Chanel perfume and a telescope. "But I told him I didn't want the telescope—and that I didn't give a damn about the perfume." Hughes gave her a present, anyway. When Lupino opened it—a pair of binoculars—he told her, admiringly, "You're not a phony." He would express his continued admiration for Lupino in years to come by paving her way as a director, making her a pioneering female filmmaker.

He dated actress Marian Marsh, who remained a platonic friend until the forties. She saw Howard undergo his transformation. "I saw him start to change," confessed Marsh, who attributed Hughes's growing girl-craziness to the company he kept.

After *Hell's Angels* put him on the map, Hughes began partying and club hopping with a crowd whose nucleus could be called the Rat Pack of the thirties. There was darkly handsome agent and hanger-on Pat De Cicco, dapper agent Johnny Maschio, and around the mid-thirties, suave Warner Brothers leading man Alex D'Arcy.

"Basically, we would go from club to club, helping Howard to get girls," remembered D'Arcy.

"He wanted quick lays," admitted Maschio.

During these wolf hunts, when he was abetted by his buddies, Hughes sometimes slept with several women each week. Not surprisingly, he became known as a notoriously indifferent lover. He was famous for leaving starlets stranded at swank Perino's on Wilshire Boulevard or at New York's Stork Club. And for interrupting sex to take a telephone call and never returning to bed.

In one example, scarlet-haired screen vamp Nancy Carroll, an actress whose sexuality would later be compared to Marilyn Monroe's, drifted into a split-second affair with Howard just weeks after his breakup with Dove. A discriminating lady who had been a much courted New York chorine at the age of eighteen, Carroll had flirted with Hughes from the sidelines of several A-list parties. But the first time he took her home to Muirfield, their foreplay was interrupted.

He served her French cuisine by candlelight before leading her up to the master bedroom. While Nancy stripped to a sensational set of black lingerie, Howard disappeared into the bathroom, with its stacks of aviation and engineering books.

He opened a World War I flying opus and began reading. Carroll waited for twenty minutes before throwing on her black-beaded dress and slamming out of Muirfield's massive double doors. She clacked off into the night in her spike heels.

When he remembered Carroll, Howard went running back to the bedroom. His sexual playmate was gone. He drove off in a fury, only to later return home alone.

Hughes was luckier with her half a dozen other nights before she disappeared for good. "I was tired of being just another plaything," she admitted to Noah Dietrich.

On his way to the Cocoanut Grove one evening in early 1932, Howard stopped by Dietrich's office to complain about an eternal subject, women. "I'm through with the actresses . . . I need to find me a nice girl outside this business and marry her."

Noah, himself a married man, nodded in agreement; he'd spent a legion of sleepless nights cleaning up the aftermath of Hughes's Hollywood escapades.

Despite what he said, however, the next woman to attract him longer than the next rosy dawn would be up-and-coming star Ginger Rogers. Had she been less levelheaded, she might have become the next lady at Muirfield. But she kept him at a comfortable distance.

A former vaudeville performer and Broadway ingenue, Ginger was less than a year away from superstardom as Fred Astaire's partner in *Flying Down to Rio*. She was a Texan, given to wisecracks, with platinum hair and a sassy, brassy demeanor. At twenty-one, she was also the precursor of a new breed of film star. Strong-willed and independent, she was far less vulnerable than the eclipsed stars of the silent era.

The night Howard met her, she was exhausted from a long day, one of many, belting "We're in the Money" in pig Latin on the set of *42nd Street*. She was dancing, appropriately enough, at the Cocoanut Grove, with her boss, producer Mervyn LeRoy.

"I looked over Mervyn's shoulder and saw a very handsome young man staring at me. He kept twirling his partner so his eyes could follow me. Our eyes met, and the young man smiled at me," Rogers recalled sixty years later. "And when he smiled, he lit up the whole room."

Hughes was dancing with the hapless Nancy Carroll, who was soon ditched. Then Howard appeared at LeRoy's table, where he wound up sitting between the producer and Rogers. "He cracked a joke and laughed," Ginger said. "He was devastatingly handsome."

When crooner Russ Columbo started singing "Street of Dreams," Howard stood and gallantly held his hand out to Ginger. Across the decades Rogers remembered his strength and the yearning quality he projected. And she recalled wondering, "What would he be like to kiss?" The next day, Hughes raved about her to Dietrich.

But to Noah she was just another starlet. Hughes insisted, "This one's different."

He was correct. Ginger Rogers blew a gust of reality into the jaded life of the young heir, told him what she thought, told him his wealth was nothing special (and meant it), and intrigued him to such an extent that he would chase her, off and on, for seven years.

A week after they met, Howard telephoned Lela Rogers, who would become known as one of Hollywood's legendary stage mothers, and asked permission to escort Ginger to the premiere of his gangster epic, *Scarface*. Answering for her daughter, Lela said yes.

For Hughes, the Los Angeles opening of *Scarface* marked a personal victory. With *Hell's Angels* he had triumphed over his own inexperience as a filmmaker as well as the day's technology for aviation stunt flying and photography. With *Scarface*, he had triumphed over the censors, though not without some concessions.

To appease the era's demanding Hays Office, which awarded movies the Seal of Approval that was essential for theatrical distribution, Hughes agreed to certain changes. A new ending showed the title character getting his comeuppance on the gallows. And the movie was subtitled *Shame of a Nation*. But Hughes also added a smug touch: an introductory disclaimer that decried gangland anarchy, which the film vividly reveled in.

With Ginger on his arm and his hat tipped cockily over his face, Hughes looked every inch the successful film producer at the Paramount Theater premiere, where a curious crowd gave the movie a standing ovation.

Ginger would keep him at bay, however, and his endless hunt for fresh faces continued. Fame and family money made Hughes a welcome presence in society circles. He would eventually squire debs in Bar Harbor, Newport, Santa Barbara, Burlingame, Fort Lauderdale, Manhattan, Palm Beach, Charleston, Philadelphia, Boston, and Stamford.

Although he was genuinely fond of several cotillion graduates, he also viewed them as trouble-free dates. As he breezily explained to Dietrich: "All I need is my tux; they even provide their own flowers—to match their dress. The hosts supply the food, and there aren't even any tips." The dates were hardly pure. Years later, Johnny Maschio said that for Hughes, the "debutramps" were "even easier than some of the starlets he dated."

In an ironic twist, he would end up wooing his former wife. Four years after Howard forced her out of his life, Ella had reinvented herself and become a major social force in Houston and a sophisticated world traveler. And she had reunited with her former paramour, James Overton Winston, who transformed himself into a rising commodities and oil broker.

Winston was visiting Ella in her suite at New York's Waldorf-Astoria when a phone call came from Howard, who was downstairs in the lobby. James watched Ella as she listened intently to what Hughes had to say. She finally agreed to meet him for a brief reunion in the hotel's tea room—neutral ground.

Howard was direct and passionate in his approach, displaying qualities Ella had never seen during their sterile marriage. He pleaded with her to remarry him, told her she could name the terms, told her it would all be different—traditional promises of a husband who has learned, too late, what he once had.

But Ella was a different person, wiser and stronger. She let him down slowly and carefully—with the grace that was her birthright. In the end, she told him that she and Winston were to be married. She had her own promises to keep. "Write me," she said, then hurried back to the man she had loved for thirteen years.

Six decades later, James Overton Winston emotionally described his own ordeal as he waited for Ella to return. "Even I wasn't sure what she would do, so my joy was great when she returned and again agreed to marry me. And Hughes, he was a fool to let a woman like that slip from his grasp."

The summer in New York following the opening of *Scarface* was a veritable rake's progress through the ranks of nubile socialites. Even so,

Howard badly needed a bachelor pad less in the public eye. Constantly slipping in and out of the sheets at the Drake Hotel soon became dangerous. Columnists lurked behind every column, hoping to catch him playing sexual tag with Gotham's most luscious debutantes.

Well-rewarded tips from industrious bellhops and prying upstairs maids landed Hughes in the gossip columns, exposing several of his secret affairs and allowing his high-toned conquests to compare notes. Another army of spies dogged his footsteps in Palm Beach, fattening the columns of his friend Louella Parsons in Hollywood and Walter Winchell in Manhattan.

He briefly considered leasing penthouse suites up and down both coasts. But instead, he purchased the sexiest yacht in the world.

It was the era of Noël Coward, who often saw to it that his heroines were bedded at sea; and Cole Porter, whose musical hit *Anything Goes* featured nooners on the high seas; and of Rogers and Astaire, whose movies romanticized the satin beds of luxury liners. Fortunately, the *Rover*, a 320-foot Art Deco steamer with a formal dining room, three master bedrooms, and a gourmet galley, was on the market.

Hughes sailed for Scotland to purchase the fifth-largest private yacht in the world. To do so, he had to evade the legal freeze Ella had placed on his assets. Though Dietrich objected, he arranged for Hughes to buy the *Rover* in installments, partially from tool company earnings in Europe.

He also hired a captain, Carl Flynn, changed the boat's name to the *Southern Cross*, and hired a crew of thirty to staff the imposing gold-and-white cruiser. He added lavish final touches in Europe, including a crystal chandelier in one of the master bedrooms and a spread of wolf skins for the enormous double bed. Then the *Southern Cross* sailed for Newport, where the debutantes du jour awaited.

Some of the most desirable women in the world would be entertained on this seagoing palace, which featured a $5,000 wine cellar, a case of Napoleon brandy, and dressing rooms with a full rack of Parisian perfume plus towels, sheets, and linens monogrammed HH by nuns in Belgium.

The *Southern Cross* became the most legendary yacht in Southern California, the grandest boat of all in a region accustomed to floating palaces. Howard used it with great effectiveness when rushing prospective conquests.

His dates were strictly disposable. He would romance a girl, lead her to believe he would marry her, and then move on. The first of what would be many cruel seductions was seventeen-year-old Manhattan debutante

Timmie Lansing, a stunning socialite who fell into Hughes's clutches on a brief trip to Los Angeles in the early thirties.

Their romance began in her suite at the Ambassador and later continued on a cruise from New York to Los Angeles through the Panama Canal. They left the boat at Acapulco and cavorted in the Mexican resort for two weeks. Then he brought the teenager to Muirfield and installed her in Ella's old rooms. "She was a captive, actually," said Dietrich. "He sent her to drama school, had the Westmore brothers [Hollywood's top beauticians] make her over from head to toe, and led her to believe they were to wed."

Eventually, Lansing caught on and made what Dietrich described as "a terrible scene, even threatening suicide." Recalled Dietrich, "Finally her parents came out and physically took her away from Hughes. She was under his spell as many others would be."

During this period Howard and the devilishly handsome William Randolph Hearst, Jr., heir to the world's largest publishing empire, became airborne cocksmen as well, using Hughes's luxuriously appointed amphibian that could seat six and, with the seats pushed back, provided makeout space for four. They scooped up showgirls, starlets, and willing debutantes and swept them off to Palm Springs, Agua Caliente, and even to Hearst's castle, the 100-bedroom Xanadu of Hearst Sr., San Simeon.

One evening, when Hearst Jr. was late for a rendezvous with Howard, Hughes called San Simeon. "Where the hell are you?" he asked. "And where are the girls?"

"What girls?"

"What do you mean, 'What girls?'" Howard bellowed. "What's the point of going out without the girls?"

Hughes heard laughter on the other end of the line.

"Mr. Hughes, this is Bill's father," said the newspaper magnate. "You've got the wrong Mr. Hearst. Knowing Bill, he will be there with the girls shortly."

Then, somewhat wistfully, Hearst said, "You know what, Howard? I wish I could be there with you."

CHAPTER 8

COMING OF AGE

IT WAS DURING THIS SAME WILD PERIOD THAT HOWARD WOULD BECOME unmoored in other ways as well. He began displaying what would later become legendary eccentricities. His phobias on health matters would grow apace. He began disappearing for days at a time. And in his desire to become a premier aviator, he would start taking more and more reckless chances.

His first step toward bizarre behavior occurred when he decided to jettison the good-time-Charlie bankroll he had flashed as a denizen of Hollywood after dark. The usual messenger came to deliver the weekly envelope of petty cash, amounting to some $2,000 in small and large bills, but Hughes turned him away.

Noah phoned him. "Howard, what the hell's going on?"

"Simple, Noah," Hughes answered. "I'm not carrying any money from this moment on, and I want everyone to know it. I'm not even going to carry enough to pay for a cup of coffee."

Dietrich was perplexed. "For God's sake, Howard, you can't go around with no money."

"Goddammit, Noah, there are people out there right now who will knock you off if you've got five hundred dollars in your pocket."

Hughes's concerns were not unfounded. In December 1932, a Los

Angeles newspaper reported that he had been the target of an extortion plot involving a beautiful blonde who telephoned him and threatened suicide. "If you don't see me at once I will kill myself on your doorstep," she taunted. Hughes gave her the address of his attorney, Neil McCarthy, then jumped in his car and headed to McCarthy's residence nearby. There, the girl threatened Hughes and McCarthy. Unless they paid her off, she would create a scene that would attract the neighbors.

Hughes was undaunted. He gave her five dollars.

Along with shedding a fat wallet, Hughes let go of his fancy Dan wardrobe. Instead of the closet full of Savile Row and Brooks Brothers suits, Hughes purchased one dark suit and one light one off the rack, two pairs of canvas tennis shoes from a sporting goods store, two pairs of khaki work pants, and a handful of moderately priced department-store shirts.

The first time Hughes strolled onto a film set in blue-collar drag, crony Pat De Cicco, who always dressed to the nines, looked him over and said disgustedly, "Howard, how can you dress like that?"

Hughes shot back, "It's okay, Pat. You be the dude; I'll do the work."

His only concession to conventionality was a tailored tuxedo, a set of summer formal wear, and a pair of severely plain evening shirts. If necessary, his entire wardrobe could be neatly tucked, and often was, in a department-store gift box. He didn't worry about accessories. He was often spotted wearing tennis shoes with his tuxedo.

His eating habits became uniform as well. A standard Hughes meal consisted of steak, green peas, and ice cream—sometimes two or three helpings of each. Meanwhile, his daily schedule became even more erratic than it had been during the filming of *Hell's Angels*. If need be, he could go seventy-two hours without sleep.

Hughes also began to display paranoia and to be ruled by irrational fears. Like his mother, he became terrified of being engulfed by unseen bacteria and viruses. He was only in his late twenties when he summoned Dietrich to Muirfield for an "emergency conference," declaring, "I'm dying. I'm certain I've already suffered one heart attack, and that the next one will finish me off."

Dietrich thought his boss was in great shape. But he played along. "Okay, Howard, let's check you into St. Vincent's Hospital and have the cardiologists give you every test in existence." Hughes submitted to a four-hour examination and was monitored for half an hour as he ran up and down four flights of stairs. The physicians found him to be in tip-top condition. But Hughes wasn't convinced. "I'll prove them wrong," he insisted.

"How?" asked Dietrich.

"When I die," said Hughes. "When I die pretty damned soon."

His phobias reached a chilling height one night in the mid-1930s. As hot Santa Ana winds gusted through the open doors at Muirfield, he carried out a bizarre ritual. Amid the swirling banyan leaves and drifts of soil he piled up ever growing heaps of garments—cashmere sweaters, linen suits, Scottish wool suits, and argyle sweaters in a muted splendor of executive colors.

Howard bounded up and down the main staircase, his arms piled with more and more clothing that he transported to the yard. He was neat and precise with the castoffs: evening gear in one pile, sweaters and jackets in another, shoes and underwear in opposite corners. Flight gear, including the jacket he wore during *Hell's Angels*, occupied the center.

Several hours earlier he had alerted Dietrich that he needed "an emergency, very discreet" crew of workers dispatched to his house. He raved about "betrayal all around him" and about a "dreadful contamination which had permeated his clothes" as well as the Egyptian cotton sheets on his bed. Howard had slept with one too many anonymous blondes, including one who had given him venereal disease.

"She had the clap, Noah!" he yelled. "She caught it from the golf pro right here at the Wilshire Country Club, and now the infectious germs are everywhere. Everything must be burned to ashes, Noah. Absolute ashes."

Then, in a calmer voice, he issued precise instructions for the destruction of his clothes and bed linens. Four tool company employees were to report to Muirfield with a dozen large canvas mail bags and a brand-new brass padlock (with only one key) for each of the sacks.

"I've already made arrangements for you to use special industrial kilns near the Long Beach oil fields. I will lock each bag as it is loaded, keeping the keys for myself. When your men bring me back the charred locks, I will know the mission has been accomplished properly."

When Howard's entire wardrobe lay in hillocks, he paced back and forth in new chinos and a white shirt from Sears, watching the young men sacking up the clothes. For their protection, he made them wear large rubber gloves. One of the young men couldn't bring himself to put the *Hell's Angels* jacket into a bag. He looked up at his boss and asked, "Can I keep it?"

Howard thought for a moment and then nodded. "But don't come back to me when you catch syphilis . . . I won't pay your hospital bills."

Once he had burned his clothes and scoured Muirfield from top to bottom, Howard felt he was safe. His mother's superstitious attitude toward germs and bacteria had been passed on. Disinfectant plus strong lye soap could cure anything. Syphilis was no exception, he believed.

But tests soon proved that he had contracted primary syphilis, a serious, sometimes fatal disease in the world before penicillin. Hughes underwent a radical treatment that was not only risky but which sometimes engendered a family of side effects, including heart disease and neurological damage—in the worst-case scenarios. Over a period of five weeks, Hughes endured a treatment known as "the magic bullet," in which low levels of poisonous mercury and arsenic were injected into his bloodstream. But in some cases, even these "heavy metals" could not completely cure the victim. Howard was one of them, a fact that Noah Dietrich hinted at in several interviews just before his own death.

Physicians at the time informed Howard that his syphilitic infection had mutated into "tertiary syphilis," a condition that was not curable then and that posed great dangers to the central nervous system. Eventually, some patients, though not all, notice marked deterioration of their thought processes. Mental confusion and grand paranoia were not uncommon.

Hughes's autopsy report revealed the "classic signs of tertiary syphilis."

According to one of Hughes's personal attorneys, the private dossier of the illness and its potential side effects was used with great efficiency to quash a number of paternity suits in the forties and fifties. But in truth, Hughes was not rendered sterile by the illness. At least three women would eventually deal with the dilemma of becoming pregnant by Howard Hughes.

It was during this period that Hughes also began staging what would become a lifelong series of vanishing acts. The Muirfield house staff would discover Howard's untouched bed and one of the cars missing from the garage. Often, the car would be located at the Inglewood Air Field, and Dietrich would discover that one of Howard's planes, either the Scout or the amphibian, was missing. No flight plan would have been filed, and wads of cash would have evaporated from the safe at Muirfield.

Much later, industrious investigators hired by the Hughes estate tracked the lost weeks and months; their tables showed that Howard was "officially" missing for thirty-one days in 1931; thirty-five days in 1932; nineteen days in 1933; forty-two days in 1934; and forty-one days in 1935. In 1932, he vanished twice.

From March 1 through March 16 of 1932, Dietrich, who needed his boss to sign several crucial documents, frantically scoured the country. Convinced Hughes was in Houston, involved in some sort of unidentified corporate spying at the tool company, Noah wired Annette Lummis. "Unable to reach Howard for some time," Dietrich told her. It would become a familiar refrain.

That September, Hughes pulled his most daring disappearing act. It began when he ambled over to the barber shop at the Ambassador Hotel to have most of his hair cut off, abandoning his rakish producer's styling for the naked-ear cut of the man on the street. Picking up a blue cotton suit from Sears and a pair of salesman's brown shoes, he took the train to Fort Worth, Texas.

He lined up with other job hunters at the regional personnel office at American Airlines. An authentic Texas driver's license and a bona fide Social Security card identified him as Charles Howard. Somehow, despite his hearing problem, he managed to get hired as a baggage handler and a candidate for the corporation's pilot-in-training program. His regular shift on American's daily flight from Fort Worth to Cleveland began at 7:30 A.M., when he checked and stowed luggage. He then occupied the co-pilot's seat as a veteran captain taught him the art of flying the large Fokker trimotor. His instant grasp of the array of levers, buttons, dials, and switches was impressive. Always with him was one of the ubiquitous notebooks that he quickly filled with details on wind velocity, navigational techniques, and the off-the-cuff observations of the pilots he flew with.

Dietrich later discussed this amusing escapade with an executive of American Airlines. The executive told Noah that Hughes had garnered "incredibly favorable recommendations." One captain wrote, "That man has the makings of a first-rate airline pilot."

"Charles Howard" also advanced rapidly from a starting salary of $115 per month to $250 three weeks later. His secret life ended when a district officer recognized "Mr. Howard as Mr. Hughes, who he had met at the New York premiere of *Hell's Angels*."

Once Howard's identity was discovered, he posed for a series of photographs in New York following his first transcontinental flight as a co-pilot.

Wearing a freshly starched uniform and pilot's cap, Hughes was snapped as he unloaded bags and peered confidently from the cockpit. The photos were distributed by Hughes's own Hollywood publicist—with captions that revealed Hughes had hired out "to gather data and atmosphere for his next film production . . . on the drama and romance of commercial aviation"— and they traveled the United Press wire. On December 6, 1932, the *New York Sun* reported on its front page that Hughes was hoping to make a movie "dealing with commercial aviation," after working for four months for American Airlines.

For this disappearance, at least, there did seem to be a reason. He was gaining yet more insights into the field that had captivated him for so long: aviation. During this time he would take marked steps toward becoming a world-renowned pilot. Professionally, Howard was restive. He ached to become a bona fide aviation hero and to carve his mark in the sky while he was still young and handsome, as Charles Lindbergh had done. Howard had yearned for such acclaim ever since Ella cabled him a breathless account of the New York ticker-tape parade celebrating Lindbergh's flight across the Atlantic in 1927.

He also sought solace in the air, flying his new Boeing Scout across the West. With a pile of notebooks beside him, Howard would occasionally glance over at a page of his aviation calculations as he rode the currents, pitched and rolled in the coast winds, spun and dived suddenly toward ground, pulling out at the very last moment.

By 1932 Hughes had flown almost every type of airplane in existence, from vintage World War I fighters to lighter-than-air biplanes, from ocean-going amphibian seaplanes to the roaring Fokkers. The rush that came when he soared or plunged exhilarated him. He soared higher and farther and faster than the limits allowed, often to the very edges of unconsciousness.

"For a man obsessed with germs and consumed by shyness, Hughes experienced no trepidation of any sort in the air," Dietrich recalled. "His joy overpowered any instincts of self-preservation."

Howard shook his fist at the sky. He never doubted that up there he was without equal. Hughes the aviator would also prove irresistible to women, and he used his flying machines as tools of seduction, as he did with his movie projects.

In fact, the first plane he created himself was perhaps the sexiest prop machine ever invented, a sleek cloud skimmer without so much as a rivet

or seam to break its clean silhouette. When he assembled a team of engineers, scientists, and mechanics and installed them in a corner of a Glendale
air field, his directive was simple: "I want you to build me the fastest airplane in the world."

Any of the major aircraft companies could easily have built a plane to
Howard's specifications. And they could have done it less expensively. But
Hughes intended to build a family of planes that would "revolutionize aviation." Even then he visualized the nucleus of an aeronautical giant—a
factory to rival Hughes Tool Company.

To head the team, Howard chose recent Cal Tech graduate Richard W.
Palmer, already famous for his radical aircraft designs. Glenn Odekirk was
selected to supervise the construction. Just twenty-seven years old at the
time, Odekirk became one of Hughes's closest friends.

Along with Palmer and Odekirk, each member of the team signed a
vow of silence concerning what the press would call "the Howard Hughes
mystery ship."

Precision welders slipped in and out, as did upholsterers wielding
strangely shaped strips of rubber padding and luxuriously tanned bolts of
leather. When the airplane, disguised by an enormous canvas shroud, was
trucked over to the wind tunnels at the California Institute of Technology,
it clocked in at 365 miles per hour, surpassing any speed ever recorded at
Cal Tech.

This racer, known as the H-1, or the *Silver Bullet,* would fly for only
forty-four hours during its entire career, but it would make Howard Hughes
a household name. Built at a cost of $120,000 over two years at his small
factory, which had been incorporated as Hughes Aircraft, the plane Howard
called "this beautiful little thing" was unveiled in early August 1935.
Hughes's goal: to set a new record for land planes by shattering the existing
mark of 314 miles per hour set by French pilot Raymond Delmotte.

Because of the dangers inherent in flying "faster than any man had
done before," Hughes told only a handful of colleagues about his plans for
the flight. Even Noah Dietrich learned of it at the last minute.

But the troublesome tool company executives had been spying on
Howard. The company's general manager, R. C. Kuldell, who had come
to loathe "this young wastrel," protested to Howard's Houston attorney,
Frank Andrews, "that this dangerous flight could leave us all high and
dry." He demanded that Howard draft a will and that he leave a large part
of Hughes Tool Company to its employees and executives.

Howard fumed at Dietrich, screamed about "obvious leaks," but sent a letter proclaiming that "the key officers had been generously provided for." Actually, he refused to write a new will.

It was Friday the 13th, September 1935, when Hughes climbed into the stubby-looking red-and-silver metal H-1. Once in the air, he headed out over the Pacific past the rocky Palos Verdes Peninsula and headed for Eddie Martin Field in Orange County, where his official speeds would be clocked.

Taking off directly behind were celebrated aviatrix Amelia Earhart, Lawrence Therkelsen of the National Aeronautical Association, and Hollywood stunt master Paul Mantz.

Before plunging down to pass the cameras and counters, Howard pulled his flight cap raffishly to one side and waved over his shoulder to Earhart. Her presence at the test testified to its importance to the aviation establishment. Not since Charles Lindbergh had such a dashing yet thoroughly serious pilot roared onto the scene. Like Lucky Lindy, Hughes had the funds and the contacts to dramatically change the course of this industry in the skies.

To gain speed, the *Silver Bullet* flew over the Santa Monica Mountains and then made an arc toward the breakers of Corona del Mar. Then Howard dived out of the sky, a blurred ribbon of silver. He flew past the trackers and photo monitors seven times, posting speeds of 355, 339, 351, 340, 350, 354, and 351 miles per hour. The record was his; he knew it. But he signaled to Earhart that he would make one more pass, this time from 1,450 feet.

The *Silver Bullet* streaked down like lightning, pulling out of the dive very late, at only fourteen hundred feet above the field. Amelia saw Howard try to pull the plane up. But Hughes's engine had died, and he was struggling with the controls, frantically trying to open a second gas tank—the first had gone dry.

But the little plane wouldn't level out and headed downward with an ominous whine. From 1,250 feet up, Earhart saw Howard disappear into a cloud of dust and debris at one hundred miles an hour.

Luck was with him. He successfully landed the *Silver Bullet* in a Santa Ana beet field. When the ground crew arrived, the aviator was climbing out of the cockpit, swearing under his breath. Odekirk ran over to him. "You okay?" he asked.

Hughes grinned lopsidedly. "She'll do better than this, Ode. She'll do three-sixty-five; I just know it."

Explaining that he at first thought of bailing out, then reconsidered because "of all the money and time I'd put on the plane," Hughes attributed the crash, which crumpled the plane's propeller, to "simple pilot error."

"I tried to switch to the auxiliary tank but just wasn't fast enough," he said while posing for a press photographer on the bent propeller. In his new blue suit, Oxford cotton shirt, and dark tie, along with his aviator's cap and goggles, he was an emerging hero in a depression-racked country hungry for heroes.

But not everyone was cheering him on. A mechanical autopsy on the racer turned up a wad of steel wool jammed into the pipe leading to the auxiliary gas tank. It was carefully held there with a small lead wire. The *Silver Bullet* had apparently been programmed to crash.

The saboteur was never discovered. But Hughes felt he had another reason to mistrust the rebellious tool company executives.

Without any advance notice, Hughes made another speed run on January 13, 1936—a race that would take him from Burbank to Newark, New Jersey. But shortly after takeoff, he lost radio control. His compass went bad north of Wichita, Kansas, when a gust of wind knocked the needle off the point. With no directional guides Hughes had to open a map, which he placed on his knees, and keep a close eye on cities below to figure where he was.

When he touched in at Newark at 12:42 A.M. he was greeted only by a timekeeper. He had beaten the existing record, but not by much. He came in at nine hours, twenty-seven minutes, and ten seconds. It was a snail's pace compared to what he had planned. As he would tell the Associated Press, "I wanted to go to New York, so I tried to see how fast I could do it in." He was a long way from the triumph of Lucky Lindy.

Later in the year, on a $50 wager with a friend, he completed another record flight. Betting that he could have lunch in Chicago and dinner in Los Angeles, he landed after eight hours, ten minutes, and twenty-five seconds. After the flight, which cost him approximately $1,000, he went out to have his dinner. He ordered roast beef and all the trimmings for 75 cents.

Despite the frivolity, the flight proved a serious training ground. "I learned more in eight hours than in the last fifteen years," Hughes admitted. While flying without any maps (because he couldn't find any in Chicago) "everything went haywire" several hours out of the city. "The airspeed indicator suddenly dropped to zero. Then the oxygen tank connections fouled. Finally, when I thought my troubles were over and California was in sight, my oil pressure sank down to nothing. I started pumping by hand." Noting that he bucked a fierce head wind and had ice on his wings for five hours, Hughes matter-of-factly added, "The only thing that worked on my ship was the engine."

CHAPTER 9

CARY AND KATE

ON A LATE FALL AFTERNOON IN 1935, A YOUNG ACTOR NAMED RANDOLPH Scott arrived at Muirfield, dressed for golf and accompanied by a thoroughly tanned, overdressed friend. Scott deposited his golf bag in the entry hall and called out for Hughes.

Scott was a familiar presence at Muirfield. He had walked into Howard's life six years earlier, with a letter of introduction from his family in Virginia. Ella had taken him in, and Hughes, with a call to Paramount mogul Adolph Zukor, had gotten him the first of many film roles.

Thanks to their mutual passion for golf, the Hughes–Scott friendship had survived Howard's divorce, and the actor's career had evolved into starring roles opposite Irene Dunne and Ginger Rogers. He would later become one of the great Western stars—and one of the wealthiest men in Hollywood.

"This is Cary Grant," Scott said, introducing his current roommate. Because Cary was in the doldrums over his recent divorce from actress Virginia Cherrill, Scott had brought him along. He had no way of knowing he was initiating a friendship that would span four decades. (Inexplicably, Scott's friendship with both Grant and Hughes was terminated in the late thirties.)

From the beginning, Hughes is said to have envied Grant's flair, his sophisticated facade, a sort of pedigreed bravado that was markedly successful in class-conscious Hollywood. Cary was at ease in all levels of Hollywood society, from actor Ronald Colman's "veddy British" set to the polo-playing philanderers who surrounded powerful 20th Century-Fox mogul Darryl F. Zanuck. The young actor's wardrobe of beautifully cut suits and dinner jackets was notorious for its elegance, but then, it was tailored by Howes and Curtis in London. Grant was the only actor who dressed himself for most of the drawing-room dramas in which he starred.

He also had a rakish reputation that stretched back to his lusty relationship with the bawdy Mae West, who handpicked Grant as her love interest in *She Done Him Wrong* and *I'm No Angel*. It was to Grant that she breathlessly uttered her personal anthem, "Come up and see me."

When he strolled into Howard's life, he had yet to achieve stardom, but it was not far in coming.

In explaining his durable friendship with Hughes, Grant once said, "We certainly weren't at all alike—maybe that's why we liked each other so much." As proof, Grant recalled their many plane trips together, during which Grant would take along "matched and monogrammed luggage," and Hughes, "would arrive with a cardboard box with a couple of shirts thrown in." If Hughes needed a tux, he would borrow one of Cary's. "One thing I know he liked about me a lot was that we were almost exactly the same size," Grant once joked.

Actually, the two men also had a number of striking similarities. Beneath Cary's sleek outer plumage, he was easily as insecure, shy, and abjectly alone as Hughes. He considered himself to be an orphan, having left his dirt-poor and disinterested parents at the age of thirteen. For the remainder of his adolescence he had eked out a living as a juggler and song-and-dance man in a touring British acrobatic troop. He bolted that job in 1920 in New York, where he eventually got his break in several light musical comedies, and from there went to Hollywood.

Like Hughes, Grant also possessed a dark, brooding side. Given to spells of melancholy and depression, he would, like Howard, be eventually pushed to nervous collapse. Like Hughes, he was also secretive—and protective of his media image.

Though Grant liked to say, "I think Howard Hughes and I were friends because he didn't want anything from me and I didn't want anything from him," theirs was a mutually advantageous friendship. Grant relished great wealth and being in the company of those who had it.

Hughes relished beautiful women, who always seemed to swirl around Grant. "Cary helped Howard to meet women. No question about it," said Johnny Maschio, a close friend of both men.

However, the friendship wasn't dependent on night life. The two men shared a quiet emotional alliance. Grant would sometimes sit silently in Howard's den while Hughes pored over the plans and speculations for his various experimental flying machines. "Howard was the most restful man I have ever been around," Grant later recalled. "Sometimes we would sit for two hours and never say a word." Hughes's housekeeper, Beatrice Dowler, recalled one long dinner in which Grant and Hughes didn't utter more than a dozen sentences.

The friendship between Hughes and Grant is perhaps the most misunderstood, misportrayed, and notorious chapter in Hughes's life, particularly in recent years.

Following Grant's death in November 1986, writers began depicting their association as a lascivious homosexual affair. Several of them claimed that Hughes and Scott were lovers. Cary and Howard supposedly fell into each other's arms when the romance between Scott and Grant cooled. But there are no direct sources to prove a Hughes–Grant affair or, for that matter, any sexual relationship between Grant and Scott. Three exhaustive studies of Howard's life found no hints of bisexuality.

"Howard had so many enemies, including the FBI, that even the most discreet homosexual encounter would have been uncovered," said Robert Maheu, the former FBI special agent who became Hughes's second-in-command in the 1950s. And Noah Dietrich told his biographers that he had heard the rumors but knew them to be false.

"Absolute balderdash," said actress Phyllis Brooks, who dated both Hughes and Grant.

Billie Dove echoed, "Howard with another man? I don't believe that for a second."

Likewise, our complete reading of the 2,059-page FBI study of Howard's private life turned up no trace of homosexuality. Nor did the 100,000-page legal, sexual, and psychological abstract ordered by the Hughes estate.

The Hughes–Grant friendship may seem odd for Hollywood, where relationships are largely fleeting. But it was genuine and lasting. It was Hughes who convinced Grant to attend the Academy Awards show in

1970 to accept his special Oscar. It was Grant who stayed in touch with Hughes in later years when so many others had abandoned the tycoon.

And it was Grant who led Hughes to one of the great romances of his life, his four-year affair with Katharine Hepburn.

From the beginning, it was a relationship marked by drama. It began one afternoon when a Boeing Scout dropped out of the offshore fog like an apparition. The sun glinted off its nose, and its wings dipped as it glided over the sand dunes and landed in a wind-swept meadow above the surf.

George Cukor, who was directing a scene from *Sylvia Scarlett*, frantically motioned for his cinematographer to stop the cameras. Then, his hands placed on his hips, he looked up, taking in the spectacle with the rest of the location crew.

Today, a plane or a helicopter landing near a film set is nothing extraordinary. But in 1935 it was wondrous. And Howard himself was a sight, in his leather flight jacket, aviator's breeches, and cordovan boots.

Katherine heard the roar and leaned out the door of her portable dressing cabin to witness the arrival of "the fastest man alive." Her red hair spilled out over a man's plain polo coat. She ducked back inside to hurry the preparations for a lavish picnic luncheon while her maid unpacked the porcelain cups and saucers necessary for high tea.

Even director Cukor, who lingered nearby, had to admit that it was some opening scene.

But the beginning of Howard's long, turbulent love affair with the Magnificent Yankee was not arranged by fate, as both Kate and Hughes would later say. It was arranged by Cary Grant.

For three years he championed the romance with all the fervor of an Eastern European matchmaker. He even arranged for this introduction on one of the most appealing sections of the California coast line, the rolling dunes of Trancas Beach, where he was completing this peculiar film, in which Hepburn spends most of the movie masquerading as a boy.

"Look, Howard," he'd said the night before, "I'm in a bind . . . you've got to come up to the set for lunch. Each of us promised to invite 'someone very interesting.' "

Hughes hesitated. "Look, I'm working on the racer every day."

"Do it as a favor to me."

Howard reluctantly agreed. "But I can't stay long."

Grant led his friend over to a blanket that Kate had spread across the top of scrub grass that grew behind the dunes. Waiting there was George

Cukor, a popular gay director who was the absolute master of bitchy Hollywood conversation. Hepburn made her entrance fashionably late, in slim gabardine slacks and a Brooks Brothers white shirt. A basket of Scottish scones was slung under one arm.

Hughes sat between Cukor and Cary while Kate reclined decorously on the blanket. True to form, Hughes remained nearly mute as Hepburn, Cukor, and Grant gossiped about Hollywood. Afterward, as they accompanied the stone-faced aviator to his plane, Kate and Cary walked a bit behind. "I thought we had an agreement to bring only 'interesting people' for lunch," she said pointedly.

"When Howard's on a project, he does clam up," Grant confessed. But, he promised, away from work Hughes could be great fun. Grant would continue to try to sell Hepburn on his friend.

For his part, Hughes would deluge her with flowers and invitations for dinner at Muirfield, and use his planes to impress her. Eventually, he wore down her resistance. The great Kate agreed to see him. When she did, she was taken aback to discover how deaf Hughes was. No wonder he had been such a dolt that day on the set of *Sylvia Scarlett*. As Hepburn would write, with some sorrow, "he was apparently incapable of saying, 'Please speak up. I'm deaf.' Thus, if he was with more than one person, he was apt to miss most of the conversation." She attributed his deafness to his eventual downward spiral. Observed Hepburn, "I think that in an effort to be on an equal basis with people, he retired further and further out of his life."

Their relationship was not played out against the gaudy backdrop of Hollywood nightclubs, which Kate detested. It took place on the greens, in the sky, and during long horseback rides through Malibu Canyon. Once, for a golf date, he landed a Scout on a narrow, pitching expanse of green at the Bel Air Country Club. To do so, he maneuvered between two majestic pine trees, which left him less than three feet on either side of the wings. Ignoring angry protests from the club's director, Hughes abandoned the Scout and played out nine holes with Kate, and then hitched a ride home in her car. The plane was later disassembled and towed back to its hangar, a $10,000 bit of bravado.

Both were impetuous. Hughes was once in the midst of a haircut at Muirfield when Hepburn stormed in and demanded they play golf. Off Hughes went, with only half his hair cut, leaving behind a befuddled barber.

"She's brilliant, she's kind," Hughes exultantly told Grant after several evenings with Hepburn. "And she's totally devoid of sham and pretense—perhaps the most totally magnetic woman in the entire world."

Kate was equally overcome. "I admired his verve and his stamina. He was sort of the top of the available men in the world and I of the women. And we both had a wild desire to be famous."

Both also came from money and were fiercely independent. Neither caved in to social conventions. Like Hughes, Hepburn didn't use clothes to impress. Her shirts were sometimes frayed, her shoes scuffed, and she was one of the first notable women who dared to wear trousers in public.

Hughes and Hepburn were also physically similar. Both were lean, with angular features. She was five-foot-seven-and-a-half, about 115 pounds, and seldom bothered to cover her copper-colored freckles with makeup. Hughes was six-foot-three, with darkly hypnotic eyes and a broad grin. Both had been freed of marriages of convenience. Hepburn was divorced from a family friend, stockbroker Ludlow Stevens.

He was thirty and she was twenty-eight; his fame was on the rise because of aviation, hers was on the wane due to a series of box office and critical disasters and an image as a rich, disdainful easterner who was only slumming in Hollywood. Columnists had dubbed her "Katharine of Arrogance" only a month before her life collided with that of Howard Hughes.

After a sensational film debut in *A Bill of Divorcement* (1931), which had earned her an Oscar nomination, she'd turned in a series of triumphant performances in films such as *Alice Adams* and *Morning Glory*, for which she won a Best Actress Oscar. But a series of pretentious commercial failures such as *Mary of Scotland* and *Quality Street* landed her on a list of stars who Harry Brandt, head of a powerful theater owners group, labeled "box office poison." Ever indefatigable and lofty, Hepburn shot back, "If I weren't laughing so hard, I might cry."

Her studio, RKO, anxious to dispense with her $2,500 per week paycheck, offered her a dismal series of scripts that they knew she would reject. They eventually won that gamble when Hepburn refused to appear in a potboiler called *Mother Carey's Chickens*. Hepburn went on suspension and opened negotiations to buy back her own contract.

Who could have predicted that the man who had dropped into her life so daringly would play a major part in the rebirth of her career?

As usual, though, Hughes was unwilling to commit himself to just Hepburn. Like so many other powerful men, Hughes saw no practical reason for being faithful to one woman. He believed in establishing a primary lover, *the* lover, such as a Billie Dove or a Kate Hepburn. But he saw no reason why this single "great affair" could not thrive alongside numerous passing affairs.

It was as if he was fleeing memories of his mother's smothering love.

"He was psychologically unable to be faithful to one woman," explained Robert Maheu. Added Hughes's former aide-de-camp, "He could tolerate the threat of death easier than that."

In fact, death would be the outcome of one of his many dates. He had been spending time with aviation buddies in the Southern California seaside resort of Santa Barbara when he met local debutante Nancy Bell Bayly, a twenty-year-old brunette who bore a resemblance to Ella Rice. "I was dancing at the Montecito Country Club when this man cut in," Nancy recalled. As he spun her on the dance floor, Hughes revealed he had seen a photograph of her in the local newspaper. She had been snapped in the surf, wearing a bathing suit.

On their dates that followed Howard was, to her surprise, the perfect gentleman. "He didn't kiss me good night, or even hold my hand in the movies," remembered Nancy, who found Hughes to be confounding. "He was taciturn, yet also very vulnerable, like a little boy who needed to be cared for. I think that was one of his great appeals to women."

The night he took her out for her twenty-first birthday, he promised her a memorable evening. She didn't know they'd make headlines.

It was cloudy and foggy on July 11, 1936, when Hughes piloted Nancy to Los Angeles. Then the couple headed for Trader Vic's, a Hollywood night spot where rainbow fishnets, an artificial rain forest, and cascades of orchids made it the most exotic dining spot in town. Howard and Nancy sipped the ice-blue drinks of strong rum and fruit juice that were the specialty of the house. "So strong that just one made me light-headed," she reflected.

Then they dropped by Muirfield. Howard ran upstairs to change his clothes while a housekeeper served martinis. Nancy poured hers into a potted palm; the rum had been enough for her. "I don't know if Howard drank his."

From Muirfield they headed for the Cocoanut Grove. Dinner and drinks followed. And Pat De Cicco dropped by their booth to say hello. Then Howard and Nancy took off, heading west to the amusement park on the Santa Monica pier, where Howard wanted to ride the roller coaster.

Around 10:45, at the poorly lit corner of Third Street and Lorraine,

Nancy saw a flash of a streetcar going by and felt the dizzy swerve of the car as Hughes tried to dodge an oncoming vehicle. She heard a loud thump as if the car had struck something. She was confused, but Howard seemed to know exactly what had happened. He stopped the car and ran over to a form slumped in the road. The man, a 59-year-old tailor named Gabe Meyer, had been killed instantly.

Whether Meyer was standing in a streetcar safety zone or had walked in front of Hughes's car has never been determined. Precise details of the fatal accident were clouded by contradictory police reports, confused witnesses, and by very successful flanking movements by Howard's lawyer, the formidable, well-connected Neil McCarthy. "He was a friend of my father's," Nancy recalled in 1994. "And he was considered the finest attorney in town.

"I never knew it happened until we came to a full stop," she added. "I had never seen action happen so fast in my life."

Hughes, with the help of an onlooker, moved the victim to the side of the street. He was startled to see that a crowd was gathering, many of them passengers who had just stepped off the streetcar at nearby Third and Wilshire.

"Suddenly, Howard whisked me out of the car, pulled my gorgeous gardenia lei that he had given me from around my neck, and directed me to the streetcar. I protested, I wanted that beautiful lei. But he said, 'No, I want you to melt into the crowd.'

"I was shoved onto the car, told to get off near Muirfield and to spend the night at his house. He said that I would be taken home to Santa Barbara the next morning."

Officer C. P. Wallace, the first cop on the scene, found Hughes slumped against his car. "I tried to stop in time," he told Wallace. "I moved my hand to his wrist to see if I could find a pulse. I couldn't feel a thing." Hughes identified himself as "a manufacturer" and gave his address as 3921 Yoakum Boulevard, Houston, Texas. But he was recognized.

Howard was driven to Hollywood Receiving Hospital, where he was pronounced sober after a sobriety test. But the doctor there noted that Hughes had been drinking.

At Central Jail, Hughes was booked on "suspicion of negligent homicide."

Detective Lt. Ralph N. Davis, suspecting intoxication, wanted details. "Do you even know what happened?"

"Yes, I do," answered Hughes. "And I will answer in the presence of my attorney, Neil McCarthy."

After conferring with McCarthy, Hughes issued a brief statement to the press, stressing this was his first accident, that he'd never before hit "even a cat or a dog." For good measure, he added, "My dad taught me to drive eighteen years ago and he was a stickler for caution. During the six and a half years I've had this car I've never even scratched the paint." He refused to give the name of the woman who had escaped into the night. He was released from jail early on July 12, with McCarthy at his side.

The story made the morning newspapers. But the reporters all but ignored the death of Meyer and focused on Hughes and "the mystery woman who had been spirited away." One headline read: MISSING BEAUTY HOLDS KEY TO DEATH.

Just after the morning papers were thrown onto the quiet yards of Hancock Park, a private detective showed up at Muirfield to drive Bayly back to Santa Barbara. Until they were out of the neighborhood, the detective made her lie down on the back seat. Hughes never would reveal her identity. It wasn't until police questioned Pat De Cicco that they were able to track down Bayly, whose picture was then splashed across front pages.

By this time a crucial witness, a United Parcel Service driver, had told police that the victim had been standing in the trolley car safety zone when Howard struck him down. Worse, he described Howard as driving erratically, and faster than he should have been.

On July 15, Howard and the still ashen Nancy testified at the coroner's inquiry. McCarthy had since reinterviewed the witness, who now changed his story. In a new version, Meyer had stepped directly in front of the Hughes vehicle. At the recommendation of District Attorney Buron Fitz, Hughes was cleared of all blame. Outside on the courthouse steps, Hughes told reporters, "The accident was not my fault. That was clear from the start. I was driving slowly and a man stepped of the darkness in front of me."

Documents in the Hughes estate would later indicate that the changeable witness might have been influenced by the Hughes pedigree and the Toolco bank account.

Meyer's family received a $20,000 settlement.

Bayly, who has always believed in Hughes's innocence that night, never saw him again.

*   *   *

Hughes renewed his romance with Hepburn in December 1936, making news as he followed her during a Theater Guild production of *Jane Eyre*. The tour opened on December 10 in New Haven and moved to Boston soon after. For the first time Hughes put his own life on hold to devote himself to another. He chased Kate to Boston, where he occupied a seat down front on opening night, and stayed in a suite not far from hers in the Copley Plaza Hotel.

He swept her off to candlelit dinners and flooded her dressing room with roses. As Hepburn once coyly put it, "the inevitable" happened. She and Hughes became lovers.

Hughes followed the tour to Detroit, Cleveland, and Chicago. "And he conducted business on the telephone," Hepburn wrote in her autobiography, *Me*. But the night Kate opened in Chicago, Hughes abruptly returned to Los Angeles. He stopped by at rehearsal and talked to her quietly for a few minutes before dashing to the airport. The reason for this exit was their secret.

Though Howard wanted to share Kate's various beds as *Jane Eyre* continued its tour across the East, he also knew that his best chance to set a coast-to-coast speed record was in January, when the westerly winds off the Pacific Ocean would speed him on his way to fame.

On January 19, at Union Airfield in Burbank, Hughes strapped himself into the cockpit of the racer, pulled on his leather cap, and waited for a radio signal from the control tower. Almost as an afterthought, he strapped on a brand-new "continuous feed" oxygen mask.

In many ways, he had been waiting for this moment since his father died. The wind billowing at his back had the power to help him create his own legacy, to carve a place for himself.

Glenn Odekirk, who was assisting from the ground, noticed that his boss seemed preoccupied, not quite paying attention to the lights and knobs, which could mean the difference between life and death. Then the signal for takeoff came, at precisely 2:14 A.M.

Hughes opened the throttle, raced down the runway, and roared into the sky, piercing the windy clouds and banking his plane over the Sierra Nevada Mountains. Darkness engulfed Hughes as he flew above the clouds. The faint radio signals from sleepy airports below were only distant guideposts.

When he crossed the edges of the Grand Canyon, a yawning black chasm below, Hughes began to feel dizzy. Then his arms grew alarmingly heavy, so paralyzed that he could barely grip the controls. Thirty seconds later he was gasping for breath and falling in and out of consciousness.

He struggled with his deadened arms, grabbing the line leading to his oxygen mask to try and shake it, to free the oxygen trapped by an air bubble. It didn't work. His hand froze in position, gripping a small section of tubing.

Howard released the controls with his still mobile hand and, using every ounce of strength, yanked off his oxygen mask and pulled the line up to his mouth. He ripped the tube open with his teeth and desperately sucked the oxygen. Slowly the paralysis receded. Later he would comment on how close he was to death. "There was a rhythm to it," he told *The Times*. "A throbbing pain followed by almost blissful dizziness. Then another throbbing pain."

Since Howard was flying at 20,000 feet, higher than anyone had ever flown, the ragged end of the oxygen system was literally a lifeline. And he sucked on it all the way to the East Coast. To ease the agonizing pressure inside his head, Hughes opened his mouth and screamed off and on for nearly five minutes. Only then could his eyes focus on the dials and lights guiding his plane.

As he headed across northern Arizona to connect with the high altitude wind system to speed him on, the radio in the *Silver Bullet* sputtered and died. He would navigate the remainder of the route by sight, aided by brief breaks in the cloud cover over Winslow, Arizona, St. Louis, and Indianapolis.

By dawn, Hughes was officially reported as missing by the National Aeronautical Association (NAA). Morning radio bulletins informed the world that radio contact "with this millionaire playboy hero of the air" had ended abruptly five hours earlier.

In Chicago, Kate thought the worst. Frantic calls were placed to Hughes's Los Angeles headquarters. But they were in the dark as well. There was nobody to dispute the headline on the extra editions of the *Chicago Daily Tribune*: AVIATION HERO LOST!

At Newark, the exhausted delegation of the NAA had just about given up on Howard when a U.S. Army Air Corps plane reported that the pilots had seen the *Silver Bullet* in the skies above Army Field in Middleton, Pennsylvania.

Still, they were amazed when the sleek silver racer shot out of the clouds at 380 miles per hour, plunging 12,000 feet in less than a minute. As the rubber wheels struck asphalt at Newark, the official NAA timer, William Zint of the Longines Watch Company, snapped his stopwatch. It was 12:42 P.M. Eastern Standard Time, seven and a half hours since Hughes left Burbank.

He had slashed 117 minutes off his own, admittedly sluggish, land plane speed record of a year earlier. He had also proved that high-altitude flying, an airship free of rivets, and retractable landing gear could pave the way for commercial aviation.

Shivering, even in his fur-lined flight suit, Hughes brushed past the small press delegation and ran to a phone booth inside the Newark terminal. His telegram to Kate Hepburn was simple: "Am down and safe at Newark. Love, Howard."

But Hepburn, already backstage for a matinee, knew he was fine. She had eagerly grabbed up the latest edition of the *Chicago Daily News* with its two-inch high headline: HUGHES SPANS THE U.S. BY AIR IN 7½ HOURS.

From that moment forward, Howard was as famous as she was, a factor of no small importance, as Kate later noted, "for two people addicted to fame."

While Howard was racing to Hepburn's side, the Cook County clerk's office in Chicago received calls from someone who identified herself "as representing Mr. Howard Hughes." The caller solemnly asked about the local requirements to obtain a marriage license. Coincidentally, someone from the front office of Chicago's Ambassador Hotel, where Hepburn was staying and Hughes was still booked, made a similar call.

Naturally a convenient tipster from the clerk's office (he was up for re-election) flooded the media with calls, and the "Kate and Howard chase" was on. Although some Chicago journalists viewed this as a publicity stunt to improve attendance at *Jane Eyre,* considerable evidence exists that Howard impulsively proposed to Hepburn after his audacious cross-country flight and that she tentatively accepted. Hughes later told Odekirk that he and Kate were "almost married early in the relationship."

But the press killed any chance the pilot and the actress would marry in the Windy City by stampeding to the theater and the Ambassador. At 2:45 A.M. on January 21, Hepburn returned from the theater—with a pack of journalists tailing her cab. In the hotel lobby, she faced an even larger mob. "Where's Howie?" screamed one reporter. "When's the wedding?" demanded another. "When're you moving to one suite?" yelled out another even more rudely.

Kate turned to face them, then thought better of it and slipped into the elevator.

The next afternoon, three thousand screaming girls braved a light snow to cheer her arrival at a two o'clock rehearsal. The radio predicted ten thousand by curtain time. At the same time, Cook County clerk Michael J. Flynn held a downtown press conference to announce that he was eagerly awaiting the arrival of America's most celebrated lovebirds. He also happily displayed a new suit and a carnation that matched his maroon tie.

But Flynn waited in vain. At 5 P.M. the concierge at the Ambassador delivered an official message from Miss Hepburn. He spoke in a monotone: "Miss Hepburn wishes to announce that Miss Hepburn and Mr. Hughes will not marry today."

Next morning, the *Chicago Daily Tribune* informed its readers that LA HEPBURN'S WEDDING DAY IS REALLY SOMETHING!

Upstairs, Hughes was trapped in his own suite, unable to remain with his lover overnight. When he made a brief stopover in her rooms at teatime, the news about the wedding that didn't happen was on the radio, and on the Associated Press wire a short time later.

But if the wedding was canceled, for reasons never made public, their relationship was stronger than ever. In fact, Hughes flew home to wait for Kate.

Muirfield was to have a new mistress.

CHAPTER 10

KATHARINE THE GREAT

IN THE SPRING OF 1937, KATHARINE HEPBURN MOVED IN THE MUIRFIELD mansion and swept away the emotional cobwebs that reminded Hughes both of his arranged marriage with Ella Rice and his affair with Billie Dove. She brought with her pieces of New England furniture, a wardrobe built around slacks, a tower of books and plays, and a wry sense of humor. There was laughter at Muirfield once again.

Hughes abandoned his small hospital-type bed for a double bed, showed up for dinner now and then, and endlessly roamed the golf links with Kate until sunset. Both strong-willed, they had learned to make concessions. She helped entertain his business and aviation contacts, including the occasional mobster. He did his best to stay monogamous. Always just offstage was Cary Grant, nudging his two friends toward matrimony.

If ever there was a golden age in the troubled life of Howard Hughes, this was it.

He had a lover who was his intellectual equal. As the recent recipient of the Harmon International Trophy—presented to him by President Roosevelt at the White House, it would remain one of his most cherished possessions—he was a genuine aviation hero. He also happened to have a fortune from a renaissance of the Hughes Tool Company, which soared just as the Great Depression began to fade.

One morning Hughes escorted Hepburn to the airfield and shoved open the hangar door to reveal a gleaming Sikorsky S-43, a twin-engine amphibian with room for six crew members and enough fuel to cross the Atlantic Ocean. With the seats removed, it became an airborne sleeper with the capacity to land on water or asphalt anywhere in the world.

Kate and Howard sat in the plane, with its smells of new leather, freshly applied enamel, and new carpeting, while he told her of his plan to circle the globe, not as a hotshot in a daredevil racer but as a pioneer in a half-million-dollar airship carrying a full crew. It would, he told her, open the skies to worldwide air travel, to airlines that would regularly carry passengers from New York to London. But first he had to put the plane through a series of extensive flight tests at wide-ranging altitudes and speeds.

Hepburn was almost as enthusiastic as Hughes, and from that moment their romance took to the skies. They flew to Santa Catalina Island and bobbed in the lagoon while flying fish leaped out of the green ocean water. They would go on to fly across the continent dozens of times while Howard piloted and Kate snuggled in a sleeping bag below. Sometimes they would talk through the night about Hollywood and aviation. "Sheer heaven!" she later exclaimed.

They toured the eastern seaboard and watched the lights of Boston, Philadelphia, and New York drift by as they headed to deserted islands off the coast of Maine. "I flew everywhere with Howard. Across the country . . . here . . . there. We took off once from under the Fifty-ninth Street Bridge in New York City," Hepburn recalled. "When we flew in the East, and it was hot, we would stop in the middle of Long Island Sound and dive off the wing to swim."

Back in Hollywood, they were oblivious to what anyone else thought. The fact that Howard's only tux had finally fallen apart and that trousers-loving Kate barely owned a dress didn't stop them. If they went out, Howard would dash off to rent dinner clothes. And Hepburn would borrow a gown.

"Their total lack of pretense was quite wonderful really," Grant said years later. "From that moment forward, Hughes didn't own a tuxedo and could literally pack all of his clothes in a large box. Kate was similarly disinterested in clothes and social conventions. They didn't want to complicate their lives."

Life at Muirfield, however, was far from simple and bucolic.

Accustomed to wealth and to satisfying their every whim, Kate and Howard populated the mansion with eight servants, including a formal valet, two chauffeurs, and a hand laundress.

Their habits were singular: Hepburn, for instance, took six showers every day, changing after each one. Howard went through four or five shirts and a couple of pairs of chinos in the same amount of time. And since each dinner was semi-formal, requiring damask table linen and monogrammed napkins, laundress Florence Foster's working day sometimes ran to nine hours.

Mirroring the Court of Versailles, Howard's guests were carefully ranked A, B, and C. The A-list, usually society blue bloods and members of the Hollywood mogul class, dined off Haviland china and crystal goblets. The B-list, usually actors and Howard's carousing buddies, were served on rose-patterned American china and cut-glass goblets. The C-list was problematic. Since it included mobsters Lucky Luciano and Bugsy Siegel as well as rough and tumble aviators, these callers dined off porcelain and glassware kept by housekeeper Beatrice Dowler in a special pantry. After some of these guests had dined, the service was then smashed and tossed in the trash.

"You know, Howard," Kate once told him, "if you picked your friends more carefully you wouldn't have this problem."

Climatic conditions fluctuated wildly at Muirfield as Hepburn, a fresh-air fiend, clashed with Howard's tendency to keep windows closed, fearing the invasion of germs. Kate frequently threw open all the downstairs windows in January to accommodate the roaring fire she had built in the sprawling colonial fireplace. Hughes huddled in a robe and house slippers.

There were few tears and recriminations in this love affair, but there were some long episodes of silence as the lovers smoldered over some slight disagreement.

Once, battle lines were drawn because of Hepburn's smoking, a habit Howard could not abide. Actress Phyllis Brooks, whose romance with Cary was then in full swing, witnessed the first salvos of the battle at the Cock 'n Bull restaurant, a tweedy industry hangout. "Kate lit a cigarette at dinner, and Howard reached over and pulled it out of her mouth. And I thought, 'My God, what's gonna happen?' But she just did her little laugh and looked embarrassed, didn't say a word." Hughes won not only the battle but the war: Hepburn eventually gave up smoking.

In the winter of 1937–38, as Howard prepared for his global flight, a year after his record-setting coast-to-coast hop, his affair with Hepburn suffered its first major breach.

When he traveled to Washington, London, and Paris to negotiate flight clearances, he failed to keep in touch for several weeks. Kate became so anxious over his whereabouts that one morning at RKO, where executives were plotting to get rid of her because of her temperament, she threw herself into a frenzy. She stepped out onto a ledge atop the two-storey makeup building and threatened to jump.

Layne "Shotgun" Britton, a makeup artist working on special assignments for Hughes, had to lean out the window and coax Hepburn off the ledge. "I sat her in a big barber chair and talked to her until she calmed down." Britton tried frantically to reach Howard but discovered he was in the air. But he did reach Cary Grant at MGM.

"Cary called me and said he had a hell of a time talking Kate out of a suicide attempt," Johnny Maschio recalled. "When Hughes was out of contact, he was *really* out of contact."

Actually, at these times he was often in the company of other women. Though Hepburn was now residing at Muirfield, he was still incapable of committing to her. Howard began straying while in London in 1938, where he was meeting with aviation officials. While he was occupying a baronial suite at the Savoy Hotel, he collided spectacularly with Woolworth heiress Barbara Hutton. At that time she was blonde, beautiful, highly sexed, and even richer than Hughes. Producer Frederick Brisson saw them at a Savoy tea dance "looking very sweet and holding hands like young lovers misty-eyed." Howard and the "poor little rich girl" spent several afternoons in Hutton's round satin bed with its ostrich feather canopy.

Hutton later recalled, with unusual candor, that "he saw I had difficulty reaching orgasm and tried desperately to make me do so the first time . . . thereafter pleasing himself and saying that 'I would not have one anyway.' If I touched myself, he angrily brushed my hand away. He could not take it when a woman lost herself in pleasure because he felt he must absolutely be in control of a situation . . ."

Hughes said nothing of the affair when he returned to Hepburn. In fact, he assured her that he wanted marriage. "I was madly in love with him and he about me," Hepburn insisted. Naturally, she introduced him to her family. This would lead to further problems.

*   *   *

Howard got his first glimpse of Old Saybrook, Connecticut, as the amphibian followed the Atlantic breakers. Then came the promontory, and a breathtaking view of Fenwick, the Hepburn family's summer home. It was just as Kate had described it: a rainbow of late spring and early summer colors. Rambling turf, pink-blossomed cherry trees, and exotic tulip trees of magenta and orange. Fenwick was easily identifiable, surrounded as it was by a fortress of coastal oaks and maples. Beyond lay ancient sand dunes and coastal marshes mottled with water willows and chartreuse algae.

That early May morning in 1938 Howard was meeting the formidable Hepburn family, which was well known in show business circles for having chased off a fair share of Kate's suitors.

The visit was mandatory, part of three resolutions he had made to himself just after the new year dawned. He would wed Katharine Hepburn in the summer, fly around the world in July, and embark on his plan to turn Hughes Aircraft into an aviation giant.

Noah Dietrich, to himself, gave Hughes "little to no odds of achieving any of the three."

Despite Hepburn's love for the impetuous Hughes, she was altar shy and obsessed with restoring her box office power, part of her "ambition before love" mandate.

His global flight dream remained mired in bureaucracy. The Air Commerce Bureau repeatedly turned him down, ruling that Hughes "had no viable reason" to make the trip. At the same time Adolf Hitler refused to let him fly over Nazi Germany, which was essential to his plan of breaking all existing speed records.

As for becoming an aeronautics magnate, the country's fledgling aviation conglomerates, American Airlines and Pan American, considered Hughes to be little more than a daredevil playboy and economic wastrel.

In fact, Hughes had packed his aviation charts and his tool company ledgers for the trip to Fenwick. But the purpose of the trip was not business. He was here to meet Kate's parents. Howard understood that he would need the approval of the unorthodox Hepburn clan before marrying its most famous member.

Nothing prepared him, however, for the reception he received from this suspicious Yankee family. Kate's father, Dr. Thomas Norval Hepburn, a prominent American urologist, was quietly reserved. Kate's mother, Katharine, a former suffragette and early birth-control activist, paid him little mind other than to make it painfully clear that she much preferred Kate's former husband, a blue blood named Ludlow Stevens, who still had a room at the summer house. Though he and Kate had been divorced for four years, it was as if he were still part of the family.

Affectionately referred to as "Luddy, our dear, sweet ex," Stevens was even on hand during Howard's visit and wittingly demolished the hail-fellow-well-met image Hughes was trying to project, a desperate charade to impress this gregarious clan. When a jittery Hughes slipped down to breakfast just after dawn to share coffee with the woman who was, secretly, his fiancée, Stevens bounded through the door to good-naturedly discuss his decade-old courtship and marriage to Hepburn. At dinner, witty, urbane, and perfectly tailored, Kate's "dear, sweet ex" monopolized the conversation while Howard sat quietly; because of his deafness, he wasn't able to participate. Luddy also undid Hughes on the greens of the Old Saybrook Country Club, the one place Hughes stood his best chance to impress Dr. Hepburn. As they teed off the first morning, Hughes was enraged to find Stevens filming every move he and Kate made. He swooped in and out with his hand-held camera with no regard to the niceties of greensmanship. Hughes's rage grew when he noticed that Hepburn was hamming gracefully for the camera. "Stop, dammit," Hughes demanded of Kate. "I can't concentrate." Stevens grinned and continued filming. Hughes protested again.

"Look, Howard," said the physician. "Luddy has been taking pictures of all of us years before you joined us, and he will be taking them long after you have left. He's part of this family. Now. Go ahead. Drive. You need a seven iron, by the way."

"In a fury, Howard drove and landed six feet from the pin," Kate recalled. "Sunk a two. Not bad in a pinch."

The Hepburns were outspoken (Mrs. Hepburn liked to grill guests about their political leanings, and she also chided conservatives) and wildly unorganized (there were no schedules at Fenwick). They celebrated the arts, not aviation. And they had raised their daughter to be a "new" woman, free of a man's control.

Clearly, Hughes was out of place at Saybrook. Hepburn family friend Sarah Clement Pease recalled he seldom dined with the others, preferring to eat on his own after they were done. According to Pease, Hepburn was patient with her famed suitor: "[She] would say it didn't do any good to get mad at him because he couldn't hear what she was saying anyhow."

Though Hughes would come to form a friendship with Dr. Hepburn, with whom he enjoyed talking about medical discoveries and treatment, he would never really warm to the Hepburns. Nor they to him.

Kate was undaunted. On May 25 and 26 she and Howard tentatively decided to marry. Louella Parsons, after a series of interviews "via phone to Connecticut," learned of the decision early on May 28. Less than two hours later, the *Los Angeles Herald* issued an extra edition with the banner headline, KATHARINE HEPBURN TO WED HUGHES. The story began: "Word was received in the film colony today that Hepburn and Howard Hughes, the millionaire flying producer, will be married soon. It was also reported that the star and Hughes planned to take an expensive wedding trip aboard Hughes's palatial yacht. But the date of the marriage is a matter of conjecture."

Dietrich pointed out, years later, that the *Southern Cross* was stocked with gourmet food the last week in May and its crew called back from vacation. The bedroom suite was even refurbished.

But the relationship was in jeopardy again by June 10, just before Howard flew back to Los Angeles and immersed himself in preparations for the global flight, by now finally approved. Hepburn later noted that their differences had to do with a career choice. "Paramount made me an inferior offer I didn't want to take. Howard wanted me to. He felt I was embarrassed by my failure and should do something about it."

For his part, Hughes at last received permission from the Air Commerce Bureau to fly his new Lockheed Lodestar around the world.

A sleek silver monoplane, the Lodestar was capable of carrying twelve passengers, 1,500 gallons of aviation fuel, 150 gallons of oil, and a veritable laboratory of aeronautical equipment. By the time it was outfitted to Hughes's specifications, it weighed close to thirteen tons. To support the weight, it was fitted with customized tires from Goodrich.

In anticipation of the flight, Hughes had made some changes to his will. After all, his friend Amelia Earhart had disappeared during her flight the summer before. Because he had decided to take the polar route, he also phoned Kate and frankly discussed the dangers he faced flying over Siberia and then the North Pole. But the risk seemed to function as an aphrodisiac. Hughes flew from Los Angeles to New York several days before the flight, secretly moving into an apartment with Kate on Fifty-second Street. They shared a romantic liaison right up until the moment he left with Kate for Long Island's Floyd Bennett Field.

Early on the morning of July 10, Kate and Howard, obscured by hats in the deep confines of Kate's Lincoln, left their secret hideaway. They were on the highway that led to the airfield when, Hepburn recalled, "all of a sudden, we heard a siren behind us."

She didn't know what her chauffeur, Charles Newhill, had done. But she didn't want to be spotted with Hughes on this particular day. Hepburn leaned forward from the back seat, saying, "Charles, don't lose your cool. Take the ticket. Take anything. He must not find out that H.H. is with us."

Her chauffeur followed instructions. "And the cop never looked into the back of the car," Kate remembered.

They entered Bennett Field by a commercial entrance. "Keep me posted," Kate said.

"You'll hear from me, kiddo."

CHAPTER 11

HIGHWAY IN THE SKY

KATE SAT IN HER LINCOLN, WATCHING HOWARD'S LANKY FORM AMBLING toward the brightly lit Lodestar and his flight into immortality, or death. His fedora was tilted jauntily, and his battered shoes, veterans of every flight he'd ever made, scuffed along the gravel. He finally disappeared from sight into an enormous hangar, where Howard's crew swarmed about the Lodestar. Hepburn watched until he was gone before telling Charles Newhill to take her to Fenwick.

Once there, she and her family clustered around a radio. For Kate, it was her only link with a lover who now commanded the attention of the entire world, as had Lindbergh a decade earlier. Hughes called her several times during the six hours it took for final adjustments on the Lodestar and its state-of-the-art instrument panel. During his final call, at 7:00 P.M., he promised, "I'll contact you from each stop—through each ship," he said. "See ya in three days."

He had fashioned Kate into an emotional partner in this, "his grand adventure," as she liked to call it. The finale, he believed, would be their wedding in late summer.

For her part, Kate was still torn by indecision, all uncertainty only heightened by Hughes's growing fame. She wondered, she later told Cary

Grant, if two such dedicated loners were capable of sharing a life together. For the moment she would settle for Howard's safe return.

Depending upon climatic conditions, the Lodestar was in danger of depleting its fuel over the Atlantic, or worse, over the inaccessible wilderness of Siberia. Aeronautical maps of the time were uncertain, underestimating the actual distances and even the height and density of mountain ranges. By the time Hughes took off, bookies in the alleys behind Broadway and on the gambling ships off Atlantic City were giving Hughes only a fifty-fifty chance of safely crossing the first leg of the journey, the eighteen hundred treacherous miles of ocean between Newfoundland and the rocky coast of Ireland.

Hughes and his four-man crew—flight engineer Ed Lund, radio engineer Richard Stoddart, Lt. Thomas Thurlow of the Army Corps of Engineers, and co-pilot Harry P. M. Connor—sat at the edge of the runway at Bennett Field and awaited their cue, which came at 7:19. Howard, milking the moment, slid back the pilot's window and waved at the crowd. Darkness was closing in, and small orange lights blinked the full length of the runway. Finally, he was off.

Kate heard it clearly on the radio—the thunderous roar of the engines, the hoarse cheer of the crowd, the announcer's description of the swirling cloud of dust left in the Lodestar's wake. Just twenty-five yards from the edge of the runway, the tail lifted . . . barely missing the cap of a sandbar.

The Lodestar was a dark shadow in the fading light, headed toward the Atlantic coast. Then it vanished from view.

The first leg of the trip looked as if it would be easy. The flight was smooth across Newfoundland. Then, at 1:30 A.M., Hughes encountered fierce head-on winds. He looked at Connor. Maybe they wouldn't make Paris, after all. Nevertheless, he dispatched his first cable to Kate via an Italian liner below: "Over the Atlantic. All is fine. Love, Howard."

At dawn, he was over Ireland. Through a hole in the clouds he glimpsed the frothy breakers sweeping over the tip of the rocky coast. He again cabled Kate: "The Irish coast is breathtaking in its beauty. Call you from Paris, Howard."

Talking to the captain of the liner *Ile de France*, Hughes quipped, "Bet we beat you to Paris." At 4:00 P.M., sixteen hours and thirty-six minutes after leaving Long Island, three thousand Parisians cheered as Hughes landed at Bourget Airport successfully, even though the Lodestar had lost a crucial piece of its landing gear.

"La Lodestar, c'est finis," said an officious French mechanic.

"We'll be back in the air in an hour," claimed Howard. But it took eight long hours in a light rain to patch up the plane, and Howard left France drastically late. This sealed a very dangerous intention; he would now have to fly directly over Nazi Germany, against Hitler's orders, with the German Luftwaffe pilots itching to get him in their sights.

German papers speculated that Hughes would not cross their territory. STERN WARNINGS TO HUGHES FROM HITLER, the *International Herald-Tribune* trumpeted across its front page.

As the Lodestar flew over Nazi airspace, an escort from Hitler's fighting Luftwaffe instantly took to the skies. *"Verboten! Verboten!"* screamed the German commander over the radio as his squadron of fighter planes flanked the Lodestar. Hughes continued grimly on.

Almost an hour later, the Lodestar was still hemmed in by Nazi war planes. Co-pilot Connor looked inquiringly at Howard. "We'll go on," Howard said. "It's night, so obviously they can't see anything." He paused and added, in his typically understated fashion, "I don't think they'll shoot us down."

All across Nazi territory the frustrated Luftwaffe captain continued his stream of *verbotens* accompanied by expletives.

The BBC informed America that Hughes had thumbed his nose at Hitler and safely negotiated his shortcut to Moscow.

The next word came from Russia: "Hello, America. This is Radio Moscow. It is four-ten A.M. here and Mr. Howard Hughes just landed. Our people are storming the plane. Cheering. Calling out his name. What a night!"

As Howard pushed on for Omsk in Siberia, "Hughesmania" was reaching a crescendo back home. CBS's Lowell Thomas, the dean of commentators, set the tone: "The whole country is captivated by this heroic young man and how he has not let himself be spoiled by inherited wealth." The Associated Press pointed out that "babies everywhere are being named after him . . . twenty-five of them today alone." (In its flight coverage, *Life* adoringly called him "A rich young Texan with a poet's face.")

In New York City, a gypsy camp of reporters and paparazzi kept Kate's town house under siege. In a matter of hours, the balance of their fame had changed dramatically. Howard was no longer her boyfriend; *she was his girlfriend*.

Near the frozen top of the world, Hughes and the Lodestar landed at

Omsk, Siberia's industrial metropolis. Caviar and chilled vodka were offered and rejected politely by Hughes, who explained through a translator that he had to "keep a clear head." Besides, Hughes's plane had been stocked with ten pounds of ham-and-cheese sandwiches, and quarts of milk with which to wash them down. More useful were the fifteen hundred gallons of fuel the Russians pumped into the plane.

When he headed out again, he saw that overgrown cabbage plants blighting the runway had caught in the plane's wheels. "Cabbages! Can you believe that!" Hughes shook his head. The Lodestar was nearly upended by vegetables.

Ten hours, thirty-one minutes, and 2,456 miles later, they flew into the remote outpost of Yakutsk in the far reaches of Siberia. "We tried to tell them that we were looking for gasoline. They couldn't speak English and we couldn't speak Russian," remembered Ed Lund. After frantic hand motions, the plane was fueled. But not before the Siberians made their own hand motions, pointing curiously at the plane's insignia that promoted the World's Fair of 1939. Laughed Lund, "They couldn't figure out why we were in 1939 and they were still in 1938."

The Lodestar pushed on. Twelve hours to American soil. At 12,000 feet Hughes and his men saw both the moon and the sun suspended above the earth. "This is beauty beyond belief. Still safe, HH," he cabled to Hepburn.

Flying through a salmon-pink sky streaked with magenta, Hughes peered through the windshield to gauge the height of the Siberian range and ordered Connor to check the only map they had been able to find of the region—a *National Geographic* foldout. The peaks' altitude was listed at 7,000 feet.

According to the instrument panel, the Lodestar was already at 7,500 feet, and heading directly into the granite faces of the rugged mountain range ahead. They nosed up to 8,000, then 10,000 feet. But the plane was still too low to make clearance. Finally, at 12,000 feet, they "barely cleared the mountains." Had it been night, Hughes later said, "we would have crashed."

From the peaks above Siberia on to Fairbanks, Alaska, Hughes fought fierce head winds. So cold was the cockpit that in order to prevent his hands from freezing, Hughes urinated into a jar, then cradled it for warmth.

During the fuel stop in Fairbanks, the well-wishers included the widow of aviation great Wiley Post, who had circled the world in 1931. But there was also a comedic mishap: someone looking to help with refueling opened the wrong compartment, and suddenly thousands of Ping-Pong balls burst out. Snatched up by the crowd as souvenirs, the hollow plastic balls had been loaded at the instruction of Hughes, who figured their buoyancy might keep the plane afloat if it went down in water.

Off again they pushed, to Minneapolis for refueling. After hearing the radio reports, Kate swept out of the house and jumped into her Lincoln. She wanted to be at her New York town house to await Hughes's return. She wasn't the only one who wanted to welcome America's newest hero. As the Lodestar coasted down toward Long Island, a control operator warned: "You're the toast of the town now, Mr. Hughes. Prepare to be mobbed."

A haggard Hughes, with four days' growth of beard, looked down at the 25,000 people surging across the runway. He calmly bypassed the designated runway, finally stopping at a more remote airstrip.

Officially, timers recorded that he landed at 2:37 P.M., July 14, 1938. It was a record-breaking flight of three days, nineteen hours and 17 minutes. And 14,824 miles. He had beaten Wiley Post's solo flight record by almost half.

As he was borne through the teeming mass, a small man in a Western Union uniform kept trying to push through to him. "I've got a message from Miss Hepburn," he yelled. But the note, and its private message of congratulations, never reached Hughes in the pandemonium. In fact, the *New York Times* reported Hughes was so weary and so flustered by the suffocating mob of reporters, that he couldn't come up with "a coherent sentence" during interviews on the airstrip.

Howard and his crew were ferried through packed New York streets to the town house of Grover Whalen, the prominent New Yorker who was chief of the 1939 World's Fair, which had sponsored the global flight. Also waiting for him were New York City Mayor Fiorello La Guardia and other Manhattan dignitaries. Hughes, who needed to clean up, took a look at the well-dressed VIPs and asked if he could change into a fresh shirt. They waited downstairs for thirty minutes before sending Whalen to fetch their hero. But Hughes had bolted.

He'd found a back entrance, slipped onto the street, and hailed a taxi to Kate's town house. When he saw the media pack, he turned back and headed to his private suite at the Drake Hotel, where he talked with his lover by phone for twenty minutes. Then he collapsed into bed.

The next morning. Howard Hughes *owned* New York. Looking boyish and embarrassed, he led a ticker-tape parade with his crew down Broadway. A million well-wishers lined the streets, and 750,000 more jammed the streets surrounding City Hall, where endless speeches awaited. Later that night, he and Kate caused a furor when they showed up, arm in arm, for Whalen's official reception on the Jersey shore.

Hughes couldn't escape the crowds. The lionized aviator and his crew were feted with parades and rallies in Washington, D.C., Los Angeles, and finally in Houston, where 250,000 people turned out for the hometown hero's welcome. Afterward, at a banquet at the Rice Hotel, where the special menu included "Ice cream à la Howard," Howard downplayed his achievement in a speech he read from a wad of notes he pulled from his pockets. Grinning broadly, he said, "If you don't believe I wrote this myself, just try to read the handwriting."

At midnight on July 30, Hughes returned to the Yoakum Boulevard mansion with its ghosts of Allene and Howard Sr. He found the friends and acquaintances of his youth waiting on the old back porch. Over watermelon, "Texas ice tea punch," and his Aunt Annette's fudge cake, they all celebrated how far this young stranger—for that's what he had become to them—had traveled since he shut his door on the old radio room upstairs and left for good.

Howard himself felt oddly out of place. As he confessed to his Aunt Annette, "I didn't think any of my friends would speak to me after Ella and I got a divorce."

As he climbed the stairs to sleep there one last time, Annette wondered about his future. "I think he's only just begun," she told the *Houston Post*.

Howard Hughes spent his first week as "America's most beloved hero" sitting in the Muirfield den waiting for the telephone to ring. He kept busy by sorting and occasionally reading the hundreds of congratulatory telegrams that cluttered his desk. But he was cranky and preoccupied.

He had proposed marriage to Katharine Hepburn one more time. She had three days in which to answer. He must have known that this would anger his proud Yankee. "I have to know where I stand," he had explained to Glenn Odekirk.

By the afternoon of the third day, Cary Grant, the original matchmaker, reinvolved himself. While Hughes and Odekirk were reviewing plans to modify the amphibian, Grant dropped by and pleaded with Hughes to call Hepburn. "You make the move, old boy," Grant urged. Hughes declined. Then Grant reached Hepburn and pleaded for her to call Hughes.

But Katharine Hepburn had already made up her mind. She would not play Howard's game. "I did not want to marry Howard. He was bright, and he was interesting," she recalled. "But I knew that somehow Howard and I had become friends and not lovers. Love had turned to water."

What sorrow Hughes felt at this, perhaps his greatest rejection, he kept to himself.

"I don't know what happened," recalled Phyllis Brooks, whose relationship with Cary Grant was still underway at the time. "I thought they were perfect for each other . . . the love affair brought out the best in both of them."

CHAPTER 12

HE'S IN THE MONEY

WHILE WRESTLING WITH MATTERS OF THE HEART, HOWARD COULD ONCE again bankroll his dreams. Hughes Tool Company's success, carefully engineered by Hughes and Dietrich, had exceeded all expectations. Profits rose to $6 million in 1935, to $9 million in 1936, and to $13 million in 1937, an incredible figure in those days. And the future economic forecast predicted $22 million annually by 1941.

Despite Howard's feigned disinterest in the company and his frequent claim that "Toolco is my father's monument," Hughes worked behind the scenes to insure his monopoly on drilling equipment. (Asked about the monopoly, Hughes once playfully pointed out that there were other options—"a pick and shovel.") He and Dietrich were a ruthless team, dedicated to pushing Toolco profits to heights never contemplated by Hughes Sr.

Even during his early days of madcap spending, Hughes had not been idle. Between 1924 and 1926, profits soared from $2.2 million to $8.4 million. He and Dietrich also streamlined the Houston plant so successfully that the firm was earning 51 cents on the dollar by 1929. By 1930, Toolco added 235 new types and sizes of bits to an already bulging catalog. Many of the drills revolutionized oil extraction. As new oil strikes proliferated in California, west Texas, Oklahoma, and overseas, Howard personally hired top-flight geologists away from Cal Tech, Rice University, the University of Arizona, and the University of California at Berkeley and ordered them to the fledgling oil fields with instructions to gauge their different needs and to design drill bits to match.

One of these new bits, the Tricone, cut drilling time in half throughout the rich Texas and Oklahoma oil depositories. Another, the Acme, cut through the granite shelves protecting California oil, which increased extraction twelvefold. The Acme was twice as long as previous bits and featured pointed teeth to push rock shards out of the way, especially in fields resistant to traditional bits.

In 1931, Hughes founded a research branch, which resembled a small think tank, devoted to improving oil production throughout the world. Two hundred scientists were hired, and Howard built a three-storey laboratory to house them, the largest private petroleum lab in the United States.

Later, Hughes hired Fred Ayers to overhaul Toolco's outdated assembly line. Ayers literally tore the plant apart, thereby quadrupling the factory's output, just as he had done for General Motors several years earlier. The price tag was $5 million.

Hughes was intimately involved even when it came to crushing his competitors. When a former Toolco scientist defected and founded a rival corporation by carefully modifying Hughes's basic bit, Howard instantly went to court and collected half a million dollars in damages. By reading thousands of pages of depositions from the trial, Howard learned that the "mock Toolco" bit performed better than the original.

He purchased one, took it back to the lab, and dissected it. He found that it used very soft lead ball bearings in place of the hard grinders favored by Toolco. Howard quickly added the soft bearings to his bits, causing sales to double within the year.

Later, with the onset of the war, profits jumped to $22 million in 1940, $33 million in 1942, and $55 million in 1948.

"Howard's success with Toolco has always been deprecated," recalled Hughes attorney Greg Bautzer. "They said he just lucked into it. But, from personal experience, he worked on it endlessly, tinkering, calculating, and jotting down dozens of ideas in one evening. On dates, he would dash to the phone and talk to Houston for hours; once he even interrupted a screening to cable a new brainstorm back to Toolco."

The renaissance in the tool company's fortunes came just in time. Howard had always dreamed of owning an airline, and in 1939 he got his chance. He targeted Trans World Airlines, which had been founded by Charles Lindbergh, the only aeronautical hero who challenged Howard in fame. Nicknamed "the Lindbergh Line," TWA's silver mail planes were an airborne advertisement for Lucky Lindy.

But the Depression hit TWA hard just as it was expanding from a glorified mail carrier into a passenger line. This allowed Hughes to purchase 200,000 shares of the airline's stock for $1.6 million at $8 a share. This gave him 21 per cent of the corporation. By early 1940 he was enmeshed in a buying frenzy. By courting small shareholders and big players, including Lindbergh, Hughes owned 78 per cent of TWA by the end of the year.

By later that year all traces of Lucky Lindy's glory had been painted over with silver lacquer.

Because Pan American World Airways and later, American, had such a lock on air travel and even cargo revenue, all of Hughes's advisers, particularly Dietrich and attorney Neil McCarthy, predicted dire consequences. Howard simply ignored them and continued to pour hundreds of thousands of dollars into TWA's coffers. Armed with the aviation secrets he acquired and with the practical know-how accumulated from his record-breaking flights, he developed a master plan for TWA, a plan that envisioned the airline as the undisputed leader in coast-to-coast flights. He promised to achieve this miracle within a decade.

TWA president Jack Frye welcomed him aboard and nicknamed him "the savior." Frye, a dashing pilot from the barnstorming era, willingly shared his power with Hughes to become what Lindbergh himself described as "the most successful team in the brief history of commercial aviation."

Some results were immediate. TWA doubled its income by 1940 and by 1941 transported 256,000 passengers a year, a 57 per cent increase since 1939. During the first two years Howard launched the first star-studded publicity flights, created the first nonstop coast-to-coast passenger service, and invented a series of electronic advances, including "power steering," larger and safer cockpits, and an amazingly advanced hydraulic system.

But Howard's finest gift, to TWA in particular and aviation in general, was his concept for a fleet of superliners, sleek airplanes that would carry sixty passengers from Los Angeles to New York in ten hours. They would also feature unheard-of comfort and air speeds of three hundred miles per hour.

He combed the aviation industry begging designers to "do the impossible" because, he explained, "almost everyone had told me my ideas are merely fantasies." But Lockheed president Robert Gross promised to turn this daydream into reality. Hughes agreed to meet with Gross personally, showing up at Lockheed's headquarters in a frayed white shirt, fresh chinos, fedora, and sandals. He kicked off the sandals and dropped to the floor, crossing his legs beneath him. Soon he had scattered all of Lockheed's blueprints all over the room and walked and crawled from one to the other. "I like 'em," he finally said. "Gimme a price."

"Four hundred and fifty thousand dollars apiece," Gross answered, expecting a roar of protest from Hughes.

"Well, goddammit, TWA can't pay for them. The damn airline is flat broke." Hughes was silent for several minutes before shouting, "Hell, I guess I'll just have to pay for them myself. Build 'em, Bob, and send the bill to the Hughes Tool Company in Houston." Then he pulled on his sandals and leisurely strolled out while eating a cheese sandwich.

Howard purchased forty airplanes for $18 million, the largest commercial order in aviation history up to that time.

Although Hughes wasn't worried about cost, he was worried about secrecy. To make sure word of the new liners wasn't leaked to other airlines, he stored the blueprints in a cabinet that required three keys to open it, one each from the key rings of Hughes, Gross, and Frye. The mock-ups were kept in a downtown Los Angeles bank vault. All communications were written in code, and the three principals were never identified by name. In correspondence on the invention, Hughes was designated as "God," Frye was "Jesus Christ," and Gross was "the apostle Paul." The plant itself was Aircraft Number 0-49. But insiders knew the real name—the Constellation.

The "Connie" more than lived up to its name. On its first test flight, the liner flew from Los Angeles to Washington, D.C., in six hours and fifty-six minutes. The *New York Times* lauded it as "the outline of things to come in the airline industry—a great silver bird, shimmering in the sun."

From 1939 until the dawn of the jet age Howard bankrolled the airline to bring comfort, regular schedules, and, especially, speed.

Gross noted that Hughes "showed great brilliance in his aviation ventures." Though he had never taken a single university course on the most basic rudiments of aviation design, experts in the field marveled at what he accomplished with sheer intuition.

Lockheed's senior vice-president, Jack Real, later a flying buddy, noted, "Howard had all the attributes of the greatest aeronautical engineer." Author Robert Sterling *(Howard Hughes' Airline)* interviewed hundreds of TWA employees and found that "every veteran traces TWA's success to one man, Howard Hughes! He shaped the line's destiny as one would mold a piece of clay."

He did not have an unblemished record of success, though.

In 1939 he also began a fierce battle with the army to transform Hughes Aircraft into a major supplier of planes in the coming world war. His hopes were riding on the D-2, a medium-range bomber constructed of wood and resin, in a secret process called Duramold that bonded thin strips of wood into a molded framework.

By the early 1940s he had expanded his aviation dream team to five hundred designers, engineers, and scientists, installing them in a new thirteen-hundred-acre facility in Culver City, a stone's throw from MGM. He had also already invested $2 million in the construction of a prototype. Another $2 million went into the construction of a modern, air-conditioned, humidity-controlled plant that attracted the envy of the aviation establishment.

The army, however, rejected the D-2 out of hand and described the team that built it as forming the nucleus "of a hobby" of a rich young man. It concluded, "the D-2 is a waste of time."

Typically, Hughes stubbornly plunged ahead, spending an additional $4 million to refine the wooden monster. He was even more obsessed with building the consummate reconnaissance plane. But the War Department ignored him. Finally, in August 1943 he would reluctantly take the low road to achieve his wartime ends. When he learned that a planeload of army brass was winging its way to the coast in search of "a dependable reconnaissance plane," Howard decided to woo them with a Hollywood orgy of booze and babes, fueled by $200,000 from the Hughes bank accounts.

To organize this spectacle, he hired a notorious, mob-related procurer named Johnny Meyer, a Tinseltown bottom feeder who had hustled girls for Charlie Chaplin and Errol Flynn. Hughes told Meyer to assemble an ample supply of the best champagne, crates of the finest caviar, and enough party girls to ambush the officers with luxury and glamour. As a head-quarters for this powder-puff assault, Meyer leased a magnificent estate on Doheny Boulevard and transformed it into a Tahitian fantasy.

Col. Elliott Roosevelt, FDR's son and the nominal head of the dele-gation, was Howard's target. A specialist in reconnaissance war machines, he was a handsome bachelor who had blazed through Washington, D.C., society for years. On Roosevelt's first day in town, Meyer scored by intro-ducing him to a tawny, blond Warner Brothers starlet named Faye Emerson, who was languishing in Hollywood long before she became the queen of early talk-show television. Sparks flew at the meeting, and soon Emerson and Roosevelt were doing the town, all paid for by Hughes cash.

On August 8, 9, and 10, Hughes hosted a trio of galas that began at the Doheny mansion, where the army brass and a stampede of Hollywood starlets dined on lobster, squab, and beef Wellington, all under a canopy of tiny white lights. (The wartime brownouts were still in effect.)

While the banquet proceeded, an array of talent performed on a small stage. During one particular set piece, swimming star Judy Cook, wearing a flesh-colored bathing suit and a couple of sequins, staged a spectacular water ballet.

Unknown to both guests and the host, a contingent of FBI agents mingled among the crowd disguised as waiters and technicians, cataloging each movement of the military delegations.

The party continued at Caraways and the Mocambo on the Sunset Strip, where the entire tab was picked up by Hughes.

Meyer saw to it that the dress-uniformed captains, majors, and colonels were never without a starlet or model to dance with. These glamour girls earned from $100 to $400 per night, depending on their beauty and, as Meyer said later, "their usefulness."

Hotel bills and meal receipts were all charged to Hughes, a move that was strictly against wartime regulations governing such top-priority delegations.

The morning of August 11, a spiffy Hughes, wearing his round-the-world jacket and the lucky fedora, personally conducted a tour of Hughes Aircraft. The flyboys were then airlifted to Harper Lake, a dry lakebed in the high desert, where the recon machine was scrutinized. Afterward, the president's son whispered to Howard, "I think we've found our plane."

On August 20, after Hughes reluctantly agreed to convert the plane from wood to metal, the army contracted for one hundred of the planes at a total price of $43 million. From that moment on, the D-2, rechristened as the XF-11, was destined to change Howard Hughes's life. But the millionaire, by hiring Meyer, had made a pact with the devil. His life would never again be free of procurers and yes men. It hadn't occurred to him that he would probably have earned the contract fair and square just by demonstrating it in the desert.

In Washington, Major General Bennett E. Meyers of the War Materiel Command looked at the paperwork and the reports, including a caustic FBI memorandum. He prophetically concluded: "There's going to be an awful smell when the background of this deal is revealed."

CHAPTER 13

THE PARADE'S GONE BY

In 1938, BITTER AND DISILLUSIONED BY KATE HEPBURN'S REJECTION, Hughes became emotionally adrift. As in the aftermath of Billie Dove's departure from his life, he would embark on a new series of conquests in retaliation. In the beginning, his women would all be Hollywood stars.

Less than forty-eight hours after Hepburn's silent dismissal, Hughes sent five dozen yellow roses to Ginger Rogers, who had usurped Kate's place as queen of the RKO lot. He followed with the usual tidal wave of orchids and gardenias, accompanied by tender love notes addressing Ginger as "my princess."

Since her brief fling with Howard five years earlier, Rogers had changed dramatically. Her films with Fred Astaire, her flair for zany comedy, and her subtle sex appeal had transformed her into a Hollywood favorite, just as Kate's star was descending. At twenty-seven, Ginger was the highest paid actress in Hollywood, taking home $300,000 a year, three times Hepburn's salary.

Howard re-entered her life shortly after Rogers filed for divorce from actor Lew Ayres, an Oscar winner for the pacifist drama *All Quiet on the Western Front* who went on to star in the Dr. Kildare movies. Savoring her new independence, she was unimpressed by Hughes's exploding wealth and power, which only made him chase her more ardently.

In a gesture aimed directly at Kate, he commenced his romantic assault with a highly publicized "whirlwind tour" of New York City, where Hepburn was ensconced in her Turtle Bay town house. Rogers and her mother whizzed across the country on the Twentieth Century Limited while Hughes flew to New York in his amphibian. Waiting for them at a dock in the Hudson River was the majestic *Southern Cross* in its ivory and gilt splendor.

Before the yacht sailed off toward Long Island Sound, Hughes tossed a bon voyage party honoring Rogers and her mother. Columnists Earl Wilson and Dorothy Kilgallen saw them off, and news cameras flashed as Hughes, in a dark and fashionable business suit, and Ginger, in jet black and furs, later toured the Sikorsky helicopter factory.

A part of Howard still wanted Kate back, though. Earlier the same afternoon, Howard paid for her return to the stage as the patrician heroine of *The Philadelphia Story*, the Philip Barry play that would become the cornerstone of a spectacular comeback. Hughes purchased a controlling interest in the play and, with Barry, an old Hepburn friend, carefully engineered his former lover's return to stardom.

Nevertheless, that same day he proposed to Rogers. "But, Howard, I'm still married to Lew," she protested.

"Nonsense," he answered, "my lawyer can get you out of that marriage in a hurry."

Ginger wouldn't be rushed. "We'll talk back in Los Angeles."

This second rejection had immediate consequences. Before Ginger's train even pulled into Union Station, he leaped into an affair with Bette Davis, the least likely of his star lovers. They collided at the Tailwagger's Ball, a canine charity close to Davis's heart. Wearing a tightly bodiced pink dress and framed by waves of lace, Bette was the star attraction in a roomful of star attractions such as Mary Pickford, Lupe Velez, and Norma Shearer.

Like Howard, Bette was on the rebound from an affair with "the love of her life," director William Wyler. Unlike Hughes, she was still very married to her childhood sweetheart, advertising man Harmon "Ham" Nelson.

Davis was also a rival of Kate's. At Warner Brothers, Davis had already streaked past her rival in the serious actress sweepstakes. In addition, she was a box office darling and would soon win her second Best Actress Oscar for playing the temptress of *Jezebel*.

Far less attractive in person than on the screen, Bette was wraithlike, with a piercing voice and boyish figure. But she possessed all earthy seductiveness, particularly in her sexy pink dress.

"I expected Hughes to look at my breasts," she recalled. "Instead, he looked directly into my eyes. I won't say there was magic, but there was warmth."

He bought "scads of raffle tickets" and arranged for the first of a series of rendezvous. Within days they were nestled in bed, listening to waves pounding outside Howard's rented Malibu hideaway. They slept together ten times during a brief but idyllic affair. "Howard brought out the maternal instinct in me, which no other man had ever done. He was such a quiet, shy man. But when we were alone, he evolved into a very romantic lover." She continued, "I used to cook for him at the beach, and as we sat by the fire, he would stroke my hair."

After one of those "fireside evenings," Harmon Nelson prematurely ended the affair. "He caught them together," said Michael "Mickey" Herskowitz, who helped Davis write her 1988 autobiography, *This 'N That: Bette Davis.* "Bette graphically described to me how Nelson and a private investigator used primitive recording equipment, connected to a sound truck outside, to tape Howard and Bette as they made love. They then burst in and caught them in bed."

Davis later paid Nelson $75,000 in hush money and then sought a divorce. But the discordant night ruined her fling with Hughes.

In the meantime, Howard pressed his rushed courtship of Ginger Rogers. But she cagily sensed that deep emotional trouble lay beneath the brash millionaire's facade. During all the dashing plane flights that followed, to pick wildflowers on the banks of Lake Tahoe or to picnic on the sugar white sands of Coronado Island, Rogers ducked commitment.

One evening he drove Ginger up a winding road to the top of a hill that overlooked the lights of Hollywood. He gestured grandly across the horizon. "I'm going to buy this hilltop for you, princess. We'll live up here by ourselves with the world far below."

"I realized he felt he was going to bring me up here and make me a prisoner," Rogers recalled. "He planned to possess me in a way I didn't want to be possessed. He wanted to build a fence all around me."

But the more Rogers avoided the subject of marriage, the more tenacious Hughes became. Despite her protests, he sent his attorney Neil McCarthy to engineer a quickie divorce in late 1938. "He was absolutely relentless and desperate in his pursuit," she recalled. She finally accepted an enormous emerald engagement ring from Hughes, a tribute to his persuasiveness. He also persuaded Rogers's mother, Lela, into the role of matchmaker. Remembered Ginger, "I would wake up in the morning to find that my day had already been planned for me by Mother and Howard. As she poured me coffee, she would announce, 'You're cruising to Catalina today. Howard will pick you up at eight-thirty.' "

She eventually confronted her mother. "Why don't you just put me on the phone so that I can tell him yes or no?"

"It wouldn't work," Mrs. Rogers responded. "Howard considers me his ally. I don't know if he could carry it off on his own. He's afraid you'll say no."

By the time Ginger secretly accepted Hughes's ring, he was already blatantly playing the Hollywood field. Indiscreetly, he set his sights on two professional acquaintances of Rogers's, Olivia de Havilland and, at the same time, her sister Joan Fontaine.

Louella Parsons virtually propelled Howard and Olivia together when she proclaimed that the actress had accepted his engagement ring after a whirl-wind courtship that supposedly began on the set of *Dodge City* in Modesto. This classic case of gossip column misinformation began when Hughes sent a plane to the set to collect buddy Errol Flynn for a party in Los Angeles. Olivia was offered a ride but declined. There was nothing more to it.

After she completed *Dodge City* and returned to Los Angeles, Hughes telephoned: "I read in the paper that you and I are engaged and going to be married." He paused, then continued uneasily, "Since we have never met, I thought we should at least look at each other before we do something so permanent."

She agreed to have tea with him. After hanging up, she turned to her mother. "One of the world's most renowned wolves has just asked me to go out, but he doesn't sound very dangerous to me."

De Havilland seemed a dubious choice for Hughes. Known for her fine, delicate features and for her serious manner, on-screen and off, she'd rarely been seen in the world of Hollywood night life. Hughes changed that. They began to show up at hot spots such as Victor Hugo's Garden Room and the Brown Derby, where they nestled in oversize booths. They also had flying dates, with Howard giving the actress instructions. Soon she was curious about his long-range plans. Would they ever marry, she asked. "I have no intention of marrying until I'm fifty," said the man who was engaged to Rogers at the moment. "There are too many things to do."

At least Olivia knew where she stood. But what she didn't know was that Hughes was two-timing her with her younger sister, Joan Fontaine. Admittedly, it was a busy time for both sisters. De Havilland was fresh from her success as Melanie in *Gone With the Wind*, and Fontaine was about to make *Rebecca* for Alfred Hitchcock.

In fact, de Havilland was rushing from one film to another when Howard shamelessly courted Joan at the party celebrating her engagement to dashing actor Brian Aherne. Worse, Hughes was hosting the affair, thrown at the Trocadero. To Fontaine's surprise, Hughes whisked her off to the dance floor and tried to talk her out of the wedding. "Forget it, you're going to marry me instead," he whispered in her ear.

"I was shocked," Fontaine later recalled. "Olivia had been seeing him steadily. No one two-times my sister."

Despite a firm rebuff, Howard edged up to Joan as she was leaving the nightclub and slipped her his private phone number. The actress decided to play along "to see what he had in mind." She called him and the two met in the garden of Trader Vic's. Hughes again proposed. "He seemed in deadly earnest," she recalled.

In a rage Joan returned home, where she told Olivia the truth. De Havilland refused to see him again. But his pursuit of both women would add to the "feuding sisters" saga that became a part of Hollywood lore.

Howard's erstwhile fiancée, Ginger Rogers, hadn't heard about his flirtation with the town's most famous sisters. But she did learn of another woman, a woman whose name she chose not to reveal during repeated interviews about her romance with Hughes. "I realized he couldn't be faithful," she said of her ultimate break with Howard.

The square-off between the lovers began one rainy afternoon in 1940. As he sped down a Los Angeles street, oblivious to the cars skidding around him, Hughes was fuming. Ginger had refused to accompany him to the dentist and refused even to take his call.

During the previous months, he had become irrational in his jealousy over Ginger, tracking her every movement and monitoring her telephone calls. He was used to having his way. Her refusal obsessed him.

A sudden jerk brought him back to reality when a sedan veered suddenly into his lane. The cars collided head on.

Hughes's head pitched forward, shattering the windshield. A shard of glass sliced across his forehead and knocked him unconscious. The concussion was so severe that he was rushed into an intensive care unit.

But when he regained consciousness late in the afternoon, Howard ignored his doctors and bellowed for Ginger. "Find her," he told Dietrich "I need her here."

Noah found her in her Bel Air mansion, seething with anger. The day before, an old friend, screenwriter Alden Nash, had telephoned: "Look, Ginger, I've got to warn you. The man you are about to marry is spending night after night with a young actress who lives across the street from me. This is none of my business, but I don't want to see a nice girl like you being two-timed by a lug like Howard Hughes."

Ginger drove over to Nash's neighborhood, where she found Howard's car parked on the street.

But she didn't mention this to Dietrich as she coolly agreed to rush to Howard's side. Dietrich would hear about it later. Before leaving home, Ginger gathered up the jewelry Howard had given her, including the emerald solitaire engagement ring, and placed it in a basket.

When she showed up at the hospital, Howard was propped up in bed, looking like a petulant schoolboy. His head was wrapped in gauze, which revealed a deep red trail from the stitches just above his eyebrows.

Rogers was civil. She intended to make it a classy finale. "How are you?" she asked.

"I'm miserable," he moaned. "And this is all because of you. When you refused to go to the dentist with me . . . I was so upset I crashed into another car."

Rogers folded her arms and let him ramble on. Then she calmly spoke her piece. At the end of her scene, she threw the jewelry into his lap. She had started for the door when she turned for one last grand gesture. Pulling the ring from her finger, she said, "And here's the emerald engagement ring . . . We are no longer engaged." She threw it at him. Ginger would later note that Howard looked up pitifully through his bandages, like a small boy caught in a lie.

When Dietrich came by the hospital on business, Hughes actually wept. "Noah, it's Ginger; she's left me."

"When it came to women he really cared for, he sabotaged himself every time," Dietrich recalled. "He simply could not be faithful."

Although neither Dietrich nor Hughes could have known it at the time, Ginger had slammed the door on an entire epoch in the romantic life of the 34-year-old millionaire. He would never again choose a lover who was his equal—or even from his own generation. The new ladies to glide in and out of his life would be increasingly younger and flashier and, with only a few exceptions, willing to bend to Howard's whims.

"He was fighting a desperate battle against loneliness," Dietrich later wrote. "First Katharine and then Ginger walked out. And Howard couldn't figure out why—didn't ever learn from his mistakes."

Shortly before Ginger jumped ship, Kate, now the hottest star of the Broadway season in the Hughes-backed play *The Philadelphia Story*, had moved into the guest house at Muirfield. It would be her headquarters in her fight to regain her movie stardom.

Most of the actresses of her generation had already stumbled badly, including Norma Shearer, Joan Crawford, Greta Garbo, and Marlene Dietrich. All were clawing at scripts in search of a comeback hit. Thanks to Hughes, Hepburn had her entrée, the screen rights to *The Philadelphia Story*.

Despite the pain it must have caused him, Hughes craftily engineered his former lover's renaissance. For help he turned to an old friend: Louis B. Mayer, MGM's all-powerful mogul and Hollywood's strongest player. With Hughes standing over him, Mayer agreed to cast Kate in the lead and to hire two stars of the first rank to support her, Howard's friend Cary Grant and James Stewart.

Kate's maid Johanna Madsen recalled that Hepburn continued to occupy the guest house until sometime in 1941, "for convenience." But if Hughes expected Kate to return as his lover, he was soon disappointed. Her second MGM blockbuster, *Woman of the Year*, co-starred Spencer Tracy, who would go on to become the love of her life.

To take his mind off his breakup with Rogers, Howard escaped into the frothy fantasy world of high society. It was an era when debs were presented in winter wonderlands, complete with Art Deco igloos and thousands of white orchids. The ballroom of the Plaza Hotel was periodically transformed; orange trees bloomed in silver tubs, and pink champagne gushed from the mouths of frozen gargoyles.

Using the splendor of the *Southern Cross* as a baronial bachelor pad, Hughes sailed up the Hudson River or anchored off Nassau, the wintering headquarters for debs and their formidable mothers.

Perhaps as an antidote to Kate and Ginger, Howard romanced two of the most fragile, artificial women to populate his life, a matching pair of debutantes named Brenda Duff Frazier and Gloria Vanderbilt. They were almost caricatures of their breed: preening young socialites as Walt Disney might have drawn them. Skin the color of snow, slashes of pomegranate red at the mouths, and midnight black hair cascading over the shoulders of their gowns.

They were the first in a new line of socialites, dubbed "celebutantes," blue-blood beauties who graduated from the society columns to the front pages and from there to headlines in the tabloids and covers of magazines like *Life* and *Vogue*.

Both were very young, just seventeen, when Hughes appeared, and both proved fairly easy conquests.

He found Frazier on the crowded dance floor of the Bahamian Club amid a sea of sundresses and madras formal wear. Hughes towered over them all, wearing white tie, a tropical dinner jacket, black cotton sailing pants, and scruffy tennis shoes. "I watched him survey the dance floor with his . . . extraordinary costume and realized he was the only real man in this room full of social swains," Frazier later told *Vanity Fair*. "He was the most glamorous man in the room."

"Everyone knew that Hughes and Brenda would find each other," said Frazier's friend Gerald Groesbeck. "All of us in the New York group just sat around and waited for the affair to happen."

Society lioness Elsa Maxwell took Howard by the hand and led him to Frazier's table. "This, Brenda dear, is the infamous Mr. Hughes, as if you didn't already know."

A painful silence followed.

Maxwell, a Hughes crony from the days of San Simeon, broke the silence. "Ask her to dance, Howard." He instantly complied.

The dance stretched to two dances, then four, and ended with a walk through the club's formal gardens and from there to the sandy beach where they talked until dawn. Early the next morning, Frazier took out her engagement book and canceled all the dates she had made for her seventeen-day stay in Nassau. Howard canceled appointments in New York, Palm Beach, and Washington, D.C.

He rescued the amphibian from its hangar and flew it to the Bahamas so that the love-at-first-sighters could picnic on a deserted island with their feet in the warm water and champagne glasses in their hands. They made love for the first time on the circular wolfskin bed in the master bedroom of the *Southern Cross.* "Three days after they met, they slept with each other," recalled Groesbeck. "It was inevitable."

Howard followed her back to New York, where the affair blazed for ten weeks, through stolen hours on the yacht or in an enormous suite at the Carlton Hotel, where room-service feasts were accompanied by candlelight and silver vases of yellow roses.

When Howard finally proposed, though, Frazier turned down "the most eligible bachelor in America." "The love making was divine," she confided to Elsa Maxwell. "But he was simply too mysterious to marry. There were too many secrets, too many things I didn't know. In the end, I wasn't even certain that I had met the real Howard Hughes."

Frazier was correct. Hughes functioned masterfully as a chameleon, becoming whatever his current environment called for. So the *Southern Cross* sailed for home while Hughes flew the amphibian to Culver City.

To his surprise, he found a replacement slumming among the palms and orange blossoms, a dreamy girl whose tragic young life had been a blitzkrieg of newspaper headlines and radio bulletins. A victim of the most bitter custody battle in the history of high society, waged by her mother and her aunt, heiress Gloria Vanderbilt had traveled west with her mother, Gloria Vanderbilt Morgan, a gorgeous fortune hunter who had landed Reginald Claypool Vanderbilt during World War I.

Hughes understood that he would have to woo the mother to gain access to the seventeen-year-old socialite. Consequently, Hughes called at their Beverly Hills villa, Maple Manor, late one afternoon. Gloria Jr., on the way to a reception at the Beverly Hills Hotel, answered the door. "His hat was tilted back on his head and he was tall, really tall, and his jacket was slung over one shoulder in a most appealing way," Vanderbilt remembered. "He couldn't think of anything to say, and I couldn't either."

Howard met with Gloria Sr.'s approval. Or rather, his bank account did. The Hughes pedigree, minus the drill bit, would not have earned him entrée into the rarefied world of the Vanderbilts. Gloria envisioned Howard as a white knight, a dream lover totally dissimilar from the dandified preppies who had surrounded her during the rites of passage in Manhattan. And she instantly understood that Hughes didn't give a damn that she was a Vanderbilt.

On a rainy, blustery night on the eve of World War II, she watched from her window as he drove up in a clunky Chevrolet, "a car no one would notice," and dashed up the steps carrying a brand-new umbrella. He would use it to protect her from the storm.

"We drove over the hills and far down into the San Fernando Valley," she recalled. "Neither of us said a word as the rain fell, hitting the car with a spattering sound."

After the emotional battering Gloria had taken from her family, Howard, with his Gary Cooper looks and masculine aura, made the young heiress feel secure, as if she were inside a romantic cocoon. "In his car, we were safe as could be, gypsies in a caravan on our way to set up camp for the night," she later wrote in her memoirs.

Their first date included a plainer than plain dinner at the Sportsman's Lodge in the Valley, where Howard ate his standard meal: steak, a baked potato, and green peas. Picky about his peas, he often used a special uten-sil—resembling a small rake—to ferret out the largest peas, which he found unappetizing.

He soon carried her off into his own dream world, the one above the clouds over Santa Catalina, Las Vegas, and the Grand Canyon. Once, while the plane darted in and out of the fog banks above Santa Barbara, Gloria took his hand and, as she described it, experienced incredibly sensual feelings for this fellow loner. The smell of his leather jacket, the roar of the engine, his intense concentration heightened the sexuality of the moment.

Then the amphibian sliced through the fog and landed near a beach. "We walked along the rocky beach—no other human being in sight—secret as can be."

Long evenings before Muirfield's roaring fireplace followed.

Neither Vanderbilt nor Hughes ever talked about the sexual side of their relationship. But Gloria was familiar with the master bedroom. She described it briefly in her diary when she wrote of seeing a photo of Katharine Hepburn next to Howard's bed: "Her eyes are so full of love for him, and he loves her. I know . . ."

Gloria believed she and Hughes were mutually in love. In a letter to her childhood nanny, Vanderbilt declared, "I've met the most wonderful man. You told me long ago I'd meet someone who would cherish me—and that's the way he makes me feel."

In the meantime, in what was a dark move on his benefactor, hand-some Pat De Cicco also began to pursue Gloria.

When informed of her ward's romances with these commoners,

Gertrude Vanderbilt Whitney, her guardian, summoned her home to the family's Long Island estate. If there were betrothals to be arranged, they would be arranged through her.

Gloria sat down in her aunt's living room, surrounded by five decades of Vanderbilt portraits, and insisted that Hughes had proposed. Mrs. Whitney erupted in anger. "Why haven't I been told of this? This man is thirty-seven years old and you are seventeen."

That evening the society lioness called Hughes in Los Angeles and talked with him for some time. What she said is unknown. But Hughes quietly backed out of Gloria's life. As Gloria put it, "Howard had dropped off the face of the earth."

She, in turn, fled to the arms of De Cicco, whom she married.

But Vanderbilt spoke to Howard one more time. Strapped for cash, De Cicco coerced Gloria to ask Hughes for $5,000. "Five thousand dollars means nothing to him."

"I can't," she answered. De Cicco continued to plead. As Vanderbilt once related, "He talked as if he were really frightened, and I felt sorry for him."

So she called. "Howard, I need five thousand dollars. I'll pay it back when I'm twenty-one." Hughes didn't answer. "Howard, Howard," she pleaded.

He answered in a measured tone, "I thought you were calling to say that you were coming back to me." Then he hung up.

Several days later Gloria received a small package from Howard. Inside was a silver medal she had given him, engraved on the back: "G.V. to H.H. 1941."

Hughes never spoke her name again.

CHAPTER 14

WAY OUT WEST

As always in Howard Hughes's hectic life, romancing was only one of his obsessions. Even as he was becoming an aviation hero in the late thirties, he had decided to return to another of his lifelong passions. He was getting back into the movies.

When he showed up at the Trocadero in December 1939, he wasn't on the lookout for girls. The occasion was a postpremiere party for *Gone With the Wind*. Hughes had gone in hopes of meeting publicist Russell Birdwell.

It was Birdwell who had come up with the clever Search for Scarlett campaign that had kept *Gone With the Wind* in the media, and the minds of moviegoers, for the past two years. Birdwell had also once flown the entire town of Zenda, Ontario (population: twelve), to Manhattan, to attend the premiere of *The Prisoner of Zenda*.

For his filmmaking comeback, Hughes felt he had to have Birdwell. He didn't want to just make a movie; he wanted an event.

When Hughes at last spied Birdwell, the publicist was basking in glory, holding court with Norma Shearer and Mary Pickford. Hughes sauntered over and stood hesitantly at Birdwell's elbow. When Birdwell didn't say anything, Hughes asked, "May I see you?"

Birdwell coolly appraised the intruder. "In a minute."

After Hughes had sulked away, Norma Shearer looked at Birdwell with a smile. "Don't you know who that is? That's Howard Hughes." Birdwell made an immediate about-face and walked across the room looking for Hughes. He found him hovering in a corner.

Hughes didn't introduce himself. He simply said, "I'm thinking about making a new motion picture. Would you be interested?"

"I might be," Birdwell replied. "At least I'll be happy to talk about it."

"You may hear from me," Hughes said. Then he turned and left.

Several months later, Birdwell was at work in his office when his secretary came in and told him, "There's a man outside who can't talk." A messenger from Hughes, the man presented the understandably curious Birdwell with a note that read, "Mr. Hughes will see you tomorrow at 3:00."

Birdwell looked at the note, then scribbled his own message: "3:00 P.M.?" The mute messenger shook his head and wrote back, "3:00 A.M." (The messenger, it turned out, was Charlie Guest, a Hughes assistant who had once been his golf instructor, and who was quite capable of speech.)

During the wee hours, Birdwell sat on a tattered couch in the dimly lit living room at Muirfield and listened as Hughes revealed his plans to make a Western that would have moviegoers talking before the characters ever saddled up. Tentatively entitled *Billy the Kid*, it would give a new twist to the saga of gunslinger William H. Bonney. This time the movie would involve sex.

In the search for the film's stars that followed, the emphasis was on an unknown to play the leading lady. The quest wouldn't rival the Scarlett campaign, but since Hughes was the man who had discovered Jean Harlow fifteen years earlier, it caused a stampede among the town's casting agents. The desks at Hughes's Romaine Street office were soon piled with eight-by-ten glossies.

After scrutinizing the stack of photos, Hughes pulled out a shot of a nineteen-year-old who stood five-foot-seven and measured 38-22-36. "Give her a test," he instructed.

The actress was brown-eyed raven-haired Ernestine Jane Geraldine Russell, soon to be known as Jane Russell. She was working as a part-time receptionist for a chiropodist when Hughes spotted the photo sent by her agent.

Hughes was nowhere to be seen the day she was summoned to his headquarters at 7000 Romaine for a screen test in the basement. Against a makeshift barn setting, which included a haystack and pitchfork, Russell and other actors acted out a scene in which a half-Mexican girl named Rio is thrown to the ground by Billy the Kid after she's tried to kill him. Billy doesn't know it, but Rio hates him because he killed her brother. In the movie the scene would end with Billy raping Rio. "Ye gods!" Russell is said to have exclaimed. But she wasn't at all flustered by her first experience in front of the cameras. "Actually, it felt very natural," she recalled.

A few days later, she was rewarded with good news. She had the role of Rio and a $50 a week contract. Also contracted for $50 a week was baby-faced Texan Jack Beutel, twenty-three, as Billy. Neither she nor Beutel could have known that *The Outlaw* was going to dominate their lives for the next decade.

Production began in the spring of 1940, some eighty miles east of Flagstaff, Arizona. Howard Hawks, who had worked for Hughes as the director of *Scarface*, was once again in the director's chair. Two weeks into filming, publicist Russell Birdwell got a 1:00 A.M. call from Hughes. "Can you get over here?" asked Hughes, who was at Romaine watching dailies that had been flown in from the set.

Hughes was running and rerunning footage when the bleary-eyed Birdwell entered the screening room. As a scene came to an end Hughes asked, "Didn't you notice something?" Birdwell had to confess that he hadn't.

"No clouds," said Hughes.

As Birdwell sat silent, Hughes continued: "Why go all the way to Arizona to make a picture unless you get some beautiful cloud effects? . . . The damn screen looks naked. Naked."

A decade earlier, Hughes had held up production of *Hell's Angels* for months in order to have clouds as a backdrop for aerial battles. Now he wanted them to grace the skies over Billy the Kid and a spitfire named Rio. The next morning Hughes told Hawks he wanted clouds, "even if you have to wait for a little while."

As if sensing that clouds would be only the beginning of their differences, Hawks said, "Why don't you finish this thing?"

"Do you think I can?" Hughes asked.

"I'll tell you after you get through with it," Hawks declared.

The day after Hawks left the project, Hughes telephoned the movie's production manager and ordered the cast and crew of two hundred and fifty to return immediately to Los Angeles. Never mind that they had traveled to Arizona in an eight-car train that couldn't quickly be turned around. "Just back it into Los Angeles," Hughes said matter-of-factly.

"And so the train came into Los Angeles, with the engine on the wrong end," recalled Russell Birdwell.

It was an apt prelude to what would follow.

Most movies then were filmed in six to eight weeks. The production of *The Outlaw* spanned nine months.

After clamoring for clouds, Hughes decided to film on cloudless soundstages at the Samuel Goldwyn Studio. Actually, he had ulterior motives. By sticking close to home, he could also oversee his burgeoning aviation empire. In order to accommodate his schedule, filming usually began in the afternoon and continued through the early morning hours.

"Nobody could believe it," groaned Russell, who remembered having to convince her boyfriend, UCLA football star Bob Waterfield, that she really was on the set during those hours.

After filming had wrapped for "the day," Hughes would often want to confer with his crew members. Screenwriter and assistant director Jules Furthman got so agitated by the odd-hour calls that he instructed his maid to answer the phone and tell Hughes, "He has a gun. He told me that if I woke him, he'd shoot me."

The schedule wasn't the only thing that was haywire. Hughes ordered so many retakes that "Let's do that one again" became a grating refrain. For Russell and Beutel, who'd never before made a movie, it made for a harrowing baptism. For veteran character actors Thomas Mitchell, as Sheriff Pat Garrett, and Walter Huston, as Doc Holliday, it was sheer boredom.

"Tommy Mitchell went crazy, yelling and screaming and swearing. I guess everyone went a little crazy, me included. But Howard was always gentle," said Russell, who described Hughes's demeanor as "almost pleading."

A graveyard scene with Huston and Beutel was shot 104 times. By the time they had done a wrap, Beutel, who'd never missed a line, was visibly shaken.

After doing one scene twenty-six times, the volatile Mitchell, who had won an Oscar for *Stagecoach* and played Scarlett O'Hara's father in *Gone With the Wind*, angrily tore off his hat, threw it on the floor, and jumped up and down on it. He stormed off the set, loudly denouncing "stupid sons-of-bitches making this bastard of a film." Mitchell later returned and pleaded, "My God, man, you can't dissect emotion like you do an airplane . . . We're trying to create a mood here, and you think it's a scientific experiment."

Mitchell's observation was correct. Hughes was directing like an engineer, attacking each scene as if it were a precise mathematical problem, including the one that led to his now-famous design for Jane Russell's brassiere.

By this time it had become clear to everyone on the set that Russell's breasts were to be considered stars in their own right. Gregg Toland, the respected cinematographer of *Citizen Kane* and *The Grapes of Wrath*, was invariably ordered to emphasize Russell's cleavage. This after Hughes's complaint, "We're not getting enough production out of Jane's breasts."

But when it came time for a scene in which the character of Rio is tied to a tree, Hughes noticed that her breasts wouldn't stay put during her struggle to get free. As she twisted about and her bosom shifted, the outline of her bra was visible beneath her peasant blouse. "Someone call the wardrobe mistress," Hughes demanded.

When wardrobe couldn't fix the problem, Hughes requested a pencil and drawing board. He explained, "This is really just a very simple engineering problem."

"What he was trying to do was get a smooth look, a no-bra look," said Russell. "And as usual, Howard was right. He was ahead of his time."

When the time came for Russell to put on the Hughes-designed bra, though, she balked. "It was absolutely ridiculous-looking. So, I threw the bra behind the bed and I put my own on and I put Kleenex over the top of it, so you couldn't see the lines through it."

The wardrobe girl was frantic. "What if we get fired?"

"Nobody's going to tell," Jane declared as she pulled her blouse on.

Off she went to stand before a silent Hughes, who looked her over for what seemed an eternity. Finally he said, "Okay."

Jane was retied to the fake tree, not knowing that in years to come, Hughes would again pull out the drawing board to deal with her bosom. Nor could anyone have guessed at the cultural significance *The Outlaw* would ultimately have. Like *Hell's Angels* in the twenties and *Scarface* in the thirties, it would become a milestone for an era.

And what a time it was. With America's eventual entry into the war, patriotism on the home front reached an all-time high—one that has never since been equaled. *Everyone* pitched in. Youngsters saved their lunch money for War Bonds; teenage girls dutifully wrote to soldiers they'd never met; senior citizens collected scrap metal; Rosie the Riveters headed for the munitions factories; and all able-bodied men headed for the recruitment centers.

Hollywood was also a valiant participant. Along with producing some of the greatest movies ever made about wartime and its effects—*The Story of G.I. Joe, Destination Tokyo, Pride of the Marines, Sands of Iwo Jima,* and countless others—filmmakers churned out hundreds upon hundreds of military training, propaganda, and other movies for the war effort. The stars also climbed aboard trains and planes to entertain the troops—and raise money for War Bonds. From 1942 to 1945 more than thirty-five hundred entertainers volunteered their time to make more than 35,000 personal appearances. Bob Hope, Joe E. Brown, Dinah Shore, and Frances Langford became fixtures on the front. At home, Bette Davis was active as founder of the Hollywood Canteen, where John Garfield could often be spotted serving up meals and Joan Crawford, Marlene Dietrich, Olivia de Havilland, and others twirled to big band sounds with homesick servicemen.

Hollywood provided inspiration of another kind—the curvaceous kind. Betty Grable's gorgeous gams, insured by Lloyd's of London for $1 million, made her the number-one pin-up girl of American G.I.s. But she had notable competition in the likes of fiery Rita Hayworth, sultry Veronica Lake, and exotic Hedy Lamarr. And *The Outlaw*'s Jane Russell.

By the end of 1942—before the movie had even been released—"better than 43,000 photographs" of Hughes's discovery had been distributed. Among them were George Hurrell's shots of Russell brandishing a six-shooter as she reclined seductively, displaying plenty of cleavage, against a haystack. Every G.I. was familiar with them. Or as Hughes liked to joke, "with both of them." *(Life* magazine had fun with the Russell phenomenon when it snapped a shot of a soldier knitting a sweater for *her.)*

Though he was by no means a great filmmaker, Hughes had an innate understanding of what the public wanted because, despite his wealth, his own tastes were those of the average worker. In the forties, when movie-going reached frenzied numbers—with nearly two-thirds of the entire country going to the movies weekly—he astutely knew that audiences would clamor to see something they hadn't yet seen on the screen. That something was sex. Hughes was determined to give it to them. It was, after all, a subject in which he had a special expertise.

CHAPTER 15

THE BLUE PRINCE

HOWARD STRODE THROUGH MUIRFIELD, LEADING HOUSEKEEPER BEATRICE Dowler from room to room, helping her to cover each chair, table, and couch with dingy cotton shrouds. It was May 1941, but this was no spring cleaning. Howard was systematically putting dust covers on relics.

Staring into the living room, which had been Kate's domain, he saw expanses of Moroccan tile upon which her furniture had once been set. He pulled the huge siesta shutters closed, plunging the once vibrant room into perpetual twilight. Pointing at Tiffany lamps and crystal decanters that dated to his marriage to Ella Rice, he told Dowler, "Wrap them up. I don't want to look at them anymore."

A handyman trailed behind, installing new door locks, each with only a single key.

In the dining room, Howard and Beatrice spread oilcloth on the Italian banqueting table where Jean Harlow, Lucky Luciano, and William Randolph Hearst had dined during a vanished era. Upstairs, Billie Dove's velvety bedroom suite was retired, along with the Venetian glass and Viennese crystal accessories, reminders of the romantic European trip Howard and Billie had taken when they were Hollywood's hottest young lovers.

In the master bedroom, he piled up his gold and silver aviation trophies, along with the honorary keys to the cities of New York, Los Angeles, and

Houston. "Wrap these up, too," he said. The tributes to his heroism were wrapped in newspaper and unceremoniously sent to 7000 Romaine.

He replaced them with a macabre artifact: the crumpled, scorched propeller that had almost decapitated him during the *Hell's Angels* crash. As he would tell Cary Grant, "It's my reminder that death is always just a second away." The propeller was also proof that he had looked death in the face and triumphed over it.

His shrunken world now consisted of the bedroom, its accompanying bath and his den—with its amplified phone system and bank of engineering equipment. Dietrich described it as a "universe of gloom where the sun never shone."

For the rest of the month, Howard sat alone in the silent rooms and brooded, a disappointed, disenchanted prince whose reputation, along with the medals and trophies, was tarnishing.

There were new, more vital heroes in the sky: the young Royal Air Force pilots who were fighting the Battle of Britain above England. Along with the rest of America, he sat by the radio and listened to the bursts from their guns as Edward R. Murrow reported from beleaguered Great Britain. There was also a new breed of young rich men cruising the Sunset Strip: actor Robert Stack, for instance, and John Fitzgerald Kennedy, with his navy ensign whites. And Howard's despised aeronautical rivals, Lockheed and Douglas Aircraft, were riding the rivets to meet the oncoming war, rich with army contracts and each boasting more than 50,000 employees.

"This was a formative period for Hughes," Dietrich recalled. "He began to feel that greatness was passing him by."

He closeted himself for weeks in his darkened bedroom—a preview of his later reclusiveness. Then, on Memorial Day, a charming fifteen-year-old named Faith Domergue walked into his life and rescued him from this well of self-pity.

She was the most beautiful of a pack of Warner Brothers starlets invited to decorate an industry cruise on the *Southern Cross*. Hughes singled her out instantly, curious about this graceful teenager with raven hair, hypnotic dark eyes, and a shyness that matched Hughes's own. As the party broke up, Hughes insisted upon driving her home in a battered Buick, in which Faith immediately fell asleep.

In front of her parents' house, he kissed her on the cheek and whispered, "I'll be seeing you . . . soon." Domergue herself was enchanted with this man, even though at thirty-six he was just a year younger than her father.

Hughes did not phone until eight weeks later, when he extended an invitation to a weekend house party in Palm Springs. Faith, with the blessing of her parents, accepted. Howard, typically, had spent more than an hour on the telephone with her mother, assuring her of his "honorable intentions." He then swept her off to a sprawling ranch in the desert, initiating a dazzling courtship and a mutual obsession that would stretch across five turbulent years in which Hughes would exert iron-fisted control of both Faith Domergue's personal and professional existence.

Their first days together were giddy with romance. They flew to the Salton Sea, where they floated in the primeval brine and feasted on cold chicken and champagne. They cruised the commercial "millionaires' row" in Palm Springs, where she left the boutiques with towering boxes of clothes. "By the end of October, all strain and shyness were gone, and we were falling in love," Domergue later recalled. "It seemed as if danger or unhappiness couldn't get close to me when I was with this man."

On October 19, after a gala at the Palm Springs Racquet Club, Howard led Faith out onto a terrace where sandstorms had created a red harvest moon and framed it with swirls of light. "I love you, Faith," Howard said. "I want to marry you." He put a diamond engagement ring in her hand.

As this naive girl slipped the emerald-cut gem onto her finger, Hughes held her tight. "You are the child I should have had." He added a possessive footnote: "Remember, you belong to me now, so don't even look at another man."

On Monday morning, Domergue danced onto the Warner Brothers lot with the diamond on the third finger of her left hand. Although Faith confided the name of her fiancé to only her drama teacher, word soon spread all over the studio and she was mobbed at lunch. Everyone wanted to see the Hughes diamond.

Late that afternoon Louella Parsons informed the rest of the world via her column.

Howard, bludgeoned by media calls, phoned a series of orders to Faith and her parents. They were to decline all interview requests and to enter and leave their house from the back alley. "And Faith, don't let them take your picture."

The next morning, in a dizzying series of maneuvers, Hughes purchased Faith's seven-year contract from a cagey Jack Warner, who took advantage of the publicity and charged $50,000, and acquired her representation pact from her agent, Henry Willson, at the Zeppo Marx Agency.

"Suddenly, my professional and emotional future were completely in his hands," Domergue recalled. "Sometimes I wasn't afraid. I had complete confidence that my 'Blue Prince' had arrived in my life."

Hughes's arbitrary control convinced Faith's parents to move to a small house on McCadden Drive, just several blocks from his Muirfield address. Obviously, some money changed hands, and Hughes was said to have rewarded both parents with a series of expensive gifts. Later the financial stakes would be higher. But for the remainder of 1941, Howard operated under a set of mutually agreeable ground rules.

Every morning a Hughes limousine collected Domergue and delivered her to a series of teachers and tutors at 7000 Romaine Street, Hughes's Hollywood headquarters. She would finish high school and begin drama lessons in the sterile, lonely building in the city's industrial neighborhood. She was also furnished with a chauffeur, provided with golf lessons at the Wilshire Country Club, and sent to fashion consultants at Bullocks and Robinson's department stores, where she was outfitted with a chic, understated wardrobe.

Like an Elizabethan-era lady-in-waiting, she would be regularly summoned to the side of her lord. Many evenings Hughes had her brought to Muirfield, where she spent quiet evenings with her benefactor, often sitting with him in the den listening to classical music. She usually drifted about while Howard fielded calls from Washington.

Like any other girl about to turn sixteen, Domergue bubbled with curiosity. She wanted to know everything about her mentor and his life. One afternoon in November, when she had finished her homework and was idly flipping through the magazines Howard had purchased for her, she daringly began to rummage through the massive antique bureaux in the bedroom. Most of the drawers were tightly locked and could be opened only by Hughes. But by trial and error she discovered that he'd left one unsecured. She was apprehensive as she pulled it open. What she discovered was a treasure chest of mementos from Hughes's romantic past.

Her fingers shaking, Faith flipped through postcards, business notes, checks, jewelry tags, and letters testifying to Howard's involvements with Billie Dove, Katharine Hepburn, Ginger Rogers, and half a dozen others. In the very back of the drawer she discovered a series of exquisitely carved angels, nesting in a matching set of wooden eggs. Tiny scrolls of writing swirled around the wings of each cherub. The delicate penmanship was in blue ink to match the color of the angel wings. To Faith it was obvious that a woman from Hughes's past had written the messages on each scroll. One of the parchment scrolls read "from C.M. to C.M." A second proclaimed "C.M. will always be scurrying along waiting for you to turn around and wink."

Faith thought back to the stories and rumors she'd heard about Hughes. Who was "C.M."?

Underneath this crypt of angels lay a small hand-painted card, upon which metallic blue fairies fled through a blue mist. It also was signed by "C.M."

Suddenly feeling like an intruder, Faith carefully put the angels back in their eggs, re-wrapped them in the scrolls, and replaced the blue card at the bottom. To her, it looked precisely as it had when she first opened it up.

A week later, though, Howard cornered her in the upstairs bedroom and accused her of investigating him "like a Pinkerton detective." She had ruffled the papers on the angels, he raged. And the card with the fairies got wrinkled when she put it back. "You read those things, didn't you?" Hughes accused. Faith anxiously nodded. "Well, those things were for good luck when I flew around the world," he said, furious.

Then he paused, struggling to regain control of his emotions. He eventually explained that the double "C.M.'s" stood for "Country Mouse" and "City Mouse"—"just friendly, funny names she and I used to call each other many years ago." What he didn't explain was that Kate Hepburn was the inimitable "city mouse," who remained in New York while the "country mouse" would not leave suburban Los Angeles.

After his outburst Howard turned soothing. "Faith," he said, "if you ask me, I'll open any drawer or room in this house. Just ask." In conciliation, he endowed Faith with her own pet name: "Little Baby."

Faith forgot about the confrontation and Howard's uncharacteristic outburst when he flew her off to a weekend in Phoenix, which was just beginning to become a sunny resort area. But the idyll was ruined when a tipster at the spa alerted Louella. Within days she filed a story that ran with an oversize photo of Faith provided by Warner Brothers. The headline questioned IS SHE MRS. HOWARD HUGHES? Parsons quoted "sources close to the couple" who vowed that Howard and Faith, along with her parents, had flown to Arizona for "a very secret wedding ceremony."

When Hughes and Faith returned to Los Angeles he locked himself in the den at Muirfield and sulked. He also pointedly ignored his teenage fiancée, passing her in the halls without a hint of recognition. For three days he was emotionally shaken, pacing and mumbling to himself about "spies in his midst." Finally, on December 4, Hughes apologized to his "Little Baby" and reaffirmed their secret betrothal. But his paranoia continued.

During their drives to the ocean or to shops in Beverly Hills, he stopped the car every half hour and jumped out to use telephone booths. "The people I'm calling, you can't call on the phone at home—might be tapped," he explained to the bewildered Faith. It seemed as if he was expecting some kind of signal.

On December 7, when Faith and Howard were returning from brunch, Howard's sign came. She watched him on the phone, moving his hands and shaking his head back and forth. He ran back to the car and loudly declared, "Faith, the Japanese have bombed Pearl Harbor. America will declare war before the day is over!"

He took her hand when he saw the fear on her face. "Come on now, Little Baby, don't be frightened."

Back at Muirfield, he built a fire, settled behind his desk, grabbed the phone, and ordered his empire to war, from the tool company (which would manufacture tank parts and gun mountings) to Hughes Aircraft (which would become the largest source of weapon machinery of the war).

For six hours, with Faith nestled into an oversize settee, he communicated with key executives in Houston, New York, and Los Angeles, formulating a master plan to convert all his assembly lines from peacetime to wartime. Strangely, the next day Hughes drove off to Romaine, where he locked himself in the editing room to continue work on what had become his own personal war: *The Outlaw.*

As in the rest of America, the holidays passed somberly at Muirfield. Faith was allowed to decorate a miniature Christmas tree. But nothing else. "Too messy and dirty," Hughes grumbled. He did reluctantly agree to take Domergue out on the town on New Year's Eve. He even let her order a new evening gown from a Beverly Hills designer.

Faith threw herself into preparations for the big night, hoping that this was to be a "coming out" before Hollywood society, for which New Year's was the primary holiday. She made reservations at Chasen's and the Mocambo and changed her hairstyle from Joan Crawford thirties to Dorothy Lamour forties. But Howard drove through the dim streets (the blackout was already in effect) in the wrong direction, away from the glitz of Beverly Hills and toward the shabby eastern edge of Hollywood.

They stopped in front of a small Italian dive, where they were the only patrons.

A fight ensued. The precise order of events on that troubled New Year's is unclear. But sometime before dawn, Domergue disappeared. Howard returned to Muirfield alone and collapsed into bed.

An hour later, his maid was awakened by repeated hammering on the front door. Faith's father was on the front steps. "My daughter's in there with your boss. Bring her down," he yelled, shaking his fist.

"Shhh," the servant said. "Only Mr. Hughes is here, and he's asleep."

Faith's father raised his voice. "I know she's here! And you know what? Mr. Hughes is going to hear from me!" Then he stomped off.

Neither he nor the maid spotted the dark sedan parked in the shadows some one hundred yards away. Inside, two FBI agents were monitoring the tumultuous private life of the man who, overnight, had become one of the country's most powerful war barons.

By February, Hughes had convinced himself that Faith's growing dissatisfaction centered not on his infidelities or his solitary ways but on Muirfield, which Faith described as a dead, gloomy museum of the past. That was the one thing Hughes could fix.

In the eighteen months since he had first encountered her on the moonlit deck of the *Southern Cross*, he had become hopelessly entangled in the sensuality of this child-woman. She had made him feel young again and erased his loneliness. Howard was ready to abandon the Muirfield mansion that afternoon, leaving behind its furniture, its art works and, most important, its servants. Whenever any of his lovers grew restive, Hughes always believed the problems could all be solved by externals: fur coats, new houses, expensive cars, and showers of jewelry.

"Because he tended to view the women in his life as 'things' to be collected, it seemed to him that he could please them by showering them with gifts," recalled Dr. Raymond Fowler, who performed the psychological autopsy on the billionaire.

"He felt he could let them sit on the shelf until he needed them. He put people, as well as things, into suspended animation," Domergue noted.

Thus, he counted on this new home, a villa actually, to solve all his problems with Domergue, a girl who had been imprisoned within Muirfield.

As soon as Domergue hopped into the car, he told her of an "incredible surprise" and then headed away from the flatlands of Los Angeles up into the hills of Bel Air. Finally, this king of California moguls was moving to the kingdom of moguls, a rambling enclave of estates with a view of the distant ocean and the scent of a thousand formal rose gardens.

"Faith was Howard's most enduring obsession," recalled Noah Dietrich. "He would have done almost anything to keep her with him."

In fact, her problem was his unfaithfulness. From the start of the relationship, Hughes had been dating the foremost sex symbols of this new wartime Hollywood era. He would eventually romance Lana Turner, Rita Hayworth, and Ava Gardner.

While he cruised Chasen's, Perino's, and the Player's Club with the glittery sex goddesses, Domergue roamed idly through Muirfield or was banished to her parents' house. Even at sixteen, Faith knew the score: Howard had other women. Grown women. But whenever she confronted him with gossip column items about Rita, Lana, and the rest, he claimed they were the fabrications of scoop-hungry columnists. He would hold up Hughes Aircraft worksheets or suspiciously convenient memos from Noah Dietrich, like a teenager with too many unexcused absences trying to cover his tracks.

Left alone by her "father-lover," as she called him, Domergue often slipped onto the greens of the Wilshire Country Club, just as Kate Hepburn had done, to walk for hours in the darkness. It was "like walking on the surface of the moon." One evening in 1942 she just kept walking, past the boundaries of the country club, past the safe confines of Hancock Park, and past Hollywood, where even the theater marquees and neon jungles were dimmed out as a wartime precaution. When she finally returned, it was to her parents' home, not to Muirfield and a frantically alarmed Hughes. He rushed over, but the teenager wouldn't talk to him. "Give her time," Mrs. Domergue cautioned. "She needs a couple of days."

"This young girl was in a terrible dilemma," Dietrich recalled. By now both Faith's father and grandfather were employed by Hughes. "She carried the security of her family on her shoulders," Dietrich recalled.

Several days later, Domergue told Hughes that the romance was gone from their relationship. Never one to analyze himself, Hughes blamed the Muirfield mansion—not his very public womanizing—for all the trouble. So he put it on the market and leased a sixteen-room estate at 619 Sorbonne Road on a hilltop ledge in Bel Air.

Hughes and Faith were on a drive when he surprised her by pulling in front of the exquisite French regency house, set in the midst of its own park. It was, he told her, their new home. "I was crying by the time he led me into the living room—so lovely with glass doors opening onto the garden."

When they were seated on the couch, Hughes took her hand. "We'll start a new life here," he told her, adding that she would never have to return to Muirfield. "That era is over."

Years later, Domergue admitted that at the time of his grand gesture, she thought Hughes was play-acting. Nevertheless she accepted the peace offering and moved into the house. But not because she wanted material possessions. "I came back because I loved him. I knew him thoroughly, of course, and there were things I couldn't accept. But I sincerely loved him, so I said, 'I'll try.' "

"Howard believed he was raising the 'perfect lover,'" Dietrich recalled. "Sexually they were very compatible . . . it was an obsession he couldn't control. On the other hand, he couldn't be faithful."

Faith was also about to become a war widow when Hughes jumped into the treacherous waters of World War II politics and tried to become a major player. He got his first chance on July 20, 1942, when he received a confidential telephone tip from a source in FDR's White House.

Reading from a classified memo, the informant described a multi-million-dollar contract that had just been awarded to metal magnate Henry Kaiser. It authorized the manufacture of a fleet of "flying boats" to ferry troops and supplies across the Atlantic. Nazi submarines were taking a terrible toll on cargo liners. Of particular interest to Hughes was the stipulation that the winged troop trains were to be constructed of wood, precisely in the manner of Howard's XF-11 bomber. The Hughes-perfected Duramold process seemed made to order.

Kaiser further appealed to Howard's boundless imagination by bragging to the press, "Our engineers have on their drawing boards gigantic flying ships more fantastic than any ever imagined by Jules Verne." What Kaiser did not have was a process that would meld wood into the structural elements required by an aircraft.

Early on the morning after Kaiser's press conference, a man phoned the industrialist's headquarters with an anonymous tip: "Did you know that Howard Hughes will soon have two hundred aeronautical engineers free? And that he developed a way to build wooden planes?"

Kaiser called Hughes the next day and convened a meeting on the morning of August 21 at San Francisco's Fairmont Hotel, where Hughes was re-editing *The Outlaw.*

Early that morning, Faith swept into the hotel lobby wearing a wine-red suit, a rope of pearls, and a full-length mink coat. A suite had been reserved for her one floor down from the Hughes penthouse.

After a perfumed bath, Howard's sixteen-year-old fiancée changed into a rose-colored skirt and a pink angora sweater woven so richly that it appeared to be decorated with swirls of blush pink whipped cream.

Hughes was waiting beside the open door of his room. "Little Baby, I really missed you. To see you now, standing there, is like showing a starving man a plate full of gourmet food." They were soon entwined in each other's arms, lying on the sofa.

The desk clerk called to say that Henry Kaiser and a gray-suited delegation were on the way up. They hugged one last time before Faith ran for the elevator. When she turned back to blow him a kiss, she doubled over in laughter. Tufts of pink angora decorated his black suit like angel hair on a Christmas tree. Howard looked down in shock: "Hell's fire! What the hell am I going to do?"

"Grab a wet towel," she giggled, before dashing to the elevator.

The first vision greeting Henry Kaiser and his formal adjutants when they reached Hughes's floor was this gorgeous starlet walking sultrily down the hall from Hughes's door—the only door at that end of the wing. She smiled broadly and tugged at the sleeves of her pink angora sweater. Then she winked.

As for Hughes, he sat through one of the most important meetings of his life in his black suit, no tie, and tennis shoes. All with pink angora accents. Because he was still dizzy from a recent bout with pneumonia, Howard also reclined against a couch. An exasperated Kaiser finally erupted. "Sit up, Howard, and let's talk about winning this war."

After much finessing and cajoling, Hughes and Kaiser agreed to build a fleet of five hundred seaplanes, with Hughes designing the prototype for the largest aircraft ever contemplated. The War Production Board, after a lobbying campaign, allotted $18 million for construction of the flying behemoths, each with eight engines, a wingspan longer than a football field, and a hull taller than a three-storey building.

Hungry as he was for any kind of recognition from the Armed Forces, Howard impulsively agreed to have the first ship operational within a year. Though the millionaire knew the goal was impossible, he signed the pledge anyway, dubbing the plane the HK-1 (for Hughes-Kaiser 1), or Hercules.

The world would eventually know it as the Spruce Goose.

As 1943 began, both Dietrich and Glenn Odekirk blessed Domergue as the single stabilizing force in Hughes's life, even though the underage Faith remained largely in hiding. "When I came over to work, she remained upstairs," Odekirk recalled. "Through those war months, I only caught sight of her once." But Faith's strong domestic influence was to be shattered by a more mature baby doll, all of twenty-one, who blew into Howard's arms in January 1943 and who kept his life in turmoil for more than a decade.

When Hughes first met Ava Gardner, she was just another gorgeous starlet, toiling in the shadow of Lana Turner, Hedy Lamarr, and Greer Garson. She was actually better known for her incendiary marriage to Mickey Rooney than for anything she had done on-screen.

The daughter of a poor North Carolina tenant farmer, Ava had made it to Metro-Goldwyn-Mayer on the strength of an eight-by-ten glossy taken by her brother-in-law. When he placed it in the window of his Manhattan portrait studio, it literally drew crowds. As beautiful as Gardner was on the silver screen, with her tigress sensuality and eyes flecked with green and gold, she was more breathtaking in person. Director John Huston, who came to know her intimately, called her "an explosion of sensuality."

Hughes first noticed Ava during one of his eternal girl hunts through the Los Angeles newspapers. The photo in question showed her standing next to her first husband, Mickey Rooney. The caption beneath it declared, "Mickey Rooney Divorces Actress Ava Gardner." The picture was not particularly flattering, depicting her without makeup and in a mousy gabardine suit. But Hughes saw something. "This runt couldn't satisfy her," he told Dietrich.

"And you can tell that from a picture?" Noah asked.

"Yep."

Two days later, Hughes aide Johnny Meyer knocked on Gardner's door. "I think you've been told of Howard Hughes's interest in you. He's anxious to meet you." The requisite roses had already arrived.

"I didn't know until much later that Meyer was there to size me up, to see if I was qualified to be a 'Hughes girl,'" Gardner recalled.

She obviously passed muster, because Howard arrived on her doorstep several days later. "He was well over six feet tall, but couldn't have weighed more than one hundred and fifty pounds," Gardner remembered. "Thin, bronzed, with a small moustache. Eyes dark and sensual. A male man. Secure. Private. He reminded me of my father."

For his part, Hughes wanted to marry Ava the moment he saw her, not so much because he loved her but because he believed her to be the ultimate bauble: the perfect wife for his arm in his new role as a global entrepreneur.

To sugarcoat one of his four proposals of marriage to Ava Gardner, he went to Cartier and returned carrying a brown paper sack stuffed with diamond bracelets, ruby earrings, an opal necklace, and a leather pouch full of loose stones. He dumped them in a pile for Ava's sister, Beatrice (Bappie) to peruse. Bappie remembered the jewels as "sparkling and unbelievable in their richness."

Another evening he sent Ava a battered shoe box containing $250,000 in cash. Ava reacted like one of the tough broads she was famed for portraying. "See this," said Gardner to her publicist David Hanna. "It means nothing to me . . . absolutely nothing."

However, a gift in honor of her birthday in 1945 earned him high romantic marks. "What would you like?" he asked. "Just name it."

Rather off-handedly, Ava asked for "a small bowl of orange ice cream," a dessert she had enjoyed as a child in North Carolina. To make her wishes clearer, she added: "And I don't mean orange sherbet . . . that watery stuff . . . but orange ice cream."

The Hughes empire swung into action, finally locating the wartime rarity at an ice cream parlor in New York's Little Italy. A TWA plane rushed the precious dessert to Los Angeles, where it was delivered to Gardner's home in a solid silver tub. She was finally impressed, "because of the imagination and the trouble involved."

From the start Hughes handled Ava differently.

All that he had cruelly denied Faith Domergue, he showered upon Gardner: flashy nights at Caraways and the Mocambo, weekends at the Palm Springs Racquet Club, formal dinners at the mansions of Darryl F. Zanuck and Samuel Goldwyn, and shopping expeditions to Mexico City and Manhattan. He set her up in a lavish apartment just off Sunset Strip, complete with accommodations for Bappie. She was, Hughes told Dietrich, "a romantic investment: I can do a lot for her; she can do a lot for me."

He hired a slick private detective named Frank Angell, who in turn brought along operatives and specialists in electronic bugging and photo surveillance, creating the nucleus of the notorious "Hughes Secret Police," which would be with him in one form or another until he died.

From the second he listened to the clandestine tapes of Ava's private telephone calls, he was addicted. No woman who went on to cross his life, however briefly, would be spared from this illegal espionage. In the case of Ava, Angell and his men delivered a bombshell a month after they were hired.

"The news got back to him that Mickey was slipping in and out of a back window" at Ava's, Dietrich recalled. "It was actually revealed by electronic surveillance. Howard was steamed that Rooney was getting past the staff of three 'bodyguards' he'd hired to follow her everywhere. Because he set her up in this place, in Hughes's mind, he owned her."

Howard's first question was predictable: "Are they sleeping together?"

"Yes, if you accept the sounds we've heard as proof," Angell replied.

Hughes raced over to Ava's apartment. Using a front door key he kept secret from Ava, Howard let himself in and crept into her bedroom. Gardner awakened with a start to see Howard standing over her. She could see the fury on his face.

"I understood what he wanted. He had wanted to sneak in and catch Mickey in bed with me. I think he even hoped for that confrontation. Trouble seemed to make him happy," Ava recalled.

But Gardner remained cool: "Howard, why don't you go downstairs. I'll put on a robe and join you at the bar." Wearing a soft peach robe, her dark hair tumbling over her face, Gardner stepped down into the sunken living room smiling deliberately, "to let him know that I abhorred being spied upon."

Furious, Hughes grabbed her by the shoulders and slapped her repeatedly. "I could feel my face swelling and my right eye closing. But mostly I was angry. I had never been hit like that in my life—and all because of his goddamned pride and jealousy."

The look on Gardner's face snapped Howard out of his rage and he stumbled backward. "I'm sorry, Little Baby," he said—using Faith's pet name. "God, I'm sorry."

His pleas for forgiveness made Ava even angrier. "I thought, 'I'm going to kill that skinny bastard,'" she said. "I groped around for something to club him with—anything would have done." Her hand closed around the handle of an authentic eighteenth-century bronze bell. She aimed directly at his head and let fly. There was a crunch as the metal sliced open Howard's forehead. He collapsed onto the floor, mumbling incoherently.

"He wasn't dead yet, and I was still determined to kill the son of a bitch. I grabbed a big hardwood chair and lurched over to smash him with it."

Just then Bappie ran through the door. "Ava! Ava! Drop it!" she said. Gardner whirled around and dropped the chair and collapsed on the couch.

Howard lost consciousness as two of the bodyguards lifted him out to the car. A deep zigzag gash leaked blood from his hairline to his bottom lip. Ava had also knocked out two teeth and splintered his jaw, which had already been pulverized years ago during the filming of *Hell's Angels*.

From his hospital bed, Hughes sent Dietrich to Faith with an elaborate tale of a car accident.

Ava was unrepentant. "You don't own me, you bastard," she said. "And don't forget it."

This latest dangerous liaison convinced Dietrich and Dr. Verne Mason, Howard's internist, that their boss had become addicted to psychodrama and danger—both real and manufactured—whether it came from staring at death behind the wheel of an untested airplane or from romancing several incendiary women at the same time.

"Why else would he promise to deliver the world's largest airplane in ten months when he knew for certain it would take more than two years?" said Dietrich. "He did things like that because he relished the trouble which inevitably ensued."

Dietrich also noticed that Howard seemed the most exhilarated when things were about to come crashing down, as they were in early 1943. Overextended professionally, emotionally, and romantically, Hughes saw his life veer drastically off course.

His cozy domestic charade with Domergue was the first to collapse.

As she approached Howard's bedroom early one morning she heard her "father-lover" whispering to another woman. "Okay, Little Baby, you be careful now." Domergue flew through the door.

"Howard, don't try and tell me that was Odekirk at the plant or Jack Frye of TWA. And don't tell me that was a business call, because I'm quite certain that you don't call any of these men 'Little Baby'!" She turned and ran down the hall, yelling, "I'm through, Howard! Did you hear that? I'm through!"

She ran downstairs, through the vast expanse of the living room and out into the rose garden, where she tore through the plants, frantically snatching blossoms from the bushes. She finally stopped, her chest heaving. When Faith looked down, she saw that the stems had shredded the flesh of her hands. "I heard his voice from the terrace behind me: 'Faith, Faith. There's no one else but you . . . there will never be anyone else in my life.'"

Howard wiped the blood from her hands with the tails of his white shirt. Then he held her tight. But he would never again call her Little Baby.

And she would no longer believe him. "I felt like a butterfly on a pin—beautiful, vibrant, and utterly trapped."

Her father, who was ill at the time, was working for Howard, as was her grandfather, who lived in a war worker's home arranged for by Howard. In addition, Faith had five more years to go on her supposed film contract with Hughes.

Later that afternoon, the seventeen-year-old girl sat in her ornate boudoir, with its antique finery, and cried out of sheer loneliness. Howard had left for an airfield. Or so he said.

To take the edge off her confused feelings, Domergue jumped into a little red roadster, a gift from Hughes, and tore off into the night, her dark hair flowing wildly. She sped up and down Sunset Boulevard, through the desert canyons and the wide Los Angeles streets toward the ocean. Then, on a hunch, she headed back toward Muirfield. Her sixth sense was correct.

Instead of being at the airfield, Hughes had escorted a gorgeously gowned Ava to Frances Langford's opening at the Cocoanut Grove. Now, driving Gardner home, Hughes was startled to see Faith's roadster coming up in the distance.

Driving a sleek, metal-gray Cadillac belonging to Hughes Aircraft, Hughes picked up speed and headed down Fairfax Avenue toward Farmer's Market. But Faith recognized his car and gunned the roadster's engine.

Hughes felt her small car bump the back of his town car. He speeded up.

Faith swerved around the side of his car, matching his speed. Now she got a good look at Ava Gardner, her dark hair piled on her head and held in place by a matching pair of diamond clips (a gift from Howard).

Hughes glanced down and was alarmed by the look on Domergue's face. He squealed into the parking lot at Farmer's Market and slowed down. Faith careened along behind.

He stopped the Cadillac, leaving its engine idling.

Domergue deliberately backed up her roadster and floored the gas pedal, crashing repeatedly into the passenger's door. Gardner screamed. "Poor Ava bounced up and down in her seat," Domergue recalled.

The front of the roadster was crumpled, spewing steam into the air.

All three sat in silence. Gardner sobbed. Hughes clenched his teeth. But Domergue just stared into his eyes. He finally leaped out, ran over to the roadster, and grabbed Faith and shook her until she cried out.

Aviation magnate Sherman Fairchild, dressed formally, pulled up at that moment. He eased Gardner out of the Cadillac and into his own car, and after whispering to Hughes, drove Ava home.

Hughes and his "Little Baby" stood in the darkness beside their crippled automobiles. Faith trembled, stung by what she had done. But Howard was unruffled. Without speaking he took Faith by the hand and pulled her into his battered Cadillac.

Back at Muirfield, Howard made more promises; uttered his now familiar apologies; offered more money ("Let me set your father up in business"), and swore he would make her a big star and "build a studio" around her.

Young, confused, and still in love with Hughes, Faith stayed on at Sorbonne.

Ava was rewarded with a two-day shopping spree in Mexico City. "I didn't own him; he didn't own me," Gardner recalled years later. "And he made life so easy for me when I wanted him to. And, most important, he backed off—when I needed him to."

"It was quite a cachet to be seen with Howard Hughes," said columnist Dorothy Manners. "And it did a lot for Ava, among others."

Soon, however, dueling lovers would be the least of Howard's problems.

CHAPTER 16

BRAINSTORMS

THE ODD LAPSES OF THE LONELY MILLIONAIRE WOULD BE NOTICED BY MANY in this pressure-filled year. A host of girlfriends would witness behavior that ranged from bizarre to downright threatening. Howard would end up being booted out of the pilot's seat during a test run for TWA. And his mental fog would be responsible for a crucial mistake that would end in tragedy.

During the troubled spring of 1943, *The Outlaw* would also help push him to the edge. He had spent more than a year editing the movie and had battled with censors for two years. Led by Hollywood's Joseph Breen, they first reacted when they saw the film's script. After seeing the finished print more than a year later, an enraged Breen fired off a letter to Will Hays, the nation's chief censor. Among Breen's complaints: "Throughout almost half the picture the girl's [Jane Russell's] breasts, which are quite large and prominent, are shockingly uncovered." Breen also balked over certain lines of dialogue. In all, Hughes was asked to make 108 cuts.

In a brilliant stroke, Hughes ordered publicist Russell Birdwell to bring a Columbia University mathematician to a meeting of the censorship board in Manhattan. When members convened, they were surprised to find the hearing room was encircled by oversize photographs of leading actresses, including Jane Russell. Birdwell introduced his special guest, who produced a pair of calipers. Then the mathematician went from photograph to photograph, measuring the amount of cleavage on display.

Hughes was later asked to make only three cuts. Still he refused. So Glenn Odekirk, under instructions from Hughes, built a lead room at Romaine where the film was stored.

But by early 1943, three years after the film started production, even Hughes had tired of the wait. After making minor concessions, he secured a seal of approval for *The Outlaw.* It would finally have its day.

By this time Jane Russell was one of the most talked-about stars in the country, receiving an estimated eleven hundred letters a week, even though no one had yet seen her in a movie. When the world premiere finally rolled around on February 5, 1943, at San Francisco's Geary Theatre, Russell and her co-star Jack Beutel were booked to perform personal appearances before each screening, even midnight shows. To further trumpet what it called "the picture that couldn't be stopped," a massive billboard of Russell outside the theater proclaimed, "Sex has not been rationed."

Actually, a real-life sex scandal took a bite out of the press corps scheduled to attend the premiere. Because the Errol Flynn statutory rape trial was underway in Los Angeles, many reporters didn't make it to the gala. In retrospect, that proved to be a blessing.

From the time the curtain went up, or rather, didn't, premiere night was a debacle.

Russell and Beutel were supposed to start the evening off by performing a scene from the movie. But as the curtain began to go up, it suddenly stopped. "This fabulous, terribly expensive, frigging curtain was stuck!" said Russell, who watched helplessly from a backstage wing. She and Beutel never did perform their scene. By the time the curtain finally rose, the audience was in laughter. Then the movie started. And the laughter continued.

As the movie began to unspool, Hughes spirited Russell and Beutel out a stage door and onto a cable car. Hughes was silent, his eyes expressionless, as the little car chugged up the hill to the Fairmont Hotel. Later, the three made small talk and sipped champagne in Hughes's suite. But he was obviously distressed.

None of them attended the special postpremiere press party that Hughes had arranged. It was for the best. One reporter was overheard to say, "In the forty years I have been going to the theater, this is the worst thing I have ever seen."

The next day Hughes awakened to find the press gunning for *The Outlaw.*

"Oh, my God, the reviews," Russell recalled.

Variety called it "almost a burlesque on all screen Westerns." The *San Francisco Chronicle*'s Dwight Whitney complained, "Nothing happens that's worth mentioning." The cruelest comments came from *Time* magazine, which dubbed it "a strong candidate for the flopperoo of all time," and claimed that the movie's horse, named Red, rode off with the acting honors. Hughes was so hurt he considered taking legal action against the magazine.

Despite the critics, *The Outlaw* really was the picture that couldn't be stopped. Russell Birdwell's ongoing publicity campaign kept the movie in the headlines, and moviegoers in the theater. Birdwell's tactics included placing anonymous calls to the San Francisco Police Department, asking for the film's suppression, and stirring up women's, parents', and religious groups. He even planted an article in the *San Francisco Chronicle* that addressed the pros and cons of the "inflammatory" western. The article quoted an unnamed sailor who came away from the movie so satisfied "I can go back to my ship for another six months!" He also quoted a women's club representative concerned about "reel number seven." The resulting furor led to the brief arrest of the manager of the Geary Theatre and a hearing in which a Hughes lawyer toted a replica of the Venus de Milo into the courtroom to better illustrate the artistic merits of the female form.

The Outlaw was in its eighth record-breaking week when Hughes, strangely, pulled it from distribution. For the next three years it sat on a shelf in the lead-lined room at Romaine.

To Noah Dietrich, it seemed as if Howard's mind was "shorting out emotionally," resulting in amnesia-like episodes of bizarre behavior. In fact, Hughes's actions were the result of an undiagnosed emotional illness—one that would become progressively worse with age.

In an era when psychological problems were only whispered about, no one in Hughes's circle foresaw the tragedy that lay ahead. Those who witnessed the frightening symptoms kept quiet about it for decades.

Ava Gardner was party to a mental collapse on a trip up the coast to San Francisco on Santa Fe's luxurious Zephyr. Although Howard had been unusually quiet when they boarded, Gardner chalked it up to exhaustion. He had been working at Hughes Aircraft all day, taking her out at night, sometimes dancing until dawn, and then returning to the airfield again.

When they reached their connecting drawing rooms, Howard seemed manic. "Get all gussied up and meet me in the club car. I've got a wonderful surprise." The invitation thrilled Ava. It was her first time in a first-class train compartment and her first visit to San Francisco.

She waded through the banks of yellow roses from Howard and pulled on a costly black traveling costume designed for her by MGM's "queen of high couture," Irene. It featured black mink at the collar and cuffs and jet black beading spilling down the front. The ensemble even included embroidered black hose with shoes and gloves to match. "I felt like a million dollars," she recalled. "I swept my hair atop my head and slipped into those tall, tall high heels . . . so high and so thin that it took me about ten minutes to reach the club car."

When the doors whooshed open, all eyes followed her as she sank into an armchair. She was the only woman in the room.

The club car terminated in a curving dome of glass that revealed a crimson sunset settling far out on the Pacific Ocean. Soon a porter arrived and handed her a battered white box wrapped with an unkempt bit of brown shipping cord. While everyone gazed at her, Ava opened the box. Inside were wads and wads of crumpled newspapers that spilled onto the carpet.

Finally, at the bottom of this trash, she found a large bottle of champagne, which was immediately popped open by a waiter. "I was furious," Gardner recalled. "But the champagne was French and soon had a magical effect on me. By the third glass, I was smiling at everybody." As the young waiter poured her a fourth, Hughes stumbled through the double doors. He had greased his hair à la Rudolph Valentino, a look that had been in vogue twenty years earlier.

His broad shoulders and long legs were crammed into an ivory ice-cream suit, the very suit that was the pride of his Rice University wardrobe in 1924. The pants were pleated and ended about four inches above his shoes. Instead of a belt, his frat boy pants were held up with a paisley tie pulled though the belt loops and knotted in front. Saddle Oxfords completed this Henry Aldrich look.

The club car was hushed as Hughes sank into the seat next to Gardner. Blushing, Ava leaned close to his ear. "Good God, Howard, what trunk did you dig that out of?" She could tell that he had no idea what she was talking about. He pouted, "This is a swell suit."

That's when she realized that Hughes was lost inside some sort of mental fog. He saw absolutely nothing wrong with his bizarre costume and was oblivious to the stares of fellow passengers. She quietly took his hand and led him back to their adjoining suites.

While they both changed, Gardner decided she couldn't risk intimacy with this "disturbed stranger." She edged over to the connecting door and twisted the lock. Howard leaned against the door. "You didn't have to do that, Ava. I'm a gentleman," he said softly.

Although Hughes had purchased a million dollars worth of jewelry, intending to place one costly treat on her breakfast tray every morning of their stay in the city by the bay, the shaken actress made him fly her back to Los Angeles after their first night's dinner.

Several weeks later, Faith Domergue noticed signs of Hughes's deteriorating psyche. They were driving through the desert toward Palmdale, where he was testing a new wooden plane, when Howard spotted a jackrabbit lying on the roadside.

Without a word he stopped the car and ran back to the small animal. He knelt down and gently placed his hand on the rabbit's neck. Then he returned sadly to the car.

"What was it, Howard?" Faith asked. "Didn't you think it was dead?"

"I wasn't sure," he answered. "If it wasn't, I couldn't leave it on the side of the roadway." She noticed that for the remainder of the journey he held his left hand out the window.

Upon reaching their leased cottage, he ran to the bathroom, turned on the hot water, and began washing his left hand with a bar of strong surgical soap he always carried with him. Moving his hands rhythmically, almost in slow motion, he performed the ritual for more than an hour until his hand was raw and bleeding. Then he tumbled into bed, leaving the contaminated hand hanging down toward the floor.

More dangerously, he began to fall apart professionally as well. The first sign was a marked erosion of his unerring control of an airplane.

In April 1943, Hughes insisted on personally testing the first Constellation when it rolled off the Lockheed assembly line. The "Connie," partially invented and perfected by Hughes, would soon be the flagship of emerging Trans World Airlines—or, as *Fortune* magazine called it, "Howard's Airline."

Technically, Hughes was in command of the flight, but Lockheed's chief test pilot, Milo Burcham, and Lockheed's chief engineer, Kelly Johnson, could commandeer the plane at any time. Sitting in the co-pilot's seat and armed with the same controls as Hughes, Burcham also rode along to monitor any irregularity during the plane's inaugural flight.

High above the desert, Howard demanded to know what it took to stall the skyliner. "It's something all TWA pilots will have to know."

Burcham maneuvered the wing flaps slightly. The Connie stalled, hung in the air for a millisecond, then recovered smoothly.

"Goddammit, man, that's no stall," Hughes taunted. Before Burcham could stop him, Howard lowered the flaps fully while the plane was flying at 225 miles per hour. The enormous plane shuddered.

"It was the only time I ever saw 'zero speed' indicated on a large plane," Johnson recalled. Burcham's face blanched. Johnson ordered, "Quick, Howard, raise the flaps!"

Hughes looked straight ahead, apparently oblivious to the danger. Johnson screamed: "Up flaps, dammit. Up flaps, now!" Howard finally obeyed, pulling out at the very last second.

During the takeoff and landing tests that followed, Hughes seemed right on target for the first five passes. Then this champion aviator, with twenty thousand takeoffs and landings to his credit, began allowing the Constellation to drift dangerously to the left, tilting the aircraft as if a giant were tugging on the wing. "Careful, Howard," Johnson advised. "Hold her steady."

On the sixth pass, the plane drifted so far to the left that it missed the Palmdale control tower by about twenty yards, rattling the windows and creating panic among the traffic controllers. "Howard, you almost crashed the plane," Johnson said evenly.

Then the Lockheed pilot seized control of the Constellation, booting Hughes back into a passenger seat. The ultimate humiliation for any flier, it was an especially crushing blow to Hughes, who never mentioned the incident to anybody, once claiming that he had never flown the Constellation. But a confidential memo was dispatched to Howard's partner, Jack Frye, the hands-on president of TWA. "Your man's losing it. We had to take control of the plane away, and even then he remained in a fog."

"We could have all been killed," Johnson later wrote. "We were lucky."

Death would be precisely the outcome of another test run a month later. On May 16, 1943, over the ink blue depths of Lake Mead, Hughes insisted on captaining a government-mandated shakedown cruise of the Sikorsky amphibian, which he had fine-tuned into aviation's finest water plane. Cost of the refinements exceeded $300,000. In hindsight, it's easy to see that Howard was on the brink of a collapse. But at the time even those closest to him, including Odekirk, protectively described him as "suffering from exhaustion."

The morning of the Lake Mead tests Howard woke up at four o'clock next to Ava Gardner in a palatial suite at the Desert Inn. He felt dizzy and disoriented, but didn't volunteer that information to Odekirk on the drive to the grubby air strip at Boulder City. Waiting for them were two Civil Aeronautics Agency fliers, C. W. Von Rosenberg and Ceco Cline, along with Howard's own engineers, Gene Blandford and Richard Felt.

Nobody paid much attention to his nervous state. He was perhaps the finest pilot in the world. And during the past six months he had landed the Sikorsky on the waters of Lake Mead 4,588 times, trying out each of the twenty design modifications Hughes Aircraft had added to the plane.

Uncharacteristically, Howard violated his own never-fail flight inventory of the plane from tail to propeller. So he failed to see that his ground mechanics hadn't loaded the weighty ballast into the tail, an essential ingredient for any safe water landing. "After all, Hughes was the expert," the CAA's Von Rosenberg later recalled. "We all felt supremely confident that we were in safe hands."

At first everything proceeded perfectly on this, Hughes's 4,589th landing. He descended smoothly toward the lake. The desert air was calm, the lake's surface as still as a mirror. The Sikorsky glided to an almost perfect touchdown, its pontoons leaving churns of water in its wake.

But when Howard tried to brake the huge airplane, its nose plunged into the lake at eighty miles per hour. The screech of tearing metal echoed across the lake. "Then the plane bounced up and down," recalled Clyde Stevenson, who was fishing nearby. "It seemed as if it were spinning like a top, losing pieces of its tail and peeling the metal skin from the fuselage, as if it were sliced with a knife." Powerless, Hughes clung to the controls, his eyes darting back and forth.

Then the left propeller snapped off and headed back toward the Sikorsky, spinning and shredding as it impacted the fuselage. Working like an out-of-control buzz saw, it sliced open Richard Felt's head and propelled Ceco Cline into the lake, sucking him down into the black water.

Hughes, Von Rosenberg, and Blandford were trapped in the plane as water boiled around them. The amphibian was swamped in less than thirty seconds. Von Rosenberg was the only one of the aviators who was fully conscious. Shaking Blandford awake, Von Rosenberg ordered him to lift the mortally injured Felt out through a hole in the roof.

Hughes was frozen at the controls, with blood gushing down his face from a gash that ran the full length of his forehead. Von Rosenberg fought his way through the churning water and unfastened Hughes's seat belt. "Hughes," he yelled, "get control of yourself!"

Howard fell forward onto the control bank, moaning incoherently about notifying Ava Gardner. Von Rosenberg grabbed and shook him. "Crawl through the window, Howard, or we're all going to drown."

Despite a fractured back and dislocated shoulder, Von Rosenberg summoned the force to push Hughes out through the pilot's side window and down into the water. Once Blandford and the comatose Felt were out of the plane, Von Rosenberg scrambled out seconds before the Sikorsky disappeared into the lake.

Rescuers rushed Von Rosenberg, Felt, and Blandford to the hospital. But Hughes insisted upon waiting for a lake patrol boat.

Odekirk, monitoring the tests from the air, found his boss in the office of the Boulder City Airport, collapsed in a chair and still bleeding from the blows to his head. The moment he saw Odekirk, he lapsed into hysteria. "It's my fault, my fault. You could see it from the air. How could I have let it happen?"

"God, Howard, let's get you to a hospital."

Hughes panicked. "No, no, no," he answered. "If I get in there they won't let me out; they'll put me in a locked ward."

Odekirk finally led Hughes to the Boulder Dam Hotel and treated his boss's cuts with alcohol and cotton batting. "I stretched the skin so that it almost covered the nasty gash and then held it together by wrapping gauze around his head," Odekirk recalled.

Knowing that Felt was dying and rambling on that "it was murder," Hughes became obsessed with his bloody clothes. "A lot of that blood belongs to Dick," he said plaintively. "I can't stand it . . . I've got to change." Then he added, "Take me to Penney's."

Ten minutes later, Hughes appeared wearing new clothes—a pair of cheap cotton pants and shirt, an outlandish pair of blue socks, and blue tennis shoes. But in his tormented state he had purchased a shirt, pants, and a jacket that were much too small for him.

"Nothing he bought was even near his actual size," recalled Ava Gardner, who later held the quaking Hughes in her arms. "But I knew better than to say anything; he literally didn't know what he was doing." She tried to convince Howard to remain at the Desert Inn until he regained control of himself. "He was in no condition to go anywhere."

He refused, lamenting, "I have to be the one to inform Dick's wife. I'm the one who killed him." With Odekirk at his side, Hughes actually flew another plane back to Culver City, communicating with Faith Domergue at Sorbonne via a radio-telephone patch.

"You're going to hear news about a plane crash," he told her. "But I'm okay, and I'll explain it all to you later." Despite the static on the radio-phone, Domergue could tell that Howard was badly shaken. "Spells of silence followed each sentence pause, which indicated to me that he was under terrible stress. I had never heard him sound so bad."

On the way to Hughes Aircraft, Domergue heard the first terse radio bulletin on the car radio: "One man was drowned, and four others, including Howard Hughes, the millionaire film producer and aviator, were hurt when an experimental flying boat crashed and sank in Lake Mead."

When Hughes jumped down from the cockpit at Culver City, his appearance alarmed Faith. It seemed to her as if he had physically shrunk. She later described him as "lifeless and stooped, looking fifteen years older than he had the day before." Recalled Domergue, "He only managed a weak smile when he saw me."

Hughes hugged her tightly. "That propeller was meant for me, Faith. I should have been killed, not Dick. My fault," he murmured, "my fault."

While Hughes was in the air, Dick Felt, a colleague and friend for more than seven years, died. The body of CAA pilot Ceco Cline was never found. A CAA commission, realizing they were dealing with a major wartime supplier, whitewashed the incident, blaming "poor communication and Hughes's ground crew." Pilot error was, conveniently, never mentioned.

But Hughes and the rest of the aeronautics world knew otherwise. It was the captain's job to check the plane inch by inch to determine if it was weighted properly. Even without the ballast, Howard at his peak would have controlled his beloved amphibian. He knew it down to its last ball bearing. "He let it get away from him," Odekirk sadly admitted.

The implication was serious: the leading pilot in America, perhaps the world, had killed two men during a routine landing that had occurred under optimum conditions. "This was an enormous psychological blow for him," concluded Captain Charles Barton, an author who spent ten years researching Hughes's aviation career.

He also suffered his seventh major head injury, this time refusing to be treated and x-rayed.

He displayed further signs of emotional collapse during his pursuit of forties screen femme fatale Jane Greer.

Hughes had caught his first glimpse of Greer as he flipped through the pages of *Life* magazine and spotted Bettejane modeling the new, chic uniform of the Women's Army Corps. Summoning his girl gofers, Charlie Guest and Johnny Meyer, he ordered, "Find this girl and sign her up, then get her out here as soon as possible."

Greer, who would become one of the predominant queens of postwar film noir, would witness Howard's slow, painful descent into what appeared to be a mental breakdown. Because he soon fell in love with her, Jane saw a side to Hughes that escaped his aides and superstar lovers.

"He was obsessed with me," Greer said. "But at first it seemed as if he were offering me a wonderful career opportunity."

After being whisked to Los Angeles, Greer and her mother remained under a kind of house arrest for five months in a specially arranged apartment. Hughes didn't phone; he didn't visit. "Finally, we just walked into Hollywood one evening," Greer recalled. "We were bored and lonely." Jane soon got the rush from Rudy Vallee, the balladeer king of the Roaring Twenties. "After our fourth date, Howard finally called."

Jane was already in bed when Charlie Guest called to tersely report, "Mr. Hughes will see you now."

"But it's so late," Greer protested.

"Look," Guest said sternly, "Howard Hughes never knows what time it is, and he never cares what time it is. People do what he wants when he wants it."

The car deposited her at the door of a deserted studio theater. "I looked down rows and rows of empty seats, all dark except for a stage light in the front row. At the bottom of the light, I saw two long legs. And I knew that must be Howard Hughes."

She heard a voice: "Come and sit next to me." When she settled into the theater seat, Hughes turned.

Finally, she got to look at him. She stared intently, studying his dark features, as he said, accusingly, "I hear you've been seeing Rudy Vallee."

"Oh, yes," Greer answered. "And he's been so nice to Mother and I."

Hughes looked perturbed. "And you've even been going *without* your mother as well."

"Sometimes, yes," she answered. "He also lets me sing in his band."

"But you were told not to meet anybody and especially not to go out. You are not to see this man ever again," Hughes continued.

"I can't do that, he's been so nice to me," she replied.

Howard grew angrier. "I'm telling you not to see him. I'm ordering you not to see him . . . never again."

Jane was undaunted. "I can't do that," she argued. "I don't see why you should pick and choose my friends, or my boyfriends for that matter."

"I see," Howard muttered. Extending his hand, he said, simply, "It's been very nice meeting you." Greer sat there for a moment, uncertain about what she should do. "I said, good night," he said.

Hughes fumed for days over Greer's acts of insubordination and even began scouring Hollywood for a Jane Greer look-alike. In the end, however, he signed her to a seven-year contract with his production company.

As 1943 turned to 1944 and still brought her no film roles Greer impulsively married Rudy Vallee and sued to end her contract with Hughes. Shortly thereafter, though, she began having marital troubles and Hughes shouldered his way back into her life—this time giving her the full Howard Hughes rush: the gardenias, the Texas charm, and tours of the nightclub circuit.

At times he courted Greer in the manner of a high school senior, taking her again and again to the neon midway of Pacific Ocean Park, the perpetual, mist-shrouded carnival that rambled along the length of the Santa Monica pier. They held hands while riding the melodious carousel, ate cotton candy, and roamed the midway. "He loved those games—like where you throw a baseball or shoot at clunky metal ducks," Jane recalled. "We took armloads of Kewpie dolls back to my mom, beginning a fabulous collection." With the eighteen-year-old Greer, Hughes became a teenager himself, as if he were "experiencing adolescence for the first time," according to her.

With Greer's help he learned how to play. One cold evening while they were holding hands at the end of the pier, Howard confessed that his mother, Allene, had robbed him of his childhood. "She overprotected me," he said candidly. "I'm doing all of this for the first time." As he compulsively played the midway games, it seemed to Greer that he was as proud of the Kewpie dolls he won as he was of the multimillion-dollar war contracts pouring into his empire.

They became lovers, using Hughes's headquarters suites at the Town House Hotel and an apartment above Sunset Boulevard as their secret hideaways. "I was inexperienced and he was very sweet—and very patient," Greer recalled. Though she didn't love Hughes, "there was a great deal of tenderness between us."

Nevertheless, she had given him the wrong signal. Hughes believed that by sleeping with him, Greer had become his property. He was now loath to let her see anyone else. He had her every move shadowed.

Not long after they became intimate, Greer endured one of Howard's emotional lapses. They were dining at midnight at the Chi Chi Club in Palm Springs when Howard excused himself to go to the bathroom.

"Howard," Jane warned, "don't make any telephone calls to any of your business associates. I don't want to be stranded out here alone while you wheel and deal." Like all of Howard's other girls, Greer had been a telephone wallflower time and again as he ran his empire from nightclub phone booths.

"Uh-huh," Hughes answered absently.

When Hughes didn't return for an hour, Greer was gunning for him. "I thought I told you not to make any telephone calls," she said angrily.

"I didn't," he replied. "I swear I didn't."

Then she noticed he was trembling with cold and that both his shirt and his tie were sopping wet. She reached up and felt his shirt. "Howard, what the hell happened?"

Hughes looked up as though he hardly comprehended what she was saying and as if a sopping wet shirt were nothing out of the ordinary. "I got a bit of chocolate sauce on me, and I had to wash the shirt and tie in the basin. Then I tried to dry them for a while."

"But, Howard, all you had to do was take a bit of water and dab the spots out. You don't take off your clothes and wash them in the sink." From the look on his face, Jane knew it was no use. He just didn't understand.

Later, at another nightclub, Greer was left stranded while Hughes waited patiently in the rest room for some other patron to leave so he wouldn't have to touch the door handle.

The shock of Hughes's bizarre behavior and fervent pleas from her estranged husband caused Jane to reconcile with Vallee. However, before she returned, she decided to go through with a final Saturday-night date with Howard.

Hughes had pleaded, "Please, please keep the date . . . you have to hear me out."

Against the objections of her mother and of Vallee, Greer agreed to spend several hours with him at what Hughes called "a surprise restaurant, a very special place." But as soon as she was in the car, Greer could see that Howard was experiencing another of his disoriented periods.

"I'm taking you to Balboa," he announced as he turned onto Crenshaw Boulevard, which stretches from Los Angeles all the way to the coast. Staring straight ahead, Howard babbled an almost incoherent fable about a small girl and her special doll, ending with the admonition that if Vallee failed her again, he would not be there to pick her up as he had been the first time.

Something in the way he talked through angry, clenched teeth frightened the eighteen-year-old Greer. She protested, "Howard, I don't think this is a good idea. Take me back home."

Hughes instead floored his battered Chevrolet, speeding through yellow lights and barely slowing for red ones. He took her out of Los Angeles, past San Pedro, the harbor city, and across the ship's channel into Long Beach. After crossing the bridge, Greer convinced Howard to stop at a pay phone so that she could check in with her mother and Vallee, who were both waiting at her house.

"They expect me back in two hours, Howard, and we haven't even reached the restaurant yet. They'll call the police, and we don't want a scandal." Howard reluctantly let her out, but to her surprise and anger, he followed her to the booth and stood in the door blocking her exit.

When Jane had both Mrs. Greer and Rudy on the phone, Hughes pushed his way into the booth and forced Jane to hold the receiver so that he could listen in on the conversation. "Everything's okay," she said reassuringly. "Howard is taking me to a very special place so we'll be gone longer than expected. But he's behaving beautifully."

"Come home, Jane. Come home now," Rudy said. "Did you know that he has a plate in his head? He can be dangerous."

"What the hell is he talking about?" Howard screamed. "Who's got a plate in his head? Not me!" He grabbed the phone and began arguing with Vallee, both of them screaming.

When Greer finally calmed them, she and Hughes continued on the way to a swank restaurant on Balboa Island in Orange County. While Howard ate his usual steak dinner, followed by ice cream with chocolate sauce, Jane grew more alarmed about his state of mind. She could tell he was eating as slowly as possible to keep her at his side. As the hours drifted by, Jane wondered how she could get home without having a fight.

Seeking some sort of control over the situation, Greer convinced Hughes to free her so that she could go to the powder room unaccompanied. She knew timing was important. If she was gone too long, he would come in after her, as he had done with Billie Dove and Ginger Rogers.

Fortunately, a middle-aged woman entered the lounge shortly after Greer.

Greer handed the stranger a dollar bill and slipped her mother's phone number along with it: "Please call this number for me. Tell them where I am and that I'm okay. But please don't try to return the change or contact me in the restaurant."

"Are you in trouble, honey?" the lady asked.

"No, I can handle it. Please, would you just make the call?"

Then Greer nonchalantly rejoined Hughes for dessert and coffee. Several minutes later, she saw her rescuer approaching the table. "She's coming over and I'm shaking my head at her. I realized that she'd talked to my mother, who by then must have been hysterical. I thought to myself, 'Now you've gone and compounded the problem.' "

Howard saw her walking toward them. "What does she want?" he demanded.

Greer thought fast: "I borrowed some change from her to use in the ladies room, and I only had a dollar. She's bringing me the rest." She took the change from her, then shook her head as if to say "thank you, thank you, thank you."

But since the woman was staring intently at Hughes, he wasn't convinced. He grabbed the stranger by the arm, demanding to know, "Who are you anyway? And what do you want?"

"You let go of me, mister," she replied. "I've got friends in here, and they're watching me."

Greer looked at the woman imploringly and said, "Please go." To Jane's relief, she did.

Jane, convinced that Hughes was losing it, sagged back in her seat. He finally noticed her unhappiness. "You're not having a good time, are you?" he asked sadly.

"No, Howard, I'm not!"

"Okay, Bettejane," Howard said. "I'll show you the surprise I have for you, and then I'll take you home."

They drove back onto Pacific Coast Highway to an amusement park located on the Balboa peninsula. Its midway was a forties kitsch of shooting galleries, magic mirrors, haunted houses, and rides. For the last time they walked hand in hand, lost among the crowd.

By the time he escorted her back to the car it was 1:00 A.M. He sped back to Hollywood, as he had promised. But as they neared her house he made a special request. "You've got to do one more thing for me. You've got to sing the aria from *Madam Butterfly*."

At first Jane thought he was joking. But he leaned closer, pleading, "Please sing 'One Fine Day' ['Un Bel Di'] for me."

So, Jane Greer, a former big-band singer, sat in the battered Chevrolet and sang Puccini's most bittersweet aria, about lost love and hope eternal that love would reappear.

When they got to Greer's house, Howard leaned over and kissed her on the cheek. Then he reached over and opened the door for her. "See ya," he said.

CHAPTER 17

THE GREAT ESCAPE

IN EARLY OCTOBER 1944, AS THE PACIFIC MIST SWIRLED AROUND THE ledge-top mansion on Sorbonne, Howard led Faith into the ornate living room and lit the fireplace. When the logs were blazing, he threw down two brocade cushions, one for himself, the other for Faith. "Sit here," he said. "I need your help with something." Then he disappeared upstairs.

Domergue had earlier heard Hughes rummaging through cardboard cartons in his study. Now he returned to the living room, clutching a bundle of letters, postcards, and telegrams, many of which dated back to World War I. Acting nervous and preoccupied, he unceremoniously dumped these yellowed documents, records of his most intimate secrets, onto the carpet beside her.

He moved the fire screen aside, stationed Faith near it, and began handing her documents to toss into the flames. As he solemnly surrendered each relic to the pyre, he told her its contents and often read brief passages, bringing to life the words and secrets of his parents, his grandparents, and others, all of them long dead.

Messages from ghosts, Domergue would later say.

First to go were the notes he had written to his mother while at the Thacher School. In one he rebuked her: "Mother, I'm writing to you twice a day—once in the morning and again before bedtime. Couldn't you write me at least once a day?" Allene's own exquisitely penned notes to her son, a painful reminder to Hughes of her iron-willed control, were bundled and tied with a red ribbon. He tossed them casually onto the logs. As they were engulfed by flames they left behind a trace of the aromatic ink so popular during the post-Edwardian era in which they were written.

In the midst of this ritual, Howard pulled out one small note and turned it over in his hands. It was a letter his mother had written to his father from her hospital bed the day before she died. Tenderly, Hughes read from it, his voice full of emotion. Halfway through, he broke down and handed it to Faith, who finished reading it aloud.

"The handwriting was so beautiful and the message so sweet that I couldn't see how he could bear to part with it," Domergue remembered. "Howard, you should save this for posterity," she urged.

"No," Hughes said. "Definitely not. I only saved it because she expresses her wish to leave her portion of the tool company to me, not to other relatives. I only kept it in case I had to use it against my relatives."

It was with some bitterness that Hughes consigned the next batch to the flames. They contained, in vast detail, his fight with his kin to gain control of the Hughes Tool Company. In a note to his paternal grandfather, Felix Hughes, Howard had written, "I feel deserted and abandoned by my own family in the death of my father. And I consider the legal battle you are waging against me to be akin to treachery."

The prize of the entire collection, Allene's letter to Howard Sr. the night before she died, was held apart from the rest. Finally, he reached for it as well.

"Darling, don't destroy this," Domergue pleaded with him. "What do you have of her that is more personal than this—to remind you of how great a lady she was."

But, stressed Hughes, "if I die, how do I know who will get a hold of these letters and papers, and who knows to what use they'll be put?" Then he gently held out Allene's letter, a present to the inferno.

Last to go was a leather portfolio labeled ELLA RICE HUGHES. Without revealing its contents, Howard sternly tossed it into the fireplace. It was as if Hughes wanted to destroy his ties to the past and move on.

What Faith could not have known was that Howard Hughes was preparing to escape not just from his past but also from his present. The responsibilities and pressures of his high-profile, high-flying lifestyle were driving him mad.

Noah Dietrich had already observed the first signs of the boss's breakdown as the mercurial Hughes became more and more difficult. In the same week Hughes cremated his past, he began repeating himself to Dietrich again and again, sometimes during the most mundane conversations.

One morning Howard needed to order a tiny amplification device for his telephone. He called Dietrich and began: "Noah, I want you to look into the matter of the amplifier. Noah, I want you to look into the matter of the amplifier. Noah, I want you to look into the matter of the amplifier . . ."

Before Noah could interject a word, Howard continued. So Dietrich started counting. Howard repeated himself thirty-three times. "Howard," Noah finally yelled, "do you realize what you are doing? You're repeating the same sentence over and over again."

"What the hell are you talking about?" Hughes countered. When Dietrich began explaining, Hughes moaned, "Oh, my God, Noah. I'm cracking up."

"It's overwork, Howard," Dietrich countered. "I think you ought to see Verne Mason [Hughes's physician] and see what he recommends . . . before you collapse entirely."

Neither Dietrich nor Faith nor good friend Glenn Odekirk was surprised when Hughes's emotional house of cards finally collapsed in the fall of 1944.

The Hughes estate psychoanalyst, Dr. Fowler, has surmised that Howard was trying to flee from the crushing weight of the first failures he had experienced in his overprivileged life. "His father's ghost was chasing him," Fowler declared. "Having been totally obsessed with the Spruce Goose, its failure would force him to view himself as a failure . . . he felt he was risking his total worth on this. So he worked himself beyond what any man can stand. And he snapped."

Dr. John Chappel, who made a thorough psychological study of Hughes's life for the state of Nevada, said at this point in time that Howard's mental spirit was broken down, "in part, because he wanted to play a part in the war, but was discounted almost every place he turned." Added Chappel, "It was during World War II that he experienced, for the first time, some major failures . . . When a person has become accustomed to success, that is a devastating experience."

Recent pressures on Hughes had been intense.

Already, 1944 had been marked by two physical mishaps. During the first Constellation demo flight from Los Angeles to Washington, D.C., Howard began acting erratically even before the plane left the ground. Hughes delayed the flight and kept a group of VIPs waiting for half an hour while he tried to convince Ava Gardner to accompany him. When she refused, he boarded the plane in a fury. When a chicly dressed TWA hostess walked by, he growled, "No women on this flight—boot 'em off." When airline vice president Jack Nichols protested, Hughes became incensed. "Goddamned Ava Gardner!" he said. "There's no reason for her to miss this flight—this is a great triumph. Why the hell wouldn't she come?"

As the fully loaded Constellation flew over the Rocky Mountains, Hughes cut off two engines to demonstrate how advanced the "Connie" was when compared to other liners. The plane shook violently, and Nichols raced to the cockpit. "Jesus, Howard, you're scaring everybody to death."

The look on Hughes's face was maniacal. "You think that's something. I'm gonna cut a third. That'll show them."

Nichols pleaded: "Look, Howard, we could crash . . . You would ruin your own airline." The warning jostled Hughes back to attention.

The second lapse was more serious. Hughes blacked out when he was driving down busy Beverly Boulevard, causing him to plow into another car, smashing the front of his Chevy and throwing his head, once again, through the windshield.

Mumbling and almost delirious, he nonetheless convinced the driver to take him to Muirfield and to accept a settlement in lieu of notifying the cops. Then he stumbled through the door of the old mansion and collapsed against a wall in the entryway.

Dietrich rushed over and picked up his bloodied boss. "Who the hell are you, and what are you doing to me?" Hughes said.

"It's me, Howard," Dietrich answered.

Hughes grabbed Noah's shirt: "You let me go." When Howard was lowered into bed and treated by Dr. Mason, he came to, briefly. "No hospitals," he said. "They'll never let me out."

But Howard Hughes was not drifting toward insanity, though he himself or the doctors couldn't have known it at the time. In fact, Hughes's repetition of the wail, "I'm cracking up!" was a dead giveaway of his true mental condition.

"We know now that Howard Hughes suffered from obsessive-compulsive disorder. In fact he's probably the most famous obsessive-compulsive in modern history," explained Dr. Jeffrey Schwartz, a professor at the UCLA School of Medicine, a scientist at the forefront of obsessive-compulsive disorder research. Schwartz's ten-year focus on Hughes's four decades of profound emotional anguish, presented here for the first time, has finally unlocked the mystery that so puzzled and saddened Howard's lovers and physicians and confounded previous biographers. During the last year scientists around the world have recognized Hughes as an epic example of OCD's emotional ravages. Studies on his thought patterns have now been done in Sweden, Switzerland, France, Japan, and Great Britain. But Schwartz states that there is no doubt "that Hughes was in no way insane or incurable." In fact, a year of therapy by Schwartz and his UCLA team might have cured Howard permanently.

Equally potent proof comes from a psychiatrist personally close to Howard, Noah Dietrich's son, Dr. Anthony Dietrich, who depicts his father's boss—whom he knew during his boyhood—as a "badly misunderstood man who was in the grip of obsessions and compulsions he could not control. Today we might treat him with Prozac." According to Dietrich, use of that drug and support therapy could have ended Hughes's intermittent agony early on, perhaps averting some of the tragedies that later engulfed him, including the ravages of his drug use.

Dietrich recalled that his father viewed Hughes's traumas as the downside of his boss's profound genius. "My father was intrigued by Howard's nonconformity and by his adventurous approach to life."

And it was Noah who first noticed the signs of OCD (obsessive-compulsive disorder).

When Howard realized he was repeating sentences, his immediate protests to Dietrich and others were typical of the cries for help from men and women trapped inside OCD's mental prison. "Howard knew he was repeating things scores of times. And when he cried out that he was going insane, he meant it," continued Anthony Dietrich. "He must have thought, 'I hate feeling like this. But what can I do?' An insane person wouldn't even have recognized the deviation. But he knew what he was doing and was crestfallen by it. This knowledge was perhaps the most painful aspect of his ailment."

"Forget everything you've heard and read about Hughes's so-called madness," said Schwartz, whose methods at UCLA are treating scores of OCD sufferers "with symptoms even worse than those experienced by

Hughes." Schwartz sees Hughes as a man who was besieged by a chemical imbalance in his brain, probably inherited directly from his "obsessive-compulsive" mother, Allene. Schwartz explained that OCD is not a neurosis but a real disease, like manic depression or epilepsy, with a biological basis, "a short circuit of the brain caused by a chemical imbalance."

In other words, all of Howard's delays on *The Outlaw*, his indecision over the construction of the flying boat, his thousands of takeoffs and landings, were all merely symptoms of an illness that today could be brought under control.

This startling research unlocks the riddle of Hughes's genius and his eventual fall from grace. But, emphasized Anthony Dietrich, "the illness was not even understood then. People just thought he was mad."

The frightening full onset of obsessive-compulsive disorder after the Lake Mead crash kept Hughes locked in his bed at the Sorbonne mansion—almost oblivious to the visitors who streamed in and out. When he made the same request for aspirin fifteen times, Dr. Mason sat on the edge of the bed and spoke frankly with his longtime patient. "Howard, get away from everything before you have to be committed. You're going to kill yourself."

Surprisingly, Howard took the advice to heart. For the next two weeks he put his projects in the capable hands of his colleagues, particularly Odekirk and Dietrich. Then he bolted—from the lovers, the night life, and his ruinous meddling into every corner of his sprawling empire.

The strangest journey ever undertaken by an American public figure began late on a mid-October evening in 1944. Howard telephoned his close associates Joe Petrali, chief of services for Hughes Aircraft, and Dick Beatie, one of his favorite flight mechanics. "Get the amphibian gassed up," he ordered. "And pack enough clothes for a long stay. I'll tell you where we're going when we're in the air."

Neither Petrali nor Beatie noted the irony of Hughes's choosing the trouble-plagued Sikorsky amphibian in which to make his escape. After the Lake Mead crash, Hughes had paid divers more than $100,000 to find and raise the ship and then spent an additional half million dollars to restore it.

Once they were airborne, he announced to Petrali and Beatie that their first destination would be Las Vegas. He added, "We'll be gone about six months." No other words were exchanged during the flight over the Sierra Nevada Mountains toward the high desert.

A wind-whipped storm was buffeting the gambling capital when Hughes dropped the Sikorsky out of the clouds toward Las Vegas. But his control was erratic, as it had been on Lake Mead. Upon touching down, the plane was caught by gusts of wind. It overshot the runway and roared into the mesquite bushes and sand hillocks surrounding the airfield. Still traveling at eighty miles an hour, the plane bounced up and down again and again before it finally flipped back onto the asphalt, coming to a reluctant stop.

When Hughes leaped out to gauge the damage, he sheepishly noted that he had crushed and buckled part of the fuselage and smashed the wheel that controlled the plane's direction. He asked Petrali, "What do you think?"

"A month," Petrali said. "We've got a month of repairs ahead."

Using a replacement plane, Howard, Petrali, and Beatie rambled through the desert for three months, from Vegas to Reno to Palm Springs and back to Vegas. They pursued a bizarre daily ritual. Each day at precisely 3:30 P.M., no matter where they were, all the bags were packed and the hotel checkout procedures completed. Then, and strictly according to Hughes's whim, they either left or checked right back into the hotel. once, in Vegas's El Rancho Hotel, they followed this procedure for twenty-two consecutive days.

As Christmas approached, both Petrali and Beatie asked for a week's leave to spend the holidays in Los Angeles with their families. Hughes balked. "I never know when I might need you." Then he added plaintively, "Besides, Christmas Eve is my birthday, you know."

This was too much for Petrali. He waited until he thought Hughes was out and then slipped a note under the door informing the boss that they'd be back the day after Christmas. They rolled out of Vegas just steps ahead of a frantic Hughes, who found the note and was determined to stop them.

Unable to head off his lieutenants, Hughes sped off in a rented station wagon through the desert, into the San Gabriel Valley, and finally to Maple Drive in Beverly Hills, where he ran out of gas. He left the driver's door open and hiked off into the night. It was Christmas Eve 1944, his thirty-ninth birthday.

When Petrali returned to Vegas on December 26, Hughes had vanished, leaving his hotel room in disarray. All attempts to trace the millionaire's steps failed. "So we just sat there in the motel waiting for some kind of word from the boss," Petrali recalled. "The days stretched into weeks." Petrali figured Hughes was shacked up with one of his many starlets.

Petrali was wrong. Hughes had been with Cary Grant.

Hughes stayed with Grant sporadically during Cary's disastrous marriage to Woolworth heiress Barbara Hutton. It was a strange trio: Hutton, Howard's former lover and a woman who lived in the glare of the nightclub set and rarely woke before one o'clock in the afternoon; Hughes, who conducted business in the early morning hours and slept from 7:00 to 9:00 A.M.; and Grant, who was bound to the soundstage from five in the morning until dark. "Hughes was as quiet as a church mouse. Barbara slept all day and I slept like a log while Howard paced the living room with his infernal phone—working with the Pentagon, with his tool company and Houston, and wooing his girlfriends," Grant recalled.

During January and early February of 1945, when Petrali was scouring the Southwest for Howard, he was helping his old friend weather the collapse of his marriage, a particularly nasty period for Cary, whose union with Hutton had jokingly been dubbed by the press, "Cash and Cary." On February 11, five weeks after his disappearing act, Hughes knocked on the door of Petrali's Las Vegas motel room while a Los Angeles taxicab waited downstairs. When Petrali opened the door, he was shaken to discover Hughes looking even thinner than when he left and "very gaunt . . . troubled . . . years older."

"He acted as if nothing had happened," Petrali recalled.

Before Hughes entered Petrali's room he looked anxiously up and down the street, as if to make sure he hadn't been followed. "Joe, I need you to go down to the cab and bring up a box," he said. "I want you to bring it up carefully, wrap it in number-four butcher paper, and tie it with tradesman's string number fifty-one. Then I'll give you instructions on how to handle it."

Petrali ran down to the cab and was astounded by the size of the box. It was six feet long and three feet wide and weighed about 150 pounds. Petrali somehow managed to get the hefty container into his room. Then, according to Howard's instructions, he headed for a hardware store. He had to go to four of them before he found the proper string and thickness of butcher paper.

At one o'clock in the morning, Howard called Petrali and said, "Be prepared to leave on a moment's notice." Then Hughes took a taxi across the desert to the tiny community of Boulder City, where he commandeered the TWA cargo office. Seated in a small accounting office, he hunched down over a typewriter, his head lowered to just a few inches above the keyboard.

The TWA man on duty, Chester McBain, noted that Hughes would break out in a sweat periodically and shake all over, sometimes gripping the arms of his chair with white knuckles. For eighteen hours the millionaire typed, discarding sheet after sheet only to start all over again on a fresh piece of paper. When McBain entered the room to offer coffee from a thermos, Hughes threw his shoulders down over the typewriter and cried out, "You can't read this! You can't even know about this! So get out of here!" He finally lurched out of the office late the next evening, but not before shredding and burning each of his practice sheets. "No one must ever know I was here," he instructed McBain.

Returning to Las Vegas, Howard immediately summoned Petrali to his motel room, where he handed him a manila envelope. Screaming at the top of his lungs, Hughes ordered Petrali to take the envelope to his room and study its contents for forty-eight hours. For two hours Hughes repeated the orders to Petrali again and again and again.

As he paced the room, Hughes's voice grew louder and nastier and his movements wilder. A man out of control, he sprang up and down in a chair and, at one point, fell backward on the bed. "You are to read these instructions in exactly this manner. Study them for two hours. Rest for two hours. Study them for two hours. Rest for two hours . . ."

Finally, Howard shook Petrali hard by the shoulders and shouted, "These instructions shall remain in force as long as you shall live!" The instructions came with a postscript. Petrali was told to wash his hands before opening the envelope.

Back in his room, the understandably shaken flight engineer opened the envelope to read the proclamation it had taken Howard eighteen hours to type. On a single sheet, it read: "Do not convey, communicate, or telephone any message from me to anyone in California unless I repeat that message ten times."

That was it! Twenty-one words!

Petrali spent the mandated two days in his hotel room, then reported back to Hughes, who now seemed even crazier. Constantly looking out his hotel suite window, he told Petrali, "The guys who are out to get me are determined to get me." Then he shifted moods. "Now about the instructions," Hughes said, "they are secret—top secret. If I bring a congressman or a senator to this room, carrying a plaque with big red ribbon and seal on it, and I say to you, 'Joe, ignore my instructions,' you answer, 'Howard, go fuck yourself.'

"Now, remember this and keep it straight."

He was yelling again: "If I come to you and tell you to call so-and-so in California, put your hands behind your back and count with your fingers. If I only tell you to do it nine times, then don't do it. When I have spoken it, letter perfect, ten times, then do it.

"By the way," he said, "we're leaving at dawn tomorrow."

At 5:00 A.M. Howard showed up at the airfield wearing a 1925 raccoon coat and a heavy blue serge suit, with patches on the arms and knees. When Petrali asked where they were headed and for a specific flight plan to relay to the tower, Hughes erupted, "I don't have to file any god-damned flight plan. Just tell 'em we're headed east. That's good enough for them."

These were dangerous instructions at the height of World War II, when the army was monitoring every plane in the skies above North America. But Petrali did as he was told, whispering to the control tower, "This is Howard Hughes, and he's on business for the army." It seemed logical enough: the Air Corps brass had painted the coveted Army Star on the plane, giving the amphibian priority over other civilian planes.

So the "great escape" was airborne again.

Passing over the Arizona desert, Hughes finally confided his destination: "Plot me a route to Shreveport, Louisiana."

"Why Shreveport?" Petrali asked. His boss shrugged. "At that moment he looked so lost," Petrali recalled, "the loneliest man in the world."

As they passed over Texas, just miles from Houston, Hughes surveyed the wilds of south Texas and emotionally crumbled. He suddenly sagged in his seat, tears running down his cheeks, and with a sob let go of the controls to bury his head in his hands. The plane lurched wildly through the air. Petrali grabbed his own controls and guided them back on course.

Still, Howard remained immobile, his head in his hands, a lost expression on his face all the rest of the way to Louisiana.

They finally landed in near darkness, fighting thundershowers and dodging spectacular shows of lightning against the blue-black bayou cloud formations. Howard appeared to be lost as Petrali helped him into a rental car and saw him safely to a room in Shreveport's rundown Inn Hotel, where he fell into a deep sleep.

Hughes rarely went out in the evenings during his wanderlust, but Petrali needed a night out, so he headed for a restaurant and a movie, figuring Hughes would sleep through the night. He was wrong. Hughes sprang awake less than an hour later and walked the rural streets in his bedraggled serge suit, tennis shoes, and fedora.

Blocks from the hotel, on a side street, Howard found a small store that was still open. He bought a loaf of bread and a quart bottle of milk. Chugging the milk, he wandered to a parking lot near a deserted gas station, where he sat on the curbside, pulled out a pad and paper, and jotted down mathematical equations for the rear tail section of the reconnaissance plane.

"It was amazing," Petrali recalled. "No matter how distracted he was, he could always pull those magical math configurations out of the depths of his brain—a mark of a true genius."

Off-duty Shreveport police officer Marvin K. Ezell glimpsed the stooped apparition as he cruised past the small stand of commercial shops. "His suit was all torn up, he had an unkempt growth of beard and, gulping down that milk, I thought he was an escapee from a nearby prisoner of war camp." Ezell put in a call to the station, and police officer O. C. Merritt arrived. Both men then quizzed the unshaven stranger. "Can I see your identification, sir?" Merritt asked. Hughes stared blankly back at him. "Could you tell me your name?" Howard remained silent, munching on a piece of bread. "Sir, if you refuse to answer me, I'll have to arrest you." Ezell noticed a flicker of anger in Howard's eyes but no other reaction.

Howard Hughes, then the fourth-richest man in America, was hauled off in a squad car to the station, where he finally spoke. "Call the Inn Hotel and ask for Petrali; he'll tell you who I am."

"Okay, buddy, I'm tossing you in jail, and we'll sort this out tomorrow."

Hughes slowly raised his head and glared arrogantly at the chief. "My name is Howard Hughes, and I'm registered at the Inn Hotel." He paused, adding, "I'm not an indigent." Then he pulled $3,500 from his pockets and dumped it on a counter before lapsing back into silence while the police hunted for the local manager of Hughes Tool Company to verify his story. Finally, the manager showed up to I.D. the boss he had never before met, bringing with him a stack of newspapers with photographs of Hughes as added proof.

Back at the seedy Inn Hotel, Petrali noticed that Howard seemed unaffected by the experience and that he "appeared to be sleepwalking." (Hughes would later tell Dietrich he knew nothing about being arrested "in Louisiana or anywhere else.") The next morning, Petrali was relieved by Hughes Aircraft flight engineer Ray Kirkpatrick, who along with Bob Martin took off with Hughes for Orlando, Florida. The three men jumped into yet another rented car and, on Howard's instructions, drove to the Greyhound Bus Station in downtown Orlando. With only a cardboard shirt box under his arm, Hughes, over protests from his companions, boarded a bus bound for Miami. He said jauntily, "You'll be hearing from me."

But not for three hair-raising months. During that period Dietrich, Kirkpatrick, and even Hughes's family in Houston scoured the country for the errant millionaire. Howard's aunt, Annette Lummis, screamed at Dietrich, "This is a conspiracy!" She added, "I wouldn't be surprised if poor Howard was dead and you have hidden his body and are running things yourself."

Noah tried to calm her. "I can't find him either, and I *really* need to find him . . . Some defense contract business is running far behind."

Dietrich received a puzzling clue to his boss's whereabouts in late April, when a test pilot called to report that Hughes was living in Fort Lauderdale, where the millionaire had rented a beachfront cottage.

"The pilot told me that, in a repeat of his earlier ritual, Hughes had built a roaring fire on the beach and burned his clothes, one article at a time, until he was nearly naked and pacing wildly around the blaze," Dietrich recalled. "Then he put on some new clothes from Penney's and re-entered his cottage. But two days later, Howard left Fort Lauderdale in the middle of the night."

Hughes finally called Kirkpatrick on May 7. "I'm in Miami," he announced casually. "And I need you to get me forty-five hundred dollars and enough war ration stamps to get me back to Orlando. Wire the money and the gas coupons to me at the Romey Plaza Hotel by tomorrow at 1 P.M. Call Washington if you need to. They'll approve the rations."

The next day, Hughes pulled into Orlando in a Chevrolet that was piled high with boxes of all shapes and sizes, each crammed with clothes purchased in Miami. There was a new dinner jacket and several presentable suits, testifying to his nighttime activities in Palm Beach. When Kirkpatrick held the swank dinner jacket aloft before stowing it on the plane, Howard said with a grin: "Debutantes!"

"File a flight plan for Newark," he said breezily.

In New York, Kirkpatrick and Martin were stationed at the Carlton while Hughes moved into a suite of rooms at the Plaza Hotel, where he again stormed Manhattan's romantic shores. On June 3, the *New York Post* announced his return: "Howard Hughes is wearing tennis shoes around town, proving something fascinating about men's fashions. If you're Howard Hughes, it doesn't matter—whatever style you sport is suddenly *au courant*."

Out at Newark Airport, where Martin and Kirkpatrick were over-hauling the amphibian, they spilled a quart of oil all over Hughes's gigantic mystery box. Suddenly, they had an excuse to finally tear it open and explore its contents.

Inside, they found piles of Sunday comics, some of them rolled, some of them tied in compressed bundles. And hidden among four years' worth of Red Rider Comics were a variety of douche bags, all varieties and sizes.

Kirkpatrick winked at Martin. "I guess we know what the boss has been doing in Manhattan."

A week later, a rejuvenated Hughes flew back to Los Angeles to begin his reign as Hollywood's pre-eminent cocksman. Ava, Rita, Lana, and the rest were awaiting his call.

CHAPTER 18

THE LONE WOLF

ERROL FLYNN AND DIRECTOR PRESTON STURGES FIRST GAVE HOWARD THE nickname of "the Lone Wolf," referring to his unparalleled success in Hollywood's bedrooms. At the time, it wasn't considered sexually irresponsible, it was a compliment to his manhood.

But his status and his success as a lover also set him apart as the first producer in film history who was also a sex symbol in his own right, a moody Hamlet whose sex appeal was grounded in danger and based, in part, on his boyish loneliness. Columnist James Bacon, Howard's friend for twenty years, ranked him as "the greatest swordsman" the town ever produced—more active than Flynn or Charles Chaplin.

Joan Crawford, who got the Hughes rush in the thirties, once said, "Howard Hughes would fuck a tree."

In recent years Hughes's sexuality has been misportrayed by an entire school of biographers and tabloid reporters. He has been depicted as a notorious closet homosexual, based on second- and third-hand sources—or interviews with sources now deceased. Because of his final mysterious years, an entire generation thinks of Hughes as a sick, derelict old man with unkempt hair and long fingernails and toenails. The image of this late 1970s recluse has splattered backward, staining Hughes even when he was at his heterosexual prime during the early and mid-forties.

Books and articles about Los Angeles in the forties also consistently type him as a tramp in dress and in manner, the very antithesis of sexuality. In fact, Howard's simple sartorial style, the cocky fedora, the clean (though sometimes frayed) white shirt and workman's slacks, endowed him with a strength and an air of mystery that Hollywood's dudes lacked.

In a town where tailors reigned supreme, Hughes projected the aura of a man who, as Cary Grant described it, "worked for a living." Explained Grant, "He just did not make time for all that stuff, and he didn't need it. Women found that very sexy."

They were also drawn to his complexity—his mix of daredevilry and wounded child. His brown eyes could flash defiant anger—and brim with pain. Women loved his eyes.

They also loved the lengths to which he would go to win them over.

Early on the morning of September 5, 1945, Hughes ignored strict regulations and flew across the border into British Columbia in pursuit of the "most alluring woman" he had ever seen. Using his top-secret military status and emergency army fuel, he landed in Vancouver, to the surprise of airport officials. The metal Army Air Corps star emblazoned on the fuselage of his DC-3 greased his path into a military docking berth, where a limousine waited. This was a risky move, and Hughes knew it. With the Federal Bureau of Investigation tracking his every step, and with both his military projects in shambles, the generals of the War Materiel Command were already after his hide.

In an affair of the heart, though, all other considerations took second place. The lady in question was sultry Yvonne De Carlo, twenty-three, who after three years of bit parts had just shimmied her way to stardom in the film *Salome, Where She Danced*. Posters for the movie, in which she delivered the dance of the seven veils, touted her as "The Most Beautiful Girl in the World."

During the seventy-two hours immediately preceding this impulsive, misguided dash across the border, Hughes sat in the darkness of his screening room and viewed *Salome* five times, obsessed with the dark beauty who so resembled his mother, Allene. He ordered Johnny Meyer to "find her and set something up." Meyer reported back that Yvonne had gone home to Vancouver for a week. "She'll be back in town by September fifteenth."

"Not soon enough," Hughes murmured. "We're going to Vancouver."

The day he flew off to win another hoped-for paramour, Hughes was still involved with Ava Gardner, Jane Greer, Rita Hayworth, and at home, Faith Domergue. Explaining his penchant for beautiful, famous women, Hughes told one reporter that they neither wanted nor needed anything from him.

Hughes favored a particular physical type: bosomy brunettes with full, luscious lips. In fact, his women tended to resemble one another. (His two wives, Ella Rice and Jean Peters, looked strikingly similar.) Many were reminiscent of his mother.

According to Noah Dietrich, Hughes also developed a quirky fondness for what he crassly called "wet decks"—women who were recently divorced, such as Ava Gardner. "I've found that sex is so much hotter, so much more intense with a new divorcée . . . especially if the girl in question wasn't all that satisfied with her husband," he told Noah.

The man who Noah suspected of having been a virgin when he arrived in Hollywood in the twenties now strove to be an eager-to-please sex partner. He told one lover, starlet Yvonne Shubert, that he had studied the intricacies of intercourse. "I ordered a lot of books on the subject. You know, the kind that arrive in a plain brown wrapper," he said with a laugh.

Yvonne De Carlo would discover that he could be downright technical in his bedroom talk.

Another Hughes lover recounted that he was particularly adept at performing oral sex on his partners—though first, he insisted that they cleanse themselves with a douche. "There was always that germ thing."

The arrangement of his sex life followed a lifetime pattern: a "stay-at-home lover," Faith; a flashy "out front" lover, Ava Gardner; a secret lover, Jane Greer; an "occasional lover," Rita Hayworth; and a "hot new flame," Yvonne De Carlo. "The boss was rampantly heterosexual," recalled D. Martin Cook, a personal attorney to Hughes. "He was absolutely driven to possess entire groups of women . . . and nothing could stop him."

He seemed sadly desperate to add De Carlo to his list of conquests, as if this perpetual girl rush would help him outrun the onset of middle age. The actress had traveled to her hometown of Vancouver to participate in Yvonne De Carlo Week, a folksy celebration of her newfound stardom. She was shocked to find Howard Hughes in her midst.

He showed up unannounced at a gala dinner party in her honor. "The mysterious Mr. Hughes came to our table looking lanky, underfed, and remarkably sad," De Carlo recalled. "I immediately felt my maternal instincts coming out." Just how much of this sadness was part of Hughes's "country boy" seduction act is open to question. But it worked; De Carlo agreed to spend the entire next day with him.

"My new billionaire friend came by to meet my whole family—even my grandmother," she later wrote in her memoirs. "And in the afternoon he took me on an airplane ride over the city." Later in the day, Hughes escorted her to a private golf club where he tried to teach De Carlo the basics of the game. "My singular lack of talent amused both of us, and it was a very good day. As we left the course, I said to myself, 'Yes, I like him; I like him very much.' "

After dinner in a restaurant overlooking the lights of Vancouver, Howard kissed her on the front porch of her parents' home. No one noticed that a Vancouver journalist had been trailing them, interviewing waiters, sales clerks, and even Howard's limousine driver. By dawn, Hughes was trapped in a public relations disaster.

In Los Angeles, columnist Harrison Carroll told his readers that Howard and Yvonne were "doing the town" in Vancouver. He went on to tantalize, asking, "Is marriage in the wind?" Others fleshed out the story. The *New York Post* trumpeted: HUGHES CHASES DE CARLO TO CANADA. The repercussions were instant.

In New York, Gerald Schultz, assistant superintendent at Newark Airport, roused Hughes's engineers Ray Kirkpatrick and Bob Martin out of bed. (They were still baby-sitting Hughes's amphibian.) "Come get your boss's plane, and get it out of here," said Schultz, adding, "The army has ejected it."

"And what do we tell Mr. Hughes?" Kirkpatrick asked.

"Show him the headline in the *New York Post,*" Schultz answered. "And, guys," he added, "I don't think your man is on an essential military mission, do you?"

At that same hour in Washington, officials of the War Materiel Command took the first steps toward stripping Hughes's personal fleet of airplanes of its military privileges and toward canceling his fuel priority. More important, the nation's intelligence community, particularly the FBI, was suddenly riveted upon Howard's private life and its direct relation to the ways the millionaire aviator was spending his fat military bankrolls.

At first J. Edgar Hoover, the all-powerful chief of the FBI, hesitated. For one thing, Hoover was aware, as the Materiel Command was not, of Hughes's secret-weapon projects in Tucson and Houston. For another, Hughes and Hoover were both superpatriots, who respected each other and shared the same fear of the communist menace in World War II Europe. But Hoover, his back to the wall during the espionage-crazed final days of the war, bowed to pressure from the army and put four agents on the "Howard Hughes matter," a pair in Los Angeles and a pair in Vancouver.

With aid from the federal police of British Columbia, Hughes's hotel phones in Vancouver were tapped, and a well-dressed FBI agent and a female companion tailed Howard and Yvonne as they dined out. When the phone taps revealed that Hughes and De Carlo planned to fly to Reno, Nevada, the afternoon of September 11, Hoover assigned a young Nevada field agent to tail them when they arrived.

While the couple were still in the air, agents arranged to tap the bed-side phone in Hughes's suite at Reno's Riverside Hotel and ordered the housekeeping staff to keep a "particularly keen eye on sleeping arrangements." In Reno, Johnny Meyer registered as "John W. Morris," Yvonne as "Yvonne Middleton" (her real surname) and Hughes as "Steve Merritt." Both the millionaire and the movie star were bunking in room 315. Which, according to FBI reports, contained "a queen-size bed."

That evening at 7:10, the eavesdroppers were treated to a boring series of business conversations about Hughes's "top-secret plan" to extend TWA's routes "to include the Pacific Ocean, and, eventually, the entire world." The young agent forwarded these conversations to Washington and the War Materiel Command, unaware of the significance the information would have in Howard's future.

Of greater interest to the spies was the housekeeping report that "two persons occupied the bed in room 315—no doubt about that."

De Carlo, who was then ignorant of the stakeout, remembered the Nevada jaunt fondly. "As we cruised southward from Vancouver, Howard spent several hours trying to teach me the basics of flying, allowing me to pilot the ship on my own for a couple of minutes." During one refueling stop, Hughes left De Carlo and sprinted into an airport operations center to make a hurried call to Los Angeles. Yvonne was curious and edged closer and closer to the door. She could hear Howard's booming voice. "He was intense and angry," she recalled. "Is that your final answer?" Hughes screamed at the party on the other end of the line. "You never cared at all, did you?" he questioned before slamming down in the receiver.

A mystified Yvonne "tippy-toed," as she put it, back to the plane before Hughes could see her. She didn't quiz Howard about his intriguing conversation.

The Los Angeles field office of the FBI could have clued her in. Their tap on an apartment telephone in West Los Angeles revealed that the lady on the other end of the line was Ava Gardner, speaking from the apartment Howard had leased for her. Once again Ava had casually returned Hughes's emerald engagement ring, accompanied by a renewed chorus of "I don't care how rich you are. I don't care how much you love me." It was the third time Howard had offered the ring.

When Hughes returned to the plane, he "managed a flickering smile." Then he grabbed the shoulders of this woman he had known for just six days. "Are you serious about me?" He seemed desperate for some sort of assurance. When she didn't answer immediately he shook her.

Yvonne answered: "Why . . . uh, yes." Howard didn't say anything. He just nodded and leaped into the plane, pulling De Carlo along with him.

On October 2, 1945, FBI Report 62-2682 indicated that, in the Bureau's opinion, De Carlo had succeeded Gardner as the millionaire's primary consort, an opinion that might have shocked not only Gardner but Faith Domergue as well.

Yvonne and Howard flew back to Los Angeles for five days, until both returned suddenly to Las Vegas, where Hughes went public with his courtship of Hollywood's newest movie star. He swept into the casinos with De Carlo on his arm, uncharacteristically dined openly at the Flamingo Hotel. He even sported a new banker's-stripe suit. As an emerging star with only one starring role under her belt, De Carlo was jittery about the media gadflies who circled them in the gambling capital. "Got it covered," Hughes reassured her.

True to his word, no further items on the Hughes–De Carlo affair emerged from the gossip corps. Yvonne was intrigued; she wondered how he did it. The FBI had the answer. In a Nevada field office report, for which agents tapped Johnny Meyer's Flamingo Hotel room, it was noted that Meyer was plying the media with "multiple gifts of very expensive Scotch whisky."

By mid-October agents were booking tables in swank Hollywood restaurants like the Florentine Gardens and Perino's so they could eavesdrop on Hughes's dinner conversations. And for the next eighteen months a stream of hearsay memos poured into FBI headquarters. Eventually, the private dossier on Howard Hughes would total more than two thousand pages.

Fortunately for Hughes and De Carlo, the FBI did not resort to installing taping equipment in Howard's bedroom. If they had, they would have discovered that Yvonne De Carlo was easily Howard's hottest affair since Kate Hepburn. With good reason. "After weeks of love and laughter, I was seriously in love," De Carlo recalled. In a deeply felt analysis of Hughes as a lover, De Carlo characterized him as "an expert who calculated to please."

The pillow talk between the millionaire and the screen's newest exotic temptress was remarkably clinical. One evening before a roaring fire at the Del Monte Lodge at Pebble Beach, Hughes spent the better part of an hour describing the mechanical differences between the male and the female orgasm. "Yvonne, the female orgasm is an 'implosion,' a reaction to the male 'explosion'—and both are totally different in their physiological engineering."

After another evening of lovemaking in Pebble Beach, Hughes coerced De Carlo into listing her past lovers, right down to physical dimensions and other specific details. He even interrogated her for snippets of conversations and sounds that accompanied her earlier experiences. "Enough," she finally said. She also grew tired of his incessant praise of Billie Dove's charms and of how he had proposed to her in the very same cottage seventeen years earlier. He did not, however, impart the reasons that Dove finally called off the wedding plans.

As the months wore on, De Carlo, like all of Howard's lovers, began questioning his faithfulness. She would have questioned it even further if she could have seen the FBI wiretap logs on Meyer's phone, some of them made during those same evenings when she spooned with Howard in the Del Monte Lodge. They also showed that Meyer worked overtime trying to procure dates for his boss with a luscious crop of new starlets, including Diana Lynn, Gail Russell, Joan Leslie, and Virginia Mayo.

When the new year of 1946 brought a world free of war, rendering obsolete the Spruce Goose and the reconnaissance bomber, Howard also opted for freedom. After admitting to the lovestruck De Carlo that they would never marry, he slipped from her side to woo 25-year-old Lana Turner, the hottest platinum blonde to hit town since Jean Harlow.

Typically, the love affair started in the screening room. MGM studio boss Eddie Mannix invited him to see a rough cut of a new Metro film, *The Postman Always Rings Twice*, the film noir classic about illicit passion and murder in a roadside diner. It's hard to imagine what MGM had in mind. Maybe they expected him to build a multimillion-dollar production around her as he had done for Jane Russell with *The Outlaw.*

Whatever the reason. Hughes was definitely interested in the blonde with the icy beauty. He pursued Lana Turner for twelve passionate weeks. The fact that Lana was recently divorced only heightened his interest.

Hughes eased his way into the Turner relationship the way he had with Ginger Rogers, by lavishing attention on Lana's forty-year-old mother. "At first I felt he was more interested in my mother than he was in me," Lana told her longtime secretary, Taylor Pero. "I would come home from the studio and find them together, chatting and laughing."

One evening she found them laughing more uproariously than ever, Hughes with a towel around his waist, and Mrs. Turner mending his pants on her sewing machine. "Why the towel?" Lana asked.

"No underwear," explained her mother. Lana frowned.

Hughes just shrugged. "Don't like 'em, I guess."

When Lana protested, her mother countered, "Leave it alone, Lana; he's a man."

Hughes and Turner were particularly mismatched. She wanted romance and security. He wanted a brief passionate affair with no ties. She put career first. He wanted a lover to be at his beck and call. He was impassioned. She was indifferent.

Nonetheless, Hughes saw her as a challenge, a strong woman who had already spurned the advances of Clark Gable and Spencer Tracy. Howard made his bid by taking her to Manhattan for a storybook tour of fancy boutiques and even fancier nightclubs.

It was April 1946, and New York was crammed with cash and returning soldiers. Lana later characterized that particular visit as "incredibly romantic with the women all dressed up and men in uniform. So glamorous . . . and it was never like that again."

On the fifth floor of the stately Sherry-Netherland Hotel, Meyer had booked five suites—one each for Hughes, Turner, Turner's young daughter Cheryl and her governess, Meyer, and Cary Grant, who was arriving from Europe. Hughes and Turner rendezvoused on April 27 in a suite full of gardenias, rare white orchids, and five dozen ivory roses, all a tribute to Turner's preferred color.

To safeguard Lana's rising superstardom, Hughes took unusual precautions in eluding reporters by traveling to her floor on a tiny room-service elevator. He also resorted to disguises. Harriet Huntoon, a senior TWA hostess who staffed Howard's private plane, caught him in full costume one afternoon when she stepped into a lobby elevator.

She heard Helen Frye, wife of TWA president Jack Frye, whispering to someone, "What the hell are you up to?" Huntoon turned around and was both startled and amused to see Howard in a corner, dressed in painter's white overalls, a paint-spattered hat, and work boots. "He had a little knapsack over one shoulder," Huntoon recalled, "so that he would look like the help." He also held a finger to his lips and said, "Shhhh."

One evening, when Turner was attending to Cheryl next door, Howard telephoned his newest love interest in Hollywood, 20th Century-Fox star Linda Darnell. Despite the fact that he had just the night before proposed to Turner, he offered his hand in marriage to Darnell. "You have no idea how much I love you," Hughes said ardently. "I cannot wait until we can get married."

Darnell promised to ask her husband, cameraman Peverell J. Marley, for a divorce that same evening. "That makes me very happy," Hughes said. "I'll see you soon."

After ten days, Howard and Lana left separately for Los Angeles with the film star considering his proposal. The only mention Turner ever made concerning her physical relationship with Hughes was a statement to Taylor Pero that Howard "preferred oral sex—to which I told him forcefully that I was not interested."

However she was apparently interested in becoming Mrs. Howard Hughes. A date was even set. One May morning, still in 1946, Lana telephoned Howard's friend, agent Johnny Maschio. "Where's Howard?" she asked.

"I have no idea," Maschio answered. "Was I supposed to hear from him?"

Turner barely controlled her anger, fuming, "Well, we were supposed to fly to Las Vegas two hours ago—to be married."

"Christ, I didn't know that," Maschio answered. "I'll see what I can do." Decades later he recounted how Lana phoned every half hour, more distraught with each call. At 3:00 P.M. she shouted, "This is my last call!"

At 4:00 P.M., a sleepy Hughes checked in with Maschio who said angrily, "For God's sake, Howard, Lana's been waiting for you since 9:00 A.M. What should I tell her?"

"Nothing," said Hughes. "Absolutely nothing."

Meanwhile, the rumor mill at Fox, the studio where Darnell was under contract and on the rise, buzzed as Darnell confided to a series of friends that she was engaged to the elusive millionaire. Darryl F. Zanuck, Fox's resident mogul, finally heard of this "engagement" and alerted Hughes, an old crony. "This girl is very, very serious, Howard," Zanuck told him.

Hughes was alarmed. But he couldn't bring himself to confront Linda. Instead, he made a dinner date with Linda's close friend, MGM dancing star Ann Miller, and asked her to tell Linda there would be no wedding.

"He was very peculiar and would kind of halfway propose to these girls. And he could be very, very convincing, leading them to believe that a wedding was just on the horizon. It could be very sad," Miller recalled. "When I told Linda what Howard said, and about all the other girls he had on the string, she was badly hurt."

He set his sights on another alluring brunette, the exotic star Gene Tierney, who became a legend as the enigmatic title character of *Laura*. Ignoring her budding affair with fashion designer Oleg Cassini, Howard filled her Westwood apartment with the inevitable gardenias and presented her with a jeweler's case overflowing with diamonds and pearls. Opening the casket he asked, "Is there anything in here you'd like?" But as much as Tierney was enthralled with Hughes's mystery, she married the more sophisticated Cassini.

Hughes told her she had "made a mistake," but later displayed gallant sportsmanship when he learned that Gene and Oleg's baby daughter was mentally retarded. He sent eminent specialists to examine the child and paid for treatment. For this, Tierney considered Howard "a saint."

Cassini wasn't so sure. He confronted Hughes at one of Jack Benny's dinner parties. "I won't have you treating my wife like all your other 'girls'!" Cassini shouted. "If you really want to marry her, I'll step aside. But, personally, I think you're a bullshit artist."

Warned Cassini, "Stay away from my wife."

The macho Cassini kept his word after catching Howard and Tierney returning from a Las Vegas trip. He appeared out of the darkness and whacked Hughes on the butt with a two-by-four, knocking him over. "I did show mercy," Cassini recalled. "I truly could have killed the bastard." Howard jumped into his car and fled, with Cassini in pursuit and Tierney screaming after them.

As Cassini suspected, Hughes soon moved on.

It was only natural that his path would cross that of the era's ultimate sex symbol, Marilyn Monroe. She was still a model appearing on the covers of such magazines as *Titter* and *Laff* when Hughes spotted a photo of her cuddling a lamb. A meeting was arranged. Though Hughes failed to sign her to a contract, Marilyn used his name to plant several column items, one of which attracted the interest of Hughes's old pal, Ben Lyon (one of the stars of *Hell's Angels*), by then casting director of 20th Century-Fox. Her stardom followed a year later. As for the Hughes–Monroe dalliance, it consisted of several flying dates and one night on the town. Monroe's drama coach Natasha Lytess recalled a morning Monroe returned home at dawn, her delicate face chaffed raw. Explained Monroe, "Mr. Hughes doesn't like to shave."

All of these women were just part of the passing and passionate parade to amuse an aging, weary Don Juan who, ironically, complained all the while that he could not find a "nice, unspoiled girl."

"When I do find one," he vowed to Dietrich, "I'll marry her."

CHAPTER 19

FALL FROM GRACE

FOR YEARS, HOWARD'S MOST CONSISTENTLY SUCCESSFUL SEDUCTION SCE-
nario had involved his airplanes. The cockpit endowed him with the flair,
the sensuality, and even the courage he lacked on land. The young actress
Jean Peters, who would come to play a pivotal role in the life of Howard
Hughes, would be equally enraptured. In her case, however, it would not
be his flying skills but his harrowing brush with death after a plane crash
that proved to be the odd start to this long-lasting relationship. Certainly it
was not according to Howard's usual game plan.

Much of his affair with Kate was played out in the amphibian. Ginger
Rogers felt a rush of fear, coupled with excitement, when the plane she
shared with Hughes appeared to nearly plunge into San Francisco Bay.
"But I didn't notice any fear on Howard's part, just enormous strength."

Unlike Charles Lindbergh, who pursued a quiet, retiring family life
after his fame in the skies, Howard traded on his status as one of America's
two great aviation heroes as a sexual lure. "I would call it ingenious,"
recalled Dietrich. "He tried to work a flight into his first date with a
woman if at all possible."

"Hughes could be Mr. Hyde outside of an airplane and Dr. Jekyll
when he was in the cockpit," said Joe Bartles, who worked for Hughes as
head of TWA's western region.

In his pursuit of the very married Ingrid Bergman in 1945, Hughes arranged for a three-day weekend in New York, where Bergman was filming *Arch of Triumph*. With Cary Grant as a chaperon, they did the town. But when Bergman called to confirm her airline reservations back to Los Angeles, where her husband, Dr. Petter Lindstrom, was waiting, she found that the flight was fully booked. "Don't worry about it," Hughes said. "I'll fly you home in a TWA liner. Just name the time."

Upon boarding, Bergman was astonished to find that she, Hughes, Cary Grant, and his date, Irene Mayer Selznick, were the only passengers. The co-pilot was also missing, his seat reserved for Bergman. "I later learned that Howard had purchased every single seat between New York and Los Angeles on that Monday," Bergman recalled. "It was all very flattering, and I imagine some women would have been very impressed." She, however, wasn't one of them.

In one extravagant gesture, Hughes spent $250,000 to coax blonde bombshell Virginia Mayo into the cockpit with him. The occasion was the February 1946 launching of the Hughes-designed TWA Constellation liner, and the ostensible purpose was to introduce America to the luxuries built into the new plane. There would have been some sort of publicity junket in any case. But Howard planned this star-studded flight to center around the romance he envisioned with Mayo, the former showgirl turned statuesque star of Samuel Goldwyn spectacles.

Howard's agent pal, Johnny Maschio, engineered the luxurious trip, which was to begin with a cocktail party in Los Angeles and to end with ten days of nightclubbing in Manhattan. The celebrities were invited in pairs, except for Mayo, who was escorted to the very first seat in the first-class section.

The trip boasted a passenger list that included Cary Grant, William Powell, Veronica Lake, Paulette Goddard, and Celeste Holm, all of whom signed on for the full ten days. When the Constellation was airborne, doors opened at the rear of the plane, where restaurateur to the stars Dave Chasen offered a buffet that began with beluga caviar and Dom Perignon and ended with baked Alaska.

When the plane encountered head winds over the Rocky Mountains, it bounced up and down, buffeted by the air currents. Crusts of ice formed on the windows. When Hughes sauntered through the plane and asked for a large tumbler of Dave Chasen's 90 proof vodka, Maschio's wife, the musical star Constance Moore, was alarmed. Grabbing her husband's arm, she asked, "My God, is Howard drinking? We must really be in trouble. Howard never, ever drinks."

Maschio headed for the cockpit, where he found Hughes de-icing the windshield with a vodka-soaked towel. Said Howard matter-of-factly, "Works every time."

The junket garnered headlines and newsreel attention. But it failed to impress Mayo, who lasted about five minutes in the cockpit. The air turbulence so affected her that she was dangerously dehydrated by the time the plane landed in New York. After seeing a physician, she immediately took a cab to Grand Central Station and a train for Los Angeles.

"I was too sick to realize that I was to have been his date," Mayo later recalled. Once back in Hollywood, she was admonished by her boss, Samuel Goldwyn. Shaking his head, he noted, "You were crazy to come back. He could have done a lot for you."

More often than not, though, Howard's cockpit courtships were successful.

Yvonne De Carlo affectionately remembered how Hughes timed a cross-country flight with such precision that they hung above the Grand Canyon at sunset, the sky a canvas of pink, crimson, and lavender. This special portrait was a gift he would go on to share with other women as well.

He wooed Linda Darnell with an equally romantic sight, an aerial view of fog wrapping around San Francisco's Golden Gate Bridge. Darnell, famous for her role as the temptress in the period epic *Forever Amber*, was twenty-four and still married to cameraman Peverell J. Marley when Howard first asked her to lunch. Howard's wolfish reputation alarmed her. Determined to pursue her budding career and maintain a spotless reputation, Darnell told her agent, Bill Schiffrin, "I really don't need this, but I'll go if you come with us."

When Hughes drove to the airport, Darnell protested. "Take me back to the studio."

"Relax," Schiffrin told her. "I'm right here. And this is Howard Hughes! Did you expect him to take you to just an ordinary, run-of-the-mill lunch?"

Darnell laughed. "Well, where are we going? Paris?" She was astounded when Hughes pulled up in front of an enormous Constellation airliner, with its props already turning. She was further fascinated to find the plane empty, though she did spy bottles of Dom Perignon chilling in ice buckets.

Howard put Schiffrin in a first-class seat before disappearing into the cockpit with Linda. He was en route to a romantic victory. Upon arrival in San Francisco, Darnell emerged hand in hand with the pilot.

A sleek midnight-blue limousine awaited and carried them to the Fairmont Hotel where Hughes had reserved the penthouse suite with its spectacular views of the bay. A full orchestra played a medley of dance tunes, and a champagne buffet was set out on a table adorned with opulent yellow tulips, Darnell's favorite. A bouquet of similar dates followed.

But still Hughes hadn't succeeded in getting her into bed. So he played his ultimate card, a proposal of marriage.

Since 1929, Hughes had proposed marriage to a succession of beauties, hoping to lure them into bed. It usually worked. "I think that was the one way he could be sure these women would sleep with him," said Dr. Raymond Fowler. "He would propose marriage, with absolutely no intention of following through. And it worked again and again."

Howard didn't just use the skies for seduction; he used them for advertising.

In the spring of 1946 a small skywriting plane soared high above the streets of Pasadena. Zipping across the sky, it left behind the words THE OUTLAW, followed by two giant circles, each dotted in the center. Jane Russell's breasts were back in the news.

Three years after it had been unceremoniously pulled from its engagement in San Francisco, The Outlaw was going to have its day—again. But Hughes's latest attention-getting ad campaign was not winning him friends in high places. Newsweek called the skywriting "literally a new high in vulgarity." In other parts of the country, gigantic billboards were erected, asking, WHAT ARE THE TWO GREAT REASONS FOR RUSSELL'S SUCCESS? Another cooed, HOW WOULD YOU LIKE TO TUSSLE WITH RUSSELL? It featured the image of a young stud cowpoke dragging a gal with ripped clothes into the barn. In smaller type, it promised TRIGGER-FAST ACTION!

The censors were once again enraged—this time over the advertising campaign. In an unprecedented move, the seal of approval that had been bestowed on The Outlaw three years earlier was removed.

A showdown was under way, and Hughes refused to blink. In April, he filed a daring lawsuit against the Motion Picture Association, charging restraint of trade. Then he did the unthinkable: he made the movie available to those theaters that would run it without the seal. The payoff was instantaneous. In Los Angeles, where a gigantic blimp promoting the movie hovered over the city the night before it opened, 100,000 admissions were sold in the first week alone. Asserted the *Los Angeles Daily News* "what packed them in was . . . an opportunity for anatomic research."

As *Time* magazine touted, BUST BECOMES BONANZA. In Atlanta, the first week's ticket sales totaled $22,413—$3,091 more than *Gone With the Wind* had earned in the same period of time. In Chicago, *The Outlaw* toppled the previous record-holder at the Oriental Theater.

Contributing mightily to ticket sales were the state-by-state attempts to ban or alter the movie as it traveled across the country. Typical of the arguments was Baltimore Judge E. Paul Mason's insistence that the ban be upheld because Russell's breasts "hung like a thunderstorm over a summer landscape." Hughes's battles over *The Outlaw* would not abate until the end of the decade. By that time *The Outlaw* had earned more than ten times its $2.5 million cost. Along the way, it enraged censors and made headlines on three continents.

In England, where the picture played to a packed London Pavilion, a playful press agent used a "psycho-galvanometer" on moviegoers. The gizmo presumably measured reaction to the movie. One sailor who had been at sea reportedly sent the needle spinning.

Hughes's refusal to give in would ultimately have major repercussions on the movie censorship system in the United States. Over the years film scholars have praised Hughes for his efforts. Murray Schumach, author of *The Face on the Cutting Room Floor: The Story of Movie and Television Censorship* noted that Hughes "brought some refreshing honesty to Hollywood's approach to sex. He made the American public laugh a little at its own prudery about the female breast."

But Hughes's determination to put *The Outlaw* before the public had more to do with his pride than concerns about free speech and artistic integrity. Jane Russell claimed that Hughes was a soul mate to the movie's Billy the Kid. "Howard patterned Billy after himself to a large degree. He always came out on top, but he was really an innocent who was pushed into tight spots through no fault of his own."

By this time Hughes was also feeling defeated professionally. For a man who vowed to be king of maritime aviation by the end of the war, he saw his fat government contracts collapse around him. First the War Materiel Command canceled its contracts for the ninety-eight XF-11 spy planes, leaving Hughes with the $4 million prototype. It had yet to be tested.

Then Washington pulled the plug on the Hercules, which its detractors had dubbed the Spruce Goose (though it was made of birch), telling both Hughes and industrialist Henry Kaiser that, at this late date, there was no longer any demand for the airborne troop carrier. The Goose wasn't ready in any case. In fact, its hulking components were still squatting on the floor in the cavernous hangar in Culver City.

In press releases, military officials hinted that the Goose would never fly, and the spy plane was too complicated to ever serve as a wartime reconnaissance tool. Naturally, this whipped Hughes into a frenzy. He was determined to get both planes airborne by the end of the year. More to salvage his reputation than anything else, he frantically accelerated work on both planes, though he knew that both planes were considered to be dinosaurs by the aviation establishment.

Hughes had by now renegotiated the $18 million contract for the HK-1, and Toolco was putting $7 million into it. But first the massive plane had to be transported to the ocean. Hughes briefly considered a scheme to get the Hercules to the sea by barge via a creek. Instead, the monumental challenge went to house movers.

Over five headline-making days in June 1946 the massive hull and the two wing sections of the biggest plane in the world traveled the twenty-six miles from Hughes's Culver City plant to Long Beach's Terminal Island, where it was later reassembled. What commenced, wrote *Herald-Express* reporter Will Fowler, was "the world's longest block party."

Moving the gargantuan, 164,000-pound load cost Hughes $60,000 and required the efforts of more than two thousand people and twenty-three different groups, ranging from utility companies to law enforcement agencies. Traffic was rerouted. Bridges and roads were checked for strength. More than three thousand trees were trimmed by the parks departments, and over twenty-three hundred utility wires were temporarily taken down. Schoolchildren were dismissed from their classes, on the condition that they watch the Hercules as it lumbered by.

When it finally reached a leased waterfront facility, the dismantled HK-1 was lowered into dry dock. Preparations were under way for a flight, but first Hughes would make news with another plane—a plane that would lead to tragedy as well as romance.

At this time he was smarting from romantic failure. He asked Noah Dietrich, "Why does everyone abandon me?"

Faith Domergue had finally summoned up the courage to leave him and had married playboy Teddy Stauffer. She later starred in the Hughes-produced *Vendetta*, a turgid period melodrama about a Corsican code of honor. Like other Hughes productions, it had a drawn-out journey to the screen, including a series of directors. And Ava Gardner ejected Hughes from her life after a bitter fight. She rebounded into the arms of oft-married big band king Artie Shaw; Ava would become the fifth Mrs. Shaw.

Though he was still half-heartedly romancing Lana Turner, Yvonne De Carlo, and after a reconciliation, Linda Darnell, Hughes spent most nights haunting the hangars of Hughes Aircraft, fiddling with refinements on the doomed airplanes. The rest of the time found him holed up in the guest room of Cary Grant's mansion or in the one habitable room in the Bel Air villa he once shared with Faith. But things were about to change.

On July 4, producer Bill Cagney, brother of actor James Cagney, convinced Hughes to attend a boating party that began at Cagney's Newport Beach home and continued with a cruise to sun-dappled Santa Catalina Island. As partygoers drifted through Cagney's glass villa and wandered out onto the sand, Hughes's attention was awakened by a phenomenally beautiful young brunette in a dazzling white bathing suit. His eyes followed her as she walked hand in hand with World War II hero Audie Murphy. The recipient of the Congressional Medal of Honor was a boyishly handsome 22-year-old trying to break into the movies.

Hughes edged over to Cagney. "Who's the girl?"

"Name's Jean Peters," Cagney answered. "A new starlet at 20th Century-Fox."

His warning that Jean was involved in a hot affair with Murphy did little to dampen Howard's interest. For the rest of the afternoon, he hung about the edges of the party, trying to talk to Peters alone. But an obviously jealous Murphy always headed him off.

When the partygoers boarded two yachts for the cruise to Santa Catalina Island, Howard saw his chance. While chatting with Murphy about his wartime exploits, Hughes helpfully volunteered to fly some of the group across the channel.

On the flight across the channel, Howard arranged it so that Audie sat in the backseat with Johnny Meyer, while nineteen-year-old Jean sat next to him in the cockpit. Hughes guided the ship over the magnificent Palos Verdes Peninsula so that his guests could see the white breakers pounding against the promontory at land's end. Then he made a wide arc over busy Los Angeles Harbor and dipped down over Long Beach before heading over the open water to Santa Catalina. While Meyer talked with Murphy, Howard drew Jean out and impressed her with his knowledge of the Hollywood establishment and "the business of becoming a star."

Jean Peters was precisely what she seemed to be—a bona fide Ohio farm girl who made her own clothes and who didn't seem to care whether or not she became a star in Hollywood. Jean had journeyed to Tinseltown to make a screen test, one of her prizes when she was named Miss Ohio State University. The test was so good that Fox mogul Darryl F. Zanuck offered her a seven-year contract less than a week later.

Hughes understood that he couldn't impress Jean in the Hollywood manner—jewels and nightclubbing were not her style. Nor could he count on his power and his wealth. She was too grounded in Midwestern reality. Instead he poured on the charm, not just with Peters but with Murphy as well, coming across as a sort of father figure to them both.

On Sunday morning, July 7, as the party was finally breaking up and the yachts sailed for home, Howard suggested that he fly Peters, Murphy, and Johnny Meyer back to Hughes Aircraft, where he was to test the XF-11 spy plane. At the airfield, Hughes saw to it that wine, chicken, and soft drinks were set out for the guests, while he jumped into the cockpit. For more than an hour, with flight engineer Gene Blandford at his side, Hughes taxied up and down the runway, testing both sets of twin counter-rotating propellers, one behind the other.

Neither Hughes nor any of his engineers knew how the plane would perform at five thousand feet or at 350 miles per hour, qualifications mandated in Hughes Aircraft's contract with the army. As he was about to begin the altitude tests, Hughes stopped the plane at the end of the runway and ejected Blandford. It would be a solo test; the danger and the glory would be his alone. The day before, he had argued furiously with veteran pilot and engineer Joe Petrali about the peril of testing the complicated aircraft without a navigator on board.

"It's suicide," Petrali told his boss. "It's just too complicated for one man to operate."

"Nonsense," said Hughes. "I've had no trouble with this plane during the runway tests, and I won't have a problem with it in the air."

Now Howard taxied the plane around, waved in the direction of Jean Peters and Audie Murphy, and lifted faultlessly into the air.

For some reason, Hughes ignored his own high standards that afternoon—much as he had during the fateful crash into Lake Mead three years earlier. First, he overloaded the XF-11 with twelve hundred gallons of fuel, double the amount mandated by army regulations. Then he charted plans for a two-hour "shakedown" flight; army regulations specifically stated that the XF-11 could fly a "forty-five-minute course on its first test." But Hughes insisted, "This plane could fly across country if it had to."

Finally, Hughes elected to test this complicated airplane over the crowded west side of Los Angeles, when his agreement with the War Materiel Command was for testing in the California desert near Palmdale. But Hughes was under the gun. He erroneously felt that the whole postwar future of Hughes Aircraft was on the line. He needed to prove that the XF-11 could fly fast enough, high enough, and long enough to photograph and survey military targets without getting chewed up by the flak guns.

Moreover, because of the Lake Mead disaster, he believed that his reputation as one of America's premier aviators was on the line. "It was a matter of pride with him," flight engineer Joe Petrali recalled. "In his mind there was no alternative." Nor did Howard anticipate anything but success.

Before climbing into the plane he had his publicists pound out a lengthy press release anticipating the completion of the test. The release noted that Hughes had successfully vindicated his spy plane by "flying it for more than an hour at altitudes as high as 5,000 feet and at speeds up to 350 miles per hour." It was not to be.

Two days earlier, Lana Turner extracted a promise from Hughes that he would not test the spy plane alone. "I had a very bad feeling," she recalled. Likewise, Yvonne De Carlo said she woke up on July 7 feeling "that something bad was going to happen to Howard. Of course I didn't know about his test flight."

Hughes himself, however, had no such concerns. This plane was his baby—"the most beautiful plane ever built." So he took off toward the breakers of the Pacific Ocean at 5.00 P.M., flying into the blinding light of the hot July sun. He swooped through the skies following a half-moon course over Venice Beach and Beverly Hills and then back toward Culver City.

He repeated this arc again and again, gaining a bit more speed each time. When his ground crew radioed that he had exceeded the army's time limit, Hughes disregarded them. The XF-11 was the fastest large plane ever built, and Hughes was exhilarated by its performance and its rush of power. So he ignored the military guidelines and flew on, hoping to remain airborne until dusk, ninety minutes later.

At 6:45 P.M., the plane's right wing suddenly dipped. Hughes said later it felt as if a giant had grabbed the wing in his hand and "refused to let loose." He unfastened his seat belt and stood erect in the tilted cockpit. Looking through the glass dome, he checked to see if the wing and tail sections were intact. "I thought something must have torn off, the pull was so great." But the spy plane was intact.

The aviator had two choices. He could head directly back to Hughes Aircraft less than five minutes away or continue on course in hopes that he could "diagnose the trouble and correct it."

"What he didn't understand was that he was losing valuable seconds in his race to save himself and the aircraft," said Capt. Charles Barton, an author who studied Howard's aviation career.

With the XF-11 whirling down like a model airplane with a lead on its right wing, Hughes crouched down in the plane, trying to adjust the right engine, which he thought was somehow malfunctioning. He dramatically increased the speed, hoping that the extra force would realign the plane. Nothing. Then he reduced power on the right engine while holding the left engine steady. The plane continued to plummet.

The XF-11's performance puzzled him; he could control the direction in which the craft traveled but not its altitude. Thirty seconds later, he knew the plane was going to crash. It was too late to reach Culver City.

He steered the plane for the only open space large enough to accommodate him—the verdant fairways of the Los Angeles Country Club. He chose the area near the ninth hole, which spread widely between stands of pine and weeping willow trees. This course carried him directly over a chunk of rich Beverly Hills real estate.

But could he make the fairway? Between Washington Boulevard and Wilshire Boulevard, a distance of about four miles, the XF-11 had plunged forty-two hundred feet. Pedestrians on the Miracle Mile stared up in apprehension as the plane, now emitting a telltale whine, roared less than eight hundred feet over their heads, toward Beverly Hills. The force of the fall pressed Howard, now without his seat belt, into the Plexiglas of the cockpit dome.

Just ahead he saw welcoming trees and nursed a slight hope that the plane could soar above the rooftops and onto the golf course. Undoubtedly, the trees would have ripped him and the plane to shreds but would also have saved the lives of those on the ground.

As he half-stood in the careening XF-11, he was too frantic to realize that his talisman, the lucky fedora, had been blown off his head and onto the floor. The plane, accelerating dramatically, had dropped to two hundred feet. Hughes realized that time had run out.

Leaning up into the canopy during these last precious seconds, he aimed the nose of the plane between houses in the 800 block of Linden Drive, a last-ditch plan to clear the residential structures. Then he braced himself by planting his feet on the instrument panel. He was about to crash.

In some ways Howard had awaited this moment for twenty years, believing, as did most of his fellow aviators, that the manner in which you died was the test of your mettle. Now he gripped the wheel with all his strength and, with no thought for his own mortality, steered for the alley.

The roar inside the plane was terrific, an ear-splitting shriek. Hughes felt an explosion as the right wing and landing gear crashed into a corner of the house at 803 Linden Drive. He was tossed about like a rag doll as the plane flipped onto its side. The XF-11 shook furiously again. What was left of the right wing, an amputated nubbin, ripped through the rear corner of the residence at 805 Linden Drive, causing what was left of the plane to roll end over end through the air.

Without his seat belt, Howard pitched around in the crushed fuselage, sliced by shards of metal and Plexiglas as the XF-11 broke into four pieces, all of them engulfed by flames. Hughes fell in a heap at the bottom of the fuselage.

He heard a series of popping explosions and then felt the intense heat as flames spread up his jacket and out onto his shoulders. Blood spurted from his nose, his ears, and his mouth, and his right hand, drenched with aviation fuel, caught fire. With an almost superhuman effort, he beat it out by slapping the hand onto the side of his jacket.

Light-headed and dizzy, Hughes grabbed up a seat cushion and tried to hoist himself up on the Plexiglas canopy that trapped him in the inferno. But he couldn't move; his left foot was entangled in the wreckage.

Nauseated by the burning fuel and weakened by the fire feeding on his own flesh, Howard collapsed back into the wreckage and drifted into semi-consciousness. About a minute later, he came to. With all that remained of his strength, he pulled himself up to the Plexiglas canopy, grabbed onto its red-hot rim, and freed his boot. He then filled his lungs and pushed on the bubble. Because its rubber seal had melted, it popped right out.

Again his strength failed, and he hunched his shoulders, halfway out of the fuselage. When he looked down, he saw a gusher of fuel pouring out

Howard Robard Hughes, Jr., age 1.
(*DIETRICH/SYGMA*)

Hughes with his mother, Allene. Their bond
would forever impact his life—especially
his attitudes toward women.
(*DIETRICH/SYGMA*)

Hughes's father, an adventurer and inventor,
succeeded in business but failed as a family
man. (*COURTESY HOUSTON METROPOLITAN
RESEARCH CENTER, HOUSTON PUBLIC LIBRARY*)

Hughes at age 12, showing off his motorized bicycle. *(COURTESY HOUSTON METROPOLITAN RESEARCH CENTER, HOUSTON PUBLIC LIBRARY)*

Hughes at 16. *(ARCHIVE PHOTOS)*

Hughes (*top row, center*), age 15, at the prestigious Fessenden School in Massachusetts. *(UPI/BETTMANN)*

By age 25, in 1930, Hughes was already a heartbreaker and Hollywood mogul. (*MARC WANAMAKER/ BISON ARCHIVES*)

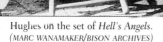

Hughes on the set of *Hell's Angels*. (*MARC WANAMAKER/BISON ARCHIVES*)

he June 30, 1930, premiere of *Hell's Angels* at Grauman's Chinese Theatre drew a crowd of thousands. (*MARC WANAMAKER/BISON ARCHIVES*)

Hughes with starlet Helen Gilbert and Errol Flynn at a Hollywood charity function in 1939.
(UPI/BETTMANN)

Hughes, with Detective Lieutenant Tom Sketchley, as he is booked on a negligent homicide charge after a July 11, 1936, car accident. A pedestrian was killed.
(AP/WIDE WORLD PHOTOS)

Hughes on the stand during an inquest the car crash. *(HEARST COLLECTION/U DEPARTMENT OF SPECIAL COLLECTION*

...es with his first Hollywood discovery, Jean Harlow. *(BETTMANN ARCHIVE)*

Hughes's two favorite stars, Jane Russell and Robert Mitchum, teamed for *Macao*. *(COPYRIGHT © RKO PICTURES, INC., 1952. USED BY PERMISSION TURNER ENTERTAINMENT CO.)*

...ne Russell in one of the famed publicity ...hots for *The Outlaw*. *(UPI/BETTMANN)*

Hughes, head of RKO Pictures, in 1948. *(MARC WANAMAKER/BISON ARCHIVES)*

Ella Rice, a genteel Houston socialite and
the first Mrs. Howard Hughes.
(COURTESY JAMES OVERTON WINSTON)

Katharine Hepburn—independent,
impulsive, and born to privilege—was a
soulmate to Hughes. *(BETTMANN ARCHIVE)*

Hughes and Ava Gardner ringside at
an August 1946 championship bout in
Yankee Stadium. *(UPI/BETTMANN)*

Hughes with Ginger Rogers at the 1933 premier
of *42nd Street*. *(UPI/BETTMANN)*

Hughes escorts Ida Lupino to the Trocadero shortly after her arrival from Britain. Lupino's mother would accompany them on their dates. *(UPI/BETTMANN)*

Billie Dove, the "American Beauty" of the silent screen, was also Hughes's leading lady offscreen. *(HEARST COLLECTION/USC DEPARTMENT OF SPECIAL COLLECTIONS)*

Hughes meeting Bette Davis at an August 1938 charity event shortly before they became lovers. *(MARC WANAMAKER/BISON ARCHIVES)*

Hughes out on the town with actress Marian Marsh in 1935. *(UPI/BETTMANN)*

Icy screen goddess Lana Turner, another of
Hughes's lovers, was left at the altar.
(BETTMANN ARCHIVE)

Sultry Yvonne De Carlo didn't know that the
FBI was listening in on her affair with
Hughes. *(BETTMANN ARCHIVE)*

Forties pinup queen Rita Hayworth, a passionate lover of Hughes.
(UPI/BETTMANN)

Jane Greer, the former Bettyjane Greer, was spotted by Hughes while modeling a WAC uniform. She became a queen of postwar film noir. *(USED BY PERMISSION TURNER ENTERTAINMENT CO.)*

Brenda Frazier, the premier debutante of the era, fell under Hughes's spell when they met in a ballroom in Nassau. *(UPI/BETTMANN)*

ust a teenager when she caught Hughes's eye, Faith Domergue was given a star buildup and the term of endearment "Little Baby." *(UPI/BETTMANN)*

Heiress-debutante Gloria Vanderbilt, 17, fell fast for the much older Hughes. But after a phone call from her guardian, Hughes backed out of her life. *(UPI/BETTMANN)*

Sallilee Conlon, the Midwestern college beauty who became part of Hughes's starlet factory. *(COURTESY SALLILEE CONLON)*

Gail Ganley, the last Hughes starlet. Her lawsuit against Hughes gave the media a glimpse inside his secret empire. *(COURTESY GAIL GANLEY)*

Singer-starlet Phyllis Applegate saw the compassionate side of Hughes, her friend and lover. *(COURTESY PHYLLIS APPLEGATE)*

Actress Joyce Taylor says of Hughes, "He had to have control." *(COPYRIGHT © TURNER ENTERTAINMENT CO., 1961. ALL RIGHTS RESERVED)*

After an eleven-year courtship, Jean Peters became Mrs. Howard Hughes in January 1957. *(UPI/BETTMANN NEWSPHOTOS)*

Kathryn Grayson, the exquisite MGM musical star, nearly married Hughes on three occasions. *(BETTMANN ARCHIVE)*

Yvonne Shubert loved the married Hughes. His aides and Jean Peters wanted her out of the picture.
(COURTESY YVONNE SHUBERT)

Terry Moore enraptured Hughes with her teenage silliness, but they never exchanged wedding rings. *(BETTMANN ARCHIVE)*

Hughes and his 1938 round-the-world flight crew are surrounded by fans during a refueling stop at a Minneapolis airport—en route to their final destination, New York City.
(AP/WIDE WORLD PHOTOS)

Hughes at 28, when he captured the Sportsman's trophy at the Miami Air Meet.
(UPI/BETTMANN)

In need of a shave after his global flight of three days, nineteen hours, and seventeen minutes, Hughes strides across New York's Floyd Bennett Field. To his left is Grover Whalen, president of New York's World's Fair. *(AP/WIDE WORLD PHOTOS*

Hughes was found working for $250 a month as a pilot for American Airlines in 1932. *(UPI/BETTMANN)*

Howard Hughes, aviation hero, in 1937.
(UPI/BETTMANN NEWSPHOTOS)

Houston welcomes a jubilant Hughes and his aide de camp, Noah Dietrich, following Hughes's 1938 flight around the world. *(COURTESY HOUSTON METROPOLITAN RESEARCH CENTER, HOUSTON PUBLIC LIBRARY)*

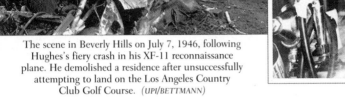

The scene in Beverly Hills on July 7, 1946, following
Hughes's fiery crash in his XF-11 reconnaissance
plane. He demolished a residence after unsuccessfully
attempting to land on the Los Angeles Country
Club Golf Course. (UPI/BETTMANN)

Hughes at the controls of the two-hundred-ton Spruce Goose during the history-
making flight of November 4, 1947—a personal triumph for Hughes. (UPI/BETTMANN)

With longtime colleague Noah Dietrich, Hughes shows signs of strain as he prepares to testify before the Senate in 1947. *(DIETRICH/SYGMA)*

During the Senate hearings of 1947, Hughes was questioned about his wartime aircraft contracts. However, Hughes triumphed and was a hero once more. *(AP/WIDE WORLD PHOTOS)*

Hughes and Hepburn: A romance made for the fan magazines. *(AUTHORS' COLLECTION)*

Hughes in the media spotlight July 19, 1948. *(COPYRIGHT © TIME INC., 1948. REPRINTED WITH PERMISSION.)*

A latter-day Hughes, sometime in the 1950s. *(COURTESY HOUSTON METROPOLITAN RESEARCH CENTER, HOUSTON PUBLIC LIBRARY)*

and running in a rivulet toward the blazing engine. Just then, through the curtain of smoke and flames, he heard a voice.

It was Marine Sergeant William Lloyd Durkin, who had sprinted into the alleyway between the homes in search of survivors. "Is anyone in there?" Durkin yelled. He heard nothing. "Is anyone in there?" he screamed again.

Sergeant Durkin finally detected a weak but steady series of thumps— a signal that someone was inside. Durkin moved cautiously toward the plane. When he was within two feet, the flames jumped toward him, lighting his shirt on fire.

Undaunted, the rescuer managed to grasp Howard under the shoulders. He was hoisting him out when a fireman appeared and helped remove the survivor. When they had smothered Hughes's burning clothes, they noted he was smiling. "Lay me on the grass," he told the two men.

Howard later remembered closing his eyes and drifting into a euphoric state, free of pain. He realized he was dying, but at least he wasn't burning to death.

Sergeant Durkin knelt beside Hughes until the medics arrived and put him into the ambulance. Hughes seemed surprisingly fragile under the dim lights of the ambulance. "That man's going to die," Durkin thought. Then he backed away from the wreckage, which was by then crawling with police and onlookers.

He didn't learn the identity of the man he had rescued until an hour later, when Los Angeles Station KRLA broadcast the report that "millionaire aviator and film producer Howard Hughes was critically injured an hour ago when the plane he was testing crashed into a Beverly Hills neighborhood. Hughes is not expected to live."

At 7:15 at the end of a glorious Fourth of July weekend, the doors of the Beverly Hills Emergency Hospital flew open, and Howard Robard Hughes was rolled into the only available operating room. The man who columnist Louella Parsons had recently described as "one of the most glamorous men in the world" had been burned on 78 per cent of his body and mangled from his forehead to below the knees.

His face was oozing blood, and his burned chest had begun to swell with huge blisters. At a glance, physicians estimated that he had sustained multiple fractures in his ribs, arms, and shins.

The physician in charge applied a stethoscope to Hughes's festering chest and listened for a few seconds. "This man's dying!" he screamed to the medics. "His lungs are filling with fluid. You've got to get him to Good Samaritan Hospital. They've got a burn unit there."

As they zipped Howard inside an oxygen tent for his race across town, he came to and feebly gestured with his hand. "I'm Howard Hughes," he said. "The aviator."

The nurses and the medics fell silent and gathered to take a look at what remained of one of the great figures of the twentieth century. The senior physician broke the silence. He snapped, "Get this man out of here! He's dying!"

Howard nodded his head at the physician and then fell back into the oxygen tent, which was the only thing keeping him alive. Later he told Glenn Odekirk that oxygen and the steady drone of the ambulance engine lulled him to sleep, but not until he had asked about the identity of the man who had pulled him from the wreckage. "See to it he's taken care of," Howard gasped before slipping into a twilight slumber. He would later recall seeing brilliant white lights before drifting off. He remained unconscious until the medics carried him into the burn unit at Good Samaritan, where doctors grimly inventoried the extent of his injuries.

He appeared to be barely clinging to life. As Hughes gulped pure oxygen, his blood pressure fell to a dangerous level. Ten of his ribs were fractured, as were his nose, left knee, and left elbow. His scalp was cleaved open—the worst of the sixty cuts on his face, shoulders, and hands. The left lung was punctured and collapsed; the bones protecting both lungs were splintered.

His chest had sustained a third-degree burn from his shoulder to just above the waist, a wound that required intensive treatment and four skin grafts to repair the damage. His left forearm and hand had been seared just as badly, prompting one of the medics to say that "it appeared as if he had plunged his left arm into a deep fat fryer and left it there for fifteen minutes."

There were fifty other separate, more minor wounds. For Hughes, they would prove to be the most important. His chin, crushed by the *Hell's Angels* crash, had again splintered apart into a soft mass of fragments. The careening XF-11 had sliced his face repeatedly, destroying much of its natural elasticity. His nose had been flattened and pushed to the right as a result of the terrific force that occurred as the cockpit hit the asphalt alleyway.

He entered Good Samaritan losing so much blood that a transfusion was administered ten minutes after the medics wheeled him in. But the force of his will was still intact. When staff doctors gathered around to begin cutting and inserting, he lifted up his hand. "I want you to wait for my doctors . . . I know they're on the way."

"But we need to get started this very second," answered a pulmonary specialist who had been called from his home.

"No," said Howard. "Wait for my own doctors."

Dr. Verne Mason, Hughes's internist for a decade, and his surgeon of fifteen years, Dr. Lawrence Chaffin, arrived within two hours after the crash. They went to work immediately.

"How am I doin'?" Howard asked Mason.

"I'm not going to lie to you, Howard. You might not live."

"Do what you can," he mumbled. "I'm prepared."

Half an hour later, Mason had drained thirty-four hundred ccs of bloody fluid from his chest cavity and ordered the second transfusion. At 4:00 A.M. the following day, after Mason, Chaffin, and a team of four other doctors had been working steadily for eight hours, Howard fell into "profound shock," and from there into a coma.

A crowd of more than two dozen reporters had gathered in the Good Samaritan lobby, where Dr. Mason announced that Hughes's condition had worsened from "critical" to "severely critical." Privately he told Noah Dietrich that he didn't see how Hughes could live, given the extent of the trauma. "Howard's a tough Texan," Dietrich declared. "If anyone can do it, he can."

By 5:00 A.M. Pacific time, teams of reporters at the *Los Angeles Examiner*, the *Los Angeles Times*, the *Houston Post*, and the *Houston Chronicle* had completed their obituaries. The *Post* and the *Chronicle* had them set in type and scores of pictures engraved. "It was like a death watch for a king," remembered Bill Feeder, who covered the story for *Daily Variety*.

Headlines reflected the bleak prognosis. Typical was the *Los Angeles Examiner's*, which screamed, HOWARD HUGHES CRITICALLY HURT IN FIERY CRASH OF TEST PLANE: GIVEN ONLY A 50/50 CHANCE OF SURVIVAL.

In the hours just before dawn, Howard summoned one of his secretaries, Alice Burns, to his bedside. "I had a phone call from Johnny Meyer," she recalled. "He told me that Mr. Hughes needed to see me and that it couldn't wait." A limousine took Burns and Meyer to the back entrance of Good Samaritan Hospital.

After they entered Hughes's darkened room, he looked at Meyer and a nurse. "Please leave," he told them.

Remembered Burns: "And so I shut the door and sat down next to his bed. Because of the oxygen mask, I couldn't quite understand everything he was trying to dictate. So I leaned on the bed, and poor Mr. Hughes gave out a slight cry. He told me, 'Pin up your hair, Miss Burns, because I don't think you can hear me very well.' "

The memos Hughes dictated that night were about the aircraft business, and how and why the XF 11 had failed. Burns felt he wanted her there to take down his painfully delivered words "because he believed he was dying."

The requisite stars milled about the hospital corridors: Lana Turner in black and crying a flood of tears; Linda Darnell, also in black and fingering a rosary; and Cary Grant, sorrowful and wearing his only black suit. Yvonne De Carlo and Ava Gardner, who understood Hughes's aversion to public displays, sent intimate personal telegrams along with white roses and red ones, respectively, but remained discreetly at home.

Louella Parsons informed her radio listeners that Hollywood had not been so riveted on a hospital drama since Jean Harlow died in 1936. When Howard awakened from his coma there was another flurry of headlines and radio bulletins. Without even inquiring about his chances, Hughes called aide Walter Reynolds to his side. "Tell them that I did my level best to keep her up . . . and that I thought, at first, that I could get her back."

An hour later he again surrendered himself to Mason and Chaffin with only one request: that Glenn Odekirk be put in the room next to him, with the connecting door between the rooms to remain open. Whenever Howard stirred, no matter what time, Glenn was instantly at his side to engage him in aviation chatter.

But he wasn't out of danger. The physicians were unable to cure the secondary problems—the burns, fractures, and dozens of open wounds—until they brought under control the primary problem, his collapsed, fluid-filled lung. It had been drained twice by the time he rallied just before dawn on July 10. For the first time since the crash his blood pressure was back to normal, and the crushed left lung began to function again.

Dr. Verne Mason felt optimistic enough to hold his first official press conference in the lobby of Good Samaritan. With flash bulbs popping and a bank of radio mikes in front of him, the physician exclaimed: "My patient is truly 'The Man of Steel,' and he is crawling back to health from injuries that would have killed most men. He's not out of danger yet, but he has a terrific will to live. That alone might save him."

Then Mason provided the ultimate photo opportunity. He held up

Howard's partly charred, somewhat-worse-for-wear lucky fedora, which had been missing since the XF-11 plunged to the ground. It had turned up on a shelf in the Beverly Hills Police Department and had been rushed to Good Samaritan in a squad car.

On July 11, Howard was able to sit up in bed and eat a cracker. Incredibly, he also put his aides to work. He was obsessed with two things. He wanted to explain why the XF-11 had crashed, so he dictated a series of memos on the subject from inside his oxygen tent. And he wanted to stake out his claim on Jean Peters.

While Noah Dietrich was bringing Peters to the hospital, Howard issued this statement to the War Materiel Command: "I am now certain that this crash occurred when the rear four blades of the right propeller reversed and pulled the plane downward. Tell the army I wouldn't wish this to happen to anyone else."

An hour later, Jean Peters achieved what Lana Turner, Linda Darnell, and Cary Grant hadn't: she was escorted to Howard's room, where he talked with her from the oxygen tent and touched her hand with two fingers of his left hand.

But later that night, his left lung failed again, sending his blood pressure spiraling out of control, plunging him into "severe nervous shock" for the second time. Just before he lost consciousness, Hughes asked Verne Mason, "Am I going to live?"

The physician looked him in the eye. "I don't know, Howard. I sure can't guarantee it."

On July 12 he hovered near death. At 10:30 P.M., his chest filled with fluid for the third time, and the large third-degree burns remained only partially treated, lowering his body temperature to a near fatal level. That same day, United Press dispatched a dramatic photo of dark-eyed Linda Darnell weeping in the hospital corridor and fingering her rosary. In the *Hollywood Citizen-News*, the photo ran beneath the headline, REFUSED PERMISSION TO SEE HUGHES.

The next day, however, he made tremendous gains, with his lung rebounding to the point that he was taken off oxygen for the first time.

Then the doctors waged war against the burns, cuts, and fractures. Since most of Hughes's skeletal and nervous system had been traumatized in one way or another, the pain was almost unbearable. Dr. Mason and Dr. Chaffin reluctantly prescribed morphine, which was at first administered by injection. When Howard learned of it, he reared up out of his bed in anger. "I don't want that stuff," he yelled at Mason. "And I don't need it."

Mason explained that he was already receiving it intravenously. "Well, stop it," Howard said. "Give it to me in pills. Something I can control." Mason complied.

To give himself a "fighting chance against this dope," Hughes had Odekirk, still ensconced in the room next door, keep track of the morphine vials. Said Odekirk, "He would read the chart at the end of his bed and order me to cut the dosage in half or sometimes to just one third of what the doctor had prescribed. He resisted it with all of his strength."

But as much as Hughes resisted taking the drugs, his obsessive-compulsive disorder soon convinced him he couldn't function without them. He was on his way to a secret addiction.

Though Jean Peters dominated Hughes's thoughts during recovery, she was not without competition. When he was still in an iron lung, Hughes called Johnny Meyer to his hospital room and told him to take down a series of very lengthy notes on the care and treatment of his lovers. For more than an hour, Howard dictated a remarkable battle plan. Meyer was to keep the women busy, with lunches, dinners, and entertainment, on a rotating basis. Hughes even matched each lover with her favorite restaurant.

"And I want you to send them all flowers, each week," Hughes told an amazed Meyer. He made it easy for Meyer by outlining each lady's preference. Meyer was also expected to give each of the lovers a beautifully crafted speech and messages from Howard, which included the special terms of endearment he had showered on each of them. Meyer was astounded to find that these varied with each of twenty women. "Be sure that you follow this precisely," Hughes cautioned, "because I don't want one of these girls to see you out with another. They'll understand immediately what is going on."

Ever mechanically minded, Hughes also called in some of his plant engineers and had them design to his specifications a special motorized hospital bed, with push buttons and hot and cold running water.

Sixteen days after the crash, following his eighth blood transfusion and a series of burn treatments and skin grafts, the press could finally report that Howard was speeding toward recovery. A day later his lung was tapped for the final time, allowing physicians to remove "a negligible amount of fluid."

Hughes remained at Good Samaritan Hospital for thirty-four days. During his recovery, he drank gallons of orange juice daily and monitored his morphine intake. He also underwent secret plastic surgery.

Glenn Odekirk was with Hughes when he gazed into a mirror for the first time during his hospitalization. Initially Hughes was emotionless as he carefully studied the reflection of his battered image. Then, with a wail, he turned to Odekirk. "Look at me," he screamed. "Just look at me." With a sob Howard declared, "I'm a monster."

Surgeons repaired much of the damage but couldn't erase an angry scar on his lip and almost imperceptible gashes across the top of his forehead. To conceal the former, Hughes grew a mustache. A hat would help to cover the lines above his eyes. But the resiliency of youth could not be restored. Friends and lovers would notice the difference.

Jane Greer, who brought him a potted plant not long after he left the hospital, said, "You could see that he had been through hell. His cheeks were sunken and his face looked incredibly tired." Actress Gene Tierney, who had dated Hughes occasionally before and after the crash, remembered that "his eyes had turned beady, and the face had tightened. Rather than adding character, the scars only aged him." Yvonne De Carlo claimed that she could see the lines of every injury and "of all the pain" etched around his eyes. "I wanted to say something, but knew that I could not."

It was during this invalid's progress that Dr. Mason switched Hughes from morphine to codeine, inadvertently triggering his slow but eventual descent into drug addiction.

Howard's physical injuries were compounded by the psychological blow the army delivered through its verdict on the cause of the XF-11 crash. After studying the accident reports and interviewing twenty witnesses, the official board of injury blamed the crash on "pilot error."

They specifically faulted Hughes for "not being sufficiently acquainted with emergency operating procedures" and for "failing to consider an emergency landing." Even worse, some of his own men agreed with the verdict. Hughes aerodynamist Carl Babberger believed, "Howard got spooked on that one. He lost it. If he had cut the power he would have been okay."

"He simply didn't check everything the way he should have," recalled hydraulics engineer Dave Grant. Even Odekirk reluctantly stated, "He should have reduced speed on *both* engines so that he could have distinguished between structural troubles or power failure."

"This accident was avoidable after the propeller trouble was experienced," noted the hoard of inquiry. The army added to his humiliation by ordering Hughes Aircraft to nominate another test pilot, "someone other than Mr. Hughes," to test the second XF-11 prototype. (Ultimately, though, it would be Hughes back in the XF-11 cockpit; he successfully tested a "twin" of the crashed plane in April 1947.)

Released from the hospital on August 12, thirty-five days after the crash, Hughes went to Cary Grant's rented villa to recuperate. He would move aimlessly from hotel to hotel and from house to house during his recovery, during which time he was deluged with feminine attention.

Lana Turner was among those who roared back onto the scene, at least briefly.

Less than a month after Hughes moved into Cary's house, Lana ran into starlet Janet Thomas and her date Johnny Meyer at a swank charity event. "Why don't we go over and see how Howard is doing?" Turner suggested.

"Why not?" answered Meyer.

"As we drove up," Thomas recalled, "I could see the outline of a woman on the shade of an upstairs room, Howard's room." Lana saw it as well.

Turner gave Meyer an indignant look. "I'm going in," she declared.

She was out of the car, dashing unannounced through the front door, before Meyer could stop her. She ran up the stairs and burst into Hughes's room. There, standing next to Howard's bed, was Jean Peters.

"Oh, Howard," Lana said, tears running down her face, "how could you? Why would you do this to me?"

Leaving Lana and Hughes to argue, Peters walked down the curving staircase. Seeing Meyer and Thomas standing at the foot of the stairs, Peters looked up and said, with aplomb, "For that performance, Lana should get an Academy Award."

Turner finally realized the hopelessness of her relationship with the millionaire. "In later years, she hardly mentioned Hughes. Even when he died," said her former secretary Taylor Pero.

For a while in 1947, Hughes carried on a torrid affair with a leading sex symbol at the sprawling Santa Monica home of Marion Davies. Arriving in his old Chevrolet, he would slip into the house through a back door. Minutes later, a woman wearing oversize sunglasses and a scarf over her head would cautiously enter the same door. Both walked down a long corridor in the 64-room villa to rendezvous in a bedroom suite. Once reserved for Greta Garbo, it had been redecorated for Hughes.

Once inside the room, Hughes threw off his coat and the mystery woman removed her sunglasses and loosened her scarf, allowing a cascade of red hair to tumble down her shoulders. It was Rita Hayworth, who had heated up the box office as the star of *Gilda*, which was dominated by her sultry rendition of "Put the Blame on Mame."

With a fire blazing in a marble fireplace and champagne chilling in a silver bucket, Howard and Rita would make love and then lie together naked. Surprised one day by an unexpected visitor, a nude Hughes tried to cover Rita's body, ordering the intruder, "Don't look." It was the most secret love affair that both Hughes and Rita would ever experience. Davies, Howard's friend since the San Simeon days, presided over these trysts, ordering servants to avoid the suite and devising a backstairs route through the villa, allowing them to avoid other guests and members of Marion's family.

Rita had to be discreet. Two teams of detectives had been following her for weeks, one deployed by her estranged husband, filmmaker Orson Welles, who was out for vengeance over her rejection, and the other by Columbia Pictures boss Harry Cohn, who was looking to invoke the "morals clause" in her contract. Hughes was vulnerable as well, desperate to keep Jean from discovering yet another affair.

Author Dan Wolfe, who visited the beach house often as a teenager and had the run of the house, encountered the lovers several times. "They seemed devoted to each other," he recalled. When that devotion led to an unexpected pregnancy, Rita underwent an abortion. Afterward, with Hughes's encouragement, she embarked on a four-month European holiday, during which Hughes's representatives catered to her every need.

Hughes also became enamored with a teenage Elizabeth Taylor. After spotting her in 1949 in the lobby of the Beverly Hills Hotel, Hughes told an assistant, "Get me an introduction to that girl." Later he cleverly visited the hotel art gallery run by Elizabeth's father, Francis. Not only did Hughes buy several paintings, but he also invited Elizabeth and her parents for a weekend getaway. They accepted, but Elizabeth was not won over by Hughes, whom she considered an old man at forty-three. But his interest didn't abate. Years later, his attorney Greg Bautzer approached Taylor's mother about an arranged marriage between the multimillionaire and the violet-eyed beauty. As a sign of his commitment, Hughes agreed to pay Elizabeth $1 million. When Elizabeth heard about the offer, she laughed out loud. Years later, following the 1958 death of her third husband, producer Michael Todd, a shaken Liz boarded a TWA plane that took her from Los Angeles to Todd's funeral, just outside of Chicago. She didn't know it at the time, but Hughes had made the plane available for the mourning widow. Three years later, when Elizabeth learned of Hughes's kindness, she called his switchboard and left the message, "Howard made a wonderful gesture after my husband was killed and I never thanked him . . ."

As the forties progressed, though, it was Jean Peters who increasingly dominated the scene. Not since Kate Hepburn had Howard found such a soul mate. Peters once recounted that as he lay in bed, during his recuperation from the crash, Howard "would talk for hours about his feelings, his dreams and his sorrows." They sometimes came with the admonition, "This is absolutely secret. Don't discuss it with anybody." Among his revelations: if it hadn't been for the great expectations forced upon him by his family and wealth, he would have been content to have worked as an aeronautical engineer or designer.

Often she sat next to his bed, making her own clothes or knitting sweaters. Jean had become a friend as well as a lover.

"I've finally found the girl of my dreams," Hughes told Dietrich.

"Then marry her," Dietrich advised. "And cut out all that other stuff."

"I should marry her," Hughes replied. "I'd be crazy not to marry her. But I can't bring myself to do it."

"Why?" asked Dietrich.

Unable to think of a reason, Howard concluded, "I just can't."

CHAPTER 20

HIDE-AND-SEEK

THE YEAR 1947 WOULD SEE A NEW SERIES OF FLYING EXPLOITS, BOTH PERSONAL and business related. Twice Hughes would disappear, gaining banner headlines both times. He would confront the government and its four years of spying on him by the FBI. And he would conduct another test run, this time putting the memories of his disastrous crash to rest.

He was well aware the FBI was closing in as the new year dawned. Federal auditors hunkered over his books to prepare for a U.S. Senate probe of his government contracts. "They're running me down like an animal," he complained to Cary Grant.

"Ditch 'em," Grant suggested from London. "I'll meet you in New York."

A day later, Hughes ducked out a rear entrance of the Town House, slipped past the feds, and piloted a Constellation toward Manhattan, where a TWA board of directors meeting, and Grant, waited. But the threat of a snowstorm grounded him in Amarillo, Texas.

The press-shy Hughes tried to hide out in offices at the airfield. But a reporter from the *News-Globe* snared a brief interview. "He shook my hand and I shook from my boots upward," admitted reporter Cal Brumley, who noted that Hughes's eyes were sunken from lack of sleep. He wore wrinkled trousers fastened "with what looked like a couple of shoe strings," a wrinkled overcoat, and a stained white shirt open at the neck.

Asked about prospects for marriage, the world's most eligible bachelor shook his head. But in fact, Jean Peters dominated his thoughts. After his TWA meeting, she would dictate his destination—and his first disappearing act of 1947. It would be an excursion of the heart. A second also loomed: it would involve the government.

On January 10, New York newsboys leaned into the winds of a blizzard as they hawked their midmorning editions. The city awakened to find that one of its tabloid heroes, Howard Hughes, appeared to be again in mortal trouble. AVIATOR HOWARD HUGHES—CARY GRANT MISSING; BELIEVED DEAD, trumpeted the *New York Daily News.*

With his heroic fight for life still a vivid memory, headline writers vied to capture the drama of this latest chapter in the endless soap opera that Howard Hughes's life had become. Had luck finally run out for the man who had risen like a phoenix from the ashes of the XF-11 accident back in July? The fact that the ultimate matinee idol of his day, Cary Grant, had flown off with Hughes added spice to an already sensational story. Just days earlier, Hughes and Grant had decorated Manhattan gossip columns as they prowled the nightclubs and luxuriated at the Plaza Hotel.

This sensational story began quietly when air-traffic controllers lost track of Howard's sumptuous DC-3 somewhere near the Mexican border. It had taken off from Ohio's Wright Field. Hughes had been genial and even waved at the control tower before taking off into the thunder and lightning of a "blue norther" winter storm. It was 6:11 on the evening of January 9. Hughes radioed his intentions to fly directly for Amarillo, high in the panhandle, his normal refueling station. From there they had charted a course over New Mexico and Arizona toward Los Angeles. During their half hour on the ground Howard and Cary had been amiable. Hughes even invited three military pilots into his "floating penthouse," as it was called, to show off its sofa bed, wet bar, and armchairs set amid the thick carpeting and draperies.

Less than an hour later, a traffic controller in Indianapolis strained to make sense of a garbled radio message Hughes had broadcast. A fury of winds throughout the Midwest made the sputtering signal impossible to decipher. By two o'clock in the morning the plane and its famous pilot had still not landed in Amarillo. The first bulletin went out over United Press shortly afterward.

Again, the Hughes obituaries were dredged out of newspaper libraries, along with those of Cary Grant, who was then at the height of his popularity. The Hughes headquarters at Romaine buzzed with activity, gearing for the word that Howard's plane had been located somewhere in the desert, felled by the wintry storm.

Actually, at that moment Hughes's flying penthouse was parked on a dark, distant runway at El Paso airfield. Its two famous occupants were inside, eating sandwiches and drinking coffee, completely unaware they were the subjects of a search. Indeed, they were on their own search—to see the newest love of Hughes's life.

After Hughes told his closest friend about his deepening affection for Jean Peters, who was then in Mexico co-starring with Tyrone Power in the swashbuckling epic *Captain from Castile*, Grant casually suggested, "Let's drop in on them."

With that, Hughes headed the nose of the DC-3 farther west toward El Paso and its border town, Juarez, Mexico. But upon arriving in El Paso, Hughes couldn't get U.S. Customs clearance until the following morning. "Hughes didn't want to attract a crowd, so he taxied the plane to the most distant runway," Cary Grant recalled. They sat until they could get their clearance. The next morning they flew into Nogales, Mexico, below Tucson, and at 6:39 A.M. on January 11, flew to Guadalajara.

In Guadalajara Grant and Howard fell into bed at the Reforma Hotel and didn't awaken until seven hours later. On their way to breakfast, they ran into an Associated Press reporter who recognized them instantly. "Hey," he said, "you guys are supposed to be dead." Or as the headline read in one Mexican newspaper, SEÑORES GRANT Y HUGHES CREYENDO MUERTO.

"Upon learning that, we stayed missing for another two days. We figured that as long as nobody knew where we were, we could enjoy ourselves in peace," Grant recalled.

For Hughes, however, 1947 would bring far more sensational headlines.

He got his first warning of trouble just a week after his jaunt to visit Jean Peters. Elliott Roosevelt, the man who had been responsible for endowing Hughes with $40 million in airplane contracts, telephoned from New York City, warning that the Senate intended to grill him about alleged "financial irregularities" involving the XF-11 and the Spruce Goose. With its new Republican majority, the Senate had targeted all projects in which the late Franklin Delano Roosevelt had been personally involved. The spy plane and the unfinished Hercules easily qualified. But where Hughes was concerned, there was a hidden agenda.

The executive suite of Pan American Airways was frantic to strip Howard's airline, TWA, of its newly won routes across the North Atlantic to Europe, where Pan Am had always held a monopoly. Through conservative Maine Senator Ralph Owen Brewster, Hughes was offered a deal. The Senate investigation would be tabled if he surrendered his North Atlantic routes or, better yet, if he agreed to merge his emerging airline with established Pan American.

Howard was outraged. During the previous seven years he had invested more than $12 million in order to transform this regional airline into a global conglomerate. He fought back, putting a team of New York detectives and corporate lawyers on the case. He discovered that Brewster had already introduced a bill that would rob TWA of what it had just won from the Civil Aeronautics Board.

Hughes's intelligence proved that this bill had actually been written by lawyers for Pan American, which only fueled his desire to make war with the Senate. He turned Brewster down. Howard suspected that Brewster was just a tool for Pan American Airways president Juan Trippe. What he did not know was that FBI agents had been dogging his every step for almost eighteen months. A few snippets from these "top-secret" FBI reports show what the millionaire was up against.

On February 12, 1947, the Los Angeles FBI field office cabled Washington that "Hughes and Jack Frye, the president of TWA, were negotiating with Russia to establish an airline in the Soviet Union." A day later, FBI Report 62-3541 sneered that "Hughes used expensive party girls to woo military officials." On March 2, FBI agents had proof "that Hughes bribed Elliott Roosevelt to get priority air service in postwar Europe." A day later, the L.A. field office noted that "Elliott took a $75,000 bribe from Hughes which should result in a federal indictment." Although the charges in this "secret dossier" were false, all two thousand pages of the two-year probe, with its reports on Howard's friends and lovers, ended up in the hands of the special Senate subcommittee.

Shortly after Brewster announced that Hughes would have to come to Washington to testify, TWA president Jack Frye urged caution. He warned: "Pan American has the biggest, most complex political machine to ever hit Washington. Trippe believes you have moved in on his territory."

Hughes was intransigent. "I'm going to fight."

When Brewster set the hearings for late July and early August, he said he would have the millionaire "dragged to Washington if I have to." He would later brag: "I want to see the whites of his lies."

"Let 'em find me first," Hughes told Dietrich.

Between July 10, when U.S. marshals stepped up their search for Hughes, and August 5, when Howard finally flew to Washington, Hughes thumbed his nose at Congress by hiding out.

In the beginning, it was fun. The media loved it. So did the average working American. Howard seemed to be saying, "I did my best for the country during the war. And now I'm getting screwed."

The U.S. Marshal's Service discovered that Hughes had vanished into the immense suburban sprawl of Los Angeles. They still had the subpoena in their hands on August 1, when Senator Homer Ferguson, chairman of the special committee, called Los Angeles in a fury. "Has he been served yet? And if not, why the hell not?"

Later that same afternoon, Howard called a couple of his favorite reporters to announce that "they haven't served me yet," adding, "They will find not the slightest hint of graft or bribes in any of my defense projects. The time just ran out. But I guarantee you that the XF-11 is the best photo reconnaissance plane ever built and that the Hercules Flying Boat will fly by the end of the year. I'm coming to Washington on my own. I don't need federal cops picking the time and the place. I have no intention of committing contempt of Congress."

"The average Joe ate this up," recalled Washington columnist Jack Anderson, who helped coach Hughes on his appearance before the committee. "In a way, he was speaking for them."

But Senator Ferguson was irate. "We're sending marshals from Washington now. You can be sure that Mr. Hughes will be served."

On August 2, Robert Clark, one of the marshal's top guns, flew to Los Angeles and held a press conference. "This time we've brought in four extra men." Then he laid his hand on the shoulder of the beefy man standing next to him. "This is George Rossinni, our super snooper."

With a smile, Rossinni said, "It's certainly Mr. Hughes's constitutional right to evade this summons, but it's our right to find him. And we will. After all, I'm the man who brought in Al Capone." With that, Rossinni waved the senatorial summons about his head.

Then he and his four men spread out across Los Angeles in search of the elusive millionaire. They made a well-publicized tour of the hot night spots on the Sunset Strip, the Mocambo, Ciro's, and the Palladium. As they swept in and out, they questioned head waiters and cigarette girls and even toured the kitchens, aware that Howard frequently dined with the kitchen help.

Hughes's cloak of secrecy was so well constructed that no marshal came within a mile of him.

Since there was no deed or even rent receipt in his name, they were unaware of his hideaway in the San Fernando Valley, his suite at the Los Angeles Town House, his apartment at 10000 Sunset Boulevard, or his "always waiting" guest room at Cary Grant's mansion. But Howard over-estimated these high-priced feds, working out an elaborate scheme to evade them. Between July 28, when they first started looking for him, and August 5, when he showed up in Washington, he slept in a different place every night.

With Jean Peters in tow, he spent one night in Grant's guest house, another in Jean's small apartment in West Los Angeles, and three nights, when he was feeling safer, at the small San Fernando Valley tract home belonging to Frank Angell, his head of security.

He even found time to pursue romance with other women. When he and Peters were safely ensconced with Angell, Hughes disappeared alone into the night "on business." Actually, he was wooing MGM dancing star Cyd Charisse. Since she lived only around the corner from Angell, he arranged to dine with her all three nights. "Nobody could find him," Charisse recalled. "He was staying in a small house in the valley only a block or so from where I was staying. He would drive his funny old car over to my place, and we would have dinner together and listen to the reports on the radio, saying that everyone was looking for him."

On the afternoon of August 1, Howard tricked the deputies who had staked out his DC-3. While they were on a lunch break, two men, one matching Hughes's description, leaped into the cockpit and took off. Surprised marshals dropped their hamburgers and ran out onto the field just as the plane lifted off. "Supersnoop" Rossinni rushed up the stairs to the control tower to seize Howard's flight plan. Typically, he hadn't filed one.

Meanwhile, at Frank Angell's, Howard made a great show of sleeping separately from Jean. His bedroom was at the rear of a long hall; hers was up front. Each night after returning from his trysts with Charisse, he waited until Peters retired. Then he tiptoed up to her door and tapped lightly on it. "Is everything okay for the night, sweetie?" he would ask, making sure Frank Angell's wife could hear him. "Okay, honey," he said. "Let me know if you need anything, anything at all."

When the house was dark, he padded down the hall to spend the night with Jean, creeping back to his own chamber at dawn.

On August 4, the day before he was to testify in Washington, Hughes showed up with Jean at the Flamingo Hotel in Las Vegas, making a point of playing the slots and dining on filet mignon. Deputy marshals in Las Vegas roared up to the hotel in two cars escorted by a Las Vegas police car, its red lights flashing and its tires screeching. They burst their way into the Flamingo, making a sweep of the public rooms and of a suite Howard had occupied for an hour or two. All they found was a half-eaten room-service order of cheese sandwiches and chocolate milk. At that very moment Hughes was airborne in the DC-3.

He landed in Los Angeles and drove immediately to Cary Grant's house, where Cary achieved a makeover for Hughes that would prove quite effective in his Washington appearances. Grant took him to a Beverly Hills Hotel hair stylist, who deemed Hughes's tousled aviator's cut hopelessly outdated. Hughes was given the latest version of the CEO cut, not a hair out of place and sealed by a drop of Brylcreem. Cary's impeccable British tailor had cut two elegant suits for Hughes, one of them a double-breasted gray suit and a blue-black pinstripe. Black brogans, four hand-tailored white shirts, and a rack of ties accessorized his new executive look.

Finally, at 2:32 P.M. on August 5, he settled into the pilot's seat of the DC-3 and, with co-pilot Earl Martyn at his side, flew across America, despite a fierce storm over the Midwest. They flew through the eye of the storm, the plane pitching up and down and zigzagging its way around lightning flashes.

At one point, after Martyn had taken over the controls, Hughes woke up from a sleep to find the DC-3's wings shuddering and tilted to the right. Still reclining back on his seat, Hughes calmly talked Martyn through the wind and lightning while monitoring the plane's "penetration speed"—not too fast, not too slow. And they made it safely to Washington.

When Hughes was installed in his Carlton Hotel suite, he got his first look at the secret dossier the FBI had gathered and provided to his nemesis, Senator Brewster. He was dumbfounded. Agents had been shadowing him for four years. Worse, they had been tailing his girlfriends, bugging his hotel suite and his telephones. More audacious still, they had crassly inspected the sheets he had slept in. He would look over his shoulder for the rest of his life.

When Noah Dietrich, who was staying at the Mayfair Hotel across town, arrived to discuss tactics, Hughes greeted him at the door with a finger up to his lips. "We can't talk here," he whispered as he led him into the bathroom and turned on the shower and the faucet as well. "This room's wired. I'm convinced of it."

He was right. On the orders of Pan American Airways, a sophisticated surveillance team had wired the Hughes suite as well as that of Noah Dietrich. Under the direction of Lt. Joseph W. W. Shimon of the Washington, D.C., Police Department, the eavesdroppers lowered tiny mikes from the air ducts and intercepted the phone wires inside the walls. It was a complicated operation that involved renting the adjacent suites and then crawling through the air crawl spaces between floors.

Since Dietrich had checked in at the Mayfair a week earlier, along with Howard's attorney Thomas Slack, Shimon's men had been in the nearby room, taking down verbatim the telephone strategy calls between Dietrich and Slack in Washington and Hughes in Los Angeles. When some of their phrasing showed up in backup materials for the Senate subcommittee, even Noah finally realized "that Hughes wasn't crazy, he was correct." Admitted Noah, "They heard our every word."

To fight back, Howard hired the powerhouse Schindler Detective Agency and sent them to wire Senator Ralph Brewster's room in the Mayflower Hotel, in a hilarious scenario in which Hughes and Dietrich listened in while the Pan American Airways detectives listened to the action in their suites. At one point, when Lt. Shimon overheard Howard and Slack discussing Brewster's private life, he commented, "Brewster will get a kick out of this."

The Schindler Agency performed another task for Howard and Dietrich by eventually removing the bugs from both suites. Therefore, Hughes felt free to host a high-level strategy session with Jack Anderson, the right-hand man to Drew Pearson, the most powerful political columnist in the country.

Pearson dispatched Anderson with the message that Hughes should go on the offensive, making Brewster the target. Pearson relayed another bit of intelligence. "Tell Hughes that Brewster is much closer to Pan Am than anyone could imagine."

At noon on August 6, the day Howard was to appear, he failed to pick up Dietrich at the appointed time. By 12:30, Dietrich was alarmed; Howard was to go on the stand at 1:00 P.M. Calls to the Carlton produced no answer. Dietrich and attorney Slack raced over to the suite. They found

Howard's door locked, and no amount of banging and yelling roused him. "He's sleeping." Dietrich confessed to Slack. "He goes for days and days without sleeping and then takes to his bed for twenty-four hours or so."

They unlocked the door with a duplicate key only to find that the chain lock was on. "Get a coat hanger," Dietrich told Slack. That did it. They broke into the room and shook Howard awake.

"What day is it?" Howard asked sleepily.

"You're on," Slack answered. "Right now."

The "new Hughes" arrived at the senatorial hearing room at 2:42 P.M., ending a waiting game that had lasted more than three weeks.

A crowd of fifteen hundred was packed into a chamber built to handle six hundred, and four hundred more were gathered in the hallway. The onlookers greeted Hughes with a burst of applause, forcing committee chairman Homer Ferguson to turn red and bang his gavel repeatedly for order. "The women spectators sighed over the 41-year-old as if he were the latest dreamboat film star," wrote Stephen White in *Look* magazine.

The first two days Hughes was on the stand, he and Brewster traded charges about Pan Am. By raising the Pan American issue, Hughes turned the spotlight away from himself and onto his senatorial adversary. He was on the stand for four days, in the end successfully defending the XF-11 and the Hercules (Spruce Goose). He was emphatic when he declared, "If the Hercules won't fly, I will leave the United States for good." He was also candid, admitting he had wined and dined the army dignitaries—along with all the other "war barons."

When Senator Ferguson abruptly adjourned the hearings three weeks early, on August 13, it was obvious that Howard had won. He exited the chamber through a curtain of klieg lights and popping flashbulbs. The cheers resounded through the chamber and spread into the hall as Hughes was pushing his way through.

In less than a week, one hundred Hughes for President clubs had formed in the major cities. The Brooklyn branch had more than five hundred members.

It has often been claimed that the specter of these hearings blackened the reputation of Hughes Aircraft in official circles. In truth, just ten days after, and continuing through the fifties, Hughes Aircraft would become the largest supplier of electronic products to the Air Force. When Hughes arrived back in Los Angeles, he stepped out of the DC-3 flushed with victory. He allowed the press to photograph him from every angle, a first for Hughes.

But he had yet to close his book on Washington. He demanded vindication.

In late October 1947, more than one hundred writers and reporters gathered at the Los Angeles Biltmore Hotel, where Howard Hughes was throwing a party. With the Senate hearings behind him, Hughes wanted to tell his side of the story, on his turf.

He had spared no expense. Carl Byoir & Associates, which handled public relations for the Hughes companies, had put together the press list of 115 persons, and Hughes himself came up with an idea for a special gift for each: gold cigarette cases with matching lighters. Account executive Bill Utley was also instructed by Hughes to find out "from each of them what their favorite booze is." Explained Hughes, "I want a case delivered to everybody's home."

But the real payoff for the press came several days later, on the chilly morning of November 2, when they were brought to a press tent on Pier E in Long Beach. Hughes had promised taxi tests of the Spruce Goose.

As the Goodyear blimp hovered overhead, spectators began to line the waterfront. Hundreds of pleasure craft dotted the harbor. The rich and famous clustered in yachts. On one was a cocktail party, thrown by Cary Grant, where the guests included Jean Peters.

Hughes had rented showman Earl Carroll's yacht, *Vanities*, for the press contingent. The deck was clustered with newsreel camera equipment. Though Hughes was insisting this would only be a taxi test and that the real flight would be next spring, there was growing anticipation that something special was going to happen. Reporters aboard *Vanities* were taking bets. Cary Grant later said, "Nobody expected him to fly." In fact, Hughes had told actress Marion Davies he had a standing offer of $1 million to anyone who'd dare to pilot the Hercules.

Now, wearing his familiar fedora, Hughes himself was taking the plane through two test runs across the choppy waters. The Goose performed so well that reporters aboard decided to abandon ship; they took a water taxi to file their stories. This left only one reporter, KLAC radio man Jim McNamara, aboard the plane for the third run. McNamara said later he felt the plane's strength building, and a sense of tension. Other reporters, filing from the deck of the *Vanities*, claimed they heard a mighty roar.

From inside the Goose, McNamara tightly grasped his microphone, telling his listeners, "Mr. Hughes is opening all eight throttles. We're hitting seventy knots . . . eighty knots . . . ninety knots . . ." Then McNamara exclaimed, "My God! We're flying!"

The flight lasted less than a minute. Hughes took the Goose up just seventy feet, for approximately one mile. But when he returned to the dock, he had the look of a victor who had just spanned the globe. Mobbed by reporters who broke out into applause, he grinned broadly. Then, in typical understated Hughes manner, he said, "Well, the airplane seems to be fairly successful."

CHAPTER 21

HOLLYWOOD CONFIDENTIAL

HOLLYWOOD WELCOMED A NEW MOGUL IN MAY 1948 WHEN HOWARD Hughes bought a controlling interest in RKO Pictures. The man who had spent eight years fighting censorship battles involving Jane Russell's breasts was now going to oversee a historic studio with a pedigree that included such titles as *King Kong*, the Astaire–Rogers musicals, *Bringing Up Baby*, and *Citizen Kane*. Ironically, the latter had started out as a project about Hughes.

Rumors had circulated for months about the possibility of a Hughes takeover of RKO, with many Hollywood observers understandably cynical. After all, it had been nearly two decades since Hughes had enjoyed the success of *Scarface* and *The Front Page*.

Bill Feeder, then with the *Hollywood Reporter*, recalled a Sunday afternoon call from Hughes, who demanded that he drive over to his office at the Goldwyn Studio, "for a front-page story." But, protested Feeder, his wife was cooking a pot roast. "Come on over and I'll also give you lunch," Hughes added. So Feeder drove over to the lot in his brand-new Studebaker, which he parked near a battered Chevrolet just outside the stairs leading to Hughes's office. "I thought the thing had been abandoned," sighed Feeder. "It didn't dawn on me, at the time, that it might belong to Hughes, which it did."

Hughes's office had an equally abandoned look, with "hardly any furniture," Feeder recalled. As for Hughes, he sat at his desk, matter-of-factly dictating the RKO news to Feeder. Hughes didn't say a word about his bare feet, and Feeder didn't mention them, either. "I could see the scars on them, from the crash. I figured he was trying to get them to heal," said Feeder.

It was Feeder who finally reminded Hughes that he had promised him lunch. "Dammit, you're right," Hughes said, reaching for the phone. A short while later, an assistant entered, delivering two boxed lunches: chicken sandwiches, cole slaw, apples, and milk in little glass bottles. "Not quite what I'd envisioned when Hughes asked me to lunch," laughed Feeder.

Nothing would be predictable during Hughes's reign at RKO.

"We were all very impressed and very frightened because he had a reputation for being an interferer and a tinkerer," remembered Richard Fleischer, a director under contract at RKO. But the studio's production chief, Dore Schary, a respected screenwriter and producer in his own right, was personally assured by Hughes that there would be no interference. Hughes claimed, "I want no part of running the studio." He lied.

Just days after assuming control of the studio, he sent for Jane Greer, who was under contract to RKO. She had since divorced Rudy Vallee, remarried, and had a child. But Hughes was still interested in her romantically. Recalled Greer, "He as much as said to me, 'You're not happy.' And I said, 'Yes, Howard, I'm very happy.' " He persisted, telling her that "down deep inside" she wasn't happy. When Greer refused to budge on the issue, Hughes retaliated. He told Greer, "Well, as long as I own the studio, you won't work." She continued getting RKO paychecks but no film roles. "And I was stuck dead in my tracks," she recalled.

Studio contractee Barbara Bel Geddes didn't have an opportunity to save her RKO career. After flipping through the file of the talented but rather ordinary-looking actress, Hughes ordered, "Fire her!"

He did, however, reveal a sense of humor when he offered a $300-a-week acting contract to his nemesis, Senator Owen Brewster. "This is twice the usual starting salary, but you are no amateur; your ability as an actor has been well demonstrated," Hughes declared.

When he pulled the plug on the war drama *Battleground*, a pet project of Schary's, the executive decided he'd had enough. "I feared . . . that he wanted a messenger boy, not a studio head," Schary later wrote. Claiming that he didn't want Schary's resignation, Hughes invited him to talk over differences during an afternoon meeting at his house. Actually, it was Cary Grant's house, but Grant was out of town. And from the looks of things, the house was all but abandoned.

As Schary entered, he was startled to find "nothing except two chairs and a sofa" in view. "There wasn't a paper, a cigarette, a flower, a match, a picture, a magazine . . ." he recounted. He did get a brief glimpse of a woman putting on a brassiere when Hughes exited from a room off the living room. The two men went on to talk studio politics, with Hughes letting Schary know that his executives would have to swallow their pride and abide by his instructions.

Hughes never did mention the unnamed woman. But before the two men parted that afternoon, he did compliment Schary on the shoes he was wearing, asking how much they cost and whether they were comfortable.

With Howard Hughes running RKO, the studio's employees found themselves plunged into a kind of netherworld.

William Fadiman met his new boss for the first time at two o'clock one morning. "I was picked up by a car, transferred to a second car, then to a third car, on the theory that no one would really know where he was," recalled Fadiman, who was finally dropped off in front of Hughes's office at Romaine.

"When I walked in he was seated at a very plain desk with nothing on it but a brown bag, which had his dinner or lunch in it. I never knew quite which meal. He always ate that way."

Hughes told Fadiman, who was executive story editor, to cut his staff of 40 by 25 per cent. When Fadiman started to protest, Hughes quickly cut him off. "I know what you're going to tell me," Hughes said. "You're going to tell me, probably, that you know someone who has cancer or someone who just got married or just had a baby, and that you can't do that to those people."

Admitted Fadiman, "Well, yes, I was going to say things like that."

"Don't tell me that, Bill. And I'll tell you why. Learn immediately, Bill. A corporation has no soul. I can't know about those things and be a corporation." With that, Hughes reached into his paper bag and began to pull out a sandwich. Then he looked up at Fadiman and said, "I want a twenty-five per cent reduction. Can you do it?"

"If you insist."

"I insist, Bill."

Fadiman, who begrudgingly cut his staff, would later go on to marvel over the personal generosities of Howard Hughes. "You may or may not know that he helped a great many people, in private. He did so many wonderful things. But he would always remember that he was a businessman first. Then a human being."

Because of his increasingly troubled emotional state, and other business pressures, Hughes was also becoming even more indecisive than usual. When filmmakers couldn't get him to make up his mind about their projects, they took them elsewhere. The RKO production slate shriveled. As a result, so did the studio's number of employees. The summer that Hughes took control, the studio payroll was cut from twenty-five hundred to six hundred. Could it be, asked a *Hollywood Reporter* gossip columnist, that Hughes, "thinks you can operate a studio on instruments like you do a plane?" Actually, his love of aviation did have an impact on RKO. Along with making the John Wayne–Janet Leigh aerial epic, *Jet Pilot*, he purchased a script that he thought was called *Pilot's Wife*. The hard-of-hearing Hughes was not amused to later discover he had actually bought the biblical drama *Pilate's Wife*.

But Hughes wasn't a complete washout as a studio chief. In the case of Robert Mitchum and his marijuana scandal, he stood solidly behind his contract player when others would have bolted. At $3,000 a week, Mitchum, whose contract was co-owned by producer David O. Selznick, was one of the biggest stars at RKO. This after his stint in the army, which followed up his Oscar-nominated performance in *The Story of G.I. Joe*.

But on September 1, 1948, Mitchum, who was known even then for his rebellious ways, was arrested for the possession of marijuana. At the time, a drug bust of any kind was considered serious—and a career killer. When he was booked at the Los Angeles jail and asked his occupation, Mitchum answered, "former actor." There was talk from civic leaders across the country of Hollywood hedonism—and a leading man whose movies should be banned. But Hughes stuck by his star.

When Mitchum was later sentenced to sixty days, Hughes even managed to get smuggled into Wayside Honor Farm, in Castaic, California, where he spent four hours. "I want you to know directly from me that we're going to keep your contract," he told Mitchum.

Mitchum recalled being taken aback by Hughes's earnestness when he asked, "Bob, do you need anything?" Mitchum was frank. He needed $50,000 to pay his attorney's fees and to buy a home for his family.

"Hughes didn't bat an eye," said Mitchum. "He got me the fifty thousand dollars at five per cent interest." Hughes also saw to it that Mitchum got vitamins and chocolate bars.

Always one to take advantage of controversy, Hughes made sure shortly after the arrest that the studio release the Mitchum film *Rachel and the Stranger.* It proved an immediate hit. And when Mitchum was released from the prison farm, Hughes put him to work in the aptly titled *The Big Steal.* But finding an actress to co-star with Mitchum was problematic: the drug bust had made him a pariah within the acting community. So, Hughes put in another call to Jane Greer, who was delighted to learn she was going back to work.

"Any other studio chief would have hung me out to dry," acknowledged Mitchum, who credits Hughes with having saved his career. Mitchum wouldn't always agree with Hughes's decisions. (Hughes nixed Columbia Pictures' request to borrow Mitchum for *From Here to Eternity.*) But he would remain a Hughes loyalist and friend. For those filmmakers and performers too afraid to confront Hughes, Mitchum was also an unofficial liaison.

Actor Jim Backus once surmised that the reserved Hughes lived vicariously through the wild Mitchum. Explained Backus, "Because of who he was, Howard's conquests were unquestionably staggering. But Bob Mitchum would have gone right on being a bum, and beautiful women would still have fallen all over him. And I think Howard was canny enough to realize that."

Mitchum believed the rapport was based on something much more basic: the deaf Howard could communicate with him. "I've got a pretty loud voice, you know. I didn't have to shout or raise my voice with Howard."

It was Mitchum who dubbed Hughes "the Phantom," a nickname that referred to the fact that in all the time he owned the studio, Hughes never publicly set foot on the RKO lot—choosing to operate, instead, from his office at the nearby Goldwyn Studio. But his presence was undeniably felt. Especially where actresses were concerned.

Hughes paramour Faith Domergue began making movies for RKO after the studio purchased her movie *Vendetta*, which Hughes had produced independently. He also ordered operations chief Sid Rogell to hire his sometime girlfriend, "the beautifully stacked" Terry Moore, for the movie *Gambling House.* When Rogell and the filmmakers balked, arguing that Moore, at twenty, was far too young to portray a social worker who reforms a world-weary gangster, played by Victor Mature, thirty-four, Hughes countered, "I don't care. I love the girl."

As the Hughes tenure continued, the RKO lot became increasingly known for its stable of big-breasted starlets, most of whom never achieved recognition—except with Hughes. "Hughes was using RKO as a whore-house," declared Norman Krasna, who was teamed with Jerry Wald in a short-lived production company at the studio. Krasna recalled how production of films would be held up because Hughes wanted better cleavage.

"So he would build up the sets again and put Vaseline between the girl's tits and shoot the scene over. Do you know how much that costs?"

When it came to Hughes's vicissitudes, no one was safe. Jean Simmons awakened one morning in early 1951 to learn her contract with the British-based J. Arthur Rank Organization had been purchased by Hughes. He had been an admirer of the beautiful brunette since her 1949 visit to the United States to promote her movie *The Blue Lagoon*. In fact, during that trip Hughes gave Simmons a party at the Beverly Hills Hotel. "It was lovely. I met all sorts of wonderful movie stars, like Ingrid Bergman, Joan Fontaine, Hoagy Carmichael, Elizabeth Taylor. I was very young and very naive and very impressed, of course." She didn't meet Hughes at the time; he was an invisible host.

So when her contract was purchased by Hughes, Simmons, who had recently garnered acclaim for her Ophelia opposite Laurence Olivier's Hamlet, was suitably anxious. "I had to be driven to the meeting and we had a long talk in a car. Which I thought was very peculiar."

The peculiarities were just beginning. When Simmons starred in RKO's picture *Androcles and the Lion*, Hughes sent the makeup department drawings of how he wanted Simmons's lips to look. "They were very luscious sort of lips, which I kind of resented." Added Simmons, "You can't draw somebody else's mouth on your own mouth." Later, for the psychological drama *Angel Face*, Hughes tried to dictate how she was to wear her hair. Simmons, then twenty-one, reacted by taking scissors and "just whacking off the front of my hair. So they had to cut it very, very short, which is absolutely what he didn't want."

All was not acrimony. After Simmons married dashing actor Stewart Granger, Hughes was a frequent visitor to their cliffside home in Bel Air. "And he would always bring drinks. He loved Mai-Tais, which he'd order from the Beachcomber. He'd have them delivered."

Granger later recalled a social gathering that also included Elizabeth

Taylor and her fiancé, Michael Wilding. Both Taylor and Simmons were busty, "And they're sitting on the couch . . . and Hughes, this very tall Texan, he's sort of trying to look down the front of their dresses." When Granger asked, "Howard, which one would you like?" Hughes replied, "Well . . . I can't make up my mind."

Hughes's control of Simmons's career would ultimately lead to a contractual dispute and wild talk from Granger of a "murder plot." Granger once told an interviewer for the BBC that he planned to mix Hughes a drink, then have him go out on the terrace with Simmons. Then she was to scream and Granger would rush out to defend her honor, toppling Hughes over the cliff in the melee. Nobody would question the incident, claimed Granger, "because Hughes has got a terrible reputation for women."

With a sigh, Granger added, "Thinking back now, it really would have been simpler if I had killed him."

The RKO career of poor Jack Beutel, aka Billy the Kid, exemplifies the general frenzy that marked the Hughes regime. He went a decade without a movie, only to star at last in a string of B titles before slipping into obscurity. Ironically, Howard Hawks originally wanted Beutel for the role that made Montgomery Clift a star in *Red River*. "But Hughes wouldn't let him do it," said Jane Russell. "Jack was crushed."

Jane Russell was luckier. Hughes allowed her to work for other studios, which is how she wound up in film favorites like *The Paleface* opposite Bob Hope and *Gentlemen Prefer Blondes*, in which she teamed with Marilyn Monroe. Russell, like Mitchum, was a Hughes favorite.

She was all the things he liked most in a woman. Big-breasted. Brunette. Gutsy. And not afraid of him. She was also paradoxical.

An outspoken Christian, she once got so tired of a reporter's questions about her religious beliefs that she quipped, "Christians have bosoms, too, you know." While *The Outlaw* was being denounced by censors and religious leaders across the country, Russell prayed to the Lord to help her through the ordeal. This after initially attempting to break away from her Hughes contract. "Howard kept me a prisoner in San Francisco for nine weeks while he tinkered with *The Outlaw*," remembered Russell, who finally decided she'd had enough of waiting. So she signed an agreement promising she wouldn't make movies for anyone else, and bolted, heading for Georgia where she married her football-star sweetheart, Bob Waterfield.

But after Jane's mother lectured her about keeping her word, Jane contacted Hughes saying she would honor her contract "if you still want me." She also quoted Psalms 15, "He that sweareth even to his own hurt and changeth not . . . This man shall never be moved." Years later, when Hughes signed Russell to a headline-making long-term pact, he quoted the verse back to her.

Off-camera, Jane shunned her glamour image for fund-raising. It was Russell who founded the post-World War II organization called WAIF, which allowed Americans to adopt foreign-born children. In fact, she and Waterfield adopted three youngsters.

Despite Hughes's obvious worship of her physical attributes, Russell kept him at a distance. "He wasn't my type," said Russell. "I liked physically big, take-charge kind of men. That wasn't Howard. He was too sweet."

Hughes made his move nonetheless, late in 1948, when Russell's husband was on the road with the Rams. Russell had gone out with Howard, Ava Gardner, Johnny Meyer, and some others for a night of dinner and dancing at the Mocambo. "We closed the place down," Russell recalled.

Afterward, Russell, Ava, and Meyer went over to Howard's for a nightcap. Jane and Johnny sat talking in the living room, while Howard and Ava sat at the bar and bickered loudly. "Oh, my gosh, the language," said Russell. "You've never heard anything like it."

It was a conversation peppered with "you fuckin' this," and "that fuckin' so-and-so," and "that fucker" until Johnny Meyer finally yelled out, "Do you two really need to use that kind of language?"

Soon, light was starting to creep in through the curtains. Howard was going to drive Ava home. Russell was going to go along and stay the night at Ava's. Hughes protested, "You won't get any sleep. You two will talk all night." He talked her into taking the guest room at his place.

She was sound asleep when Meyer came in, "drunk as a skunk," and proceeded to make unwelcome advances. Russell was screaming and throwing things at Meyer when Hughes burst in. He admonished Meyer, who was too loaded to know what was going on, and then escorted Russell to his bedroom—which had a pair of large beds. She would sleep in the one opposite his.

She was asleep for a second time when she awakened to find Hughes standing beside her bed. He complained that he was "freezing," that he'd caught a chill driving Ava home. "Can I get in with you?" She reached out and felt his hand. It was "like an ice cube." Okay, said Russell, "but no funny business."

After a while, Hughes reached his hand out and carefully slid it around Russell's waist.

"All right, that's it! Get out, Howard!"

He was peeved. "I'll go. But let me get out when I decide."

Despite all Hughes put Russell through professionally, she was an amazingly good sport.

Consider the movie *Macao*. Set in "the Monte Carlo of the Orient," *Macao* teamed Russell and Mitchum in a tale of waterfront intrigue. But the real star of the picture was Russell's bosom. Writing in the *New York Times*, Bosley Crowther noted, "It is remarkable how often Miss Russell, in an assortment of low-cut sweaters and gowns, is directed to lean toward the camera." It was no coincidence. Wherever possible, Hughes had dictated, he wanted her wearing clothes that were low-necked, "and by that I mean as low as the law allows." Hughes labored over how Russell's breasts should be depicted in *Macao*. In a single-spaced, four-page memo he addressed everything from the contour of her breasts to a potential dilemma involving a dress she was to wear in which, he feared, it might result in a look of "multiple nipples." The dress was made of a fabric with tiny raised bumps.

With *His Kind of Woman*, another Russell–Mitchum entry, Hughes tampered with everything: plot, settings, lines (Hughes himself wrote new dialogue for one of the villains), and even casting. The filming ran so long that co-star Vincent Price threw a party on the set to mark the first year of shooting.

With its strategically placed 3-D cameras, *The French Line*, which featured Russell in skimpy costumes, including a then-startling bikini, and an ad campaign that promised, "It'll knock *both* your eyes out," led to yet another showdown between Hughes and the censors. Once again Hughes refused to make changes. He opened the movie in December 1952, in St. Louis, without benefit of a Seal of Approval. Days before the film's premiere, the city's 473,000 Catholics were warned they faced the "penalty of mortal sin" if they attended.

About the romantic adventures of a Texas millionairess who sets sail for Paris on the liner *Liberté*, *The French Line* opened to SRO audiences; sixty thousand tickets were sold in the first five days. Associated Press reported that opening night "went off without a hitch . . . Although three members of the police morality squad were in the audience."

There was a hitch involving Russell, though. She was originally going to attend the premiere, but when she learned Hughes was releasing the movie without a Seal of Approval, she jumped into the fray, telling Associated Press reporter Bob Thomas that she disapproved of Hughes's decision. As Russell explained, "I've been years shaking off the bad publicity on *The Outlaw*, and I decided this time I wasn't going to keep quiet."

She also let it be known that her costumes in *The French Line* were modest compared to what she was originally handed. "You should have seen what he tried to stick me with at first, a jeweled G-string. I was so upset I was off the picture for a whole week, arguing over it."

Hughes was unshaken by his leading lady's stance. Reached in Las Vegas, he mused, "You never know what she's going to say." But he was upset when theaters wound up balking over showing the movie sans seal. He ultimately bowed to the censors, making minor changes. "After our battle over the bikini costume, Howard promised me I would never have to appear in another picture that didn't obtain the Seal of Approval," said Jane. But after making this promise, Hughes added, with a wink, "If you ever tell anyone of this promise I will deny it." Then he offered another perk: director approval from that time forward.

Like *The French Line*, the Russell movie *Underwater* also racked up mountainous press, this time for the publicity junket concocted by RKO publicist Perry Lieber and his staff including Edith "Edie" Lynch who recalled, "Hughes absolutely loved it." Groaned Russell, "It was stupid."

To promote the 1954 title RKO transported two hundred journalists "and screen personalities," via TWA Constellation flights, to Silver Springs, Florida. There the press was wined and dined and outfitted in bathing suits, fins, and Aqua-Lungs. Then they were taken twenty-five feet beneath the surface of a small lake. "We literally had underwater seats and a projection room down there," said Lynch. There they saw *Underwater*, with Russell as a Cuban treasure hunter. Or at least they tried to. Several journalists kept bobbing to the surface.

Along with the waterlogged screening, there were photo opportunities with the movie's stars, including Russell, as well as starlets who happened to be on hand, like Debbie Reynolds. The press also got to meet a platinum blonde "unknown," named Jayne Mansfield, who strode into view wearing a bikini. Waxed *Variety*, "How she got on the junket from L.A. nobody knows, but she proved worth her weight in cheesecake."

CHAPTER 22

SEPTEMBER SONG

HOWARD TOOK JEAN PETERS BY THE HAND AND LED HER ACROSS THE SAND dunes and into the still midnight of the California desert, stretching endlessly in every direction. With the wind whistling around them and the lights of Palm Springs at their backs, Howard and Jean quietly talked about their dreams and their troubles.

He rambled on somewhat guiltily about the burdens of wealth and "of doing something really important with it," and she talked about the difficulties of finding her way through the unreality, shallowness, and envy that saturated her life as a movie star.

This 24-year-old had accomplished in two years what two decades of supercharged lovers had failed to do. She had transformed Hughes, forty-three, into a romantic.

Most of Hollywood wondered what Jean had that all the other glamour girls lacked.

For Noah Dietrich, it was simple: "She was the first one who wasn't interested in him for his stature, his money, and his fame. She saw him as an average man, an average man she fell in love with. It was as if all that other never existed." Added Dietrich, "But I also feel that his confrontation with death after the XF-11 made him take stock of his life. And when he did, he was amazed by its emptiness."

On that walk in Palm Springs, when Hughes offered a magnificent engagement ring, he also analyzed his own life. "I feel that it's immoral for one person to have such a huge amount of money," he told her. "I find it ironic that fate endowed me with this fortune when I would rather have spent my life working in a shop, inventing and testing airplanes."

Jean tried to point out his accomplishments: the world flight, Hughes Aircraft, the government work. "But he was very critical of himself for having permitted worries, commitments, properties, and deep business involvement to happen," Peters recalled. "He told me his goal was to straighten his life out, set up a medical institute, and to return to aviation."

Shortly after Hughes and Peters returned to Los Angeles, columnists began pressing her to name a wedding date. The ubiquitous Louella Parsons cornered her one afternoon at Fox: "When are you going to marry Howard Hughes?" she asked.

Jean replied nonchalantly, "Louella, I'm not one to kick fate in the teeth. I have elected to be an actress, and I don't think I could be married and do both things well." Then Jean added, "But I do think he's wonderful."

That's the story Louella printed. But she knew that Jean and Howard had been living together since late 1947. Howard rented a house for Jean and her family on Veteran Avenue in Westwood, while he also maintained two bungalows at the Beverly Hills Hotel and kept two adjoining apartments in the Los Angeles Town House. There was also an apartment at 10000 Sunset Boulevard, a hideaway in the San Fernando Valley, the rented villa in Palm Springs, and a small house in Las Vegas.

Howard, along with Jean, Jean's maid, and Hughes's chauffeur, trekked from one location to the other, like a king on a royal progress, toting linens, clothes, Hughes's special amplified telephones, and a towering load of Kleenex crates. "I never saw that man without a Kleenex in his hand," recalled the maid, Macy Todd. "He could walk through every room and there would be a box of Kleenex. He used them instead of towels, to answer the telephone, to open doorknobs, even to pick up a newspaper or a magazine. He fitted them onto his hands like gloves so that he never had to touch the magazine itself."

In 1948 Howard wrote the first of his many Kleenex directives to his aides, maids, and chefs—a tissue tort that ran almost one thousand words long and described how the Kleenex is to be employed in the bathroom:

First use six or eight thicknesses of Kleenex pulled one at a time from
the slot in the box . . . then fit them over the door knob and open the

bathroom. Please leave the bathroom door open so there will be no need to touch anything when leaving. This same sheaf of Kleenex may be employed to turn the spigots so as to obtain a good force of water.

A particularly amusing segment of the same memo detailed the Kleenex protocol when aides escorted Jean Peters to screenings on the Goldwyn lot.

When escorting Jean Peters to the movies, if it is necessary to open the doors entering the theater, do so with the feet and not the hands. If you need to lower the seat for her, do so with Kleenex.

The Veteran Avenue house, Cary Grant's house and the Beverly Hills bungalow were all equipped with special toilets and bathtubs to accommodate Howard's height, and with giant, made-to-order beds. "The sheets were so mammoth that it was impossible for one person to change them," Macy Todd recalled. Special triple-thick "blackout" curtains were installed as well, to allow Howard to sleep whenever he desired, usually from about 3:00 A.M. until the early afternoon.

Except for the two or three evenings a week Howard spent with Jean, Hughes continued his normal pattern; working from early afternoon until about 9:00 P.M. and then visiting one, sometimes two, ladies during the evening. It would be years to come before Peters realized the extent of Howard's womanizing, which is why he encouraged her to remain at Fox, which was building her into a major star. While Jean was teaching Howard how to call time-out and enjoy each day, he used those lessons to great effect with his continuing parade of lovers, including MGM dancing star Cyd Charisse, MGM soprano superstar Kathryn Grayson, and young starlet Terry Moore.

Raven-haired Charisse was, ironically, introduced to the millionaire by one of her own beaux, singer Tony Martin. Hughes intuitively understood that Charisse cared very little about the café circuit. So he wooed her with simple, elegant dinners and midnight drives through Malibu or up the mountain to Mulholland Drive, where the lights of Hollywood spread into the distance. Often Hughes brought ham-and-cheese sandwiches along with chilled bottles of milk, an argyle blanket, and candles to brighten the darkness.

Hughes also brought Charisse into his most secret world, the laboratories and designing studios at Hughes Aircraft. Years later, guards recalled

Hughes, in his chinos, white shirt, and fedora, and Charisse with a black lace gown from an MGM movie, strolling in the darkness hand in hand. They even toured the enormous Spruce Goose and sat in its cavern, which could accommodate seven hundred, and talked far into the night.

The day Charisse broke her leg during a studio rehearsal, Hughes reached her via phone even before MGM president Louis B. Mayer. "I don't know how he found out about it, but he did and offered his help instantly," Charisse related.

When it was safe to move the dancer, Hughes began arriving every afternoon. "He would bundle me up and carry me out to his car, not his usual car, but a limousine to accommodate my injured leg." Howard offered her an airplane and emerald earrings. "But I turned them down," she recalled. "It was my Amarillo morality kicking in."

Soon pitched battles erupted between Howard and Tony Martin, both of them exuding charm but only one of them, Martin, offering marriage. "When I tried to see her on a weekend, I'd find out that Hughes had swept her up to San Francisco for lunch and on to Las Vegas for dinner and a show," Martin wrote in his memoirs.

One morning Tony found a fat envelope shoved under his apartment door. "It contained two round-trip, first-class tickets on TWA for anywhere in the world," Martin said. "I believe he thought I would pick up some dolly and go scooting all around the world and thereby eliminate me from the Charisse chase." It was Martin who won the race to the altar, in a marriage that has lasted until the present day. Howard meanwhile was exhausted by the rigors of balancing the intense demands of the two young women he had promised to marry, Jean Peters and starlet Terry Moore.

His relationship with Terry was the antithesis of the quiet, mature life he lived with Peters. Three years younger than Jean, she blew into Howard's world like Tinker Bell, and yanked this "old man" (which was the way Terry's mother viewed him) out of his reclusive tendencies. With her childlike valentines, her lengthy teen-talk conversations, she coaxed him into the hip postwar universe.

Howard had spotted Moore four years earlier, at fifteen, wearing a bathing suit, in an issue of *Look* magazine. "Get her over to RKO," Hughes told Johnny Maschio, who was acting as a casting agent for the studio. "I'll meet her at the studio." Terry's mother, Louella Koford, wary of Hughes's reputation, refused and insisted instead that they meet in the well-lit, overcrowded Brown Derby.

Moore had already received a better offer from 20th Century-Fox. But Hughes began courting her assiduously. "Less than a week later, Howard invited me to go to the Racquet Club," recalled Maschio. "Terry was along, and it became a big romance, real quick."

So quick, in fact, that they were spending every other weekend together, either in Palm Springs or on the magnificent *Southern Cross*.

Hughes, pleading urgent business in Washington, left Jean Peters stranded in Westwood with her sewing machine and geranium garden. Since he used the enormous switchboard at Romaine, it was impossible to know the origin of Howard's calls. He telephoned Jean every evening no matter where he was in the United States.

Despite the cruises and the resort bungalow nights, Terry refused to sleep with Hughes until they were married. But he was determined to find a way through this virginal barrier. One night he got dressed up and even borrowed one of the sleek cars belonging to Hughes Aircraft. He presented her with a corsage when he picked her up.

They then drove to one of the lovers' points on Mulholland Drive, which meanders atop the foothills above Bel Air, Beverly Hills, and Hollywood. Hughes stopped just above Beverly Hills. With Moore standing beside him, he gestured broadly. "Terry Moore, under the moon and stars, I, Howard Hughes take you for my wife." Then he placed a ruby and diamond ring on her finger.

As they headed down one of the swirling streets toward the Beverly Hills Hotel, Terry asked, "Where are you taking me?"

"Home to the bungalow at the Beverly Hills Hotel. We're legally married now."

"Turn this car around, Howard. We may be married spiritually, but we sure aren't married legally. So take me home to Glendale."

Several weeks later, in November 1949, Howard took Moore and her mother to the *Southern Cross* for a cruise down the California coast, and from there to the waters off Baja California. While they were anchored out in international waters, Hughes whipped out what appeared to be a bona fide marriage license. "We can get married out here in international waters," Hughes told Moore and her mother. "That way we can avoid the publicity which could ruin your career."

An hour later, the two appeared on the upper deck of the *Southern Cross*, where they were joined by Captain Carl Flynn, a Scotsman Hughes had inherited when he purchased the yacht. "I possess the authority to marry you and the boss," intoned Captain Flynn, who went on to "join" the couple in "holy matrimony." Both Terry and her mother bought this line.

This "wedding," and the question of its legality, became the most contentious claim in a flurry of claims in the battle for Howard's estate after his death in 1976. And though Moore received a settlement, most of the twenty attorneys involved in the postmortem warfare privately declared that the event never happened. Of the aides, attorneys, and even other women who knew Hughes, few believe the ceremony took place though nearly all admit that Hughes and Moore were very close.

Dr. Raymond Fowler, who conducted the psychological autopsy on Hughes, believes the ceremony did occur but "it simply wasn't legal." As Fowler noted, "Hughes promised marriage to a long list of women to get them to sleep with him. And, in this case, he staged an actual marriage ceremony to convince her." Further evidence comes from James Wadsworth, one of Howard's attorneys at the time. He noted that on certain occasions, as when checking into motels, Hughes would introduce Terry as his wife.

"It's clear that Moore believed they were married and that some sort of ceremony took place on that yacht," said Suzanne Finstad, one of the lawyers involved in the battle for the Hughes empire. "In Terry's mind a legitimate wedding took place."

Moore finally slept with Hughes the night of the "ceremony." Years later she described him as a "generous, gentle lover." As Moore once told New York columnist Earl Wilson, "I had a lot of loving, but not a lot of lovers. And Howard was the best. He was gentle and kind."

Terry made Howard feel young again, sending him sweet cards every day and talking baby talk during their daily phone conversations, which went on for hours. When Moore was on location in Germany, Howard's Romaine headquarters logged more than five hundred calls to and from the lovers, at all hours of the day and night.

Often, these calls would begin and end with Hughes and Moore imitating alligator love calls. Howard performed the courting sounds of the male gator, deep and guttural, and she responded with the softer hoot and clicking sound of the female. This swamp-style billing and cooing often ended with the two of them laughing uproariously.

During the months that followed, Terry began recording her conversations with her "husband." "I intended to use them to get rid of Jean Peters," Moore admitted to lawyers involved in the estate battle. "I knew he was having a relationship with Jean and lots of other women, but Jean was the only one that disturbed me. The others were fly-by-night and would soon disappear." These conversations, which were submitted to Houston Superior Court during the estate battle, are remarkable because of what they reveal about Howard's attraction to Terry Moore. They illuminate an endearing side to a man widely perceived as distant and humorless.

One of the tapes was made after Moore had married West Point gridiron great Glenn Davis. Hughes seems to be trying to talk her out of her current relationship and back into his arms. "Why don't you decide you need somebody to take care of you?" he said soothingly. "And why don't you let me have the job?"

"Oh, Howard," Terry answered, "you want it? You mean that, don't you? "

"Yes."

"Oh, I love you, you can have the job. And you can have it real soon if we get this annulment," Terry replied, apparently referring to her legal battle to end her then-stormy marriage. Minutes later, Terry pouted and asked Hughes to curtail his workload so that he could spend more time with her. "What would happen if you left your work alone?" she asked.

"Well, that would be a dereliction of duty and I just cannot do it. I've got sixty thousand stockholders. I'd wind up with a stockholders' suit that would have me in court for five years."

In one exchange, Terry pleads: "Hey, Howard, I can have an engagement ring, can't I?"

"Oh, I don't think so . . . that would be in very poor taste."

But, Terry protested, "Who's going to know except you and me?"

"You can't keep a thing like that a secret."

"Please let me have the ring. I'll put it away in a box."

Howard, obviously exasperated, spoke like a father. "Baby, don't you know that once an engagement ring is put on, it should never be taken off?"

As their relationship continued, Hughes grew sensitive to the age difference between them. When Hughes was forty-four, he actually looked ten or fifteen years older. Terry, who was then twenty, looked far younger. At a big Hollywood party one evening, the actor Mike Connors came over to the Hughes table and shook Howard's hand. "May I dance with your daughter?" he said. Howard pretended not to hear. "I promise I'll bring her directly back to the table." Howard shook his head no and was in a fury for the rest of the evening.

While Terry was in Florida making *Beneath the Twelve Mile Reef*, gossip columnists stumbled all over themselves trying to cook up a love affair between Terry and her handsome leading man, Robert Wagner. Hughes and his longtime friend and business associate Walter Kane were listening to Louella Parsons on the radio one evening when she declared that "wedding bells might ring for Terry and Bob once the picture is completed." Several minutes later, the Associated Press announced that Wagner and Moore were already engaged.

Hughes turned to Kane and smiled. "Well, that lets me off the hook, doesn't it?"

Terry called shortly after, promising Hughes "that it was just a publicity scheme cooked up by the studios." Then she begged him to join her in Florida. "It's beautiful here," she said. "You'll love it."

"Absolutely not," Hughes shouted. "If I came down there, people would say, 'There's this rich old fellow coming down here and breaking up a romance between these young people.' " Still, after Terry's return, the rich old fellow continued to date his nymphet and to sleep with her off and on at the Beverly Hills Hotel.

According to Moore, their relationship led to a pregnancy—and the birth of a daughter who survived only twelve hours. Moore said she delivered the child in the early fifties in Germany during the location filming of *Man on a Tightrope*, in which she co-starred with Fredric March and Gloria Grahame. No medical records exist to back up this allegation, but the son of Hughes's physician has recalled a medical trip his father made to Germany, on behalf of Moore, during that period. Dr. Verne Mason, Jr., said his father "had seen and taken care of Terry . . . She had a very serious infection and damn near died from it. Those were essentially his words."

Not all girls were easily impressed by Hughes. For instance, though he used every trick in his book to woo MGM star Janet Leigh, she was singularly unimpressed.

A discovery of thirties star Norma Shearer, Leigh was given a PR buildup that heralded her for having "the most exquisite face in pictures." She also had an exquisite figure—something else Hughes couldn't resist. She possessed as well an engaging, bouncy charm. All of this was put to effective use in a series of romantic comedies.

Twice married by the time she came to Hollywood, Leigh was wary of the much older Hughes—and his intentions. During meetings with him, she liked to inform him that her father was outside, waiting for her in the car. "I always let him know Daddy was there," she remembered.

Her first date with Hughes took place, much against her wishes, when her agent, Richard Ingersoll, suggested she have lunch with Hughes. "Just this one time. I promise you'll like him."

Leigh doubted it. "He was the same age as my father," she recalled. "I just didn't find him romantic in the least. But I agreed to go. We were to drive down to Balboa Island, but we headed in the wrong direction and ended up in Culver City."

Ingersoll explained, "Howard felt it would be more convenient to fly instead of the long drive in traffic."

One thing led to another, and Janet found herself in a plane that would ultimately land near the Grand Canyon. When she saw a limousine waiting for them, she realized this odyssey had been planned for in advance. "I guess he expected me to be so dazzled that I would just pass it off lightly. Well, they had the wrong girl this time. I felt manipulated, angry, and not just a little scared."

Leigh was relieved when they took off for home. "When I saw the lights of Los Angeles in the distance, I started to relax. But the closer we got, the less it looked like L.A. And, no wonder, because we touched down at Las Vegas, for dinner!" Leigh remembered feeling out of place, in her shorts and casual blouse, which would have looked perfect during an afternoon in Balboa, as she walked among the dressy crowds in the casino.

After a somber dinner in Vegas, Howard finally took Leigh home. "My prayer was answered. We actually landed at Culver City, *California!*"

Still, Hughes went on to lure her to one rendezvous or another and arranged to be conveniently near her at dinner parties and receptions. Leigh finally had enough. She confronted Hughes during one of these pre-arranged meetings. "Aren't you man enough to ask me for a date? You always arrange to be at a dinner I go to, or the party. But why don't you come out and ask me like a normal person?"

Hughes paused, and then said quietly, "All right, will you have dinner with me?"

"No, never!" Leigh replied.

She instantly regretted the tone of her answer. "I saw both fear and rejection in his eyes; it was terribly crushing." So, Janet added, " 'Sure, we'll go to dinner with my mother and father.' And we did. I have to admit he was charming to both of them." But the night out led nowhere as far as Leigh was concerned.

Still Hughes persisted. He had a plan, apparently believing repeated meetings would win her over. Using his strong contacts at MGM, he borrowed her for three films at RKO.

The first of these was *Holiday Affair*, a rather sweet Christmas picture in which she starred opposite Robert Mitchum. Shooting came and went without a hitch. *Jet Pilot* was another, more convoluted story. Billed as "the thundering story of a man . . . a jet . . . and a woman he couldn't forget!" it began filming in 1949. Scenes were still being filmed in 1951. Because of Hughes's indecisiveness, he couldn't stop tinkering with the aviation sequences. By the time *Jet Pilot* was released in 1957, the jet scenes looked outdated. As did Leigh and John Wayne, in the story of a female Russian jet pilot who strays into American territory and catches the heart of a gruff colonel.

Leigh's final film for RKO was *Two Tickets to Broadway*. A throwback to MGM-type musicals about "kids" trying to break into the business (which, in this case, turned out to be television), it represented Hughes at his most scheming. Rehearsals went on for months at RKO sound stages, with Leigh being coached by the best, Marge and Gower Champion. But there were no director and no co-stars. After a while Leigh began to suspect that Hughes was using the movie to get close to her. Her suspicions were confirmed during a weekend yachting party with the Champions, at which Hughes suddenly showed up. He kept eyeing Leigh, but she had brought along a date, her *Two Tickets* rehearsal dance partner, Robert Scheerer.

When Scheerer continued to date Leigh as rehearsals droned on, he was visited by "a Hughes minion," who told him to leave Janet alone. When Scheerer refused, Hughes had him taken off the picture. "I guess he thought I was getting in his way . . . I was young enough and headstrong enough that I couldn't care less about him," remembered Scheerer.

Tony Martin, meanwhile, had finally come aboard as Leigh's leading man. But as the film's production schedule dragged on, spanning nearly two years, Martin told Hughes, "My fans are going to forget who I am."

Two Tickets was released at last in late 1951. After the experience at RKO, Leigh never again spoke to Hughes.

His obsession with the resistant Janet Leigh ushered in a new era for Howard. Beautiful women had always been his weakness. But now when he wanted a woman, he was ruthless in pursuit. All methods, no matter how low, were excused. And to wage this warfare, he needed help.

CHAPTER 23

SECRET POLICE

ONE MORNING IN 1947 AVA GARDNER WAS AWAKENED FROM A DEEP SLEEP by the shrill rings of her phone. It was 3:00 A.M. It could be only one person. Picking up the receiver, she said huskily, "Hello, Hughes."

"So Artie Shaw has left you," he said smugly. Gardner sat up in bed. Shaw had only told her that afternoon, and she'd only made one call about it, to her sister Bappie.

Howard continued: "When's he gonna marry that author, Kathleen Winsor [*Forever Amber*]?"

"Bastard!" said Ava as she slammed down the receiver.

Just on a hunch she edged over to the window and pulled aside the curtains. As she suspected, there was a car parked just down the block with one man in the front and another in the back. "Howard could be a cruel and ruthless man," Ava remembered. "With his own security and spy system, he knew about my breakup with Artie the day it happened."

Not long after, Hughes summoned Jane Greer, who was under contract to RKO, into his presence. "You're knocked up, Bettejane," said Hughes, who never used her stage name.

"What?" she said, unnerved.

"You're pregnant. You tested positive."

Greer was amazed. "He knew before I did."

There wasn't much she could do about it; Howard was still upset over her second marriage, to entertainment attorney William Lasker. "Who was powerful enough to stop him?" she asked years later.

While Jane Greer and Ava Gardner were merely angry, Janet Leigh was shaken. "One morning when I was completing a picture for Hughes at RKO, he summoned me to his office and handed me a sheaf of papers." Glancing over the thick bundle, she was astonished to find a minute-by-minute account of her movements and conversations for the past two weeks.

Another bulging dossier included condensations of Janet's telephone conversations for a six-month stretch including the full texts of recipes, details on a dress Leigh was having made, and a verbatim version of gossipy girl talk concerning Elizabeth Taylor's love life. Conversations between Leigh and her mother, however, were merely logged, without analysis.

"I was so stupefied I couldn't speak," Leigh recalled. "Howard had hired detectives to follow me. Why? What did it all mean? And I was frightened. Was there a veiled threat to all this craziness?" When she reported this to her home studio, the brass at MGM shrugged it aside. It was merely Hughes being Hughes. After all, at that moment he was running investigations on Cyd Charisse, Kathryn Grayson, and Elizabeth Taylor.

In the fifties, Howard continued building his corps of secret police to include bugging experts and legmen to keep an eye on his friends, his enemies, and his employees, as well as his lovers or any beautiful woman who captured his attention. The fifties was the decade of the spy, an era in which the Central Intelligence Agency rose to its power and in which spies were the ultimate heroes at the movies or on television.

Howard's own infatuation with spy tactics had begun during his battle with the Senate in the forties, and he would remain an information junkie until his final days. His agents and electronic listening devices fed him a continuous glut of information, all filtered through the sinister-looking headquarters at 7000 Romaine.

This private army of detectives had another, more practical mission as well: to seal him off from the waves of process servers that were endemic to a man of his position. The sole purpose of this guerrilla band was to protect him from the world, even if it meant hiring, coaching, and launching lookalikes and setting up dummy residences and apartments as costly decoys. The sudden growth of his empire, which now stretched to every corner of the globe, and his love for Jean Peters, who refused to sanction his dalliances, made security a priority for Hughes.

So Howard fused his professional security force and his private body-guards into one massive force. As chief of security, he hired Jeff Chouinard, who had once worked for private eye Frank Angell. Hughes provided the dashing ex-fighter pilot with $2 million a year, a fleet of cars and trucks, and a generous expense account to purchase state-of-the-art eavesdropping devices.

By 1952, Chouinard presided over a private army of detectives and guards who were augmented by 50 drivers, many of them college students. Between 1950 and 1954, the homegrown CIA compiled case histories of more than one hundred women, including Gina Lollobrigida, Susan Hayward, Elizabeth Taylor, Mitzi Gaynor, Barbara Payton, and the French ballet star Zizi Jeanmaire.

Chouinard also assembled a bugging team to install microphones in most of the homes and apartments used by Hughes's growing club of lovers, allowing him to read a running account of each woman's day. Another daily bulletin recounted the gist of each telephone conversation.

Chouinard's most frequently used tool was a bugging radio, usually installed in bedrooms so that Hughes, if he wished, could tell when his girlfriends went to bed and could calculate their "sleep time." Howard liked to offer fatherly lectures to his girlfriends about the need to get enough sleep. Infrequently, the bugs picked up the sound of lovemaking between the ladies and boyfriends they snuck into their apartments and hotel rooms.

One of Jeff's bugs picked up the grunts and groans of a Hughes driver making love to one of the women he was hired to chauffeur around. Another surveillance discovered that a particularly handsome young driver, a former college football player, was sleeping with statuesque Swedish actress Anita Ekberg.

Occasionally, physical surveillance was used to augment the mikes and telephone taps. Chouinard and his men donned telephone repair garb and climbed the power poles to obtain birds-eye views inside the apartments and houses and frequently discovered secret lovers who lived in the same building or who had used rear entrances or the back alleys.

Once, when Howard was watching over a very young Elizabeth Taylor as a favor to her parents, he sent his old friend Pat De Cicco to escort the star to dinner and a movie. As backup, Chouinard stationed a detective high up on the power pole behind her Sunset Boulevard flat. The man shimmied up on the pole, where he stayed for more than ninety minutes while Taylor and De Cicco had a nightcap and listened to the radio. Then the apartment was suddenly plunged into darkness.

With a pair of detectives covering the front and rear, and a shivering agent clinging to the light pole until dawn, they were able to report that De Cicco didn't leave Elizabeth's side until seven in the morning. Hughes raged, "God damn that bastard!" when he received the dossier during breakfast. "That's the last time I give such an important job to a friend."

Hughes often sent Chouinard off to conduct totally nonsensical operations. In 1950, for instance, he became maniacal over Terry Moore's fondness for sweets, particularly her addiction to hot fudge sundaes, with nuts, whipped cream, and "three extra maraschino cherries." Forgetting that she was still a teenager, Howard logged her consumption of ice cream, cookies, and another favorite, salted peanuts. He presented these statistics to Moore with the admonishment, "This will ruin your figure and your career."

Cleverly, Ava Gardner often used the team of operatives to satisfy her slightest whims. One cold winter evening, she walked out to Howard's spymobile and tapped on the driver's window. "I feel like a bowl of pistachio ice cream," she said. Without a word the detective raced off into the night to fulfill her sudden craving and searched for two hours before producing a carton.

Ava's publicist, David Hanna, was with her when she received the carton and casually tossed it into her freezer. "Ava, what was that all about?" he asked.

"I don't even like pistachio. Every once in a while I do something like this. It makes their life more interesting. And that's what they're here for."

Hughes's police squad was so thorough he knew the precise minute one of his paramours initiated a new love affair. When Hughes learned that Ava Gardner had started sleeping with Howard Duff, he used the discovery to his advantage. Several days earlier, Gardner had telephoned Hughes asking for the return of a gray Mercedes he had given her two years earlier. When she married Artie Shaw she had given it back. "It's been here so long," said Hughes, "that I thought it was mine."

"Well, it isn't," Ava answered. "I'm coming over to get it."

Then came Ava's "infidelity dossier" and Howard's revenge. With the aid of two Hughes Aircraft engineers, Howard cleverly loosened all the major components of the Mercedes.

After Gardner came over to pick up the car, he watched in amusement as Gardner, with Howard Duff following her in another automobile, headed down the twisting road leading from his estate. Gardner had driven several blocks when the car began to self-destruct. As metal parts rolled down the hill, Ava and Duff stopped and ran after them.

"You bastard!" Gardner screamed later on the phone. "Why did you do that?"

"Why did you jilt me for Howard Duff?" Howard answered just before he slammed down the receiver.

On New Year's Eve, 1951, Howard's old buddy William Randolph Hearst, Jr., realized how bad things had gotten. He flew into town and invited Hughes to a party at Mike Romanoff's restaurant. "Wait a second," Hughes said. "This telephone isn't safe. I'll call you back in a couple of minutes."

About five minutes later Howard rang through. In a hushed voice he said, "I'll meet you about nine o'clock tonight. Get your car and park in front of the hotel. I will come by driving a dark Chevrolet. I'll flick my lights twice. If you see me, then flick your headlights once. I will keep going, but you stay where you are." He continued: "I will drive around the block once or twice to make sure nobody is following me. I will pass again but this time follow me. I will park a few blocks down and you wait behind me. I will get out of my car and dash into yours. But the minute I slip inside, drive off so that nobody will see us."

"What the hell is going on, Howard?" Hearst asked. Hughes didn't understand the question and repeated the instructions all over again. "That was my first inkling of Hughes's deterioration," Hearst recalled. "Howard began imagining dangers everywhere."

He was especially frightened about the dangers he couldn't see: the billions of germs that were "ready to attack . . . at any time."

"Germs are death, Noah!" he shouted one evening. "I want to live longer than my parents, who were killed by germs when they were still relatively young. I do not intend to let this happen to me."

Hughes went so far as to form a battle plan to insure a "germ-free environment." Some of his directives on the subject ran to ten thousand words or longer. For instance, one Hughes memorandum cautioned the aides against contaminating his supplies, which were kept in his various Beverly Hills Hotel bungalows.

It is extremely important to me that nobody ever goes into any room, closet, cabinet, drawer, bathroom or any other area used to store any of the things which are for me—either food, equipment, magazines, paper supplies, Kleenex—no matter what. It is equally important to me that nobody ever opens any door or opening to any room, cabinet or closet or anything used to store any of my things, even for one-thousandth of an inch, for one-thousandth of a second. I don't want the possibility of dust or insects or anything of that nature entering.

The nine-step program for opening a can of peaches, without drenching them with germs, filled three single-spaced pages and is equally specific, and includes the admonition:

Be sure that no part of the body, including the hands, be directly over the can or the plate at any time. If possible, keep the head, upper part of the body, arms, etc. at least one foot away from the can of fruit and the sterile plate at all times. During the procedure, there must be absolutely no talking, coughing, clearing of the throat, or any movement whatsoever of the lips.

In Howard's "Operating Manual for Taking Clothes to HRH," he wanted to be sure that nobody else's germs "somehow leaped onto my clean clothing." An excerpt:

He wants you to obtain a brand new knife, never used, to open a new box of Kleenex using the knife to open the slot.

After the box is open you are to take the little tag and the first piece of Kleenex and destroy them; then using two fingers of the left hand and two fingers of the right hand take each piece of Kleenex out of the box and place it on an opened newspaper and repeat this until approximately 50 sheets are neatly stacked.

You then have a paddle for one hand. You are then to make another for the other hand, making a total of two paddles of Kleenex to use in handling these three boxes.

Mr. Hughes wanted you to remember to keep your head at a 45-degree angle from the various things you would touch, such as the Kleenex box itself, the knife, the Kleenex paddles.

The thing to be careful of during the operation is not to breathe upon the various items.

Howard initiated these precautions so that "the killer bacteria" would not reach him on a slip of paper, a telephone receiver, or from the "aura of germs" that surrounds each person "like a poison capsule." He quit talking to many of his friends and business associates because he felt that bacteria might be transmittable via telephone lines.

He was even terrified of "tiny organisms" that might conceivably be passed on by his agents out in the field. To prevent this, all employees working at the Romaine headquarters had to wear white cotton gloves to type and process the memos and logs that were forwarded to him at the Beverly Hills Hotel. These cotton gloves were changed twice a day. Discards were burned in Romaine's basement incinerator. Jeff Chouinard started to collect checks to pay for his "secret police" by appearing outside of Romaine at an appointed time. A second-storey window would open, "just a very small crack." Then a deep-sea-fishing line was lowered down. "I would attach my statements to the fish hooks which they reeled up into the business office."

Since Howard only authorized the use of the fish hooks to "receive memos and statements," the checks themselves would be thrown out the window. "If it was a windy day, I'd be chasing money down the street," Chouinard recalled.

Eventually, Hughes's surveillance reports and transcripts of phone conversations filled an entire room at the Romaine headquarters, which had been transformed into a massive listening post and nerve center, the conduit for all Howard's personal and professional contacts. To reach him one first had to call OL-4-2500, the number of the hotel-size switchboard at Romaine.

The communications center also had a radio room to co-ordinate all the cars and drivers and to patch through to Hughes if he was in the air. The co-ordination could be tricky. Sometimes the chauffeurs took half a dozen of Hughes's women to Los Angeles restaurants on the same night. Chouinard had to make sure that none of these women ate in the same place and that they would never run into each other. Every so often the messages flying back and forth were personal and spicy. For instance, when Robert Mitchum was starring in a film with Ava Gardner, he telephoned Howard to report that Ava was "putting the moves" on him. "Should I sleep with her?" asked Mitchum.

Howard's reply was pragmatic. "If you don't, they'll think you're a fag."

To run this nerve center, Hughes hired a 27-year-old Brigham Young University graduate named Frank William (Bill) Gay, who had been a secretary to Hughes's assistant Nadine Henley. Gay was a member of the Church of Latter-Day Saints, the Mormons. Gay agreed to try it out for three months "to see if I like it." Two decades later he ruled the entire Hughes empire.

The "secret police," and the efficient young Mormon and his staff, would soon play a key role in establishing a remarkable kingdom of love nests and overseeing the women to occupy them.

CHAPTER 24

GIRLS, GIRLS, GIRLS

IN 1950, THE MOTHER OF THE REIGNING MISS ORANGE COUNTY, CALIFORNIA, received a telephone call from a Los Angeles talent agency. Howard Hughes had spotted a photograph of her daughter, wearing a bathing suit and a winning smile, in the *Los Angeles Times.* He wanted to talk to her about a possible movie contract.

"My mom asked me if I wanted to go, and I did," said Helen Weir, who was then a long-legged dishwater blonde of seventeen, who was often told she resembled Terry Moore. Added Weir, "I was very naive."

A meeting time was arranged, and Weir was instructed to wear "something very plain, something black, no jewelry." On the appointed day, she and her mother climbed into a limousine, which had been sent to the family home in Anaheim, and were taken to Los Angeles. First on the agenda was a meeting with the agents. They wanted to know Weir's height, her weight, her measurements. And because she was about to become a high school senior, they wondered about her "goals." Would she like to move to Hollywood? And she was asked, "How far would you go to be a starlet?"

Said Weir, "I didn't know what they meant . . . and they jumped in and said, 'Well, would you be interested in being available to accompany stars to premieres? That kind of thing?' "

She and her mother, who wasn't pleased with the line of questioning, were then sent to a photographer's studio, where Weir was photographed in a form-fitting black sweater and skirt, with her hair worn full. Then they were driven to the Samuel Goldwyn Studio, where they were escorted to an office "that was very bare, with a wooden table and a few dinky chairs, nothing fancy."

It was there that they met the 44-year-old Hughes, who also quizzed Weir about her "goals." "He was nice. And nice looking," said Weir, who confessed she was "sitting there, scared speechless," during the encounter. Hughes wrapped up the meeting by telling Weir he thought she should finish high school and, when she was ready to go out on her own, contact him about a possible contract. "It was like he didn't want my mom to be around," Weir recalled.

As she and her mother were leaving, her mother turned and "caught Hughes peeking his head out the doorway, watching us," said Weir. "As soon as we got outside, my mom said, 'Well, I know what was going on in there!'

"But I didn't know. I really had no idea," laughed Weir.

As the fifties progressed, and as Hughes himself approached fifty, he would concentrate on starlets, and would-be starlets, rather than "names." RKO was the perfect calling card. Under Hughes it became an assembly line of young female hopefuls—almost all of them voluptuous.

"It was a time when women were flaunted," reminded actress Dana Wynter, who was married to Hughes attorney Greg Bautzer. Times were changing. It was *cool* to think of women as "playmates." For Hughes, who had romanced the greats, the fifties were like a giant frat party brimming with sorority girls. He was living a fantasy, to the bemusement of everyone in town except, undoubtedly, Jean Peters. "*Les Girls* were one thing he would never talk about, although their names were well known in Hollywood and in the gossip columns everywhere," was how columnist Sheilah Graham put it.

Hughes couldn't even resist making a pass at the daughter-in-law of his longtime physician, Dr. Verne Mason. He met Patricia Mason one night at the family home. When she was out of earshot of her husband, Verne Mason, Jr., Hughes said, "When you get tired of the kid, call me," and flipped her his phone number.

"I thought that he was quite possibly the all-American shit," remembered Patricia.

Hughes's modus operandi was to entice young women with the

prospect of a contract with his Hughes Productions, for which various Hughes aides acted as wranglers. Their job: both to keep the women from straying and maintain them on a regimented schedule. Scores of women were processed through Hughes's intricate star-making program, but few would find stardom.

Howard's interest in some of the starlets was purely platonic, as if he were acquiring the sisters—or the daughters—he never had. Sally Bliss was just fifteen when Hughes spotted her on the cover of *Parade* magazine. An ingenue with a New York theater company, the petite, brown-eyed brunette was put under contract and, with her parents' permission, moved to Hollywood. She lived with associates of Hughes and was given a regimen of dramatic classes and studies. "There was never anything romantic. Ours was like a father-daughter relationship. Howard could be very paternal," Bliss recalled. He sometimes took Bliss to lunches and relied on her to relate conversations back to him. "I would enunciate very carefully, and he would watch my mouth," said Bliss.

Unaware that Hughes had an undiagnosed medical condition, Bliss came to believe that it was largely Hughes's hearing problem that led to his often strange behavior. "He never quite understood what people were saying to him. I know that was a disappointment to him in his business dealings. He told me there was a constant ringing in his ears. It must have been awful for a man like that—a man who had to be a winner."

Bliss eventually underwent a professional name change—to Carla Balenda. "He wanted me to have a European-sounding name," said Bliss, who eventually starred in four movies for Hughes at RKO—but only after a nine-year wait and countless heated arguments over her stalled career. "He kept promising me roles and movies that didn't happen. One day he told me he'd bought a movie for me that I knew someone else had just bought. I said, 'Howard, you're lying.'

"He said, 'Sally, it's bad taste to call a man a liar.'

"I said, 'Howard, it's worse taste to lie.' "

But lie he did. As a result, many of the women found themselves entrapped. Like Gina Lollobrigida. After she was named Miss Rome and Miss Italy, Hughes spotted a photograph of her in a magazine. She was wearing a then-shocking bikini.

An agent for Hughes contacted her representative in Rome. In July 1950, Lollobrigida, who spoke very little English, came to Hollywood, where Hughes signed her to a contract and had her ensconced in the Town

House Hotel on Wilshire Boulevard. Jerry Wald, a producer working with Hughes at the time, revealed that Lollobrigida was told "not to leave the place unless Mr. Hughes sent orders." He would sometimes show up around two in the morning and escort Lollobrigida down to the hotel's supper club, where he had hired the orchestra to perform only for them. They would have the dance floor to themselves.

Though she was married, Lollobrigada was initially entranced. "I said to myself, 'This tall, dark and handsome American, I could fall in love with him.' I almost did."

She didn't fall for Hughes's overprotectiveness, however. When he had Jeff Chouinard post a man outside her door twenty-four hours a day—so she wouldn't venture out—she reacted by throwing things at her guard and by screaming out tirades in Italian and broken English. After six weeks, she packed her bags and headed home, bad-mouthing Hughes along the way.

Other Hughes imports included Mara Lane, dubbed "England's answer to Marilyn Monroe" (she wasn't put under contract) and Germany's Ursula Thiess (she was). Hughes also sent one of his photographers to Rome to shoot a young Sophia Loren. There was no contract offer. "He didn't like her nose," remembered Jeff Chouinard.

For Hughes, girl-finding became yet another magnificent obsession. He scoured dozens of magazines, ripping out pages of girls he liked. Just days after she appeared on the cover of *Life* in May 1953, Indiana University student Sallilee Conlon was contacted by RKO Pictures. Then came a photographer, followed by an offer to come to Los Angeles with her mother. After meeting with Walter Kane they flew to Las Vegas, where Conlon met with Hughes. "And he was absolutely stunning looking," said Conlon, who played Hughes tape recordings of her singing.

She and her mother remained in Las Vegas for six months, with Hughes playing escort.

The last time she saw Hughes he showed her the sunset from the parking lot of the Desert Inn. Then she and her mother went back to Los Angeles, where they were put up in a house and Sallilee was given voice lessons. She took the lessons for five years and abided by the various Hughes organization rules, including no dates. And off and on, she spoke with Hughes by phone. All the while she waited for a movie role or a singing offer. The Hughes people kept telling her to be patient. She will never forget the day she found out from her vocal coach that Hughes had countless young women like herself under contract. All of them waiting.

Hughes kept track of car shows, hairdressers' conventions, and beauty pageants across the country. He would also scrutinize movies, looking for extras with that extra something. As aide Ron Kistler once explained, "Sometimes he would call the projectionist and say, 'I am interested in the gal sitting at the third table from the left top part of the screen.' " Then the guys at the Romaine headquarters, or "Operations," would be off and tracking.

One of Hughes's photographers, usually Jack Christy, was sometimes dispatched to the girl's hometown to do a photo session. During one five-week period in the early fifties, eleven women were photographed for Hughes. Hughes aide Raymond Glen Brewer said that of the girls photographed, "maybe one out of fifty would get a screen test. And maybe one out of one hundred and fifty would get lessons." The regimen went this way: if Hughes liked the results of the photo session, there would be a trip to Los Angeles, yet another photo session, a screen test, and sometimes a personal meeting or telephone conversation with Hughes. Then, possibly, a contract.

Afterward, the girls would learn what it was like to be part of a modern-era harem.

"They had a very well-regimented schedule to make sure that their time was wholly occupied," said Ron Kistler. That schedule would include drama lessons, photography sessions, and specially arranged screenings of movies that were approved by Hughes. And they were escorted by Hughes's aides during their lunches and dinners out.

"The whole idea was that Hughes wanted them for himself. He didn't want them to have any other men in their lives," Chouinard explained. For that reason Hughes's various associates were strictly forbidden to fraternize. But not all obeyed.

When a Hughes driver named Bob Miles ran off with RKO contractee and former Miss America runner-up, Vera Ralston, who later became known as actress Vera Miles, Hughes was so enraged he requested that all future drivers be homosexual. But this was one Hughes dictate that was too unrealistic for its time. Said Chouinard, "There weren't a lot of guys, in the fifties, talking about that."

Because of Hughes's rampant possessiveness, none of the aides, not even the growing cadre of Mormons, ratted on the young driver who proved irresistible to a Scandinavian screen bombshell he was transporting for Hughes. She turned out to be a nymphomaniac who startled her driver by performing oral sex on him as he negotiated the Los Angeles freeway system. "Oh, Jesus, he thought he was going to rear-end someone," said Chouinard.

Scandinavian imports aside, there was an entire manual of rules for the care and feeding of Hughes's harem. For example, the girls were allowed just one ice-cream cone a day. Also, they were not to be jarred as the aides drove over speed bumps and the like. "We were told if there was any such obstruction in the road to immediately slow to two miles an hour," said Kistler. Hughes insisted they take the precaution because he believed the sudden motion, and pull of gravity, could tear at the muscles of the girls' breasts. In addition, the girls were not to be told that there "might be others like [them], under contract to Hughes Productions," said Kistler.

Hughes sometimes personally dispensed beauty advice, such as how to sleep (without moving the neck, which is prone to wrinkling), and the dos and don'ts of breast care.

Rules were customized for certain girls. Sometimes Hughes asked them to quit shaving their legs. One fifteen-year-old was so busty that she was instructed "to wear a bra at all times." Food restrictions also varied from girl to girl, depending on whether or not Hughes intended to sleep with them. "We could always tell which ones he was having sex with," said a longtime Hughes associate, adding, "Hughes hated to be in bed with women who had gas. So he wouldn't let them have any pork products, things like that."

All the women were initially sent to the dentist. The papers in the Hughes estate include a lengthy list of dental appointments and treatments of the Hughes contractees. They also reveal that dental x-rays were imperative. "He wanted a woman to be perfect in every way," explained one Hughes aide.

The women didn't always know it, but they were also put under twenty-four-hour surveillance. Sometimes their phones were tapped. Their movements were recorded in copious daily logs, kept by Operations. These logs also carried Hughes's instructions.

A typical listing looked like this:

12:40 a.m.   *Whoever is on in the morning should call [Miss X] at*
             [phone number] at 7:30 a.m. Say that you are from Mr.
             Hughes' office and that we would like very much to make
             some photos of her and have her work with our drama
             coaches. Tell her that we have something coming up—a

> *part—and we may be able to use her in it . . . Keep her in*
> *our clutches all day. Don't tell her, but I would like to have*
> *her available so I can see her in the late afternoon. Don't*
> *tell her that I am going to see her. Tell her we'll have a car*
> *pick her up.*

Hughes had a getaway playboy pad located on Sunset Boulevard. Actually, it was Walter Kane's apartment, which was located above the photo studio of Paul A. Hesse, famed for his color portraits of stars. Hesse's studio became an unofficial adjunct of Hughes's "talent" operation. Wallace Seawell shot the sessions. "We used to call Hughes 'Pappy' when he wasn't around. We'd say, 'I wonder who Pappy's sending us today,' " recalled Seawell, who became a leading color photographer of the fifties and sixties.

The women were clothed for the photo sessions—Hughes didn't want nudes. But he did like cleavage. He also wanted profile shots in order to see the outline of the bust. Most of the subjects were there just to be photographed. But some wound up being entertained by Hughes and Kane in the apartment.

According to Chouinard and other Hughes associates, some of the young women had aggressive mothers who fairly pushed their daughters into Howard's lap. The mother of the busty fifteen-year-old "worked and worked to get them together," said Chouinard. But when Hughes bedded the teenager during a weekend in Palm Springs, the mother caught him. "She was screaming, 'You dirty bastard! I'm going to sue the hell out of you!' " Chouinard recalled. Instead, Hughes agreed to a payoff of what some sources said was close to $1 million.

Phyllis Applegate, age nineteen, was in Florida in the winter of 1952 when she got a call from RKO Pictures. Howard Hughes had seen some photographs of her, taken in Las Vegas, where she had appeared in a revue. Would she be interested in doing a screen test? Hughes sent a photographer to shoot her.

"They told me to wear a tight sweater and a tight skirt," Phyllis remembered. "They told me to stand to the side for a profile. Then stand straight on. Oh, and I was told no makeup. And to wear my hair long. I was a brunette."

Hughes liked the photos that were taken. Applegate was summoned to

Los Angeles and put up at the Westwood Manor. "And I just sat there. And I'm not the quiet type. I started to complain." After several weeks of doing nothing but shopping, on Hughes's money, she was told to pack her bags for Las Vegas. She was given a suite at the Desert Inn. And once again she waited.

In April 1953 she was whisked into Hughes's room by his aides. "I'd wanted to get dressed up," said Applegate, who was in corduroy pedal pushers, a sweater, and white moccasins, "and no makeup," when she found herself staring across a desk at Hughes, then forty-seven.

He took her out that night for dinner. And for the next two weeks. "We saw every show in town. He always had a ringside seat. At the Desert Inn, the Thunderbird, the Frontier. We made the rounds. Sometimes we'd see the same show again."

Then Applegate was sent back to Los Angeles, where she began drama lessons with acting coach Florence Enright. She also got nightly calls from Hughes, who always knew exactly what she'd been doing. "I finally realized that probably everyone at the hotel was a spy," said Applegate.

After a year at the hotel, Applegate moved to an apartment in Beverly Hills. Hughes paid the rent. She also continued to get a paycheck, though she never made a movie for RKO. But she continued with her lessons, and she watched the movies arranged for her by Hughes. Nine months after they met, they began a sexual relationship.

"It was a mutual thing," said Phyllis, who had previously been married. "The time was right. And it was very pleasant. Don't believe that talk about impotence. He was just fine. Sometimes he could go on for about a half an hour."

She added, "Thinking back on it, he must have been able to go on and on because of drugs. He was using some medication for his back pain, so it would take him a long time to climax." Hughes, who liked to sleep with a single night-light by the bed, talked with Applegate about past girl-friends. He admitted that to get some women in bed, he'd use a ploy: he would pretend to marry them. "There's a cross up on a hill in Hollywood. He would take the girls there, by the light of the moon. And he had a little book which he'd read from. And he'd say, 'I'm going to marry you, in the eyes of God.' And that would make them feel so secure that they would go to bed with him.

"It was considered a sin to have sex then if you weren't married," she reminded.

She also saw a side to Hughes that he tried to keep hidden: his compassion. "He took care of medical bills for so many people. He would read about them in the newspaper, or hear about them in Hollywood, and he would get tears in his eyes. And he would make arrangements to care for them. He loved to do things like that."

In fact, Hughes sent Applegate's younger sister to the best physicians and facilities for lifelong problems that had resulted from a bad fall. "My mother never forgot what he did for us."

Applegate's relationship with Hughes ended with her 1955 marriage. But they remained in touch by phone into the sixties. She recalled that he telephoned her just before he married Jean Peters. "He said, 'I'm finally going to get married.' I laughed and teased him, and said, 'You mean for real, or in front of the cross?' And he laughed and thought that was funny, because he'd done that so many times. I told him, 'Be happy. I hope you're happy.' "

Joyce Taylor was anything but happy during the seven years she was under contract to Hughes. She was just fifteen and, despite her tender years, already a veteran of the nightclub circuit when she sang on Walter Winchell's television show, wearing a skirt, sweater, and bobby sox. When the show ended, Winchell took a call from Walter Kane, who said, "Howard Hughes wants Joyce." She met with Hughes one afternoon in Los Angeles. "There was nothing at all odd about it," said Taylor, who found Hughes "charming, warm, and nice—and normal." As the head of RKO Pictures, he also promised movie roles. A second meeting took place in the early morning hours in an empty sound stage on the Samuel Goldwyn lot.

Taylor entered to find Howard "standing in this dark place, with a light nearby." He held out his hand and motioned for her to sit down. She did—and discovered she was in the light. When Hughes sat opposite her, she couldn't see him. He reached out to hand her a pen. "And suddenly I felt very uneasy."

After she had signed her contact, she looked up "and I saw this look in his eyes. It was scary and dark. It was an 'I own you, you're mine' look." Taylor ran from the sound stage, turning back only once. "And Howard Hughes was gone."

She was put up at the Westwood Manor Hotel. But she didn't want to live there alone, so Hughes flew out her mother and sisters. Eventually the family was placed in a home in Bel Air. Taylor was not permitted to date or arrange her own day's schedule. "Every morning I woke up and got myself perfectly groomed. Every hair in place. And I went to drama lessons. At night, I watched movies Howard Hughes forced me to see. By myself. That was my life for the first six or nine months." Taylor went on to suffer a nervous breakdown. Hughes sent birds of paradise. "That was his flower for me."

To her great anger, Hughes made an ally of her mother, who encouraged Joyce to go out with Hughes. Accompanied by chaperons, she went with him to Palm Springs and to Florida. It was in Florida that she incurred his wrath because she dived into a pool. "He was yelling when I came up out of the water," recalled Taylor, who had done what Hughes considered the unthinkable—jostled her breasts with the dive.

Taylor never had a physical relationship with Hughes. "I hated him too much." She remembered the time he touched her shoulders. "And I shouted at him, 'No! Don't you ever, *ever* touch me!' " And he never did.

She recalled that Hughes once told her, "I play chess with people." He explained: "In a chess game, you see how long you can keep a person in a certain move."

According to psychiatrists Jeffrey Schwartz and Anthony Dietrich, Howard's catalog of girls was one of the most intriguing aspects of his obsessive-compulsive disorder. "He was a collector," recalled Dietrich, who learned from his father about Hughes's inventories of planes, cars, executives, and women. "He was as impelled to collect women as he was to collect the planes. And quite often he had no idea what to do with them once he had them stockpiled. Once, right after World War II, Hughes imported whole groups of German scientists, but left them sitting idly by for years. It was enough that they were there."

With the women—the endless variety of women, the multiple fiancées—Schwartz believed Hughes was desperately trying to recapture the rapt, thrilling love he had received from his mother. "When Allene compulsively checked and rechecked Howard's body, his temperature, his every move, she was actually making love to her beautiful son. And Howard grew dependent on that intense form of love. So, for the rest of his life, he went from lover to lover trying to recapture the all-encompassing passion he felt for his mother."

After studying three hundred depositions and the surveillance reports on "Howard's girls," for his psychological autopsy on Hughes, Dr. Raymond Fowler came to believe that Howard, like many of the super-rich, was a maniacal collector of women, and that once they were his, he viewed them with a cool, calculated, and detached attitude. Like Liz Taylor's diamonds, Alfred Vanderbilt's cellar full of brandy, and Malcolm Forbes's Fabergé eggs, these women, said Fowler, were collectibles. They "belonged to Hughes."

Added Fowler, "I have always thought there was a parallel between Howard's collecting girls and his collecting planes. Like the planes, they were guarded twenty-four hours a day; and like the planes, they were often forgotten and left to rot away.

"He might romance them for a few days and then withdraw. But the girls were expected to be there 'in case he needed them again.' "

Hughes's girl-craziness reached comic proportions in April 1953 when *Confidential* magazine ran a story about Hughes and his collection of starlets, headlined PUBLIC WOLF NO. 1. In it, a Hughes "colleague" revealed that "at last count," Hughes had "164 girlfriends stashed" around town. *Confidential*, the most scandalous publication of its day, also speculated that Hughes suffered from "a mother complex."

The day the magazine came out, Hughes's staffers were ordered to traverse the newsstands of Los Angeles, Hollywood, and surrounding cities to buy up every copy they found.

CHAPTER 25

TYCOON

HOWARD HUGHES SWAYED BACK AND FORTH ON THE CROWDED DANCE floor of the Harbor Lights, a Greek tavern near the Houston docks. Dancing around him were rowdy bands of merchant marines from distant countries: Portuguese in blue uniforms with gold piping, rowdy Brits in dazzling whites, and Greek sailors lined up arm-in-arm dancing *Zorba the Greek* style. Howard towered above them all, his fedora clearly visible despite the crush of revelers.

"He danced all by himself. And he never talked to anybody," remembered Koula Dadinis, who helped her late husband Harres run the popular night spot.

A Greek native, Koula wasn't familiar with Hughes or his reputation. The first time he sat down at the bar she mistook him for a transient.

"He says to me, 'I'm hungry. Can I have something to eat? But I don't have no money.'"

Her husband told her to give the stranger what he wanted. He ordered fried shrimp and a beer, which he drank carefully—wrapping the beer can with a Kleenex. When he had finished eating, he asked Koula, "Can you call me a taxi?"

"How do you like that!" she told her husband. "He don't have no money to pay for the food and drink, and now he wants me to call a taxi."

The stranger laughed, then began to encircle Koula. "Take everything out of my pockets," he told her. With her husband urging her on, Koula reached inside the pockets of his baggy khakis and found a $100 bill. "Take it," said the man, who smiled as he sauntered out the door and into the humid Houston evening in late 1948.

After the cab sped away, Koula's husband clued her in. "That's Howard Hughes," he said. "He's one of the richest men in the world."

Off and on into the 1950s the industrialist made occasional anonymous visits to the Harbor Lights. Always alone, he would sit and watch the dancers on the crowded dance floor. When he left, he often ambled up the road to nearby Bornell's Lounge. Like the Harbor Lights, it was within walking distance of Hughes Tool Company.

Though Hughes hadn't made a public visit to his hometown since 1938 in the aftermath of his famed flight, he made periodic clandestine visits over the years. He sometimes flew in during the wee hours, met with associates, slept at the downtown Rice Hotel, where he kept a suite under an assumed name, and then slipped back to the airport. There were also discreet visits to Manhattan, Georgetown, and Florida, where "handshake deals" were negotiated between Howard and the postwar power brokers from the Pentagon. His casual demeanor and his reputation as the man whose bravado derailed the 1947 Senate hearings gained him crucial audiences with the men who authorized defense contractors. The legacy of "Mr. Hughes Goes to Washington" allowed him to duck the failure of the Spruce Goose and the doomed XF-11 reconnaissance plane. It also allowed him to continue his relationship with the Department of Defense as well as to cultivate a new allegiance with the Central Intelligence Agency. Over the years, his CIA ties would result in $7 billion in espionage contracts with the spy agency.

Hughes believed that the future for most defense contractors depended upon newer, slicker weapons control systems. He had already learned that some of his competitors were disinterested. The profit margins were beneath consideration.

"Hughes was ahead of his time," Lockheed's Robert Gross recalled. "By plunging into military electronics, which many established contractors were ignoring, he founded one of the most advanced and diverse aeronautics corporations in the world. Until Hughes these advances were only pipe dreams."

One of Hughes Aircraft's early successes, a seek-and-find radar system that automatically hunted down its target, revolutionized air warfare. But Hughes obtained this pact only because he was willing to go out on a financial limb to secure it. His little electronics laboratory of one hundred scientists was bidding against the giant of the field, General Electric. Hughes, certain of his design and guided by intuition, agreed to build the test model with his own money. If it worked, Hughes Aircraft's future was secure. If not, General Electric triumphed. Howard's creation, the Falcon missile, was embraced enthusiastically. Because it could follow its target, it became a staple of modern warfare.

The air-to-air missile chased the target by emitting radar impulses. Six feet long and 110 pounds, the Falcon floored top Pentagon brass and opened up the financial floodgates for Hughes Aircraft. Less than three years later, the corporation boasted $8 million in Air Force contracts alone. The workforce jumped from one hundred to ten thousand, including thirty-three hundred Ph.D.s. He also triumphantly raided General Electric, Bell Labs, and Convair, coming away with some of the best minds in the industry.

By the outbreak of the Korean War in 1950, Hughes Aircraft was far ahead of everyone else in military electronics. Less than a year earlier, the corporation won a design competition for supersonic interceptors with the F-102, the first in a series of interceptors that would increase the Hughes Aircraft profits tenfold.

By 1953, Hughes Aircraft was into its fifth year of phenomenal growth. Its military contracts totaled $200 million a year, its workforce was seventeen thousand strong, and its two plants in Culver City and Tucson, Arizona, were grossing $1.7 million a day—swollen by lucrative pacts with private industry as well as the military. So vast was Howard's military catalog that former President Truman had described him as "the human linchpin of America's air defenses."

In addition, millions of dollars per week were pouring into Hughes's coffers from the Central Intelligence Agency, which had already ordered more than $250,000 in espionage equipment so advanced that the CIA summaries of its dealings with the elusive billionaire are still classified documents. The agency referred to Howard as "the spook of American aviation."

Hughes Aircraft's greatest strength was the mysterious chemistry between Howard and the world-class scientists who worked for him. He pursued a laissez-faire style of leadership, ruling from afar by conversing with his executives from a series of pay telephones scattered across the Southwest.

"He made them think they were the most important scientists in the world working on the most important scientific projects in the world," Noah Dietrich recalled.

After Howard's death, it became journalistically fashionable to depict him as an ultra-rich dilettante who had little or nothing to do with the awesome achievements of the companies he founded. "Of course, that's a ridiculous idea," said Howard's latter-day aide-de-camp Robert Maheu. "In many cases he was the front man, dealing directly with generals and politicians at the Beverly Hills Hotel." Maheu, who helped his boss mold Hughes Aircraft, has physical proof of the boss's involvement: hundreds of yellow tablets filled with Howard's handwritten instructions.

"Howard was often integrally involved with intimate scientific details," Dietrich said in 1972. "He showed his brilliance by providing the inspiration for hundreds of electronic advances. And he was brilliant at finding the greatest scientists and convincing them to fulfill his dreams. He cast a spell over them."

He also meddled incessantly. For years the scientists and aerospace executives were tolerant, lulled by fat salaries, ideal working conditions, and state-of-the-art laboratories and assembly lines. However, the honeymoon ended abruptly in 1953 when seventeen of these renowned scientists mutinied and threatened to leave the corporation. It was an act of protest against Hughes's eccentricities. Their complaints, forwarded to Air Force headquarters in Washington, charged Howard with dallying for months before making even the most basic of decisions. Moreover, they claimed that he talked "gibberish" when they finally reached him.

The scientific revolt soon spread to the plants in Culver City and Tucson.

Since Hughes Aircraft was now the third-largest supplier of weapon delivery systems, the Air Force brass were alarmed by the portrait of a badly faltering Hughes. They now questioned his obviously irrational handling of his electronics industry.

The Pentagon ordered the FBI to find out what was wrong. So FBI agents in both Las Vegas and Los Angeles took to the field in one of the most unique probes in the history of domestic espionage—to diagnose the emotional health of the richest man in America. Their report, number 62-1476-4, advised the army brass, "Mr. Hughes has become a paranoid, vengeful, and emotionally disturbed man, whose mind has deteriorated to the point that he is capable of both suicide and murder."

A second, more secret analysis of Hughes's troubles was commissioned personally by J. Edgar Hoover in 1970. Its analysis was never sent to the Air Force. That study detailed Hughes's growing "codeine habit, noting that the billionaire is making most of his decisions in a drugged state." This was the first documentary proof that Howard's use of opiates, first prescribed after the 1946 crash, had become an addiction. FBI Memorandum 64-1996-6 claimed that Hughes was taking "at least six codeine tablets per day even though the subject has no therapeutic reason to ingest codeine."

In fact, Howard was in great pain, particularly in his pelvis and thigh bones. In addition, the residue of his neurological syphilis caused agonizing pain that ran down to his knee. "I continued prescribing codeine because Mr. Hughes needed it," Dr. Verne Mason explained later.

The FBI was unaware that his obsessive-compulsive disorder was becoming so crippling that it led to indecision and dysfunctional thinking. But the Pentagon wasn't really interested in an explanation. Its officials wanted the scientists to go back to work. In 1953 Secretary of the Air Force Harold E. Talbott went to Los Angeles for a showdown with Hughes and Noah Dietrich.

Talbott raged at Howard. "You have wrecked a great industrial establishment with gross mismanagement! I don't give a damn what happens to you, but I am concerned for this country. The United States is wholly dependent on Hughes Aircraft for vital defense systems." Added Talbott, "It was a terrible mistake entrusting the nation's security system to an eccentric like you."

Then he delivered an ultimatum to Hughes. "Either sell Hughes Aircraft to Lockheed or accept a new management that I myself will designate."

Hughes sat in his chair, stunned and staring down at the floor. For three minutes the silence continued. It must have been one of the most traumatic moments of Hughes's life. If the Air Force called him eccentric, he undoubtedly believed that there were others who questioned his sanity.

It was Noah who finally answered. "Look, give us ninety days to get the corporation back in order." Talbott agreed. But he said he would permit no more than ninety days.

Exactly ninety days later, Hughes solved the problem by publicly donating Hughes Aircraft to the Howard Hughes Medical Institute, a charity he had conceived four years earlier. By putting control of Hughes Aircraft in the hands of a major charity, Howard believed the United States government would not dare to cancel the contracts. As window dressing, he imported a top-level panel of executives to run the electronics program.

The Pentagon capitulated.

In Los Angeles, Hughes's public relations man Perry Lieber advised the media of Howard Hughes's magnanimous gift, "the mark of a great philanthropist." Touted Lieber, "During the coming fifty years, medicine will realize a sensational windfall from this gift. It will support research on a scale never attempted before." Both Associated Press and United Press helped to spread the word. Even President Dwight D. Eisenhower announced from the Oval Office, "Howard Hughes has created a high water mark for American philanthropy."

Actually, the gift was one of the craftiest financial flimflams ever conceived.

If anyone in the Pentagon or the Internal Revenue Service read the fine print in the 330-page contract between the institute and Hughes Tool Company, they would have seen that the original gift amounted to just $36,463. A second clause required the institute to purchase certain assets of the aircraft division for $74.6 million. And since the new Hughes "charity" had no money, it assumed more than $56 million in Toolco liabilities. In order to pay for the $18 million difference between the liabilities and the $74 million the institute "paid" for the Hughes Aircraft assets, the institute signed a promissory note for the $18 million difference.

Since Hughes retained the buildings and the land of Hughes Aircraft, the institute was to pay $26 million in rent back to Hughes, over a decade.

In other words, Hughes created an ingenious tax dodge and was allowed to keep running Hughes Aircraft any way he wished, since he was the "sole trustee" of the institute.

For every million the institute gave to medical research, it gave $2.5 million to Howard Hughes. Even more important, the Pentagon called back its dogs. They could no longer even comment about the administration of Toolco, since it was the sole support of a major philanthropic organization.

A one-time stroke of brilliance, however, was not what was required to keep two other business concerns profitable. Both his movie studio,

RKO, and his beloved airline, TWA, were suffering from his mental deterioration.

RKO was in disarray. Movies were sitting on shelves; producers were fleeing, actresses by the score were being paid for doing nothing. With so many things on his mind, including his burgeoning aircraft industry and TWA, Hughes treated RKO like a neglected stepchild.

In September 1952 he attempted to unload RKO by putting his shares of stock, 25 per cent of the company, on the market. And there was some interest. But his attempt backfired when the *Wall Street Journal* revealed that the five-man syndicate of buyers had ties to organized crime. When the buyers backed out of the deal, Hughes was back in control. In the meantime, a flurry of lawsuits had been filed by RKO stockholders angry with Hughes's management. There were so many headlines involving lawsuits that actor Dick Powell, who directed movies at RKO during the Hughes reign, joked, "RKO's contract list is now down to three actors and one hundred and twenty-seven lawyers."

In February 1954 Hughes came up with a curious antidote to his RKO troubles: he bought out all the other shareholders, becoming the first and only man in history to solely own a studio. But he still wanted out. What had once been a giant toy had turned into a giant headache.

Already, Hughes's unabated patriotism and paranoia had led to controversies at RKO involving the Red Menace—communism. In the era of communist-bashing Senator Joseph McCarthy, Hollywood had a strong anti-red brigade, led by the powerful Hedda Hopper, as well as Lela Rogers, the mother of Ginger Rogers and a frequent date of FBI director J. Edgar Hoover. Hughes got caught up in the battle, becoming one of its most fierce warriors.

"He bugged the studio offices at RKO and fired some of the filmmakers he thought were pro-communist," said Jeff Chouinard.

When RKO screenwriter Paul Jarrico refused to tell the House Un-American Activities Committee (HUAC) if he was a communist, Hughes fired him. He also removed Jarrico's credit from the Jane Russell movie *The Las Vegas Story*. The act brought praise from Richard M. Nixon, then junior senator from California. In a statement inserted in the *Congressional Record*, Nixon said Hughes had taken a stand "which deserved the attention and approval of every man and woman who believes the forces of subversion must be wiped out." The reclusive Hughes was so fired up over the communist threat that he made a surprise appearance at an April 1952 meeting of the Hollywood Post of the American Legion.

He also took apart what was said to be a perfectly watchable thriller, directed by esteemed production designer William Cameron Menzies, called *The Whip Hand* in order to change scenes originally involving Hitler into a scenario about germ warfare and the communists. "When we saw what had happened to the film, we couldn't believe it. It no longer made any sense," admitted Sally Bliss, who starred in the movie under her stage name, Carla Balenda.

Hughes also publicly denounced Charles Chaplin's movie *Limelight*, and asked the RKO theater chain to ban it because of Chaplin's refusal to testify before HUAC five years earlier. The tidal wave of publicity that followed led to Chaplin's decision not to return to the United States from England, where he had earlier fled.

But if Hughes wanted out of RKO, he could not bear to part with his beloved Jane Russell. He wrapped up his RKO epoch by signing her to a new twenty-year contract worth $1 million. Russell's agent, Lew Wasserman, was so startled he asked, "Oh, my God! Are you sleeping with him?" She went on to earn $1,000 a week for the next two decades, for movies she never made.

The Hughes-RKO saga was also climaxed by the 1955 release of *Son of Sinbad*. Ostensibly starring Dale Robertson and Vincent Price, it was really an excuse to showcase some one hundred starlets, many of whom were rumored to be involved with Hughes. Sally Forrest, who co-starred as a slave girl who was secretly a member of the all-girl forty thieves gang, recalled coming to the set each day and discovering her costume had become smaller. "The brassiere got so small they finally had to paste it to my breasts," she laughed.

In the Hughes tradition, the movie was condemned by the Legion of Decency and heavily promoted. The Sinbadettes, four young women dressed as Persian harem maidens, made a three-week transcontinental tour to promote the movie.

Hughes finally sold RKO in 1955, but his legacy continued for several years thereafter with the 1956 release of the ludicrous *The Conqueror*, starring John Wayne as Genghis Khan opposite Hughes's one-time flame Susan Hayward. *Jet Pilot* was released in 1957—eight years after production began. It was ridiculed for its obsolete depiction of aviation.

Trans World Airlines was the first part of Howard's empire that began to collapse under the weight of his mental and physical ailments. Since he had built TWA from a small mail carrier to one of the world's great international airlines, Howard took the decline personally. "If Hughes truly loved anything, he loved TWA," recalled Robert Gross, one of the line's major executives. "So it was tragic when that dream began to shatter."

Ironically for Hughes, it was the onset of the jet age—a supersonic era he had helped to create—that eventually undermined his leadership and iron-fisted control of the airline.

In 1952, Hughes had the first crack at a new fleet of jetliners just coming off the assembly line of the DeHavilland plant in Great Britain. He passed. "There will be jets far more sophisticated than these," he told Noah Dietrich. But Dietrich, who was then on the board of TWA, was worried. He knew that TWA's competitors, United, American, and Pan American airlines, were already scouring the world for "just the right jet."

In early 1954 Boeing unveiled the jet the aviation world had been seeking, a long-range luxury liner version of Hughes's beloved Constellation, the 707. Douglas Aircraft was right behind with the swank DC-8, soon to become one of the most popular liners in the sky.

Still Hughes dallied. He hunkered down in his shadowy bunker in the Beverly Hills Hotel, toying with miniature jet planes and sketching his own fanciful concepts onto large blueprint sheets. The advancing symptoms of his syphilitic dementia and the worsening of his obsessive-compulsive disorder had greatly diminished his powers of judgment. "He insisted upon tampering with all of the proposed designs and agonizing over his choice for two years," Dietrich recalled. "He seemed lost in a daydream."

Meanwhile, TWA's major rivals rushed to greet the jet age by ordering fleets of DC-8s, putting them far ahead of TWA. Still, Howard tinkered. He filled notebooks with algebraic and geometric calculations, part of his latest obsession, which was to build his own jets and then sell them back to his own airline at a profit.

Howard finally awakened from his dream in 1956 to confront a nightmare. By then TWA was headed for disaster in the jet sweepstakes, and Hughes knew it. But he was typically paranoid. "Unknown forces are trying to steal my airline," he wailed to Dietrich after learning that the airline executives were ready to mutiny over the boss's indecision.

Hughes reacted instantly and hysterically by ordering half a billion dollars worth of airliners, 188 Boeing 707s and 30 Convair 880s. "This was a frantic, unthinking act," said Dietrich. "And he consulted no one."

Dietrich drove to the Beverly Hills Hotel to confront Hughes: "Where are you going to get the four hundred and eighty-seven million dollars?"

Hughes answered, "It's not true. I promise you I haven't ordered jets costing four hundred and eighty-seven million dollars or anything like it."

"I added it up, Howard. In fact, I'll send you the bills which have arrived on my desk."

Hughes screamed back, "Get out! You can send me anything you goddamned please. But I didn't buy that many jets!"

But Hughes had, of course, signed for the jets, and neither he nor TWA had the cash to pay the bill. Hughes and TWA were caught in financial quicksand.

Already decimated emotionally by his psychological ailments and his increasing dependence on codeine, the millionaire would spend two years scurrying to raise the half a billion dollars he needed. He became so desperate at one point that he sent his personal army of security agents to Convair's San Diego plant to surround the partly finished jets. At gunpoint, they confronted the workers who wanted to finish the jets. As long as the planes were incomplete, Hughes didn't have to pay for them.

In 1959, he would be forced to turn to a consortium of Wall Street financiers to get the half a billion dollars to pay for the jets he had ordered so impetuously. In return, they forced Hughes to put his stock (78 per cent) in a nonvoting trust. "I've lost my airline," he said prophetically. A year later the bankers who controlled his stock sued him for mismanagement, seeking $187 million. TWA had lost $438 million between 1958 and 1959.

To initiate the court action, the bankers sought a deposition from Howard. When he refused, the bankers hired detectives to hunt him down, which caused him to run faster—until he became the most famous fugitive of his era.

At the height of the war for control of TWA, its beleaguered former president Jack Frye despaired over his failure to reach Hughes, once a valued friend. So he was delighted the night he spotted Hughes across the room from him in a Miami restaurant.

Frye jumped up, still carrying his napkin, and began walking toward Hughes. But Hughes saw Frye coming and, with the wild-eyed look of a trapped animal, got up from his table and broke into a run. "Howard!" shouted Frye. He wound up chasing Hughes through the restaurant's kitchen and out a doorway leading to an alley, where Hughes disappeared.

Hiding would become a way of life for Howard Hughes and for the women who loved him.

CHAPTER 26

WEDDING BELL BLUES

HOWARD'S DOMAIN OF OPULENT HOTEL SUITES AND MANSIONS WAS WORLDS away from the quiet, hidden beauty of the Riviera Country Club, where old-money families hid from the extravagance to the east (Bel Air) and the west (Malibu). Set on a slight peninsula that juts toward the Pacific Ocean, this hidden preserve was where Kathryn Grayson made her home. And it was to Grayson that Hughes fled for comfort when he felt the world closing in on him.

There was an equally deep abyss between most of Howard's lovers and Grayson, the MGM singing superstar then at the top of her career. She had starred in *Show Boat* and *The Toast of New Orleans*. Just ahead was *Kiss Me Kate*. A genteel beauty who had distanced herself from the Hollywood set, Grayson left the sound stages every night and retreated to her Tudor mansion, with a backyard that meandered down the hill to the Riviera's golf course.

Hughes had seen Grayson performing under the blue lights of the Hollywood Bowl, a vision with dark brown hair and a sensational figure. He pursued the buxom soprano for months, showing up at dinner parties and premieres, where he always managed to position himself conveniently nearby. "Honey, he was impassioned," related Grayson's friend and MGM co-star, Ann Miller. "It finally got so bad that he leaped over her fence to get to her."

One evening Grayson looked down from a second-story window to see Hughes below, pacing back and forth in the moonlight, gazing up at her window. "After he came over the gates, my father got his rifle out and said, 'No womanizing SOB is going to come near my daughter.' And my mother said, 'No, Dad, you can't do that. That man is Howard Hughes and think of the horrible publicity for Kathryn,' " Grayson recalled.

"Daddy hated him on sight. He told me that I had already endured two womanizing husbands and that there was not going to be a third."

Kathryn's father told her, "You stay up here; I'll go down and take care of this." Hours later, when Grayson came downstairs to leave for MGM, she found her father and Hughes talking about inventions and engineering.

A day or so later, Grayson told Hughes that she just was not interested.

The next morning, twelve dozen roses were delivered to her door. "Do you know how many twelve dozen roses are?" she said. "We spent hours just getting them into vases."

A long, tender relationship developed between this aging, exhausted millionaire and Hollywood's most vibrant soprano. Soon Howard was a regular in the Grayson home. "Many nights he slept in the guest room," she recalled. "It was safe for him, a hideout nobody knew existed since we never, ever did the town, and no publicity was ever published about the relationship."

Sometimes Kathryn would awaken after midnight to watch Howard walking the pathway on the estate, apparently talking to himself about his troubles with TWA and Hughes Aircraft. To her, he seemed to be "the loneliest man in the world." Soon she was inviting him in more often, where the guest room was waiting.

She would sometimes come home from MGM to find Hughes sitting in her den, holding and rocking her little daughter, Patty. "I realized then how painful it was for him to have missed out on a family."

When Grayson was on location, Hughes moved into the guest room for weeks at a time, working and looking out over the golf course to the Santa Monica Mountains in the distance. "Sometimes, I had to call his deputy, Bill Gay, because he didn't want to leave. But eventually, we would get him back to the Beverly Hills Hotel."

Howard's outrageous pursuit of Grayson became the talk of the MGM lot, where his roses regularly arrived at her dressing room. It reached the apex during the filming of *Show Boat*, the musical blockbuster that made her one of the top box-office stars of 1951.

When the town buzzed about the electric chemistry between Grayson and her dashing baritone co-star, Howard Keel, Hughes erupted in jealousy. During the filming of a lavish wedding scene between Grayson and Keel, Hughes took to the air in his noisy amphibian and swooped down over the riverboat set just as Grayson and Keel were to be joined in make-believe wedlock. "He got it through his head that this 'pretend wedding' would somehow result in a romance between Keel and myself," Grayson said with some amusement. "And you know, they never used that expensive sequence . . . maybe he did ruin every take."

When Hughes repeated his flyby on the second and third days, Grayson noticed that her co-star Ava Gardner was "shooting daggers" at her. Gardner had just rejected Hughes again but must have had second thoughts about surrendering him to the younger, more sophisticated Grayson.

One afternoon when Kathryn returned from the studio, Hughes, who had been asking her about marriage, handed her a case containing $2 million in jewelry. "I want you to have these," he said quietly. "For all you have done for me and to show how much I love you."

Grayson wouldn't even look at them. "I put them in a plain, brown grocery bag and sent them to my lawyer, so he could return them. I didn't want anyone to know what was inside, that there were two million dollars worth of gems."

Howard called her the next morning. "You are mean!" he said. "You are just mean! Those were gifts and you are not supposed to return gifts."

Grayson replied, "Well, I am not going to accept your proposal of marriage, so I shouldn't keep the gifts." Hughes told her he could take a hint. "You won't have to worry about me anymore." But that same night she looked down and saw him sitting in an arbor on her lushly landscaped grounds. There he felt contentment and security—which he so desperately needed.

Havens such as Grayson's became indispensable to Howard by the mid-fifties, when the Los Angeles night was no longer safe for the most notorious nocturnal dweller the city had ever known. Disgruntled boyfriends and process servers had all, in their turn, ferreted out his hiding places and confronted him. His kept women, his increasing troubles with TWA, and his callous treatment of RKO artisans had made him a marked man. Because he was involved in more than twenty lawsuits, several of them paternity actions, he changed all his patterns and habits.

Instead of sleeping until 2:00 P.M. and working until 2:00 A.M., he slept until 4:00 P.M. and worked to dawn. He even abandoned his familiar screening theater on the Samuel Goldwyn lot and switched to Martin Nosseck's screening room in a run-down part of West Hollywood.

Because he now suffered from blinding migraine headaches and spells of confusion, after-effects of the 1946 crash, he no longer prowled the city alone like a tomcat. One of Chouinard's men once tailed his circuitous route, from Kathryn's house to Cary Grant's to a motel in the Valley, where he met Terry Moore, then back to the Beverly Hills Hotel, where he collapsed into bed at the height of the lunch hour.

Instead of one bungalow at the Beverly Hills Hotel, he now had two cavernous cottages with blackout curtains on the windows and triple-locked doors. Two additional suites in the regular hotel wing served as the staging area for his guards and his growing cadre of crew-cut Mormon aides.

On really perilous excursions Chouinard himself drove backup. One night in May 1952 Chouinard was instructed to follow "the Old Man," as he and the aides called Hughes (though not to his face), to a dark parking area adjacent to the Warner Brothers studio. Howard waited for more than half an hour before Louella Koford, Terry Moore's mother, drove up beside him. Koford and Hughes talked earnestly for about two hours, with Terry's mother nodding her head now and then.

When Moore's mother drove off, Hughes came over to Jeff's car and handed him a plain manila envelope containing Terry's wedding ring from Glenn Davis, the football star she had married in February 1951 after a month-long courtship. "Here," he said to Chouinard. "See that this ring is handed directly to Davis. Give it to him personally."

Hughes was going to help Terry with her ensuing divorce, as he would later do with the marriages of Ava Gardner and Jean Peters. Moore was also counting on Hughes to marry her, in a church wedding, when the divorce was final. But Hughes wasn't counting on Davis's temper. According to classified FBI documents, just after the wedding ring was returned to Davis, he cornered Hughes and "beat the hell out of him."

The 190-pound Davis re-fractured all the ribs that Hughes had injured in the 1946 crash. His left eye was swollen shut and part of his chin shattered. "They put Howard on a plane and flew him to San Francisco for treatment," Chouinard recalled. "If he'd been treated in Los Angeles, there would have been an avalanche of publicity."

Hughes called Louella Parsons, Hedda Hopper, the Associated Press, and United Press to douse the hottest Hollywood news story of the year. But gossip about it spread through the industry and made it into the scandal sheets, including *Confidential* magazine. Jean Peters learned of it while on a film set and was said to have become hysterical over the fact that Hughes was again involved with Terry Moore.

Rumors continued when it was announced, on the heels of the beating, that an injury would keep Davis from playing on the Rams another season. In fact, the Football Hall of Famer slipped into obscurity. Today, Davis will not speak about what he said was "not one of my prouder moments." But he wound up having fans over at Romaine, where some of the aides felt Hughes had gotten what he deserved.

As his personal problems escalated, Hughes decided to escape from his tainted Los Angeles haunts and take refuge in Las Vegas, a city that he had frequented off and on for several decades. He had always liked the atmosphere of the city, where time seemed to have no meaning. In Las Vegas everyone was up at all hours. Hughes, the ultimate night crawler, was right at home in the gambling capital, which didn't really come to life until long past midnight.

"He used to cruise the 2:30 A.M. show at the Silver Slipper—it was the celebrity show," said Las Vegas columnist Bill Willard, who used to perform with a variety revue at the casino. The players frequently ad-libbed about some of the big celebrities who'd show up for the show—including Humphrey Bogart and Lauren Bacall, Tallulah Bankhead, and Frank Sinatra and his pals. "But when Hughes came in, we weren't to mention that he was in the house," said Willard.

During one night on the town with Jean Peters and John Wayne, who was then making pictures for RKO, Hughes balked at going into the Desert Inn. "Everybody will be looking at me," he complained. Wayne brought him down to earth. "You asshole!" said the Duke. "You are with the most beautiful woman in the world. And John Wayne! And they're gonna look at you?" Hughes was so upset by that retort that for months afterward he wouldn't talk to Wayne.

For three years Hughes roamed from hotel suite to hotel suite; from the El Rancho to the Flamingo and from the Desert Inn's penthouse to a five-room cottage he finally leased from the Desert Inn and furnished in 1953. The brigades of gorgeous showgirls and dealers provided him with an almost endless supply of one-night stands.

Hughes would install himself tables that executives at the Desert Inn and the Flamingo kept open for him twenty-four hours, from which he could girl-watch. When he saw one he liked, he would have one of his lackeys relay an invitation from Hughes, "the business leader."

"He was definitely on the lookout," recalled Willard. As a press representative for the exotic dancer Kalatan, he was once approached by Hughes who asked, "Is she available?" Willard shot back, "For what?" Hughes hastened to add that he was casting an opulent *Arabian Nights* movie and needed bountiful stars. (Kalatan wound up appearing in Hughes's *Son of Sinbad*.)

During this Vegas sojourn, he sometimes invited Kathryn Grayson, Jean Peters, or Terry Moore to join him. Hughes also stayed in touch with them by (germ-free) phone. He had to retain control.

Despite his promiscuity in the gambling capital, he regularly accused all three women of infidelity. In long conversations with Kathryn Grayson, he sometimes screamed as he accused her of cheating on him. "The fighting between Kathryn and Howard became quite bitter," said Chouinard, who maintained wiretaps on Grayson's phone and Howard's as well.

When the MGM soprano took her lavish show to one of the major hotels, Hughes circled her protectively. One evening, by eavesdropping on her phone conversations, he learned that MGM executive Benny Thau, who was romantically interested in Grayson, was flying in to meet her. "Howard would not believe it was business involving the studio," Grayson later recalled. He raged and pouted all that afternoon.

At 7:00 P.M., an hour before she was to appear, Hughes called to tell her that her brother was very ill and that he had a plane ready to carry her to Los Angeles. "I was worried—frantic, in fact," Grayson said. "So I took off my costume and drove with him to the airport."

But once he got Kathryn in the air, he didn't head for Los Angeles. He simply circled over Vegas again and again, admitting that he was merely jealous and wanted to "save her" from Thau. Grayson was so incensed that she didn't speak to Hughes for almost three months.

So busy had Hughes been on other romantic fronts that he didn't realize that Jean Peters was finally fed up. Out of nowhere came a bolt of lightning: she was going to marry someone else!

Louella Parsons phoned the Romaine headquarters early one morning in May 1955. She had to talk to Hughes. When Romaine wouldn't put her through, she telephoned Greg Bautzer, Howard's personal attorney. He handled business dealings involving Hughes's various female associates. So, he quickly got in touch with Hughes, who reached Parsons half an hour later.

"Jean's going to be married this week," said Parsons. "Were you aware of it?" Hughes was floored. He had been so enmeshed in other affairs, including TWA turmoil, that he never got around to formally welcoming Jean back from Rome, where she had filmed *Three Coins in the Fountain*. The movie followed three American career women in Rome, where each tossed a coin in the Trevi Fountain in hopes of finding love. For Peters, the film had proved prophetic.

She met Texas oilman Stuart Cramer III during filming. "They're getting married," Parsons told Howard.

Both Jeff Chouinard and Hughes's key aide, Bill Gay, were shocked at the boss's reaction to Parsons's news. "He didn't rage or cast blame or fall into one of his depressions," recalled Chouinard. "He kept his pain hidden."

Despite word that Jean was marrying someone else, Hughes spent two days concentrating on TWA, furiously writing almost five hundred pages of instructions, solutions, and ideas about how to solve the financial crush and end the constant threats of mutiny among the seventeen thousand scientists, engineers, and factory workers at Hughes Aircraft. Then he stampeded into action on the personal front.

After dressing up, he drove over to the Grayson home, where he formally proposed to Kathryn with a beautiful speech that was aimed at her parents as well. He was probably thunderstruck when she sweetly accepted and even acquiesced to his timetable. They would be married in Las Vegas on Memorial Day weekend. Though the arrangements were still tentative, Howard apparently planned to move into Grayson's Tudor showplace on the Pacific Palisades peninsula.

If Jean could get married, so could he.

Weary of waiting and of spending most of her evenings alone at the house Howard leased for her, Jean was susceptible to the attentions of the handsome Cramer, an executive at Lockheed. They were married on May 29, 1954, in Washington, D.C. It would be the first marriage for both. But not the last.

While Kathryn Grayson was being fitted for an elegant suit for what she thought would be her wedding ceremony, Hughes summoned Jeff Chouinard to the Beverly Hills Hotel and told him to set the dogs after the newlyweds. "I want to know as much about that relationship as possible. If there's a way to do physical surveillance, then do so." He then phoned Washington contacts, professional lobbyists, and asked them to name the hottest new private eye in the business, a man who could discreetly handle the toughest of assignments.

Both men recommended Robert A. Maheu, an FBI veteran who had just formed Robert A. Maheu Associates. Hughes phoned Maheu that night, beginning a relationship that was to last fifteen years. "I want you to get me all the dirt on Stuart Cramer III," Hughes told him. "Among other things, check to see if he's working for the CIA. I've heard rumors."

Hughes didn't know it at the time, but he had contacted the right man. Maheu had also been a CIA operative.

Maheu's report was on Howard's desk a week later. It turned out Cramer was a real blue blood with an enormous fortune and, yes, he had some CIA ties within the massive Lockheed aviation empire.

Howard filed the information away for later use. He next sent Chouinard to Miami, where Peters and Cramer were living. Chouinard wound up with an eyeful. While playing Peeping Tom outside the couple's residence, he watched as Peters and Cramer sat cozily alongside one another. Then they began to kiss and embrace, and slid to the floor. When they stood up, back in view of the spying Chouinard, they were naked.

Per protocol at Romaine, Chouinard was supposed to give his written surveillance reports to Bill Gay, who then relayed the information to Hughes. "No way," said Jeff. "The Old Man won't want to hear this second hand."

After listening to Chouinard's report, Hughes sighed and said, "Well, I'll be damned."

Memorial Day weekend was looming. Howard intended on seeing through his proposal to Grayson, unlike the aborted Lana Turner nuptials eight years earlier.

But Grayson, who has long been a believer in spiritualism, woke up on the appointed day with a strange foreboding. "Whenever I closed my eyes, I saw a little blond head sinking in a whirlpool. Something terrible was going to happen to a child. And I believed it would involve my daughter." She tried but couldn't find Howard, who was already at Hughes Aircraft, arranging for a flight to take them to Las Vegas. By the time she did reach him, a limousine was already waiting outside her house.

"I can't do it, Howard," said Grayson. Then she told him about her strange premonition.

"That's craziness," he said soothingly. "It's just nervous jitters."

Grayson couldn't be persuaded. Johnny Maschio's wife, Connie, later called her. "You are crazy, Kathryn. This man is in love with you and wants to marry you. Do you know how many other women have wanted to be in your place?"

Grayson was in tears. "I can't. I just can't."

Less than five hours later, Grayson found out that her nephew Timmy had drowned in her brother's swimming pool.

When Jean Peters married Stuart Cramer she didn't tell him about her relationship with Hughes. "It had never been mentioned," Cramer later said. But he learned of it directly from Hughes, who called him and requested, "Please come and hear me out."

"Jean tried to get away from Howard, but it just wasn't possible," said actress friend Jeanne Crain. When Hughes wanted something, added Crain, he could be "overpowering."

After Cramer flew in from Miami, he was chauffeured to the Beverly Hills Hotel. Then he was escorted to Hughes's bungalow, where Hughes was frank about his intentions. "I am in love with your wife and have been so for many, many years," said the 48-year-old millionaire. He further stunned Cramer when he added, "And she is completely in love with me. Now, if she will confirm this, will you give her an uncontested divorce?"

Cramer said later that he felt his legs collapsing beneath him. "I had to fight to keep from fainting."

When Cramer returned to Miami, Jean admitted to her ties with Hughes but, no, she didn't want a divorce. According to Noah Dietrich, though, Jean was distraught over the situation. "She was racked with grief," he said. All the same, she refused Hughes's calls. So Hughes called Cramer and audaciously used Peters's distress as a trump card, pointing out that if Cramer truly cared for her, surely he would let her go.

"You must have some sort of lingering affection for this girl," Hughes told him.

Cramer is said to have fought back tears as he insisted, "Mr. Hughes, I'm still completely in love with this wonderful girl."

Hughes wouldn't back down. "Cramer told me that Howard provided some sort of marital promissory note," Noah remembered. It was on the strength of that promise that Jean Peters agreed to divorce Cramer to marry Hughes. But Cramer told Peters, "I really love you, remember that.

If the year passes and he doesn't marry you, I will take you back, on any terms."

Cramer later noted, "If your wife is going to get a divorce, you might as well let her marry someone who can afford to support her. It's the cheapest way out."

There is an odd footnote to this already odd scenario: in 1959 Stuart Cramer married . . . Terry Moore.

Once Peters left Cramer, Hughes again put her in exile, installing her in one of his leased houses on Los Angeles's west side, where she was surrounded by aides, drivers, and maids. "I overheard Howard telling Jean he was too busy to marry her at that moment," Dietrich recalled.

Yes, Hughes was busy. There were other women to romance.

For a while he began to see Grayson again. But as their relationship matured, he appeared less frequently in her moonlit courtyard.

Then came two red-hot affairs. They would be the grandest of finales for Howard Hughes.

At thirty-seven, Susan Hayward was Hollywood's pre-eminent red-headed beauty. Temperamental and smoky-voiced, she had come to Hollywood in 1937 to vie for the role of Scarlett O'Hara in *Gone With the Wind*. When Hughes caught up with her, she was a three-time Oscar nominee, with a Best Actress award in her future (for her role as executed murderess Barbara Graham in *I Want to Live!*). She was also just escaping her marriage to B-movie actor Jess Barker, whose career had been eclipsed by hers.

Hughes had made a play for her more than a dozen years ago. Now she was receptive. She was so self-assured, in fact, that she told her boss, 20th Century-Fox chief, Darryl Zanuck, "I might become the next Mrs. Howard Hughes." Like many others in Hollywood, she was not aware of Howard's continuing relationship with Jean Peters.

Hughes so swept her off her feet that she introduced him to her sons, Timothy and Gregory, as "Mr. Magic." He put planes at her disposal, filled her dressing room with roses every morning, and talked with her for hours at a lovers' lookout above Beverly Hills. But it wasn't Hayward, with her beauty and Hollywood status, that posed a threat to Jean Peters, then twenty-nine. It was an eighteen-year-old former beauty queen.

Yvonne Shubert had come to Hughes's attention one morning in early 1955 when Walter Kane handed a picture to Hughes as they flew to Las

Vegas. Occupied by the flight, Hughes gave only a quick glance to the image of the fifteen-year-old schoolgirl. "Gorgeous," he said. "Sign her up."

Kane quickly sought out the girl and delivered his song and dance about making her a star. All that was needed, Kane explained to the girl's mother, was to deliver her daughter into Howard Hughes's hands. Yvonne Shubert listened intently. The teenager had never heard of Howard Hughes and had no idea why he was interested in *her* when Hollywood was packed with starlets already.

But Kane, the Hughes talent scout, was persuasive, and Yvonne, along with her mother, entered Howard's harem and was given "the big treatment: dance lessons, drama coaching, and vocal lessons."

At first there was no reason to believe this girl would be different from any of the others. Then Hughes ordered Kane to "handle her personally" rather than putting her in the care of the usual aides. Screenings, usually double features, were scheduled in the Goldwyn screening room. Sitting near Kane and her mother, Yvonne was enthralled that someone would show films just for her. She didn't learn until later that a tall man huddled against the back wall and watched her night after night.

But, finally, she was asked to come without her mother. Not long after, the tall man moved through the empty room and sat near her. Still later, Kane quietly slipped away, leaving Yvonne alone with the stranger. At the end of the screening, Hughes signaled that he would like to talk to Yvonne, who nodded, "Sure."

"Now here's what we will do," he said. "You go in that office right there and I'll go down the hall to another one. You just wait by the phone." A minute later, the phone in Yvonne's darkened office rang. It was Hughes. They talked for about an hour.

For months their relationship was conducted on the telephone. "Some nights we'd talk for four or five hours," Yvonne recalled. "We just had that instant rapport. We discussed everything, new films, current events, and about his professional woes. In that way we were not only friends but totally involved emotionally before we became intimate." They played an interesting cat-and-mouse game: Hughes, always fearful of rejection, tried incessantly to gauge Yvonne's commitment before he let down his romantic guard. "He tried again and again. He wished me to expose my feelings for him."

"How do you feel about me?" he asked early one morning.

"I think I have a kind of love," she responded warily.

"What do you mean a *kind* of love?" Hughes prompted.

"Well, certainly not as a lover," she answered.

Howard was crestfallen. "Like a father, I suppose."

Yvonne shook her head no.

"Well what then?" he said in disgust. "Like a grandfather?"

Shubert protested that she hadn't meant that at all, though Hughes, at age forty-nine, was old enough to be her grandfather. He was deeply hurt.

The teenager and the millionaire struggled for months to find a common ground strong enough to support their problematic relationship, now a budding love affair. "He was guiding me, carefully leading me into the affair," she recalled, adding, "He was by now my friend, a good friend, and I really didn't know what real love between a man and a woman was at that point."

By the time Yvonne and Howard's physical relationship commenced, Hughes had promised to marry her several times. It was never a case of whether they would be married, he said, but when. Since the aides kept her in seclusion, Shubert knew nothing about Jean Peters or any of the starlets linked to him in the gossip columns. But Howard wasn't lying to Shubert. "This was a major love affair," recalled Robert Maheu. "He became obsessed with her."

His plan to lure Yvonne into intimacy was identical to maneuvers he had used earlier with starlets like Faith Domergue and even Jean Peters. After winning her over, he told her he had to leave town for a week on business—ostensibly to New York. "I had become so attached to him that I felt a sense of loss at his leaving," Yvonne remembered.

Hughes actually remained in a Beverly Hills Hotel bungalow just fifty yards from Shubert's, and his diaries show that he called her first to say he was in New York, then in Chicago, and finally in Denver and headed home. Then he rang to say he'd just arrived at Hughes Aircraft and had planned a gala dinner for the two of them to celebrate his return.

When Hughes finally arrived at Shubert's room, she was fairly glowing with anticipation. For the first three hours the two discussed films, Howard's business troubles, and plans for Shubert's singing career. At midnight, Howard turned off the lights and made love with the teenager. Years later she recalled, "I had strong religious convictions regarding premarital intimacy. I wouldn't have slept with him if he hadn't promised marriage."

Howard installed Yvonne in a rambling home in Coldwater Canyon, a rustic area dotted with cliffside houses that hang above the San Fernando

Valley. He also provided her with a permanent suite in the Beverly Hills Hotel, in one of the wings that looked down on his bungalow.

Because Howard was so infatuated with her, and because Yvonne and Hughes conducted their affair right under Jean's nose, Chouinard and Gay assigned four men to watch over her full-time. In addition, both her house and hotel suite were bugged, and the phones tapped.

There was also a peephole, which had been drilled by Chouinard's men, in the wall that separated her room from his. The peephole became a front-row seat for the boss's extracurricular swan song. Some of the guards would take turns playing voyeur on what Chouinard called a "near perfect sexual relationship."

"Of all those girls, I was the only one who really loved Howard," Yvonne recalled. "And he was aware of that." It was because of her love for him, she added, that "all of the aides despised me."

But Jean Peters despised her as well. When she found out that Hughes had spent $250,000 trying to make Yvonne a singing star, and that he had taken her to Vancouver and the Bahamas while Peters was left at home, she initiated a campaign to get rid of the girl. It would take four years.

In the meantime, these three Hughes consorts, Peters, Shubert, and Hayward, participated in a New Year's Eve adventure in 1956 that could have been in a Marx Brothers movie. Jeff Chouinard learned of the "New Year's caper" earlier in December when a stern and worried Bill Gay summoned him to the Romaine headquarters.

"The Old Man has decided he wants to greet the New Year by dining at midnight with three women, none of whom know about the other two," said Gay. The ambitious dinner plans were to unfold at the Beverly Hills Hotel.

Howard had spent three weeks arranging this mad scenario—weeks in which he was at the height of his troubles with TWA.

Maybe it was a diversion, a return to the anything-goes days of the thirties. Maybe it was intended to be a magnificent finale for the twentieth century's busiest Casanova. Whatever the reason, Hughes planned the night with the precision of Napoleon preparing for battle. As the line commander, Chouinard, backed up by a dozen assistants, was to preside over this gambit by stationing lookouts throughout the hotel complex.

Jean Peters was established in the hotel dining room, where Dom Perignon and a dozen gardenias awaited her. Susan Hayward was to occupy the "prestige, center-stage table" of the Polo Lounge, the haunt of the rich and famous. She was also to be presented with a nosegay of roses when she arrived and, as an added trinket, an emerald bracelet from Cartier. Yvonne Shubert was to greet the New Year in a specially decorated bungalow in the hotel's rambling tropical garden.

The evening commenced when Hughes, in a tuxedo, sat down with Peters in the main dining room. But after ordering drinks and kissing her hello, Hughes was suddenly called away for an emergency "telephone call" from the Hughes Tool Company. "Go ahead with your cocktail, Jean," he said. "I'll be back as soon as I can."

Jean was easily the standout in a room of beauties that night, wearing a white sequined gown, her dark hair piled on top of her head. She had high expectations that tonight Hughes would finally set a date for their marriage.

He strode into the Polo Lounge and settled in the chair across from Hayward, who was wearing an Edith Head confection, strapless, with mink at the neck and thousands of jet beads decorating the skirt. Again, there were greetings and an order for champagne. And another phone call for Hughes, who left the room to take it.

He literally ran from the hotel to Shubert's bungalow, where dinner of beef stroganoff, asparagus in hollandaise sauce, and out-of-season raspberries, all prepared by Howard's own chef, had already been delivered in sterling silver braziers. "He dashed in and out, but I didn't think it at all unusual," said Shubert. "He always had business to attend to, day or night."

While Peters and Hayward would suffer through the night, the teenage Yvonne Shubert gloried in her role as Cinderella. She even wore a special gown of understated chiffon and silk brocade made especially for her by MGM costume designer Michael Woolfe. Even before Hughes appeared at the bungalow, a florist filled the room with yellow roses, iced two bottles of Dom Perignon, and lighted a generous stand of holiday candles.

All the while, Jeff's men, in tuxedos and armed with binoculars and walkie-talkies, were spread throughout the grounds.

For a while it looked as if Hughes was going to succeed with his preposterous charade. He managed to make a full circle. When the next "emergency phone call" arrived suspiciously on cue, Susan Hayward watched Hughes retreat once again. "There was something in his demeanor that made me wary," Hayward confided to columnist Earl Wilson the next day. "After all, how many people work on New Year's Eve?"

So Hayward grabbed her mink coat and tailed him. She caught him at Jean Peters's table.

"What the hell is going on?" Hayward demanded of Hughes. Then she added, "Hello, Jean. You're date number two, aren't you? Well, I'm date number one." Peters and Hayward, both in a fury, turned their backs on Howard and walked out the front entrance of the hotel. Separately.

To this day, Yvonne remembers the night as "incredibly romantic." At the time she knew nothing of Peters and Hayward, since it was she who Howard kissed as the clock struck midnight. She has come to believe Hughes set up the threesome to prove he could carry it off. "He did it as much for the aides as anything else. He wanted to show them that he could get these three women and they couldn't. He loved showing off for them, in a macho kind of way."

CHAPTER 27

SHOTGUN WEDDING

WHEN KATHRYN GRAYSON RETURNED TO HER RIVIERA COUNTRY CLUB mansion late on the afternoon of January 6, 1957, she found Howard in the den, cradling her daughter as he rocked her back and forth in an antique rocking chair. Hughes seemed at peace, totally engrossed in the child.

Appearances were deceiving. As soon as the child went to bed, Hughes began pressing Kathryn to marry him immediately, within twenty-four hours if possible. Grayson, exhausted from a day on the set and from rehearsals for a major concert tour, put him off. "Not now, Howard," she answered wearily.

"No," he declared. "It must be now." Then he yelled: "Kathryn, I have a very, very good reason for asking you to do this, and to do it now!"

They had pursued this same argument for three days, ever since Grayson had agreed to marry a surprisingly ardent Hughes, and accepted his engagement ring for the third time. But she refused to cancel her prestigious concert tour, set to begin three days later in New York City.

Kathryn couldn't understand the rush. Nor could the millionaire's staff, which was scurrying about making hotel reservations and arranging for "a secret ceremony." For most of 1956 Howard had been seriously involved with four women: Grayson, Fox star Susan Hayward, starlet Yvonne Shubert, and Jean Peters. Though all four had received somewhat vague marriage proposals, none was aware that the others had, too.

As Hughes continued his rage, Kathryn decided to ignore him. "Look, Howard," she said calmly, "I'm leaving for New York tomorrow, and we can discuss this when I return."

He whirled to face her. "It has to be now," he said before striding across the room and slapping her—hard across the face.

Grayson was stunned. "He'd never shown the slightest sign of violence before," she recalled. "I stood there for a minute, trying to control my temper, which was worse than his." Instinctively, she picked up a small stool and raised it over her head, ready to clobber him. But reason prevailed and she dropped the stool.

Recalling the incident in 1995, Grayson admitted, "I was mystified. Why the rush? I just thought he was being irrational."

It wasn't until decades later that she connected Howard's hysteria that night with a phone call she had received a few days earlier. Several of Hughes's aides at the Romaine Street headquarters had offered her a "confidential tip" to pass on to Howard. "They asked me to tell him that Noah Dietrich was planning to have him committed," she remembered. But she kept the curious message to herself.

Saddened by Howard's desperate emotional state and haggard appearance, Grayson was also certain that this meant the end of their eight-year relationship. "I would never tolerate any sort of violence," she recalled. "And I wasn't about to make an exception for Howard Hughes."

So that night she gathered up her suitcases, called for her driver, and walked out the front door of the Tudor mansion. Hughes was hunched down in the rocking chair—alone in the darkened living room. He didn't look up. "I want you out of here when I come back," she told him.

She would never see him again.

Once she was safely installed in her suite at New York's Hampshire House, she telephoned Hughes's Romaine Street headquarters. "I want Howard out of my house when I return."

"Is there any message?" asked one of the Hughes aides.

"No," Grayson answered. "Just let him know he's not welcome there any longer."

Puzzled and disillusioned, she proceeded with the concert tour. She couldn't have known that Howard was caught up in a web of plots and counterplots within his vast industrial empire, all of them centering on the state of his sanity. Nor could she have known that Hughes believed marriage was the only thing that would keep him out of a mental institution.

Being fed rumors by his aides and operating through an increasing haze of paranoia, Hughes believed that Noah was planning to commit him and then seize control of his then $500 million empire. Actually, Howard's instincts were astute; he just targeted the wrong man.

Several weeks earlier, two of Hughes's physicians, apparently Dr. Verne Mason and an unidentified specialist from the Hughes Medical Institute, asked for a private, "urgent" meeting with Dietrich at his home. Noah reluctantly agreed.

They arrived with a battery of test results and a commitment form they wanted Dietrich to sign. "They explained that Howard's syphilis hadn't been totally eradicated," recalled Mary Dietrich, Noah's widow. In fact, she explained, the venereal disease had mutated into "neurosyphilis," which was attacking his brain, his spinal cord, and his central nervous system. The physicians further explained that Hughes, for some years, had suffered from "paresis" and "locomotor ataxia," and that in their opinion the industrialist should be committed.

Never revealed before, this diagnosis explains the avalanche of emotional woes that crashed down on Hughes in 1957 and 1958. According to Dr. Per-Anders Mardh, a Swedish scientist who is at the forefront of syphilis treatment today, "general paresis (also called dementia paralytica) and its companion, ataxia, hit patients when they are in their fifties." Howard was fifty-one when the diagnosis was presented to Dietrich. "Unfortunately, the damage to the brain is irreversible," Mardh continued.

UCLA's Dr. Jeffrey Schwartz notes that as many as 30 per cent of those infected with syphilis during that era ended up with neurosyphilis. "The mercury treatment wasn't very effective, obviously."

The symptoms of paresis and ataxia included irritability, difficulty in concentrating, defective judgment, memory deterioration, delusions of grandeur, and a marked erosion of hygiene and grooming habits. Hughes would experience all of these during the coming decade.

But Noah would not concede to the doctors that his boss was insane, and he angrily escorted the physicians to the door. Privately, though, he admitted that he wasn't surprised by the diagnosis. For more than a decade he and Dr. Mason had shared a secret. Following the 1946 plane crash, when Hughes was still fighting for his life, his syphilis had recurred, this time attacking his central nervous system. Because of the catastrophic nature of his injuries and the enormous array of drugs flowing through his body, physicians were unable to treat this outbreak of secondary syphilis. For more than a year, it attacked his brain and spinal cord.

Both Dietrich and Hughes's private secretary, Nadine Henley, discussed this subject "off the record" with Don Williamson, a senior reporter for both *Time* and *Life*. While this information was placed in Hughes's background file, it never appeared in print. Author Dan Wolfe, Williamson's stepson, recalled being told "that Howard had been given such amounts of penicillin and other drugs that he had developed a resistance to them. Therefore, they were unable to control the syphilis."

A confidential letter written by Raymond Cook, who handled Howard's estate matters for the legal firm of Andrews and Kurth, said Dietrich told him that he had been approached by two people, including Dr. Verne Mason, about possible commitment. Fearful that his aides and attorneys might lock him up, Hughes, with the help of Hollywood attorney Greg Bautzer, researched the California statutes governing mental illness. He seized upon the provision that stated that the decision to institutionalize rests solidly with the husband or wife.

This resulted in the frantic proposal to Kathryn Grayson, and when she declined, to Jean Peters, the woman he had been living with off and on for twelve years. Before orchestrating a second wedding, he asked Jean, "You wouldn't commit me, would you?"

She answered indignantly, "No. Of course not."

"It isn't that he didn't love Jean," said Noah Dietrich. "In fact, I believe he loved her more than any woman since Katharine Hepburn. But he was dead set against marriage, period." Glenn Odekirk agreed. In a videotaped interview with Jane Russell's brother, Jamie Russell, Odekirk said "the fear of being locked up pushed [Howard] into that wedding, no doubt about it."

For Jean, the blessing was mixed. After years of patiently waiting, she became Mrs. Howard Hughes. But she would not be a traditional bride. There would be no flowing gown; no posh Hollywood reception, no notices in the newspaper. The ceremony would be carried out in utmost secrecy. Noah was not told, nor was Howard's longtime aide, Nadine Henley. Instead, Howard enlisted the help of attorney James Arditto, who arranged for the couple to be married in Nevada using assumed names.

Attorney D. Martin Cook and aide George Francom were alerted by Hughes personally. Using a pay telephone in Beverly Hills, he ordered them to assemble duck hunting outfits and to await his phone call. "This is a top-secret journey," he said. "Don't leave your house; don't use your telephones; just await my next call."

The calls came at four o'clock on the morning of January 12, 1957. Hughes, using a different phone booth for each call, told Arditto, Cook, and Francom, "Get your hunting clothes on and meet me at Hughes Aircraft in forty-five minutes. Don't shave; remember you're duck hunters."

At the airfield, Cook was astonished to find a brand-new gleaming Constellation, the largest liner in the TWA fleet, waiting to carry them off to a yet unnamed destination. As he noted, "No matter the destination, four duck hunters, one of them a gorgeous film star, were bound to create a stir as they arrived in a commercial jet designed to carry one hundred and twenty passengers."

When they were airborne, Hughes told them their destination was Tonopah, Nevada, a dusty, partly deserted settlement surrounded by out-croppings of slag gray granite and dreary expanses of mud-colored sagebrush. Early in the century it had been a boomtown for miners who pulled millions worth of silver out of the granite outcroppings; in 1951 the region was selected as an atomic testing site.

The plane landed on a small runway, an airfield built to handle military traffic. The huge liner dwarfed the runway as it finally came to a stop on a sandy patch of desert surrounded by cactus and ocotillo trees.

Because the airport didn't have a stair ramp, the plane's passengers had to climb down a knotted hemp rope. A disguised Hughes wore a camou-flage vest and battered hat; corporate attorney Arditto, the only one of the group who actually hunted, was in fisherman's pants, an old canvas hat, and a genuine duck hunter's padded jacket. Cook and Francom had impro-vised. "He called before dawn and directed us to come to Culver City on a special mission," recalled Cook, one of Howard's twenty-five attorneys. "We were supposed to look like we were going hunting. So I did my best with jeans, an old flannel shirt, and a fairly beat-up jacket."

Jean was dressed in a suit with high-heel pumps as she gingerly came down the rope. She had been willing to make certain concessions, such as marrying under an assumed name, but she had her limits. She had told Hughes she would not be married in disguise—certainly not as a duck hunter.

The troupe converged on the Mizpah Motel, located on the town's Main Street, where several rooms had been reserved and a justice of the peace was waiting. In a simple ceremony conducted by Walter Bowler, G. A. Johnson (Hughes) married Marian Evans (Peters), slipping a ruby ring on her finger as their "friends" watched. Afterward, remembered Cook, Hughes embraced Peters "with a proud look on his face."

The bridegroom and his bride didn't spend their wedding night in Tonopah. They returned to the airport instead and took their Constellation back to Los Angeles. On the return flight, Howard acted like a lovestruck college boy. He and Jean held hands and put their heads close together as they whispered to one another.

Back in Los Angeles, the newlyweds were dropped off at the house where Jean had been living. But before going inside, Hughes did something uncharacteristic. "He shook hands with each of us, breaking his long-standing taboo of not touching anyone," remembered Cook.

Then Hughes and Peters walked up the lawn, into the house and a new epoch.

Three days later in New York, Trans World Airlines publicity director, Walter Mehnke, knocked on the door of Kathryn Grayson's suite at the Hampshire House. He solemnly explained that "rumors are flying that Howard has married Jean Peters.

"But Howard wants me to assure you that there is no truth to these reports, no matter where you read or hear them. He's in love with you." Then he backed out of the suite.

Kathryn Grayson never heard from Howard Hughes again, not even in March when his own representatives announced to Louella Parsons that Peters was indeed Mrs. Howard Hughes.

Left behind were "memories of a warm and wonderful relationship," Grayson recalled.

Hughes's veil of secrecy was remarkably effective. Although Hollywood buzzed with rumors of the marriage, nothing appeared in print until eight weeks later. The first news break came in the *Los Angeles Mirror-News* on March 16. "Howard Hughes, Hollywood's most eligible bachelor for more than twenty-five years, has secretly married Jean Peters," the paper announced. But reporters had the date wrong, March 12, and the location, claiming the pair had been married at sea on the Hughes yacht anchored off Miami Beach.

Two days later Hearst columnist Florabel Muir wrote, "Green-eyed actress Jean Peters and millionaire Howard Hughes were secretly married three days ago." Muir noted that the site of the marriage was "still unknown." She added: "I happen to know that they plighted their troth in an auto parked in 'lovers lane' atop the Santa Monica mountains overlooking the twinkling lights of film land."

Because reporters were unable to find a marriage certificate, many Hollywood insiders refused to believe that the marriage was legal. Adding to the rumor mill was the fact that shortly after marrying, Hughes and Jean were on their way to living separate lives. But first they embarked on a brief honeymoon at a secluded ranch near Palm Springs, where Hughes stationed a cordon of guards and ordered them to pace around the property, military style, twenty-four hours a day.

The newlyweds rarely left the house, nor did they raise the blinds or open the dark Spanish shutters on the windows. The guards caught only one glimpse of Jean and Howard as they strolled hand in hand just before dawn on a Sunday morning. They were leaning against each other as they gazed at the moon.

Hughes was jumpy and paranoid throughout the brief idyll. He was convinced that Noah had betrayed him and had directed TWA's process servers to his hideaway. When a jeep roared out of the sagebrush and tried to plow through the fence, Hughes blamed it on Noah. Though the intruders were chased away by guards "firing their guns in the air," Hughes and Jean evacuated the love nest. "We're not safe here anymore," he said.

A week after he returned to the Beverly Hills Hotel, Hughes received "proof of Noah's mutiny." Raymond Cook, one of his battery of Houston attorneys, informed his boss that Dietrich had actually admitted that he had met with Verne Mason to discuss seizing the empire.

Already distrustful of his longtime aide, Howard now treated him with disdain. One early morning at two o'clock he summoned Noah to Las Vegas and grilled him for hours about the state of Hughes's finances. Dietrich was forced to stand between chalk marks on the floor. A light was directed at his face, and he couldn't see his boss, seated in a dark space behind his desk.

Then, on May 12, 1957, Howard telephoned Noah at 2:00 A.M. He was brusque: "You're to leave for Houston at once and do everything you can to inflate the profits."

Dietrich replied that he would go under one condition. "I want a capital gains guarantee, signed and delivered to me within eight hours."

Hughes screamed his answer: "Noah, you're holding a gun to my head. You will be provided for. Don't worry!"

"I've been living on your promises for years, Howard. It's over," Noah responded.

"Nobody holds a gun to my head!" Hughes yelled.

"Forget it," said Dietrich. "I'm through as of this moment. Don't call me again. Just reach me through my attorneys."

Then Hughes cried out, "Noah, I cannot live without you!"

"These were the last words I ever heard from Howard Hughes," Dietrich recalled. "And it was the first time in thirty-two years that he paid me such a compliment."

Dietrich's widow, Mary, heard her husband's side of the conversation—and his slamming down of the receiver, which ended one of the most successful business partnerships in the twentieth century. She wasn't surprised. "I think something would have happened anyway, because William Gay and all the other aides were united against him. Noah stood in their way, and he wasn't going to let them grow rich off of Howard." She added, "Shortly after, these drivers were suddenly executives, vice presidents and so forth."

Like everyone else, Yvonne Shubert read the news accounts of Howard's marriage.

Brandishing copies of the newspaper articles, she confronted him one night when he came to visit her in her Beverly Hills Hotel bungalow. "What's this about?" she asked.

"False reports," he answered. "You know how the press operates. I'm still seeing Jean, because you don't just shut somebody out of your life. You have to let them down easily." Then he renewed his promise to marry Shubert "as soon as the time is right."

"He was very convincing," she recalled. "I would have left him if I'd believed he was married."

Because of Shubert's age and innocence, Hughes had been sexually cautious with her, preferring the "withdrawal" method of contraception—withdrawal before ejaculation. It didn't faze him that, even then, physicians considered this remarkably ineffective. She was seventeen when she discovered she was pregnant—a fact that left Hughes shaken. He knew he was the father, since the aides had accounted for every second of her time for two years. But he hesitated before arranging for an illegal abortion because Shubert was three months into the pregnancy. Both Howard and Yvonne knew there could be serious complications.

"He arranged for it to be done in a doctor's office," she remembered. "Dr. Norman Crane set it up, but for legal reasons, he wouldn't even ride in the car with me. I think we may have even changed cars once to throw anyone off the trail."

Fortunately, the operation was a success. But Yvonne's innocence was shattered. Shortly after, she had a frightening dream that left her so upset she began beating on the door of the bungalow where Hughes was conducting a business conference. When he came to investigate the commotion, he found Shubert in hysterics, leaning against a rail wearing nothing but Howard's old white shirt. "He was angry at first, but a short time later calmed me down."

Yvonne's residences were always chosen by Hughes, who set her up at the Beverly Hills Hotel, the Beverly Hilton Hotel, and finally in a large house in Coldwater Canyon. But she constantly chafed under his requirements.

Her screening schedule was plotted day by day for four years. For instance, on a Tuesday night in 1958, Howard made her watch the movies *Slim Carter, Ride a Crooked Trail, Fraulein,* and *The Thing That Wouldn't Die.*

When Howard sent her on a trip to New York to record an album (he was determined to turn her into a "queen of pop") he told the aides not to let her visit Central Park. "Avoid this at all costs," he said. "The park is out. I do not want the word ever mentioned in her presence, and at no time should she be driven by the park or taken to a restaurant which overlooks the park."

As soon as Howard plunged into the financial hurricane surrounding TWA, his preoccupation with Shubert abated. Since he kept her isolated from others her own age, he tried to placate her. He showed up at her door one evening with a tiny French poodle under his arm. "Honey, you gotta have this dog. This little dog is just what you need. Its name is Kesha," Hughes said proudly. "I selected him personally." But when Shubert made a place on her bed for Kesha, Hughes declared, "Absolutely not!"

He explained, "Kesha must have his own room. And his own bed because he absolutely cannot sleep with you."

"He was simply jealous of everything," Shubert said. "He could not deal with that tiny little dog sleeping with me." So Kesha moved into an executive suite three doors down from Yvonne's room. Kesha's room ran

$45 per night (compared to $18 for Yvonne's) and included a view of Beverly Hills, a wet bar, and coffee nook.

Yvonne, meanwhile, was giving way to a wild streak that asserted itself more with each year she lived in the gilded prison Howard had erected around her. At first she practiced escaping from the guards who shadowed her day and night, to the point of bugging her telephone. It got so bad in the house on Coldwater Canyon that Chouinard had his men climb light and telephone poles so they could see into her bedroom and den.

Then, in 1959, Yvonne met a young man named Johnny Rand. He was young and exciting and they began a telephone relationship that was duly tape-recorded and brought to the attention of Hughes. Not long after, she invented a series of disappearing acts—so she could be with Johnny.

Rand was convinced she was a prisoner who needed freeing from Howard's spell. She, in turn, had been told by the aides that he had a criminal past. Ultimately, Rand talked her into meeting him. When the two drove off together, the Hughes detectives roared up behind them, but Yvonne and Johnny lost them on the crowded freeway. "And we switched cars three times," Yvonne recalled.

Later that same day she and Rand went to a shooting range where he wanted to test a gun he had purchased for protection. When he tried to line up the barrel with the sight, the gun accidentally discharged. A bullet ripped through Rand's head, killing him instantly.

Shubert was taken to a hospital in shock. "The tragedy helped me see the emptiness of the life I led with Howard," said Yvonne, who returned to live with her parents.

Hughes, meanwhile, had been advised of the shooting. He was sure Maheu had somehow carried it out. "Bob, I knew you were good, but I didn't know you were this good. Now let me ask you this, can it be traced back to you—to us—in any way."

Maheu soothed him. "It was an accident, Howard. The guy shot himself." But Howard was convinced that Maheu had used his considerable contacts in the LAPD to have it declared an accidental death. "He thought I was this super tough guy, an FBI agent with a gun and the guts to do whatever was necessary," Maheu mused.

To end any police speculation that Hughes was involved, Maheu had the police science lab do extensive tests on the gun used by Johnny that proved without a doubt that it was an accident. "There was talk in the law enforcement world that Hughes had ordered a 'hit' because of his involvement with this beautiful teenager," Maheu remembered.

This allowed the aides, under the direction of Bill Gay, to end Shubert's reign as a royal thorn in their side.

At 5:00 A.M. on the morning after, these instructions were given to the Romaine switchboard: "Yvonne Shubert is to be treated as a total stranger. If she calls us, we are not to recognize her voice or her name—but not to be rude either—but treat her as we do any of the hundreds of 'strangers' who call here every day."

Shubert admits there was no love lost between herself and the aides. "They hated me from the beginning because they had no power over me. I dealt directly with Howard, and he kept them in the dark. They also knew that I informed him when they were slacking off or ripping him off. And he listened to me."

She remembers them as desperate little men. "They all stood around and took this abuse from Howard for years.

"I was their worst nightmare, because I was a close friend of Howard's, and anyone who was a friend had to be disposed of. After the incident with Johnny, I was easy to get rid of. They had been planting seeds of doubt in his mind for years."

So they won. Hurt and disillusioned, Shubert was finally free of Hughes and the isolated lifestyle she'd endured for five years. "I never expected to hear from him, no longer wanted to hear from him. He was not the man I thought he was," she recalled.

Howard began phoning again several weeks after Shubert escaped. She refused all calls but eventually agreed to meet him early in 1960 "more to say good-bye than for any other reason."

She found Howard in Bungalow 4 at the Beverly Hills Hotel. He was lying back on the bed with a smug expression on his face, wearing nothing but a blue dress shirt. "He offered no greeting but launched into a conversation which began, 'Now that Johnny's dead, we've cleared the air,' " Shubert recalled.

Hughes spoke of the death in a cavalier manner. "He talked about it as if it meant nothing; as if it were a joke."

"How can you be so cruel?" she screamed.

With no warning, he sat up in bed and began slapping Yvonne, as he had done to Kathryn Grayson when she refused to marry him. After the second blow she tried to hit back, but Howard retreated to the bathroom and locked the door.

Somewhat sadly, Shubert walked out of the hotel room and out of the life of the man who for five years had dominated her life as lover, friend, and surrogate father.

It was over. But it also ended an era for Hughes. Yvonne Shubert was the last lover in a romantic career that stretched back to the silent era. "He never got over the loss of Yvonne," said Maheu. "Those affairs had added adventure to his life. Now he retreated into the darkness and into drugs." And into one of the oddest marriages in the annals of Hollywood.

The married Hughes returned to his blacked-out bungalow at the Beverly Hills Hotel (BHH Number 4). And Jean was given her own bungalow (BHH Number 9).

The Beverly Hills Hotel was one of the most glamorous hostelries in the world. During the four years Howard and Jean lived there, their neighbors included Marilyn Monroe, Elizabeth Taylor, the Empress of Iran, Yves Montand and his wife, Simone Signoret, Ethel Merman, and the Duke and Duchess of Windsor. But this meant little to Mr. and Mrs. Howard Hughes.

Jean retained the Beverly Hills Hotel furniture but imported a sewing machine and a dress dummy so that she could continue making her own clothes. She gave herself home permanents. And to Howard's irritation, she smoked constantly. She also surrounded her porch and veranda with a family of flowers, most of them growing in old coffee cans.

In all, Howard rented eight of the bungalows that sprawled throughout an imperial garden. The additional bungalows were needed to house the ten full-time guards and aides who catered to the wishes of these odd royal recluses.

Obsessed by the most trivial details, Howard kept strict control of his food and that of his wife. This preoccupation with his food and its preparation had begun decades earlier when, as a child, he sat in his mother's kitchen and watched her scrub and scald and scour not just the pots and pans, but the meat and vegetables as well. So the adult Howard feared that hordes of germs could attack him through ill-prepared nutrients.

If Hughes had been a Renaissance prince instead of a modern-day tycoon, he would have undoubtedly procured a taster. Instead, he spent weeks devising ways to insure that his meals were sanitary and cooked to exact specifications. Even with his drug abuse still far in the future, Howard's obsessive-compulsive disorder produced full-blown food fetishes. Suddenly, he was fixated on the minutes it took to open a can in a sterile manner, the exact thickness of roast beef, the shapes of stew vegetables, the precise number of chocolate chips in a batch of the "germ-free" cookies, and the conditions of the vats that Kellogg's used to prepare his favorite breakfast cereal.

His hand-picked executives at TWA were kept dangling while Howard drafted his baroque instruction manual. Consider just one entry, from 1960, entitled, "The Proper Way to Wash a Food Tin."

> *The man in charge turns the valve of the bathtub on, using his bare hands to do so. He also adjusts the water temperature so that it is not too hot nor too cold. He then takes one of the brushes, and, using one of two special bars of soap, creates a good lather and then scrubs the can from a point two inches below the top of the can. He should first soak and remove the label, and then brush the cylindrical part of the can over and over until all particles of dust, pieces of paper label, and, in general, all sources of contamination have been removed. Holding the can at all times, he then processes the bottom of the can in the same manner, being very sure that the bristles of the brush have thoroughly cleaned all the small indentations on the perimeter of the bottom of the can. He then rinses the soap from the cylindrical sides and bottom of the can.*

When he ordered his special beef stew, the vegetables had to be pared into perfect half-inch squares, with "each and every corner cut off at a precise forty-five-degree angle." He kept a slide ruler on his TV table to measure any suspiciously inexact pea or carrot.

A plate of his chocolate chip cookies had to have a precise number of chips per dozen. And Hughes could gauge the amount just by balancing the cookies in one hand. Too few or too many chips and the cookies were rushed back to the crestfallen chef. He even devised an exact way of folding the chips into the batter "so that they would not be bruised."

"All this is classic obsessive-compulsive behavior," said Dr. Jeffrey Schwartz. "He was absolutely driven to these procedures," he said. "But what was originally believed to be a form of insanity was only a rather mild symptom of OCD."

Even though they lived only fifty yards apart, Jean and Howard communicated mostly by memo and by telephone. All calls, messages, and menus went through a central clearing house set up in Bungalow 7. During their tenure at the sprawling pink hotel, aides typed up more than 100,000 pages of reports, menus, logs, and messages that in themselves indicate the sort of relationship the famous lovers endured. There were distinct rules for preparation and delivery of room service orders, which were prepared by Howard's staff of chefs, not the hotel staff.

Howard's rules governing breakfast orders sent to his wife went like this:

Any food that goes to [her] is not to be cooked in any frying pan or grill. Now waffles are OK providing they are cooked on a waffle iron where only waffles are cooked. Now it is not alright to have french toast, fried eggs, pancakes, wheat cakes, buck wheat cakes, or anything like that because they are usually cooked in a frying pan or skillet in which sausage or bacon has been cooked. Now they might say that the former has not been cooked in them, but I just don't believe them so it is best not even to question them.

In fact, everything Peters ate and drank went into an indexed surveillance report that was presented to Howard. Some examples:

Wed., 6/19/57

info   *At 8:52 a.m., JP ordered 1 coffee, 2 milk and papers for 10A.*

info   *At 10:18 a.m., JP ordered breakfast for 3 in Bung. #19: eggs benedict, 2 large orange juice, 4 bottles of milk packed in ice, 2 orders of sweet rolls, 2 large pots of coffee, 3 bottles of Poland water, 1 packed in ice.*

Howard also had to know where Jean was at all times. The following exchange was filtered through the switchboard at Romaine.

Thur., 3/20/58

5:05 a.m.   *Have you heard from her yet? No sir.*

5:50 a.m.   *Have you heard from her yet? No sir.*

6:45 a.m.   *Have you heard from her yet? No sir.*

6:58 a.m.   *Have you heard from her yet? No sir. You're positive? Positive!*

7:50 a.m.   *Tell Mr. Hughes I'll be ready in about 15 minutes.*

8:10 a.m.   *Have you heard yet? Yes sir. (message given) OK.*

These log entries demonstrate the frustrating nature of Jean's life and how difficult it was to even talk to her husband by phone.

Tue., 5/3/60

10:25 a.m. *Have you heard from Mr. Hughes? (Not since I came on this morning.) Will you tell him I'm up.*

3:00 p.m.   *Inquired again.*

4:30 p.m.   *HRH advised.*

5:50 p.m.   *HRH had been sleeping too long. I am going down to try to wake him up. (Johnny alerted per BG and sent to stop her from going in B#6.)*

info   *(Per aide 6:30 p.m.) ordered 3 steaks, 1 baked potato, 1 Hamburger steak, 1 creamed spinach, 9 Chinese peas, 1 cream of pea soup, 1 sliced tomatoes, 8 milk, 3 orders cheese.*

9:45 p.m.   *I would like to talk to HRH as I have to go to bed soon.*

3:10 a.m.   *Tell Mr. Hughes I am sick and tired of waiting for him to call and I'm going to bed. Please give him that message whenever he deigns to call in!*

7:00 a.m.   *HRH advised.*

After just eleven months of this strange existence Howard Hughes pulled yet another one of his disappearing acts. This time, though, a handful of aides knew where he was.

CHAPTER 28

REFUGE

HOWARD DRESSED CAREFULLY THAT DECEMBER EVENING IN 1957. HE rummaged around for his newest white shirt, slipped into gabardine slacks, and pulled brand-new brown brogans from a shoe box. Then he paced around his bungalow for about ten minutes searching for a twenty-year-old address book. He rifled through a stack of old newspapers, tossing them through the air in every direction before he finally located the book beneath a pile of Hershey bars. He grabbed the candy as well, and then ran out of his bungalow into the alley behind the Beverly Hills Hotel. An aide, Ron Kistler, already had the Chevy running, with its passenger door open. Howard leaped in. "Quick," he said. "Let's get outta here."

As they drove through the empty boulevards of Beverly Hills, Hughes kept looking over his shoulder, certain they were being followed. By the time they pulled up to the back entrance of Nosseck's Studio, Hughes had calmed down a little. "We made it," he sighed with relief.

Inside the dingy compound, which had first been used in the days of silent films, Howard headed straight for the screening room, a dank enclosure about the size of a studio apartment. Though paint was peeling from the walls and the floor tilted downward toward the movie screen, Hughes considered it a haven.

Sitting in the middle of the room was his white leather recliner with a TV tray next to it. Howard lowered himself into the chair and stacked the Hershey bars into seven little piles. He looked them over, picked them all up again, and arranged them into ten stacks. "The piles were too high," he explained to Kistler. "Start the film," he said.

The lights were lowered. What followed was a 1941 bullfighting adventure, *Blood and Sand*, starring Tyrone Power and two of Hughes's former lovers, Linda Darnell and Rita Hayworth. But Hughes registered no emotion; his eyes stared blankly at the screen, and his fingers tapped rhythmically on the arms of the lounge chair. He was expressionless as the movie ended.

The projectionist ran another film. And another. When the screen at last went blank, aide Johnny Holmes asked the boss if he was ready to leave. Hughes looked down at his hands and whispered, "I'm not leaving. I'm staying right where I am. And, by the way, I want you to come back in the morning, early, and bring with you a case of Hershey bars, three cartons of homogenized milk, and six unopened boxes of Kleenex. And remember, I don't want these boxes mixed in with the Kleenexes I use to take my food or to pick up my bottle. These boxes are to remain sealed up."

Hughes spent the night in the screening room.

Early the next morning, the aides found him in the same chair eating a breakfast of six Hershey bars and a half pound of Texas pecans. Any pecans that weren't totally intact were rejected by Hughes, who flicked them onto the floor. "Mr. Hughes, can we get you anything?" said Ron Kistler. Howard continued to stare straight ahead.

Kistler pressed on: "Is there anything you need? Do you have instructions for us?"

Howard wheeled around in his chair. "As long as I'm here, don't speak to me unless I ask you a question or make a comment. Each morning and each evening you will bring me a fresh bag of halved pecans, ten Hershey bars, and a quart of milk. Don't speak to me when you deliver it. Just come over and stand next to me. I want Johnny [Holmes] to bring me the supplies when at all possible."

Looking Holmes in the eye, he continued, "Walk around and stand in front of me when I raise my left thumb up. Then you may roll back the edges of the bag and hold it before me at a forty-five-degree angle. At which time, I will take five layers of Kleenex and extract the items one by one. I want no deviation from this procedure. If I am watching a film . . . stand and wait quietly behind my chair."

More rules followed. "When I ask you a question which requires a yes or no answer, do not speak. Just nod your head for yes and shake your head back and forth for no. Sometimes I will need to present you with more complicated questions. In that case I will use a number fourteen grease pencil and scrawl the question on one of my yellow legal pads. Once that is done, do not speak, just write the answer on your yellow pads which are over there," he said, pointing at a theater seat ten feet away.

"This is the last word you will hear from me," said Hughes, folding his hands behind his head. And it was, for five terrifying months, months in which Howard remained trapped in a fight with insanity. Untreated and unchecked, Hughes's obsessive-compulsive disorder had become psychotic.

The combined effects of his head injuries only intensified his fears and his irrational behavior. In breakthrough OCD research in Great Britain, three psychologists, Joseph F. McKeon, Peter McGuffin, and Paul H. Robinson, have proved that obsessive-compulsive victims they studied plunged deeper and deeper into the grip of their neuroses after they suffered major trauma to the skull.

Dr. Jeffrey Schwartz says Hughes was actually a victim of medical ignorance not just about OCD but about the effect of his head injuries. "They viewed him as insane and probably believed the accidents pushed him further over the edge. But OCD had not even been diagnosed at that point; there was no hope for Howard."

After the first week inside Nosseck's, Hughes began to use the screening room telephone, which was tapped into the Romaine switchboard. With movies flickering on the screen and the room illuminated by a single lamp at Howard's side, he made as many as one hundred calls a day to lawyers, tool company officials, Yvonne Shubert, and William Gay, who, now that Noah had departed, was running the Romaine operations center.

But Hughes didn't contact Jean Peters. She was left to wonder where her husband was as an army of aides dashed in and out of the Hughes storage bungalows, loaded down with balance sheets and yellow pads. Not that she ever asked.

There had always been a gulf between Mrs. Hughes and the Mormon aides, some of whom had lost power when the boss finally married. In retaliation, they froze her out of the information network.

On the tenth morning Howard began taking the boxes of Kleenex and arranging them in ever changing geometric patterns. Some mornings they would all be standing on end, a tower of cardboard that reached to his waist. Sometimes he would lay them flat, moving and twisting them for eight or nine hours at a time. Depending on his mood, the boxes would either be neat and lined up like soldiers or careening all over the floor at the foot of his white leather chair. Many days he hunched over the boxes and hummed softly to himself his own atonal versions of songs from the thirties, his heyday.

When aides rushed off to fulfill Howard's latest strange whim, they returned to find that he had urinated against the wall or in a corner. The first time it happened, Kistler was shocked. Hughes, who was particularly attuned to Kistler, picked up his grease pencil and scrawled the message, "The bathroom's in the lobby. And as you know, I cannot touch the door handle."

Kistler wrote back, "Call me if that happens again." Howard nodded. He finally discovered that he could open the door by wrapping his hands in twenty-five thicknesses of Kleenex.

Six weeks later, Howard signaled Kistler to walk with him to the bathroom and stand beside the open door while Howard remained hunched on the toilet for twenty-six hours. During another toilet experience, Hughes suddenly went into a frenzy, grabbing up armloads of paper towels and unfurling them up and down the length of the lobby until six rolls were expended. Then, crawling on his hands and knees, he spent five hours wrapping every porcelain fixture in the bathroom, mummy-style, binding even the spigots.

By early March, more than two months after he'd entered Nosseck's, Howard's clothes were filthy and tearing at the seams. They also reeked of urine. The white shirt was now gray with grime and sweat and splotched by stains from the Hershey bars, which he sometimes drooled all over himself and onto the white leather chair.

By the third month Hughes had discarded his clothes. He remained naked for months.

Filth was now everywhere, except on the telephone, his conduit to the world and to sanity. Every morning he took Kleenex and scrubbed the phone up and down, sideways, and in a circular motion until tissues were strewn around him like dirty snow. On good days, it took an hour to clean the telephone; on a bad day, four hours.

Since the guards were often nearby for ten- to twelve-hour shifts, they needed the use of a bathroom. But as decreed by one of the rules he scrawled onto the pads, they had to use Howard's discarded milk cartons. "Please put them outside when you are through," he wrote to the aides.

After three months, Jean Peters Hughes became understandably alarmed. Howard had written her that he was sick and being treated in a medical center. Now Peters began telephoning centers in search of him. She questioned everyone at the Romaine headquarters. Nadine Henley, Hughes's longtime associate, told Howard that he needed to placate Jean. Hughes responded by sending her a vague message about an "undiagnosed illness." If she was to visit him, she could become contaminated.

In one of his thousands of memos to Jean, his diminishing mental capacity is apparent.

Wed., 9/10/58

8:20 p.m. *Darling, I just came to sorta—if this is what the chinamen go for I don't understand it. I think the same effect could be achieved much better by asking your wife to hit you over the head with a heavy book. Maybe the camphor spoiled it, and maybe that is why they put it in—so the old folk won't grow to like it. I know it must be late. I tried to stand up and I feel awful shaky. Lloyd says it is only 7:30 pm but I feel as if I have been out for a week. Anyway since it is this early I am sure I should have no trouble navigating long before the navigator's time check. I will stay conscious long enough to receive a reply from you. I wish you would send me a nice bulletin include particularly how you feel, how you like the show. After I receive your reply I will give in to natures forces for awhile longer, and call you the minute I feel better. Obviously it was not a cold but instead emanated from the same system that has been the source of my recent troubles. I send my love and please let me know if everything is all right and did you send Rennie the flowers. Love again, Howard.*

During the five months at Nosseck's, it seemed to his aides that he was taking inventory of his mind to see how it functioned, to gauge its condition as if he were testing an airplane. And he soon realized that his mind had shut down.

"If you can afford to arrange your own asylum, you do so," said Dr. Raymond Fowler. "And I think that's simply what he did. Gradually, as the world became more and more painful to him, he built an asylum to occupy for the rest of his life." His nudity was also symptomatic. "I really think he was so mentally disorganized at times that putting on clothes would have taken more organization than he had." In addition, noted Fowler, Hughes was a man who typically rejected many of society's norms and niceties. In his shaky mental state, clothing would have been an obvious rule to ignore.

But his core illness, obsessive-compulsive disorder, was greatly accentuated by the fourteen head injuries he had suffered since 1929. "As the brain suffers more and more trauma, you end up with a punch-drunk person who can't function at the level he had before," said Dr. Fowler. "It's not that he loses intelligence; he loses the ability to organize his thoughts. Which is what happened to Hughes."

Finally, in the spring of 1958, Howard had his aides bring him some fresh clothes. He bathed himself in the Nosseck's sink, dressed himself, and asked to be returned to the Beverly Hills Hotel. Though he got in touch with Jean by phone, he did not see her again for months.

Back in Bungalow 4, he had the windows blacked out with thick paint so that no spot of light would penetrate his world. Once again he took off his clothes and sat down in a leather chair and inaugurated what he called a "germ-free zone." When the aides entered, he sometimes placed a Kleenex over his genitals, but not always. No one was permitted to come within four feet of him. He would remain in that perpetual "germ-free zone" for the remainder of his life. No matter where he resided, Howard's life pattern was now fixed. The light of the sun was blocked out; his clothes were largely banished; television, movies, and the telephone were the only intruders.

He became a disembodied voice on the phone, an electronic Wizard of Oz.

CHAPTER 29

THE MASK OF SANITY

IT WAS CHRISTMAS EVE, 1960, BUT THE TIME OR DATE MEANT LITTLE TO the three men stationed at the garden entrance to the Beverly Hills Hotel. In their midnight-blue uniforms they hung back against the bushes, their eyes riveted on a station wagon parked in the alley. Inside, a man was hunched in the back seat.

French film star Simone Signoret strolled by and was so fascinated by what she saw that she circled the hotel again, trying to find the source of long black hoses that emerged from one of the bungalows and snaked along the grass and into the car's windows. "I traced the hoses back toward the bungalow where a friendly man was amused by my curiosity.

" 'They're feeding the car with refrigerated air,' he told me. 'It's just for this one night.' " Signoret nodded. She didn't need to inquire about the identity of the man in the car. Legends about Howard Hughes had enhanced her stay at the hotel. She'd been trying to catch a glimpse of the recluse for weeks. Unfortunately, the dim lights in the wagon only illuminated a shadow, an outline of a tall, thin man writing furiously on yellow tablets.

"It must have been 3 A.M.," Signoret said later. "And he was wide awake, concentrating utterly on his writing."

Signoret couldn't have known it, but she had witnessed the first stirrings of a rebirth for Howard Hughes, who had hauled himself out of his sick bed and his codeine haze for one last power lunge. At age fifty-five, Howard faced uphill battles on several fronts. In the strung-out months since he exited his self-enforced asylum, he had watched his marriage to Jean Peters slowly crumble. Like a princess in a tower, Mrs. Hughes finally rebelled. Either they lived together as husband and wife, or their marriage was over. To save this relationship, Hughes rallied, and actually flew around California in search of a house.

With Jean's approval, he chose a hilltop ranch-style house in San Diego County's exclusive Rancho Santa Fe. They were to move in on Christmas Day, to spend their first night together under the same roof since their wedding three years earlier.

The days of carousing were behind him. Even the days of girl-collecting.

He had recently ended that era with a last hurrah that turned into a slapstick comedy. It started when Hughes saw televised coverage of a Miss Universe pageant, held in Long Beach, California. Particularly taken with Miss Belgium, Hughes also liked Miss France, Miss Switzerland, Miss USA, and at least a dozen others. Hughes put in a call to Walter Kane, who called Jeff Chouinard. The boss wanted the beauty contestants.

Chouinard, who'd thought this kind of surveillance had gone out with Yvonne Shubert, got together his men and off they went. Bob Maheu, too. At the start, they tailed the girls. Then, using a dummy film production company as a cover, they tried to sign the girls to contracts. Six or seven were actually established in apartments. But after less than a week the confused young women, who were growing uneasy at the surveillance tactics, took off. All except one: Miss Belgium, Carolyn Lecerf.

Her mother, meanwhile, began to get worried. Carolyn should have returned home to Belgium by now. So Madame Lecerf alerted the Belgian Embassy and the FBI. Lecerf didn't know it, but her letters to her mother were never mailed. All the while Miss Belgium proceeded through Hughes's girls' program: photos, lessons, screenings. But she refused to sign the contract that was perpetually brandished before her. She had occasional phone conversations with a man she assumed to be Hughes, who knew her every movement. He promised they would meet, face-to-face, as soon as she "mastered English." The meeting never took place.

Six months later, Miss Belgium bolted. But not before she blabbed to *Confidential* magazine telling all about the "nightmare" of having been a prisoner of "jailer" and "tormentor," Howard Hughes.

Meanwhile, one more starlet was still being kept, secretly, under contract.

As Hughes struggled to keep Jean, he was also valiantly attempting to fight another battle. After three straight reversals in court, he thought he saw a way to regain control of TWA, which had been wrested from him several months earlier by a consortium of banks.

The airline he built into a global giant sued him for mismanagement and was seeking $483 million in damages. Hughes, who still held 78 per cent of the stock, and attorney Chester Davis thought the TWA battle could be turned around if Hughes would fight his case by personally showing up in the courtroom.

Hughes's physicians by now had him on a potent dosage of Ritalin, a central nervous system stimulant used on hyperactive children. It acted like an amphetamine for Hughes. Not only had he found the home in Rancho Santa Fe in record time, but he himself would drive his wife there on Christmas morning when the streets were deserted. His constant working and reworking of strategies, scrawled on the legal pads, excited Howard's staff. It also revitalized Jean, now called "the Richest Wife in America." But beneath the *Saturday Evening Post* headlines and the gossip column items, Peters was actually a widow. She had been replaced by drugs.

When the aides escorted Peters to the station wagon for the drive up the coast, Hughes sat behind the wheel, seemingly excited at the prospect of living in a house for the first time in four years. The house boasted spectacular views of the rolling hills and the beaches of Cardiff-by-the-Sea. Jean and Howard moved into the expansive master bedroom to occupy queen-size beds that were shoved together. Howard even permitted his wife to open the curtains, flooding the room with light.

The Ritalin kept him propped up in bed for days, as he schemed of ways to recapture his beloved airline. But after losing round after round in the Manhattan court system, he sank into a quagmire, caught in an undertow of codeine.

He re-established his private asylum. Windows were closed tight. Rooms darkened. But Jean put up a fight. Chouinard recalled an evening when she stormed into the bedroom and began opening windows to the ocean breezes. "No! No!" Hughes shouted. "Close those windows this minute. Don't you realize how dangerous that is? Contagious diseases travel through the air!"

"There was total fear in his voice," noted Chouinard, adding, "The boss had slipped again." But this time he had slipped even further than usual.

His fear of germs escalated. Maids were no longer allowed to clean the master bedroom at Rancho Santa Fe. "Can't happen," he told Peters. "That would be foolhardy."

When dust balls had accumulated around Howard's bed and the floor was caked with food debris, Jean stormed in, brandishing a vacuum cleaner hose. But, she stressed to Howard, "I'm only bringing the hose in; I'll leave the actual vacuum in the hall." Because Hughes kept the room plunged in darkness, aide Johnny Holmes had to crawl along the floor, shining a flashlight into the corners and up under the bed, so Jean could vacuum the filth. She also wasn't permitted to get near the television. "Don't touch the TV!" Hughes shouted. "I turn those knobs . . . I don't want them contaminated."

Because Hughes often worked all night, the aides would come into the master bedroom at all hours, taking dictation while kneeling at the head of Howard's bed. Jean was an amazingly good sport about all the activity at the bed next to hers. But she hated the way Howard clicked his long toenails, which he refused to trim. She finally inserted tissues between Hughes's toes each night. Thereafter, she slept in peace.

It was at Rancho Santa Fe that Howard's temper tantrums began. They would eventually become deadly serious. But the first series of Hughes's memos from the mansion were humorous in their detail. When Jean's cat, Nefrite, wandered off and didn't return, Hughes put the entire power of his empire into the search. A day later, Nefrite was still at large, leading to this memo:

This is not the jungle; this is not the Everglades; this is not New York City with the dense population. It is thinly populated and it is no problem at all to question all the people here and have them questioned by somebody and get at the truth and not permit somebody to conceal the truth just because they are afraid of being sued or something like that. Proper questions by people skilled in questioning could have been had. The animal could have been searched for by a team of people skilled in the ways of animals of this type. I know one thing; if a zoo had lost some valuable animal in this area there would have been twenty-five or thirty men scouring the countryside, men skilled in the habits and ways of an animal of this kind and would have found it by now.

Two days later, Jean's cat showed up at the back door, screaming to be let in. (As a result of her outdoor escapade, Nefrite subsequently gave birth to three kittens.)

Memos flew hourly over yet another missing cat—a battered one-eared tom that Jean had befriended. "Goddamn it, I don't care if you have to fly the best animal trapper in Africa over here to hunt for it," wrote Hughes. "Find that cat or you're all fired!" It took two days for Chouinard's security men to locate the feline. But by then Jean didn't think she could keep it. So at Hughes's instructions, the cat was sent to an expensive "hostelry for cats" where it was given its own room—with television. So it would not be lonely, one of Chouinard's men was assigned to write the cat a monthly letter.

Five months after Howard moved to Rancho Santa Fe, he increased the Ritalin drastically, trying to stay awake for three and sometimes four days to work on the TWA problems. He soon began hallucinating. "Look! Look!" he screamed. "Look at the things crawling up on my arms . . . get them . . . get them!" His physicians determined that the Ritalin had spawned a shocking sensation that ran up and down his arms. One night he began pulling hair off his forearms, clawing himself so badly that angry red sores appeared, sending him into another fury. When the Ritalin was discontinued, Hughes again fell into a stupor.

On November 1, 1961, pipes in the kitchen burst, creating such damage that a team of plumbers was summoned by the landlord. "No, no," Hughes said. "They can't come in. Don't let them in here." He finally decided to abandon the house rather than risk contamination from the repairmen. So, on Thanksgiving morning, 1961, Howard, Jean, and the aides piled into cars and drove back to Los Angeles, where a Bel Air mansion had been leased for them.

Jean Peters sat quietly in the back seat of her chauffeured car as it wound up into the verdant hills. The vegetation, mostly palms, flowering jasmine, and bougainvillea, had been planted decades earlier and obscured the mansions that clung to ledges carved into the Santa Monica Mountains. The automobile stopped before an electric gate. It opened to reveal Jean's dream house—fulfilling a promise Hughes had made eleven years earlier.

It was a French regency villa with a spreading rock terrace, rose garden, and an inevitable azure swimming pool. Jean's reaction, though, was wary and guarded. There had been too many promises and too many heart-breaking disappointments. Just months earlier, she had learned that the beloved Rancho Santa Fe ranch house had not been purchased for her, as Hughes had said. When Hughes first led her up to it, he gestured grandly and proclaimed, "Here's your house. You own a home of your own." But one afternoon that lie was unmasked when a law officer arrived on the property. Jean thought he had discovered she had an illegal compost heap. But he was there to serve a lien on the property owner—who was leasing the home to Hughes.

Jean would later admit a sense of betrayal. "I became a doubting Thomas." Her faith would not be restored by the house on Bel Air Road. For despite pleas from Greg Bautzer and Robert Maheu, Howard refused to pay the $500,000 asking price. Instead, he leased it for nine years at a cost of $50,000 per year, a figure just short of the purchase price.

Bel Air soon became yet another asylum for Howard.

Jeff Chouinard had had guards stationed at the house and its grounds for months prior to Hughes's arrival. "You know, to keep it germ-free," remembered Chouinard. According to Chouinard, Jean was brought to the house first. Later that night a Chevrolet drove up and parked in front of the dark villa. The driver, carrying cardboard boxes, entered the house first. Chouinard, whose suspicions had gotten the best of him, was spying from the bushes. He watched through the windows as the driver proceeded through the house, wiping each exposed surface to determine if it was "properly sanitized."

Moving closer to the house, Jeff peered into the Chevrolet. There, on the floor of the back seat, lay one of the richest men in the world, hiding beneath a blanket. Howard cowered there for more than three hours while the germ hunt continued. Finally, when it was deemed safe, Howard stood up in his pajamas and shuffled into one of the most beautiful homes in Bel Air.

Under Hughes's instructions, the house was literally divided into two camps: Jean's in the south wing and his in the north. It was clear that Howard intended to lock himself away in what was little more than a bunker. Hughes's domain of sixty square feet included a bed, a dilapidated lounge chair, a small table, and a television set. Guard stations were built and double doors were added—the better to lock out everyone, including Jean.

Soon she fought a daily battle even to visit with her husband for twenty minutes. Her phone calls were likewise limited. The Hughes surveillance logs show that she penetrated the domain only when the aides could work her into the millionaire's appointment calendar. Hollywood insiders soon called her "the prisoner of 1001 Bel Air."

For the first year or so, Howard tried to see her for at least twenty minutes a day, usually before he ate his dinner, now his only meal. Since he slept until three in the afternoon, Jean was often rushed in and out, particularly if he had a business call or was about to receive his codeine, Valium, Seconal, or Librium. The drug habit was hidden so successfully that twenty years later Jean solemnly testified that she had not known of or even suspected any of her husband's addictions.

Soon life in the Bel Air mansion revolved around three titanic struggles: Howard's avoidance of his marital obligations to Jean, the daily battle to keep Hughes supplied with drugs, and the tangle of the TWA lawsuits.

Hughes's obstinacy over TWA spawned an entire family of suits, countersuits, and injunctions that involved fifteen corporations, fifty-six lawyers—with Hughes's team headed by Chester Davis and Greg Bautzer— $25 million in legal fees, and the court systems of eleven states. It was this battle that led to the "search" for the reclusive Howard Hughes.

Beginning on February 11, 1961, when a Maryland bailiff stood up and asked three times, "Is Howard Hughes present?" Howard was a marked man. Representatives for TWA, Maryland Superior Court, and three financial institutions all raced to deliver subpoenas into the hands of this "phantom millionaire."

TWA, which offered a $50,000 bonus to anyone who could produce Hughes, dispatched a young Ivy League attorney named Frederick Furth to Los Angeles and teamed him with former FBI agent Alfred E. Leckey. Hughes's reclusiveness puzzled them; neither Furth nor his bosses at TWA could imagine that a handsome multimillionaire in the prime of life would not leave his darkened bedroom. They were also no match for Robert Maheu. By this time Maheu's private agency, based in Washington, D.C., was one of the slickest in the burgeoning world of corporate spying.

The pros from New York faced a distinct disadvantage in this "war of the subpoenas," for Maheu and Chouinard found a decoy, a double for Howard Hughes, who was deployed with great effectiveness. Jeff discovered the dead ringer sitting at a counter in Schwab's Drugstore, the Hollywood hangout for aspiring and out-of-work performers who hoped to be discovered there. Chouinard introduced himself and listened to the actor's tale of woe. He wasn't getting any work precisely because he looked like Hughes. He was very available.

"This guy, Brucks Randell, looked so much like Hughes that from across the room, you couldn't tell the difference," remembered Chouinard.

Jeff outfitted Randell in replicas of Howard's rumpled, well-known wardrobe, and took him to the Romaine Street headquarters for "acting lessons." Chouinard and Maheu taught him how to walk and talk like their Texan boss, and even shipped him out to stage a carefully orchestrated series of "Hughes sightings." Thanks to deliberate press leaks, Howard was sighted on the banks of Lake Tahoe, walking the dusty streets of Tijuana, gambling in Las Vegas, and riding a cable car in San Francisco, where a Hughes aficionado, columnist Herb Caen, caught a glimpse of the Hughes facsimile and devoted a column to him. *Newsweek* was taken in, as was Los Angeles's KTLA television station and the newspapers in Reno, Nevada.

The lawmen from the East scattered across the Southwest but failed to detect that this was the work of a double. They always seemed to arrive several steps behind Randell as he went from city to city. At one point, TWA became so frustrated that it pondered launching a probe to see if "Howard Hughes was still alive."

All this allowed Howard to remain where he was at his most comfortable—in his own Bel Air bedroom, where it soon became clear that they had found Randell just in time. Howard was collapsing under the weight of an accelerating addiction to codeine.

It's impossible to pinpoint the exact moment that Hughes's physicians and keepers learned that his thirst for codeine was not an addiction as such but rather a compulsion. However, they understood this by the time he closeted himself in the mansion. They soon saw that Howard was compelled to take codeine and Valium, according to some desperate schedule he had conceived, at precisely the same second three times a day. Likewise, the dosage could not vary and was measured in liquid form down to the hundredth of an ounce.

He was equally obsessed with his hoard of painkillers. Just as he insisted upon having an exact number of yellow pads at his side and a constant inventory of Poland water in his storeroom, Hughes panicked if his inventory of pure codeine tablets, Empirin No. 4 (with codeine), and injectable codeine varied so much as one grain.

According to Dr. Jeffrey Schwartz, the ritualistic nature of Hughes's drug consumption qualifies it as a compulsion rather than a true addiction. "Hughes was not taking these drugs to 'get high,'" agreed Dr. John Chappel, who studied Howard's drug records for the state of Nevada during the probate hearings involving the Hughes estate. "Because of the constant, unrelenting pain, a legacy of the 1946 crash, his codeine merely made the pain bearable, made him feel normal," Chappel concluded.

Following Hughes's death, the Drug Enforcement Administration investigated his drug use by surveying ten years of "drug statistics and logs" kept by the physicians and aides. Officials demonstrated in a 355-page report that the doctors and aides systematically increased Hughes's intake of codeine until he was totally in their thrall. By counseling that he needed ever more opiates, they played upon his obsessive fears, keeping him in a constant state of panic over his continued supply.

During the last six years of his life, his codeine intake would accelerate to near fatal levels. In 1969, Hughes was taking about 2,300 dosage units of codeine per year—approximately the amount a physician would prescribe for a person in constant debilitating pain.

By 1975, the doctors were administering 5,500 dosage units of codeine to their reclusive patient—about 481 milligrams per day, as compared to the 240-milligram dosage prescribed for a critically ill cancer patient. During one nine-month period, Roxbury Pharmacy in West Los Angeles filled one thousand prescriptions for codeine and Valium under the names of the aides to deflect suspicion that they were for Hughes. A year before Howard's death, Dr. Wilbur Thain and his aides-de-camp administered 8,200 dosage units to their practically comatose patient. Hughes also injected 550 one-grain Seconal tablets, 1,000 Valium and, occasionally, Librium.

The DEA also showed that the Hughes retainers realized that he wasn't a true addict who faced dangerous, life-threatening withdrawal when his dosages where changed. In fact, again and again the codeine was reduced when the aides wished to force Hughes to do their will. "When they wanted him to fire me and to move from Las Vegas, they cut him off," recalled Robert Maheu. "Then they flooded him with codeine just before he signed the proxy ousting me."

CHAPTER 30

ORPHAN OF THE STORM

GAIL GANLEY STOOD OUTSIDE THE ROMAINE STREET FORTRESS AND LOOKED up to see a string being lowered from the second-storey window. "Excuse me! This is not going to work!" the starlet hollered to an aide who hovered out of view, near the window. "This is a chocolate cake I've got here!" she yelled. For a moment nothing happened. Then another string dropped down and dangled before her.

Incredulous at the thought of hoisting up a cake in that manner, Gail shouted, "I don't think this is going to work, guys!"

Then the unthinkable happened. A voice from above directed her to the back of the building. "You'll see a door," she was told. Cake in hand, Ganley rushed to where she was directed and stood, holding her breath.

From inside she could hear a lock turning. Then the door opened a crack and a pair of eyes peered out. There followed a pair of hands—reaching for the plate in Gail's hands.

"Please, can't I just take a peek?" begged Gail. The man inside hesitated. Then the door to Romaine opened wider and Gail Ganley—the last starlet under contract to Howard Hughes—moved forward. She squeezed inside for a look down a hallway that opened into a series of rooms. Some appeared to have no furniture; in one she spied a piano.

"Okay. That's it," said the aide, who led her back out the door.

In 1961 it was a coup for anyone outside of the Hughes retinue to gain entrance to Romaine. But Ganley would have still another distinction. For in 1962 the 22-year-old starlet, who had grown tired of promises never kept, dared to sue Hughes for failing to put her to work. The lawsuit led to revelations about Hughes's starlet factory, helping to open the doors further to the increasingly strange world of the man who was now dubbed "the Phantom" by the media.

Initially contacted by a Hughes representative in 1958, Ganley was put through the usual motions—lessons, trips to the dentist, meals out with the aides. And there were several phone conversations with a man who said he was Hughes. But she never met him in person.

She thought she might when—at the aides' instructions—she dined alone at Perino's, night after night, wearing a specially requested red dress. Three tables opposite Gail were always empty. "I kept thinking maybe 'He' would come in and sit down," remembered Gail, who resembled a young Elizabeth Taylor. But no one ever came to sit beside the young woman the Perino's waiters had come to call "the lady in red."

Gail eventually received an out-of-court settlement from Hughes's filmmaking entity, Hughes Productions. But she remained mystified by her treatment at the hands of Hughes, who, she had been told, was planning another return to movies.

She couldn't have known that he was incapable of carrying out any such dream. Or that his life was no longer solely his own.

Hughes's staff had by now erected human barriers as formidable as the concrete and steel mausoleum that was Romaine. With Noah Dietrich's departure, Nadine Henley, who started with Hughes in the forties as a secretary, had assumed more control, sharing it with Bill Gay, the Mormon she had hired in 1947. Both Henley and Gay would ultimately take part in a coup involving the Hughes empire. And Gay would help to create Hughes's so-called Mormon Mafia.

According to one Mormon aide, Hughes's penchant for having Mormons on his staff stemmed from a phone call to Romaine one New Year's Eve. Hughes suspected everyone would be out partying, but a young man answered the phone. Why was he working? And sober? The young aide in question replied he was a Mormon—and that Mormons didn't drink or smoke. Hughes, who had become a teetotaler and was vehemently against smoking, applauded those virtues.

Most prominent among the aides from the 1950s until Hughes's death in the 1970s were Roy Crawford, Howard Eckersley, George A. Francom Jr., Kay Glenn, John Holmes, Levar Beebe Myler, James H. Rickard, and Chuck Waldron. Of the group, only Holmes was a non-Mormon (and a cigarette smoker). A former salesman, he had come aboard Hughes Productions in 1949, acting as a driver and chaperon to the various Hughes starlets.

Most of the aides had done some job-hopping before landing their Hughes assignments. Rickard, for instance, was a former drive-in movie theater manager and former logging and sawmill operator. After dropping out of college, Myler operated a burr-and-milling machine. Kay Glenn was "a little farm boy" who graduated from Utah State College and then, on a tip from a fraternity brother, applied for a job with Hughes. He became Gay's chief assistant.

Many of them started as drivers or bodyguards. Others went on to cater to Hughes's increasingly bizarre food and germ fetishes. But all of them signed contracts that forbade them to discuss their association with their employer. Hughes himself insisted on the confidentiality; ironically, the shroud of secrecy would ultimately affect his own well-being. For the aides came to assume a power of their own.

The power-hungry Mormon aides had been scheming against Jean Peters since the end of the Nosseck breakdown. Since she was the only person they could neither control nor deny access to, she was a stumbling block to their goal of total control over the richest man in the world. They had succeeded beyond their hopes. In 1961, 1001 Bel Air was a divided camp with Jean on one side and Howard and his aides on the other.

Unaware of the internal dramas, the media concentrated on the external picture. Choppers buzzed above the hilltop home, hoping for a chance to photograph Jean sunbathing or working in her garden. Reporters for the news magazines sometimes camped out on the street. Howard Hughes had become such an enigma that art began to imitate life: Harold Robbins's lurid 1961 best-seller *The Carpetbaggers* was about a Hughes-like titan with a ravenous appetite for women. The inevitable movie version starred George Peppard as the rakish movie mogul–plane manufacturer.

It was during the Bel Air period that Jean Peters at last began to realize that her marriage, such as it was, could not be salvaged.

Then, on July 10, 1966, all hell broke loose within the sealed rooms of the Hughes bunker. Howard rose up out of his depression, cut back his codeine consumption, even to the point of refusing what the aides offered him, and shook off the heavy load of depression.

He shortly beckoned Jean back into his life and met her halfway, in the sunny living room that stretched between their distant dominions. He promised that they would find another house, not a fortress this time, but a house back East where they would live without the barricade of Mormon aides. Peters was wary. She'd heard these promises before.

He revealed his plan. First, he told her, he had to flee California before the taxes could be extracted from his TWA windfall. So he was headed to Boston to look for their dream home. "No," Jean said. "We're going together . . . [to] look together."

Hughes promised she could trust him. He would find the place and then she would join him.

The impasse continued for several days, until relations were strained again. According to Jeff Chouinard, Jean gave him an ultimatum: they either moved together, preferably to a farm, or they split forever.

"He told her he was going to a clinic in Boston and that he would arrange to start looking for a farm, much like that belonging to his attorney Chester Davis."

Peters did not believe him.

On the morning of July 15, Hughes told Robert Maheu to arrange for transportation; he was leaving California the night of July 17, via train. Maheu was to arrange for two of the finest private cars available. "One for you and Jean, the other for the aides?" Maheu asked. "Mrs. Hughes will not be coming," Howard said stonily.

Around noon on July 17, the aides began moving Howard's crates and filing cabinets out of his quarters. As she passed through to her garden, Peters noticed that her husband was also removing his battered lounge chair, his air purifier, his projection equipment, and his telephone amplifier. The implication was clear; he was not coming back to 1001 Bel Air.

As darkness fell, Howard gathered up his boxes of clothes and his lucky hat and waited outside the mansion for the aides.

Jean heard both limos start up and move into the driveway. From the windows on her side of the house, she could see her husband waiting with his pitifully few possessions. Then she drew a symbolic line in the sand. If he turned back around to say good-bye, she'd come into the living room, their emotional no man's land.

Half an hour passed as Johnny Holmes and the others packed up the limos. Finally, without a look back over his shoulder, Hughes got into the back seat of a limousine, which drove down the hill and out of the gate.

Mrs. Hughes was alone at 1001 Bel Air, waiting for a phone call or a message, some sort of farewell.

After the last of her husband's retainers departed 1001 Bel Air, she was consumed with sorrow and stung by both Howard's emotional brutality and his personal betrayal. As she wandered the empty rooms of the hilltop mansion and tried to unravel the psychiatric puzzle of her twenty years with Howard Hughes, she wondered: had his professions of love for her been a cold and calculated charade?

For years Mrs. Hughes had been tormented by Howard's determination to treat her like a Barbie doll, a wistful, beautiful presence who decorated his life and was there, waiting patiently, for when he "needed her." A decade later Jean pursued a bachelor of arts degree at UCLA, possibly to prepare for the teaching career she'd originally planned back in Ohio.

Jean would finally come to terms with the emotional holocaust her marriage to Hughes had left behind. "I eventually realized that he was a sociopath, a man utterly incapable of understanding the needs of another person," she recalled. "I believe it is a very appropriate definition of the man I was with for twenty years.

"He was very manipulative even though he was just darling and charming at the same time. And even though he was affectionate in some ways . . . and totally persuasive, it was a charade, I guess. I'll just say that my faith in him was eroded."

Look magazine editor Leslie Midgley once observed Hughes close up when he was trying to placate Jean after the explosion of publicity surrounding his reunion with Ava Gardner. Hughes was in a small room at the Flamingo Hotel in Las Vegas when he called Peters during the early morning hours. "Just listening to him talk on the phone made me realize . . . what a charmer he was," said Midgley. "He came across so sincere, caring, and loving that who could resist? He could be infuriating but also irresistible when he so chose."

The railroad cars, originally built for William Randolph Hearst, Sr., were already hooked up to the train when Hughes arrived and was greeted by nods from a phalanx of five guards from the Bel Air Patrol. Other passengers who were boarding were alarmed to see the guards' firearms, including a submachine gun.

At 10:20, the City of Los Angeles Express pulled out, carrying Hughes away from California, his home state for four decades, the scene of his greatest triumphs and worst degradations. As the train sped east, Howard banished the aides from his luxurious private coach and sat down with a pen and his yellow legal pads.

Guilt overcame him. Hughes broke down over leaving Jean alone in the darkened, stripped Bel Air mansion. He wrote frantically, trying to find the correct words for the woman he had loved ever since the first day he met her, two decades earlier, when the world was simpler and when he was still dashing and handsome.

In his heavily slanted handwriting, he began, "Jean Darling, originally, I had not the faintest thought of proceeding. At the last minute, you started wearing a long face. I said why? You said because I would goof out like the last time."

Howard was undoubtedly referring to his promise two days earlier that he would find a house for them to share, a retreat, and that he would end their "telephone marriage." Peters reminded him he had made that same promise before they moved to Bel Air; a promise to live together in the same set of rooms minus the ever-present aides.

By sneaking out of 1001 Bel Air Road, he confessed, "I broke our pact of reconciliation." He continued: "At the last minute I could not face the possibility of reverting to a telephone relationship, so I delayed [finding a house]. You let me know that the closeness and trust we had once achieved was destroyed.

"The crux of the whole deal is that, if you come, we have no option or choice. From that point on we are committed to the place where we land. But if I go alone, either of us can look around, describe what we see, what is available and where it is available. Then the die is cast until the other arrives."

Panicked that he had lost Peters irrevocably, Hughes reminded her of an earlier conversation in which he had promised they would look for the dream house together; that they would find a "rose-covered bower" to purchase. No aides, no locked doors, no distant telephone logs.

"I had to go," he wrote plaintively. "I told everybody we were leaving and I did not want to fail. But I will not leave you upset." He signed the draft, "love, yours, Howard."

Then he decided to add a postscript. "My adorable wife," he began. Then, with a slash of red ink he crossed it out.

"Honey," he continued. "I want to do what you want me to do. I am boxed into a corner. I have the distinct feeling you don't want me to go ahead with any of this. But if I stop now, I feel this may not be what you want either. I will be quitting once more." Then, in capital letters, he wrote: I HOPE THIS IS THE START OF THE ROAD BACK FOR US. Down at the bottom of the pad, he scrawled a note to himself, a note not intended to be transcribed by the aides. In capital letters, he wrote, CUT YOUR HEAD OFF.

Howard stopped the train at San Bernardino, where he dispatched a courier to his abandoned wife. He also dictated a shorter version of this farewell apology.

However, neither the short version of this message nor the long one, which was to have been edited and telegraphed from Boston, ever reached Jean Peters. The Mormon contingent wasn't about to let the boss restore his marriage, a marriage they had helped destroy. More than anything else, this miscommunication ruined Howard's only surviving relationship with another human being. He was now totally alone.

During the estate trial in Houston, aide John Holmes remembered taking down the shorter message. "I don't remember the exact words, but it was something about loving her dearly, and that he would get back there; and would welcome the day when they were back together." On the same witness stand, Peters denied receiving any such message.

By the time the luxurious Pullmans entered Boston two days later, newspapers around the world were trying to prove that the mysterious passenger was Howard Hughes.

On Saturday, July 23, the *Los Angeles Herald-Examiner* ran a front-page photo of Howard under the headline: GUESSING GAME: HOWARD HUGHES? The report discussed a "well-guarded itinerary" and Pullman cars "under heavy security guard" when the cars were switched in Chicago to the New York Central Railroad for the journey to Boston. "Throughout the cross-country trip, food was ordered in writing and placed outside the door of the two special cars," continued the account. Once in Boston, a bearded man wearing what appeared to be an overcoat over pajamas quickly exited the train and entered a waiting limousine.

On that same day, the *Boston Globe* declared that a mysterious guest had checked into the Ritz Carlton Hotel, "and it might be Hughes. Adding to the mystery is the presence at the hotel of Robert Maheu, now the right-hand man of Howard Hughes."

The millionaire commandeered the entire fifth floor of the Ritz Carlton, sealing it off with guards at the elevator and the fire doors. The eastern press below spun wild stories of strange illnesses and of a private army "prowling the hotel."

When Jean Peters Hughes arrived five months later, it was reported in the *Boston Globe* that her husband was near death. Actually, Jean had given him one more chance to repair the marriage.

From behind closed doors, the aides could hear raised voices and more promises. Later that evening Hughes told Maheu that "Bill Gay and his men have ruined my marriage."

During the third and final week of the visit, Howard promised to purchase an estate in Westchester, New York, and to buy "an enormous yacht" to cruise up and down the East Coast. "It will be as we always dreamed," he told his wife.

"He spun a fairy tale; it was all very glowing and lovely," Jeff Chouinard remembered. Everyone noticed a complete change in Jean's mood. But it was a cruel and brutal farce, because "the Man," as his aides often called him, was already plotting his invasion of Las Vegas.

Three months later, Hughes summoned Maheu to his bedside and announced his intention to move to Las Vegas and become a casino baron. He'd finally decided how to spend that half billion dollars from his TWA windfall. He also declared he would become "the largest single property owner in the gambling capital." Further, he told Maheu there was to be a changing of the guard. Top aide Bill Gay was out; Maheu was in. "The gang from Romaine has ruined my life. I want that Hollywood crowd out."

Maheu jumped at the chance to become chief adjutant. For years he had believed the Mormon Mafia was a gang of profiteers dedicated to controlling Hughes and his enormous fortune. So he accepted.

A civil war followed, with Maheu on one side and William Gay, who ran Romaine, on the other. Hughes had become a pawn whose life and health depended on the outcome.

Maheu rented the top floor of the Desert Inn and ordered the two Pullman cars to carry Hughes to the desert. But the train broke down in Ogden, Utah. Although it required only four hours to fix, Howard reared up from his bed. "We're in trouble, Bob," Howard said. "We're going to arrive in Las Vegas after dawn. That cannot happen; I can't and won't arrive at a time anyone can see me."

Maheu burned up the telegraph lines, searching for a locomotive to pull the cars into Vegas before dawn. He finally found one in nearby Salt Lake City and hired it at a cost of $17,000.

Therefore it was pitch black when Hughes, on a stretcher, was carted off the train, still in his blue pajamas, and ferried to the Desert Inn at 4:15 A.M., November 27, 1966.

The caravan pulled up to a back entrance and whisked Howard up a service elevator to the ninth-floor penthouse, where the windows had already been sealed and fitted with blackout drapes. Two eighth-floor suites became the new nerve center for the millionaire's vast empire.

Hughes and Maheu announced their intention to buy the Desert Inn a month later, negotiating with its mob ownership. It was to be the cornerstone of his "kingdom in the desert," as Maheu depicted it.

Although Maheu had advised Hughes to inform Jean of the move to Las Vegas, he did not heed the warning. "She'll follow me here," he confidently predicted. "I know she doesn't really care where we live, just that we live together."

At 1001 Bel Air, Mrs. Hughes learned of the move from a television news team that camped on her doorstep. "When she found out he went to Vegas, she flew into a fury," remembered Chouinard, whose men were still guarding the mansion.

Both men stationed at the gate to the estate heard a blast of gunfire coming from within the house, followed by an eerie silence. The men believed Mrs. Hughes might have committed suicide, so Jeff called the Romaine operating center.

They were relieved when she answered the private line at her bedside. "She was so angry over the Vegas move that she began drinking and shot up the $150,000 copper roof," Chouinard recalled.

When the report was teletyped to the Desert Inn, Howard was again overcome with guilt and sent Maheu on a shopping spree. "Find the two finest houses out here and buy them," he said. "You know what Mrs. Hughes wants, something traditional and with enough room to house the staff and aides." Then Hughes turned to the business of buying up Las Vegas—and changing it.

He vowed to end the old empire of thousand-dollar-a-night call girls, mobsters in gaudy silk suits, and its overtone of "the boys from Detroit." Howard imagined a different Las Vegas, one where gambling and neon would be merely the foundation for an empire of magnificent hotels, five-star dining rooms, and ornate playgrounds for children. As Hughes put it in a memo to Maheu, "I like to think of Las Vegas in terms of a well-dressed man in a dinner jacket and a beautifully jeweled and furred female getting out of an expensive car." But Howard faced dangerous enemies whose power rested with the Chicago mob, headed at that time by Sam Giancana, and upon the insidious influence of mob-affiliated Teamster boss Jimmy Hoffa.

"Howard's plan was a long shot," recalled journalist James Phelan. "Until he showed up, no person had ever wholly owned a resort-casino. And Howard eventually intended to buy them all."

He had the assets. As he was hoisted up a back elevator of the Desert Inn to begin his desert reign he was worth, according to the conservative *Fortune* magazine, $1.4 billion. But that did not include the windfalls still to come from his TWA deal. In a memo he confided that his empire was "worth more than two billion dollars."

Hughes was touchy about this. When a tabloid in 1966 referred to him as a "paranoid, deranged millionaire," he erupted, "Goddammit, I'm a *billionaire!*"

Between 1966 and 1968, Hughes built the greatest Vegas kingdom ever assembled. His investments in the city soon made him the largest single investor in the history of the gambling capital. His Vegas buying spree began with the $13.25 million purchase of the Desert Inn on March 31, 1967. Four months later he bought the Sands for $23 million. Then came the Castaways ($3.3 million, October 26, 1967), the Frontier ($23 million, December 28, 1967) and the Silver Slipper ($5.4 million, April 30, 1968). With the purchase of the latter, which was located across the street from the Desert Inn, rumors circulated that Hughes planned to dismantle the casino's gigantic spinning high-heel slipper—aglow in red lights, come nighttime—because it kept Hughes awake in his penthouse suite. But the slipper kept spinning.

And Hughes continued buying. His deal for the Stardust ($30.5 million) was never closed, but later he bought the Landmark ($17.3 million) and Harold's Club in Reno ($10.5 million).

He bought the Las Vegas television station KLAS, a CBS affiliate, for $3.6 million—after frequently complaining to his aides about the station's policy of going off the air during the wee hours. Hughes wanted movies to be run all night. Moreover, he wanted his favorite pictures to be shown. With the Hughes purchase, all-night movies were a mandate.

Hughes's Las Vegas acquisitions also included the two posh estates that he'd hoped would lure Jean to the desert. The Riddle estate was located in an exclusive area where the neighbors included comic Buddy Hackett and Phyllis McGuire of the singing McGuire Sisters (and Sam Giancana's mistress). Farther out of town, toward picturesque Red Rock Canyon, was the 518-acre Krupp ranch, which had been owned by Vera Krupp, wife of German munitions titan Alfried Krupp. The two properties cost Hughes $1 million. Jean never visited either.

Hughes, meanwhile, continued to gobble up real estate and businesses. In a year he had gambled $65 million on his newest obsession. Hughes's hotels had a total of nearly two thousand rooms, approximately 20 per cent of the accommodations on the Strip. In a town full of players, Hughes was the biggest of them all.

As Nevada's biggest property owner, he had his representatives contact not only the Atomic Energy Commission but President Lyndon Johnson, personally, to express his concerns about underground nuclear testing in Nevada. The media went on to question whether Hughes's fears were based on financial interests—or resulted from his personal phobias. In retrospect, Hughes's concerns, whatever the motive, were well founded. Once again he was ahead of his time.

His eccentricities, however, escalated. Particularly when it came to mealtime. For a while, he habitually dined on Swanson TV frozen dinners; the turkey entrée was his favorite. But Hughes didn't like the mix of white and dark meat, and would have preferred that peach cobbler came with the meal, instead of apple. Summoning an aide, he asked that Swanson be contacted. "Have them switch the peach cobbler to the turkey dinner and take out the dark meat." But before the brazen request was ever put through, the fickle Hughes discovered another food fetish: roast beef sandwiches from the Arbie's fast-food chain. When that appetite subsided, Hughes switched to very thin cuts of filet mignon, which he ate with potatoes and peas, which he dutifully raked with his special utensil, in order to weed out the too large peas he deemed inedible.

For dessert, Hughes's tastes ran to cake and ice cream—but not just any cake or ice cream would suffice. At the Desert Inn, the hotel chef was implored to make sure Hughes's chocolate cake was cut in a perfect square; Hughes himself sometimes used a ruler to make sure the cake had been cut to specification. If the measurements were off, the cake was returned to the kitchen.

Hughes's love of Baskin-Robbins banana-nut ice cream led to a debacle, of sorts, for the Desert Inn kitchen. It happened when Hughes learned that his then-favorite flavor was being discontinued. So, per his instructions, a special order was put in—and filled. The result: 350 gallons of

Baskin-Robbins banana-nut ice cream, which had to be stored in the hotel kitchen refrigerator. When Hughes shifted to a new flavor, French vanilla, the Desert Inn's restaurants relentlessly promoted the banana-nut flavor. In fact, casino customers who hit jackpots were sometimes given unexpected bonuses—pints of Baskin-Robbins banana-nut ice cream. It took the Desert Inn a year to unload Hughes's frozen folly.

But if he was Las Vegas's most talked-about resident, he remained an invisible odds maker. Since his arrival, no one had seen him publicly. A powerful consortium suddenly questioned whether Howard was alive. Slightly more than a year after Hughes came to town, Governor Paul Laxalt, who had exempted Howard from personal appearances before the Gaming Control Board, was now under fire.

"What if Hughes isn't even up there? What if he has been replaced by an impostor?" Laxalt asked. "Can you imagine the national scandal which would result?"

Laxalt pleaded with J. Edgar Hoover for help from the FBI. "Some effort should be made to enable Nevada state facilities to know for certain that Howard Hughes actually is alive and that we are licensing a 'live' individual."

The FBI, after spending ten days on the case, informed Nevada that they could "not guarantee that Howard Hughes is alive or that he is the man on the ninth floor of the Desert Inn." Hoover recommended that Laxalt "find some way to speak with Hughes" and judge for himself. This demand was relayed through Robert Maheu and had immediate impact on the team of aides in the Desert Inn. For Howard was in no condition to see anyone.

"In fact, if they do meet with me, all of my petitions will be denied," Hughes warned. Again, through Maheu, a telephone conference was set up.

After lowering Howard's codeine and Valium doses for forty-eight hours and preparing a carefully written script for him to recite, the aides set up a phone call between Hughes and Laxalt on January 5, 1968. Thanks to the quality of the script and the calmness of Howard's demeanor, Laxalt was convinced "for the moment."

However, the echo-chamber effect of Hughes's amplification device totally unnerved the governor. "The conversation was weird, a strange sound and quietly unsettling," Laxalt recalled. The governor determined to set a face-to-face meeting as soon as he could.

But Hughes, in his increasingly drugged state, was not up to personal meetings.

The first week in March 1967, Howard had given himself three injections of codeine, took three of his "blue bombers"—the aides' nickname for blue ten-milligram Valium tablets—and invited Jean to spend the weekend with him "to discuss buying a house." Peters, who still nursed a hope for reconciliation, flew out two days later. By then Hughes couldn't rouse himself sufficiently to meet with her.

"It must have been terrifying for him, to drift in and out of lucidity and not be able to control it," Dr. Raymond Fowler said. "It was the same with the thousands of memos he drafted from his seclusion. He would scrawl dozens of pages of psychotic dribble and then twenty pages of lucid, inspired instructions only to sink back into his torpor."

Jean had waited patiently in her suite for four days, drowned in memos and reports from the Mormon aides. Finally, discouraged and angry, she returned to 1001 Bel Air Road. Because her husband had hidden all his problems from her, Jean knew only that Howard was backing further and further into a place she could not reach. She had no idea that he was seriously addicted to drugs. Nor did she understand the consequences of taking Empirin with codeine. Years later she related that the only drug she ever saw Howard take was Empirin, "a painkiller-like aspirin."

Hoping to ease the pain of the lonely lady of 1001 Bel Air, Howard telephoned her 114 times during the Vegas years, usually late in the afternoon when he was semilucid.

Three years later, in 1970, Jean Peters Hughes announced that she was seeking a divorce.

Hughes tried to dissuade her by touting the magnificent Krupp ranch. But Jean said she would not move in until he himself was physically in the house, proving that he was returning to a "more normal lifestyle."

Howard pleaded with Jean that he could not make the first move but that he would move in "a month after you arrive."

Jean Peters Hughes read between the lines. Vegas would be just another "telephone marriage," with Hughes barricaded at the Desert Inn and she isolated far out in the Vegas wilds.

So she filed for divorce. Her demands were quite simple; she wanted her freedom and $70,000 a year. Hughes was thunderstruck, offering to give her millions. But Jean stood her ground.

As the divorce action proceeded, Howard refused to give up hope, call-ing and writing her two or three times a week. He even leased the house across the street from 1001 Bel Air and staffed it with guards, who were directed to send reports, twice weekly, to the Desert Inn. When Jean began dating Stan Hough, a 20th Century-Fox executive, Hughes received a thoroughly detailed report of that love affair. "How can we stop it?" he screamed to Bill Gay. "She's still living in my house." The die was cast, though. Peters eventually married Hough.

CHAPTER 31

THE CAPTIVE

THE HIERARCHY OF AIDES LEARNED EARLY ON THAT THE WAY TO ERECT A barrier between Howard and Maheu, who was becoming more important every day, was to encourage Hughes's paranoia and that the foolproof way to foster paranoia was by feeding him more codeine and Valium. By tracing the highs and lows of Howard's codeine consumption, particularly its variations in potency, detectives for the Hughes estate and officers of the Drug Enforcement Administration were able to show "gross manipulation" of the man on the ninth floor.

One outburst of madness involved the annual Desert Inn Easter Egg Hunt, which drew the pillars of the community, select members of the social hierarchy, and the media. It had always been the photo opportunity of the season.

Maheu, a man of considerable executive and political skills, erupted in anger when Howard directed him to "cancel or move" this "dangerous event." Maheu fought back. "This is a harmless but very important event for the D.I.," Maheu wrote. "It would be a grave mistake to cancel it."

Pumped up with five times his usual amount of codeine, Hughes pleaded with Maheu, "Please, Bob, don't declare war on me so early in the day, and I'm well aware that this Easter egg hunt is not anything that is important to you, but merely something you were pressured into doing by certain groups here."

Bob appealed again, asking Hughes to consider "the children, if nothing else."

Two more codeine injections later, with almost twenty grains pumping through his blood, Howard grew angrier and angrier at Maheu. He began stacking and restacking, sorting and resorting his yellow pads.

For their common good, the aides encouraged rather than discouraged this thinking as Hughes muttered under his breath about "enemies everywhere; foiled at every turn; nobody on my side." Memos flew, with Hughes claiming "that although there are a number of people in Las Vegas who favor this event, there is a more powerful group who are dedicated to discrediting me." Added Hughes, "This second group will stop at nothing." In Hughes's increasingly clouded mind, stopping at nothing meant no less than a "juvenile riot."

Hughes's detachment from the world at large was further exemplified when he asked Robert Maheu to host a lavish seafaring party, off the coast of Florida, to celebrate the looming Apollo 13 launch, and to underscore Hughes Aircraft's contribution to the mission—a lunar observer which sent messages to earth from the moon's surface. Strolling the deck of the 150-foot yacht were VIPs including Vice President Spiro Agnew, TV newscaster Walter Cronkite, and the astronauts and their wives. Maheu didn't get back to his hotel room until two in the morning, Florida time. No matter. Hughes still wanted a complete run-down over the phone. "Tell me all about it, from the very beginning . . ." Hughes said eagerly.

As Maheu talked, Hughes sometimes interrupted him to exclaim, "How I wish I could have been there!" After a nearly three-hour conversation, Maheu finally hung up the phone, telling his wife, "Honey, I was just talking to the poorest man in the world."

In 1970, the bitter civil war between Maheu and the Mormons reached a bloody conclusion. Ironically it was Howard's secret alliance with the CIA, who had worked with Maheu when he was an FBI agent, that sealed Maheu's doom. Because Hughes personally enjoyed espionage and because he had worked with the CIA before and was a major equipment supplier to their espionage community, the CIA hierarchy believed Howard to be the perfect front man in a top-secret operation (code named Project Jennifer) to raise a Russian submarine that sank in the northwest

Pacific Ocean. The CIA wanted the sub's data on nuclear weaponry, targeting, and codes. But who could provide the best entrée to Hughes?

Memos between the CIA and the FBI show that they ruled out Maheu from the start. "Too risky and too involved in past projects," according to one report. So they went through Bill Gay, head of the Mormon contingent.

Howard was ecstatic with the new contract; one of his dreams was to become an integral part of the American spy establishment. In his mind, Gay had succeeded where Maheu had failed.

Hughes agreed to construct a huge oceangoing device that, ostensibly, would be used to mine the ocean floor. Called the *Glomar,* it would eventually cost $250 million.

The billionaire rose from his sick bed on November 13, 1970, the day the contract was signed between the Hughes Tool Company and the CIA. Hughes delegated his financial adviser, Raymond Holliday, to guarantee to the agency that he "was perfectly willing to act as the cover for the spy station—and that it would remain a classified secret."

The humiliating rejection of Maheu by the CIA was a windfall for William Gay. CIA Director William Colby had rejected Maheu at the first mention of his name. "He's a bad risk," Colby told the CIA agents involved in what became publicly known as the *Hughes Glomar Explorer.*

When Hughes's aide Raymond Holliday briefed Howard on Colby's opinion of Maheu, Hughes's opinion was shaken as well.

Hughes also blamed Maheu for screwing up a lavish "weekend entertainment of blondes and booze," Howard threw for Senator Edward Kennedy. The senator, in town for a political speech, was to "have anything and everything he wants—and that includes the most beautiful blonde chorus girl you can find." Maheu carried out the orders to the letter, providing a blonde who was so beautiful that people gasped when she came down the stairs of the Desert Inn floor show.

Unfortunately, a tabloid reporter was following Teddy through the neon jungle in hopes of catching the senator in the act. "Teddy and the Well-Stacked Blonde," made the front page of a tabloid in Great Britain and migrated across the Atlantic, where he was featured prominently in the *New York Post.*

"Maheu has single-handedly ruined what should have been a coup," Hughes wrote to Bill Gay. The day after Hughes signed the secret agreement with the CIA he stopped taking Maheu's calls. All messages now were filtered through the Mormon aides, many of them undelivered.

Maheu refused to accept the silence and finally wrote a blistering memo to his boss. He challenged Hughes, the man he had served for fourteen years without ever having met face-to-face: "I sometimes think the time has come for you to either walk down the nine flights of stairs, or more conveniently, utilize the elevator so as to face the world once and for all. Perhaps then you might have at least one more ounce of sympathy for someone else who is constantly facing the world in your behalf and who is about ready to go to bed one more evening finding himself on a damned lonely island."

On Thanksgiving Eve, November 25, 1970, Hughes and his gang of aides vanished. Nobody answered the ninth-floor phones. Gay had installed a new line and routed it through the Romaine headquarters.

After waiting a week to hear from Howard, the former FBI man journeyed to the ninth floor and was amazed by what he found. All the desks and security stations were gone—picked up by a moving company five days earlier. The rooms were unlocked, the beds unmade. But the most telling change was the emptiness of Howard's suite. Gone were the hospital bed, the mountains of yellow pads, the locked strongbox full of drugs, and his tower of movie canisters.

"Oh, my God," Maheu thought. "The old man's gone. What the hell could have happened to him? How could he have escaped from this huge hotel without being seen?"

Nor had there been any calls to the suite for the past seven days, no room service orders or traffic in and out of the Hughes wing. Maheu could only conclude that Hughes had been kidnapped by the William Gay faction.

Maheu reported the disappearance to Hank Greenspun, publisher of the *Las Vegas Sun*, the field office of the Federal Bureau of Investigation, and Nevada Governor Paul Laxalt. For the moment, "the kidnapping" was hidden from the Las Vegas Police Department and the press, a course of action recommended by FBI director J. Edgar Hoover, "until you have more evidence."

The FBI field office initiated a nationwide search for the billionaire, concentrating on places he frequented in the past—Hollywood, Palm Springs and Florida. On December 5, the field office reported: "We have been advised that H. M. Greenspun, publisher of the *Las Vegas Sun*, is of the opinion that Hughes was abducted and transported out of the state—possibly to gain control of the huge business complex. He plans to break this story on December 6."

Greenspun was true to his word. On December 6 the *Sun* ran a banner headline: HOWARD HUGHES VANISHES! MYSTERY BAFFLES CLOSE ASSOCIATES. In his own column the publisher suggested that the billionaire had been drugged, kidnapped, and was perhaps even dead. The news was relayed around the world, creating a tornado of media reports. But a journalist finally reached Howard Hughes himself, who was by then ensconced in the Britannia, a luxury hotel in the Bahamas.

Shortly after, on December 8, Maheu was stripped of all power. Howard called Governor Laxalt, who in turn alerted the FBI. An agency report stated: "Governor Laxalt talked with Hughes last night, and assures us that Hughes has relocated to the Bahamas and that he had indeed authorized the takeover of Hughes's Nevada operations by Bill Gay."

Hughes told the governor he had left the Desert Inn on Thanksgiving Eve. Unable to rise from his bed that evening, he had been tied to a stretcher and carefully lowered to the ground by the strongest of his aides.

Robert Maheu believes to this day that "Howard lost control of his life to Bill Gay and his minions the night he left here, because his every move was dictated by the group of aides surrounding him."

There is also a cadre of conspiracy theorists who maintain that Hughes never left Nevada alive. Author Marjel De Lauer, who worked for Hughes's Las Vegas television station, is among those who feel Hughes may have been murdered by persons out to get control of his empire.

Three days after Hughes and his men vacated the Desert Inn, De Lauer telephoned her longtime friend Jane Russell. "I think Howard's in great danger," Marjel warned. Jane, who had already heard "terrible things" about the aides from Hughes associate Nadine Henley, picked up the phone and called Jean Peters.

Peters herself was shocked at the news of Hughes's disappearance. If Hughes had in fact fled Las Vegas, he hadn't bothered to inform his former wife. Using her network of contacts in the Hughes empire, Peters determined that her ex-husband was safe. "She told me he was fine and that no one should worry," said Russell.

But De Lauer wasn't entirely convinced, believing that the aides might have simply lied to Peters as they had done for more than a decade. She still believes Hughes was somehow killed in 1970 and replaced by a carefully coached double. She isn't alone. Other former Hughes associates believe he was killed. And for a brief time, Washington columnist Jack Anderson suspected that an actor was portraying his old friend.

The blacked-out suite in the Britannia, a hotel known for its sweeping views of the Caribbean, was just another hole for Hughes to crawl into, a private opiate den that supplied him with euphoria and all the movies he wished. The entrance and exits to the penthouse were blocked by hefty guards while another guard paced about on the roof with two attack dogs.

Wall Street Journal reporter Michael Drosnin, who had access to more than ten thousand documents about the latter-day Hughes, pointed out, "Hughes was no longer his own prisoner. With Maheu gone, his Mormon attendants were firmly in control, determined to keep their boss bedridden and befuddled."

In *Citizen Hughes,* his 1985 book based on his six-year study of the documents, Drosnin noted, "Hughes we know was now completely cut off from the world, thousands of miles from his empire. The Mormons now controlled all lines of communication. Hughes still dictated his memos and asked voluminous questions, but he knew only what the aides wanted him to know."

One of the aides, George Francom, recalled that "control of Mr. Hughes's communications began to tighten . . . I observed many messages to and from Howard being held up by all of the other aides."

Howard's days now followed a ritual that never varied, as if Howard had stumbled into the most expensive nursing home in the world. Sleep. Food. Drugs. Movies. The aides came to know every line of the Rock Hudson movie *Ice Station Zebra,* about submarine commanders caught up in cold war intrigue at the North Pole. ("If we watched it once, we watched it a hundred times," groaned one of the aides.) And every detail was laboriously entered into a log which eventually filled 100,000 pages.

Consider the entries for a sample day:

Sunday *6:55 a.m.* *Asleep*
        11:15 a.m. *Awake B/R (Bathroom)*
        11:35 a.m. *Chair, screening "SITUATION*
                       HOPELESS BUT NOT SERIOUS"
                       (completed all but
                       last 5 min. reel 3)

1:30 p.m.	10/C [10 grains codeine]
1:50 p.m.	B/R
2.10 p.m.	Chair, resumed screening "THE KILLERS"
3.30 p.m.	Food. Chicken only.
4.20 p.m.	Finished "SITUATION HOPELESS BUT NOT SERIOUS" Screening "DO NOT DISTURB" (OK to return)
6.45 p.m.	B/R
7.00 p.m.	Chair
7.45 p.m.	Screening "DEATH OF A GUNFIGHTER" (1 reel only)
8.25 p.m.	B/R
8.45 p.m.	Chair
9.00 p.m.	Screening "THE KILLERS"
9.35 p.m.	Chicken and dessert. Completed "THE KILLERS"
11.25 p.m.	B/R
11.50 p.m.	Bed. Changed bandages. Not asleep

He would still rise occasionally from his stupor, though. On December 7, 1971, the McGraw-Hill book company announced with great fanfare that it would soon publish *The Memoirs of Howard Hughes: His True Life Story as Told to Clifford Irving*.

A moderately successful novelist, Irving claimed he had been given lengthy interview time with Howard during the previous two years. He had materials in Howard's own writing to prove it. His coup electrified the book world. For more than three decades Hughes had sought to control his life's story. When Dell Publishing printed a magazine biography following the world flight, Hughes bought all 175,000 copies, which were then burned at Hughes Aircraft. In more recent years he had used teams of high-priced lawyers and bribes to quash at least seven biographies, some of them by respected authors. A typical Hughes ploy was to put writers under contract to write the "authorized" story, and then allow the deal to languish.

He also had his minions attempt to quash stories by newspaper and magazine reporters. James Phelan, who spent twenty years writing about Hughes for publications including the *Saturday Evening Post* and the *New*

York Times, was once offered a new car and lifetime passes on TWA for himself and his family, in exchange for dropping a story. Phelan passed on the offer. As did Vernon Scott, who was offered "cars, money, you name it," when he wrote about the curious Hughes–Jean Peters marriage for *Ladies Home Journal*. (For his exposé, Scott used the nom de plume D. L. Lyons.)

Spokesmen at both the Hughes Tool Company and at Hughes Aircraft denounced the Irving autobiography as a forgery. Even Cary Grant, once Howard's best friend, got into the act, telling reporters that "Howard would never even remotely be involved in such a ridiculous project. He is a very private man."

Neither McGraw-Hill nor Clifford Irving backed down. William Gay and attorney Chester Davis were astounded that the book world would not accept letters of refutation that had been drafted at the Britannia and then hand-delivered to both McGraw-Hill and *Life*, which was planning to serialize the book.

"We'll have to produce Hughes," Davis finally told Gay. "Stage some sort of press conference."

Hughes balked. "I will not go on television. I don't want anybody to see the state I'm in."

A compromise was reached. After fifteen years in hiding, Howard Hughes was going to meet the press—in a conference conducted by telephone. Though the Hughes aides were nervous, they believed his remarkable memory would pull him through.

On January 7, 1972, seven newsmen—six of whom had known Hughes in earlier years—met at the Sheraton-Universal Hotel near Hollywood for a two-hour-forty-minute marathon interview session with a man who was speaking from three thousand miles away in the Bahamas.

Howard disposed of Irving right off: "I don't know him. I never saw him. I never even heard of him until days ago when this came to my attention."

But the press wasn't interested in hearing about Irving; they needed to prove whether they were actually speaking with Howard Hughes. Roy Neal of NBC acted as moderator for the conference and asked many of the questions.

"One question we have from the outset is, where are you speaking from right now, sir?"

"Paradise Island," Hughes answered. "Nassau seems to be a more widely known name." The voice was clear and strong.

"There was no mistaking that voice, which was one of the most famous in the world because of his exploits," said Hollywood columnist James Bacon. He spoke directly to Hughes: "I have heard your voice so many times, and the minute you started talking, I knew it was Howard Hughes." The other reporters came to agree with Bacon.

Though Hughes had some memory lapses during the dialogue— especially when it came to identifying names of associates from the past—he never faltered on queries about aviation, including the Lockheed Constellation and the Spruce Goose. Nor did he dodge questions about his physical condition and appearance.

At the time, a grotesque image of Hughes had made its way into popular myth—and the media (he was often the subject of cartoonists). "If I had toenails eight inches long I couldn't walk. If I had fingernails eight inches long, I couldn't write my name," stressed Hughes. As to how his health was, he shrewdly replied, "Well, how the hell is anybody's health at sixty-six years of age? I certainly don't feel like running around a track at UCLA and trying to break a record, I can tell you that. But my health is tolerable, that's certain. And probably better than I deserve."

He also conceded that for all his wealth, his life lacked a key element. Admitted Hughes, "I'm not very happy."

The Hughes press conference made the front pages. Though Clifford Irving and McGraw-Hill initially denounced the press conference as a fraud, Irving's carefully orchestrated hoax was toppling. Within the month he acknowledged that he had perpetrated the literary heist of the decade. *Time* magazine dubbed Irving "Con Man of the Year." He was later to serve prison time.

The day after the press conference Hughes sat up in bed and confided to aide Mell Stewart, "I don't know how many summers I have left, and I don't intend to spend them holed up on a BarcaLounger in the middle of a dark hotel room."

Somehow, without the knowledge of his coterie, Howard had accumulated a stash of yachting brochures, which he displayed to Stewart. "You know, Mell," he said, "the choice of boats in Miami is at its peak right now. And a couple of preferred boats are in Europe. Who knows? I may spend the summer on the Mediterranean."

The aides reacted hysterically to these innocent conversations. They conducted an organization-wide search for the man who let the yacht brochures reach Howard's hands. Two of them ordered Stewart out and confronted Howard. "Look, Mr. Hughes," said one of them, "Robert Maheu has already tried to kidnap you—right here in this hotel. On a yacht you would be a sitting duck. We cannot protect you."

According to Stewart, these "scare tactics" sent Hughes scurrying back to his bed, where the level of codeine and Valium in his system increased to forty times the prescribed dosage. "Don't encourage him," one aide warned Stewart.

From that day on Hughes's mail was intercepted and censored. "They routinely pulled out whatever they didn't want him to see," said Stewart.

During his press conference, Hughes had also talked of returning to Las Vegas to resume control of his hotel and casino operation. In fact, he was about to embark on a strange, country-to-country odyssey, triggered by the government in Nassau, which believed Hughes's presence brought the country adverse publicity, a deterrent to tourism. They discovered that his residency permit had expired, and police were immediately dispatched to root him out.

Tipped by a government source, the aides managed to sneak Hughes out of the Britannia by tying him to a stretcher and carefully taking him down the fire escape. Hughes and the aides fled the Bahamas in a private yacht, the *Cygnus*. Howard was wearing a bathrobe.

Certain that the Bahamian authorities were on their trail, the aides forced the captain to sail directly into the eye of a Caribbean squall, causing the boat to pitch and plunge through the twenty-foot waves. The aides pumped Howard full of Valium and Dramamine for the twenty-two-hour crossing. Rolling around a small bed, Hughes mumbled again and again, "I don't understand. Where are we going?"

Captain Rob Rehak caught a brief glimpse of Hughes as he invaded the small stateroom to strap down furniture and later told reporters that the once-handsome Hughes was now a wizened old man. "He looked thirty years older than his actual age. His hair was shoulder length and filthy. His skin resembled parchment." As the boat slipped sideways, the sheet slipped off Howard's naked body. He looked up pitifully at Rehak, who averted his eyes. "He was down to skin and bones with long, curling fingernails," he told reporters. "He hadn't bathed in months."

The captain's verbal portrait, broadcast around the world and converted into newspaper sketches and magazine illustrations, convinced the public that Howard was indeed a dirty, drug-ridden old man. Because Hughes's syphilis and its neurological fallout were hidden even from his aides and associates, no one connected the lapse in hygiene and grooming habits with locomotor ataxia, yet it is the first outward symptom of degenerative neurosyphilis.

The depiction of the once handsome swashbuckler as a filthy bum has prevailed to this day.

After being taken by the *Cygnus* to Key Biscayne Bay in Florida, Hughes and the aides boarded a leased jet. Their destination: Managua, Nicaragua, and the eighth floor of the Intercontinental Hotel. The twenty-five-day Nicaragua trip climaxed with a headline-making meeting between Hughes, President Anastasio Somoza, and Turner B. Shelton, the United States ambassador to Nicaragua.

But this time Hughes was well groomed—with short hair and a neatly trimmed Vandyke beard. He had also showered (and had even had his toenails cut). Hughes's aide Mell Stewart had done the makeover just forty-eight hours before the historic encounter. Afterward, Somoza reported that except for using a hearing aid, Hughes appeared in good health. He said Hughes told him he regretted he had become a recluse "because I haven't met anybody in twenty-three years outside of the people in my close circle."

From Nicaragua the Hughes contingent headed for Vancouver, where Hughes displayed a burst of independence. When his limo pulled to the front entrance of the Bayshore Inn, surrounded by dramatic vistas of bay and ocean, Howard hoisted himself from the automobile and walked into the lobby. "Wait, Mr. Hughes, wait," said Gordon Margulis as he struggled to unfold the boss's wheelchair.

"Oh, never mind about that," he replied. "Don't bother, I'm going to walk in." To Margulis's amazement, the boss walked through the front doors and surveyed the inn's luxurious lobby. "Hey, this is pretty nice." An elderly lady walked right up to him, grabbed his arm, and grinned, saying, "Hi, how are you?"

Margulis was startled. "Normally, such an encounter would have thrown Mr. Hughes into a panic. But he just smiled." A senior aide appeared behind Margulis. "Get him back into that wheelchair and take him upstairs. And do it now."

Upstairs, Howard rose from the wheelchair and strolled about the expansive suite. He approached the picture windows with their sweep of the Vancouver skyline and pressed his face against the glass, entranced by the sight of a seaplane shining across the water. Hughes gestured toward the windows.

"Gordon, we're not going to black these out; I'd like to make this into a sitting room."

"I think that would be a great idea," Margulis answered. But a senior aide vetoed the idea instantly, convincing Hughes that helicopters would have easy access, able to fly by at any time, taking pictures and beaming their lights through the glass. So Hughes was marched into his bedroom—and the windows throughout the suite were blacked out. Five ten-milligram Valium tablets were pressed into his hand just before they put him to bed. "They wanted him in bed, where they could control him," Margulis recalled.

By August 1972, Hughes had been spirited back to Nicaragua and its Intercontinental Hotel. Now the aides exercised such iron-fisted control over the ailing billionaire that they tricked him into selling the Hughes Tool Company, the rock upon which his fortune rested. He issued only a pitiful whimper of protest as they gathered around his bed and told him, erroneously, that he had to "sell in order to pay off the looming TWA judgments." They knew this wasn't true and that attorney Chester Davis was already "certain of overturning those penalties."

In a landmark power play, the triumvirate of Davis, Hughes's New York counsel; Raymond Holliday, president of Toolco; and William Gay retained the Wall Street firm of Merrill, Lynch, Fenner and Smith to offer corporate stock on the market at $30 a share. But the top executives of the brokerage firm were suspicious and demanded a notarized proxy.

At first Hughes indignantly refused to sign—a temporary setback that was soon corrected by the aides. In late August they increased Howard's drugs to four injections of codeine and twelve "big blues," the billionaire's nickname for ten-milligram Valium tablets, twenty times the recommended dosage. Enveloped in a euphoric chemical haze, he scrawled his approval to what his friend Jack Real described as "the financial rape of the twentieth century."

In Washington, D.C., the Securities and Exchange Commission demanded an "on-site interview to prove that Mr. Hughes is alive and well." Merrill, Lynch sent senior broker Julius M. Sedylmayr to secure "verbal approval" of the sale from the reclusive billionaire. The aides immediately detoxed Hughes and summoned aide Mell Stewart to cut his beard, hair, and fingernails so he would be presentable to this "outsider." They decided upon "the distinguished gentleman look" for the historic September 24 meeting.

Hoping to frighten this "sober Howard" into selling, the aides told him that the tool company could not be sold in the same year he paid the TWA penalty, which loomed in early 1973. With the aides on hand to prompt him, a shaky Hughes confirmed the sales agreement. But Hughes also weakly protested that he didn't "think this was the correct time to sell." Told that his father's company would be offered publicly for $30 a share, he mumbled, "That's a bit low, isn't it?" No one answered.

Both Hughes and Real were correct. The stock, with its bargain-basement price, sold within hours on the stock exchange, netting $140 million. Five months later, the shares went for $90 a share or $500 million. Howard lost a third of a billion dollars.

But Gay, Davis, and Holliday gained mightily. Holliday became president of the new independent tool company in a deal that gave him hundreds of thousands in stock options; Gay took control of the Summa Corporation, the new entity that ran the remaining empire; and Davis earned substantial legal fees. By selling Toolco out from under Hughes, they effectively destroyed his control of the far-flung empire.

When the U.S. Supreme Court overturned the TWA judgment against Howard twenty-seven days after the sale, as Davis had predicted all along, it became obvious that there had been no reason to sell. Howard did not learn about the Summa Corporation until December 21 when he was handed incorporation pages to sign. "What the hell is Summa?" he asked. "And how the hell do you pronounce it?" Several days later he ordered his aides to change the name. "Call it HRH Incorporated." But his orders were ignored.

Hughes might have remained in Central America for years, sliding toward death, were it not for the catastrophic earthquake that struck Managua at 12:30 A.M. on December 23, 1972, leveling six hundred square blocks of the downtown area, killing six thousand people, and igniting ten thousand fires that burned out of control for hours.

Hughes was tilted back in his BarcaLounger watching *Goldfinger* when he heard a deafening boom. The skyscraper hotel swayed as if it had been caught in a hurricane. A heavy standing lamp crashed down onto Howard, and a stereo speaker shook loose from the wall and grazed his forehead as it flew through the air. Then the hotel plunged into total darkness.

"Don't panic," Hughes said calmly to his aides. "It's only an earth-quake. If you make it through the first jolt, you're going to be okay." At that moment the hotel shuddered from the effects of thirteen aftershocks that rumbled beneath Managua. "Just aftershocks, boys," Hughes said soothingly. The boss's words were no comfort to aide James Rickard, who was propelled about the hotel suite as if he were a rag doll.

When Rickard reached the lounger and tried to carry Hughes to safety, the old man wouldn't budge. "Never mind, I'll be safer right here in my room than I would be on the street." But the aide could see the orange towers of flame that surrounded the hotel and called for help. It took three of them to dress Howard, strap him to a stretcher, and lower him inch by inch down nine flights of stairs.

They stumbled out onto the street and faced a hellish sight. Clouds of black soot raced through Managua's central core, obscuring the twisted shells of a thousand buildings. Wearing his cotton undershorts and wrapped in a woolen blanket, Howard was eased into the backseat of a Mercedes limo. He looked straight ahead as the sleek car sped toward the safety of the hilltop suburbs.

Their destination was President Somoza's villa, but Hughes soon panicked as dust from the rubble obscured their vision. "Take me back!" he screamed. "Take me back to the hotel!" He gestured toward the dust storm. "It's this dust that will kill you. It's full of germs. Please take me back."

"We can't, boss," Rickard protested. "It's been condemned."

To calm Howard, the aides cruised about Managua's dust-free foothills for three hours before finally reaching a compromise with their recalcitrant boss. They took him to President Somoza's summer house, a Spanish-style villa perched atop a distant hill overlooking the city.

But when they reached the hideaway, Hughes refused to enter the mansion. Instead, he climbed into the back of the presidential limousine and huddled there until dawn, watching the city burn. At 7:00 A.M., Howard's chartered jet was the only private plane allowed to leave Nicaragua.

Managua was still ablaze when the Hughes jet pierced the black clouds and made first contact with the FAA in Miami. Learning that Howard Hughes was aboard, the feds ordered the pilot to land in Fort Lauderdale to "submit to a U.S. Customs check." This maneuver was directed by the United States Treasury Department, which had been shadowing Howard for months, hoping he could return to America long enough to be served an IRS subpoena, part of an investigation of his tax dodges.

When his jet landed at 2:15 A.M. on Christmas Eve, U.S. Treasury agents surrounded the aircraft and directed it to an empty hangar, where customs officers awaited Hughes's arrival. Aide Chuck Waldron stepped out to greet and hopefully divert G. T. Register, the Internal Revenue Service's top man in Florida.

Register stepped forward. "We'd like an interview with Howard Robard Hughes." He handed Waldron the federal authorization allowing Register and his armed deputies to detain Hughes until they were satisfied.

Waldron disappeared inside the jet, and Register could hear angry voices, followed by a plaintive appeal. "No, no. I can't do this. They can't do this to me. Tell them to call the president of the United States. Tell them to call Chester Davis in New York."

During a three-hour standoff, Hughes's own army of detectives stood before the plane with their hands fingering shoulder holsters. Treasury agents were no less menacing.

In Manhattan, Chester Davis used his connections to the White House, and the IRS was told to back off. "It was an interesting power play," Washington columnist Jack Anderson recalled. "Only the power of the Hughes name and his well-cultivated ties to the Nixon and Ford administrations could have achieved such a surrender by the IRS and the United States Justice Department." The federal agents were called off.

But Register, known for his toughness in confronting "IRS violators," was furious and insisted upon a concession. "We should at least use this opportunity to prove that Howard Hughes is still alive," he told Washington. "Yes," he was told. "You may do that."

So, at 3:10 A.M., a U.S. Customs agent boarded the plane and aimed a flashlight at the gaunt form huddled in a filthy blanket. Caught in the beam was a black-hatted man with a scarf obscuring most of his face. He was starvation-thin with long, greasy hair and a beard that cascaded onto his chest. "He looked as if he were ninety years old and was smudged with dirt," one of the agents noted in his report.

"Are you Howard Robard Hughes?" the agent asked. "Yep," Hughes mumbled as he pulled the blanket up to his nose. The official IRS report described Hughes as "emaciated, filthy and unkempt—like a derelict." The report concluded: "This man could barely state his own name."

Saved from public humiliation, Howard sank back onto the floor of the jet and headed to London and sanctuary.

In London, at the Inn on the Park, he requested the latest aviation magazines, ordered new clothes from British tailors, and sent aide Gordon Margulis to procure a replica of his old lucky fedora. This alarmed the aides and the phone lines buzzed between the Inn and the Romaine Street headquarters in Hollywood.

When Nevada governor Mike O'Callaghan met Hughes a short time later, he was greeted by "an alert, intelligent, enthusiastic man with a commanding personality." Added O'Callaghan, "There was no doubt in my mind that he was telling the aides what to do. When he disagreed with them his voice rose accordingly."

Hughes also drastically altered the status quo by adding a dynamic new executive to his retinue. Jack Real, a former fighter pilot, former Lockheed official, and a longtime flying buddy, moved into a suite just down the hall from Hughes. When Real began closeting himself with the boss each afternoon, the aides were helpless to interfere. Real had gone to work for Hughes in 1971, hired personally by the billionaire. According to James B. Steele of the *Philadelphia Inquirer*, "Real was not an aide; he was simply there because Hughes specifically asked for him. His presence in London annoyed Gay and the other aides because he was totally free of the Romaine Street power brokers. They could only isolate Real as much as possible, allowing him into the bedroom only when Hughes demanded to see him."

And "Get me Jack" was becoming Howard's most frequent command. A senior aide was sent to warn Real, "You're encouraging him to get up. He's easier to take care of when he's in bed and medicated." But Real ignored them and reported directly to Hughes.

On May 12, 1973, Howard bounded from his bed and announced that he was ready to fly again. "Jack's got it all set up." *Empire* co-authors Donald L. Barlett and James B. Steele noted, "[Hughes's] staff was stunned. If Hughes began to venture forth, Romaine Street might lose control." A second deputation of aides hiked down to Real's quarters. "Go home!" one of them yelled. "You're getting him *alive*."

Real pressed ahead. Because Howard had let his pilot's license lapse thirteen years earlier, Real pulled strings and arranged for him to "test fly" a brand-new Hawker-Siddeley 748, a hefty, twin-engine turboprop. Tony Blackman, chief test pilot for Hawker-Siddeley, agreed to serve as co-pilot. But the turboprop sat idly on the runway for two weeks while Hughes "sobered up."

It was a joyous, enthusiastic Hughes who made his own way down to the lobby of the Inn the morning of May 12, dressed in new clothes and clutching his new lucky fedora. Considering the stories he had heard,

Blackman was amazed by the sober, professional flier he met in a military hangar on the outskirts of London. He appeared to be drug-free. Conveniently for the aides and for the Romaine Street leadership, they claimed to have kept no drug records during the British sojourn, perhaps to cover up the extent of Howard's detoxification.

When he was in the cockpit, however, Howard shed his light blue shirt, unzipped and took off his slacks, and dropped his drawstring shorts. Naked and smiling, the fedora tilted rakishly upon his head, he eased into the pilot's seat, fired up the engines, and taxied down the runway.

Between early May and late July, Howard completed four extensive flights, one of them across the English Channel to Ostend, Belgium. After the final flight, Real noted that "Howard was in complete control. This was his best day in the four years I spent with him."

But this was only an interlude. On August 19, Hughes fell in the bathroom of his hotel suite. Shortly after British surgeons inserted a pin in Hughes's left hip, the drug regimen was reinstated, including high levels of codeine. Whatever the cause of the mishap, Hughes returned to his bedroom, crawled into the battered hospital bed, and never left it again other than to travel from hotel to hotel.

As Cary Grant told *The Times*, "The soul and the mind were dead."

Only the ravaged body was left.

CHAPTER 32

HOWARDGATE

ONE MORNING WHEN HOWARD WAS IN LONDON THE HEADLINES OF A tabloid newspaper astounded him. HOWARD HUGHES BANKROLLED WATER-GATE declared the *Daily Mirror*.

"What the hell is Watergate, and how am I involved in it?" His aides mumbled a few unsatisfactory answers. So Hughes furiously scribbled a memo to his New York attorney Chester Davis. "What have I to do with this mess?" Later in a telephone conversation he demanded to know what he could have possibly done to imperil his favorite president. Weeks would pass before Davis replied.

The twisted, paranoid trail that allowed an incapacitated billionaire to bring down an American president was incredibly complicated, hinging, as it did, upon Nixon's fear of Hughes and upon the intensification of Howard's obsessive-compulsive disorder. It also depended upon the river of drugs Hughes's doctors and aides had begun pumping into his system in 1968, the year the scandal was born.

Starting early that year, Hughes made campaign contributions totalling $400,000, divided among a series of both Nevada candidates, including Nevada governor Paul Laxalt, and presidential candidates, including Hubert Humphrey, Lyndon Johnson (before he decided not to seek another term), and Richard Nixon. This largesse to competing presidential candidates made perfect sense to Howard.

"Look, I expect Dick Nixon to win," he explained to Maheu. "But I'm hedging my bets." In any case it was Nixon who pocketed the real windfall, $200,000 over a two-year period.

The most significant contribution was a briefcase full of cash Hughes had secretly delivered to influential Nixon aides. It was earmarked for a political slush fund and was never reported as a campaign contribution. Nixon could do as he wished with the money; a later investigation hinted that the president employed this money to enlarge his estate in San Clemente, California. Nixon associate Richard Danner was a go-between for Hughes and the White House.

The $100,000 under-the-table donation would eventually help change the course of American history and involve Howard in the greatest scandal in the history of the presidency. So would his hiring of Larry O'Brien.

Hughes cast the first stone from the penthouse at the Desert Inn in July 1968, less than an hour after Sirhan Sirhan assassinated presidential candidate Robert F. Kennedy. "Kennedy could have gone on to be the president," Hughes mused as the tragedy played out on his television screen. It was the horror of that possibility that led to Hughes's hiring of O'Brien, former Democratic strategist and campaign aide for Robert Kennedy and Hubert Humphrey among others. O'Brien was to assist the billionaire in lobbying for his interests in Washington, D.C.

In a memo to Robert Maheu, Hughes scrawled, "The Kennedys have been a thorn relentlessly at my side for decades. We must put a candidate in the White House who knows the facts of life." Just what Hughes meant by that statement is unclear. What is clear is that O'Brien went to work for Hughes through his consulting firm, O'Brien Associates of Washington, D.C. He was paid a retainer of $15,000 per week and was told to await instructions from Hughes.

Richard M. Nixon, then in the midst of a run for the presidency, learned of the alliance five days earlier from a contact in the Central Intelligence Agency. "What is Howard Hughes up to?" the unnamed informant questioned. "It could place your candidacy in great danger."

Robert Maheu, who served as Hughes's liaison with Larry O'Brien, said that the Democratic chairman's work for Hughes began and ended with major aid on guiding the Hughes empire through labyrinthine tax legislation and federal antitrust regulations. "But Nixon was very, very frightened, and he imagined that O'Brien held all sorts of information in confidence."

Added Maheu, "Nixon wouldn't even have had to telephone Hughes. How ironic that a breach of confidence concerning funds could have been laid to rest with a simple phone call to me. His men had a history of dealings with me. Instead, the history of the United States, and the presidency, was altered forever."

In fact, Nixon became riddled with paranoia. The very man who had engineered his defeat by John F. Kennedy was now working for the most unpredictable, uncontrollable figure in America's power structure. Adding to Nixon's trauma was the realization that an unpaid loan of $205,000 from Hughes to his brother F. Donald Nixon had cost him the 1960 election.

The loan to Nixon's brother had been made back in 1956, when Donald Nixon was running a financially shaky restaurant chain that boasted the "Nixonburger." The loan came to Donald Nixon through his mother, who received the money in two payments from an attorney. Coincidentally, just a few months after the loan was made, Hughes was granted a tax break by the Internal Revenue Service that was worth millions. Richard M. Nixon was then the vice president.

News of the loan was made public in 1960—when Richard Nixon was campaigning for the presidency. But the cagey Nixon wasn't answering questions about his brother's loan. Election Day was nearing when Nixon visited San Francisco's Chinatown for some grandstanding. Unbeknownst to Nixon, Democratic prankster Dick Tuck had already left his mark . . . in Chinese.

When Nixon obligingly posed for photographers before a gigantic banner with Chinese characters, he had no idea that they read WHAT ABOUT THE HUGHES LOAN? Still later that day, at a luncheon with the Chinese community leaders, Nixon was addressing the crowd when laughter broke out. The reason: the fortune cookies had been passed out, each one of them containing the message, "Ask him about the Hughes loan."

The Hughes loan led to Nixon's defeat—not just for the presidency but also for governor of California in the 1962 race. In his book *Nightmare: The Underside of the Nixon Years,* J. Anthony Lukas noted that "ever since, [Nixon] had been extremely sensitive about his brother's ties with the Hughes organization."

In a brilliant maneuver, O'Brien had traded upon the loan from Hughes to Donald Nixon to taint Nixon as "a man nobody can trust."

In late 1968, when Nixon was president-elect and while O'Brien was still on retainer to Hughes, Howard passed $100,000 in cash—a political slush fund—to Nixon through his millionaire pal, Key Biscayne banker Charles "Bebe" Rebozo. The billionaire placed no ties on the cash, and Nixon never declared it as a campaign contribution. This gusher of cash apparently quelled Nixon's fear of O'Brien.

Then in January 1971, O'Brien jumped into the fray again, vowing to put George McGovern in the White House, riding a wave of protest against the Vietnam War and trading upon Nixon's closet full of "dirty tricks." Nixon was frightened that O'Brien must know of the slush fund and of the fact that some of the cash had been used to remodel his winter retreat in Key Biscayne.

On January 14, 1971, when Hughes was little more than a prisoner in the Bahamas, Nixon sat back in his Air Force One armchair and dictated a memo to his chief of staff, H. R. Haldeman: "It's time that Larry O'Brien is held accountable for his retainer with Hughes."

Privately, the president added: "We must neutralize O'Brien."

"Larry had beaten him in 1960; the specter was raised again," wrote Michael Drosnin in *Citizen Hughes.* "Now Nixon wanted revenge."

Haldeman later said that Nixon "often lost all balance when it came to Howard Hughes and the president's estimation of his power."

Nixon's irrational fears intensified when he finally received a president's-eyes-only memo on Hughes that had been requested by presidential aide John D. Ehrlichman. J. Edgar Hoover replied personally to the White House aide: "Hughes is considered by many to be an unscrupulous individual who possesses a highly unstable nature, is ruthless and capable of almost anything."

"O'Brien is not going to get away with it this time," Nixon wrote Haldeman a day after returning to Washington. Later that afternoon Nixon confided to Haldeman that he believed Hughes to be the "most powerful man in the world."

Nonetheless, Nixon won the election handily, and neither O'Brien nor McGovern had even hinted at the clandestine financial dealings between Hughes and the president of the United States. A month later, however, someone else did.

When McGraw-Hill announced the publication of the Clifford Irving book, Nixon was as shaken by the news as Hughes himself. Using the services of the CIA, Nixon obtained a condensation of the Irving material along with an unsigned note that stated: "The Irving-Hughes book is very damaging to the president." Irving himself made this clear a month after the re-election. "Howard Hughes paid Nixon four hundred thousand dollars to fix the TWA case," the writer told breathless reporters. In fact, the Federal Court of Appeals had overturned the judgment against Hughes and vindicated the billionaire.

Howard's telephonic press conference from the Bahamas failed to quell Nixon's fear. The tycoon lied convincingly and slickly about the charges. "I never passed any money to President Nixon through Bebe Rebozo," he claimed. He added that he'd never "had any dealings" with the president's mysterious millionaire crony.

"Now, regarding Mr. Nixon," said Hughes in an irritated tone, "I have tried not to bother him since he's been in office, and I have made no effort to contact him."

Reading a transcript of the press conference later, Nixon indicated to Haldeman that he didn't trust Hughes, stating, in fact, that Hughes might have something up his sleeve.

On January 31, 1972, yet another book entered the fray. This time it was a bona fide memoir, as Haldeman reported in his diary.

> *Attorney General called today about the Howard Hughes problem. He's gotten a report from the United States Attorney in New York, who has a draft of the Noah Dietrich book, that indicates that Hughes apparently contributed, or made a gift of, $195,000 to Nixon, after the '60 election, and said it could be considered a belated campaign contribution. Mitchell's concerned that we get the background on that.*

O'Brien and the Democrats remained silent, however.

But Nixon couldn't let the matter drop—telling his aides again and again, "O'Brien had to be neutralized." Finally, on March 30, U.S. Attorney General John Mitchell ordered a team of secret operatives (called "the plumbers") to invade O'Brien's office in the Watergate building. They were to look for the chairman's file on Nixon, to bug his phone, and to "seek out financial data tying O'Brien to Howard Hughes." The operation, under G. Gordon Liddy and E. Howard Hunt, was only partially successful.

Though the plumbers easily penetrated the Democratic headquarters, they failed to activate the listening device properly, and they forgot the Hughes files. The careless gang was sent back to finish the job early on Saturday morning, June 17. And this time Jeb Magruder, a top Nixon aide, ordered them to "photograph O'Brien's shit file on Nixon."

They never got the chance. A security guard had noticed the break-in. As the burglars were prying open O'Brien's file cabinet, the "F to H" drawer, the police rushed in.

Though Nixon could not have known this, Hughes was as isolated by his corporate aides as the president was by his "palace guard." A single phone call between the leader of the free world and the richest man in America could have prevented the disaster that followed. Instead, the president and all his men were embroiled in a cover-up during the next six months. If Nixon had even checked with his highly placed sources within the CIA or the FBI, he would have learned, as a March 1972 FBI memo noted, that "Howard Hughes is no longer in a position to run *any* of his businesses, particularly those in Las Vegas."

On June 20, 1972, the president summoned Haldeman to the Oval Office for a conversation about Watergate matters, including the Hughes loan.

Counting the 1956 unpaid loan to Donald and another $150,000 undeclared contribution, Nixon's financial obligation to the world's most notorious recluse had topped half a million dollars. After postulating on "Howardgate" to Haldeman, Nixon speculated that there was a weak link within the plumbers: Charles Colson, his special counsel. "I'm worried about Colson," Nixon told Haldeman. "Colson can talk about the president and, if he cracks . . . you know I was on Colson's tail for months to nail Larry O'Brien on the Hughes deal."

This conversation would become famous as the eighteen and a half minutes missing from the Watergate tapes, having been erased by Nixon's secretary, Rosemary Woods. This erasure would become the last straw that unseated a president.

Hughes's fateful connection with Watergate didn't end in the Oval Office. It extended into the scandal's media arena as well. The new Hughes man in Washington, ironically replacing O'Brien, was a former CIA agent by the name of Robert Foster Bennett—who many believe was "Deep Throat," the D.C. insider who leaked details of the cover-up to Bob Woodward and Carl Bernstein, who uncovered the scandal for the *Washington Post* and, later, in their book-turned-film, *All the President's Men*.

Though Bennett has repeatedly denied this, he was working out of Robert Mullen and Company, a CIA front, and he later told his CIA case officer, Martin Lukasky, that he was "feeding stories to Bob Woodward and others."

The leaks convinced President Nixon that "Bob Bennett is 'Deep Throat,' " as he told Haldeman. He also voiced concern that "Hughes and the CIA are plotting together to bring me down." This claim would have astounded Hughes, who finally received his report from Chester Davis.

It was remarkably benign and uninformed:

We are involved in the Watergate affair to this extent:

1. E. Howard Hunt, convicted for the Watergate break-in, was employed by Bob Bennett (our current Washington representative). In addition Bennett was maintaining liaison with the White House through Chuck Colson, who was deeply involved in the Watergate cover-up.

2. Bennett Ralph Winte (employed by us re: security matters) and Hunt are involved in plans to burglarize Greenspun's safe, and even though those plans were rejected and never carried out, investigators see political motivation related to Watergate.

3. The political contribution . . . to Rebozo . . . [is] claimed to be an effort for influencing Governmental decisions, including an alleged change in rulings of the Department of Justice.

4. Payments made to Larry O'Brien and his employment has been claimed to have been part of the possible motivation for the Watergate break-in because of White House interest in that arrangement as a possible means of embarrassing O'Brien and the Democrats.

5. The massive political contributions supposedly made by Maheu, particularly those made in cash, is part of the over-all Watergate investigation dealing with the need for reform.

According to Robert Maheu, the entire scandal was unnecessary. "Larry O'Brien never knew of the slush fund."

There was a sad postscript to the "Hughes connection."

Shortly before Howard gave President Nixon another $150,000 in 1972, his aides asked the president's men for only one thing: could the president please call him on Christmas Eve, "and wish him a happy birthday"?

The call never came.

CHAPTER 33

EVIL UNDER THE SUN

ACAPULCO, MEXICO, MARCH 30, 1976

AT 4:00 P.M. HOWARD FINISHED DRINKING EIGHT OUNCES OF MILK. IT HAD taken him eight hours, interrupted by doses of his real nourishment, 150 milligrams of liquid Valium, and an injection of his milky white codeine solution.

He almost choked on the last sip, and the glass fell from his hand onto the floor. He was frighteningly gaunt—his ninety pounds barely covering his bone structure. His eyes were blank as he stared at the garish ceiling, with its glitter of mica chips and flecks of fool's gold.

It was a lovely, windy day as clouds pushed in by the trade winds turned the water midnight blue, the waves creating frothy ruffles of white-caps. "Like lace over blue velvet," recalled the aide George Francom.

It would surely have reminded Hughes of the days off Santa Catalina Island when he swam in equally blue waters with Katharine Hepburn and yachted with Billie Dove and, in later years, Ginger Rogers, Ava Gardner, and Yvonne De Carlo.

But the old man had drifted away from the outside world, its amusements, its vanities.

His vast empire was bringing in $75,000 an hour; his kingdom possessed the most luxurious of Las Vegas gambling palaces; satellites he manufactured orbited the earth and beamed television to India and Australia; he had known presidents and world leaders; he had courted and made love to some of the world's most beautiful women. But Howard Hughes's world was now confined to this murky suite. Where it would end.

Hughes had arrived in Acapulco from the Bahamas just before dawn on February 11 accompanied by six aides, two doctors, two orthopedic beds, two electric-powered wheelchairs, and enough medical equipment to fill a suite of the pyramid-shaped Acapulco Princess.

From the twentieth floor of his spacious penthouse apartment, the rich old man could have viewed the lush palm and bougainvillea-dotted lawns of the hotel golf course. But once again sheets of plywood and cardboard were plastered across the windows, which were covered with blackout curtains. Soundproof panels further isolated him, muffling the sounds of life outside his suite.

Gaping bedsores, untended, scoured his back; sheets served as his only clothing. A warped, tilting bedside table was cluttered with the only life-line he had left—codeine, small bowls of Valium tablets, bottles of Librium, and a scatter of hypodermic syringes and needles.

As the opiate sated his blood late that afternoon, as he drifted in and out of a drug induced slumber, Howard Robard Hughes began talking about his life as it once was. As the old man's aides and physicians slipped in and out of the suite, they paused to hear his whispered memories. For them it was a historic day. Howard Hughes had seldom spoken of his private life. Now he talked in bursts of words, as if to unburden himself, as if to ease his guilt.

He spoke of his two marriages and the two women he had so thoughtlessly tossed aside. To his second wife, Jean Peters, he sent a message: "Tell her I loved her to the end . . . that I always loved her." To George Francom, perhaps his favorite aide, he spoke of his mother, Allene, an "angel on earth," and of his father, Howard Robard Hughes, Sr., "one of the most brilliant men who ever lived."

Gulping another dram of Valium, he grasped the arm of his old friend, aviation industrialist Jack Real, and spoke of his days as this century's most prolific Don Juan. "Jack, you have got to help me. When I'm gone the biographers are going to flock around, and I don't want them to dwell on the girls and the movies." The old man added, "I want to be remembered for only one thing—my contribution to aviation."

Several minutes later, with tears in his eyes, he recalled a Christmas in his hometown of Houston when the century was just beginning. His mother had put red candles on the Christmas tree. And a shiny red bicycle was in front of it. "How I loved that Christmas. How I loved her."

Then, as happy as his aides had seen him in years, he fell asleep.

By April 1, the reminiscences ceased, smothered by near-lethal doses of codeine being pumped into his body by the aides and doctors. But at 3:00 A.M. the following morning, he reared up from his comatose state and beckoned Francom to lean forward.

He had one last lament. "George, I suppose I should have been more like other men; I was not nearly as interested in people as I should have been. But I'm not a robot, as some called me. I was merely consumed by my interest in science."

Then he fell back into the hospital bed, which had been his "home" for ten years, lugged from one hotel room to another, from one blacked-out penthouse to another, in what had become his shadow world.

"But what an incredible life you have led," said Francom as he reassuringly gripped Hughes's hand. Hughes shook his head ruefully. "If you had ever swapped places in life with me, I would be willing to bet that you would have demanded to swap back before the passage of the first week."

Then the codeine pulled him in, buying a bit more sleep and contentment for a man who had fought sleep and contentment for seventy years.

At 6:00 A.M. on April 5, Dr. Victor Montemayor entered the Acapulco Princess, pushed his way through a crowd of vacationers waiting to check in, and tugged the sleeve of a liveried clerk.

He held his medical bag aloft. "Quick, can you take me to Howard Hughes's suite? I'm Dr. Montemayor." The clerk held up one finger, and a bellboy ran over.

"Here's the key to the twentieth floor," he said. "They're expecting him."

Dr. Montemayor tried to catch his breath in the express elevator. He wasn't sure whether he was jittery from his run up the beach or from fear of treating one of the most famous and wealthy men in the world.

He had read about Hughes's hotel bill at the Princess—$2,000 per day. Who hadn't? He'd heard about his reclusive ways and his private army of aides. Who hadn't? But not until half an hour earlier had he heard that Howard Hughes was mortally ill.

The aide who called him had said, "Get here as quickly as you can. There isn't much time left."

On the twentieth floor, the elevator opened to reveal a massive, stern guard. "You go," he told the bellboy. "Right this way, Doctor," he said to Montemayor.

The physician was led past more guards, past a cluster of worried-looking men, and finally, to the double doors of the master suite. The guard knocked three times and then opened the door and pointed toward a bed in the far corner. Then the guard backed out, shut the door, and plunged the room into a disturbing darkness.

Two well-dressed men came over to him and shook hands. "We'd like you to take a look at Mr. Hughes," said one of them. "He's been unconscious for a while."

Jack Real introduced himself and, with a look of deep concern, led Montemayor to Howard's bed.

Nothing in his entire medical background prepared Montemayor for what he confronted in that murky room, the most expensive in the most expensive hotel in Acapulco.

Barely clinging to life amid all the splendor was a frail old man of seventy who looked ten years older. He was nude beneath a pastel sheet. Tracks of drug injections straggled across his bone-thin arms. His stomach was swollen from malnutrition; his skin fell down his cheeks in folds, and his body was skeletal.

The physician knelt down by Howard's bed with his stethoscope and barely touched it over his heart. His fingers brushed the skin, which felt like parchment. "How long has this man been unconscious?" Dr. Montemayor asked the men.

"Three days," one of them answered.

"Three days? Three days and you haven't put him on an IV drip? This man is dying."

"We didn't trust Mexican IV solution," said one of the men.

Montemayor winced but calmly continued his examination. "This man is suffering from dehydration, kidney failure, malnutrition, and severe shock," he said. "I ask you again, why haven't you taken him to a hospital?"

The eldest of the aides replied, "Mr. Hughes will not go voluntarily to a hospital even in America . . . he would put up quite a fight."

"Nonsense, he would put up no fight. He is unconscious."

"Look, we'll do anything, anything to save him," said another aide. "What made him this ill?"

"Neglect," said Montemayor. "Total neglect and poor medical treatment. You get this man to a hospital right now!"

On his way out the door, one aide whispered to Dr. Montemayor, "What about the codeine? Could that kill him?"

"What codeine?" asked Montemayor.

"He gets it every day."

"Injections?" asked the doctor.

The aide nodded his head. "And pills sometimes."

Jack Real walked over to thank the physician. "Look," he said. "I just flew down here, but I want you to know we'll have him on a plane as soon as possible."

Montemayor was both agitated and concerned that this neglect might add up to manslaughter under Mexican law. To this day he wonders at what he witnessed: "The richest man in America—ill, starving, and neglected as if he were a derelict on the streets."

Jack Real felt the same way. Two days earlier, he had telephoned Dr. Wilbur Thain, Hughes's chief physician, and told him to rush down from Logan, Utah, "before it's too late." Explained Real, "I don't want to play doctor, Wilbur, but your patient is dying."

"Well, goddamn, you are playing doctor. Why don't you mind your own business?"

"Wilbur, you need to be here," Real pressed.

"I've got a party in the Bahamas, and I'll come over after that," Thain said with what Real later described as a cavalier attitude.

Once Dr. Thain finally arrived in Acapulco with his chartered jet, there were even more delays. Roger Sutton, who piloted the jet, says they landed about 6:00 A.M. and were told to wait for the imminent arrival of "the ill Mr. Hughes and his retinue."

Hughes was already in a coma before Thain arrived, and accounts vary as to what happened next. But according to Jack Real, Thain didn't immediately tend to Hughes. He wrote a new prescription, which was quickly filled. Then, said Real, Thain injected Hughes several times with the medicine. (Thain would later be acquitted on charges that he improperly dispensed medicine to Hughes.) Afterward, aides scurried off to check on the airplane and its medical equipment.

Flanked by the hotel's security guards, Hughes was taken down the service elevator in a stretcher covered with a yellow sheet. An IV dangled from his arm; a plastic oxygen mask covered his face. The cadaverous figure was then loaded into an ambulance that screamed off toward the airport. Hughes, Dr. Thain, Dr. Lawrence Chaffin (who had cared for Hughes following the 1946 crash), and aide John Holmes climbed aboard with Hughes.

The chartered plane left Acapulco for Houston shortly after 11:00 A.M. The city's Methodist Hospital was on the alert that a mysterious emergency case—involving one "J. T. Conover"—was en route.

But at 1:27 P.M. Dr. Thain reported that he no longer heard a heartbeat. Dr. Chaffin remembered that the plane had just passed over the Gulf of Mexico into Texas. They were just twenty minutes outside of Hughes's hometown.

Thain advised Sutton not to hurry. "He's gone."

Yet there are contradictory reports about precisely when Hughes died. Despite the widespread and legally accepted opinion that Howard died in the air over Texas, the Mexican attorney general's office noted, "Hughes died no later than 10:00 A.M. and probably earlier."

"He died in Acapulco. No doubt about it," said Dr. John Chappel, a psychiatrist who probed all the death reports. A source in Houston who saw Howard's body confirmed the reports by the Mexican attorney general and Dr. Chappel.

"He looked very close to death, if not dead, to me," pilot Roger Sutton recounted.

When the plane landed in Houston and Hughes was being taken off, his arm fell on Sutton, who remembered, "It felt extremely cold."

In a Mexico City press conference shortly after Hughes was taken home to Houston, Dr. Montemayor concluded: "Howard Hughes died of an illness called neglect."

Rick Harrison, the deputy Texas attorney general who handled the case, concluded: "I definitely think that he was mistreated and allowed to die. There was not a reason in the world for the man to have died when he did. He was terribly neglected that last six weeks of his life in Mexico."

His arrival in Houston was no different than his arrivals had been over the last two decades: no one was sure it was really Howard Hughes.

Despite objections from the family, fingerprints were taken and turned over to the FBI. A U.S. Customs agent asked for identification of the body. (Dr. Thain provided a photostat of Hughes's birth certificate.) Then

Hughes's body was taken by ambulance to the morgue at Methodist Hospital for a two-hour "private autopsy," which was an option Texas families had in those days.

The autopsy showed that the man who had once weighed 150 pounds and stood six-foot-three had shrunk two inches in height and withered to a mere 93 pounds. But only parts of the autopsy were released. The conclusion was that he died of chronic renal disease—kidney failure. Other, more incendiary revelations about Hughes's physical condition would not be made public until much later.

But the coroner, Dr. Joseph Jachimczyk, said he was surprised at "the extent to which the brain cells had degenerated." The tertiary syphilis and Howard's fourteen crashes, both auto and airplane, had left physiological testimony.

A sleek black Cadillac hearse rushed Howard Robard Hughes to the Geo. H. Lewis & Sons Funeral Home. His shriveled body was immediately taken to the embalming room. It required just three sixteen-ounce bottles of embalming fluid.

Hughes's cousin, William Rice Lummis, the son of his Aunt Annette—who had been a boy during his only meeting with Howard—chose the casket. Another family member brought a blue suit for Howard to wear.

The switchboard at the funeral home was deluged with calls. "Mostly from the press and curiosity seekers," explained funeral director Norman Lewis. In fact, except for Jean Peters, no one who had known Hughes bothered to call and inquire about services.

Though a policeman was hired by the family to sit outside the door of the private stateroom where Hughes's body lay, it was not necessary. No one came to visit.

Howard Hughes was buried on April 7 in the family plot at historic Glenwood Cemetery, sixty-five acres dotted with moss-draped oaks in the shadow of downtown Houston.

Surviving family members, headed by Annette Lummis and her son, Will, sought to keep the affair private. But the press was camped outside the funeral home and formed a caravan behind the hearse that carried Hughes's body to its final resting place.

There was only a scattering of persons present at the graveside service, most of them cousins who had had little or no contact with Howard. Cemetery superintendent Otis Jeffocat would later surmise, "I just figured that there were a whole lot more friends he had who just couldn't make it that day."

During his ten-minute memorial, the Reverend Robert T. Gibson, dean of Christ Church Cathedral, read from Chapter 14 of the Book of John, "We brought nothing into this world and it is certain we can carry nothing out." When the thousand-pound, seamless silver-and-copper coffin was lowered into the grave, photographers and TV camera crews moved forward, their cameras whirring and snapping.

Gravediggers took just twenty minutes to cover the coffin. Then came the flowers, including red roses from an anonymous sender and a five-foot-high airplane-shaped arrangement made of five hundred white pompons. Sent by a Southern California fitness club, it was adorned with a red-white-and-blue ribbon that read HE CAME, HE SAW, HE CONQUERED.

Fresh flowers continued to adorn Howard's final resting place for weeks afterward.

Jean Peters sent them.

LEGACY

EVEN BEFORE HOWARD WAS BURIED, SPECULATION WAS RAMPANT THAT HE had died without leaving a will. An army of attorneys and the remaining aides turned the vast empire upside down in frantic searches that sent detectives scurrying from coast to coast. When no valid bequest turned up, the estate even hired psychic Peter Hurkos, who combed the spirit world while caressing one of Howard's shirts and a pair of shoes found in the basement of 7000 Romaine.

"Nothing. I find nothing," said Hurkos. "Mr. Hughes never wore these clothes."

The medium was correct: the clothing samples had come from a closet of untouched clothing found in a vault. Hurkos reluctantly bowed out when the estate couldn't produce a garment actually worn by Hughes. (Howard's box of pajamas had been burned in Acapulco.)

A federal judge in Houston declared that the billionaire, the second-richest man in America (after J. Paul Getty), had died intestate without a legal will. More than ninety lawyers accepted this as the signal for the longest, costliest estate battle in American history. The case would spread to courtrooms in four states: Texas, Nevada, California, and Delaware. The race was on to determine the rightful heirs and Howard's legal domicile—the place he called home.

Both questions were clouded.

Houston genealogist Mary Smith Fay, a paid consultant to the estate, worked from 1977 to 1981, hacking through the tangled family tree. She eventually "certified" twenty-two heirs, mostly maternal and paternal first cousins—all of whom closed ranks behind Will Lummis and his mother, Annette Gano Lummis. These united heirs sued for legitimacy in all four states.

While the legion of lawyers searched for a proper bequest, a hastily scribbled "last will and testament of Howard Robard Hughes" was discovered under mysterious circumstances at the Salt Lake City headquarters of the Mormon church.

Handwritten on three sheets from a yellow legal tablet (Hughes trademarks), and comprising 261 words, riddled with misspellings (not a Hughes trademark), the bizarre document bequeathed substantial amounts to the Hughes Medical Institute, Ella Rice Hughes (now Mrs. James Winston), and Jean Peters (now Mrs. Stan Hough). And one-sixteenth of the estate— a multimillion-dollar share—was left to Melvin Dummar, a Utah gas station operator.

Dummar soon went public, telling a wild yet strangely believable tale of his brush with the phantom billionaire. He claimed to have picked Howard up on a deserted Nevada roadside in 1968 and to have driven him to Las Vegas, where the industrialist borrowed a quarter and was dropped off behind the Sands Hotel, which Hughes owned.

Although the so-called "Mormon will" was soon unmasked as fraudulent, the story became what author James Phelan described as "another fabled folk tale of Hughesiana."

Charges were never filed against the conspirators behind the Mormon will. And Melvin Dummar's story became a part of Americana. As befits folk-hero status, his story was enshrined by Hollywood in the 1980 film *Melvin and Howard*, starring Jason Robards as Hughes. Dummar even played a cameo role.

To this day there are those who believe Dummar's naive tale. The real story was much more insidious. Those who were closest to Hughes—including Jean Peters—insist that he left a will. But no legal document was ever found.

Suzanne Finstad, who spent six years sorting out the authentic Hughes relatives as a clerk in a Houston law firm, chronicled the resulting feeding frenzy in her book, *Heir Not Apparent*. She believes that there was a will, "and that it was ultimately suppressed or destroyed or conveniently lost."

She added, "This man was too preoccupied with will making and too concerned with where his fortune was going. I mean, he started writing them when he was a teenager.

"Money is a great corrupter, and obscurer of the truth."

Money also led to the fight for the estate and, as a result, the truth, at last, about the way Hughes lived and died.

Then came autopsy results, which Will Lummis and his mother sought to suppress. They revealed chronic renal disease along with signs of tertiary syphilis. And x-rays showed broken-off hypodermic syringes in Hughes's shriveled, needle-tracked arms.

At first forensic scientists couldn't find a cause of death. They echoed statements by Mexico's Dr. Victor Montemayor that "this man should not have died." "Hughes was literally starving to death," says Houston pathologist Dr. Jack Titus, who searched frantically through the toxicological and morbidity reports on the billionaire, seeking a clear-cut answer. But malnutrition was obvious. When Will Lummis was called in to identify the body, he blanched. "This is Howard Hughes?"

The man on the steel table was such a gaunt apparition that his elbows and knee caps had torn through their wispy flesh coverings. Teeth were hanging from his gums; a raw and ugly cavity split his forehead where a tumor had earlier festered; there were bed sores on his back and needle tracks on his arms and thighs.

Privately, all three physicians involved in the autopsy told journalists that Howard Hughes needn't have died since his heart, lungs, liver, and even kidneys were not severely wounded by either disease or neglect.

Nevertheless, Dr. Titus listed "kidney failure" as the "supposed" cause of death.

Upon learning of the diagnosis, Mexico's Dr. Montemayor, the last physician to treat Hughes, uttered, "Nonsense." Said Montemayor, "His kidneys were weak, they were causing him trouble, but they did not kill him. I could have saved him if he'd just been taken to an Acapulco hospital in time."

Actually, Hughes died as a result of a massive injection of codeine "administered six to eight hours before his heart stopped beating." One-point-four micrograms of codeine is deadly; Hughes's bloodstream had "something higher than 1.9 micrograms" of the painkiller. But this wasn't apparent at first. To begin with, the Hughes aides had deliberately misled investigators about the level of the boss's addiction. Then the toxicological report at Houston's Methodist Hospital "mis-stated" the initial codeine reading. Four years later, Dr. Titus testified in court that "the codeine in his bloodstream was one thousand times greater than I originally thought . . . a massive difference."

Despite all written evidence to the contrary, Howard was killed by this single lethal injection of codeine. Since Howard had been unconscious for twenty-six hours, the codeine could have had no therapeutic value. According to UCLA toxicological expert Dr. Forest Tennant, who completed an eighteen-month study of Hughes's drug abuse for the estate, "Someone administered a deadly injection of the painkiller to this comatose man . . . obviously needlessly and almost certainly fatal." Tennant and Titus estimate the strength of the final dosage at from forty-five to fifty grains of pure codeine.

Dr. John Chappel, who prepared a "psychological autopsy" of Hughes for the state of Nevada, noted, "The level of codeine in Mr. Hughes's body exceeded that in any of the other codeine fatalities in the standard scientific work on codeine poisoning. He had the highest clinical level ever recorded."

The implication was that someone, perhaps an aide or one of the physicians, killed Hughes—accidentally or deliberately. Texas attorney general Rick Harrison later authored a book proposal entitled *Some Dare Call It Murder.* Chief deputy Burt Pluyman concurred, telling federal investigators that, at the very least, the aides should have been charged with manslaughter.

Looking back over two decades of study devoted to Hughes's final years, it seems possible that the billionaire's aides administered the final jolt of codeine to silence the single witness to their abuse and negligence. When they realized they would finally have to take their emaciated charge to a hospital, their only recourse was to render him mute.

"It was apparent to me that the people around him were waiting for him to die," says Dr. Montemayor. "It's true, he was in critical condition, but he had a good, strong heart and clear lungs. If I were one of his aides or physicians at the end, I would have hired a lawyer."

The Mexican government agreed. Shortly after the death plane headed toward the wilds of Texas, a high-level meeting occurred in Acapulco, chaired by Mexico's first assistant attorney general, Dr. Alexander Gertz Manero, who was connected via long-distance to the Mexican Ministry of Justice. A temporary bill of indictment was drawn up, charging a series of "John Does" with "kidnapping and murder."

But action by the Hughes estate, the state of Texas and the United States government intervened.

Complaints by Will Lummis and the state of Texas pulled the Drug Enforcement Agency into the fray. In March 1978 a Las Vegas federal grand jury returned an indictment against Dr. Norman Crane and chief aide John Holmes. They were charged with illegally supplying drugs to Hughes for twenty years. They pleaded "no contest" and were given probation. They also testified against Dr. Wilbur Thain, brother-in-law of Bill Gay and the chief drug supplier for the last two years of Hughes's life. The Mormon physician was tried and acquitted in Utah. Thain also wound up a defendant in a $50 million suit brought by the Summa Corporation, which charged a conspiracy by Bill Gay, Chester Davis, Nadine Henley, Kay Glenn, and the aides and doctors who were hired to care for Hughes. An out-of-court settlement was eventually reached.

According to Food and Drug Administration guidelines, the maximum codeine dose allowed is 471 milligrams per day. During the final five years of his life, Hughes often ingested 1,171 milligrams daily, plus seven Valium, three Librium capsules, and occasionally Seconal. During one four-year period Dr. Thain wrote 5,500 prescriptions, and Hughes's consulting physician, Dr. Norman Crane, wrote 1,006 for codeine and Valium. Most of these drug orders were placed in the names of the aides.

When Will Lummis and the united heirs sued the aides, their complaint charged that the high levels of drugs were given to persuade Hughes to sign orders, checks, and proxies—proxies that allowed the aides, under Bill Gay, to control the Hughes empire with no interference from "the Old Man."

During the five years following Howard's death his principal aides-de-camp, his principal attorney, Chester Davis, and his beloved secretary (since 1943) Nadine Henley, depicted themselves as "unwilling participants" in the network that supplied the tycoon with an uninterrupted flow of drugs. Henley even told documentary filmmaker Jamie Russell that she "had absolutely no idea" of the extent of her boss's drug addiction. She also told her friend Jane Russell that William Gay and the aides kept her away from Hughes.

In this story, the true villains are hard to identify. But there is no dearth of bad judgment.

Jane is convinced that Henley knew nothing of "the drug war." Moreover, she attributed Henley's eventual health problems, a stroke and incapacitation, to the fact that she was included in the legal action brought about by the estate. But other accounts place Henley at the scene of the manipulative final years.

The top aides kept Hughes drugged and pliable through a calculated master plan orchestrated during a "narcotics summit conference" held at the Romaine headquarters a year before Hughes died. Dr. Norman Crane, who had supplied Hughes's codeine for years, refused to write any more "unnecessary prescriptions."

With the help of Dr. Wilbur Thain, the aides arranged to have massive supplies of opiates and Valium delivered to Hughes's hotel rooms every eight weeks. Dr. Thain ordered the drugs directly from pharmaceutical houses in New York and then ferried them to Hughes in large satchels. For instance, six weeks before the billionaire died, the aides accepted delivery of ninety-five hundred doses of injectable codeine, one thousand ten-milligram Valium tablets, and five hundred Seconal tablets.

"The Mormons were determined to keep their boss bedridden and completely befuddled," said *Wall Street Journal* reporter Michael Drosnin, who described Hughes as "a prisoner in solitary confinement."

Estate consultants Dr. Frederick Meyers and Dr. Forest Tennant claimed in a deposition that "Dr. Thain gained a $300,000 medical services contract by infusing Hughes's system with a plethora of codeine and Valium."

Lummis charged in his suit that his uncle "was forced" to approve employment contracts for members of the palace guard (where the salaries had risen to $100,000 per year) because the doctors threatened to cut off Howard's codeine.

While Howard floated about in his private opium den, the aides gave themselves a $10 million package of wage hikes, bonuses, and perks, including such items as vacation homes in Florida, a fleet of private jets, chauffeured limousines, and a swank new headquarters in a sleek new sky-scraper in the San Fernando Valley.

Further, Lummis charged that this bizarre "feast and famine" administration of drugs allowed Gay, the longtime Romaine Street aide, to gain control and push Robert Maheu out as Hughes's lieutenant.

"Davis and Gay controlled Hughes in the name of an incompetent and drug-addicted old man," the suit continued.

An extensive study by the Drug Enforcement Administration came to the same conclusion.

Between 1966 and 1976 the Hughes hierarchy pillaged the vast empire, often without Howard's approval. In the late sixties, the Romaine Street headquarters instituted a system of "verbal approval." Instead of obtaining the boss's signature, the aides were ordered to seek "verbal approval" for major expenditures and enormous "purchase orders" involving millions of dollars. The aides would describe the transactions to Howard and ostensibly gain his approval. They, not Hughes, signed the orders.

Will Lummis later charged that many of these transactions were never even presented to the billionaire.

But cash spewed from all branches of the empire.

From 1970 until Hughes's death, the triumvirate ruling the Summa Corporation spent $367,579 per day on dubious acquisitions, unwise investments, and wasteful operating costs. During those same years, Summa lost more than $100 million at the rate of $137,000 per day. At the same time, a billion dollars in cash, government securities, and savings certificates disappeared from Hughes's bank accounts.

Five days before Hughes died, and following euphoric doses of codeine and Valium, the aides drew up two more proxies to sign. The first would have allowed them total access to Howard's safety deposit boxes, one of which contained a collection of diamonds. The second would have allowed additional aides to sign checks on Howard's personal checking account.

Lummis's complaint also stated that Gay was moving to quash a palace coup then under way, involving Jack Real. According to several of his aides, Howard informed them he was thinking of dividing up the Summa Corporation into western and eastern divisions. Real would have headed the eastern territory, thereby cutting Gay's empire in half.

George Francom, the aide who personally tended to Howard's food and other needs, recalls, "We were all jumpy because some sort of palace coup was under way, regarding the company . . . all kinds of last-minute power plays. Things got so bad that even the doctors were afraid."

Although both the DEA and the estate refrained from calling Hughes's death a "murder," Walter Kane, who worked with Hughes for thirty-two years, wasn't shy about it. In a Las Vegas press conference, Kane, entertainment director for the Frontier, the Sands, and the Desert Inn, angrily told journalists, "Howard Hughes was murdered and the people around him had been planning it for years."

The longtime Hughes associate also charged that the Mormons had tried to enlist his help in supplying Hughes with drugs. "They wanted me to make a connection and deliver drugs to him in Mexico, but I told them, 'I'm not getting involved in narcotics.' "

The Howard Hughes estate was finally settled after fourteen years. Initially, twenty-two Hughes heirs were designated. But by 1990 more than one hundred people shared the remainder of the Hughes estate. Though Jean Peters said that Hughes always intended his monies to go to the medical institute—a claim backed up by aides and other associates—the Howard Hughes Medical Institute did not benefit from the will.

Texas was deemed Hughes's legal domicile and received $50 million of the estate in taxes. Lawyers also made out nicely; more than $10 million has been paid in attorneys' fees.

In death, Howard Hughes, one of this century's true Renaissance men, was at first reduced to nothing more than a series of entries in a thousand financial ledgers, his legacy obscured by dollar signs. Washington, D.C., columnist Jack Anderson lamented, "The man I knew and admired has disappeared behind a cloud bank of greed."

His reputation was also marred by a flurry of adjectives—especially *eccentric*, and *crazy*. But one thing is certain: there was never anyone quite like him. His legacy is in the skies and in Las Vegas and on the screen. To Hughes, the skies were there to conquer; the desert was a frontier, not a wasteland; and movie censorship codes were something to fight, not fear.

He also left behind a stunning medical bequest. Though it was initially created as a shrewd tax dodge, the Howard Hughes Medical Institute, which was endowed with funds from the sale of Hughes Aircraft in 1985, is today the country's largest private sponsor of biomedical research. (At present there are 280 scientists and their staffs working for HHMI, which spent $366 million on research for fiscal year 1995.) This is especially fitting, since Hughes, at 25, drafted a will that designated the bulk of his fortune for medical research. It is also ironic, given Hughes's own slide into mental and physical deterioration.

Above all, Howard Hughes was a paradox.

HOWARD HUGHES: AVIATION HIGHLIGHTS

1920   At age fourteen, takes his first flight in a Curtiss flying boat.

OCTOBER 1927   Begins filming World War I flying epic, *Hell's Angels*; spends $500,000 for more than forty vintage fighter and scouting aircraft, world's largest private air force.

JANUARY 7, 1928   Receives pilot's license.

JANUARY 30, 1930   *Hell's Angels* premieres in Hollywood; aviation sequences remain unequaled.

SPRING 1932   Founds Hughes Aircraft Company in Glendale, California.

SEPTEMBER 1932   Under the pseudonym "Charles Howard" gets a job as a baggage handler for American Airlines; advances to co-pilot within weeks.

JANUARY 14, 1934   Wins first-place air trophy in Miami in a modified Boeing.

1934   Develops and tests the first retractable landing gear and flushed rivets to streamline airplane designs of the future.

SEPTEMBER 13, 1935   Sets new land speed record of 352.46 m.p.h. at Santa Ana, California, in the *Silver Bullet*, the world's fastest plane, built by Hughes Aircraft. (Made a forced landing in a beet field, during final run, at 100 m.p.h.)

1935   Proves, in a series of death-defying flights over the Sierra Nevadas, that high-altitude flying greatly increases air speed, opening a new frontier for commercial aviation.

JANUARY 14, 1936   Sets new transcontinental speed record from Los Angeles to Newark of nine hours, twenty-seven minutes. "All I did was sit there. The engine did the work," he explains.

1936   Designs and perfects an oxygen feeder system that enhances pilot safety during high altitude flights.

JANUARY 19, 1937   Makes the world's greatest long-distance speed flight, setting a new transcontinental record from Los Angeles to Newark, New Jersey, of seven hours, twenty-eight minutes.

MARCH 3, 1937   Receives the prestigious Harmon International Trophy—as world's outstanding aviator for 1936—in ceremony at the White House. President Franklin D. Roosevelt presents the trophy, given by the *Ligue Internationale des Aviateurs*. Hughes is only the third American to receive the honor, following Charles Lindbergh and Wiley Post.

JULY 10–14, 1938   Flies around the world in three days, nineteen hours, and seventeen minutes. With his four crewmen, in a Lockheed Model 14 twin-engine transport, Hughes establishes a new record and returns home a ticker-tape hero.

1939   Perfects power-booster radio receivers and transmitters in contemporary aircraft.

1941–1943   Designs revolutionary ammunition feed chutes for fifty-caliber machine guns, doubling the rate of fire.

JULY 7, 1946   Survives fiery near-fatal Beverly Hills crash of the XF-11, which is designed for photo reconnaissance. He later redesigns propeller configuration for next prototype.

1946–1949   As principal shareholder of TWA he designs the first cost-effective routes to Europe and the South Pacific.

APRIL 5, 1947   Climbs back into the XF-11 for a successful test flight.

NOVEMBER 2, 1947   Proves his critics wrong with surprise test flight of the Hercules, aka the HK-1, popularly known as the Spruce Goose. The Long Beach, California, flight lasts less than sixty seconds, but it reinvents Hughes as an aviation hero and remains one of the most famous flights ever.

1940s   Builds Hughes Electronics into the single largest supplier of weapons systems to the United States Air Force and Navy.

1941–1956   Builds Hughes Aircraft from a four-man operation into an eighty-thousand-employee powerhouse that includes Hughes Electronics and Hughes Helicopters. (Company develops thirty-three hundred Ph.D.s)

1949   Develops the "all-weather Interceptor," an electronic weapons control system with a combined radar set and computer, capable of finding and destroying enemy planes day and night and in any sort of weather.

1950–1956   Conceives and manufactures the "air-to-air missile," which seeks out its target and then locks in through a fail-proof system of radio impulses. Deadly and quick this guided missile was considered to be the most important contribution to the defense of North America since radar.

1950–1956   Invents, then mass produces, the navigational control system for the F-102 interceptor—the backbone of American Air Defense Strategy in the fifties and sixties.

1959–1964   Revolutionizes the nation's wartime helicopter capability through $440 million in government contracts. Builds the TH55A helicopter—the forerunner of maneuverable choppers for battle conditions.

1960s   Pioneers and produces the unmanned satellite prototypes, virtually clearing the way for the onset of today's satellite era.

DECEMBER 14, 1973   Inducted into the Aviation Hall of Fame in Dayton, Ohio. Officials there hoped that the elusive Hughes would show up to accept the honor, but he instead sent Ed Lund, the only other surviving member of the 1938 around-the-world flight.

FILMOGRAPHY

As a producer, unless otherwise indicated:

Swell Hogan (1926)—Directed by and starring Ralph Graves, an old friend of Howard Hughes Sr. About a Bowery Bum, it was so bad it was never released.

Everybody's Acting (1926)—Written and directed by silent era stalwart Marshall Neilan, this lightweight comedy about five actors who adopt a baby girl was a surprise hit—helping to pave Hughes's way in Hollywood.

Two Arabian Knights (1927)—Two World War I doughboys break out of a German prison camp and wind up in an Arabian harem. Director Lewis Milestone received an Academy Award as best director of a comedy.

The Racket (1928)—Underworld drama directed by Lewis Milestone, it was a critically acclaimed forerunner to *Scarface*. Remade by Hughes at RKO in the fifties.

The Mating Call (1928)—Based on a popular novel of the day, about a marriage of convenience that leads to love.

Hell's Angels (1930)—Hughes was just twenty-five when he directed this saga of two brothers in the Royal Air Force (James Hall and Ben Lyon) who face uncertainty in the skies and vie for the same woman—Jean Harlow, a Hughes discovery. She became a star with the line "Would you be terribly shocked if I slipped into something more comfortable?" The aerial sequences remain unsurpassed.

The Age for Love (1931)—A "modern picture based on the day's most common problem—should the young wife work?" A vehicle for beautiful Billie Dove, the former Ziegfeld showgirl turned silent-movie queen, who became Hughes's paramour and contract player.

Cock of the Air (1931)—Billie Dove plays a French temptress in love with a handsome American aviator.

The Front Page (1931)—Pat O'Brien became a star, opposite Adolphe Menjou, in this saga of Chicago newspapermen, faithfully adapted from the hit play by Ben Hecht and Charles MacArthur.

Sky Devils (1931)—Leftover *Hell's Angels* footage went into this slapstick service comedy starring a young Spencer Tracy.

Scarface (1932)—Paul Muni shot his way to fame as a vicious, manic gangster who, per *Variety*, is so tough he could "make Capone his errand boy." George Raft likewise found stardom. Directed by Howard Hawks, written by Ben Hecht, loosely based on the saga of Al Capone. Hughes battled censors for two years to get the picture released. It remains one of the era's great films.

The Outlaw (1943)—The notorious Western starring Hughes's most famous discovery, Jane Russell, and Jack Beutel as Billy the Kid. When Howard Hawks tired of his interference, Hughes took over as director. With its emphasis on cleavage and sexuality, the movie riled the censors for a decade. (For one scene, Hughes redesigned Russell's brassiere.)

The Sin of Harold Diddlebock (1947)—Silent comedian Harold Lloyd came out of retirement to reprise his madcap character. Written and directed by Preston Sturges, with whom Hughes was briefly teamed in a production company. Reissued during Hughes's RKO epoch as *Mad Wednesday*.

Hughes acquired control of RKO Pictures in May 1948. During his reign he became the only man to solely own a film studio, which he finally sold in July 1955. Among the RKO titles that bear Hughes's signature are the following:

The Big Steal (1949)—Crime caper with Robert Mitchum (just after his marijuana bust), Hughes's favorite actor and good friend, and Jane Greer, on whom Hughes was fixated.

Holiday Affair (1949)—Romantic comedy with Janet Leigh, another Hughes obsession, and Robert Mitchum.

Outrage (1950)—Ida Lupino (a teenager when she dated Hughes in the thirties) became a pioneering female director with this then-daring drama of a young rape victim (Hughes contract player Mala Powers) trying to start life anew.

Stromboli (1950)—Never one to miss an opportunity to capitalize on scandal, Hughes had RKO launch a major publicity campaign for this Italian-made Ingrid Bergman movie—her first after she fled the States when it was discovered she was pregnant with the child of director Roberto Rossellini. Ad copy featured a volcano on the island of Stromboli spurting lava, with lines such as "Raging Island . . . Raging Passions!"

Vendetta (1950)—Long in production (shooting began August 1946), this film traversed three different directors and cost more than $3 million. Produced by Hughes, this period saga stars his girlfriend Faith Domergue and contract actor George Dolenz (whose career stalled under Hughes), in a story of Corsican honor and revenge. Produced by Hughes.

Where Danger Lives (1950)—Hughes's lover Faith Domergue as a psychopath who dupes Robert Mitchum.

Best of the Badmen (1951)—After ten years under contract, Jack Beutel (*The Outlaw*) gets a second film. (A year later, he starred in RKO's *The Half-Breed*.)

Double Dynamite (1951)—The title refers to Jane Russell's endowments. Implausible comedy about bank clerks Russell and Frank Sinatra, who get romantic tips from . . . Groucho Marx.

Flying Leathernecks (1951)—The first of three RKO-Hughes titles starring friend and fellow patriot John Wayne, about the war in the South Pacific. Bears the credit "Howard Hughes Presents."

Gambling House (1951)—Hughes ordered the filmmakers to cast "the beautifully stacked" Terry Moore, his girlfriend, as a social worker who reforms tough guy Victor Mature.

Hard, Fast and Beautiful (1951)—Ida Lupino directs Sally Forrest, who plays a young tennis champion. "When Howard heard I didn't know how to play tennis, he wanted me to take lessons at his house—at night," recalls Forrest. She turned him down—and eventually bailed out of her contract with Hughes.

His Kind of Woman (1951)—"Howard Hughes Presents" Jane Russell and Robert Mitchum in a romantic adventure set at a Mexican resort.

My Forbidden Past (1951)—Ava Gardner, with whom Hughes had a lengthy relationship, opposite Robert Mitchum, in a period drama set in nineteenth-century New Orleans.

Roadblock (1951)—Joan Dixon, a former beauty queen discovered by Hughes, as a femme fatale.

Two Tickets to Broadway (1951)—Musical starring Janet Leigh and Tony Martin; it was in production so long that Martin worried that his fans would forget who he was.

The Whip Hand (1951)—When Hughes began fighting Hollywood communists he re-edited this drama: a plot about Hitler and Nazi criminals was turned into a story of communists and germ warfare. Stars Carla Balenda (real name Sally Bliss), a Hughes contract player, who recalls, "It was such a good little picture, until Howard got involved."

The Las Vegas Story (1952)—More of Jane Russell, this time teamed with Victor Mature.

Macao (1952)—Jane Russell, reunited with Robert Mitchum. Film triggered Hughes's famed four-page memo regarding Russell's breasts and the design of her brassiere.

One Minute to Zero (1952)—The U.S. Army co-operated with the making of this movie but retaliated during its release due to a scene in which

Robert Mitchum, as a colonel, orders artillery fire on South Korean refugees because he believes North Koreans are among them. With Ann Blyth as a United Nations worker who falls for Mitchum.

Androcles and the Lion (1952)—Jean Simmons, who "awoke one morning to find I had been bought by Howard Hughes" (who bought her contract from Britain's Rank Organization), made her American film debut in this sand and toga tale, playing a Christian opposite Roman soldier Victor Mature. To spice up the story, Hughes had a "Vestal Virgins" sequence added, after production had wrapped. But the scene was ultimately scrapped.

Angel Face (1953)—Psychological drama, starring Jean Simmons. To spite Hughes, Simmons took scissors to her hair during preproduction, thus her very chic short haircut. Co-starring Robert Mitchum; directed by Otto Preminger, one of Hollywood's most fearsome directors.

The French Line (1954)—Shipboard silliness with Jane Russell—in 3-D— as a Texas oil gal who wears lots of barely-there costumes. Censors were not amused.

Susan Slept Here (1954)—Comedy with Dick Powell as a middle-aged screenwriter who falls in love with runaway teenager Debbie Reynolds. Hughes so admired Reynolds that he later insisted she be hired to perform at his Las Vegas hotels.

Son of Sinbad (1955)—*Arabian Nights* tale starring a bemused-looking Dale Robertson and Vincent Price, and forty gorgeous, well-endowed women as the forty thieves. To promote this movie, the Sinbadettes toured the country.

Underwater (1955)—Another Jane Russell entry, this time involving sunken treasure. More exciting than the movie was the press premiere, actually held underwater.

The Conqueror (1956)—A miscast John Wayne as Genghis Khan, and former Hughes lover Susan Hayward as the Tartar beauty he wants. ("This Tartar woman is for me and my blood says take her!") "A Howard Hughes Presentation" that had the critics howling. Hughes liked it so much he bought the movie outright.

Jet Pilot (1957)—Hughes's biggest RKO failure, it was in production so long that by the time of its release, the aviation sequences looked dated—and Hughes was no longer at the controls of RKO. With John Wayne as the all-American airman in love with Soviet pilot Janet Leigh. "A Howard Hughes Presentation."

THE WOMEN IN HUGHES'S LIFE

(A PARTIAL LIST OF FRIENDS/LOVERS/DISCOVERIES)

PHYLLIS APPLEGATE Singer, dancer, Hughes starlet—and Hughes lover. When he at last married, she told him, "Be happy." A resident of Los Angeles, she works for an ophthalmologist.

CARLA BALENDA Real name Sally Bliss, she was a Hughes discovery who virtually grew up under his thumb, starring in films for RKO and later appearing on TV.

PHYLLIS BROOKS Lovely brunette actress of the thirties who dated Howard but preferred his friend Cary Grant, to whom she became engaged.

NANCY CARROLL Scarlet-haired star of early talkies, she was left waiting in Howard's bed.

CYD CHARISSE Premier dancer of MGM musicals who was courted avidly by Hughes but eventually chose singer Tony Martin over the billionaire.

SALLILEE CONLON Virginal Indiana co-ed who chanced to be on the cover of *Life* magazine; a week later, she was in Las Vegas with Hughes. Went on to work behind the scenes in TV news.

JOAN CRAWFORD Though she was married, Hughes still pursued her, promising her a "big" gift in return for a date. The former flapper (who came to Hollywood after winning a Charleston contest) was famed for portraying strong, aggressive roles (like her Oscar-winning *Mildred Pierce* of 1945) and for her parenting skills, or lack thereof, according to her author-daughter Christina in the biographical *Mommie Dearest* (1978).

LINDA DARNELL Naive, darkly sensual star of *Forever Amber* and *The Mark of Zorro*. She left her cameraman husband Peverell J. Marley and was ready to drop her career to order to marry Hughes. Then, he unceremoniously dropped her.

BETTE DAVIS Fiery Warner Brothers actress and two-time Oscar winner, she shared a summer of Malibu idylls with Hughes—until her husband, and a private eye, caught them together. It was not until her latter years that she admitted the depth of her affair with Hughes.

YVONNE DE CARLO Perpetually cast as a saloon girl, the former dancer—who shimmied to fame in *Salome, Where She Danced*—trysted with Howard for two years in the mid-forties. Known to TV viewers for her role as Lily Munster in *The Munsters*.

OLIVIA DE HAVILLAND Warner Brothers actress who dated Hughes—until she learned he had no plans for marriage. She matured into a two-time Oscar-winning dramatic star (1946's *To Each His Own* and 1949's *The Heiress*) but will be forever known as Melanie in *Gone With the Wind* (1939). Counted herself lucky to have spurned Hughes's attention.

FAITH DOMERGUE Raven-haired, with haunting eyes, she was just a teenager when she caught Hughes's eye. He romanced her until she was twenty. Under Hughes she starred in the overwrought *Vendetta* (1950). After Hughes she starred in low-budget titles, including the science-fiction favorite *This Island Earth* (1955).

BILLIE DOVE "The most beautiful girl" in the history of the Ziegfeld Follies. Engaged to Hughes, with whom she had a lengthy relationship, she later married rancher-developer Robert Keniston and became a philanthropist and artist.

JOAN FONTAINE Olivia's younger sister, she was pursued by Hughes while he courted de Havilland. An Oscar winner for *Suspicion* (1941).

BRENDA FRAZIER The "Debutante of the Century," she was romanced by Hughes in Palm Beach and Manhattan.

GAIL GANLEY The last starlet under contract to Hughes, who allowed her promising career to languish. Her ensuing lawsuit blew the lid off Hughes's bizarre lifestyle. After appearing in small roles in a spate of films she became an in-demand sound-effects artist.

AVA GARDNER Smoky-voiced and blatantly sexy onscreen and off, she was lured into a lusty relationship with Hughes when she was on the rebound from husband Mickey Rooney. (She was also married to band leader Artie Shaw and Frank Sinatra.) Her friend-lover union with Howard lasted twenty years. In her 1954 film *The Barefoot Contessa*, Humphrey Bogart played a Hughes-inspired character.

KATHRYN GRAYSON MGM's reigning soprano and one of the studio's most beautiful, buxom stars (in titles including 1951's *Show Boat* and 1953's *Kiss Me Kate*), she was allied with Howard for eight years; she almost married him three times. Still active onstage, she remembers Hughes fondly and continues to live in the Tudor-style mansion Howard loved.

JANE GREER The sloe-eyed forties film noir femme fatale who was brought to Hughes for star-making. She married crooner Rudy Vallee instead, enraging the jealous Hughes. Today she occasionally appears on television.

JEAN HARLOW The original blonde bombshell and a brief Hughes fling, she soared to fame as the star of his *Hell's Angels*. But Hughes unwisely sold her contract to MGM, which made her one of the immortals. Following her untimely death at age twenty-six, Hughes remained close to Harlow's mother.

SUSAN HAYWARD Oscar winner (1958's *I Want to Live*) and indestructible redhead who thought she might be the next Mrs. Hughes. He pursued her for seven years; she dropped him after his New Year's Eve caper.

RITA HAYWORTH She was still married to filmmaker Orson Welles when she pursued a blazing affair with Hughes at Marion Davies's Santa Monica beach house. One of the great beauties of the 1940s—a Hayworth pinup was attached to the A-bomb dropped on Bikini Island—she displayed sultry sexuality in such films as *Gilda* (1946). Her husbands included jet-setter Prince Aly Khan.

KATHARINE HEPBURN The quintessential patrician actress; fiercely independent and one of the most talented Hollywood has ever produced—a four-time Oscar winner. Hughes and Spencer Tracy were the great passions in her life. (Hughes kept her love letters in a safe deposit box, where they were found after his death.)

BARBARA HUTTON The "Poor Little Rich Girl" who tumbled into bed with Hughes when he was engaged to Hepburn; their affair lasted just ten days. Hutton died like Hughes—wasting away and neglected in a hotel suite.

ZIZI JEANMAIRE The willowy star of the Roland Petit ballet company who attracted Hughes's attention during a Hollywood Bowl revue. He paid the bills for the entire company to remain in Los Angeles while he sought her favors.

DOROTHY JORDAN Briefly engaged to Hughes, the MGM star of the thirties later married filmmaker Merian C. Cooper (*King Kong*).

TIMMIE LANSING New York debutante who was wooed and virtually held prisoner by Hughes. She later married famed cartoonist Peter Arno (*The New Yorker*).

JANET LEIGH Fresh-faced MGM musical comedy star who spurned Howard's advances but ended up working for him at RKO. Famed as Alfred Hitchcock's leading lady in *Psycho* (1960)—and as the mother of actress Jamie Lee Curtis, she recounts her adventures with Hughes with great humor.

GINA LOLLOBRIGIDA She was on her way to becoming an Italian sex symbol when Hughes imported her from her homeland. When she refused to become a conquest, he kept her from making American films for seven years, using an obscure provision in her contract.

IDA LUPINO Known for playing tough, no-nonsense "broads," she was just sixteen when she dated Hughes. "My mum went along," she claimed. He was later instrumental in her move to directing.

MARIAN MARSH Delicate leading lady of Hollywood melodramas, she saw Howard change as a result of the company he kept in the 1930s. Active today as a community leader in Palm Desert, the California city she and her late husband (aviation pioneer Cliff Henderson) co-founded.

VIRGINIA MAYO Blonde bombshell (she was Dana Andrews's philandering wife in 1946's *The Best Years of Our Lives*) who resisted a wild fling with Hughes in New York—because she got airsick.

MARILYN MONROE Hughes was enthralled with her when he saw one of her earliest films, *Don't Bother to Knock*.

TERRY MOORE Pert perpetual starlet, she co-starred with a gorilla in *Mighty Joe Young* (1949) before going on to solid dramas such as *Come Back Little Sheba* (1952) and *Peyton Place* (1957). During the battle for the Hughes estate she claimed to have married Howard at sea. She received a settlement. Detailed her alleged Hughes exploits in the 1984 memoir *The Beauty and the Billionaire*; now at work on Hughes's "autobiography," which she says is being channeled through her.

JEAN PETERS Homespun but gorgeous 20th Century-Fox star who lived with Hughes off and on for a decade before he finally married her in 1957. Among her best-known films are *Captain from Castile* (1947) with Tyrone Power, *Viva Zapata!* (1952) opposite Marlon Brando, and *Niagara* (1953), which starred Marilyn Monroe. After divorcing Hughes in 1971 she married film executive Stanley Hough; their marriage lasted until his death in 1992. Active in charity work, Peters declines to give interviews about her years with Hughes.

GINGER ROGERS Graceful leading lady of the thirties and forties; partnered with Fred Astaire onscreen; with Hughes, off. When she left Howard he wept.

JANE RUSSELL Though he never succeeded in getting her into bed, Hughes loved her for her down-to-earth demeanor, her independence, and her fabulous figure, especially the breasts he enshrined in *The Outlaw*. Star of numerous fifties films, she credits Hughes with her stardom, which endures today.

YVONNE SHUBERT Just fifteen and an aspiring singer when she caught the eye of the fifty-year-old Hughes, she was his last hurrah and, she says, the only one of the many "Hughes girls" who truly loved him. She gave Jean Peters her toughest competition. Pursued an intermittent singing career that continues today.

JEAN SIMMONS Genteel leading lady of films including *Guys and Dolls* (1955) and *Spartacus* (1960), she saw her early career stall when Hughes bought her contract, "and put me in the toilet." She retaliated with a lawsuit. She now considers her Hughes histrionics as "part of a silly period."

ELIZABETH TAYLOR Just a teenager when she caught Hughes's eye as she strode through the Beverly Hills Hotel, she and her parents were quickly whisked off to Las Vegas for a weekend with the millionaire.

JOYCE TAYLOR Teenage songstress who looked and acted older than she was. Hughes put her under contract in the fifties, then put her contract on hold. She resurfaced, starring in science fiction and horror titles such as *Atlantis, the Lost Continent* (1961) and *Beauty and the Beast* (1963). Now makes her home in Colorado where she writes poetry. "I used to hate Howard. In retrospect, I feel sorry for him."

GENE TIERNEY One of the screen's most spectacular beauties and star of the classics *Laura* (1944) and *Leave Her to Heaven* (1945), she dated Hughes before and during her marriage to fashion designer Oleg Cassini. Though Hughes clearly had an agenda during his pursuit of her, Tierney remained ever grateful to him because of the medical attention he provided for her mentally retarded daughter.

LANA TURNER The "Sweater Girl" who became Howard's fiancée until he stood her up at the altar. Her icy blonde beauty and smoldering sexuality were especially effective when she teamed with John Garfield to murder her spouse in *The Postman Always Rings Twice* (1946). In her 1988 auto-biography she tried to minimize her liaison with Hughes. (Turner's many ex-husbands include band leader Artie Shaw, whose many wives also included Hughes's paramour Ava Gardner.)

GLORIA VANDERBILT Delicate, wistful debutante from one of America's most famous families. Briefly engaged to Hughes, who dropped her when she began dating his friend Pat De Cicco. After she became a queen of the fashion industry she wrote about Hughes in her memoirs.

SOURCE NOTES

By the time Howard Hughes died in Acapulco, numbed as he was by drugs and tired of suffering, there was one thought that comforted him. He fervently believed that his personal and intimate story—one of the most astounding in modern history—would die with him. He had always had a Garboesque philosophy about his fame, believing a man's legend is enhanced and engraved upon the hearts of humanity if it remains cloaked and mysterious.

So Hughes, beginning in the late sixties, launched a battle plan to see that his secrets died with him.

Executives, aides, lovers, and even his wife, Jean Peters, were coerced into signing vows of silence concerning their relationship with the complicated, tormented genius who changed the twentieth century. Further, in his long drafts of the last will and testament he began writing in 1965—with the help of his assistant Nadine Henley, attorney Greg Bautzer, and others—he provided for the total obliteration of the massive collection stored in the Romaine Street headquarters.

According to Henley, there were even provisions withholding money until the 200,000 pages of Hughes documents were first shredded and reduced to ashes.

And that might easily have happened, if the will and all drafts of it had not disappeared sometime before his death.

When the will vanished, so did Hughes's hopes of eternal secrecy.

Because his empire straddled six states, three of them laying claim to Hughes as a legal resident, Romaine was invaded by lawyers, deputy attorney generals, and court officers from Texas, Nevada, and California, who rifled through documents and personal effects detailing Hughes's life, from his infancy in Texas to that last, fatal codeine dose in Mexico.

Most of this intensely personal data was consigned to information hell until all the suits and countersuits made their way through the courts in Texas, Nevada, California, and Delaware.

In 1992 and 1993, through a prodigious effort that involved hundreds of letters, even more phone calls, two trips to Texas, and countless trips to Nevada, we finally gained access to most of this mountain of data. Much of it is presented here for the first time.

Yet, as valuable as the data was, it did not serve as the heart and soul of our personal biography of Hughes. Serving in that capacity were the interviews—hundreds of them, drawn from fifteen states as well as Mexico, Canada and Europe—of Hughes associates, and the authors, doctors, attorneys and others who had surveyed his life.

Although the notes that follow detail the origin of each claim and anecdote, some of the sources demand special recognition. Among the standouts:

- The 10,000 pages of single-spaced logs detailing many of Hughes's movements, meals, phone conversations, and meetings from 1930 through his death. They have never been available in their complete form until now.
- The letters and telegrams between Hughes and his first wife, Houston socialite Ella Rice Hughes, which helped to solve the mystery surrounding Hughes's first marriage.
- The surveillance logs, which Hughes's private detectives, Frank Angell and Jeff Chouinard, kept on all Howard's women, from Ava Gardner to his second wife, Jean Peters; from starlet Terry Moore to his final lover, Yvonne Shubert.
- The formerly sequestered FBI file on Hughes, which began when agents started tailing him in 1942 and continued through the Watergate scandal. Obtained under President Bill Clinton's more flexible Freedom of Information Act guidelines, the clandestine file, which runs above twenty-one hundred pages, includes blushingly

personal data obtained when agents bugged Howard's love nests and telephones.

- The Jamie Russell video archives, assembled for a documentary that Russell (brother of actress Jane Russell) is putting together on Hughes's life. The dozens of candid, lengthy video interviews with long-dead Hughes associates, such as Glenn Odekirk and Nadine Henley, was made available for us by Miss Jane Russell. Through this footage, we unearthed some of our first breakthrough revelations about Hughes.
- A multiple series of interviews, scores of hours in length, with former Hughes security chief, Jeff Chouinard, who was able to re-create—often, day-by-day—Howard's relationships with his lovers, both famous and unknown. With Chouinard's help, we were able to locate some of the starlets Hughes had kept at his beck and call during the fifties.

The complete source notes follow.

PROLOGUE

THE ROMAINE BREAK-IN LAPD interview with Mike Davis from Los Angeles Police Department (LAPD) Reports 17602-11, June 8, 1972; Davis's statement to the LA Grand Jury, July 18, 1972; LAPD Final Report, July 17, 1972. Additional details from Drosnin, *Citizen Hughes*; Barlett and Steele, *Empire*; Maheu, *Next to Hughes*.

DETAILS OF ROMAINE SECRETS Personal interviews, Robert Maheu, Kay Glenn, Jane Russell, Carla Balenda (aka Sally Bliss); depositions during battle for Hughes fortune, Kay Glenn, Nadine Henley, William Gay, John Holmes, Noah Dietrich, Hughes family papers (Hughes Estate) collection, Houston.

DETAILS OF CIA-FBI; WATERGATE SECRETS Jack Anderson columns of July 9, July 11, July 12, 1972; Senate Watergate Hearings, Book 21, p. 9947; memorandums of U.S. Congress, House Hearings on Judiciary Committees, Book 5; testimony of Mike Davis, *Los Angeles County Superior Court of California v. Donald Roy Woolbright*.

1 CROWN PRINCE

ON HOWARD'S BIRTH Dr. Norsworthy, oral history, University of Texas; January 19, 1981; deposition, Annette Lummis, Estate archives; "A Boy Who Began at the Top," *American*, April 1932; "Hughes, Record Breaker," *Liberty*, Feb. 6, 1937.

NORSWORTHY *Houston Post*, August 1938.

HOUSTON AT THE TIME Personal interview, Houston historian Marguerite Johnston; Johnston, *Houston: The Unknown City*; Fehrenbach, *Lone Star: A History of Texas and the Texans*; Frantz, *Texas: A Bicentennial History*; *New Encyclopedia of Texas* (1926).

ON HOWARD SR. AND ALLENE Harvard Class of 1897 report; deposition, Annette Lummis, Estate archives; oral history interview transcript, Granville A. Humason, Barker History Center, Austin; *New Encyclopedia of Texas*.

HISTORY OF THE DRILL BIT Oral histories of nineteen Texas oil pioneers, Barker History Center, Austin; *New Encyclopedia of Texas*; Presley, *A Saga of Wealth: The Rise of the Texas Oilmen*; "The Howard Hughes Nobody Knows," *West*, March 19, 1972; accounts of Toolco origins in *Los Angeles Times*, Dec. 17, 1970; *Las Vegas Review Journal*, Feb. 2, 1972; *Las Vegas Sun*, Dec. 13, 1970; *Fortune*, Dec. 1973; *Houston Chronicle*, Dec. 24, 1948.

ALLENE'S PREOCCUPATION WITH HUGHES'S HEALTH Barlett and Steele, *Empire*; Drosnin, *Citizen Hughes*; Keats, *Howard Hughes*; personal interviews, Dr. Raymond Fowler, Dr. John Chappel, Dr. Jeffrey Schwartz.

THE "PSYCHOLOGICAL AUTOPSY" Dr. Fowler, Estate archives.

HUGHES'S BOYHOOD Personal interviews, Mary Cullinan Cravens, Elva Kalb Dumas, Priester "Jack" Muckelroy; Johnston, *Houston: The Unknown City*; Helenthal, *The Keokuk Connection*; Nicholson, *William Ward Watkin and the Rice Institute*; Fowler, "Psychological Autopsy," Estate archives; letter, Prosso Academy director James R. Richardson to Hughes family, Estate archives; Estate trial testimony, Dudley Sharp, Estate archives; also re. Sharp, "Howard Hughes Was My Close Boyhood Friend," *National Enquirer*, Oct. 17, 1974; "Can the Real Howard Hughes . . . Still Stand Up?" *Playboy*, Dec. 1971; *American*, April 1932; *Liberty*, Feb. 6, 1937; also,

Houston Chronicle, July 14, 1946, July 10, 1983, Sept. 14, 1986, March 1, 1992; *Houston Post,* April 7, 1976.

EARLY PSYCHOLOGICAL PROBLEMS Personal interviews, Dr. Fowler, Dr. Chappel, Dr. Schwartz, Dr. Anthony Dietrich; Fowler, "Psychological Autopsy," Estate archives.

ODD RELATIONSHIP WITH MOTHER Personal interviews, Dr. Fowler, Dr. Schwartz; deposition, Annette Lummis, Estate archives.

HUGHES AT DAN BEARD CAMP Letters between Hughes Sr., Allene, Hughes Jr., and Dan Beard, 1916, 1917, Daniel Carter Beard collection, Library of Congress.

HUGHES'S MYSTERIOUS AILMENT Fowler, "Psychological Autopsy," Estate archives; personal interviews, Dr. Fowler, Dr. Chappel, Dr. Schwartz; deposition, Annette Lummis, Estate archives; Howard Sr. wire to Rockefeller Center, Estate archives; "Snapshots of Sonny," *Dallas Morning News,* April 3, 1977.

HUGHES'S HEARING DIFFICULTIES *Dallas Morning News,* April 3, 1977; Katharine Hepburn, ABC's *Good Morning America,* Nov. 8, 1984; Faith Domergue and Noah Dietrich reminiscences, Estate archives.

AT FESSENDEN Letters between school officials and Howard Sr., Estate archives.

2   SHADOW OF DEATH

HOWARD AT THACHER SCHOOL Letters, telegrams between Hughes Sr. and Thacher, Estate archives; "Psychological Autopsy," Estate archives; deposition, Annette Lummis, Estate archives; *Liberty,* Feb. 6, 1937; Dr. Chickering-Howard Sr. letters, Estate archives.

ALLENE'S TRAGIC DESERTION Personal interviews, Dr. Fowler, Dr. Chappel; deposition, Eleanor Boardman, Estate archives; Noah Dietrich's reminiscences, Estate archives.

THE SECRET OF ALLENE'S SURGERY Noah Dietrich's unpublished reminiscences, Estate archives.

ALLENE'S DEATH *Houston Chronicle,* March 30, 1922; *Liberty,* Feb. 6, 1937; deposition, Annette Lummis, Estate archives; Thacher–Hughes Sr. correspondence, Estate archives; personal interview, Dr. Fowler.

THE MERRY WIDOWER Barlett and Steele, *Empire*; Keats, *Howard Hughes*; Foxworth, *The Romance of Old Sylvan Beach*; Graham, *The Garden of Allah*; deposition, Annette Lummis, Estate archives; Dietrich and Faith Domergue reminiscences, Estate archives.

HOWARD SR'S. DEATH *Houston Chronicle*, Jan. 15, 1924; *Houston Press*, Jan. 17, 1924; *Houston Post*, Jan. 17, 1924; *Petroleum World*, February 1924; deposition, Annette Lummis, Estate archives.

THE UNSIGNED WILL Dietrich, Domergue reminiscences, Estate archives; Barlett and Steele, *Empire*.

SHOWDOWN WITH RELATIVES Depositions, Annette Lummis, Jean Peters, George A. Francom, Dudley Sharp, Estate archives; Dietrich, Domergue reminiscences, Estate archives; personal interviews, Jane Russell, Kathryn Grayson; order of Judge Walter Montieth, Harris County Court, Dec. 26, 1924.

3 THE BARTERED BRIDE

WEDDING DETAILS *Houston Chronicle*, June 2, 1925; personal interviews, Mary Cullinan Cravens, Laura Kirkland Bruce; deposition, Dudley Sharp, Estate archives; certified copy of marriage license, Harris County Court, May 29, 1925.

ELLA RICE HUGHES BIOGRAPHY personal interviews, James Overton Winston, Elizabeth Rice Winston, Laura Kirkland Bruce, Mary Cullinan Cravens, Betsy Parrish, Shelby Hodge.

THE FAKED ILLNESS Letters, Kitty Callaway to Howard Hughes, Estate archives; Noah Dietrich, "The Howard I Remember," *Life*, Feb. 25, 1972; Dietrich reminiscences, Estate archives.

HOWARD'S PREMARITAL RESEARCH Dietrich, Domergue reminiscences, Estate archives; Hughes's letters to attorneys, Estate archives.

HOWARD'S WILL DRAFT Estate archives.

ARRIVAL IN HOLLYWOOD Dietrich reminiscences, Estate archives; Adela Rogers St. Johns, BBC television, April 1978; personal interview, Billie Dove.

ELLA IN HOLLYWOOD Depositions, Eleanor Boardman, Annette Lummis, Dudley Sharp; personal interviews, James Overton Winston, Laura Kirkland Bruce,

Elva Kalb Dumas, Suzanne Finstad; Finstad, *Heir Not Apparent*; Bellamy, *A Darling of the Twenties*; Miller, *The Memories of Patsy Ruth Miller*.

NOAH DIETRICH'S APPEARANCE Dietrich reminiscences, Estate archives; Dietrich and Thomas, *Howard: The Amazing Mr. Hughes*.

HOLLYWOOD AND THE FILM INDUSTRY IN THE 1920S Heimann, *Out With the Stars*; *Motion Picture News*, 1926.

HOWARD'S FIRST (UNRELEASED) FILM Barlett and Steele, *Empire*; Thomas, *Howard Hughes in Hollywood*; MacAdams, *Ben Hecht: The Man Behind the Legend*; "The Man Who Has Everything," *New York Sunday News*, Jan. 19, 1936; Dietrich reminiscences, financial statements, Estate archives.

HOLLYWOOD ESCAPADES Dietrich reminiscences, Estate archives.

LIFE AT THE AMBASSADOR Dietrich reminiscences, Estate archives; Burk, *Are the Stars Out Tonight?*

WESTERN UNION CAPER Dietrich unpublished reminiscences (including the steam car and early film efforts), Estate archives.

TWO ARABIAN KNIGHTS Louella Parsons column items and stories, *Los Angeles Examiner*, various dates, 1926–27; *Variety*, Oct. 26, 1927; Astor, *A Life on Film*; Stine, *Stars and Star Handlers*; Thomas, *Howard Hughes in Hollywood*.

REJECTION OF ELLA RICE HUGHES Interviews, James Overton Winston, Laura Kirkland Bruce, Elva Kalb Dumas, Marguerite Johnston, Elizabeth Rice Winston, Betty Ewing, Dr. Chappel, Dr. Fowler; Ella–Howard letters, telegrams, Estate archives; deposition, Annette Lummis, Estate archives; Estate trial testimony, Dudley Sharp, Estate archives; Miller, *The Memories of Patsy Ruth Miller*.

4   GOING HOLLYWOOD

HELL'S ANGELS Dietrich reminiscences; Dietrich and Thomas, *Howard: The Amazing Mr. Hughes*; Dwiggins, *Hollywood Pilot: The Biography of Paul Mantz*; Wynne, *The Motion Picture Stunt Pilots*; Louella Parsons columns 1927–30, Louella Parsons collection, Margaret Herrick Library, Los Angeles; "Young Howard Hughes: Reminiscences by a Survivor of Hollywood's Golden Era," *Views and Reviews*, September, 1973; "Howard Hughes's Maiden Flight," *American Film*, Nov. 1981; "When the War Birds Invaded Hollywood," *Cavalier*, Nov. 1961;

"4 Million Dollars and 4 Men's Lives," *Photoplay*, April 1930; various production accounts, including *Film News*, Nov. 11, 1927; *American Cinematographer*, Jan. 1930.

HELL'S ANGELS CRASH Personal interviews, Dr. Fowler, Dr. Schwartz; deposition, Noah Dietrich, Estate archives; official Hughes autopsy report, Harris County, Texas.

ELLA–HOWARD BREAKUP Howard and Ella correspondence, 1924, Estate archives; personal interviews, James Overton Winston, Laura Kirkland Bruce, Mary Brewer Dietrich, Dr. Fowler, Dr. Schwartz, Dr. Chappel; Dietrich reminiscences; deposition, Annette Lummis.

JEAN HARLOW DISCOVERY, AFFAIR WITH HUGHES Deposition, Ben Lyon, Estate archives; Shulman, *Harlow*; Golden, *Platinum Girl*; Stenn, *Bombshell*; Stine, *Stars and Star Handlers*; *New York Sunday News*, Jan. 19, 1936; *Look*, March 23, 1954; *American Film*, Nov. 1981; Dietrich reminiscences; personal interview, Johnny Maschio.

5   AN AFFAIR TO REMEMBER

BILLIE DOVE AFFAIR Numerous personal interviews with Billie Dove; Billie Dove deposition, Estate archives; reminiscences, Noah Dietrich; "Billie Dove: An American Beauty," *Films in Review*, April 1979; personal interviews, Dr. Fowler, Laura Kirkland Bruce.

ELLA'S DISASTROUS RETURN Howard Hughes's telegrams, logs, communications, Estate archives; deposition, Annette Lummis; Howard's personal instructions to Western Union, Estate archives; Dietrich reminiscences; Louella Parsons radio broadcast transcripts; personal interview, Dorothy Manners.

DIVORCE SETTLEMENT William Farish letters, Estate archives; Hughes–Rice settlement document, Ella Rice Hughes petition and unfinished draft of the first petition, Estate archives.

NEVADA FARM CAPER Interview, Billie Dove.

DOVE–WILLAT DIVORCE Interview, Billie Dove; Louella Parsons collection, Margaret Herrick Library, Los Angeles; *Los Angeles Examiner*, Jan. 2, 1930; *Hollywood Citizen-News*, Jan. 2, 1930.

6 APPLAUSE

THE STRESS OF *HELL'S ANGELS* Dietrich reminiscences; "Psychological Autopsy"; Dr. Verne Mason medical records, Estate archives.

DAWN PATROL ASSAULT Wallis, *Starmaker*; Wynne, *The Motion Picture Stunt Pilots*; *Los Angeles Herald*, July 31, 1930.

HARLOW AFFAIR Deposition, Ben Lyon, Estate archives; Shulman, *Harlow*; personal interview, Johnny Maschio; American Movie Classics' background research for the 20th Century-Fox film *Harlow*.

HELL'S ANGELS PREMIERE Lincoln Quarberg collection, Louella Parsons collection, Margaret Herrick Library, Los Angeles; Dietrich reminiscences; Shulman, *Harlow*; Goodman, *The Fifty-Year Decline and Fall of Hollywood*; newspaper accounts of May 28, 1930, including *Los Angeles Examiner*, *Los Angeles Evening Express*, *Los Angeles Times*, *Los Angeles Evening Herald*; newsreel footage, Jamie Russell collection; official premiere program, Margaret Herrick Library, Los Angeles; *Hell's Angels* memorabilia, author's private collection.

HOWARD'S FILMS Thomas, *Howard Hughes in Hollywood*; Lawrence, *Actor: The Life and Times of Paul Muni*; Hecht, *A Child of the Century*; *Photoplay*, June 1931; McBride, *Hawks on Hawks*; personal interviews, Dr. Fowler, Billie Dove; Dietrich reminiscences.

THE FRONT PAGE O'Brien, *The Wind at My Back*; Hecht, *A Child of the Century*; MacAdams, *Ben Hecht: The Man Behind the Legend*; *New York World-Telegram*, March 20, 1931; *New York Times*, March 20, 1931; *Los Angeles Express*, March 21, 1931; *Los Angeles Examiner*, Oct. 8, 1930; personal interview, Tony Rogell.

FINANCIAL COLLAPSE Dietrich reminiscences; William S. Farish letters, Estate archives; the "forced settlement" document with Ella, Estate archives; record of Hughes's financial experiences, Estate archives; Harris County Superior Court Order.

7 ADRIFT

BILLIE DOVE BREAKUP Personal interviews, Billie Dove, Dorothy Manners, Johnny Maschio; Louella Parsons–Dorothy Manners columns, 1929–30; background, Louella Parsons collection, Margaret Herrick Library, Los Angeles; Dietrich reminiscences, Estate archives; "Billie Dove: An American Beauty," *Films in Review*, April 1979.

HUGHES'S DEAFNESS Personal interviews, Billie Dove; Dietrich reminiscences; numerous documents from Hughes's private papers, Estate archives.

TRIP TO EUROPE Personal interviews, Billie Dove; deposition, Billie Dove, Estate archives.

THE DOVE FILMS Lincoln Quarberg collection, marketing and publicity kits for *Sky Devils, Cock of the Air, The Age for Love*, Margaret Herrick Library, Los Angeles; personal interview, Dove; "Billie Dove: An American Beauty," *Films in Review*, April 1979; "The Flight of the Elusive Dove: Billie Dove Looks Back," *Classic Images*, June 1994; Dietrich reminiscences.

ON THE PROWL Personal interviews, Ida Lupino (through assistant Mary Ann Anderson), Marian Marsh, Johnny Maschio, Alex D'Arcy; deposition, Pat De Cicco, Estate archives; Rappleye and Becker, *All American Mafioso*; Dunne, *Take Two: A Life in Movies and Politics*; Fairbanks Jr., *The Salad Days*; Bodeen, *More from Hollywood*; *New York Sunday News*, Jan. 19, 1936.

HUGHES TRIES TO WIN BACK ELLA Personal interview, James Overton Winston.

NANCY CARROLL SEXCAPADE Dietrich reminiscences.

GINGER ROGERS Personal interview, Ginger Rogers; Rogers, *Ginger: My Story*; deposition, Rogers, Estate archives; Dietrich reminiscences.

SCARFACE MacBride, *Hawks on Hawks*; Lincoln Quarberg collection, Los Angeles; Hecht, *A Child of the Century*; Stine, *Stars & Star Handlers*; Lawrence, *Actor: The Life and Times of Paul Muni*; Parish and Pitts, *The Great Gangster Pictures*; *Los Angeles Examiner*, April 21–22, 1932; *Baltimore Sun*, Jan. 15, 1947.

DEBUTANTE ADVENTURES Dietrich reminiscences; Glenn Odekirk video interviews, Jamie Russell collection; Barton, *Howard Hughes and His Flying Boat*; Hearst Jr., *The Hearsts: Father and Son*; personal interviews, Johnny Maschio, Alex D'Arcy.

THE YACHT Dietrich reminiscences; Hobart, *A Steady Digression to a Fixed Point*.

8   COMING OF AGE

SHUNS SOCIAL CONVENTIONS Dietrich reminiscences; deposition, Pat De Cicco, Estate archives; personal interviews, Dorothy Lee, Marian Marsh; *Los Angeles Herald*, Dec. 21, 1932.

HOWARD'S VANISHING ACT Hughes's logs, Estate archives; deposition, Annette Lummis.

AMERICAN AIRLINES Barlett and Steele, *Empire*; Gerber, *The Bashful Billionaire*; *New York Sun*, Dec. 6, 1932.

THE SILVER BULLET Barton, *Howard Hughes and His Flying Boat*; Smith, *From Jennies to Jets*; Dwiggins, *Famous Flyers and the Ships They Flew*; *Santa Ana* [Ca.] *Daily Register*, Sept. 14–17, 1935; *New York Times*, Sept. 14, 1935; *Time*, Sept. 23, 1935; *Los Angeles Examiner*, Sept. 19, 1935.

SABOTAGE ON THE H-1 *Houston Post*, Sept. 15, 1935.

AVIATION HERO Dietrich reminiscences, actual aviation logs, Estate archives; Barton, *Howard Hughes and His Flying Boat*; Cochran, *Jackie Cochran*; Dwiggins, *Famous Flyers and the Ships They Flew*; Barlett and Steele, *Empire*; Glenn Odekirk video interviews, Jamie Russell collection.

VENEREAL DISEASE Dietrich reminiscences; personal interviews, Mary Brewer Dietrich, Dr. Anthony Dietrich, Dr. Raymond Fowler, several anonymous sources, including a key Hughes attorney who was involved in half a dozen paternity cases; Howard R. Hughes unabridged autopsy report; "Sexually Transmitted Diseases," National Center for Disease Control, 1972.

9   CARY AND KATE

RANDOLPH SCOTT AND HIS HUGHES INTRODUCTION Letter of introduction from Scott family, Estate archives; Barlett and Steele, *Empire*.

CARY GRANT "Grant Guy," *Chicago Tribune*, Sept. 18, 1949; "The Touch of Class," *Parade*, Sept. 22, 1985; "Keeping the Promises of Youth," *Liberty*, Winter 1975; "Cary Grant Talks About His Friend Howard Hughes," *National Enquirer*,

March 26, 1972; Harris, *Cary Grant: A Touch of Elegance*; Nelson, *Evenings With Cary Grant*; Wansell, *Haunted Idol*; Hepburn, *Me*; depositions, Beatrice Dowler, Dietrich, Estate archives; letters, memos re. Grant, Estate archives.

INTRO, KATE–HUGHES Harris, *A Touch of Elegance*; Hepburn, *Me*; Edwards, *A Remarkable Woman*; Carey, *Katharine Hepburn: A Hollywood Yankee*; Lambert, *On Cukor*; depositions, Johanna Madsen, Johnny Maschio, Estate archives; personal interview, Johnny Maschio.

KATHARINE HEPBURN Hepburn, *Me*; Edwards, *A Remarkable Woman*; Carey, *Katharine Hepburn: A Hollywood Yankee*; *Current Biography*, 1942; "Well! Well! So This Is Hepburn," *Photoplay*, Aug. 1933; "Hepburn: Another Scarlett?" *Photoplay*, Aug. 1938; "The Hepburns," *Life*, Jan. 22, 1940; "Young Kate, 1928–1937," *Blackhawk Film Digest*, April–May, 1980; deposition, Johanna Madsen, Estate archives.

THE CRASH Interview, Nancy Bell Bayly; official accident report and special investigative report from Hughes's attorney, Neil McCarthy, Estate archives; Dietrich reminiscences; *Los Angeles Times*, *Los Angeles Examiner*, *Santa Barbara Daily News*, *Pasadena Star-News*, *Houston Chronicle*, July 12–17, 1936.

RECORD-BREAKER *Newsweek*, Jan. 25, 1936; *Time*, Jan. 27, 1936; *The Literary Digest*, Jan. 25, 1936; *New York Times*, Dec. 4, 1935; *New York Times*, Jan. 20, 1937; *Los Angeles Examiner*, Jan. 20, 1937; *Time*, Feb. 1, 1937; *Popular Mechanics*, April 1937; Cochran, *Jackie Cochran*; Barton, *Howard Hughes and His Flying Boat*; Barlett and Steele, *Empire*; Associated Press, Jan. 14, 1936; Glenn Odekirk video interviews, Jamie Russell collection; Dietrich reminiscences.

KATE, HOWARD AND JANE EYRE Hepburn, *Me*; Carey, *Katharine Hepburn: A Hollywood Yankee*; Edwards, *A Remarkable Woman*; Dickens, *The Films of Katharine Hepburn*; "Hepburn Reconsidered," *The Dial*, March 1981; "The Hepburn Story," *Saturday Evening Post*, Jan. 3, 1942; *Hartford Courant*, Dec. 27, 1936; *Chicago Tribune*, Jan. 19–23, 1937.

10   KATHARINE THE GREAT

KATE AT MUIRFIELD Dietrich reminiscences; Hepburn, *Me*; deposition, Johanna Madsen, Estate archives; personal interview, Johnny Maschio.

HOWARD'S TROPHY *New York Times*, March 3, 1937; Barton, *Howard Hughes and His Flying Boat*; Dwiggins, *Famous Flyers and the Ships They Flew*.

THE LOVE AFFAIR Deposition, Johanna Madsen, Estate archives; personal interviews, Johnny Maschio, Phyllis Brooks; Edwards, *A Remarkable Woman*; Hepburn, *Me*.

HEPBURN'S ATTEMPTED SUICIDE Personal interviews, Layne "Shotgun" Britton, Johnny Maschio.

HOWARD IN LONDON Heymann, *Poor Little Rich Girl*.

HOWARD AT KATE'S Edwards, *A Remarkable Woman*; Dietrich and Thomas, *Howard: The Amazing Mr. Hughes*; Hepburn, *Me*; Gerber, *Bashful Billionaire*; Carey, *Katharine Hepburn: A Hollywood Yankee*; Dietrich reminiscences; *Las Vegas Review-Journal*, April 8, 1976.

MARRIAGE PLANS Glenn Odekirk video interviews, Jamie Russell collection; Dietrich reminiscences; Louella Parsons's radio show transcripts; *Los Angeles Herald*, May 28, 1938.

11   HIGHWAY IN THE SKY

AROUND THE WORLD Heckscher, *When LaGuardia Was Mayor*; Ingells, *The Plane That Changed the World*; Hepburn, *Me*; Barton, *Howard Hughes and His Flying Boat*; Leaming, *Katharine Hepburn*; Dwiggins, *Famous Flyers and the Ships They Flew*; *New York Times*, *Houston Post*, *Houston Chronicle*, *Los Angeles Times*, *Los Angeles Examiner*, July 5–15, 1938; extended video footage, newsreel, and Ed Lund interview, Jamie Russell collection; series of press releases from New York World's Fair, Inc., 1939.

RETURN TO HOUSTON *Houston Chronicle*, *Houston Post*, July 31, 1938; *Houston Press*, July 30, 1938; official program, "Houston Welcomes Howard Hughes—July 30"; deposition, Annette Lummis, Estate archives.

KATE'S REJECTION Glenn Odekirk video interviews, Jamie Russell collection; Dietrich reminiscences; personal interviews, Harriet Parsons, Phyllis Brooks; deposition, Johanna Madsen, Estate archives.

12   HE'S IN THE MONEY

HUGHES TOOLCO RENAISSANCE Noah Dietrich reminiscences; Barlett and Steele, *Empire*; Barton, *Howard Hughes and His Flying Boat*; Gerber, *Bashful Billionaire*;

Serling, *Howard Hughes' Airline*; "The View From Inside Hughes Tool," *Fortune*, December 1973; various articles on company history, *Las Vegas Review-Journal*, *Los Angeles Times*, *Houston Chronicle*; historic Hughes Toolco brochure, Estate archives.

THE WAR PARTIES Senate War Hearings, Vols. 7–17; "Duel Under the Klieg Lights," *Time*, Aug. 18, 1947; hearings coverage by *New York Times*, *New York Daily News*, *New York Journal American*, *New York News*, *New York Daily Mirror*, *Houston Chronicle*, *Los Angeles Times*, *Los Angeles Daily News*, *Los Angeles Examiner*, *Los Angeles Herald-Express*, *Hollywood Citizen-News*, *Hollywood Reporter*, July–Nov. 1947, approximately 175 articles; personal interview, Myrna Dell.

13 THE PARADE'S GONE BY

GINGER ROGERS ROMANCE Personal interview, Ginger Rogers; Rogers, *Ginger: My Story*; depositions, Ginger Rogers, Johanna Madsen, Estate archives; Dietrich reminiscences.

BETTE DAVIS AFFAIR Spada, *More Than a Woman*; Quirk, *Fasten Your Seat Belts*; Considine, *Bette & Joan*; Leaming, *Bette Davis*; Hyman, *My Mother's Keeper*; Stine, *I'd Love to Kiss You . . .* ; complaint for divorce, *Harmon Oscar Nelson, Jr. v. Ruth Elizabeth Nelson* [Bette Davis], Superior Court, Los Angeles County, Dec. 1938; *Los Angeles Times*, *Los Angeles Daily News*, *Los Angeles Examiner*, Nov. 23, 1938; personal interviews, Ruth Bailey, Anne Nelson, Lawrence J. Quirk, Michael "Mickey" Herskowitz.

OLIVIA DE HAVILLAND AND JOAN FONTAINE Keats, *Howard Hughes*; Fontaine, *No Bed of Roses*.

ROGERS BREAKUP Personal interview, Ginger Rogers; Rogers, *Ginger: My Story*; Dietrich reminiscences.

SAVING KATE'S CAREER Geist, *Pictures Will Talk*; Davidson, *Spencer Tracy*; McGilligan, *George Cukor*; Carey, *Katharine Hepburn: A Hollywood Yankee*; Edwards, *A Remarkable Woman*; Hepburn, *Me*; Dickens, *The Films of Katharine Hepburn*; Dietrich reminiscences; Johanna Madsen deposition, Estate archives.

DEBUTANTES Barton, *Howard Hughes and His Flying Boat*; Diliberto, *Debutante*; Goldsmith, *Little Gloria . . . Happy at Last*; Friedman, *Gertrude Vanderbilt Whitney*; Vanderbilt, *Black Knight, White Knight* and *Woman to Woman*; Glenn Odekirk video interviews, Jamie Russell collection; personal interview, Billy Livingstone; *Vanity Fair*, July 1978.

14 WAY OUT WEST

THE OUTLAW Leff and Simmons, *The Dame in the Kimono*; Sarf, *God Bless You, Buffalo Bill*; Schumach, *The Face on the Cutting Room Floor: The Story of Movie and TV Censorship*; Gardner, *The Censorship Papers*; Keats, *Howard Hughes*; Thomas, *Howard Hughes in Hollywood*; Russell, *Jane Russell*; "Howard Hughes and That Tussle With Russell," *American Classic Screen*, Fall 1979; "The Case Against the Outlaw," *Photoplay*, September 1946; "Jane Russell Rides Again with the Bust That Shook the World," *Village Voice*, July 19, 1976; Russell Birdwell reminiscences, *Variety*, May 26, 1965; personal interview, Jane Russell; extended video footage of Russell, the Jamie Russell collection.

THE ERA Morella, Epstein, and Griggs, *The Films of World War II*.

15 THE BLUE PRINCE

FAITH DOMERGUE Depositions, Noah Dietrich, Johanna Madsen, Estate archives; Dietrich reminiscences; Louella Parsons columns, radio transcripts; personal interviews, Jeff Chouinard, Charles Bennett, Ben Kamsler, Dr. Raymond Fowler, Dr. John Chappel; Barton, *Howard Hughes and His Flying Boat*; Glenn Odekirk video interviews, Jamie Russell collection; Domergue recollections, Estate archives.

AVA GARDNER Personal interviews, Johnny Maschio, Jane Greer, Myrna Dell, Robert Mitchum, Jeff Chouinard, Kathryn Grayson, Dorothy Manners, Alex D'Arcy; Wayne, *Ava's Men*; Rooney, *Life Is Too Short*; Rockwell, *Sinatra: An American Classic*; Torme, *It Wasn't All Velvet*; Wilson, *Sinatra*; Marx, *The Nine Lives of Mickey Rooney*; Daniell, *Ava Gardner*; Kelley, *His Way*; Finstad, *Heir Not Apparent*; Keats, *Howard Hughes*; deposition, Beatrice (Bappie) G. Cole, Estate archives; *Los Angeles Mirror*, *Hollywood Citizen-News*, Aug. 14, 1954.

16 BRAINSTORMS

THE OUTLAW See *Outlaw* sources cited, Chapter Fourteen. Also, "Hughes's Western," *Time*, Feb. 22, 1943; *San Francisco Chronicle*, Feb. 5–25, 1943; *Variety*, June 1, 1964; Faith Domergue reminiscences, Estate archives.

THE BREAKDOWNS Gardner, *Ava*; deposition, Noah Dietrich, Estate archives; Dietrich reminiscences; Barton, *Howard Hughes and His Flying Boat*; Serling, *Howard Hughes' Airline*.

LAKE MEAD CRASH Personal interview, Charles Barton; Barton, *Howard Hughes and His Flying Boat*; Barlett and Steele, *Empire*; FAA-CAB Reports, "Lake Mead Crash," 1943; Glenn Odekirk video interview, Jamie Russell collection; Faith Domergue recollections, Estate archives; Gardner, *Ava*; John Leyden, "Facing Death with Howard Hughes," *Horizons*, Oct. 1971.

PRESSURES OF TWA Dietrich reminiscences; Serling, *Howard Hughes' Airline*; Barlett and Steele, *Empire*.

HOWARD AND JANE GREER Personal interview, Jane Greer; video interview, Jane Greer, "Howard's Way" segment of BBC RKO Pictures documentary series; Vallee, *Let the Chips Fall*; Parrish, *The RKO Girls*; "Jane Greer: Out of Her Past," *Los Angeles Times*, March 4, 1984; Jane Greer, "How I Broke Into the Movies," *Los Angeles Daily News*, May 20, 1953.

17 THE GREAT ESCAPE

MAN ON THE RUN Noah Dietrich reminiscences; Petrali, "O.K. Howard," *True*, February and March 1975; Faith Domergue recollections, Estate archives; personal interviews, Dr. John Chappel, Dr. Raymond Fowler, Charles Barton; Barton, *Howard Hughes and His Flying Boat*; Serling, *Howard Hughes' Airline*; Houston Draft Appeal and Draft Board correspondence, Estate archives.

SHREVEPORT INCIDENT Noah Dietrich reminiscences; Petrali, "O.K. Howard," *True*, February and March 1975; personal interview, arresting officer Marvin K. Ezell; Shreveport booking sheet #19067-21; notebook entries, Shreveport Police

Department, Estate archives; *Shreveport Journal*, March 24, 1945 and April 6, 1976; *Shreveport Times*, April 2, 1984.

OBSESSIVE-COMPULSIVE DISORDER Multiple personal interviews, Dr. Jeffrey Schwartz; Dr. Anthony Dietrich; Judith L. Rappaport, et. al., "Obsessional-Onset Obsessive Compulsive Disorders," *Journal of Obsessional Disorders*, December 1992; McKeon, McGuffen, and Robinson, "Obsessional-Compulsive Neuroses Following Head Injury," *British Journal of Psychiatry*, July 1984; W. A. Lishman, "Brain Damage in Relation to Psychiatric Disability After Head Injuries," *British Journal of Psychiatry*, May 1968; E. Hillborn, "After Effects of Brain Injuries," Pamela King, "The Chemistry of Doubt," *Psychology Today*, October 1989; Jeffrey M. Schwartz, M.D., *Manual Cognitive-Bio Behavioural Self Treatment for Obsessive-Compulsive Disorder*, a ten-year study for the UCLA Department of Psychiatry and Behavioral Sciences.

18   THE LONE WOLF

ROMANCE WITH YVONNE DE CARLO Noah Dietrich reminiscences; Petrali, "O.K. Howard," *True*, February and March, 1975; De Carlo, *Yvonne: An Autobiography*; "Salome on Rye," *Colliers*, May 5, 1945; "Meet the Most Beautiful Girl in the World," *Hollywood Citizen-News*, Oct. 4, 1944; Sidney Skorsky column, *Hollywood Citizen-News*, March 24, 1944; Dorothy Manners column item, International News Service, Aug. 21, 1946.

FBI SURVEILLANCE The Federal Bureau of Investigation reports on Howard Hughes come from a remarkable collection on Hughes running more than two thousand pages and obtained under the Freedom of Information Act (aided by more liberal guidelines instituted by President Bill Clinton). The FBI reports about Hughes's affairs came mostly from illegal wiretaps.

SEXUAL PREFERENCES Dietrich reminiscences; De Carlo, *Yvonne: An Autobiography*; Turner, *Lana: The Lady, The Legend, The Truth*; personal interviews, Yvonne Shubert and anonymous "Hughes girls."

LANA TURNER AFFAIR Personal interviews, Taylor Pero, Johnny Maschio, Janet Thomas; Turner, *Lana: The Lady, the Legend, the Truth*; Pero and Rovin, *Always, Lana*; Morella and Epstein, *Lana: The Public and Private Lives of Miss Turner*; column items, Louella Parsons collection, Margaret Herrick Library, Los Angeles.

HOWARD IN NEW YORK Deposition, Glenn Odekirk, Estate archives; Petrali, "O.K. Howard," *True*, February and March, 1975; Barton, *Howard Hughes and His Flying Boat*; Hughes documents, Estate archives; personal interview, Harriet Huntoon.

AVA GARDNER Gardner, *Ava*; Hanna, *Ava: Portrait of a Star*; Artie Shaw video interview, Arts and Entertainment Network, *Biography* episode about Ava Gardner.

GENE TIERNEY Cassini, *In My Own Fashion*; Tierney, *Self-Portrait*; United Press International, March 28, 1979.

MARILYN MONROE Natasha Lytess's unpublished memoirs, *My Years With Marilyn* (twenty-eight-page manuscript), Maurice Zolotow collection, Humanities Research, University of Texas at Austin; Summers, *Goddess: The Secret Lives of Marilyn Monroe*.

19 FALL FROM GRACE

THE ROMANTIC SKIES Barton, *Howard Hughes and His Flying Boat*; Bergman, *My Story*; Davis, *Hollywood Beauty: Linda Darnell and the American Dream*; Serling, *Howard Hughes' Airline*; personal interviews, Kathryn Grayson, Janet Leigh, Ginger Rogers, Ann Miller, Sallilee Conlon; Dietrich reminiscences; "The Girl Who Said 'No' to Howard Hughes" (Gina Lollobrigida), *Top Secret*, Summer 1954; "Airport '44" (Virginia Mayo), *People*, May 31, 1976.

RETURN OF *THE OUTLAW* Motion Picture Association press release, "Highlights from Judge Bright's Opinion Re. *The Outlaw*," Margaret Herrick Library, Los Angeles; Russell, *Jane Russell*; Keats, *Howard Hughes*; Gerber, *Bashful Billionaire*; Schumach, *The Face on the Cutting Room Floor*; Sarf, *God Bless You, Buffalo Bill*; Barton, *Howard Hughes and His Flying Boat*; personal interview, Jane Russell; 1946 rerelease coverage in *Photoplay*, *Hollywood Citizen-News*, *Liberty*, *New York Times*, *Time*, *Newsweek*, *Motion Picture Herald*, *Variety*, *Hollywood Reporter*, *Mademoiselle*, *Los Angeles Times*, *Los Angeles Daily News*, *Los Angeles Examiner*, approximately 48 articles.

CANCELLATION OF CONTRACTS Hughes Aircraft cancellation orders, Estate archives; deposition, Jean Peters, Estate archives; Senate War Hearings, vol. 17; message by Dr. Verne Mason to Col. E. T. Kennedy, FX-11 File, Pentagon; memorandum, Col. George E. Price to Commanding General, Wright Field, Records of Army Air Forces.

JEAN PETERS Deposition, Jean Peters, Estate archives; Dietrich reminiscences; Simpson, *Audie Murphy: American Soldier*; Graham, *No Name on the Bullet*; personal interview, Janet Thomas.

THE 1946 CRASH Glenn Odekirk and Alice Burns video interviews, Jamie Russell collection; Barton, *Howard Hughes and His Flying Boat*; depositions, Glenn Odekirk, Jean Peters, Estate archives; Dietrich reminiscences. Fifty stories about the crash and Hughes's recovery, from publications including *Los Angeles Times*, *Los Angeles Examiner*, *Los Angeles Herald-Express*, *New York Times*, *New York Daily News*, *New York Journal-American*, *Houston Chronicle*, *Senior Scholastic*, July 8–August 7, 1946. Edited copy from never-published obituaries, *Houston Post*, *Houston Chronicle*, etc., Houston Public Library; letter from Dr. Verne Mason re. Hughes's injuries, Estate archives; official resolution, Supervisors of the County of Los Angeles, re. Hughes's "courageous battle for recovery," July 1, 1946, Estate archives.

Also, re. the crash: Report of the XF-11 Accident Investigation Board Hearings: p. 24507; statement of Charles E. Blandford, pp. 24523–5; Hughes's account of the flight, p. 24505; Verne R. Mason, p. 24508; Unsigned memo from Propeller Laboratory to chief, Aircraft Projects Section, Engineering Division (TSESA-5), Crash of Hughes XF-11 Airplane, dated "Approx. 16 August 1946," "F-11 Case History"; Contract W-33-038 AC-1079. Model XF-11 Airplane, Safety Inspection, April 24, 1946; Files of the assistant chief of Air Staff Materiel and Services (A-4) Research and Development Branch, Case Histories 1941–46; U.S. Congress, Senate: Special Committee to investigate the National Defense Program Hearings, 80th Congress, 1st session, Part 40, *Aircraft Contracts (Hughes Aircraft Co. and Kaiser-Hughes Corp.)* (Washington, D.C.: Government Printing Office, 1947. Part 43).

DRUG ABUSE Personal interviews, Robert Maheu, Kathryn Grayson, Layne "Shotgun" Britton, Dr. Lawrence Chaffin, D. Martin Cook; 1,111 relevant pages of the FBI-CIA Investigations of Howard Hughes, 1943-1964.

THE LANA–PETERS ENCOUNTER Personal interview, Janet Thomas.

RITA HAYWORTH ROMANCE AND ABORTION Personal interview, Dan Wolfe; Leaming, *If This Was Happiness*.

INFATUATION WITH LIZ TAYLOR Fisher, *My Life, My Loves*; Kelley, *The Last Star*; Maddox, *Who's Afraid of Elizabeth Taylor?*; Reynolds, *Debbie: My Life*; Waterbury, *Elizabeth Taylor*; transcript of Liz Taylor's phone call to Hughes, Estate archives; personal interview, Jeff Chouinard.

20 HIDE-AND-SEEK

IN AMARILLO *Amarillo Daily News*, Jan. 4, 1947.

CARY AND HOWARD Harris, *Cary Grant: A Touch of Elegance*; Glenn Odekirk video interview, Jamie Russell collection; *New York Daily Mirror*, *New York Daily News*, *New York Sun*, *El Paso Herald-Post*, *Amarillo Sunday News-Globe*, Jan. 11–12, 1947.

JEAN PETERS ON LOCATION Glenn Odekirk video interview, Jamie Russell collection; Hedda Hopper, "Hollywood's Mystery Girl," fan magazine, date unknown; *Variety*, March 6, 1947; *Captain from Castile* press book, Margaret Herrick Library, Los Angeles.

SENATE HEARINGS Personal interviews, Jack Anderson, Jeff Chouinard, Robert Maheu, Harriet Huntoon; FBI Surveillance and Bugging Reports on Howard Hughes, forty-three pages; Washington, D.C., Metropolitan Police Reports on Illegal Bugging of the Hughes Suites; Dietrich reminiscences, Estate archives.

ON THE RUN Martin and Charisse, *The Two of Us*; deposition, Walter Reynolds, Estate archives; Reynolds interview by Noah Dietrich; Dietrich reminiscences; personal interview, Jeff Chouinard; bills and statements, the Schindler Detective Agency, Estate archives.

ON THE STAND Drew Pearson, *Diaries: 1949–1959*; *New York Journal-American*, Aug. 1, 1947; recording, CBS Radio Newscast, Aug. 4, 1947; Petrali, "O.K. Howard," *True*, February and March, 1975.

SPRUCE GOOSE Barton, *Howard Hughes and His Flying Boat*; Dwiggins, *Famous Flyers and the Ships They Flew*; Maguglin, *Howard Hughes*; MacDonald, *Howard Hughes and the Spruce Goose*; Odekirk, *Spruce Goose: HK-1 Hercules*; FBI documents, "The Hughes Hercules"; Bureau of Budget, "The United States at War," Government Printing Office; Senate War Hearings, vols. 6–12.

21 HOLLYWOOD CONFIDENTIAL

BUYS RKO Personal interviews, Bill Feeder, Jane Greer, William Fadiman, Tony Rogell; Greer video interview, "Howard's Way" segment of BBC RKO Pictures documentary series; Fleischer, *Just Tell Me When to Cry*; McGilligan, *Backstory*; Zimmer, *With a Cast of Thousands*; Dore Schary, *Heyday*; Schary, "I Remember Hughes," *New York Times Magazine*, May 2, 1976; *Time*, May 24, 1948; *Motion Picture Herald*, June 19, 1948; July 17 and 23, 1948; *Los Angeles Times*, July 10, 1948; Dorothy Manners, *Los Angeles Examiner*, July 18, 1948; *Motion Picture Herald*, July 17, 1948.

MITCHUM DOPE BUST Personal interviews, Robert Mitchum, Jane Greer; Mitchum video interview, Jamie Russell collection; Greer interview, "Howard's Way" segment of BBC RKO Pictures documentary series; Eels, *Robert Mitchum*; Tomkies, *The Robert Mitchum Story*; "New Dope Arrests Due in Hollywood Cleanup," *Los Angeles Examiner*, Sept. 2, 1948; "Mitchum Goes to Jail Farm," *Los Angeles Examiner*, Feb. 14, 1949; "Robert Mitchum's Story," *New York Sunday News*, Feb. 20, 1949; "Tempest Over a Tea Party," *Entertainment Weekly*, Sept. 4, 1992.

JEAN SIMMONS Personal interview, Jean Simmons; Simmons and Stewart Granger video interviews, BBC documentary; Granger, *Sparks Fly Upward*; "Jean Simmons on RKO Roster," *Los Angeles Examiner*, March 5, 1951.

RKO NETHERWORLD Personal interviews, William Fadiman, Robert Mitchum, Tony Rogell, Jane Russell; "Forgotten Man," *Photoplay*, Aug. 1950; Beutel obituary, *Los Angeles Times*, July 1, 1989.

PUTTING THE MOVE ON JANE Personal interview, Jane Russell; Russell, *Jane Russell*.

MACAO Bosley Crowther, *New York Times*, May 1952; Dietrich and Thomas, *Howard: The Amazing Mr. Hughes*.

HIS KIND OF WOMAN Personal interviews, Jane Russell, Robert Mitchum; Fleischer, *Just Tell Me When to Cry*; Williams, *The Complete Films of Vincent Price*.

THE FRENCH LINE Personal interview, Jane Russell; Russell, *Jane Russell*; Keats, *Howard Hughes*. Approximately 120 articles re. the film's controversy and release, *Variety*, *Los Angeles Times*, *Los Angeles Daily News*, *Newsweek*, and others.

UNDERWATER Personal interviews, Jane Russell, Edith "Edie" Lynch; "The Damp Art of Movieselling," *Saturday Review*, Jan. 29, 1955; "Movies Are Wetter Than Ever," *Life*, Jan. 10, 1955; "Way Down Under," *New Yorker*, Jan. 22, 1955; *Variety*, Jan. 11, 1955.

22 SEPTEMBER SONG

JEAN PETERS Depositions, Macy Todd, Jean Peters, Estate archives; Kleenex and cleanliness rules, Howard Hughes's personal logs and instructions, Estate archives.

CYD CHARISSE Martin and Charisse, *The Two of Us*; deposition, Walter Reynolds, Estate archives; Dietrich reminiscences; personal interview, Jeff Chouinard.

TERRY MOORE Depositions, Terry Moore, Dr. Verne Mason Jr., Patricia Mason, Estate archives; transcripts, Moore–Hughes recordings, provided by anonymous source; Moore, *The Beauty and the Billionaire*; personal interviews, Dr. Raymond Fowler, Dr. John Chappel, Suzanne Finstad, Walter Kane, James Wadsworth, Jeff Chouinard; Dietrich reminiscences; Finstad, *Heir Not Apparent*.

MOORE'S "PREGNANCY" Depositions, Dr. Verne Mason Jr., Terry Moore, Estate archives; Moore, *The Beauty and the Billionaire*; Finstad, *Heir Not Apparent*.

JANET LEIGH Personal interviews, Janet Leigh, Robert Scheerer; Leigh, *There Really Was a Hollywood*; Martin and Charisse, *The Two of Us*.

23 SECRET POLICE

SECRET POLICE Multiple personal interviews with Hughes security chief Jeff Chouinard, whose cover name was Mike Conrad; Gardner, *Ava*; personal interviews, Jean Simmons, Robert Mitchum, Jane Greer, Robert Scheerer, Janet Leigh; Leigh, *There Really Was a Hollywood*; Granger, *Sparks Fly Upward*; surveillance logs and reports from the Chouinard years were surveyed in their entirety; also, re. Janet Leigh, *Los Angeles Examiner*, Aug. 21, 1946.

24 GIRLS, GIRLS, GIRLS

ON THE PROWL Personal interviews, Helen Weir, Dana Wynter, Jeff Chouinard, Robert Maheu, Wallace Seawell, Joyce Taylor, Sallilee Conlon, Phyllis Applegate, Sally Bliss, Mary Brewer Dietrich; depositions, Ron Kistler, Raymond

Glen Brewer, Patricia Mason, Estate archives; "'Public Wolf No. 1," *Confidential*, April 1953; Sheilah Graham, "Chasing Howard Hughes," *Ladies Home Journal*, July 1974; Hughes organization's surveillance logs on more than thirty young women, including names, dates, places, Estate archives; dental appointment logs for various Hughes starlets, Estate archives.

IN PURSUIT OF GINA "The Girl Who Said 'No' to Howard Hughes," *Top Secret*, Summer 1954; Canales, *Imperial Gina*; memo re. Howard Hughes's Lollobrigida employment contract, dated Aug. 17, 1955, Estate archives; "Red Hot Lollobrigida Strictly a Deep Freeze Item to Howard Hughes," *Variety*, Sept. 15, 1954; personal interview, Jeff Chouinard.

SUNSET BOULEVARD LOVE NEST Personal interviews, Jeff Chouinard, Wallace Seawell; deposition, Robert Andre Poussin, Estate archives.

HUGHES HAREM Personal interviews, Phyllis Applegate, Joyce Taylor, Sallilee Conlon, and anonymous "Hughes girls."

WHY HE "COLLECTED" GIRLS Personal interviews, Dr. Anthony Dietrich, Dr. Jeffrey Schwartz.

25   TYCOON

BACK TO HOUSTON Personal interviews, Koula Dadinis, Betty Ewing, Marguerite Johnston; Serling, *Howard Hughes' Airline*.

GROWTH OF HUGHES AIRCRAFT Barlett and Steele, *Empire*; Gerber, *Bashful Billionaire*, Barton, *Howard Hughes and His Flying Boat*; Drosnin, *Citizen Hughes*; Serling, *Howard Hughes' Airline*; Dietrich and Thomas, *Howard: The Amazing Mr. Hughes*; Dietrich reminiscences; depositions, Kay Glenn, Nadine Henley, Estate archives; deposition, Robert Maheu; Maheu personal interviews; "The Problem of Howard Hughes," *Fortune*, January 1959.

FOUNDS MEDICAL INSTITUTE Barlett and Steele, *Empire*; *Baltimore Evening Sun* five-part series, April 1986; also various articles, *Las Vegas Sun*; *Las Vegas Review-Journal*; *Los Angeles Times*; Dietrich reminiscences.

BATTLES COMMIES AT RKO Personal interviews, Jeff Chouinard, Sally Bliss; Graham, *Hollywood Revisited*; Navasky, *Naming Names*; more than fifty stories re. Paul Jarrico case, including "Hughes Defies Film Writers," *Los Angeles Times*,

March 28, 1952; "Hughes Asks RKO Chain to Cancel *Limelight*," *Variety*, Jan. 28, 1953.

FATE OF *THE WHIP HAND* Personal interview, Sally Bliss.

SON OF SINBAD Personal interview, Sally Forrest; RKO press releases re. publicity tour of the Sinbadettes, author's private collection; "Price Recalls Filmmaking with Hughes," Associated Press, Nov. 25, 1979; Williams, *The Complete Films of Vincent Price*.

TWA WOES Dietrich reminiscences; Serling, *Howard Hughes' Airline*.

26 WEDDING BELL BLUES

LOOKING FOR LOVE Personal interviews, Kathryn Grayson, Ann Miller, Jeff Chouinard, Jane Russell, Bill Willard, Marjel De Lauer; Chouinard's security logs; Stuart, *The Pink Palace*; Signoret, *Nostalgia Isn't What It Used to Be*; Hearst Jr., *The Hearsts, Father and Son*; FBI Reports on Hughes's "Occupation of the Beverly Hills Hotel" and the "Glenn Davis Incident"; the "Germ Backflow Manuals," by Howard Hughes, Estate archives; Ed Smart interview, re. John Wayne in Vegas, Jamie Russell collection.

JEAN'S WEDDING Finstad, *Heir Not Apparent*; Hedda Hopper, "Hollywood's Gorgeous Mystery Girl," *Chicago Tribune Magazine*, July 11, 1954; personal interview, Raymond Strait, also, Strait's *Mrs. Howard Hughes*, including original unedited manuscript; personal interviews, Jeff Chouinard, D. Martin Cook, Kathryn Grayson; Louella Parsons collection, Margaret Herrick Library, Los Angeles; various memos, Estate archives.

THE STUART CRAMER CRACK-UP Personal interviews, Jeff Chouinard, Robert Maheu; FBI Report on "Jean Peters–Stuart Cramer–Howard Hughes."

YVONNE SHUBERT Personal interviews, Yvonne Shubert, Jeff Chouinard, Robert Maheu, Kay Glenn; Chouinard's detailed surveillance reports on Shubert, Estate archives.

NEW YEAR'S DATE Personal interviews, Jeff Chouinard, Yvonne Shubert; Mathison, *His Weird and Wanton Ways*; Hughes's Beverly Hills Hotel security logs, Estate archives.

27 SHOTGUN WEDDING

FEAR OF BEING COMMITTED Glenn Odekirk video interviews, Jamie Russell collection; Dietrich reminiscences, Estate archives; personal interviews, Kathryn Grayson, Jeff Chouinard, Mary Brewer Dietrich.

FALL-OUT WITH NOAH DIETRICH Dietrich reminiscences; Dietrich and Thomas, *Howard: The Amazing Mr. Hughes*; personal interviews, Mary Brewer Dietrich and Dr. Anthony Dietrich.

NEUROSYPHILIS Personal interviews, Mary Brewer Dietrich, Dr. Anthony Dietrich, Dr. Per-Anders Mardh, Dr. Jeffrey Schwartz, Dan Wolfe; Dietrich reminiscences.

TO TONOPAH Personal interview, D. Martin Cook; deposition, Jean Peters; Jeff Chouinard security logs and memos; news accounts, Louella Parsons collection, Margaret Herrick Library, Los Angeles; copy of certificate of marriage, dated Jan. 12, 1957, G. A. Johnson (Hughes) and Marian Evans (Peters), Nye County, Nev.; "Howard Hughes Weds Secretly," *Los Angeles Mirror*, March 16, 1957; stories of marriage (with incorrect date, purposely leaked by Hughes sources), *Los Angeles Times, Hollywood Citizen-News, Los Angeles Herald-Express, New York Daily News, Newsweek*.

BACK WITH YVONNE Personal interviews, Yvonne Shubert, Jeff Chouinard, Robert Maheu, Kay Glenn; surveillance reports of Yvonne Shubert, Estate archives.

ACCIDENTAL SHOOTING Personal interviews, Yvonne Shubert, Jeff Chouinard, Robert Maheu; Mathison, *His Weird and Wanton Ways*.

28 REFUGE

ASYLUM Kistler, *I Caught Flies for Howard Hughes*; depositions, John Holmes, Ron Kistler, George A. Francom, Estate archives; affidavit of Kay Glenn, *TWA v. Howard Hughes*; General Instructions, Romaine Street Procedures Manual, 1949, 1951, and 1952 "editions"; "How a Great Corporation Got out of Control," *Fortune*, January, 1962.

JEAN PETERS MEMOS Day-to-day memos, 504 pages; Estate archives.

29 THE MASK OF SANITY

BEVERLY HILLS HOTEL Stuart, *The Pink Palace*; Signoret, *Nostalgia Isn't What It Used to Be*; personal interviews, Jeff Chouinard, D. Martin Cook, Dr. Anthony Dietrich.

THE MISS WORLD DEBACLE Maheu and Hack, *Next to Hughes*; Mathison, *His Weird and Wanton Ways*; personal interviews, Jeff Chouinard, Robert Maheu; "How Howard Hughes Gets His Kicks," *Confidential*, June 1969.

TWA SUIT Tinnin, *Just About Everybody vs. Howard Hughes*; Serling, *Howard Hughes' Airline*; Maheu and Hack, *Next to Hughes*; Barlett and Steele, *Empire*; "The Problem of Howard Hughes," *Fortune*, January 1959; "The Bankers and the Spook," *Fortune*, March 1961; depositions, Noah Dietrich, Bill Gay, Estate archives.

RANCHO SANTA FE Personal interview, Jeff Chouinard; depositions, George Francom, John Holmes, Estate archives; "Backflow of Germs—the Robert Gross Memos," Estate archives; Barlett and Steele, *Empire*; "America's Richest Wife," *Ladies Home Journal*, Nov. 1968.

BEL AIR HOUSE Personal interview, Jeff Chouinard; author's tour of the house during interview with current owner, Zsa-Zsa Gabor.

PETERS–HUGHES RELAXATIONS Personal interview, Jeff Chouinard; deposition, John Holmes, Estate archives.

THE HUGHES DOUBLE Personal interviews, Jeff Chouinard, Jack Anderson; deposition, Brucks Randell, Estate archives; Drosnin, *Citizen Hughes*.

DRUG FLOW Depositions, Jean Peters, Dr. Verne Mason, Roy Crawford, Nadine Henley, Dr. John Chappel, Estate archives; personal interviews, Dr. Chappel, Dr. Fowler.

30 ORPHAN OF THE STORM

GAIL GANLEY AT ROMAINE Personal interview, Gail Ganley; "Riddle of an Embattled Phantom," *Life*, Sept. 7, 1962; "The Starlet Who's Suing Hughes for

$553,000," *Hush-Hush*, February 1963; "Gail Ganley Settles Case with Hughes," *Hollywood Citizen-News*, May 17, 1963.

THE PHANTOM Personal interview, Jeff Chouinard; "Riddle of an Embattled Phantom," *Life*, Sept. 7, 1962; "The Hunt for Howard Hughes," *Newsweek*, May 21, 1962; "The Bankers and the Spook," *Fortune*, March 1961; "Is Howard Hughes the Real Hero of *The Carpetbaggers?*" *Confidential,* Nov. 1962; Wood, *Confessions of a PR Man*; Dmytryk, *It's a Hell of a Life But Not a Bad Living.*

THE AIDES Barlett and Steele, *Empire*; Mathison, *His Weird and Wanton Ways*; depositions, John Holmes, Kay Glenn, George Francom, Levar Myler, James Rickard, Chuck Waldron, Roy Crawford, Howard Eckersly, Estate archives; personal interviews, Kay Glenn, Robert Maheu, Jeff Chouinard, D. Martin Cook, James Rickard.

DESERTION OF JEAN Depositions, John Holmes, Kay Glenn, Jean Peters, Estate archives; personal interviews, Jeff Chouinard, Robert Maheu, Michael Drosnin; "Train Mystery Solved; Howard Hughes Aboard," *Los Angeles Times*, July 23, 1966; accounts of "mystery train," *Los Angeles Herald Examiner*, *New York Times*, *Boston Globe*, *Newsweek*, *Time*, July 23–Aug. 1, 1966.

IN LAS VEGAS Personal interviews, Jeff Chouinard, Robert Maheu, Bill Willard, James Phelan, Oran Gragson; deposition, Robert Maheu, Estate archives; lawsuits, *Maheu v. The Hughes Tool Company* and *United States of America v. Hughes Tool Co.*; "Howard Hughes Reportedly Ill at Las Vegas Hotel," *Los Angeles Times*, Dec. 1, 1966; "Can the Real Howard Hughes . . . Still Stand Up?," *Playboy*, Dec. 1971; *Las Vegas Sun*, *Las Vegas Review-Journal*, 1966–72; Hank Greenspun *Sun* columns, 1966–72; transcripts of Nevada Gaming Control Board, 1966–72; Barlett and Steele, *Empire*; Drosnin, *Citizen Hughes*; memos from Hughes to Maheu, Estate archives.

FOOD FETISHES Phelan, *Howard Hughes: The Hidden Years*; depositions, Mell Stewart, Gordon Margulis, John Holmes, Estate archives; personal interviews, Robert Maheu, Kay Glenn.

DRUG "ADDICTION" BEGINS Daily drug logs, 1966–76, including 22-page report on Howard's drug suppliers commissioned by Hughes's nephew William Lummis and the Hughes Estate; "White Paper on the Aides-Suppliers," Drug Enforcement Administration, 1978–80, Las Vegas DEA Bureau; depositions, John Holmes, Kay Glenn, Jean Peters Hughes, Estate archives; personal interview, Robert Maheu.

CIA TIES LAPD, CIA, FBI reports on documents stolen in Romaine Street break-in; U.S. General Services Administration, "The Hughes Glomar Explorer," undated brochure; deposition, James H. Rickard; CIA memorandums, Feb. 20, March 9, Feb. 11, 1975; personal interview, Robert Maheu; *Los Angeles Times*, March 19, 1975; *Washington Post*, March 19, 1975; *Business Week*, April 7, 1975.

31 THE CAPTIVE

DRUG MANIPULATION Drug Enforcement Administration report on the Hughes Aides and Drug Administration, 355 pages; complaint of William Lummis and the Hughes Estate, 22 pages; "Guilty Pleas," by John Holmes and Dr. Verne Mason, DEA "Disposition Report"; prescription and drug logs, including dosages and records of the contraband drug shipments, Estate archives; official complaint against aides, Eighth Judicial District Court.

EASTER EGGS AND ASTRONAUTS Personal interview, Robert Maheu; Maheu and Hack, *Next to Hughes*; Drosnin, *Citizen Hughes*.

WHERE'S HUGHES? Personal interviews, Robert Maheu, Jane Russell, Marjel De Lauer; FBI reports on "The Disappearance of Howard Hughes" 1970 71; FBI secret report to J. Edgar Hoover, Dec. 3, 1970, the FBI Files; *Las Vegas Sun* and *Las Vegas Review-Journal* articles re. the disappearance, Nov. 30, 1970–June 1971; official Hughes logs, schedules, screening lists, menus, Estate archives.

CLIFFORD IRVING AFFAIR Fay, Chester, and Linklater, *Hoax*; Drosnin, *Citizen Hughes*; transcript of Hughes telephonic press conference; personal interview, James Phelan; Phelan, *Scandals, Scamps and Scoundrels*; "Con Man of the Year," *Time*, Feb. 21, 1972; "Clifford & Edith & Howard & Helga," *Time*, Feb. 7, 1972; "The Hughes Affair, Starring Clifford Irving," *Life*, Feb. 4, 1972; account of phone interview, excerpts from transcript, *New York Times*, Jan. 10, 1972.

HISTORY OF CONTROLLING LIFE STORY Memos, personal correspondence between Hughes and staff and various authors, Estate archives; personal interviews, James Phelan, Vernon Scott.

DELL PUBLISHING BUY-OUT Memos, ledgers, buy-out statements from Hughes representatives to Dell Publishing, Estate archives.

IN MANAGUA Depositions, James Rickard, Mell Stewart, Chuck Waldron, Estate archives; personal interviews, Robert Maheu, James Rickard, Jack Anderson; FBI

Hughes files, 1970–73, including J. Edgar Hoover memos, Dec. 6, 1971, Dec. 11, 1971, and February 3, 1972; "The Great Hughes Airlift," *Time*, Feb. 28, 1972; numerous articles, *Los Angeles Times*, *Los Angeles Herald-Examiner*, *Las Vegas Sun*, *Las Vegas Review-Journal*.

VANCOUVER Depositions, Chuck Waldron, Mell Stewart, Ron Kistler, Estate archives; Barlett and Steele, *Empire*; Drosnin, *Citizen Hughes*.

SALE OF TOOLCO Barlett and Steele, *Empire*; Drosnin, *Citizen Hughes*; *Los Angeles Times*, Oct. 17, 1972, *Los Angeles Herald-Examiner*, Oct. 22, 1972; "The View from Inside Hughes Tool," *Fortune*, December 1973.

FORT LAUDERDALE STOPOVER Personal interview, Jack Anderson; Anderson column of March 25, 1977.

LONDON Depositions, Jack Real, Chuck Waldron, John Holmes, Estate archives; Barlett and Steele, *Empire*; Drosnin, *Citizen Hughes*; Jack Anderson columns of August 3, 1977, Dec. 11, 1978, and May 20, 1978.

32 HOWARDGATE

HUGHES LEARNS OF WATERGATE Deposition, Jack Real; Watergate Files, Chester Davis memo, Estate archives; personal interview, Robert Maheu; Maheu memos, Maheu collection, Las Vegas; Haldeman, *The Haldeman Diaries*; Drosnin, *Citizen Hughes*; Ehrlichman FBI memo on Howard's ruthlessness, FBI Doc. 94675-99; Haldeman, *The Ends of Power*; Chester Davis's report on Watergate, Estate archives; personal interviews, John Ehrlichman, G. Gordon Liddy.

FORTUNE-COOKIE CAPER Pilat, *Drew Pearson: An Unauthorized Biography*; Associated Press articles on Donald Nixon loan, Jan. 17, 1972, Feb. 19, 1972; Mankiewicz, *Perfectly Clear: Nixon from Whittier to Watergate*; Lukas, *Nightmare: The Underside of the Nixon Years*.

33 EVIL UNDER THE SUN

DEATH IN ACAPULCO Depositions, Dr. Victor Montemayor, John Holmes, George Francom, Jack Real, Charles Waldron, Howard Eckersly, Estate archives; report on the death of Howard Hughes, Federal Police; indictment, *United States of America v. Dr. Norman F. Crane and John Morrison Holmes*, United States District Court, Las Vegas, Nevada; personal interviews, Dr. Raymond Fowler, Dr. John Chappel, Jack Anderson, Texas deputy attorney general Rick Harrison.

FLIGHT TO HOUSTON Deposition, Roger Sutton, Estate archives; various newspaper accounts including *Los Angeles Times, Los Angeles Herald-Examiner, Houston Chronicle, Houston Post, Las Vegas Review-Journal, Las Vegas Sun*, April 7, 1976; *Time, Newsweek*, April 19, 1976.

BURIAL *Los Angeles Times, Los Angeles Herald-Examiner, Houston Chronicle, Houston Post, Las Vegas Review-Journal, Las Vegas Sun*, April 7, 1976; *Houston Chronicle*, Aug. 29, 1976 and Sept. 21, 1981; Barlett and Stēéle, *Empire*; personal interview, R. A. Jones.

EPILOGUE

SEARCH FOR THE WILL AND RACE FOR THE MONEY Rhoden, *High Stakes*; Barlett and Steele, *Empire*; Finstad, *Heir Not Apparent*; "The Billion Dollar Conspiracy" (series), *Las Vegas Sun*, August 3–8, 1980; personal interviews, Suzanne Finstad, Kathryn Grayson, various attorneys who requested anonymity.

DRUGS AND LAWSUITS Personal interviews, Jack Anderson, Rick Harrison, O. Theodore Dinkins, Suzanne Finstad, Dr. Forest Tennant, Dr. John Chappel, Jane Russell; depositions, George Francom, Dr. Victor Montemayor, Walter Kane, Gordon Margulis, Estate archives; Acapulco, Mexico, police reports of March 31, April 2, April 6, 1976 and six reports, Sept. 1–20, 1976; U.S. Drug Enforcement Agency Report, Las Vegas Field Office, August 1978, 355 pages; Las Vegas Court documents, *William Lummis et al. v. Bill Gay, Chester Davis et al.*; Burt Pluyman memorandum to Rick Harrison, undated; Hughes Estate trial testimony by Dr. Raymond Fowler, Jack Real, Dr. Chappel, Nadine Henley; special documents, the Jack Anderson collection; Barlett and Steele, *Empire*; Drosnin, *Citizen Hughes*; "Kane Cries Murder," *Las Vegas Sun*, Sept. 5, 1980.

BIBLIOGRAPHY

BOOKS

ADLER, BILL. *Sinatra: The Man and the Myth*. New York: Signet, 1987.

ALLEN, OLIVER E., AND THE EDITORS OF TIME-LIFE BOOKS. *The Airline Builders*. Alexandria, Va: Time-Life, 1981.

ALLGOOD, JILL. *Bebe and Ben*. London: Robert Hale, 1975.

AMORY, CLEVELAND. *Who Killed Society?* New York: Harper & Brothers, 1960.

ANDERSON, CHRISTOPHER P. *A Star, Is a Star, Is a Star! The Lives and Loves of Susan Hayward*. New York: Doubleday, 1980.

———. *Young Kate*. New York: Henry Holt, 1988.

ANDERSON, JACK, WITH JAMES BOYD. *Confessions of a Muckraker: The Inside Story of Life in Washington During the Truman, Eisenhower, Kennedy and Johnson Years*. New York: Random House, 1979.

ARCE, HECTOR. *The Secret Life of Tyrone Power*. New York: William Morrow, 1979.

ARDMORE, JANE. *The Self-Enchanted: Mae Murray, Image of an Era*. New York: McGraw-Hill, 1959.

ASTOR, MARY. *Mary Astor: A Life on Film*. New York: Delacorte, 1967.

AUTRY, GENE, WITH MICKEY HERSKOWITZ. *Back in the Saddle Again*. New York: Doubleday, 1978.

BACON, JAMES. *Hollywood Is a Four-Letter Town*. New York: Avon, 1977.

————. *Made in Hollywood*. New York: Warner, 1977.

BARLETT, DONALD L., AND JAMES B. STEELE. *Empire: The Life, Legend and Madness of Howard Hughes*. New York: W. W. Norton, 1979.

CHARLES BARTON. *Howard Hughes and His Flying Boat*. Fallbrook, Calif.: Aero Publishers, 1982.

BELL, JERRY, WITH GAY BURK. *Howard Hughes: His Silence, Secrets & Success*. Utah: Hawkes, 1976.

BELLAMY, MADGE. *A Darling of the Twenties*. New York: Vestal, 1989.

BERG, A. SCOTT. *Goldwyn: A Biography*. New York: Knopf, 1989.

BERGMAN, INGRID, AND ALAN BURGESS. *Ingrid Bergman: My Story*. New York: Dell, 1981.

BODEEN, DEWITT. *More from Hollywood: The Careers of 15 Great American Stars*. New York: Barnes, 1977.

BOLLER, PAUL F., JR.: *Hollywood Anecdotes*. New York: Ballantine, 1987.

BOWERS, RONALD. *The Selznick Players*. New York: Barnes, 1976.

BROOKS, LOUISE. *Lulu in Hollywood*. New York: Knopf, 1982.

BROWN, DAVID. *Let Me Entertain You*. New York: Morrow, 1990.

BROWN, PETER H. *Kim Novak: Reluctant Goddess*. New York: St. Martin's, 1986.

————. *Such Devoted Sisters: Those Fabulous Gabors*. New York: St. Martin's, 1985.

BROWNLOW, KEVIN. *Behind the Mask of Innocence*. New York: Knopf, 1990.

————. *The Parade's Gone By*. New York: Knopf, 1969.

BURK, MARGARET TANTE. *Are the Stars Out Tonight?* Los Angeles: Round Table West, 1980.

BURK, TONY. *Palm Springs: Why I Love You.* Palm Desert, Calif.: Palmesa, Inc., 1978.

BURLSON, CLYDE W. *The Jennifer Project.* Englewood Cliffs, N.J.: Prentice-Hall, 1977.

BURNHAM, DAVID. *A Law Unto Itself: Power, Politics and the IRS.* New York: Random House, 1989.

CAHN, WILLIAM. *Harold Lloyd's World of Comedy.* New York: Duell, Sloan and Pearce, 1964.

CALVET, CORINNE. *Has Corinne Been a Good Girl?* New York: St. Martin's, 1983.

CANALES, LUIS. *Imperial Gina: The Strictly Unauthorized Biography of Gina Lollobrigida.* Boston: Branden, 1990.

CAREY, GARY. *Katharine Hepburn: A Hollywood Yankee.* New York: St. Martin's, 1983.

CARPOZI, GEORGE, JR. *The John Wayne Story.* New York: Arlington, 1972.

CASSINI, IGOR. *I'll Do It All Over Again.* New York: Putnam's, 1977.

CASSINI, OLEG. *In My Own Fashion: An Autobiography.* New York: Simon & Schuster, 1987.

CEPLAR, LARRY, AND STEVE ENGLUND. *The Inquisition in Hollywood: Politics in the Film Community, 1930–1960.* New York: Anchor Press/Doubleday, 1980.

CHAPLIN, CHARLES. *My Autobiography.* New York: Pocket Books, 1966.

CLARK, JAMES A., AND MICHEL T. HALBOUTY. *Spindletop.* New York: Random House, 1952.

CLARKE, GERALD. *Capote: A Biography.* New York: Simon & Schuster, 1988.

COCHRAN, JACQUELINE, AND MARYANN BUCKNUM BRINLEY. *Jackie Cochran: The Autiobiography of the Greatest Woman Pilot in Aviation History.* New York: Bantam, 1987.

COLMAN, JUANITA BENITA. *Ronald Colman: A Very Private Person*. New York: William Morrow, 1975.

CONSIDINE, SHAUN. *Bette & Joan: The Divine Feud*. New York: Dutton, 1989.

CONWAY, MICHAEL, AND MARK RICCI. *The Films of Jean Harlow*. New York: Cadillac, 1965.

CROCE, ARLENE. *The Fred Astaire & Ginger Rogers Book*. New York: Outerbridge & Lazard, 1972.

CURCIO, VINCENT. *Suicide Blonde: The Life of Gloria Grahame*. New York: Morrow, 1989.

DALLEK, ROBERT. *Lone Star Rising: Lyndon Johnson and His Times, 1908–1960*. New York: Oxford University Press, 1991.

DANIELL, JOHN. *Ava Gardner*. New York: St. Martin's, 1982.

DARDIS, TOM. *Keaton: The Man Who Wouldn't Lie Down*. New York: Scribner's, 1979.

DAVENPORT, ELAINE, AND PAUL EDDY, WITH MARK HURWITZ. *The Hughes Papers*. New York: Ballantine, 1976.

DAVIDSON, BILL. *Spencer Tracy: Tragic Idol*. New York: Dutton, 1987.

————. *The Real and the Unreal*. New York: Lancer, 1961.

DAVIES, MARION. *The Times We Had: Life with William Randolph Hearst*. Indianapolis: Bobbs-Merrill, 1975.

DAVIS, BETTE. *The Lonely Life*. New York: Lancer, 1962.

DAVIS, BETTE, WITH MICHAEL HERSKOWITZ. *This 'N That: Bette Davis*. New York: Berkley, 1988.

DAVIS, DONALD L. *Hollywood Beauty: Linda Darnell and the American Dream*. Norman, Okla.: University of Oklahoma, 1991.

DAVIS, ELLIS A., AND EDWIN G. GROBE. *The New Encyclopedia of Texas*. Dallas, Tex.: Texas Development Bureau, 1926.

DEAN, JOHN W. III. *Blind Ambition: The White House Years*. New York: Simon & Schuster, 1976.

DE CARLO, YVONNE, WITH DOUG WARREN. *Yvonne: An Autobiography*. New York: St Martin's, 1987.

DEMARIS, OVID. *The Director: An Oral Biography of J. Edgar Hoover*. New York: Harper's Magazine Press, 1975.

DICKENS, HOMER. *The Films of Katharine Hepburn*. New York: Citadel, 1971.

DIETRICH, NOAH, AND BOB THOMAS. *Howard: The Amazing Mr. Hughes*. Greenwich, Conn.: Fawcett, 1972.

DILIBERTO, GIOIA. *Debutante*. New York: Pocket Books, 1987.

DMYTRYK, EDWARD. *It's a Hell of a Life but Not a Bad Living*. New York: Times Books, 1978.

DOLENZ, MICKEY, AND MARK BEGO. *I'm a Believer: My Life of Monkees, Music, and Madness.* New York: Hyperion, 1993.

DROSNIN, MICHAEL. *Citizen Hughes: In his own words—how Howard Hughes tried to buy America*. New York: Holt, Rinehart and Winston, 1985.

DUNNE, PHILIP. *Take Two: A Life in Movies and Politics*. New York: McGraw-Hill, 1980.

DWIGGINS, DON. *Famous Flyers and the Ships They Flew*. New York: Grosset & Dunlap, 1969.

————. *Hollywood Pilot: The Biography of Paul Mantz*. New York: Doubleday, 1967.

————. *Howard Hughes: The True Story*. Santa Monica, Calif.: Werner, 1972.

EDMONDS, ANDY. *Hot Toddy: The True Story of Hollywood's Most Shocking Crime—The Murder of Thelma Todd*. New York: Avon, 1989.

EDWARDS, ANNE. *A Remarkable Woman: A Biography of Katharine Hepburn*. New York: Pocket Books, 1985.

EELS, GEORGE. *Hedda and Louella*. New York: Warner, 1973.

————. *Robert Mitchum*. New York: Franklin Watts, 1984.

EVANS, PETER. *Ari: The Life and Times of Aristotle Onassis.* New York: Summit, 1986.

FAIRBANKS, DOUGLAS, JR. *The Salad Days.* New York: Doubleday, 1988.

FAY, STEPHEN, LEWIS CHESTER, AND MAGNUS LINKLATER. *Hoax: The Inside Story of the Howard Hughes–Clifford Irving Affair.* New York: Viking, 1972.

FEHRENBACH, T. R. *Lone Star: A History of Texas and the Texans.* New York: Macmillan, 1968.

FERNETT, GENE. *American Film Studios: An Historical Encyclopedia.* Jefferson, N.C.: McFarland, 1988.

FINSTAD, SUZANNE. *Heir Not Apparent.* Austin, Texas: Texas Monthly Press, 1984.

FISHER, EDDIE. *My Life, My Loves.* New York: Harper & Row, 1981.

FLEISCHER, RICHARD. *Just Tell Me When to Cry: A Memoir.* New York: Carroll & Graf, 1993.

FOXWORTH, ERNA B. *The Romance of Old Sylvan Beach.* Austin, Tex.: Waterway, 1986.

FRANTZ, JOE B. *Texas: A Bicentennial History.* New York: W. W. Norton, 1976.

FRENCH, PHILIP. *The Movie Moguls: An Informal History of the Hollywood Tycoons.* Chicago: Henry Regnery, 1971.

FRIEDMAN, B. H. *Gertrude Vanderbilt Whitney.* New York: Doubleday, 1978.

FRIEDRICH, OTTO. *City of Nets: A Portrait of Hollywood in the 1940's.* New York: Harper & Row, 1986.

GARDNER, AVA. *Ava: My Story.* New York: Bantam, 1990.

GARDNER, GERALD. *The Censorship Papers: Movie Censorship Letters from the Hays Office, 1934 to 1968.* New York: Dodd-Mead, 1987.

GARNETT, TAY WITH FREDDA DUDLEY BALLING. *Light Your Torches and Pull Up Your Tights.* New York: Arlington House, 1973.

GARRISON, OMAR. *Howard Hughes in Las Vegas*. New York: Dell, 1970.

GEIST, KENNETH L. *Pictures Will Talk: The Life and Films of Joseph L. Mankiewicz*. New York: Scribner's, 1978.

GENTRY, CURT J. *Edgar Hoover: The Man and the Secrets*. New York: W. W. Norton, 1991.

GERBER, ALBERT B. *Bashful Billionaire: An Unauthorized Biography of Howard Hughes*. New York: Lyle Stuart, 1967.

GOLDEN, EVE. *Platinum Girl: The Life and Legends of Jean Harlow*. New York: Abbeville, 1991.

GOLDSMITH, BARBARA. *Little Gloria . . . Happy at Last*. New York: Knopf, 1980.

GOODMAN, EZRA. *The Fifty-Year Decline and Fall of Hollywood*. New York: Simon & Schuster, 1961.

GRAHAM, DON. *No Name on the Bullet: A Biography of Audie Murphy*. New York: Viking, 1989.

GRAHAM, SHEILAH. *The Garden of Allah*. New York: Gown, 1970.

————. *Hollywood Revisited: A Fiftieth Anniversary Celebration*. New York: St. Martin's, 1985.

————. *The Rest of the Story*. New York: Coward-McCann, 1964.

GRANGER, STEWART. *Sparks Fly Upward*. New York: Putnam's, 1981.

GRIFFIN, MERV, AND PETER BARSOCCHINI. *Merv: An Autobiography*. New York: Pocket Books, 1980.

GUBERNICK, LISA REBECCA. *Squandered Fortune: The Life and Times of Huntington Hartford*. New York: Putnam's, 1991.

GUILES, FRED LAWRENCE. *Marion Davies: A Biography*. New York: McGraw-Hill, 1972.

————. *Norma Jean: The Life of Marilyn Monroe*. New York: Bantam, 1970.

GUSSOW, MEL. *Don't Say Yes Until I Finish Talking: A Biography of Darryl F. Zanuck*. New York: Garden City, 1971.

GUTHRIE, LEE. *The Life and Loves of Cary Grant.* New York, London: Drake, 1977.

HALDEMAN, H. R. *The Haldeman Diaries: Inside the Nixon White House.* New York: Putnam's, 1994.

———, WITH JOSEPH DIMONA. *The Ends of Power.* New York: Times Books, 1978.

HANNA, DAVID. *Ava: A Portrait of a Star.* New York: Putnam's, 1980.

HARRIS, MARLYS J. *The Zanucks of Hollywood: The Dark Legacy of an American Dynasty.* New York: Crown, 1989.

HARRIS, RADIE. *Radie's World: The Memoirs of Radie Harris.* New York: Putnam's, 1975.

HARRIS, WARREN G. *Cary Grant: A Touch of Elegance.* New York: Doubleday, 1987.

HATFIELD, DR. DAVID. *Howard Hughes* [sic] *H-4 'Hercules.'* Los Angeles: Historic Airplanes, 1972.

HAYS, WILL H. *The Memoirs of Will H. Hays.* New York. Doubleday, 1955.

HEARST, WILLIAM RANDOLPH, JR., WITH JACK CASSERLY. *The Hearsts: Father and Son.* Niwot, Colo.: Roberts Rinehart, 1991.

HECHT, BEN. *A Child of the Century.* New York: Primus, Donald I. Fine, 1985.

HECKSCHER, AUGUST, WITH PHYLLIS ROBINSON. *When LaGuardia Was Mayor: New York's Legendary Years.* New York: W. W. Norton, 1978.

HEIMANN, JIM. *Out with the Stars: Hollywood Nightlife in the Golden Era.* New York: Abbeville, 1985.

HELENTHAL, FRANCIS J. *Howard Hughes: The Keokuk Connection.* (Pamphlet.) Texas: Francis J. Helenthal, 1976.

HEPBURN, KATHARINE. *Me: Stories of My Life.* New York: Knopf, 1991.

HESS, ALAN. *Viva Las Vegas: After-Hours Architecture.* San Francisco: Chronicle, 1993.

HEYMANN, C. DAVID. *Poor Little Rich Girl: The Life and Legend of Barbara Hutton*. New York: Random House, 1983.

HOBART, ROSE. *A Steady Digression to a Fixed Point: The Autobiography of Rose Hobart*. Metuchen, N.J.: Scarecrow, 1994.

HYMAN, B. D. *My Mother's Keeper*. New York: Berkley, 1985.

INGELLS, DOUGLAS J. *The Plane That Changed the World: A Biography of the DC-3*. Fallbrook, Calif.: Aero, 1966.

IRVING, CLIFFORD. *The Hoax*. New York: Permanent Press, 1981.

JACOBSON, LAURIE. *Hollywood Heartbreak: The Tragic and Mysterious Deaths of Hollywood's Most Remarkable Legends*. New York: Simon & Schuster, 1984.

JENKINS, DON. *Johnny Moss: A Portrait of the Finest Poker Player of Our Time*. Nevada: JM, 1981.

JENNINGS, DEAN. *Barbara Hutton: A Candid Biography*. New York: Frederick Fell, 1968.

JEWELL, RICHARD B., WITH VERNON HARBIN. *The RKO Story*. New York: Arlington House, 1982.

JOHNSTON, MARGUERITE. *Houston: The Unknown City, 1836–1946*. College Station, Tex.: Texas A & M University Press, 1991.

KANIN, GARSON. *Hollywood*. New York: Limelight, 1967.

———. *Tracy and Hepburn: An Intimate Memoir*. New York: Viking, 1971.

KATZ, EPHRAIM. *The Film Encyclopedia*. New York: Thomas Y. Crowell, 1979.

KEATS, JOHN. *Howard Hughes*. New York: Random House, 1966.

KELLEY, CHARLES J., JR. *The Sky's the Limit: The History of the Airlines*. New York: Coward-McCann, 1963.

KELLEY, KITTY. *Elizabeth Taylor: The Last Star*. New York: Simon & Schuster, 1981.

KEYES, EVELYN. *Scarlett O'Hara's Younger Sister: My Lively Life In and Out of Hollywood*. New York: Fawcett, 1977.

KISTLER, RON. *I Caught Flies for Howard Hughes*. Chicago: Playboy Press, 1976.

KLURFIELD, HERMAN. *Winchell: His Life and Times*. New York: Praeger, 1976.

KOBAL, JOHN. *People Will Talk*. New York: Knopf, 1985.

KONOLIGE, KIT. *The Richest Women in the World*. New York: Macmillan, 1985.

KOTSILIBAS-DAVIS, JAMES, AND MYRNA LOY. *Myrna Loy: Being and Becoming*. New York: Knopf, 1987.

LAGUARDIA, ROBERT, AND GENE ARCERI. *Red: The Tempestuous Life of Susan Hayward*. New York: Macmillan, 1985.

LAMARR, HEDY. *Ecstasy and Me: My Life as a Woman*. New York: Fawcett, 1966.

LAMBERT, GAVIN. *Norma Shearer*. New York: Knopf, 1990.

———. *On Cukor*. New York: Putnam's, 1972.

LAMOUR, DOROTHY, AS TOLD TO DICK MCINNES. *My Side of the Road*. Englewood Cliffs, N.J.: Prentice-Hall, 1980.

LAMPARSKI, RICHARD. *Lamparski's Hidden Hollywood: Where the Stars Lived, Loved, and Died*. New York: Fireside, 1981.

———. *Whatever Became Of . . . ?* Second Series. New York: Crown, 1973.

———. *Whatever Became Of . . . ?* Fourth Series. New York: Crown, 1973.

LASKY, BETTY. *RKO: The Biggest Little Major of Them All*. Santa Monica, Calif.: Roundtable, 1989.

LASKY, VICTOR. *It Didn't Start with Watergate*. New York: Dial Press, 1977.

LAWFORD, LADY, WITH BUDDY GALON. *Bitch: The Autobiography of Lady Lawford*. Brookline Village, Maine: Branden, 1986.

LAWRENCE, JEROME. *Actor: The Life and Times of Paul Muni*. London: W. H. Allen, 1975.

LAYTNER, RON. *Up Against Hughes: The Maheu Story*. New York: Quadrangle, 1972.

LEAMER, LAURENCE. *King of the Night: The Life of Johnny Carson*. New York: William Morrow, 1989.

————. *As Time Goes By: The Life of Ingrid Bergman*. New York: New American Library, 1986.

LEAMING, BARBARA. *Bette Davis: A Biography*. New York: Simon & Schuster, 1993.

————. *If This Was Happiness: A Biography of Rita Hayworth*. New York: Ballantine, 1989.

————. *Katharine Hepburn*. New York: Crown, 1995.

LEFF, LEONARD J. *Hitchcock and Selznick: The Rich and Strange Collaboration of Alfred Hitchcock and David O. Selznick in Hollywood*. New York: Weidenfeld and Nicolson, 1987.

————, AND JEROLD L. SIMMONS. *The Dame in the Kimono: Hollywood Censorship and the Production Code from the 1920s to the 1960s*. New York: Grove Weidenfeld, 1990.

LEIGH, JANET. *There Really Was a Hollywood: An Autobiography*. New York: Doubleday, 1984.

LENZNER, ROBERT. *The Great Getty: The Life and Loves of J. Paul Getty— Richest Man in the World*. New York: Crown, 1985.

LEROY, MERVYN, AS TOLD TO DICK KLEINER. *Mervyn LeRoy: Take One*. New York: Hawthorn, 1974.

LINET, BEVERLY. *Susan Hayward: Portrait of a Survivor*. New York: Atheneum, 1980.

LOVELL, MARY S. *The Sound of Wings: The Life of Amelia Earhart*. New York: St. Martin's, 1989.

————. *Straight on Till Morning: The Biography of Beryl Markham*. New York: St. Martin's, 1987.

LUKAS, J. ANTHONY. *Nightmare: The Underside of the Nixon Years*. New York: Viking, 1976.

MACADAMS, WILLIAM. *Ben Hecht: The Man Behind the Legend*. New York: Scribner's, 1990.

MADDOX, BRENDA. *Who's Afraid of Elizabeth Taylor?* New York: Jove/HBJ, 1978.

MADSEN, AXEL. *Gloria and Joe: The Star-Crossed Love Affair of Gloria Swanson and Joe Kennedy*. New York: Arbor House, 1988.

———. *John Huston*. New York: Doubleday, 1978.

MAGUGLIN, ROBERT O. *Howard Hughes: His Achievements & Legacy: The Authorized Pictorial Biography*. Long Beach, Calif.: WCO Port Properties, Ltd., 1984.

MAHEU, ROBERT, AND RICHARD HACK. *Next to Hughes: Behind the Power and Tragic Downfall of Howard Hughes by His Closest Advisor*. New York: HarperCollins, 1992.

MANKIEWICZ, FRANK. *Perfectly Clear: Nixon from Whittier to Watergate*. New York: Quadrangle, 1973.

———. *U.S. v. Richard M. Nixon: The Final Crisis*. New York: Quadrangle, 1975.

MANSFIELD, STEPHANIE. *The Richest Girl in the World: The Extraordinary Life and Fast Times of Doris Duke*. New York: Putnam's, 1992.

MARTIN, TONY, AND CYD CHARISSE, AS TOLD TO DICK KLEINER. *The Two of Us*. New York: Mason/Charter, 1976.

MARY, ARTHUR. *The Nine Lives of Mickey Rooney*. New York: Stein and Day, 1986.

MARX, SAMUEL, AND JOYCE VANDERVEEN. *Deadly Illusions: Jean Harlow and the Murder of Paul Bern*. New York: Random House, 1990.

MATHISON, RICHARD. *His Weird and Wanton Ways: The Secret Life of Howard Hughes*. New York: Morrow, 1977.

MCBRIDE, JOSEPH. *Hawks on Hawks*. Berkeley: University of California Press, 1982.

MCCLELLAND, DOUG. *Susan Hayward: The Divine Bitch*. New York: Pinnacle, 1973.

McCracken, Robert D. *Tonopah: The Greatest, the Richest, and the Best Mining Camp in the World*. Tonopah, Nev.: Nye County Press, 1990.

McDonald, John J. *Howard Hughes and the Spruce Goose*. Blue Ridge Summit, Pa.: Tab, 1981.

McGilligan, Patrick, Editor. *Backstory: Interviews with Screenwriters of Hollywood's Golden Age*. Berkeley: University of California Press, 1986.

————. *George Cukor: A Double Life*. New York: St. Martin's, 1991.

McIntosh, William Currie, and William Weaver. *The Private Cary Grant*. London: Sidgwick & Jackson, 1983.

Messick, Hank. *The Beauties and the Beasts: The Mob in Show Business*. New York: David McKay, 1973.

————. *John Edgar Hoover: An inquiry into the life and times of John Edgar Hoover, and his relationship to the continuing partnership of Crime, Business, and Politics*. New York: David McKay, 1972.

Midgley, Leslie. *How Many Words Do You Want? An Insider's Story of Print and Television Journalism*. New York: Birch Lane, 1989.

Miller, Frank. *Censored Hollywood: Sex, Sin & Violence on Screen*. Atlanta: Turner, 1994.

Miller, Patsy Ruth. *The Memories of Patsy Ruth Miller*. London: O'Raghailligh, 1988.

Mitchum, John. *Them Ornery Mitchum Boys. (The Adventures of Robert and John Mitchum.)* Pacifica, Calif.: Creatures at Large, 1989.

Moore, Terry. *The Beauty and the Billionaire*. New York: Pocket Books, 1984.

Morella, Joe, and Edward Z. Epstein. *Lana: The Public and Private Lives of Miss Turner*. New York: Dell, 1971.

————. *Paulette: The Adventurous Life of Paulette Goddard*. New York: St. Martin's, 1985.

————, and John Griggs. *The Films of World War II*. Secaucus, N.J.: Citadel, 1973.

MORLEY, SHERIDAN. *Tales from the Hollywood Raj: The British, the Movies and Tinseltown*. New York: Viking, 1983.

MOSELEY, ROY. *Bette Davis: An Intimate Memoir*. New York: Donald I. Fine, 1989.

MOSLEY, LEONARD. *Lindbergh*. New York: Dell, 1976.

NASS, HERBERT E., ESQ. *Wills of the Rich & Famous: A Fascinating Look at the Rich, Often Surprising Legacies of Yesterday's Celebrities*. New York: Warner, 1991.

NAVASKY, VICTOR S. *Naming Names*. New York: Viking, 1980.

NELSON, NANCY. *Evenings with Cary Grant: Recollections in His Own Words and by Those Who Knew Him Best*. New York: William Morrow, 1991.

NICHOLSON, PATRICK J. *William Ward Watkin and the Rice Institute*. Houston: Gulf, 1991.

NIVEN, DAVID. *The Moon's a Balloon*. London: Hamish Hamilton, 1971.

NORMAN, BARRY. *The Story of Hollywood*. New York: New American Library, 1987.

O'BRIEN, PAT. *The Wind at My Back: The Life and Times of Pat O'Brien*. New York: Doubleday, 1964.

ODEKIRK, GLENN E. *Spruce Goose: HK-1 Hercules: A Pictorial History of the Fantastic Hughes Flying Boat*. [USA]: Frank Alcanter, Inc. 1982.

OUDES, BRUCE, Editor. *From: The President. Richard Nixon's Secret Files*. New York: Harper & Row, 1989.

PARKER, JOHN. *Five for Hollywood*. New York: Birch Lane, 1989.

PARRISH, JAMES ROBERT. *The RKO Girls*. New York: Arlington House, 1974.

———, AND MICHAEL R. PITTS. *The Great Gangster Pictures*. Metuchen, N.J.: Scarecrow, 1976.

PARSONS, LOUELLA. *Tell It to Louella*. New York: Putnam's, 1961.

PASTOS, SPERO. *Pin-Up: The Tragedy of Betty Grable*. New York: Putnam's, 1986.

PAYTON, BARBARA. *I Am Not Ashamed*. Los Angeles: Holloway House, 1963.

PERO, TAYLOR, AND JEFF ROVIN. *Always, Lana*. New York: Bantam, 1982.

PFEIFFER, LEE. *The John Wayne Scrapbook*. New York: Citadel, 1991.

PHELAN, JAMES. *Howard Hughes: The Hidden Years*. New York: Random House, 1976.

————. *Scandals, Scamps and Scoundrels*. New York: Random House, 1982.

PILAT, OLIVER. *Drew Pearson: An Unauthorized Biography*. New York: Harper's Magazine Press, 1973.

PREMINGER, OTTO. *An Autobiography*. New York: Doubleday, 1977.

PRESLEY, JAMES. *A Saga of Wealth: The Rise of the Texas Oilmen*. New York: Putnam's, 1978.

QUIRK, LAWRENCE J. *Fasten Your Seat Belts: The Passionate Life of Bette Davis*. New York: Signet, 1990.

RAPPLEYE, CHARLES, AND ED BECKER. *All-American Mafioso: The Johnny Rosselli Story*. New York: Doubleday, 1991.

RASHKE, RICHARD. *Stormy Genius: The Life of Aviation's Maverick, Bill Lear*. Boston: Houghton Mifflin, 1985.

REILLY, ADAM. *Harold Lloyd: The King of Daredevil Comedy*. New York: Collier, 1977.

REYNOLDS, DEBBIE, AND DAVID PATRICK COLUMBIA. *Debbie: My Life*. New York: William Morrow, 1988.

RHODEN, HAROLD. *High Stakes: The Gamble for the Howard Hughes Will*. New York: Crown, 1980.

RICKENBACKER, EDWARD V. *Rickenbacker*. Englewood Cliffs, N.J.: Prentice-Hall, 1967.

ROCKWELL, JOHN. *Sinatra: An American Classic*. New York: Random House/Rolling Stone, 1984.

ROEMER, WILLIAM F., JR. *Roemer: Man Against the Mob*. New York: Donald I. Fine, 1989.

ROGERS, GINGER. *Ginger: My Story*. New York: HarperCollins, 1991.

ROONEY, MICKEY. *Life Is Too Short*. New York: Ballantine, 1991.

RUSSELL, JANE. *Jane Russell: An Autobiography*. New York: Franklin Watts, 1985.

RUSSELL, ROSALIND, AND CHRIS CHASE. *Life Is a Banquet*. New York: Random House, 1977.

SAMPSON, ANTHONY. *Empires of the Sky: The Politics Contests and Cartels of World Airlines*. New York: Random House, 1984.

SARF, WAYNE MICHAEL. *God Bless You Buffalo Bill: A Layman's Guide to History and the Western Film*. Rutherford, N.J.: Fairleigh Dickinson University Press; Cornwall Books, 1983.

SARLOT, RAYMOND R., AND FRED E. BASTEN. *Life at the Marmont*. Santa Monica, Calif.: Roundtable, 1987.

SCHARY, DORE. *Heyday: An Autobiography*. Boston: Little, Brown, 1979.

SCHATZ, THOMAS. *The Genius of the System: Hollywood Filmmaking in the Studio Era*. New York: Pantheon, 1988.

SCHORR, DANIEL. *Clearing the Air*. Boston: Houghton Mifflin, 1977.

SCHUMACH, MURRAY. *The Face on the Cutting Room Floor: The Story of Movie and TV Censorship*. New York: Morrow, 1964.

SCHWARTZ, MILTON L, AND ROBERT O. MAGUGLIN. *The Howard Hughes Flying Boat*. Long Beach, Calif.: WCO Port Properties, 1983.

SERLING, ROBERT. *Howard Hughes Airline: An Informal History of TWA*. New York: St. Martin's/Marek, 1983.

SHAPIRO, DORIS. *We Danced All Night: My Life Behind the Scenes with Alan Jay Lerner*. New York: William Morrow, 1990.

SHEPPARD, DICK. *Elizabeth: The Life and Career of Elizabeth Taylor.* New York: Warner, 1974.

SHEVEY, SANDRA. *The Marilyn Scandal.* New York: Jove, 1990.

SHULMAN, IRVING. *Harlow: An Intimate Biography.* New York: Dell, 1964.

SIGNORET, SIMONE. *Nostalgia Isn't What It Used to Be.* New York: Harper & Row, 1978.

SILVERMAN, STEPHEN M. *The Fox That Got Away: The Last Days of the Zanuck Dynasty at Twentieth Century-Fox.* Secaucus, N.J.: Lyle Stuart, 1988.

SIMPSON, COL. HAROLD B. *Audie Murphy: American Soldier.* Hillsboro, Tex.: Hill Junior College, 1975.

SMITH, ELINOR. *Aviatrix.* New York: Harcourt Brace Jovanovich, 1981.

SMITH, SALLY BEDELL. *In All His Glory: The Life of William O. Paley, The Legendary Tycoon and His Brilliant Career.* New York: Simon & Schuster, n.d.

SMITH, VI. *From Jennies to Jets: The Aviation History of Orange County.* Fullerton, Calif.: Sultana, 1974.

SOLBERG, CARL. *Conquest of the Skies: A History of Commercial Aviation in America.* Boston: Little, Brown, 1979.

SPADA, JAMES. *More Than a Woman: An Intimate Biography of Bette Davis.* New York: Bantam, 1993.

SPOTO, DONALD. *Madcap: The Life of Preston Sturges.* Boston: Little, Brown, 1990.

STACK, ROBERT, WITH MARK EVANS. *Straight Shooting.* New York: Berkley, 1980.

STAUFFER, TEDDY [MR. ACAPULCO]. *Forever Is a Hell of a Long Time: An Autobiography.* Chicago: Henry Regnery, 1976.

STENN, DAVID. *Bombshell: The Life and Death of Jean Harlow.* New York: Doubleday, 1993.

———. *Clara Bow: Runnin' Wild.* New York: Doubleday, 1988.

STINE, WHITNEY, WITH BETTE DAVIS. *Mother Goddam: The Story of the Career of Bette Davis*. New York: Berkley Medallion, 1974.

―――. *Stars & Star Handlers: The Business of Show*. Santa Monica, Calif.: Roundtable, 1985.

STINE, WHITNEY. *I'd Love to Kiss You . . . Conversations with Bette Davis*. New York: Pocket Books, 1990.

STRAIT, RAYMOND. *Mrs. Howard Hughes*. Los Angeles: Holloway House, 1970.

STUART, SANDRA LEE. *The Pink Palace*. New York: Pocket Books, 1978.

SUMMERS, ANTHONY. *Goddess: The Secret Lives of Marilyn Monroe*. New York: Onyx (New American Library), 1986.

THOMAS, BOB. *Liberace: The True Story*. New York: St. Martin's, 1987.

―――. *Selznick*. New York: Doubleday, 1970.

―――. *Thalberg: Life and Legend*. New York: Doubleday, 1969.

THOMAS, TONY. *Howard Hughes in Hollywood*. Secaucus, N.J.: Citadel, 1985.

THOMSON, DAVID. *Showman: The Life of David O. Selznick*. New York: Knopf, 1992.

TINNIN, DAVID B. *Just About Everybody vs. Howard Hughes: The Inside Story of the TWA–Howard Hughes Trial*. New York: Doubleday, 1973.

TODD, MICHAEL, JR., AND SUSAN McCARTHY TODD. *A Valuable Property: The Life Story of Mike Todd*. New York: Arbor House, 1983.

TOMKIES, MIKE. *The Robert Mitchum Story: "It Sure Beats Working."* New York: Ballantine, 1972.

TORME, MEL. *It Wasn't All Velvet*. New York: Viking, 1988.

TOSCHES, NICK. *Dino: Living High in the Dirty Business of Dreams*. New York: Doubleday, 1992.

TURNER, LANA. *Lana: The Lady, The Legend, The Truth*. New York: Pocket Books, 1982.

VALLEE, RUDY. *Let the Chips Fall*. Harrisburg, Pa.: Stackpole, 1975.

VANDERBILT, GLORIA. *Black Knight, White Knight*. New York: Knopf, 1987.

———. *Woman to Woman*. New York: Doubleday, 1979.

VAN DOREN, MAMIE, WITH ART AVEILHE. *Playing the Field: My Story*. New York: Putnam's, 1987.

VARNER, ROY, AND WAYNE COLLIER. *A Matter of Risk: The Incredible Inside Story of the CIA's Hughes Glomar Explorer Mission to Raise a Russian Submarine*. New York: Random House, 1978.

WALLIS, HAL, AND CHARLES HIGHAM. *Starmaker: The Autobiography of Hal Wallis*. New York: Macmillan, 1980.

WANSELL, GEOFFREY. *Haunted Idol: The Story of the Real Cary Grant*. New York: William Morrow, 1984.

WARRICK, RUTH, WITH DON PRESTON. *The Confessions of Phoebe Tyler*. Englewood Cliffs, N.J.: Prentice-Hall, 1980.

WATERBURY, RUTH. *Elizabeth Taylor*. New York: Popular Library, 1964.

WAYNE, AISSA, WITH STEVE DELSOHN. *John Wayne: My Father*. New York: Random House, 1991.

WAYNE, JANE ELLEN. *Ava's Men: The Private Life of Ava Gardner*. New York: St. Martin's, 1990.

———. *Crawford's Men*. New York: Prentice-Hall, 1988.

———. *Gable's Women*. New York: Prentice-Hall, 1987.

———. *Marilyn's Men*. New York: St. Martin's, 1992.

WAYNE, PILAR, WITH ALEX THORLEIFSON. *John Wayne: My Life with the Duke*. New York: McGraw-Hill, 1987.

WHITEHOUSE, ARCH. *The Sky's the Limit: A History of the U.S. Airlines*. New York: Macmillan, 1971.

WHYTE, EDNA GARDNER, WITH ANN L. COOPER. *Rising Above It: An Autobiography*. New York: Orion, 1991.

WILKERSON, TICHI, AND MARCIA BORIE. *The Hollywood Reporter: The Golden Years*. New York: Coward–McCann, 1984.

WILKIE, JANE. *Confessions of an Ex-Fan Magazine Writer*. New York: Doubleday, 1981.

WILLIAMS, LUCY CHASE. *The Complete Films of Vincent Price*. New York: Citadel, 1995.

WILSON, EARL. *Hot Times: True Tales of Hollywood and Broadway*. Chicago: Contemporary Books, 1984.

––––––. *The Show Business Nobody Knows*. New York: Bantam, 1973.

––––––. *Sinatra: An Unauthorized Biography*. New York: Macmillan, 1976.

WINCHELL, WALTER. *Winchell Exclusive: "Things That Happened to Me—and Me to Them."* Englewood Cliffs, N.J.: Prentice-Hall, 1975.

WINTERS, SHELLEY. *Shelley: Also Known as Shirley*. New York: William Morrow, 1980.

––––––. *Shelley II: The Middle of My Century*. New York: Simon & Schuster, 1989.

WOOD, ROBERT J., WITH MAX GUNTHER. *Confessions of a PR Man*. New York: NAL, 1988.

WOODY, JACK. *Lost Hollywood*. Altadena, Calif.: Twin Palms, 1987.

WOODWARD, BOB, AND CARL BERNSTEIN. *The Final Days*. New York: Simon & Schuster, 1976.

WYNNE, H. HUGH. *The Motion Picture Stunt Pilots and Hollywood's Classic Aviation Movies*. Missoula, Mont.: Pictorial Histories, 1987.

YABLONSKY, LEWIS. *George Raft*. New York: McGraw-Hill, 1974.

YEAGER, GENERAL CHUCK, AND LEO JANOS. *Yeager: An Autobiography*. New York: Bantam, 1985.

ZIEROLD, NORMAN. *The Moguls*. New York: Coward–McCann, 1969.

ZIMMER, JILL SCHARY. *With a Cast of Thousands: A Hollywood Childhood*. New York: Stein and Day, 1963.

MAJOR MAGAZINE AND NEWSPAPER ARTICLES

A note about these materials: due to the secrecy that enshrouded Howard Hughes during and after his lifetime, it was sometimes the tabloid-type publications that lifted the veil, providing hitherto unseen glimpses of the so-called Phantom. Because they frequently broke stories first, and because we found sources who later verified their reports, we utilized some non-mainstream publications for this biography.

AMORY, CLEVELAND. "The Touch of Class." *Parade*, September 22, 1985.

ANDERSON, JACK. "Hughes Loaned Nixon Kin Cash, Got 'Break.'" *Las Vegas Review-Journal*, February 9, 1972.

―――. "Hughes-Nixon Connection Scenario." *Las Vegas Review-Journal*, February 6, 1974.

―――. "Hughes Political Moves Revealed." *Las Vegas Review-Journal*, August 6, 1971.

ANKERICH, MICHAEL. "The Flight of the Elusive Dove: Billie Dove Looks Back." *Classic Images*, June 1994.

BEATTY, JEROME. "A Boy Who Began at the Top." *American*, April 1932.

BOYNE, WALT. "Speed Merchant." *Airpower*, September 1977.

―――. "The Most Elusive Hughes . . . The D-2/F-11 Recon. Bomber." *Wings*, June 1977.

BODEEN, DEWITT. "Billie Dove: An American Beauty." *Films in Review*, April 1979.

BROWNLOW, KEVIN. "Howard Hughes's Maiden Flight." *American Film*, November 1981.

BROWNSTEIN, M., M.D. AND L. SOLYOM, M.D. "The Dilemma of Howard Hughes: Paradoxical Behavior in Compulsive Disorders." *Canadian Journal of Psychiatry*, vol. 31, April 1986.

CARROLL, JIM. "Famous Hughes-tonian." *The Houston Press*, March 8–10, 1937.

"The Case of the Invisible Billionaire." *Newsweek*, December 21, 1970.

CHANDLER, JOHN. "Star-Studded Palmdale." *Los Angeles Times*, December 21, 1992.

DELL, MYRNA. "The Howard Hughes I Knew." *Hollywood Studio Magazine*, February 1991.

DROSNIN, MICHAEL. "The Great Hughes Heist." *New Times*, January 21, 1977.

DUBOIS, LARRY, AND LAURENCE GONZALES. "The Puppet . . . Uncovering the Secret World of Nixon, Hughes and the CIA." *Playboy*, September 1976.

FLEMING, THOMAS J. "He Can Make Anybody Famous for the Right Fee." *Cosmopolitan*, August 1961.

FRANK, GEORGE M. "Inside Howard Hughes' Harem." *Top Secret*, October 1957.

GOLDEN, CHARLES. "The Strange Secret Life of Howard Hughes." *National Enquirer*, February 20, 1972.

GONZALES, LAURENCE, AND LARRY DUBOIS. "Howard Hughes: Inside His Secret Files." *Playboy*, April 1977.

GRANGER, STEWART. "Which girl do you prefer, Howard? I can't make up my mind, Hughes said." *New York Post*, October 6, 1981.

GREENSPUN, HANK. "Where I Stand." *Las Vegas Review-Journal*, columns of December 2, 1966, and September 10, 1967.

GREER, JANE. "How I Broke into the Movies." *Daily News* (Los Angeles), May 20–21, 1953.

GROSS, LINDA. "Jane Greer: Out of Her Past." *Los Angeles Times*, March 4, 1984.

GUNSTON, BILL. "Howard Hughes's Amazing Aircraft." *Aeroplane Monthly*, May 1973.

HAMILTON, SARA. "Well! Well! So This Is Hepburn!" *Photoplay*, August 1933.

HEARST, WILLIAM RANDOLPH, JR. "Another Insight into Howard Hughes." *Los Angeles Herald-Examiner*, January 16, 1972.

"*Hell's Angels* Completed." *American Cinematographer*, January 1930.

HILL, DAVID. "Bernstein: Hughes Tied to Watergate." *Las Vegas Review-Journal*, November 9, 1976.

HILL, GLADWIN. "No-Man in the Land of Yes-Men." *New York Times Magazine*, August 17, 1947.

HUDSON, DON. "Howard Hughes Was My Close Boyhood Friend." *National Enquirer*, October 17, 1974.

"The Hughes Legacy: Scramble for the Billions." *Time*, April 19, 1976.

HUGHES, RUPERT. "Howard Hughes—Record Breaker." *Liberty*, February 6 and February 13, 1937.

"Hughes's Western." *Time*, February 22, 1943.

"In Search of the Invisible Man." (London) *Observer Review*, December 31, 1972.

JENNINGS, DEAN. "Hollywood's Late-Blooming Redhead." *Saturday Evening Post*, July 1, 1959.

LECERF, CAROLYN, AS TOLD TO LUCIEN BERGERAC. "How Howard Hughes Gets His Kicks." *Confidential*, June 1969.

LEYDEN, JOHN. "Facing Death with Howard Hughes." *Horizons*, October 1971.

LYONS, D. L. "America's Richest Wife." *Ladies Home Journal*, November 1968.

MARCH, JOSEPH MONCURE. "Young Howard Hughes: Reminiscences by a Survivor of Hollywood's Golden Era." *Views and Reviews*, September 1973.

McDOWELL, RIDER. "Allah Be Praised." *Premiere*, April 1992.

McKEON, JOSEPH, PETER McGUFFIN, AND PAUL ROBINSON. "Obsessive-Compulsive Neurosis Following Head Injury: A Report of Four Cases." *British Journal of Psychiatry*, 1984.

"The Mechanical Man." *Time*, July 19, 1948.

MILES, MARVIN. "Hughes Talks: Plans to End Recluse Life and Return West." *Los Angeles Times*, January 10, 1972.

MOORE, THOMAS W. "The Day Howard Hughes Almost Bought ABC." *TV Guide*, September 25, 1976.

MUIR, FLORABEL. "Hughes Secretly Signs Jean Peters as Bride." *New York Daily News*, March 16, 1957.

PETRALI, JOE, AS TOLD TO MAURY GREEN. "O.K., Howard." *True*, February and March 1975.

PHELAN, JAMES R. "Howard Hughes, Beyond the Law." *New York Times Magazine*, September 14, 1975.

"Putting on the Ritz," *Newsweek*, November 28, 1966.

"Rashomon, Starring Howard Hughes." *Time*, January 24, 1972.

REYNOLDS, RUTH. "The Man Who Has Everything." *New York Sunday News*, January 19, 1936.

ROGERS, BOGART. "4 Million Dollars and 4 Men's Lives." *Photoplay*, April 1930.

RYON, RUTH. "Howard Hughes in Hancock Park: His Happiest Years Were Spent Here." *Los Angeles Times*, July 12, 1981.

SALEMI, DOM. "The Amazing Life and Times of Mamie Van Doren." *Filmfax*, October 1990.

SAMMIS, FRED R. "The Case Against The Outlaw." *Photoplay*, September 1946.

SARRIS, ANDREW. "Jane Russell Rides Again with the Bust That Shook the World." *Village Voice*, July 19, 1976.

SAVOLI, TOM. "When Howard Hughes Wanted to Marry Gina Lollobrigida!" *Hush-Hush*, September 1959.

SCHARY, DORE. "I Remember Hughes." *New York Times Magazine*, May 2, 1976.

"The Secret World of Howard Hughes." *Newsweek*, April 19, 1976.

SEDERBERG, ARELO. "Howard Hughes Empire Rising with Purchases in Las Vegas." *Los Angeles Times*, September 17, 1967.

SHIPLER, GUY. "The Shadow Emperor." *Nevada*, January/February 1986.

SHIPP, CAMERON. "Susan Hayward." *Redbook*, February 1956.

"Shootout at the Hughes Corral." *Time*, December 21, 1970.

SIMMONS, FOSTER L. "Why Howard Hughes Said 'Yes' to Jean Peters." *Behind the Scene*, July 1957.

STAR, JACK. "Why Is Howard Hughes Buying Up Las Vegas?" *Look*, January 23, 1968.

ST. JOHNS, ADELA ROGERS. "Unmarried Millionaires: The Howard Hughes Story." *The American Weekly*, April 13, 1947.

STUMP, AL. "The Rich Man's Game." *Golf*, December 1991.

THOMAS, CARSON L. "How Howard Hughes Got His Girls," *On the QT*, July 1956.

TORME, MEL. "When the War Birds Invaded Hollywood." *Cavalier*, November 1961.

TURNER, WALLACE. "All the Hughes That's Fit to Print." *Esquire*, July 1971.

———. "Howard Hughes: A Peek at How the Man Lives." *New York Times*, December 13, 1970.

VAN PETTEN, O.W. "The Howard Hughes Nobody Knows." *West*, March 19, 1972.

WARD, ROBERT. "Mr. Bad Taste and Trouble Himself: Robert Mitchum." *Rolling Stone*, March 3, 1983.

WECHSBERG, JOSEPH. Howard Hughes. *Liberty*, December 28, 1946.

WHITE, STEPHEN. "The Howard Hughes Story." *Look*, February 9, 16, and 23, 1954.

WISE, T.A. "The Bankers and the Spook." *Fortune*, March 1961.

The authors also utilized miscellaneous articles from the following publications, some of which are cited in the text and source notes:

After Dark
The Arizona Daily Star
Associated Press Biographical Service
The Baltimore Sun
Beverly Hills Citizen
Beverly Hills Independent
Blackhawk Film Digest
Boxoffice
Bridgeport (Conn.) Post
Cavalier
Chicago Tribune
Cine Revue
Collier's
Coronet
Cosmopolitan
Cue
Current Biography
The Dallas Morning News
Detroit Free-Press
The Dial
Drama-Logue
El Paso Herald-Post
El Paso Times
Entertainment Weekly
Esquire
Exhibitors Herald-World
Family Weekly
Film Daily
Film Fan Monthly
Film News
Films in Review
Fortune
Fort Worth Star-Telegraph
Good Housekeeping
The Hartford Courant

Hollywood Citizen-News
Hollywood News
The Hollywood Reporter
Hollywood Spectator
Hollywood Studio Magazine
Houston Business Journal
Houston Chronicle
The Houston Post
Houston Press
Hughes News (of Hughes Tool
  Company)
Inside Story
Interview
The Knoxville Journal
Ladies Home Journal
Las Vegas Age
Las Vegas Entertainment
Las Vegas Israelite
Las Vegas Review-Journal
Las Vegas Scene
Las Vegas Sun
Literary Digest
Los Angeles Daily News
Los Angeles Examiner
Los Angeles Express
Los Angeles Herald
Los Angeles Herald-Examiner
Los Angeles Herald-Express
Los Angeles Magazine
Los Angeles Mirror-News
Los Angeles Reader
Los Angeles Record
The Los Angeles Times
Los Feliz Hills (Calif.) News
Mademoiselle

McCall's

The Miami Herald

The Milwaukee Journal

Modern Screen

Monthly Film Bulletin (of the
    British Film Institute)

Motion Picture Exhibitor

Motion Picture Guide

Motion Picture News

The Nation

The National Enquirer

The Nevadan

Nevada Report

Nevada State Journal

Newark Evening News

The New Republic

New Statesman & Nation

Newsweek

New York Magazine

New York Daily News

The New Yorker

New York Journal-American

(New York) Post

New York Telegram

The New York Times

The New York Times Book Review

New York Sun

New York World Telegram and Sun

Observer

Orange County Register

Pacific Film Archives

Pageant

Palm Springs Life

Parade

Pasadena (Calif.) Star-News

People

People Today

Photoplay

Quick

Rave

Rolling Stone

The San Diego Union-Tribune

San Francisco Chronicle

Santa Ana (Calif.) Daily Register

Santa Barbara (Calif.) Daily News

The Saturday Evening Post

Saturday Review

Screen Guide

Screen & TV Guide

Senior Scholastic

Shreveport Journal

(St. Louis) Post-Dispatch

This Week

Time and Tide

Tonopah Times-Bonanza and
    Goldfield News (Nev.)

Top Secret

True

Tucson Daily Citizen

USA Weekend

Us

Valley Times (Las Vegas)

Variety

The Village Voice

The Wall Street Journal

The Washington Post

Westways

Women's Wear Daily

ACKNOWLEDGMENTS

First and foremost, we wish to recognize the foresight and courage of our editor, Michaela Hamilton, who enthusiastically backed this book even though there had been more than a dozen previous books on Hughes—some of them dealing with specific aspects of his life, several of them strictly corporate, and others with specific agendas. Michaela had faith that we could be the first to get the intimate, personal, heartbreaking story of this billionaire. For that, we will be ever grateful.

Major credit must also go to our agents, Mitch Douglas of International Creative Management, and Alice Martell, of the Martell Agency—both of whom never doubted that we could crack the awesome barrier of secrecy Howard Robard Hughes had erected around himself.

Without Hamilton, Douglas, and Martell, who stood by with advice and help during the three arduous years it took to produce *Howard Hughes: The Untold Story*, this book would never have reached fruition.

Needless to say, without the dedicated support and help of our spouses, Pamela Brown and James Broeske, there would have been no book at all. Both became involved in our byzantine rigors of research, and both often assisted as well. Writers are difficult to live with, and often, even to be around. Both Pam and Jim were saints when it came to putting up with the two of us during the high points, and low points, in our frustrating but ultimately rewarding creation.

Of course, we wouldn't have teamed at all were it not for Irv Letofsky. We met through Irv during his tenure as Sunday Calendar editor at the *Los Angeles Times*. We consider ourselves lucky to have worked for him, to have learned from him, and to always be able to call on him for advice—and for editing!

Putting together a book of this scope was in itself a learning process. We thank our researchers and assistants for their patience—and their diligence. Barbara Peterson helped us organize our dozens of boxes of articles and documents, and with her brother Rick Haefele, assisted us in research as did Fawn and Hollie Coles, Terry Trahan, and Hazel Hague (who took on the task of reading stacks of nonindexed books in search of Hughes material). In New York City, Mildred F. Buglion scoured six decades of Manhattan newspapers. Margaret Jamison did the same for us in Houston. In Hollywood, ace private investigator Cathy Griffen helped in locating hard-to-find Hughes associates. Brian Zoccola did tape transcriptions and read through the entire manuscript. Sandy Hague assisted with early research and frequently bailed us out of computer problems. Claudia Hirsch helped in the organization of our mountainous source materials. Carole Huntington helped us bring it all together with her lightning-fast transcription. A special thanks, also, to Barbrah Messing, whose inside knowledge of Hollywood was invaluable, as was her advice on content. And to Penguin USA's Jory Des Jardins, for her patience and efficiency. And thank you, John M. Wilson, for your editing assistance, astute suggestions, and your friendship.

Our book's research had its origins in Hughes's hometown of Houston, where Betsy Parish of the *Houston Post* and Shelby Hodge of the *Chronicle* kindly provided advice—and introductions. Former *Chronicle* writer Betty Ewing personified southern hospitality when she welcomed us to her home the very day we telephoned.

While in Houston we met with James Overton Winston, Jr., who—in spite of illness and weakened condition—gave us more than two hours of interview time in order to finally lay to rest the cruel and inaccurate reports involving his late wife, Ella Rice, during her marriage to Howard Hughes. Mr. Winston passed away shortly afterward; we count ourselves lucky to have met him and to have heard the true story.

Special thanks to Jeff Chouinard (aka Mike Conrad), Hughes's former security chief, who made himself available to us for three full days; to Robert Maheu, former head of Hughes's Nevada empire, for his time in Las Vegas and Newport Beach and frequent telephone follow-ups; to D. Martin Cook, the Hughes attorney who provided the first eyewitness account of Hughes's bizarre wedding to Jean Peters; and also to Hughes attorney James L. Wadsworth, not only for his revelations but for his thoughtful analysis of the much misunderstood and maligned Hughes.

We are especially indebted to Hughes's most famous discovery, Jane Russell. She not only welcomed us as house guests but also gave us hours of interview time—and access to rare video footage shot by her brother, Jamie Russell. Jane Russell also introduced us to her longtime friend and co-star Robert Mitchum. Both proved as memorable offscreen as they are on.

We are privileged that silent-era actress Billie Dove broke her decades-long silence to speak with us about her love affair with Hughes. And we are deeply appreciative for Kathryn Grayson's hours of recollections about her memorable, sometimes stormy relationship with Hughes.

Ginger Rogers was a patient, repeat interview subject even during illness. And Janet Leigh was ever gracious. We were also greatly assisted by the reminiscences of Jane Greer and Jean Simmons.

Some of the best and most insightful revelations about Hughes came from women whose names are not readily recognizable. As starlets under contract to Hughes during the most tumultuous, troubling period of his life, most saw their Hollywood career opportunities slip away while Hughes played puppet master. Who knows what might have happened had things been different for Joyce Taylor, Sallilee Conlon, Myrna Dell, Yvonne Shubert, Sally Bliss (aka Carla Balenda), Phyllis Applegate, Gail Ganley, and scores of others. Their contributions to our book were significant.

One of the major breakthroughs in this book involves proof that Hughes was not insane or even emotionally disturbed, and that he was not a junkie—his intake of codeine was due to other circumstances. Beverly Beyette, "Around Town" columnist for the *Los Angeles Times*, selflessly made available to us data she has assembled for what is bound to be a trail-blazing book on the little understood obsessive-compulsive disorder, from which Hughes suffered. In addition, her co-author, Dr. Jeffrey J. Schwartz of the UCLA School of Medicine shared the most astounding discoveries from his ten-year study of Hughes's OCD syndrome. He gave multiple interviews, as did Dr. Anthony Dietrich, Noah Dietrich's son, and another scientist at the forefront of OCD studies. Additional thanks goes to Dr. Judith Rappaport of the National Institute of Mental Health, who helped us put this in proper perspective. Dr. Forest S. Tennant, one of the country's top addiction experts, shared his lengthy study of Howard's drug problems. We are also grateful to Dr. Raymond Fowler and Dr. John Chappel, both of whom did exhaustive psychological studies of Hughes, following his death.

During Hughes's lifetime, no journalists covered Hughes and his empire as aggressively as did columnist Jack Anderson and investigative reporter James Phelan. We deeply appreciate their time, and support, for our own Hughes exposé. We also count ourselves lucky that we went to Tucson to meet with former Hughes associate turned writer Marjel De Lauer. And we are grateful for the Hollywood recollections of columnist Dorothy Manners.

Veteran columnist and author Bob Thomas provided insight into Noah Dietrich, whose book he co-authored. Raymond Strait, the biographer of Jean Peters, generously provided us with his original unedited manuscript. And newsman-biographer Mickey Herskowitz helped us to untangle the complicated scenario involving Bette Davis and her affair with Hughes. Longtime Las Vegas correspondent Bill Willard shared with us his decades-old collection of Hughes clippings, as well as his memories and insight.

Other fellow writers/editors who provided their time/support include: Jane Ardmore, James Bacon, Charles Barton, Marilyn Beck, Judy Brennan, Kevin Brownlow, Margaret Burk, Joan Cohen, Marge Crumbaker, Lawrence Dietz, Bill Donati, Michael Drosnin, Bill Feeder, Joe Finnigan, Suzanne Finstad, David J. Fox, Mary Fuschi, Lee Grant, Leonard Klady, Michael Fitzgerald, Omar Garrison, Luis Gasca, Jan Herman, Marguerite Johnston, Roderick Mann, Stephanie Mansfield, Todd McCarthy, Patrick McGilligan, Maggie Murphy, James L. Neibaur, Cable Neuhaus, Ted Newsome, Ted Okuda, Lee Pfeiffer, Cheryl Pruett, Tom Pryor, Lawrence J. Quirk, David Ragan, Chris Robbins, Hugh Trevor Roper, Vernon Scott, Stephen M. Silverman, Bill Sloan, Liz Smith, Stacy Jenel Smith, Michael Sneed, David Sorensen, Donald A. Stanwood, Jeannine Stein, Lawrence Van Gelder, Jane Ellen Wayne, Tom Weaver, Dwight Whitney, Jane Wilkie, and Dan Wolfe.

Special, special thanks to colleagues Patricia Towle and Lucy Chase Williams. And to Dennis McDougal who provided Pat with a "hot line" for panicked writers.

A book of this nature could also not have been done without assistance/encouragement of our friends and families. Assisting us in our Las Vegas trips was ever-accommodating Steve Easley. Thanks, too, to Las Vegans Jimmy Chachas, Bessie Chachas, and Barbara Jones Webber. Coloradans Dan, Sylvia, and Sean Wybrant provided computer consultation, even in the wee hours! And we could always count on the computer savvy of Terry Anderson. Gina Lubrano, ombudsman editor of the *San Diego Union-Tribune*, served as an experienced sounding board; her judgment and perspective were appreciated. And for their unwavering support, thanks to Don and Ruth Broeske, Sheryl and Charlie Mather, Genevieve Lewis, Sharon McDougal, Steve Kroh, Adrienne and Arnie Weiss, Rudy and Merlin Sorensen, Steve Sorensen—and the rest of the family!

We utilized the resources of a myriad of agencies, libraries, historical societies, and other organizations and their representatives. Our thanks to Yvonne Brooks of the Library of Congress, the staff of the Office of Freedom of Information at the FBI; the Los Angeles City Hall Archives; Linda Meher and her staff of the Margaret Herrick Library, the Academy of Motion Picture Arts and Sciences (Los Angeles), especially Sam Gill, of the Academy's Special Collections, who went out of his way to allow us to view rare memos and interviews; the Louis B. Mayer Library, American Film Institute (Los Angeles); the Santa Ana (California) Public Library; the Centennial Room, Pasadena Public Library; the Pasadena Historical Society; the Burlew Medical Library, St. Joseph's Hospital, Orange (California); and the Biomedical Library, University of California at San Diego.

Also, Carolyn Kozo Cole, manager of photo collections, and the staff of the Los Angeles Public Library; Dace Taube, curator, Regional History Center, University of Southern California; the Department of Special Collections, Stanford University; the Museum of Flying, Santa Monica; the Motion Picture Editor's Guild, Los Angeles; the library at the University of Nevada, Las Vegas; director Sally McManus and the Palm Springs Historical Society; Orange County (California) Fair community relations representative Lynda Conway; the Nye County (Nevada) Recorder's Office; the Central Nevada Historical Society; the Nevada State Museum and Historical Society; the Keokuk Public Library (Iowa); the Fessenden School (Massachusetts); the Bentley Historical Library, University of Michigan; the Ava Gardner Museum (North Carolina); the Audie Murphy

Room, Greenville Public Library (Texas); the Newark Public Library (New Jersey); Roman Hryniszak of the All About Marilyn Fan Club (Los Angeles); the New York Public Library; the Coordination and Information Center, Department of Energy, Las Vegas; director Christopher La Plante, archivist Tony Black, and other staffers—especially Eddie Williams—at the Texas State Archives, Austin; the Eugene C. Barker Texas History Center, University of Texas at Austin; the Houston Metropolitan Research Center, Houston Public Library; the Howard Hughes Medical Institute; and Judy Soles of Diversified Information in El Paso.

We were also assisted by the libraries of the *Amarillo Globe-News* and *American Daily News* (Texas); the *Arizona Daily Star*; the *Shreveport Times* (Louisiana); the *Houston Post*; the *Houston Chronicle*; the *San Diego Union-Tribune*; the *Las Vegas Sun*, and by the *Las Vegas Review-Journal* and its librarian, Padminnie Pie.

For their assistance in helping us to put together the puzzle of Hughes's extraordinary life, we would also like to thank the following: Merry Anders, Mary Ann Anderson, Charlotte Austin, Ruth Bailey, Nancy Bell Bayly, Charles Bennett, Orin Borsten, Sybil Brand, Layne "Shotgun" Britton, Phyllis Brooks, David Brown, Laura Kirkland Bruce, Corinne Calvet, Esme Chandlee, Dr. Lawrence Chaffin, Joyce Compton, Jeanne Crain, Mrs. Rorick Cravens, Arthur Crowley, Peggy Cummins, Koula Dadinis, Alex D'Arcy, O. Theodore Dinkins, Yolande Donlan, Betsy Drake, Elva Kalb Dumas, Buddy Ebsen, John Ehrlichman, William Fadiman, Sally Forrest, Paul Freese, Helen Gilbert, Kay Glenn, Alex Gordon, Oran Gragson, Tom Gray, Sidney Guilaroff, Rick Harrison, Harriet Huntoon, R. A. "Bob" Jones, Ben Kamsler, Evelyn Keyes, John Krier, Dorothy Lee, G. Gordon Liddy, Billy Livingston, Ida Lupino, A. C. Lyles, Edith "Edie" Lynch, Dr. Pers-Anders Mardh, Marian Marsh, Johnny Maschio, Harry Medved, Ann Miller, Priester "Jack" Muckelroy, Anne Nelson, Dr. Patrick Nicholson, Gerald Owens, Robert H. Parrish, Harriet Parsons, Taylor Pero, "Mousie" Powell, Mala Powers, Harvey Prever, Browne Rice Jr., James H. Rickard, Tony Rogell, Robert Scheerer, Wallace Seawell, Janet Thomas, Ruth Warrick, Helen Weir, Ren Wicks, Elizabeth Rice Winston, Michael Woulfe, and Dana Wynter.

INDEX

A

Age for Love, The (film), 73, 74, 81, 389

Agnew, Spiro, 345

Aherne, Brian, 136

Air Commerce Bureau, 115, 117

Alice Adams (film), 103

All Quiet on the Western Front (film), 73, 132

All the President's Men (Woodward and Bernstein), 4, 366–67

Amarillo News-Globe, 225

American Airlines, 115, 128, 283

American Airways, 93–94

Anderson, Jack, 229, 232, 349, 358, 383

Andrews, Frank, 30, 94–95

Androcles and the Lion (film), 241, 392

Angel Face (film), 241, 392

Angell, Frank, 161, 230, 258

Anything Goes (musical), 86

Applegate, Phyllis, 270–72, 394

Apollo 13 launch, 345

Arbuckle, Fatty, 45

Archbald, Judge Henry R., 64

Arch of Triumph (film), 205

Arditto, James, 303–4

Arno, Peter, 397

Associated Press, 121, 227, 244–45, 253, 280, 289

Astaire, Fred, 83, 86, 132

Atomic Energy Commission, 340

Ayers, Fred, 127

Ayres, Lew, 132

B

Babberger, Carl, 221

Backus, Jim, 240

Bacon, James, 193, 352

Balenda, Carla, 266, 282, 392, 394
Barefoot Contessa (film), 396
Barker, Gregory, 294
Barker, Jess, 294
Barker, Timothy, 294
Barlett, Donald L., 359
Barry, Philip, 133
Bartles, Joe, 204–5
Barton, Capt. Charles, 173, 213
Battleground (film), 237–38
Bautzer, Greg, 127, 223, 265,
    290–91, 303, 326, 327
Bayly, Nancy Bell, 104–6
Beard, Daniel Carter, 15–16, 17
Beatie, Dick, 185, 186
Beauty and the Billionaire, The
    (Moore), 398
Bel Geddes, Barbara, 237
Bellamy, Madge, 42
Bell Labs, 277
Beneath the Twelve Mile Reef (film),
    253
Bennett, Constance, 42
Bennett, Robert Forster, 4, 366–67
Bergman, Ingrid, 205, 241, 390
Berlin, Irving, 57
Bernstein, Carl, 4, 366
Best of the Badmen (film), 391
Beutel, Jack, 145, 146, 166, 242,
    389, 391
Big Steal, The (film), 240, 390
Bill of Divorcement (film), 103
Birdwell, Russell, 143–44, 145, 146,
    165–66, 167
Blackman, Tony, 359–60
Blandford, Gene, 171, 172, 211
Bliss, Sally (Carla Balenda), 266,
    282, 392, 394
Blood and Sand (film), 316
Blue Lagoon, The (film), 241
Blyth, Ann, 392

Boardman, Eleanor, 23, 30
Boeing 707, 283
Bogart, Humphrey, 396
Bond, Lillian, 82
Bonney, William H. (Billy the Kid),
    144
Boston Globe, 336, 337
Bow, Clara, 53
Bowler, Walter, 305
Brando, Marlon, 398
Brandt, Harry, 103
Breen, Joseph, 165
Brewer, Raymond Glen, 268
Brewster, Ralph Owen, 228–29,
    231–32, 232, 237
Bringing Up Baby (film), 236
Brisson, Frederick, 114
Britton, Layne "Shotgun," 114
Brooks, Phyllis, 100, 113, 125, 394
Brown, Joe E., 148
Brown, S. P., 28
Brownlow, Kevin, 72
Bruce, Laura Kirkland, 33, 52
Brumley, Cal, 225
Bryan, Dyess and Colgin, 34
Bryson, Robert, 13
Burcham, Milo, 169–70
Burns, Alice, 217–18

C

Caddo Rock Drill Bit Company of
    Louisiana, 41, 72
Caen, Herb, 328
Cagney, Bill, 210
Cagney, James, 73, 210
California Institute of Technology,
    26, 40, 94, 126
Callaway, Kitty (cousin), 26, 34
Capone, Al "Scarface," 73, 229,
    389

Captain from Castille, The (film), 227, 398
Carl Byoir & Associates, 234
Carmichael, Hoagy, 241
Carpetbaggers, The (Robbins), 332
Carroll, Earl, 234
Carroll, Harrison, 72, 196
Carroll, Nancy, 82–83, 84, 394
Cassini, Oleg, 202, 399
Castaways Hotel, 339
Central Intelligence Agency, 257
  contracts with, 276, 277
  documents stolen, 3–4
  and Glomar project, 3–4, 345–47
  and Lockheed, 292
  and Nixon, 362, 365
  and Watergate, 367
Chaffin, Dr. Lawrence, 217, 218, 219, 373
Champion, Gower, 255
Champion, Marge, 255
Chaplin, Charlie, 38, 42, 130, 193, 282
Chappel, Dr. John, 182, 328–29, 373, 379
Charisse, Cyd, 230, 248–49, 257, 394
Chasen, Dave, 205
Cherrill, Virginia, 98
Chicago Daily News, 109
Chicago Daily Tribune, 110
Chickering, Dr. H. T., 18, 22
Chouinard, Jeff, 258–59, 262, 267, 268, 269, 270, 281, 288–89, 290, 291, 297, 309, 322, 323, 324, 325, 327–28, 333, 337, 338
Christy, Jack, 268
Chrysler company, 75
Citizen Hughes (Drosnin), 349, 364
Citizen Kane (film), 236

Civil Aeronautics Association (CAA), 173
Civil Aeronautics Board, 228
Clark, Robert, 229
Clarke, Frank, 50
Clift, Montgomery, 242
Cline, Ceco, 171, 173
Cock of the Air (film), 73, 81, 389
Cohn, Harry, 223
Colby, William, 346
Collyer, June, 54
Colman, Ronald, 99
Colson, Charles, 366, 367
Columbo, Russ, 84
Confidential magazine, 274, 289, 322
Congressional Record, 281
Conlon, Sallilee, 267–68, 394
Connon, Hal, 44
Connor, Harry P. M., 120, 121
Connors, Mike, 252–53
Conquerer, The (film), 282, 393
Constellation ("Connie", Aircraft Number 0–49), 129
  demo flight, 183
  launched, 205–6
  test flight, 169–70
Convair, 277
Cook, D. Martin, 195, 303–5
Cook, Judy, 131
Cook, Raymond, 303, 306
Cooper, Merian C., 82
Coward, Noël, 86
Crain, Jeanne, 293
Cramer, Stuart, 111, 291–94
Crane, Cheryl, 200, 201
Crane, Dr. Norman, 308, 380, 381
Cravens, Mary Cullinan, 12–13, 43
Crawford, Joan, 42, 82, 138, 148, 193, 394–95
Crawford, Roy, 332
Cronkite, Walter, 345

Cukor, George, 101–2
Cutton, Rudolph, 75
Cygnus (yacht), 353, 354

D

Dadinis, Harres, 275
Dadinis, Koula, 275–76
Daily Mirror, 361
Daily Variety, 217
Daniels, Bebe, 55
D'Arcy, Alex, 82
Darnell, Linda, 316, 395
  affair with HRH, 201–2, 206–7,
    210
  and XF-11 crash, 218, 219
Davies, Marion, 36, 56, 57, 222,
    223, 234, 396
Davis, Bette, 133–34, 148, 395
Davis, Chester, 323, 327, 333, 351,
    355, 356, 358, 361, 367, 380,
    381
Davis, Glenn, 252, 288
Davis, Mike, 1
Davis, Lt. Ralph N., 105–6
Dawn Patrol, The (film), 73
DC-8 (plane), 283
De Carlo, Yvonne, 368, 395
  affair with HRH, 194–99, 210
  and aviation, 206, 212
  bugged by FBI, 3
  love letters, 2
  and XF-11 crash, 218, 221
De Cicco, Pat, 82, 89, 104, 106,
    258–59, 399
  marries Vanderbilt, 141, 142
"Deep Throat," 4, 366–67
Defense, Department of, 276–80
De Havilland, Olivia, 135–36, 148,
    395
De Lauer, Marjel, 348–49

Dell Publishing, 350
Delmotte, Raymond, 94
De Mille, Cecil B., 57
Desert Inn, 339, 340–41, 344–45
Depression, 74–75, 77
Destination Tokyo (film), 148
Dietrich, Dr. Anthony, 184, 185,
    273
Dietrich, Marlene, 138, 148
Dietrich, Mary, 302, 307
Dietrich, Noah, 30, 34, 150
  and aviation, 68–69, 93
  and goals of HRH, 40–41, 115
  and *Hell's Angels*, 48, 50, 53, 71,
    72
  hired, 36–37
  and Hughes Tool, 77, 126–27
  informs HRH he's broke, 74–77
  and lovers and wives of HRH,
    41–44, 195
    Domergue, 156, 157, 209–10
    Dove, 57, 60, 61, 62, 81
    Ella Rice Hughes, 44, 46, 51,
      52, 54, 55, 59–60
    Gardner, 159, 160, 161, 162
    Hepburn, 117
    Peters, 224, 246, 293, 294, 303
    Rogers, 137–38
  and mental problems of HRH,
    167, 182, 183, 184, 185
    disappearances, 91–92, 191
    first mental collapse, 66–67
    hypochondria, 89–90
    paranoia, 88–89
    plan to have committed, 301–3
  and movies, 74–75
  and Nixon, 365
  on personality of HRH, 39–40
  quits, 306–7, 331
  on scientists and defense contracts,
    278, 279

and Senate investigation, 229,
    231–33
and sexuality of HRH, 100
and *Silver Bullet* plane, 94–95
and spending by HRH, 40–41
and TWA, 128, 283–84
and womanizing by HRH, 83, 84,
    85, 87, 203, 204
and XF-11 crash, 217, 219, 302–3
Dixon, Joan, 391
Dodge City (film), 135
Dolenz, George, 390–91
Domergue, Faith, 2, 296
    and Ava Gardner, 159–64
    career, 240, 390, 391, 395
    and deafness of HRH, 18
    discovers mementos, 152–53
    leaves HRH, 209–10
    meets and engaged to HRH,
        150–58, 159
    and mental collapse of HRH, 169,
        173, 180–82
    and womanizing, 195, 198
Double Dynamite (film), 391
Douglas Aircraft, 150, 283
Dove, Billie, 2, 36, 100, 149, 152,
    178, 368, 389, 395
    affair with HRH, 52–53, 56–65, 68
    contract bought, 73–75
    divorce, 61–65, 67, 75
    and Harlow, 69
    and HRH's success, 71, 72
    leaves HRH, 78–81, 199
Dowler, Beatrice, 66, 100, 113, 149
Drosnin, Michael, 349, 364
Drug Enforcement Administration,
    329, 344
    report on death, 380, 381–82
D-2 bomber (*later* XF-11), 130–31
Duff, Howard, 259–60
Dumas, Elva Kalb, 12, 45

Dummar, Melvin, 377
Dunne, Irene, 98
Durkin, Sgt. William Lloyd, 215

E

Earhart, Amelia, 95
Eckersley, Howard, 332
Ehrlichman, John D., 364
Eighteenth Amendment
    (Prohibition), 38
Eisenhower, Dwight D., 280
Ekberg, Anita, 258
Emerson, Faye, 130–31
Empire (Barlett and Steele), 359
Enright, Florence, 271
Europa (ocean liner), 78
Everybody's Acting (film), 41, 388
Ezell, Marvin K., 190

F

Face on the Cutting Room Floor, The
    (Schumach), 208
Fadiman, William, 238–39
Fairbanks, Douglas, 38
Fairchild, Sherman, 164
Falcon missile, 277
Farish, Libby Rice (sister-in-law),
    32–34, 43, 46, 51, 52–53, 55,
    59–60, 62
Farish, William Stamps, 10, 32,
    52–53, 62, 74, 76
Fay, Mary Smith, 377
Federal Bureau of Investigation
    (FBI), 100
    and death, 373
    files stolen, 3
    and Maheu, 345–46
    mental health report, 278–79
    and Nixon, 366

Federal Bureau of Investigation –
  (cont.)
  and proof HRH alive, 341
  search for HRH, 347–48
  surveillance of HRH, 155,
    194–95, 196–99, 225, 228–29,
    231–32, 288
  and XF-11 bomber sale, 131
Feeder, Bill, 217, 236–37
Felt, Richard, 171–72, 173
Ferguson, Homer, 229, 233
Fessenden, Frederick James, 19
Finstad, Suzanne, 27, 251, 377–78
Fitz, Buron, 106
Fleischer, Richard, 237
Flexner, Dr. Simon, 18
Flying Down to Rio (film), 83
Flying Leathernecks (film), 391
Flynn, Carl, 86, 250–51
Flynn, Errol, 130, 135, 166, 193
Flynn, Michael J., 110
F-102 (supersonic interceptors), 277
Fontaine, Joan, 135, 136, 241, 395
Food and Drug Administration, 380
Forbes, Malcolm, 274
Ford, Gerald R., 358
Forever Amber (film), 206
Forrest, Sally, 282, 391
42nd Street (film), 83
Foster, Florence, 113
Fowler, Dr. Raymond, 15, 43, 155,
  182, 207, 251, 273–74, 320, 342
Fowler, Will, 209
Francom, George A., Jr., 303–4,
  332, 349, 368, 369, 370, 382
Frazier, Brenda Duff, 2, 139–40,
  395
French Line, The (film), 244–45, 393
Freud, Sigmund, 38
From Here to Eternity (film), 240
Frontier Hotel, 271, 339

Front Page, The (film), 73, 236, 389
Frye, Helen, 201
Frye, Jack, 128, 129, 162, 170, 201,
  228, 284
Furth, Frederick, 327
Furthman, Jules, 146

G

Gable, Clark, 73, 200
Gambling House (film), 240–41, 391
Ganley, Gail, 330–31, 396
Gano, Annette (aunt), 7, 10, 15, 23
  and buyout, 30, 31
  and death of Howard, Sr., 29
  marries Lummis, 28
  raises HRH, 24–28
  See also Lummis, Annette Gano
Garbo, Greta, 38, 138, 223
Gardner, Ava, 156, 195, 368, 391,
  396, 399
  breaks off affair, 210
  bugged by FBI, 3, 198
  divorce, 288
  on HRH, 164
  love letters, 2
  meeting and affair with HRH,
    159–64, 243, 287
  and mental collapse of HRH,
    167–69, 171, 172–73, 183
  and Peters, 334
  returns engagement ring, 198
  surveillance of, 161–62, 256,
    259–60, 262
  and XF-11 crash, 218
  wealth thrown at, 5
Gardner, Beatrice (Bappie), 160,
  162
Garfield, John, 148, 399
Garson, Greer, 159
Gay, Frank William (Bill), 263, 286,

291, 292, 297, 307, 310, 317
  battle with Maheu for control,
    337, 346–48
  and Irving biography, 351
  kidnaps HRH, 347–50
  and Las Vegas operations, 348
  and death of HRH, 380, 382–83
  and Peters, 337
  takes over HRH empire with
    Mormons, 331–32, 343, 359,
    380–82
  and Toolco sale, 355–58
General Electric, 277
Gentlemen Prefer Blondes (film), 242
Getty, J. Paul, 376
Giancana, Sam, 339–40
Gibson, Rev. Robert T., 375
Gilbert, John, 53
Gilda (film), 223
Glenn, Kay, 332, 380
Glomar Project (operation to raise
  Russian submarine), 3–4, 346
Goddard, Paulette, 205
Goldwyn, Samuel, 160, 206
Gone With the Wind (film), 136,
  143, 294
Grable, Betty, 148
Graham, Sheilah, 265
Grahame, Gloria, 253
Granger, Stewart, 241–42
Grant, Cary, 200, 210, 394
  becomes friend of HRH, 98–103,
    150
  and Hepburn romance, 101–3,
    111–14, 119–20, 124–25, 138
  house used by HRH, 187, 238,
    248, 288
  on HRH and clothes, 194
  and Ingrid Bergman, 205
  and Irving biography, 351
  on last days of HRH, 360

and Peters, 234
and Senate investigation, 225–27,
    230, 231
and XF-11 crash, 218, 222
Grant, Dave, 221
Graves, Ralph, 37–38, 388
Grayson, Kathryn, 2, 248, 396
  ends involvement, 305
  pursued by HRH, 285–88, 290,
    294
  marriage proposal, 291–93, 300–2
  spied on, 257
Greenspun, H. M. "Hank," 347–48,
    367
Greer, Jane, 195, 221, 390, 396
  and mental breakdown of HRH,
    174–79
  RKO career killed, 237, 240
  spied on, 256–57
Greer, Mrs. (Jane's mother), 177
Groesbeck, Gerald, 139, 140
Gross, Robert, 128–29, 276, 283
Guest, Charles, 144, 174

H

Hackett, Buddy, 339
Haldeman, H. R., 4, 364, 365, 366,
    367
Hall, James, 53, 389
Hamilton, Dr. Gavin, 23
Hanna, David, 160, 259
Hard, Fast and Beautiful (film), 391
Harlow, Jean, 2, 144, 149, 218, 396
  affair with HRH, 69–70
  in Hell's Angels, 54, 71, 72, 389
  stardom, 72, 73
Harmon International Trophy, 111
Harold's Club (Reno), 339
Harrison, Rick, 373, 379
Havoc (film), 42

Hawks, Howard, 73, 145, 242, 389
Hays, Will, 165
Hays Office, 73, 84
Hayward, Susan, 2, 282, 393, 396
  dates HRH, 294–99, 300
  spied on, 258
Hayworth, Rita, 148, 156, 195, 316, 396
  abortion, 223
Hearst, William Randolph, Jr., 44, 87
  on HRH's deterioration, 260–61
Hearst, William Randolph, Sr., 36, 56, 69, 87, 149, 334
Hecht, Ben, 36, 73, 389
Heir Not Apparent (Finstad), 377–78
Heller, Wilson, 69–70
Hell's Angels (film), 2, 3, 58, 78, 90–91, 389
  converted to talkie, 53–55
  cost of, 53, 67
  crash, 150
  finished, 67–70, 79
  HRH makes and directs, 48–51
  premiere, 70–72
Henley, Nadine, 263, 303, 319, 348
  and death of HRH, 380–81
  and Mormon aides, 331
Hepburn, Dr. Thomas Norval, 115–16, 117
Hepburn, Katharine, 80, 303, 368, 396–97
  affair and near marriage to HRH, 107–20
  and aviation, 112, 204
  as "C.M.", 152–53
  comeback, 133, 138
  and deafness of HRH, 18, 102, 116
  family, 115–16
  and global flight, 119–24
  love letters, 2
  meets HRH, 101–103
  refuses to marry, 124–25, 132–33
Hepburn, Katharine (Kate's mother), 115–16
Herskowitz, Michael "Mickey," 134
Hesse, Paul A., 270
His Kind of Woman (film), 244, 391
Hitchcock, Alfred, 136, 397
Hitler, Adolf, 115, 121
Hoffa, Jimmy, 339
Holiday Affair (film), 255, 390
Holliday, Raymond, 346, 355, 356
Hollywood Citizen-News, 64, 219
Hollywood Examiner, 64
Hollywood Reporter, 236, 239
Holm, Celeste, 205
Holmes, John "Johnny," 316–17, 332, 333, 373, 380
Hoover, J. Edgar, 3, 196–97, 279, 281, 341, 347, 364
Hope, Bob, 148, 242
Hopper, Hedda, 281, 289
Horner, Jack, 14
Hough, Stan, 343, 377, 398
House Un-American Activities Committee (HUAC), 281, 282
Houston Chronicle, 35, 217
Houston Post, 13, 28, 124, 217
Houston Press, 29
Houston Superior Court, 252
Houstoun, Janet Gano (aunt), 31, 34
Howard, Charles (pseudonym), 92–93
Howard Hughes' Airline (Sterling), 129
Howard Hughes Medical Institute, 280, 377
Howard R. Hughes Medical Research Laboratories, 34–35
Hughes, Allene Gano (mother)

and birth of HRH, 6–7, 8
childhood of HRH, 10–12,
    14–21, 22, 175
death of, 23–24
and death of HRH, 369
emotional problems, 22–23
letter before death, 29–30, 181
lovers resemble, 195, 273
marries Howard, Sr., 7–8
obsessive-compulsive disorder, 185
Hughes, Ella Rice (first wife), 4, 93,
    98, 181, 377
divorce, 59–60, 62–63
divorce payments deferred, 74–75,
    76
marriage nears divorce, 51–55
marries HRH, 31–36
moves to LA with HRH, 35–36,
    44–45
and other women in HRH's life,
    195
and personality of HRH, 39
rebuffed by HRH, 42–43, 45–46
and will of HRH, 35, 377
and womanizing, 46
wooed after divorce, 85
Hughes, Felix (grandfather), 181
Hughes, Felix (uncle), 16
Hughes, Howard Robard, Jr.
aides (Mormon Mafia)
    claim to find will, 377
    and confidentiality, 332
    conspiracy suit against, 380
    control HRH with drugs, 329,
        337, 349–50, 352–54,
        359–60, 381–83
    and death in Mexico, 368–74
    destroy marriage to Peters,
        331–38, 342
    and FBI search for HRH,
        347–50

force Hughes Tool sale, 353–58
Gay takes control as Maheu
    ousted, 337, 344–48
murder theory, 378–83
and psychotic episode at
    Nosseck's, 315–20
reason hired, 331–32
scare tactics of, 353
transport HRH to Bahamas,
    Nicaragua, Vancouver and
    London, 349–60
auto accidents
and blackout, 183–84
and concussion, 136–37
death of pedestrian, covered up,
    104–6
aviation
bomber sales to War
    Department, 130–31
breaks altitude record, 107–9
builds Silver Bullet, first plane,
    93–97, 107–9
buys TWA and transforms
    commercial air travel,
    127–30
disappears and works for airlines
    becoming co-pilot, 92–94
early love of, 19, 27
flight school as youth, 26–27
Harmon International Trophy,
    111
highlights of career, 384–87
last flight piloted by, 359–60
makes movie about, 47–51
mental lapse and deaths during
    test of amphibian, 169–74,
    185
near-fatal crash, 211–20
planes collected, 274
record-breaking global flight,
    114, 115, 117–24

Hughes, Howard *(cont.)*
    and Spruce Goose, 159, 182,
        199, 209, 234–35
    stunt flying, 49–50, 68–69
    ticker tape parade, 124
    tours with Hepburn, 112
    and womanizing, 204–7
    XF-11 contract cancelled, 209
    WWII sales, 157–59, 182
    beat up by Moore's husband,
        288–89
    biographies and, 350–51, 369–70
    Irving hoax, 350–52
    birth of, 6–9
    bizarre behavior *(see also*
        disappearances; mental
        problems)
    banana-nut ice cream, 340–41
    clothes and eccentric dress, 89,
        194, 320
    Egg Hunt cancelled, 344–45
    fear of germs, 176, 195, 247–48,
        260–62, 320, 324, 326
    first appears, 88–94
    food fetishes, 89, 141, 311–14
    and grotesque image of, 352,
        353–54, 358
    increases during WWII years,
        165
    Kleenex directives, 247–48,
        260–62, 316–18
    childhood, 10–20
    Aunt raises after mother's death,
        24–25
    camp in Poconos, 15–16, 17
    inventions and talent, 12–14
    and communist threat, 281–82
    death of, 368–74
    autopsy, 374, 378–79
    funeral, 374–75
    murder theory, 378–80, 382–83
    rumors of murder, and double
        hired, 348–49
defense contracts, 209
    for Air Force, 233–34, 277–279
    for CIA, 3–4, 345–47
    first bomber, 130–31
    problems with scientists, 276–80
    secret-weapon projects, 196
    and WWII, 157–59, 182
disappearances
    anonymous visits to Houston,
        275–76
    arrest of, in Louisiana, 190
    double hired to evade Senate
        subpoenas, 327–28
    early fascination with
        masquerades, 63
    escapes to Louisiana and Florida
        after breakdown, 185–92
    first, to work for airlines, 91–93
    with Grant and Peters in 1947,
        225–27
    Las Vegas officials require proof
        he is alive, 341–42
    FBI search for, 347–50
    and need to hide, 287
    during *Outlaw* filming, 149–50
    and psychotic episode at
        Nosseck's, 315–20
    roams LA followed by security
        forces, 287–88
drug abuse, 184
    aides use to control fortune,
        344–48, 350, 353, 355,
        380–83
    begun with morphine given
        after crash, 219–21
    codeine, 221, 323, 327, 328–29,
        341–42
    and death, 368, 369, 372,
        378–83

detoxifies for last flights, 359–60
discovered by FBI, 279
and inability to meet with Las
Vegas officials, 341–42
and OCD, 328–29
and psychosis after marriage to
Peters, 312, 323–29
Ritalin prescribed, 323, 325
and sex life, 271
and syphilis, 279
tries to quit, 332–33
Valium, 328, 329, 341, 342
education, 11, 17, 19–22, 25,
26–27
estate battle after death, 376–83
and drug abuse report, 379
legal, sexual and psychological
abstract for, 100
and "marriage" to Moore, 251,
252
and manipulation by Mormons,
344
message to Peters interception,
336
settlement, 383
family
background, 6–10
fortune, 10–12
heirs, 377
father
death of, 28–29
relationship with, 10, 12–16,
18–20, 27
will, 29
finances
broke during Depression, 74–76,
86
at death, 368–69
and estate settlement, 383
and first marriage, 34
and first successes in movies, 4

fortune stolen by aides, 382–83
and Hell's Angels, 53, 72
and Hepburn, 113
and Hughes Toolco recovery, in
1930s, 126–27
and military contracts, 277, 280
and payoff to Dove's husband, 62
and stock market, 40, 75
and TWA's decline, 284
and wild spending, 37–41, 75
and windfall from TWA, 339
friendship with Cary Grant,
98–103
goals, 40–41, 115
and Granger murder plot, 242
health
aviation accidents damage brain,
50–51, 150, 171–74, 214–22
auto crashes and concussions, 68,
136–37
as child, 11, 14–18
deafness, 18, 78–79, 102, 116,
266
feigned paralysis or polio as
child, 17–19
hypochondria becomes
exaggerated, 89–90
"neurosyphilis" paresis and
ataxia, 302–3, 354
secret plastic surgery, 221
spinal meningitis, 58–59
syphilis, 90–91, 279, 302–3,
353–54, 374
syphilis treatments, 90–91
and Hollywood society, 36, 38–39,
45, 55, 56–57, 82–83
homes
Agua Caliente, 2, 39, 69, 87
Bel Air, 323–29, 334
Krupp ranch, 340, 342
Muirfield, 111, 149–50, 155–56

Hughes, Howard *(cont.)*
  Sorbonne Road estate, 156–57
  Hughes Tool
    buys out relatives after father's
      death, 30–31
    drill bit developed, 127
    management of, 126–27
    sale, 353–58
    takes control and builds
      company, 74–77
  interviews
    with IRS agent, 358
    refuting Irving, 351–52
    with Somoza, 354
    with SEC, 355–56
  Las Vegas
    Desert Inn Easter Egg Hunt
      cancelled, 344–45
    Desert Inn purchase, 339, 340–41
    plans to change, 338–42
    as refuge, 289–90
  lawsuits against, 287
  legacy of, 375
  letters and papers stolen, 2–5
  love affairs
    with Ava Gardner, 159–64, 210
    with Bette Davis, 133
    with Billie Dove, 52–53, 56–65,
      69, 74–75, 78–82
    with Brenda Frazier, 139–40
    with Faith Domergue, 150–64,
      209–210
    with Ginger Rogers, 83–84,
      132–39
    with Gloria Vanderbilt, 140–42
    with Jane Greer, 174, 237
    with Jean Harlow, 69
    with Jean Peters, 210–11,
      225–27, 230–31, 246–48,
      290–94
    with Joan Fontaine, 136
    with Katharine Hepburn,
      101–3, 107–20, 124–25, 138
    with Kathryn Grayson, 285–88
    with Lana Turner, 199–202
    letters stolen, 2–3, 4
    with Linda Darnell, 201–2
    with Liz Taylor, 223–24
    with Marilyn Monroe, 202–3
    with Rita Hayworth, 223
    with Terry Moore, 249–53
    with Yvonne De Carlo, 194–99
    with Yvonne Shubert, 307–11
  "marriage" at sea to Moore,
    250–51
  marriage proposals
    to Gardner, 160
    to get women to bed, 207, 271
    to Grayson, 291–93, 300–2
    to Hepburn, 109–10
    to Rogers, 133, 134–35
    to Shubert, 296
    simultaneous, to Turner and
      Darnell, 201–2, 207
  marriage to Ella Rice
    arranged, 31, 32–36, 39
    difficulties, 43–47, 51–55
    divorce, 58–63
    woos after divorce, 85
  marriage to Jean Peters, 272,
    303–7, 311–14
    divorce from Peters, 342–43
    Mormon aides destroy, 331–38
  mental problems
    addiction to psychodrama and
      danger, 162
    caused by head injuries and
      OCD, 317, 320
    collapse into psychosis at
      Nosseck's, 315–20
    condition worsens after plane
      crashes, 165, 167–74

and defense contracts, 276–80

Dietrich's attempt to have committed, 301–3

and first aviation crash, 51

first emotional collapse, 66–67

neurotic dependence on infirmity, as child, 17–18

noted by Hearst, 260–62

obsessive-compulsive disorder (OCD) onset, 180–92

OCD and drug habit, 328–29

OCD and food fetishes, 312–14

OCD and girl collecting, 267–68, 273–74

OCD becomes psychosis, 317–20

probed by FBI, 278–79

psychological profile, 15

and drug abuse during marriage to Peters, 323–29

and pursuit of Jane Greer, 174–79

and RKO disarray, 281–82

and syphilis, 91, 302–3

temper tantrums begin, 324–25

and treatment of first wife, 43

and treatment of women, 155, 273–74

and TWA problems, 281, 283–84

mother
  death of, 23–26
  emancipated from, 20–22
  last letter, 181
  unhealthy relationship with, 10–12, 14–20, 180–81

moves
  to Bahamas hideout with aides, 349–54
  to Boston leaving Bel Air mansion, 334–338

  to Houston from California as teen, 27–28
  to Las Vegas, 337–42
  to London after Managua earthquake, 356–60
  to Los Angeles with first wife, 35–36
  to Nicaragua, 354–58
  to Southern California after mother's death, 26–27
  to Vancouver, 354

movies
  becomes producer, 36, 37–38, 41
  buys RKO Pictures, 236–45
  censorship system broken, 208, 244–45
  company launched, 41
  costumes for Harlow, 69
  costumes for Russell, 244–45
  directs Hell's Angels, 47–51, 53–55, 68–72
  early color lab, 73
  early interest in, 26, 27
  filmography, 388–93
  financing difficulties, 74–77
  and Harlow discovery by, 54
  produces and directs The Outlaw, 143–48, 158, 165–67, 242
  and RKO disarray, 281–82
  and Russell's career, 242–45
  and Scarface, 73–74, 80, 84–85

murder of Johnny Rand, 309–10

nicknamed "the Phantom", 240

paranoia, 88–91
  and Faith Domergue, 154
  FBI on, 278–79
  used by aides to control, 344–48

personality
  "avoider" syndrome and hypochondria, 14–15

Hughes, Howard (cont.)
    loneliness as child, 12–14
    obsessive nature, 39–40
  pregnancies of lovers, 91
    of Hayworth, 223
    of Moore, 253
    of Shubert, 307–8
  Romaine Street fortress
    acquired, 73
    as communications center,
        262–63, 313–14
    controlled by Mormons, 331
    mementos sent to, 150
    raid and theft, 2–6
  Senate investigation of, 228–33
  sexuality and appeal of, 193–94,
        199, 201
    homosexuality rumors, 100, 193
  spied on
    by CIA, 3–4, 345–47, 362, 365,
        367
    by D.C. police, 232
    by FBI, 4, 131, 155, 194–99,
        225, 228–29, 231–32,
        278–79, 288, 341
  spies on lovers and enemies, 3, 4,
        161, 256–63, 267, 269–74
  Watergate, 4–5, 361–67
  will
    controversy, 376–78
    written before first marriage,
        34–35
  womanizing
    advances on Jane Russell,
        243–44
    during affair with Domergue,
        156
    during affair with Hepburn,
        103–6, 114
    during affair with Peters, 230,
        248–55, 294–99

and aviation, 204–7
co-ordinated by private
    detectives, 262–63
and debutantes, 138–42
after Dove leaves, 78, 81–87
early Hollywood, 41–42
and first marriage, 42–46
girlfriend killed, 44
and harem of starlets, 5, 266–74,
    282, 295–99, 322–33,
    330–31
in Las Vegas, 290
list of, 394–99
love nests bugged by FBI, 3
and Miss Universe pageant,
    322–23
pattern of, 195
and pregnancies and paternity
    suits, 91
and pursuit of Janet Leigh,
    253–55
and RKO, 241
and secret party house, 46, 81
and starlets, 264–74
after XF-11 crash, 220–24
Hughes, Howard Robard, Sr.
    (father)
and Allene's death, 23–26, 29–30
and Annette, 28
birth of son, 6–7, 8–9
business and wealth of, 7–10, 11,
    22–23, 28–29
death and will of, 10, 28–31
demands HRH return home after
    mother's death, 25–27
drill bit patent, 9–10
HRH on, 369
indulges HRH, 26–27
marries Allene, 7–8
relationship with HRH as child,
    10, 12–16, 18–20

sends HRH away from mother,
    17–22
womanizing, 10, 14, 22–23, 27, 30
Hughes, Rupert (uncle), 7, 18,
    22–24, 25, 27, 41
    showdown with, 30–31
Hughes Aircraft, 115, 130, 171, 210,
    212, 213, 222, 233–34, 249,
    345, 351
    defense contracts, 276–80, 291
    donated to Howard Hughes
        Medical Institute, 280
    incorporated, 94
Hughes Productions, 269, 331, 332
"Hughes Secret Police"
    begun, 161, 256–63
    follows Peters and Cramer, 291–92
    and "harem," 267, 268–70, 297
    and New Year's triple date, 297–99
Hughes Tool Company (Toolco),
    11, 27, 28, 38, 41, 52–53, 351
    anonymous visits to, 276
    buys Lockheed planes for TWA,
        129
    and Depression, 74–75
    Dietrich hired to manage, 36–37,
        44
    and Hell's Angels, 48, 53, 74–75
    HRH buys out relatives, 30–31,
        181
    and HRH's first plane, 94–95, 96
    and HRH's will, 34
    and Hughes Aircraft, 280
    mortgaged to finance films, 75–77
    recovery after Depression, 111,
        126–27
    research branch, 127
    sold, 355–58
    and Spruce Goose, 209
Humason, Granville A., 9
Humphrey, Hubert, 361, 362

Hunt, E. Howard, 365, 367
Huntoon, Harriet, 200–1
Hurkos, Peter, 376
Hurrell, George, 148
Huston, John, 159
Huston, Walter, 146
Hutton, Barbara, 114, 187, 397

I

Ice Station Zebra (film), 349
I'm No Angel (film), 99
Ingersoll, Richard, 254
Internal Revenue Service (IRS),
    357–58, 363
International Herald-Tribune, 121
Irving, Clifford, 350–51, 352,
    364–65
I Want to Live! (film), 294

J

Jachimczyk, Dr. Joseph, 374
Jane Eyre (play), 107
Jarrico, Paul, 281
J. Arthur Rank Organisation, 241
Jeanmaire, Zizi, 258, 397
Jeffocat, Otis, 374–75
Jet Pilot (film), 239, 255, 282, 393
Jezebel (film), 133
Johnson, Kelly, 169–70
Johnson, Lyndon B., 340, 361–62
Johnston, Marguerite, 35
Jordan, Dorothy, 82, 397

K

Kaiser, Henry, 157–58, 209
Kalatan (exotic dancer), 290
Kane, Walter, 253, 267, 270, 272,
    294–95, 322, 382

Keaton, Buster, 38, 53
Kebbele, agent, 60
Keel, Howard, 287
Keniston, Robert, 395
Kennedy, Edward, 346
Kennedy, John F., 150, 363
Kennedy, Robert F., 362
Kilgallen, Dorothy, 133
King Kong (film), 236
Kirkpatrick, Ray, 190–92, 196
Kistler, Ron, 268, 269, 315, 316, 318
KLAS (TV station), 339
Koford, Louella, 249–50, 288
Korean War, 277
Krasna, Norman, 241
Krupp, Alfried, 340
Krupp, Vera, 340
Kuldell, Col R. C., 28, 76, 94
Kumnick, Miss, 60

L

La Guardia, Fiorello, 123
Lake, Veronica, 148, 205
Lamarr, Hedy, 148, 159
Landau, Arthur, 54
Landmark Hotel, 339
Lane, Mara, 267
Lang, June, 82
Langford, Frances, 148, 163
Lansing, Timmie, 87, 397
La Rocque, Rod, 42
Lasker, William, 257
Las Vegas Story (film), 281, 392
Las Vegas Sun, 347–48, 382
Laura (film), 202
Laxalt, Paul, 341, 347, 348, 361–62
Lecerf, Carolyn, 322
Leckey, Alfred E., 327
Lee, Dorothy, 69

Leigh, Janet, 239, 390, 392, 393, 397
    rejects advances, 253–55
    spied on, 257
LeRoy, Mervyn, 83
Leslie, Joan, 199
Lewis, Norman, 374
Liddy, G. Gordon, 365
Lieber, Perry, 245, 280
Life magazine, 121, 148, 174, 303, 351
Limelight (film), 282
Lindbergh, Charles, 127–28, 204
Lindstrom, Dr. Petter, 205
Lloyd, Harold, 53, 390
Lockheed, 128–29, 150, 169, 292
Lollobrigida, Gina, 258, 266–67, 397
Lombard, Carole, 54
Look magazine, 233
Loren, Sophia, 267
Los Angeles Daily News, 208
Los Angeles Examiner, 153, 217
Los Angeles Herald, 72, 117
Los Angeles Herald-Examiner, 336
Los Angeles Herald-Express, 209
Los Angeles Mirror-News, 305
Los Angeles Police, 2
Los Angeles Times, 72, 217
Luciano, Lucky, 113, 149
Lukasky, Martin, 367
Lummis, Annette Gano (aunt, *formerly* Annette Gano), 79, 92
    and estate controversy, 374, 377, 378, 381, 382
    and global flight, 124
    and HRH's disappearance, 191
    and HRH's first marriage, 33–34, 44, 45, 46, 52, 55, 74
Lummis, Dr. Frederick (brother-in-law), 25, 28, 46, 52

Lummis, William Rice (nephew), 374, 377, 378, 380
Lund, Ed, 120, 122
Lupino, Ida, 82, 390, 391, 397
Lynch, Edith "Edie," 245
Lynn, Diana, 199
Lyon, Ben, 45, 53, 54, 55, 69, 203, 389
Lyons, D. L. (Vernon Scott), 351
Lytess, Natasha, 203

M

Macao (film), 244, 392
MacArthur, Charles, 73, 389
McBain, Chester, 188
McCarthy, Joseph, 281
McCarthy, Neil, 37, 43, 44, 62, 63, 64, 75, 89, 105, 106, 128, 134–35
McCloud, Michael, 59, 60
MacDonald, Jeanette, 82
McGovern, George, 364
McGraw-Hill, 350–51, 352, 364–65
McGuffin, Peter, 317
McGuire, Phyllis, 339
McKeon, Joseph F., 317
McNamara, Jim, 234–35
Madsen, Johanna, 138
Mad Wednesday (film), 390
Mafia, 339
Magruder, Jeb, 366
Maheu, Robert, 100, 322, 326
  discovers HRH missing, 347–48
  fired, 329, 348, 381
  hired, 292
  on HRH as businessman, 278
  on HRH's womanizing, 104
  and Mormon aides, 344–48
  and move to Boston, 336

  and move to Las Vegas, 337–39, 341
  and Nixon, 362–63, 367
  and Peters, 333
  on Shubert, 296, 309–10
  and TWA suit, 327–28
Manero, Dr. Alexander Gertz, 379
Manners, Dorothy, 57, 61, 164
Mannix, Eddie, 199
Man on a Tightrope (film), 253
Mansfield, Jayne, 245
Mantz, Paul, 48, 49, 50, 68, 95
March, Fredric, 253
March, Joseph Moncure, 54, 67–68
Mardh, Dr. Per-Anders, 302
Margulis, Gordon, 354–55, 358–59
Marley, Peverell J., 201, 206, 395
Marsh, Marian, 54, 82, 397
Martin, Bob, 190–92, 196
Martin, Tony, 248, 249, 255, 392, 394
Martin, Earl, 231
Marx, Groucho, 391
Mary of Scotland (film), 103
Maschio, Connie, 293
Maschio, Johnny, 57, 69, 81, 82, 85, 100, 114, 201, 205–6, 249, 250, 293
Mason, Judge E. Paul, 208
Mason, Patricia, 265
Mason, Dr. Verne, 58–59, 162, 182, 183, 185, 217, 218–20, 253, 265, 279
  and HRH commitment plan, 302–3, 306
Mason, Dr. Verne, Jr., 253, 265
Mating Call, The (film), 72, 388
Mature, Victor, 241, 391, 392
Maxwell, Elsa, 139, 140
Mayer, Louis B., 138, 249
Mayo, Virginia, 199, 205–6, 397

Mehnke, Walter, 305
Me (Hepburn), 107
Melvin and Howard (film), 377
Memoirs of Howard Hughes, The (Irving), 350–51
Menjou, Adolphe, 73, 389
Menzies, William Cameron, 282
Merman, Ethel, 311
Merrill, Lynch, Fenner and Smith, 355
Merritt, O. C., 190
Mexico, and murder charges, 379–80
Meyer, Gabe, 105–6
Meyer, Johnny, 130, 131, 159, 174, 194, 197, 198, 199, 200, 210, 211, 217, 220, 222, 243
Meyer, Maj. Gen. Bennett E., 131
MGM, 199
Midgley, Leslie, 334
Miles, Bob, 268
Miles, Vera, 268
Milestone, Lewis, 41, 73, 388
Miller, Ann, 202, 285
Miller, Patsy Ruth, 45
Mitchell, John, 365, 367
Mitchell, Thomas, 146–47
Mitchum, Robert, 239–40, 242, 244, 255, 262, 390, 391, 392
Monroe, Marilyn, 202–3, 242, 311, 398
Montand, Yves, 311
Monteith, Judge Walter, 31
Montemayor, Dr. Victor, 370–72, 373, 378, 379
Moore, Colleen, 81
Moore, Constance, 205–6
Moore, Terry, 240–41, 288, 398
    affair with HRH, 248, 249–53, 290
    career, 391
    divorce from Davis, 288–89
    love letters, 2
    marries Cramer, 294
    "marries" HRH at sea, 250–51
    pregnancy, 253
    records calls, 251–52
    spied on, 259
Morgan, Gloria Vanderbilt, 140
Morning Glory (film), 103
Mother Carey's Chickens (film), 103
Motion Picture Association, 207–8
Muire, Florabel, 305–6
Muni, Paul, 73, 389
Murphy, Audie, 210–11
Murray, Mae, 23
Murrow, Edward R., 150
My Forbidden Past (film), 391
Myler, Levar Beebe, 332

N

Nash, Alden, 137
National Aeronautical Association (NAA), 108
Nazi Germany, 115, 121
Nazimova, Alla, 23
Neal, Roy, 351
Nefrite (cat), 324–25
Negri, Pola, 42
Neilan, Marshall, 48, 388
Nelson, Harmon "Ham," 133, 134
Nevada Gaming Control Board, 341
Newhill, Charles, 118, 119
Newsweek, 207, 328
New York Post, 191, 196, 346
New York Times, 123, 129, 244
Niagara (film), 398
Nichols, Jack, 183
Nightmare (Lukas), 363
Nissen, Greta, 53
Nixon, F. Donald, 363–64, 366
Nixon, Richard M., 3, 4, 5,

281–82, 358, 361–67
Norsworthy, Dr. Oscar L., 6
Nosseck, Martin, 288
Novarro, Ramon, 42, 82

O

O'Brien, Larry, 362–63, 364, 365,
  366, 367
O'Brien, Pat, 73, 389
O'Callaghan, Mike, 359
Odekirk, Glenn, 94, 95, 107, 109,
  124, 159, 162, 166, 171, 172,
  173, 182, 185, 216, 218, 220,
  221, 303
Olivier, Laurence, 241
"Operating Manual for Taking
  Clothes to HRH," 261–62
"Operation Nevada," 63–64
Outlaw, The (film), 389, 398
  censored, 165–66, 207–8, 245
  produced, 144–48, 154, 158, 242
  pulled out of circulation, 165–67,
    185
  reissued, 207–8
Outrage (film), 390

P

Painted Angel, The (film), 61
Paleface, The (film), 242
Palmer, Richard W., 94
Pan American World Airways, 115,
  128, 228–29, 283
  wires HRH's room, 232
Parsons, Louella, 36, 47–48, 53,
  54–55, 56, 57, 60–61, 64, 67,
  86, 117, 135, 151, 153, 215,
  218, 247, 253, 289, 290–91, 305
Pearl, Ralph, 382–83
Pearson, Drew, 232

Pease, Sarah Clement, 116
Pentagon, 276–80
Pero, Taylor, 200, 201, 222
Peters, Jean (second wife), 4, 195,
  398
  attends college, 334
  and aviation, 204, 234
  and death of HRH, 374, 375
  divorces HRH, 342–43
  engaged to HRH, 246–48, 289,
    290
  and food fetishes, 313–14
  on HRH and marriage, 334
  and HRH's disappearances, 226,
    227, 230–31, 348
  and HRH's drug use, 342
  and HRH's private army, 257,
    291–92
  and HRH's womanizing, 250,
    252, 265, 289, 297
  and Las Vegas, 338, 340, 377
  married life with HRH, 311–14,
    323–29, 332–33, 351
  marries and divorces Cramer, 288,
    290–94
  marries Hough, 343
  marries HRH, 272, 300–1, 303–7
  meets HRH, 210–11
  message from HRH at death, 369
  Mormons scheme against, 317–20,
    322, 332–38
  and New Year's triple date, 294–99
  surveillance of, 313–14
  and XF-11 crash, 211–12, 220,
    221, 222, 224
Petrali, Joe, 185, 186–90, 211, 212
Phelan, James, 339, 350–51, 377
Philadelphia Inquirer, 359
Philadelphia Story, The (film), 138
Philadelphia Story, The (play), 133,
  138

Photoplay, 69

Pickford, Mary, 36, 38, 56, 133, 143

Pilate's Wife (script), 239

Pluyman, Burt, 379

Porter, Cole, 86

Post, Mrs. Wiley, 122

Post, Wiley, 123

Postman Always Rings Twice, The
    (film), 199, 399

Potts, Martha (cousin), 12

Powell, Dick, 281, 393

Powell, William, 205

Power, Tyrone, 227, 316, 398

Powers, Mala, 390

Preminger, Otto, 393

Price, Vincent, 244, 282, 393

Pride of the Marines (film), 148

Prisoner of Zenda, The (film), 143

Prosso Academy, 11, 12

Q

Quality Street (film), 103

Quarberg, Lincoln, 71

R

Rachel and the Stranger (film), 240

Racket, The (film), 72, 388

Raft, George, 389

Ralston, Vera (Vera Miles), 268

Rand, Johnny, 309–10

Randell, Brucks, 328

Real, Jack, 129, 355, 356, 359–60
    and death of HRH, 369–70, 371,
    372, 382

Rebecca (film), 136

Rebozo, Charles "Bebe," 364, 365,
    367

Reckless Sex, The (film), 42

Red River (film), 242

Reed, Luther, 48

Register, G. T., 358

Rehak, Rob, 353

Reynolds, Debbie, 245, 393

Reynolds, Walter, 218

Rice, Laura (sister-in-law), 33

Rice, William Marsh, 33

Rice University, 27, 31, 33, 126

Richardson, James R., 12

Rickard, James H., 332, 357

Riddle estate, 339–40

RKO Pictures
    disarray, 281–82
    films by HRH, 390–93
    HRH buys and collects starlets,
        236–45

Roadblock (film), 391

Robards, Jason, 377

Robbins, Harold, 332

Robert Mullen and Company, 367

Robertson, Dale, 282, 393

Robinson, Paul H., 317

Rodeo (yacht), 61, 75, 81

Rogell, Sid, 240

Rogers, Ginger, 2, 5, 86, 98, 152,
        178, 368, 398
    affair and break up, 132–39
    and aviation, 204
    meets HRH, 83–85

Rogers, Lela, 84, 135, 281

Rogers St. John, Adela, 36, 69, 72

Rooney, Mickey, 159, 161, 396

Roosevelt, Elliott, 130–31, 227, 228

Roosevelt, Franklin D., 111, 227

Rosselli, Johnny, 82

Rossellini, Roberto, 390

Rossinni, George, 229, 230

Rover (yacht), 86

Russell, Gail, 199

Russell, Jamie, 303, 380

Russell, Jane, 281, 348, 398

bra, 147
cast in *Outlaw*, 144–48, 166, 207, 389
and censorship of *Outlaw*, 165
and Henley, 380–81
on HRH, 208
love letters, 2
RKO career, 242–45, 391, 392, 393
20-year contract, 282

S

Salome, Where She Danced (film), 194, 395
Sands Hotel, 339
Sands of Iwo Jima (film), 148
San Francisco Chronicle, 167
Scarface (film), 73, 80, 84–85, 236, 389
Schallert, Edwin, 72
Schary, Dore, 237–38
Scheerer, Robert, 255
Schiffrin, Bill, 206–7
Schindler Detective Agency, 232
Schultz, Gerald, 196
Schumach, Murray, 208
Schwartz, Dr. Jeffrey, 184, 273, 302, 312, 317, 328
Scott, Randolph, 98, 100
Scott, Vernon, 351
Sears, Rev. Peter Gray, 29, 33
Seawell, Wallace, 270
Securities and Exchange Commission, 355–56
Sedylmayr, Julius M., 355
Selznick, David O., 239
Selznick, Irene Mayer, 205
Sharp, Dudley, 10, 12, 13–14, 17, 30, 33, 36
Sharp, Walter, 9, 10, 11

Sharp-Hughes Tool Company *(later Hughes Tool Company)*, 10, 11
Shaw, Artie, 210, 256, 259, 396, 399
Shearer, Norma, 133, 138, 143–44, 253
She Done Him Wrong (film), 99
Shelton, Turner B., 354
Shimon, Lt. Joseph W. W., 232
Shore, Dinah, 148
Show Boat (film), 286
Shubert, Yvonne, 195, 294–301, 317, 322, 398
abortion, 307–11
Siegel, Bugsy, 113
Signoret, Simone, 311, 321–22
Silver Bullet (H-1 plane)
developed, 94–97
breaks altitude records, 107–9
Silver Slipper Hotel, 339
Simmons, Jean, 241–42, 392, 398
Sinatra, Frank, 391, 396
Sin of Harold Diddlebock, The (film), 389
Sirhan, Sirhan, 362
Sky Devils (film), 73, 389
Slack, Thomas, 232–33
Some Dare Call It Murder (Harrison proposal), 379
Somoza, Anastasio, 354, 357
Son of Sinbad (film), 282, 290, 393
Southern Cross (yacht), 86, 117, 133, 138, 140, 150, 155, 250
Spruce Goose (HK-1, Hercules), 249
contract cancelled, 209, 276
Senate investigation, 227–28, 233
successful tests, 234–35
Stack, Robert, 150
Standard Oil, 10, 52
Stardust Hotel, 339
Stauffer, Teddy, 210

Steele, James B., 359
Sterling, Robert, 129–30
Stevens, Ludlow, 103, 116
Stevenson, Clyde, 171
Stewart, James, 138
Stewart, Mell, 352–53, 354, 355
Stoddart, Richard, 120
Story of G.I. Joe, The (film), 148, 239
Stromboli (film), 390
Sturges, Preston, 193, 390
Summa Corporation
  conspiracy suit, 380, 383
  formed, 356
  theft by aides, 382
Susan Slept Here (film), 393
Sutton, Roger, 372, 373
Swanson, Gloria, 36, 42, 56
Swell Hogan (film), 37–38, 41, 388
Sylvia Scarlett (film), 101

T

Talbott, Harold E., 279
Taylor, Elizabeth, 5, 241–42, 274, 311, 399
  affair, 223–24
  spied on, 257, 258–59
Taylor, Francis, 223
Taylor, Joyce, 272–73, 399
Tennant, Dr. Forrest, 379
Thacher, Sherman Day, 21–24, 25
Thain, Dr. Wilbur, 329, 372, 373–74, 380, 381
Thau, Benny, 290
Therkelsen, Lawrence, 95
Thiess, Ursula, 267
This 'N That: Bette Davis (Davis and Herskowitz), 134
Thomas, Bob, 245
Thomas, Janet, 222

Thomas, Lowell, 121
Three Coins in the Fountain (film), 291
Thurlow, Lt. Thomas, 120
Tierney, Gene, 202, 221, 399
Time magazine, 167, 208, 303, 352
Times, The, 108, 360
Titus, Dr. Jack, 378, 379
Todd, Macy, 247, 248
Todd, Michael, 224
Todd, Thelma, 54
Toland, Gregg, 147
Tracy, Spencer, 73, 138, 200, 389, 397
Trans World Airlines (TWA), 204
  battle for, against deteriorating HRH, 284, 291, 297, 308
  bought by HRH, 127–30
  collapse of, and HRH's mental problems, 282–84
  and Constellation, 169, 183
  and FBI, 197
  fight with Pan Am, 228–29
  penalties, and Hughes Tool sale, 355–58, 365
  suit against HRH, 323, 325, 327–28
  windfall from buyout deal, 339
Trippe, Juan, 228
Tuck, Dick, 363
Turner, Lana, 156, 159, 292, 399
  affair, 199–202, 210
  bugged by FBI, 3
  love letters, 2
  and XF-11 crash, 212, 218, 222
Turner, Roscoe, 48, 71
Two Arabian Knights (film), 41, 73, 388
Two Tickets to Broadway (film), 255, 392

U

Underwater (film), 245, 393
Underwood, Aggie, 80
United Air Lines, 283
United Press, 219, 280, 289
U.S. Air Force, 233–34, 277, 278, 279
U.S. Army, 130–31, 208–9, 221–22
U.S. Customs, 373–74
U.S. Marshal's Service, 229–30
U.S. Senate
  HRH spies on, 257
  investigation, 227–34, 276
U.S. Supreme Court, 356
U.S. Treasury Department, 357–58
University of Arizona, 126
University of California at Berkeley, 126
Utley, Bill, 234

V

Valentino, Rudolph, 38, 42
Vallee, Rudy, 174, 175, 176–77, 237, 396
Vanderbilt, Alfred, 274
Vanderbilt, Gloria, 2, 139, 140–42, 399
Vanderbilt, Reginald Claypool, 140
Vanities (yacht), 234
Vanity Fair, 139
Variety, 72, 167, 245
Velez, Lupe, 133
Vendetta (film), 210, 240, 390–91
Vista Del Arroyo hotel, 26
Viva Zapata! (film), 398
Von Rosenberg, C. W., 171–72

W

Wadsworth, James, 251
Wagner, Robert, 253
WAIF, 243
Wald, Jerry, 241, 267
Waldron, Chuck, 332, 358
Wallace, C. P., 105
Wall Street Journal, 281, 349
War Department, 130–31
War Materiel Command
  cancels XF-11, 208–9, 212, 219
  strips HRH of privileges, 196–97
Warner, Jack, 151–52
Warner Brothers, 75
War Production Department, 158–59
Washington Post, 4, 366
Wasserman, Lew, 282
Waterfield, Bob, 146, 242–43
Watergate scandal, 4, 361–67
Wayne, John, 239, 255, 282, 289, 391, 393
Weir, Helen, 264–65
Welles, Orson, 223
West, Mae, 99
Whale, James, 69
Whalen, Grover, 123, 124
Wharton, Mrs. John (mother's cousin), 18
Where Danger Lives (film), 391
Whip Hand, The (film), 282, 392
White, Stephen, 233
Whitney, Dwight, 167
Whitney, Gertrude Vanderbilt, 142
Wilding, Michael, 242
Willard, Bill, 289
Willat, Irvin, 56, 58, 60, 61–62, 63, 64, 75
Williamson, Don, 303
Willson, Henry, 152

Wilson, Earl, 133, 251, 298
Winchell, Walter, 86, 272
Wings (film), 47, 72
Winsor, Kathleen, 256
Winston, Ella Rice, 377
Winston, James Overton, 34, 45,
    85
Winte, Ralph, 367
Wolfe, Dan, 223, 303
Woman of the Year (film), 138
Woods, Rosemary, 366
Woodward, Bob, 4, 366
Woolfe, Michael, 298
World War II, 147–48, 154, 157–59,
    182
Wu, Butterfly, 72–73
Wyler, William, 133
Wynter, Dana, 265

X

XF-11 bomber (*formerly* D-2
    bomber), 157–58
    Army contract cancelled, 208–9,
        221–22
    Army contract for, 130–31
    crash, 211–20, 246
    Senate investigation, 227, 229,
        233, 276

Z

Zanuck, Darryl F., 99, 160, 201–2,
    211, 294
Zimmerlee, agent, 60
Zint, William, 109
Zukor, Adolph, 98